Letters of H. P. Lovecraft

LETTERS TO ALFRED GALPIN AND OTHERS

Edward H. Cole

H. P. LOVECRAFT

LETTERS TO ALFRED GALPIN AND OTHERS

Edited by
S. T. JOSHI AND DAVID E. SCHULTZ

Hippocampus Press

New York

Published by Hippocampus Press
P.O. Box 641, New York, NY 10156.
www.hippocampuspress.com

Cover design and Hippocampus Press logo by Anastasia Damianakos.
Cover production by Barbara Briggs Silbert.
Photograph of Alfred Galpin on page 400 courtesy of Scott Connors

First Edition
1 3 5 7 9 8 6 4 2

ISBN 978-1-61498-291-3

Contents

Introduction

Lovecraft's early involvement in amateur journalism—he joined the United Amateur Press Association (UAPA) in April 1914 and the National Amateur Press Association in 1917—led to his acquaintance with several colleagues who became lifelong friends, among them Maurice W. Moe, Rheinhart Kleiner, and W. Paul Cook. One of these—Edward Harold Cole (1892–1966), who lived most of his life in various suburbs of Boston—is among the least-known of Lovecraft's correspondents, chiefly because his work rarely appeared outside the realm of amateur journalism. Cole accumulated a distinguished record as an amateur journalist. He joined the NAPA in 1905, at the instigation of Paul J. Campbell, at which time he published a small paper named the *Hustler* with Jacob Golden. This was succeeded by the *Olympian,* of which thirty-six numbers have been published. Cole served as official editor of the NAPA in 1911–12 and president in 1912–13. Lovecraft states that Cole was a teacher of English and American history at Chauncy Hall School (now the Chapel Hill–Chauncy Hall School) in Waltham, Massachusetts.[1]

Lovecraft's first letter to Cole dates to 9 November 1914. Soon thereafter, Cole was helping to establish the Providence Amateur Press Club (for which see below) and came down to Providence in late November or early December to meet both Lovecraft and the members of the club. He thus became one of the first amateurs to meet Lovecraft in person. Cole's first impression of Lovecraft was not entirely favorable, but they soon became fast friends:

> My first impression of Howard when I met him in 1914 was that he was sheer intellect and very little "human." When our real friendship developed during the twenties and the thirties, he had altered greatly—had become thoroughly human and cherished friendships and personal contacts without sacrificing his intellectual interests, and increasingly I gained the impression that he was really rather lonely and avidly desired companionship.[2]

In 1917, Cole married Helene E. Hoffman (1893–1919). Hoffman was at the crux of the disputed 1912 UAPA election that led to the establishment of two separate organizations, the UAPA and the UAPA of America, the latter based largely in Seattle. Lovecraft joined the former organization in 1914; at the time he may not even have been aware of the other. In his various writings on the subject (e.g., "The Pseudo-United," 1920), Lovecraft suggests that the UAPA of America was the breakaway organization; but in fact, histories of amateur journalism regard the Hoffman faction (Hoffman served two consecutive terms as president, in 1912–14) in that light.

---

1. HPL to E. Hoffmann Price, 4 May 1935 (ALS, JHL).
2. EHC to August Derleth, 19 December 1944 (ALS, Wisconsin Historical Society).

Helene Hoffman Cole died in the spring of 1919, shortly after giving birth to a son, E. Sherman Cole (1918–1988). Lovecraft wrote various pieces about her at this time, including the essay "Helene Hoffman Cole— Litterateur" (*United Amateur*, May 1919) and the poem "Helene Hoffman Cole: 1893–1919: The Club's Tribute" (*Bonnet*, June 1919). Lovecraft's letters to Edward H. Cole appear to be missing for this period, so it is not clear how he expressed his condolence to the widower. Before Helene Hoffman Cole's death, Lovecraft wrote several owlish letters to her infant son.

When the extant correspondence resumes in 1923, the focus was on the turmoil that was engulfing the amateur movement at the time. William J. Dowdell, who had been elected president of the NAPA at the 1922 convention, resigned a few months later (Lovecraft later states that Dowdell "ran off with a chorus girl in 1922"),[3] and Lovecraft was persuaded to take over as president for the remainder of the term. He had already been selected to assist Samuel Loveman in handling the NAPA's Bureau of Critics (equivalent to the UAPA's Department of Public Criticism), but resigned this post to take over the presidency; Cole took Lovecraft's place. Cole later attempted to persuade Lovecraft to run for a full term as president for the 1923–24 term; but Lovecraft blanched at the idea, since he disliked administrative duties of this sort. Instead, he threw his support to Hazel Pratt Adams, who in fact became president for that term.

Lovecraft often visited Cole on his various trips to the Boston area, beginning as early as 1920. When Lovecraft moved to New York in the spring of 1924, after marrying Sonia H. Greene, his correspondence with Cole apparently lapsed. In a letter of 24 February 1925, he apologizes to Cole for his uncharacteristically long delay in replying to Cole's letter of the previous August. This is the only extant letter to Cole in the period 1925–30. Lovecraft met Cole frequently during his trips to Boston in the 1930s.

E. Sherman Cole himself was later to join amateur journalism, and also became president of The Fossils. He made the following observation about his father's long membership in the movement:

> As I studied the accumulated exchanges of sixty years, I became aware of several disquieting aspects: (1) Edward H. Cole had been the confident [*sic*] of just about every amateur journalist in this century, (2) there was more hanky-panky rampant in a.j. than in Peyton Place and (3) the indiscretion of the writers was only matched by the recipient's saving the letters. Marion and I consigned them to the rubbish . . .[4]

---

3. HPL to Lillian D. Clark, 27 July 1925; *Letters to Family and Family Friends* 1.322.
4. *Fossil* (April 1979): 5), in Ken Faig, Jr., "Lavender Ajays of the Red-Scare Period: 1917–1920," *Fossil* 102, No. 4 (July 2006): 5–17, quotation on p. 8.

Cole was one of the few friends to attend Lovecraft's funeral on 18 March 1937. Cole not only wrote a lengthy and touching memoir, "Ave atque Vale!" (*Olympian*, Autumn 1940), but revived his *Olympian*—which had been in abeyance since 1917—to publish an entire issue devoted to Lovecraft, with memoirs by W. Paul Cook, James F. Morton, and Ernest A. Edkins. Little is known of Cole's later life. He does not appear to have come into contact with August Derleth of Arkham House at the time Derleth was soliciting Lovecraft's correspondents to send him their letters for transcription; no letters to Cole appear in *Selected Letters* (1965–76), and the sixty-seven letters and cards included in this volume constitute the first publication of these documents (with one exception; see bibliography).

Not all early correspondents of Lovecraft remained in touch with him in later life; one of the most distinctive of these was John Thomas Dunn (1889–1983). Lovecraft's correspondence with Dunn is perhaps unique in his epistolary corpus. This correspondence, dating to the years 1915–17, is one of the relatively few surviving groups of letters from the period preceding his marriage and his brief stay in New York (1924–26). It thereby offers invaluable insight into Lovecraft's most extensive involvement with amateur journalism (1914–25) and sheds light on his early political views as well.

Lovecraft was at this time still thrilled with the discovery of amateur journalism, seeing in it both a means for expanding his own literary and social horizons and for acting as tutor to less well educated persons. This tutorial function was an early interest of Lovecraft's: at the age of sixteen he attempted to educate a Swede whom he had encountered in the Providence Public Library (see pp. 199–200). Much of his wide correspondence, from the beginning to the end of his life, had as its primary goal the imparting of information in such areas as philosophy, history, literature, and science. The amateur world, with a handful of exceptional intellects but a large number of crude, ill-educated, but eager members young and old, formed a natural field for the implementation of Lovecraft's educational goals.

Several such opportunities emerged very early in Lovecraft's involvement with amateurdom. In November 1914, only a few months after his joining of the UAPA in April, he was appointed chairman of the Department of Public Criticism. This function required Lovecraft to write lengthy critiques of every amateur paper published during the period covered by the UAPA's official organ, the *United Amateur*. In July 1915 he was elected second vice president, in which capacity he was responsible for discovering new recruits for the UAPA. It was at this time that he wrote his recruiting pamphlet, *United Amateur Press Association: Exponent of Amateur Journalism* [1915].[5] In April 1915

---

5. HPL to Arthur Harris, 23 August 1915: "As Vice-President, I have had the privilege of writing the United's recruiting circular this year, & in so doing I have

Lovecraft began issuing his own paper, the *Conservative,* of which he published thirteen issues; this journal was not so much educational in purpose as polemical and controversial, providing Lovecraft with a forum for the expression of his early opinions on literature, politics, and the amateur world.

The formation of a group called the Providence Amateur Press Club presented Lovecraft with an opportunity to fulfill his tutorial function very close to home. This organization—one of many such local groups in the UAPA and the rival NAPA—was formed sometime in 1914 by John T. Dunn and Caroline Miller at the suggestion of Edward H. Cole;[6] Lovecraft apparently became involved at a fairly early stage. The group consisted, in addition to Dunn, "of seven or eight other students [who] attended a night class at a high school"[7] in North Providence. Lovecraft would come to their gatherings on occasion and was clearly involved in the publication of two issues of the *Providence Amateur,* the club's paper.[8] Necronomicon Press reprinted both issues (in 1976 and 1977), and their contents are of some note.

---

tried to be unusually comprehensive. This is now in the press, & when issued I will send you several copies" (ALS, JHL).<RK>

6. L. Sprague de Camp, "Young Man Lovecraft," in *Ave atque Vale: Reminiscences of H. P. Lovecraft,* ed. S. T. Joshi and David E. Schultz (West Warwick, RI: Necronomicon Press, 2018), 172.

7. de Camp 172.

8. HPL to Arthur Harris, 1 July 1915: "I am . . . sending herewith under separate cover two publications of mine; *The Providence Amateur* and *The Conservative.*" He later mentions to Harris (14 July 1915): "I trust you have received my latest *Conservative* as well as *The Providence Amateur,* a club paper which I supervise" (ALS, JHL). As Chairman of the Department of Public Criticism, HPL published favorable reviews of both issues: "*The Providence Amateur* for June introduces to the United another local press club of great enthusiasm . . . The editorials by John T. Dunn are both frank and fearless. We detest a shifty club whose allegiance wavers betwixt the United, the Morris Faction and the National, and so are greatly pleased at Mr. Dunn's manly and open stand for the one real United" (*United Amateur* 15, No. 2 [September 1915]: 24); "*The Providence Amateur* for February is worthy of particular attention on account of Mr. Peter J. MacManus' absorbing article on 'The Irish and the Fairies' . . . The prose style of Mr. MacManus is very good, being notable alike for fluency and freedom from slang, whilst his taste is of the best . . . Edmund L. Shehan contributed both verse and prose to this issue. 'Death' is a stately poem on a grave subject, whose sentiments are all of suitable humility and dignity . . . The prose piece by Mr. Shehan well describes a visit to a cinematograph studio . . . In the verses entitled 'A Post-Christmas Lament', Mr. John T. Dunn combines much keenness of wit with commendable regularity of metre. Mr. Dunn is among the cleverest of the United's humorous writers" (*United Amateur* 15, No. 9 [April 1916]: 115).

The first issue (unpaged) of the *Providence Amateur* 1, No 1 (June 1915) contained the following:

"To the Members of the United Amateur Press Ass'n from the Providence Amateur Press Club" (poem), by Lovecraft, [1–3];
"Our Candidate" (essay) (unsigned, but probably by Lovecraft), [3–4];
"Exchanges" (comments on amateur journals) (unsigned, but probably by Lovecraft), [5–6];
"Editorial" by Dunn, [7–8];
"On Acknowledgements" (essay) by Dunn, [8–10];
"For Historian—Ira A. Cole" (essay) (unsigned, but probably by Lovecraft), [10–11];
List of members of the Providence Amateur Press Club, [11];
Colophon, [12].

The second issue of the *Providence Amateur* 1, No. 2 (February 1916) contained the following:

"Death" (poem) by Edmund L. Shehan, (1–2);
"The Irish and the Fairies" (essay) by Peter J. MacManus (with "Editor's Note" by Lovecraft, [2–3]), (3–5);
"A Post-Christmas Lament" (poem) by Dunn, (6–7);
"The Making of a Motion Picture" (essay) by Edmund L. Shehan, (7–8);
"Editorial" by Lovecraft, (9–13);
"To Charlie of the Comics" (poem) (unsigned, but by Lovecraft), (13–14);
"The Bride of the Sea" (poem) (unsigned, but by Lovecraft), (14–16).

For the first issue, Dunn is listed as official editor, with Lovecraft as "Literary Director"; for the second issue Lovecraft is official editor. Other members (listed only in the first issue) are as follows: Victor L. Basinet, President; Eugene M. Kern, Vice President; Caroline Miller, Secretary-Treasurer; Edmond L. Sheehan [*sic*], Fred A. Byland, Mildred Metcalf, Peter J. McManus [*sic*]. For the first issue, the "Office of Publication" is given as 83 Commodore St., Providence, R.I., Dunn's residence; for the second issue Lovecraft's residence, 598 Angell St., is given. Both issues were printed by the Lincoln Press, Cambridge, Mass.[9]

It is clear that Lovecraft and Dunn were the principal writers in the group; their contributions form the entirety of the first issue and a good proportion of the second. Lovecraft's association with Dunn presumably began

9. Albert Sandusky's The Lincoln Press also printed at least four issues of HPL's *Conservative* 1, No. 2–2, No. 1 (July 1915–April 1916).

at the very outset of the organization's formation in 1914,[10] although their actual correspondence only began in July 1915 (assuming that the first extant letter is the first written by Lovecraft), just after the appearance of the first issue of the *Providence Amateur*. The entire correspondence has not survived intact; three letters (dated c. 16 August and 20 November 1916, and 21 January 1917) are known to be lost, as only the envelopes survive; and certain large gaps in the sequence of Lovecraft's letters—e.g., that between the first (20 July 1915) and the second (25 October 1915), and between the second and the third (10 June 1916)—may suggest that other letters have also been lost. It is, of course, possible that the correspondence was suspended during those occasions when Lovecraft attended the group's meetings in person,[11] as he must have done around the time of the publication of the second issue of the *Providence Amateur* in February 1916.

Lovecraft's early amateur interests emerge vividly in the surviving correspondence. As a staunch supporter of the UAPA, he reacted violently to Dunn's evidently fleeting suggestion that the *Providence Amateur* be associated with the NAPA. The election of UAPA officers, held in late July at the annual UAPA convention, exercised Lovecraft considerably, and he urged Dunn to send in proxy ballots supporting the candidates he favored. Many other important particulars about Lovecraft's early involvement with amateur journalism are illuminated by this correspondence.

While Lovecraft dealt with Dunn amicably as an amateur journalist, the relations between the two men were in other ways not so cordial. Dunn was at this time emphatically pro-Irish, while Lovecraft was just as emphatically

---

10. HPL's name first appears in the published UAPA membership list for May 1914 (*United Amateur* 13, No. 5 [May 1914]: 113). Four months later the R.I. membership included Victor L. Basinet and John T. Dunn (*United Amateur* 14, No. 1 [September 1914]: 19). HPL probably would have had some contact with them soon thereafter. In January of 1915 the names of Edmund L. Shehan and Guy H. Kelso were added to the Providence contingent (*United Amateur* 14, No. 3 [January 1915]: 54).

11. HPL first publicly mentions both Basinet and Dunn in the *Conservative* 1, No. 3 (October 1915): 14–15: "When Victor L. Basinet's new paper, *The Rebel*, shall appear, the amateur public will have an opportunity to behold the workings of a very extraordinary mind. Mr. Basinet is [in] some respects a true genius, blessed with an almost instinctive perception of the delicate and the artistic, and possessing a rhetorical style of remarkable vigour. But superadded to these qualities is such a strange point of view on social problems and systems, that the rational reader will stand aghast at the thoughts revealed . . . Another amateur whom the CONSERVATIVE has met several times in person is Mr. John T. Dunn, the Irish Patriot. Mr. Dunn is a man of undoubted talent, being now the editor of *The Providence Amateur*, yet his anti-English views are such that they call for correction" (*CE* 1.76).

pro-British. From the very outset of World War I, he lambasted the Germans—not so much for their aggression but because they were waging a sort of suicidal racial civil war with their Anglo-Saxon brethren in England—and excoriated the pacifist and non-interventionist policies of President Woodrow Wilson. When Dunn entered upon Lovecraft's horizon, another volatile issue began to engage his attention: the issue of Irish independence.

Lovecraft's correspondence with Dunn covers the most critical period in modern Irish history. Since the late nineteenth century, Irish politicians and voters had been split into three main factions: those who (like Lord Dunsany in the early part of the twentieth century) supported union with Great Britain, with Irish representation, in relatively small numbers, in the British Parliament; those who supported Home Rule, or the establishment of a separate Irish Parliament that would have power over many aspects of local life but would still be subordinate to the British Crown; and those who wanted outright independence from Britain. These distinctions are still evident today, with the counties of what is now Northern Ireland remaining predominantly Unionist and the rest of Ireland split between those who wish some ties with Britain and those who wish none.

Irish and English politicians alike had been moving toward Home Rule throughout the latter part of the nineteenth century, and a Home Rule Act was finally passed in September 1914, with the six counties of Ulster, who were vehemently Unionist, being exempted from its conditions; but World War I caused a temporary suspension of its operation. The war itself proved a great strain in Anglo-Irish relations, as the more radical groups—including Sinn Fein, the Irish Republican Brotherhood (later to become the Irish Republican Army), and the Irish Volunteers—urged immediate independence from Great Britain. This volatile situation was exacerbated by the Easter Rebellion of 1916.

This movement, which sought to take over the government in Dublin on Easter Sunday with the aid of arms sent by Germany, was organized by a small and confused band of politicians, revolutionaries, and poets including Padraic Pearse, Joseph Plunkett, Sir Roger Casement, and others. By and large it had no popular support and was a spectacular failure: the German transport ship carrying arms was intercepted by the British navy, and the rebellion itself was put down within a week by the British army, with much loss of life on both sides (450 revolutionaries and civilians, more than 100 British soldiers). The principal revolutionaries were executed for treason.

John Dunn evidently supported the rebellion, as did many Irish-Americans of the time, who tended to be more revolutionary than their counterparts in Ireland. Lovecraft, naturally, felt that suppression of the rebellion was essential to British security: he did not wish an independent Ireland to serve as a potential base of operations for a German flank attack. This fear was not entirely unreasonable in the light of some rebels' associations with

German political and military figures, but in the end it proved illusory. Lovecraft was, of course, at a very extreme position in the controversy, averring that Ireland should never be independent and unleashing dubious arguments on the racial superiority of the Anglo-Saxons of England over the Celts of Ireland. And yet, his ultimate argument for a strict union of the British Isles was that there were no clear-cut racial distinctions between the various nationalities: "I deny any material line of racial cleavage between the various British elements. English, Irish, Scotch, & Welsh are all Teutono-Celtic in varying proportions; though in some individuals & localities one blood or the other may be most pronounced." There is little evidence of Lovecraft's response when Ireland did indeed become independent in 1921; but it is not likely to have been favorable.

As for Dunn, his fate was very unfortunate, as Lovecraft details in a letter to Alfred Galpin:

> I am sorry that modesty caused you to refrain from telling your early experiences in "uplifting the public," for I am sure they must be interesting. My last attempt was in 1914–16, when I laboured with a "literary" club of Micks who dwelt in the dingy "North End" of the city. The brightest of them was an odd bigoted fellow named Dunn, two years older than I. He hated England & was a violent pro-German—& I was foolish enough to waste time trying to convert him—as if an Irishman could reason!! Even after I gave up the club as hopeless, I continued corresponding with this fellow, for he was well-meaning & quite intelligent in his way. But in 1917 came events which caused me to drop him. He took the war very badly, & wrote treasonable letters by the score. When the draft came, he refused to register, & was arrested by government agents. In July he was drafted, but refused to respond to the summons—hence was court-martialled & sentenced to 20 years in the Atlanta Federal Prison—where he still languishes, I presume. I am done with Dunn![12]

Dunn did not in fact spend twenty years in prison, but was released shortly after the end of the war. He thereupon attended a seminary and became a priest in the Catholic Church (de Camp 144). He died on 24 May 1983, having ended his days as chaplain emeritus of Mercy Hospital in Portsmouth, Ohio.[13]

---

12. HPL to Alfred Galpin, 29 August 1918. There is also a long discussion of Dunn in HPL's letter to Arthur Harris, 12 January 1918.

13. Fr. Dunn's obituaries, in the *Portsmouth Daily Times* (25 May 1983) and the *Columbus Catholic Times* (27 May 1983), indicate that he became a plumber after his release from two years in federal prison. He appparently worked at that trade until he entered Mount St. Mary's College and Seminary, Emmitsburg, MD, where he earned bachelor's and master's degrees before being ordained on 29 May 1930. He was assigned to the Diocese of Columbus, OH, where, after holding various

The letters to John T. Dunn offer a unique portrait of Lovecraft as a young man: the correspondence ends just as he is embarking upon his mature fiction-writing career with "The Tomb," written in June 1917. Sequestered, unworldly, and dogmatic as Lovecraft appears in these letters, it is evident that he paid very close attention to world events, and he must have read the newspaper very thoroughly to be as up-to-date on political and military events of 1915–17 as he appears to be. The image of Lovecraft as an "eccentric recluse" falls to the ground even for this early period, for he was clearly very much a part of the early twentieth century in spite of the extremism of his views. Later years would bring a mellowing of Lovecraft's dogmatism and, in some cases, a reversal of his opinions as he encountered new facts and new experiences; but the questing intellect was there from the beginning.

It is unfortunate that the long and complex relationship of Lovecraft and Alfred Galpin (1901–1983)—spanning nearly two decades and covering the entire period of Lovecraft's mature creative career—is exhibited only fragmentarily in their surviving correspondence; for around 1930 Galpin, apparently ashamed of some of his youthful enthusiasms, destroyed many of Lovecraft's letters up to that time.[14] In any case, it is evident that Lovecraft valued this relationship highly, attributing to Galpin the development of his philosophical outlook at a critical period in his maturation. Lovecraft remained cordial to Galpin to the end of his life, although it is clear that by the 1930s Galpin had outgrown the role of "adopted grandson" and had matured into but one of Lovecraft's many congenial colleagues with whom he enjoyed exchanging points of view.

Because of the fragmentary nature of the correspondence, it is not certain when the two first became acquainted. In his autobiographical notes Galpin variously dates their first epistolary contact to 1916 or 1917;[15] but elsewhere he states that the earliest extant letter (26 January 1918) was perhaps the second he received. Lovecraft clarifies the matter somewhat in a letter to Anne Tillery Renshaw dated 24 August 1918, where he states: "Galpin

---

positions at St. Vincent's Orphanage, St. Ann's Hospital, and St. Joseph's Cathedral, he served as Catholic Chaplain at Mercy Hospital, run by a community of Franciscan Sisters, from November 1932 until his retirement in October 1969. He remained as a permanent resident at Mercy Hospital, where he occasionally spoke out in support of Vietnam War draft-resisters, until his death.

14. Biographical information on Galpin is chiefly derived from his own writings, including his memoir of Lovecraft ("Memories of a Friendship," 1959) and several unpublished documents at JHL (titled "HPL" [1971], "Native's Return" [1975?], "Old Friends and New Horizons" [1976], and "A. G. (II)" [1979]).

15. The original ms. of "Memories of a Friendship" (at JHL) bears the title "1916–1937: Memories of a Friendship."

first dawned above my horizon a year ago . . ."[16] Lovecraft had been elected president of the UAPA in September, and he sought a promising high-school student to be fourth vice-president (at the time the third and fourth vice-presidents were not elected but were appointed by the president) to lead efforts at recruiting young people to join the United. Galpin had entered high school in 1915 and had quickly become a fixture in the Appleton (Wisconsin) High School Press Club, headed by Lovecraft's colleague Maurice W. Moe. It was not Moe, however, who brought Galpin to Lovecraft's attention, but Joseph Harriman, a recent graduate of Appleton High School.

The two quickly engaged in copious correspondence—one far more intellectually substantive than many others in Lovecraft's early career. From the first, Lovecraft was impressed, even awed, by Galpin's precocity. As early as 1918 he wrote: "It is hard for me to realise that eleven years separate me from Galpin, for his thoughts fit in so well with my own. I am convinced that he has a mighty future. He is passing me already in the intellectual race, and in a few years will have left me behind completely."[17] Three years later he supplied a definitive account of Galpin's influence upon him:

> It is odd that an old man should be so much influenced by a kid so vastly his junior, but it remains a fact that no other one human creature has moulded my thought and opinions as extensively as has that Alfredus child. The secret is this: that he is intellectually *exactly like me* save in degree. In degree he is immensely my superior—he is what I should like to be but have not brains enough to be. Our minds are cast in precisely the same mould, save that his is finer. He alone can grasp the direction of my thoughts and amplify them. And so we go down the dark ways of knowledge; the poor plodding old man, and ahead of him the alert little link-boy holding the light and pointing out the path.[18]

Taking into account the wry exaggeration and excessive modesty characteristic of Lovecraft at this time, this assessment is very likely true, though it is difficult to document. For example, Galpin probably introduced Lovecraft to the great iconoclastic German philosopher Friedrich Nietzsche, well before he published his perspicacious essay, "Nietzsche as a Practical Prophet," in 1921. Galpin admitted that his father raised him an atheist, but he never subscribed to what he mischaracterizes as Lovecraft's "dogmatic monism"; and in a startling shift, he converted to Roman Catholicism a year after Lovecraft's death. But their early anticlericalism—and no doubt both of them used the pious Maurice W. Moe as a foil in this regard—helped to establish an intellectual bond. Galpin's skepticism regarding the vagaries of modern poetry

---

16. *Letters to Elizabeth Toldridge and Anne Tillery Renshaw* 358.
17. *Letters to Elizabeth Toldridge and Anne Tillery Renshaw* 359.
18. HPL to Rheinhart Kleiner, 23 April 1921; *Letters to Rheinhart Kleiner* 202.

(see his essays "Some Tendencies of Modern Poetry" and "Form in Modern Poetry," as well as the parody "Two Loves," published in Lovecraft's *Conservative*) may have assisted Lovecraft in honing his own arguments against the Imagists and Modernists.

In many ways, Galpin reminded Lovecraft of his own boyhood. His delight in Galpin's various schoolboy crushes—manifested in numerous poems, such as "Damon and Delia, a Pastoral" (*Tryout*, August 1918) and "Damon—a Monody" (*United Amateur*, May 1919)—became mortifying to Galpin in later years. The evidence points to one Margaret Abraham (who, oddly enough, shared Galpin's birthday, 8 November) as his chief inamorata, and the whole business led to Lovecraft's send-up of Elizabethan tragedy, *Alfredo* (September 1918). Galpin paid homage to Lovecraft in his own literary works, including the story "Marsh-Mad" (1918)—which led the diffident Lovecraft to postpone writing his story "The Tree" for three years because he felt that Galpin had anticipated his use of the "living tree" idea—and the poem "Selenaio-Phantasma," an affectionate tribute to Lovecraft's "Nemesis" (1917). Galpin does not seem to have had any overwhelming enthusiasm for weird literature, but he doubtless appreciated Lovecraft's early macabre tales—more so than the later, longer, more complex works that did not meet his favor and that led to a gradual cooling off of their friendship.

In the early years of their association—roughly the period 1917–24—amateur affairs were largely on their agenda. After his fourth vice-presidency in 1917–18, Galpin served as first vice-president in 1918–19; Rheinhart Kleiner was president during this term, and Lovecraft had resumed his chairmanship of the Department of Public Criticism, a position he had held in 1915–17. The next term (1919–20) Galpin himself was chairman of the Department, retaining that office until 1922. Anomalously, Galpin simultaneously held the presidency of the UAPA in 1920–21. Lovecraft, for his part, was official editor for 1920–22 and 1924–25. It could well be said that Lovecraft and Galpin were among the stars of the UAPA for the entire period. Galpin's literary contributions were not as extensive as Lovecraft's, and he produced only one number of his own publication, the *Philosopher* (December 1920)—a choice issue for its several contributions by Galpin and the first appearance of Lovecraft's story "Polaris" and his poem "The House."

Galpin states that much of his correspondence with Lovecraft during the period 1918–22 was embodied in the so-called Gallomo, the round-robin correspondence cycle including Galpin, Moe, and Lovecraft. Only seven Gallomo letters are now extant of perhaps dozens that were written; but they are among the most illuminating of Lovecraft's letters of the period. In what seem less like letters than rambling stream-of-consciousness essays or autobiographical vignettes, Lovecraft expounds at length upon his bizarre dreams (including the one that led directly to the writing of "The Statement of Randolph Carter"), provides a wondrously illuminating account of the genesis of his early fiction, pontificates on the world political scene (in particular the establishment of the League of Nations and the Anglo-Irish conflict of the early 1920s), and relates at length his gradual emergence from the hermitry of 598 Angell Street (especially following the death of his mother on 24 May 1921), as he ventures to Boston and elsewhere to socialize with amateur writers. Galpin himself was at this time undergoing changes in his scholastic life: he had graduated from Appleton High School in 1919 and entered Lawrence College in Appleton; two years later he transferred to the University of Wisconsin, from which he graduated in 1923.

In the summer of 1922 occurred the first and, as it proved, the last meeting of the two associates. Galpin, having struck up a friendship with Samuel Loveman, decided to spend the summer in Cleveland, and persuaded Lovecraft to join him. Lovecraft did so, taking the long train ride from Providence on 29 July and arriving in Cleveland the next day. He stayed more than two weeks, leaving on 15 August. It was a critical trip in many ways: not only did Lovecraft meet Galpin and Loveman (the latter of whom he had first met in New York only a few months earlier), but he also met George Kirk, Hart Crane, and Crane's numerous cronies, and also began writing to Clark Ashton Smith after Galpin and Kirk had lent him some of Smith's early volumes of poetry. All these men (except Crane, whom Lovecraft met sporadically up to 1930) became close and lifelong associates of Lovecraft. Naturally, the visit is not recorded in their surviving Lovecraft correspondence to Galpin, but echoes of it can be found in letters to others.

In 1923 Galpin became a fellow in Romance Languages at the University of Chicago. On 23 June 1924 he married a Frenchwoman, Lillian M. Roche (whom he called "Lee"), a junior at the University of Chicago. In June 1925 Galpin left for France, ostensibly to study French; but by this time he was becoming enraptured by music, and he devoted much of his time to its study. Lee objected to this change in Galpin's intellectual horizons and decided to return to Appleton; it was on her way home that she stopped off in New York, briefly meeting Lovecraft and his wife and later complaining that the room in which she was lodged for a night—an apartment in the boarding house at 169 Clinton Street where Lovecraft dwelt—was infested with bedbugs.

By this time the two men's friendship had cooled somewhat. Lovecraft, in 1927, expressed a certain bewilderment at the change in Galpin's interests when he noted, "The boy for whom I predicted the quickest success—a veritable infant marvel whose cerebral gymnastics left me beaten and amazed—has dropped literature altogether and is desperately studying *music* in an effort to become a composer . . ."[19] When Galpin returned from France in 1926, he became an instructor in French and Italian at Northwestern University; but

19. HPL to Zealia Brown Reed Bishop, 28 August 1927 (*SL* 2.161).

he remained devoted to music, notably piano and composition. In 1930 he obtained his M.A. in music at Northwestern, then spent a year (1931–32) in Paris; but this time when he returned, in the midst of the Depression, he found no position available to him at Northwestern, so he went on to Appleton and took a job at Lawrence College.

Galpin reports that the letters from 1932 onward probably survive in their entirety. It was at this time that Galpin, although having destroyed many Lovecraft letters a few years earlier, decided to reestablish contact. He found Lovecraft a changed man, and one gains the impression that Lovecraft found Galpin changed also—and perhaps not entirely for the better. The philosophical discussions of 1933–34 seem to reveal an impatience on Lovecraft's part at Galpin's growing mysticism and emotionalism, a far cry from the steely intellectual sharpness that Galpin had exhibited a decade earlier. As with many other correspondents, Lovecraft expatiated upon the economic and political situation in the nation and the world, but there is little here that we do not find in other letters of the period. Galpin continued to display intellectual vagaries, producing in 1936 a detective novel—first titled *Death in D Minor* and later *Murder in Montparnasse*—as a means of gaining income while continuing to pursue his musical studies. Although August Derleth—then already a published author of mysteries—reviewed the manuscript and suggested several changes that Galpin evidently made, it was submitted to only one publisher and then shelved when it was rejected. The manuscript does not appear to survive.

Galpin was working on several musical compositions when he learned of Lovecraft's death in March 1937. Accordingly, he titled one of these pieces "Lament for H.P.L." Set in the unusual key of B major, it is a haunting and touching rhapsody. In 1977 Galpin, by then having moved to Italy and married an Italian woman, played the composition during the course of an international conference on Lovecraft. It is, certainly, one of the most distinctive tributes to Lovecraft's passing that any of his colleagues ever paid.[20]

The Lovecraft–Galpin relationship is unique not only for its intellectual substance but also for the literary works that it spawned. Aside from the "Damon" poems, "Nathicana" (a poem on which the two associates apparently collaborated), and *Alfredo*, we must cite Lovecraft's "Old Bugs" (1919), a whimsy written to warn Galpin not to indulge too strongly in liquor prior to the onset of Prohibition. For Galpin's part, we have "Marsh-Mad," "Selenaio-Phantasma," and one installment of "The Vivisector," a column published under the house-name Zoilus in the *Wolverine*. (The other four installments were all written by Lovecraft, as correspondence between Lovecraft and Hor-

20. The piece has now been recorded (in a performance by Daniel Evan Walczak) on the CD *Fungi from Yuggoth* (Nampa, ID: Fedogan & Bremer, 2015).

ace L. Lawson, editor of the *Wolverine,* makes clear.[21]) Galpin's Zoilus column
discusses Lovecraft's "Facts concerning the Late Arthur Jermyn and His
Family" at length, and is one of the more insightful early assessments of
Lovecraft. About a year later Galpin became embroiled in the heated contro-
versy between Lovecraft and amateur writer Michael Oscar White over the
merits of Samuel Loveman's poetry, contributing a pungent article, "A Critic
of Poetry," to the *Oracle* (August 1923). Galpin's devotion to Clark Ashton
Smith's work impelled a substantial review of *Ebony and Crystal* (1922) and
Sandalwood (1925), published in the *United Amateur* (July 1925) under the title
"Echoes from Beyond Space."

Alfred Galpin may not have achieved the fame Lovecraft once predicted
for him, but he remains one of the most astute and perceptive of Lovecraft's
colleagues, and his writings—particularly his memoirs of his association with
Lovecraft—attest to his perspicacity and creative fertility. His accomplishments as writer, philosopher, teacher, and musician are far from insignificant,
and he would deserve remembrance even if he had done nothing else than to
inspire the engaging letters contained in this volume.

Adolphe de Castro (1859–1959) was no amateur associate of Lovecraft; he
came into contact with him only in the mid-1920s, and as a consequence of
Lovecraft's work as a professional "revisionist." Many purported facts about
de Castro's long life have proven to be erroneous, chiefly because of his own
exaggerated claims, some of which are reflected in his letters to Lovecraft.
But pioneering work by Chris Powell[22] has illuminated several aspects of his
life that had remained obscure.

De Castro was born Abram Dancygier in Poland on 6 November 1859,
the son of Sephardic Jews. Exactly when he adopted the name Gustav
Adolph Danziger is unknown, but in 1883 he emigrated to the United States,
and by late 1884 he had settled in San Francisco. At some point over the next
few years he came in touch with Ambrose Bierce, then the leading journalist
and critic on the West Coast, who was writing both his chilling tales of supernatural and psychological horror (as well as his acclaimed stories of the
Civil War) as well as fulminating against politicians, poetasters, and other tar-
gets in an array of articles in the *San Francisco Examiner.*

Danziger persuaded Bierce to engage in a number of collaborative ventures, few of which ended successfully. First, he presented Bierce with a
rough translation of Richard Voss's novella "Der Mönch von Berchtesgaden"
(first serialized in *Vom Felz zum Meer* in 1890–91 and later published as a

---

21. "I enclose Galpin's review of *The Wolverine,* written at your request." Horace
L. Lawson to HPL, 19 September 1921 (ms., JHL).
22. See Chris Powell, "The Revised Adolphe de Castro," *Lovecraft Studies* No. 36
(Spring 1997): 18–25.

book). Bierce saw promise in the work but felt Danziger's English was in substantial need of revision, and so he undertook to correct the text. *The Monk and the Hangman's Daughter* was serialized in the *San Francisco Examiner* on three consecutive Sundays (13, 20, and 27 September) in 1891, then published as a book in October 1892 by the Chicago firm F. J. Schulte & Co.

Danziger then persuaded Bierce to join him in establishing the Western Authors Publishing Company. This venture proved to be little more than a vanity press for the two writers, as it issued Bierce's first poetry collection, *Black Beetles in Amber* (1892) and Danziger's story collection *In the Confessional and the Following* (1893). But the two partners quickly fell out over the slim profits of the enterprise, and Bierce soon walked away from it. Although Bierce and Danziger had some relations over the next decade or so, Bierce refused to engage in any business dealings with his erstwhile colleague; George Sterling remarks pungently that on their last meeting (probably around 1903), Bierce broke a cane over Danziger's head.[23] Lovecraft, who had his own frustrations with Danziger, was endlessly fond of repeating this anecdote.

Danziger was fond of making much of his influence in the realm of politics and diplomacy. And while he did serve as vice-consul of the United States in Madrid in 1903–04, that was pretty much the extent of his official functions in the U.S. government. In 1921 he legally changed his name to Adolphe de Castro, taking the surname from a remote Portuguese ancestor. The suggestion that he changed the name to ward off prejudice because of his German-sounding name is rendered unlikely by the three-year gap between the end of World War I and the name change.

In late 1927 de Castro established contact with the bookseller Samuel Loveman, and in response to de Castro's plea that he needed someone to revise certain literary projects Loveman directed him to Lovecraft, as he had done for Zealia Bishop a few months earlier. Among the projects de Castro asked Lovecraft's help on was the revision of several stories in his *In the Confessional* collection. Lovecraft found de Castro's fiction quite poor but could not turn away the prospect of much-needed revenue, even if (as in this case) the revision amounted to wholesale rewriting. That winter he revised the story published in *In the Confessional* as "A Sacrifice to Science." Lovecraft retitled it "Clarendon's Last Test," and it was published in *Weird Tales* (November 1928) as "The Last Test." Lovecraft remarked acidly that "I nearly exploded over the dragging monotony of [the] silly thing,"[24] but his own version is not

---

23. ". . . he once broke a cane over the head of a friend who had become a friend no longer." George Sterling, "Introduction" to *In the Midst of Life: Tales of Soldiers and Civilians* (New York: Modern Library, 1927), v. Later (p. x) Sterling explicitly identifies this "friend" as Danziger.

24. HPL to Frank Belknap Long, [December 1927] (*SL* 2.207).

without monotony and prolixity of its own. To add insult to injury, Lovecraft received only $16 for the revision, whereas *Weird Tales* paid de Castro $175.

Even before Lovecraft had finished work on "The Last Test," de Castro was urging him to help him with a book-length memoir of Ambrose Bierce. De Castro had spent the years 1922–25 in Mexico, editing a weekly newspaper. Bierce had disappeared in Mexico in late 1913, and de Castro began informal investigations as to what might have happened to him, actually speaking to Pancho Villa (then one of the three political and military leaders involved in the bloody Mexican Civil War) and soliciting some ambiguous comments from him about the fate of the American writer. On the basis of this and other information, de Castro wrote the article "Ambrose Bierce as He Really Was" in *American Parade* for October 1926 (see Appendix).

Exactly how much of de Castro's memoir of Bierce was actually written at this time is unclear. The revision of such a document was a much more difficult proposition than merely revising a story, and Lovecraft was properly reluctant to undertake the task without advance payment of $150. De Castro, being hard up for cash, could not assent to this; so Lovecraft turned him over to Frank Belknap Long, who was getting into the revision business himself. Long offered to do the revision for no advance pay if he could write a signed preface to the volume. De Castro agreed to this, and Long did what appears to have been a very light revision—he finished the work in two days. This version, however, was rejected by three publishers, so that de Castro came back to Lovecraft and pleaded with him to take over the project. Lovecraft again demanded that de Castro pay him $150 in advance, and once again de Castro declined. He appears then to have gone back to Long. The book did in fact come out—with how much more revision by Long, or anyone else, is unclear—as *Portrait of Ambrose Bierce,* published by the Century Company in the spring of 1929 and with a preface by "Belknap Long." Lovecraft claimed to take a sardonic satisfaction in the bad reviews the book received.

By this time Lovecraft had revised a second story from *In the Confessional,* entitled by de Castro "The Automatic Executioner" and retitled (and entirely rewritten) by Lovecraft as "The Electric Executioner." It is not clear how much Lovecraft received for this revision, but it was published in *Weird Tales* in August 1930. Both of these stories include references (mostly whimsical) to Lovecraft's evolving myth-cycle; in "The Electric Executioner" the names are slightly altered (e.g., Yog-Sototl) to reflect the Mexican or Mayan setting of the tale. At some point Lovecraft revised a third de Castro story, "In the Confessional," but this revision has been lost.

Lovecraft continued corresponding with de Castro for the remainder of his life, although he refused to engage in any revision. In 1934 de Castro had grandiose plans for a treatise on Christianity entitled *The New Way;* but Lovecraft, examining de Castro's notes to the volume, rightly criticized it for being far out of date in terms of its scholarship on central issues in the development of early Christianity.

Lovecraft had one last personal contact with de Castro in the summer of 1936, when the latter, still mourning the death of his second wife, Georgina Sterling McClellan (1880–1935), came to Providence to seek solace from Lovecraft and the young R. H. Barlow, who was visiting at the time. On 8 August the three men went to St. John's Churchyard off Benefit Street to write acrostic poems (not sonnets, as the poems only had thirteen lines) on the name of Edgar Allan Poe. All three poems have their merits, but de Castro industriously sent his to *Weird Tales*, where it was published in the May 1937 issue. Lovecraft and Barlow then sent in their poems, but the editor, Farnsworth Wright, only wished to publish one such poem. Their own poems appeared in fan magazines.

Adolphe de Castro comes across as something of a charlatan; but, for all his occasional boasting of imaginary accomplishments, he was a man of real learning (he knew five or six languages) and, in at least one instance, sound scholarship. E. P. Dutton published *Jewish Forerunners of Christianity* in 1903, apparently an authoritative book on the subject. De Castro continued occasional publishing ventures on his own, including books of poetry and other matter, with the Western Authors Publishing Company as late as 1950. He died, about eight months short of his one hundredth birthday, on 4 March 1959.

—S. T. JOSHI
DAVID E. SCHULTZ

A Note on the Texts

The texts of the letters to Alfred Galpin are derived from manuscripts at the John Hay Library of Brown University. The postcards herein are held privately. Seven known postcards to Galpin are noted, based on a listing of them at the Wisconsin Historical Society. The actual postcards have not been found. Two of the three letters to Alfred Galpin and Frank Belknap Long, Jr., exist only in the form of transcripts of Lovecraft's letters prepared by Arkham House for use in publishing *Selected Letters*. Apparent transcriptional errors in the latter have been silently corrected. Seven letters to the Gallomo will appear in another volume.

Lovecraft letters to John T. Dunn, Edward H. and E. Sherman Cole, and some of those to Adolphe de Castro, as well as de Castro's letters to Lovecraft, are all held by the John Hay Library.

The works by Galpin derive chiefly from the amateur publications in which they first appeared; the manuscripts of unpublished items are found in the John Hay Library.

Acknowledgments

The editors and publisher are grateful to Robert C. Harrall, of Lovecraft Holdings, LLC, for permission to publish the letters by Lovecraft contained in this book, and to the John Hay Library for granting permission to publish autograph letters by Lovecraft and unpublished works by Galpin. They also wish to thank Mike Horvat, Jean Rainwater and Christopher Geissler of the John Hay Library, Patrick Harrigan, and Brian Showers for their assistance in locating information in rare publications. We are also grateful to Stefan Dziemianowicz, Douglas Ellis, Kenneth W. Faig, Christopher M. O'Brien, J.-M. Rajala, and David Tribby for their assistance. Special thanks to Martin Andersson for his rigorous proofreading.

Abbreviations

AdC	Adolphe de Castro
CE	Lovecraft, *Collected Essays*
CF	Lovecraft, *Collected Fiction*
EHC	Edward H. Cole
JTD	John T. Dunn
LL	S. T. Joshi, *Lovecraft's Library: A Catalogue*, rev. ed.
SL	*Selected Letters* (Sauk City, WI: Arkham House, 1965–76; 5 vols.)
ALS	autograph letter, signed
AHT	Arkham House transcripts
JHL	John Hay Library, Brown University (Providence, RI)
NAPA	National Amateur Press Association
TLS	typed letter, signed
UAPA	United Amateur Press Association

Edward H. Cole

Letters to Edward H. and E. Sherman Cole

[1]   [TLS]

598 Angell St., Providence, R.I.,
November 9, 1914.

Mr. Edward H. Cole,
    Somerville, Mass.,
Dear Sir:—

    Permit me to thank you for the large bundle of OLYMPIANS[1] and other papers received this morning. Since joining the United Amateur Press Association[2] I have met with frequent references to your scholarly work, and lamented the fact that I had seen no specimens of it.

    After a perusal of your critical and historical prose, it is with difficulty that I can refrain from fulsome comment. The uniform force, clearness, and dignity of your style place it above any other amateur prose which I have ever seen, and offer a pleasing contrast to the affected familiarity and almost clownish levity of the majority. I sincerely hope that you will place my name on the mailing list of your truly admirable magazine.

    The article on criticism in the March OLYMPIAN[3] is just now of particular interest to me, since I am soon to enter on my duties as official critic in the United, possibly as Chairman of the Board of Public Criticism.[4] It is not likely that my first efforts on the critical board will attain the high standard which you set, yet I hope that I may not win your unqualified condemnation. My aim shall be for justness, simplicity, and charity, rather than for brilliancy or the display of literary attainments, and I shall look upon your own luminous reviews rather as models than as objects of rivalry.

    While I can scarcely expect my laboured prose and ponderous heroic couplets to meet with approbation from one so correct in his tastes, I shall await with eagerness the impartial verdicts of the REVIEWER on several literary attempts of mine which are shortly to appear in various amateur publications. My ideal in English literature is the restoration of eighteenth-century dignity and regularity both in prose and in verse; an ideal which very few share with me, and which will probably provoke much caustic sarcasm from critics both official and unofficial.

    Most of my writing is outside the domain of amateur journalism. I am an ardent amateur astronomer, and contribute a regular monthly article on the heavens to The Providence Evening News.[5] I enclose two recent specimens, which I hope will not offend your exacting eye, though no doubt they fall sadly short of excellence.

    Trusting that you will pardon this tedious letter from one unknown to you, and hoping that I may in future be favoured regularly with THE OLYMPIAN,
    I remain

Yours truly,
H. P. Lovecraft

Notes

1. One of several of EHC's amateur journals.
2. On 6 April 1914.
3. EHC, an installment of his "The Reviewer's Club."
4. UAPA President Dora M. Hepner appointed HPL to replace the previous chairman of the Department of Public Criticism, Ada P. Campbell, who had resigned. His first column was "Department of Public Criticism," *United Amateur* 14, No. 2 (November 1914): 21–25 (*CE* 1.14–18). The issue appeared a month or so after the cover date.
5. HPL contributed 53 columns to the [Providence] *Evening News* from January 1914 to May 1918, as well as columns to other papers; HPL probably enclosed "The October Sky," 45, No. 113 (30 September 1914): 6, and "The November Sky," 45, No. 139 (31 October 1914): 10.

[2]   [TLS]

598 Angell St., Providence, R.I.,
November 23, 1914.

Mr. Edward H. Cole,
    Somerville, Mass.,

Dear Mr. Cole:—
            It was with the keenest enjoyment that I received your letter of yesterday, and learned of your desire to meet the Providence amateurs in person. I am sure that the members of the local club will be highly gratified by a visit from one so distinguished in the art which they have just commenced to cultivate. The new club intends to hold its meetings at the close of each month, so that it will probably assemble within the present week. I am by this post notifying Pres. Basinet of your intended visit, and instructing him to supply you with all necessary details regarding the time and place of meeting; which I myself do not know as yet. For my own part, I shall be delighted to meet you face to face; my knowledge of the prominent amateurs has hitherto been only through correspondence, so that I have come to consider them almost as impersonal or abstract beings.
    I sincerely hope that you will not be disappointed by the local organisation. As Miss Hoffman has doubtless informed you, the members are recruited from the evening high school, and are scarcely representative of the intellectual life of Providence. Their environment has been distinctly plebeian, and their literary standards should not at this time be criticised too harshly. Most of the members seem very much in earnest, and filled with a sincere thirst for

knowledge. I regret very much that I cannot take a more active part in their affairs, and emulate Mr. Moe's work in connection with the Appleton Club;[1] but I am practically a nervous wreck, unable to attend to anything regularly, or to keep definite engagements. The easy irresponsibility of the letter-writing amateur's lot is largely what renders the press association so suitable for me. I have offered to criticise privately all the work of the local members, and to assist them in preparing their credentials for entrance into the U.A.P.A., but they seem rather slow in responding. Since they are as yet almost complete strangers to me, residing in distant and unfamiliar parts of the city, I have not been very closely in touch with them.

Their President, Victor L. Basinet, is a socialist of the extreme type, whose opinions have been formed through contact with the most dangerous labour agitators in the country. He is, however, a man of much native intelligence, and I strongly hope that the influence of the press association may help to modify his conception of society. The Official Editor, John T. Dunn, is a wild Irishman with the usual offensive Popish and anti-English views; but he is of very fair education, and fired by real literary ambition. Of course, there is much frivolity in some of the members, which detracts slightly from the dignity of the meetings. Both Basinet and Dunn are deeply interested in the history of amateur journalism, and I can give assurance that you will have an appreciative audience if you choose to favour them with remarks on that subject.

The circular of the National Association which you enclosed in your letter increases my respect for that body. I notice that in THE OLYMPIAN you are inclined to place it much above the United in dignity and merit, yet I have been told that the latter is animated by a far kindlier spirit, and is now largely freed from the feverish political activity that formerly distracted both associations. Politics is my especial bane. Some amateur journals I have seen are more like campaign pamphlets than literary magazines. I joined the United through Mr. Daas, who, though unknown to me, probably found my name attached to some stray piece of verse in the back of a magazine. After some correspondence he asked as a favour that I refrain from entering the National till I should acquire more information concerning the history of amateur journalism; wherefore I remain as yet strictly a United man.

I find the Critical Bureau of the United in a disheartening state of chaos. No reviews have been published since last March, and no critic save myself has been definitely appointed. My position as Chairman depends on the probable resignation of last year's Chairman. I have had no instructions whatsoever, but have independently attacked the problem in wholesale fashion, sending to The United Amateur five closely typewritten pages covering every amateur journal in my possession which appeared since March. Under such conditions, I must ask the indulgence of my brother reviewers if my first attempt be no more than what Ovid calls

"————rudis indigestaque moles;
Nec quidquam nisi pondus iners; congestaque eodem
Non bene junctarum discordia semina rerum".[2]

Some of my creaking couplets have this day appeared in "The Pinfeather",[3] published by the new club at Rocky Mount. When I view them with my critical eye, I find difficulty in abstaining from that severity which I usually deplore in reviewers. One might be inclined to wonder why I try to dabble in numbers when I can produce no better results than this, but I suppose a strain of native perversity is responsible for such futile pursuit of the Nine.

Asking your pardon for the length of this tiresome letter, and hoping to behold you in person at the next meeting of The Providence Amateur Press Club,
I remain
Yours very truly,
H. P. Lovecraft

Notes

1. HPL's colleague Maurice W. Moe had organized the Appleton High School Press Club in Appleton, Wisconsin.
2. Ovid, *Metamorphoses* 1.7–9. As a youth, HPL translated these lines as "a raw unfinish'd mass / Of ill-join'd seeds, congested in one place" (*AT* 25).
3. "To the Members of the Pin-Feathers . . ."

[3]   [TLS]

598 Angell St., Providence, R.I.,
December 14, 1914.

Mr. Edward H. Cole,
    Somerville, Mass.,
Dear Mr. Cole:—

I was much disturbed by my failure on Saturday evening to establish the truth of my contention, that the urban life and language of pre-English Britain was thoroughly Roman in character. I have since ransacked my library in search of evidence on this question, and feel impelled to make known to you the result of my recent researches.

Two text-books, Quackenbos' "Composition and Rhetoric", and Spalding's "English Literature", completely sustain your opinions, whilst Prof. Lounsbury in his "History of the English Language" adopts a less decisive tone, and states of the Latin tongue in Britain, that "It was without doubt chiefly confined to the educated classes, and to the dwellers in cities".[1]

The preponderant mass of evidence, however, seems to favour my original view, and to suggest that the speech of southern Britannia would have been a Romance language, had not the Teutonic invaders eradicated every trace of the native or Romano-Celtic institutions. The following citations which I have marshalled up in my defense are all from acknowledged authorities whom I think you will consider deserving of attention. The underscorings are mine.

(I.) FROM THE ENCYCLOPAEDIA BRITANNICA, ART. "ENGLISH LANGUAGE" (9th Edition) By Sir James A. H. Murray, LL.D., Editor of the "New English Dictionary".

"The long occupation of South Britain by the Romans (43–409 A.D.)—a period, it must not be forgotten, equal to that from the close of the Middle Ages to the present day, or to the whole duration of Modern English—familiarised the provincial inhabitants with Latin, *which was probably the ordinary speech of the towns.* Gildas, writing nearly a century and a half after the renunciation of Honorius, addressed the British princes in that language; and the linguistic history of Britain *might have been not different from that of Gaul, Spain, and the other provinces of the Western Empire, where a rustic Latin giving birth to a neo-Latinic language finally superseded the native one except in remote and mountainous districts,* when the course of events was entirely changed by the Teutonic conquests of the 5th and 6th centuries."[2]

(II.) FROM THE "HISTORY OF THE ENGLISH PEOPLE", By John Richard Green, M.A. (Vol. I.)

"The work of civilisation followed fast on the work of the sword. To the last indeed the distance of the island from the seat of empire left her less Romanised than any other province of the west. The bulk of the population scattered over the country seem in spite of imperial edicts to have clung to their old law as to their old language, and to have retained some traditional allegiance to their native chiefs. But Roman civilisation rested mainly on city life, *and in Britain as elsewhere the city was thoroughly Roman.* In towns such as Lincoln or York, governed by their own municipal officers, guarded by massive walls, and linked together by a network of magnificent roads which reached from one end of the island to the other, *manners, language, political life, all were of Rome.'*[3]

(III.) FROM SHAW'S "OUTLINES OF ENGLISH LITERATURE".

"Such of the Celts as submitted to the yoke of their invaders acquired a considerable degree of civilisation, *learned the Latin language, and became a Latinised or provincial race,* similar to the inhabitants on the other side of the Channel. The other portion of the Celts, namely, those who inhabited mountainous regions, inaccessible to the Roman arms, and those who, refusing to submit to the invaders, fled from the southern districts to take refuge in their rugged fastnesses, retained, we may be sure, with their hostility to the invaders, their own language, dress, customs, and religion."[4]

I desire to call particular attention to the extract from Dr. Murray's article in the Encyclopaedia Britannica. My opinion is there upheld in every detail by a scholar and lexicographer whose decisions have meant much to the world of letters.

The other disputed matter, that of the literary propriety of the climax of "Her Wish",[5] has also claimed my attention. You will remember that I insisted on having met with a tale of similar conclusion in Poe; I have now definitely recalled the instance. It is "The Masque of the Red Death".

A party of revellers, shut up in the castle of the Prince Prospero to escape the plague, or Red Death, are holding a masked ball; when they suddenly behold a strange masquerader whose hideous costume is that of a victim of the dreaded pestilence. Animated by mingled emotions of fear and detestation, they pursue the apparition through the various chambers of the strangely furnished castle, till they overtake it in a black-draped apartment containing a huge ebony clock. Here the thing turns savagely upon the company, and the Prince falls dead. The assembled guests lay violent hands on the figure which proves to be no more than an empty mask and an untenanted bundle of grave-cerements.

"And now was acknowledged the presence of the Red Death. He had come like a thief in the night. And one by one dropped the revellers in the blood-bedewed halls of their revel, and died each in the despairing posture of his fall. And the life of the ebony clock went out with that of the last of the gay. And the flames of the tripods expired. And Darkness and Decay and the Red Death held illimitable dominion over all".

I here find no mention of any surviving witness, yet Poe has in some occult manner gained the fullest particulars of the gruesome tragedy. I think this story well establishes the right of the author of fiction to the possession of an unqualified omniscience.

In conclusion, I must express my sincere appreciation of your recent visit to Providence. Personal conversation with so active an amateur journalist has aroused in the local members a keener realisation of the nature and functions of the press associations, and has shewn to them an example which they may emulate, though they may not hope to equal. I trust that the acquaintance thus formed may from time to time be renewed.

Trusting that this continuation of the historical and critical discussions of Saturday may not prove too great a bore,

I remain

Yours very truly,

H P Lovecraft

Notes

1. The quotation is from p. 15 of Lounsbury's book.

2. 8.390–91.

3. I.32.

4. This passage is not in Shaw's *Outlines of English Literature* but can be found in *A History of English Literature*, p. 2.

5. Helene E. Hoffman, "Her Wish," *Olympian* (August 1914). HPL remarks of it in "Helene Hoffman Cole—Litterateur": "This brief tragedy of a Serbian and his bride is perhaps one of the very first tales written around the World War" (*CE* 1.229).

[4]   [ALS]

> 598 Angell St.,
> Providence, R.I.
> Dec. 28, 1914.

My Dear Mr Cole:—

I was pleased at receiving your letter of the 25th. inst., and shall await with interest the facts regarding Roman Britain which you may obtain from the most recent authorities. I shall not be idle on this matter, and intend to make a thorough canvass of the public library for more modern evidence. I remember a volume on the English Language by Prof. Skeat,[1] which ought to afford some illumination of these obscure points.

In considering your estimate of "Her Wish", I am less inclined to claim the victory. Certainly, there was no attempt at the wild unreality of Poe. However, the element of the supernatural seems suggested by the extreme *timeliness* of the fatal bolt. Otherwise we have mere melodrama.

I wonder if this story was suggested by the well-known incident of the death of the two lovers, John Hewit and Sarah Drew, in 1718, by the same bolt of lightning. This remarkable calamity, you will remember, inspired Pope to write the epitaph beginning:

> "When eastern lovers feed the fun'ral fire,
> On the same pile the faithful pair expire"—etc.[2]

I shall write more when I have consulted the volumes at the library, & shall meanwhile look for your own results.

Wishing you a very prosperous New Year,
I remain
    Your obedient Servant,
        H P Lovecraft

Notes

1. Walter William Skeat (1835–1912), English philologist. HPL probably refers to *An Etymological Dictionary of the English Language* (1882).
2. Alexander Pope, "On Two Lovers Struck Dead by Lightning" (ll. 1–2).

[5]   [ALS]

598 Angell St.,
Providence, R.I.
Feb. 4, 1915.

Mr Edward H. Cole,
    Editor, *The Olympian,*
My dear Mr Cole—

I must thank you sincerely for the latest "Boston Bundle" which centres around the Sept.–Feb. *Olympian.*

Your "confession of faith"[1] certainly leaves the reader with a very favourable impression of the N.A.P.A., yet you must admit that through Mr Moe's efforts, the United seems likely to receive a valuable influx of educators, & thus be still further removed from the domination of petty politicians.

The verses "To Hortense"[2] are immensely amusing. When I first looked at the second set of rhymes, I thought you had adopted "simplified" spelling, as exemplified in certain other amateur papers.

By the way—regarding the language of Romanised Britain, I find that the 11th edition of the Britannica (1910) retains Dr Murray's paragraph (as quoted by me) without change, proving that no very revolutionary discoveries can have been lately made in this field.

Thanking you again for *The Olympian* et al.
    I remain
        Very sincerely yours,
            H P Lovecraft

Notes

1. See Bibliography. HPL later wrote "A Confession of Unfaith" (1922).
2. Apparently a poem by EHC.

[6]   [ALS]

598 Angell St.,
Providence, R.I.,
May 13, 1918.

My dear Mr. Cole:—

My tardiness in replying to your welcome communication of 21st ult. has not, as you may imagine, been a retaliatory measure prompted by a similar sin on your part. It is, instead, the result of a most unfortunate combination of accumulated work and execrable health. Up to a week ago there lay before me a mountain of unanswered mail dating back to the middle of March. Since then, however, a transient wave of physical improvement has given me some mastery of the situation, and enabled me to indulge in epistolary pleasures hitherto denied.

I share your satisfaction at the present state of peace in amateur journalism, and hope it may not be confined to the present year and the present administration. Mr Davis[1] has been the only potential menace to inter-associational amity, and whatever harm he might do has been largely neutralised by the obvious air of eccentricity which permeates his utterances. One instinctively discounts what he has to say. His most singular attack in the "Summer" *Lingerer*[2] was made quite futile by its very absurdity, and though more than one person strongly advised me to answer it, I refrained from doing so—deeming the fallacies it contained a sufficient argument against the points it upheld. It refuted itself. I appreciate the consideration Mr. Davis has shown in abstaining from further warfare, and do not doubt his good intentions regarding the amateur cause as a whole. Other officials of the National are to be commended with unreserved enthusiasm, and I hope I may claim that the United has met them half way in a joint effort to abolish all friction. Each association has a great deal to concede. The United cannot logically deny the historical place of the National, nor can the National reasonably ignore the quality and standards of the United as maintained during the past half dozen years. *The United Amateur* this year is an irrefutable argument. I firmly believe that if the literary celebrities evolved by both branches of amateurdom since the "Halcyon Days" be carefully and impartially compared, the United will not suffer either qualitatively or quantitatively. But I must not wax controversial, or unwittingly mar the very peace of which I have just been boasting!

I regret that you cannot accept the critical post, but must of course defer to prior claims on your time & energy. The very boorish and puerile attack on the critical department made last year by Mrs. Haughton,[3] is yet echoing in the United. Miss McGeoch has sought to censor the reviews wherever she thought frankness got the better of amenity; and as a result of the discussion which ensued, Mr. Moe has decided that all amateur public criticism is vain, ineffective, and superfluous. He points out that the ordinary mind can never be influenced by mere advice, more or less mingled with flattery; and that on the other hand, real criticism arouses so much antagonism on the part of the subject that its purpose is entirely defeated. His reflections leave him but one conclusion—that official criticism should be abolished. I am slow to agree with a view so radical, and shall certainly take no steps to destroy the critical bureau. I am puzzled over the future—for I cannot possibly see how a satisfactory staff of critics can be assembled next year. The most willing are the least qualified.

My views on the survival and war-time maintenance of amateur journalism coincide in every detail with your own, as given in the *Bema*, your letter, and your still more recent contribution to the *National Amateur*.[4] I am making this matter the prime subject of my May official message, to be published in the *United Amateur*,[5] and may dilate upon it further in a special editorial I have been asked to contribute to the July *United Amateur*.[6] To call the institution of amateurdom a needless non-essential at a time when the very lightest & least purposeful forms of relaxation & amusement are patronised as psychological necessities, is a breach of logic too evident to require more than the simplest refutation. But as you say, the outward aspect of things must be altered. The soul and nucleus of the institution must be re-defined and distinguished from certain superficial trappings which many mistake for the vital fabric. For my own part—I believe I go further than you in this modification of conception. I believe that an amateur literary world might survive almost wholly without publications—correspondence, circulating MS. magazines, & the like serving to keep the Pierian flame in existence. However—we are not yet reduced to these straits.

If were [*sic*] are about to bid farewell to elaborate publications, the recent efforts of Mr. W. Paul Cook make the farewell a splendid one. I have never seen a recent publication more ambitious than the new June *Vagrant,* of which you have doubtless received a copy. A July issue—of lesser magnitude—will follow close on its heels.[7] I had the pleasure of a personal call from Mr. Cook not long ago, as he passed through this city on his return from the Fossils' annual banquet in New York. His devotion to the cause is certainly quite unsurpassed.

I note a marked revival in British amateurdom whose quality a few of the leaders are energetically seeking to elevate. Through Mr. McKeag I have joined the "Amateur Press Club", amongst whose members I design to circulate a typewritten MS. magazine.[8] As yet the literary tone of the society leaves much to be desired.

With best of wishes to you, to Mrs. Cole, and to the "new recruit", I have the honour to subscribe myself

Yr most obt humble Servt

H P Lovecraft

Notes

1. HPL refers to [Francis] Graeme Davis. See Glossary.

2. See JTD 14 and n. 2.

3. See AG 4n8.

4. *Bema* (January 1918) contained EHC's "The Current Year" and "Mutatis Mutandi."

5. "President's Message," *United Amateur* 17, No. 5 (May 1918): 96–97.

6. "President's Message," *United Amateur* 17, No. 6 (July 1918): 127–28.

7. *Vagrant* No. 7 (June 1918) contained HPL's "Nemesis" (pp. 41–43) and "The Beast in the Cave" (pp. 113–20); the July issue (No. 8) issue his "The Poe-et's Nightmare" (pp. 13–23).

8. This was *Hesperia*. HPL published Ernest Lionel McKeag's "The Prodigal" in the *Conservative* (July 1918).

[7]   [ALS] [To E. Sherman Cole]

598 Angell St.,
Providence, R.I.,
Jany 16—1919.

E. Sherman Cole. Eſq.,
East Dedham, Maſs.

My dear Sir:—

I beg to acknowledge with gratitude yʳ favour of 24ᵗʰ ult., & to
expreſs my regret at yᵉ tardineſs of my reply. It gratifies me to hear that *The
Martian*[1] is to become a permanent inſtitution, & I will venture to hope that a
ſecond number may reach me before Spring.

I note with much intereſt yʳ dietetick programme, and congratulate you
upon yʳ fortitude in continuing to exiſt without much Sugar; a commodity
whoſe abſence wou'd cauſe me to ceaſe eating altogether. Let me warn you
againſt partaking of any products ſo Hunniſh as "zwiebacks".[2] Who knows
but that theſe dry and choaking victuals are inſidious poiſons; prepar'd by yᵉ
Enemy to deſtroy our riſing generation?

Accept, Sir, my ſincerest ſympathy on yʳ ill-tim'd viſit to this planet. Verily, we are fellow-ſufferers in having arriv'd hither during so dull an age. In
one reſpect I am luckier than you; for my ſomewhat earlier birth enables me
to recall a time when free-verſe was ſcarce dream'd of, & ſimplify'd ſpelling
unknown. In another reſpect, however, you poſseſs yᵉ advantage of me; for
ſince my own choſen aera is irrevocably loſt in yᵉ departed paſt, yours lyes in
yᵉ future, & you have the chance of attaining it thro' the obſcure proceſses of
metempſychoſis or reincarnation.

Permit me to ſympathize alſo upon yᵉ queſtion of Celtick barbarity. The
leading characteriſtick of yᵉ Hibernian mind is unreaſoning inſolence; & I am
not ſurpriz'd that yʳ former landlord fought to impoſe upon you & yʳ father.
May you have better luck with his ſucceſsor!

Equal in inſolence to yᵉ Hibernians, yet favouring more of decadence
than of barbariſm, is that ſpecies known as *semi-homo aeſtheticus,* which dwelleth
upon yᵉ ſub-Arctick banks of yᵉ St. Lawrence. Many naturaliſts affirm, upon
evidence not altogether to be ignored, that this ſingular animal is a deſcendant
of yᵉ human race; even hinting that it is a degenerate branch of the Caucaſian
ſtock; but this latter ſtatement I conſider an unwarranted ſlander upon our
part of mankind. Personally, I am of opinion, that this rare genus (of which
but a ſingle pair is known to exiſt) is merely a variant of ſome obſcure quad-
rumanous ſtock, with morbid & unuſual cerebral development.

Permit me to congratulate you upon yʳ new molar, which will doubtleſs
prove of great ſervice to you for ſeveral years. You will need teeth very much
if you are to become a literary critick; since the preſent ſtate of literature calls
for much gnaſhing on yᵉ part of thoſe who ſurvey it.

I am flatter'd by the reception accorded yᵉ *Coöperative*[3] by you & yʳ gifted parents, & hope yᵉ next number may be view'd with equal leniency. 'Twill contain the beginning of a highly heated controverſy betwixt Prof. P. B. McDonald & my ſelf, regarding the claſsical element in modern literature.[4] McDonald hath not ſufficient reſpect for yᵉ legacy of antiquity, & muſt be vigorously combated, left his lax precepts undo all that hath of late been accompliſh'd in amateur journaliſm. The April *Conſervative* is likewiſe a practical certainty. The leading article will be a long eſsay by Mʳ· Jas. F. Morton, Jr., who hath lately been transferr'd from the status of an antagoniſt to that of a friend; whilſt the poetry of Samˡ Loveman, & poſsibly of A. Goodenough, will help give the journal yᵉ character of an "old-timers' number". Mine own contribution will probably be a lately-writ elegy on yᵉ greateſt man of this age; which will alſo appear (if yᵉ editor is kind) in yᵉ *Cambridge Tribune.*[5]

Speaking of my immortal works, I am moſt eloquently curſing Cook, Moloney, or whatever compoſitor ſet up my Roman eſsay & notes in yᵉ recent official organ.[6] In yᵉ main ſection yᵉ word *as* is left out betwixt yᵉ words *enjoyment* & *of* in yᵉ final paragraph; whilſt yᵉ notes fairly teem with Try-outiſms[7]—*Heroids* for *Heroides, Thiſtia* for *Triſtia, A. Livius* for *T. Livius, Rumianus* for *Ammianus, Severinno* for *Severinus,* &c. &c. This eſsay hath been mangled editorially, but yᵉ unabridg'd original will appear ſerially in yᵉ prohibition weekly, *The National Enquirer,*[8] whoſe associate editor, O. W. Stewart, ſhares my enthuſiaſm for yᵉ Eternal City & its civilization.

But I muſt cloſe, truſting that you enjoy'd a Merry Chriſtmas & Happy New Year, & hoping to ſee another *Martian* in yᵉ near future.

       Yʳ moſt oblig'd humble Servᵗ·

          H. Lovecraft

16ᵗʰ Jany. 1919.

over

P.S. Kindly convey to yʳ parents my ſincere appreciation of their recent work in *United* & *National Amateurs.* Yʳ father writes comprehenſively & pleaſingly of amateurdom's paſt, whilſt yʳ mother expatiates eloquently of yᵉ rhetorical virtues of Tully.

          H. P. L.

Notes

1. The *Martian* (1918–19) was a paper nominally edited by six-month-old E. Sherman Cole but in fact edited by his parents. See HPL's review of the October 1918 issue in "Department of Public Criticism" for November 1918 (*CE* 1.210–11); two later issues were reviewed in "Department of Public Criticism" for May 1919 (*CE* 1.233).
2. *Zwieback* means "twice-baked." It is a type of crisp, sweetened bread, made with eggs and baked twice, that originated in East Prussia.
3. *United Co-operative,* ed. by HPL, Winifred Virginia Jordan, and others. Three issues appeared: 1, No. 1 (December 1918); 1, No. 2 (June 1919); 1, No. 3 (April 1921). The ref-

erence here is to the first issue.

4. "The Case for Classicism," a rebuttal to an article, "A Criticism of Amateur Journalism," by Philip B. McDonald, a professor of Engineering English at the University of Colorado, appearing just previous to HPL's article (pp. 2–3).

5. There was no *Conservative* for April 1919, but an issue appeared in July. It contained "Song" by Samuel Loveman (p. 1), James Ferdinand Morton's "Touching on Euphuism" (pp. 1–4), and Arthur Goodenough's "The Joy of Books" (p. 6). Although HPL published four pieces by himself, none appears to be the "elegy" he described. HPL's "Theodore Roosevelt: 1858–1919" appeared in *United Amateur* 18, No. 3 (January 1919): 52. It is unknown whether the poem appeared in the *Cambridge* [MA] *Tribune*. HPL's uncle Edward F. Gamwell edited the *Tribune* from 1901 to 1912, but at this time he was no longer editor and had divorced HPL's aunt, Annie E. P. Gamwell. The paper did, however, publish HPL's elegy on his cousin in January 1917.

6. "The Literature of Rome."

7. I.e., typographical errors. Charles W. Smith's NAPA paper the *Tryout* was particularly plagued with such errors.

8. The essay did not appear in the *National Enquirer*, a temperance paper that did publish several of HPL's poems.

[8]   [ALS] [To E. Sherman Cole]

598 Angell St.,
Providence, R.I.,
March 19, 1919.

E. Sherman Cole, Eſq.,
        East Dedham, Maſs.

My dear Sir:—

        Pray accept my congratulations for the two meritorious iſsues of *The Martian* which I have just received, and which exhibit your literary & editorial genius as shining with accustomed splendour. I particularly appreciated your portrait, which reveals the brilliancy one might expect from a perusal of your published works.

        Allow me to express my unstinted approbation of your verbal predilections, as indicated in the most recent *Martian*. I have ever favoured the longer and more classical words of our language, & am delighted to find a kindred spirit so much my junior; who may effectively carry on the sesquipedalian tradition long after my generation shall have perished.

        Kindly convey to your mother my appreciation of *The Hellenian*, & to your father my regret that an *Olympian* did not accompany it. Typographically, editorially, & literarily, *The Hellenian* is a decided triumph, whose reviewing will afford the Department of public criticism much pleasure.[1] In reply to a query in the article "Two Americans", please transmit to the author my contrite admission that I have *not* perused Prof. Matthews' "These Many Years".[2] I am, however, highly appreciative of his work & genius apart from hetero-graphical monomania, & have frequently recommended his treatise on versi-fication to aspiring suitors of the Nine.[3] Should I summon up sufficient ener-gy amidst the prevailing worry caused by my mother's ill health,[4] I shall examine "These Many Years", and see what the veteran litterateur has to say for his attempt at linguistic deformation.

But I must close, lest I encroach too considerably upon your hours of studious retirement.

Accept, Sir, the renewed assurances of exalted consideration which can but inadequately be expressed by the feeble pen of

Your moſt humble, moſt Obedient Serv't

H. Lovecraft

Notes

1. HPL refers to the *Hellenian,* a paper edited by Helene Hoffman Cole (1893–1919). HPL reviewed the Autumn 1918 issue in "Department of Public Criticism" for May 1919 (*CE* 1.232–33).
2. "Two Americans" was a review by EHC and Helene Hoffman Cole of Brander Matthews's *These Many Years.*
3. *A Study of Versification.*
4. HPL's mother, Sarah Susan Lovecraft, was taken to Butler Hospital on March 13, 1919, after suffering what appears to have been a nervous breakdown; she would die there two years later.

[9]   [ALS]

598 Angell St.,

Providence, R.I.,

March 29, 1919.

My dear Mr. Cole:—

I have just been informed by Mr. Kleiner of the over-whelming bereavement which you have suffered, and feel impelled to offer without delay the deepest & sincerest sympathy.[1] Though words are at such a time inadequate, it may be at least a slight consolation for you to know that all amateurdom is unanimous in its realisation of the magnitude of your loss, and in its condolence with you for the grief which must be yours. The keenness of my personal sympathy is augmented by the present grave illness of my moth-er—which is teaching me to feel subjectively what I could hitherto but imag-ine objectively.

Such were the qualities & attainments of Mrs. Cole, that amateurs will re-gard her passing as a public calamity; feeling a profound independent sorrow in the loss of so valued a friend & so important a writer & co-worker. Her place in our circle was one not easily to be filled.

I trust that the shock may not affect your nervous system as adversely as

Kleiner's bereavement has affected his; for in your case a future extends ahead, demanding all the poise & vitality which you can command. In your son you possess a living demand for a recuperation as complete as is humanly possible, in order that you may give him that care & affection without which his mother would not wish him to be.

With renewed expressions of a sympathy deeper than language may convey, I remain

Most sincerely yours,
H P Lovecraft

Notes

1. EHC's wife Helene died on 25 March.

[10]   [ALS]

598 Angell St.,
Providence, R.I.,
April 8, 1919.

My dear Mʳ· Cole:—

I received your note of the 28ᵗʰ, which evidently crossed my own note to you, of similar date. I appreciate very much your thoughtfulness in writing at a time when the extremity of recent grief must have made any effort almost impossible; and shall welcome the longer communications of later date which you promise.

Seldom has any news more genuinely shocked & pained me than that of Mrs. Cole's death, as hastily sent by Mʳ· Kleiner. That one so plentifully endowed with talent and versatility should be taken so suddenly & at such an untimely age, seemed almost too tragic for credence. The shock, indeed, is shared by every correspondent who has learned of the event; and I doubt if amateur journalism has ever before been moved to sorrow more unanimously and profoundly.

The May issue of the *United Amateur* will be a special memorial number dedicated to Mrs. Cole; and will be filled with tributes both in prose & verse, from the pens of those best acquainted with her or with her work. The planning of the issue is the first real piece of activity on Kleiner's part since his own terrible bereavement destroyed most of his initiative, and its preparation will call forth the best efforts of many members. Among those requested to furnish contributions are Misses Owen & Hyde, Mrs. Adams,[1] Mrs. Jordan,[2] & myself. Kleiner will be represented by a poem, & perhaps by a brief prose article. I have been assigned a critical appreciation of Mrs. Cole's literary work as a whole, which will enable me to call attention to its author's unusually varied gifts & attainments, and wide range of reading.[3] No other amateur of this generation, I think, has delved into a greater number of little-known literary fields, such as that of South America. As a reviewer of books, none has deserved or received greater praise. It seems melancholy to receive in my mail, yesterday, a letter from a Western high-school teacher, who has not heard of the loss; whose chief theme was an encomium of the review in the recent *Hellenian.*

I trust that you are as well as might be expected under the circumstances, & that your small son is also keeping in good health. It would be needless for me to reiterate the sympathy which I feel for you both—I say both, because I am convinced that infants can suffer from a maternal loss far more than is generally realised. Not knowing what residential changes may be occurring, I am addressing this note to 36 Tower St.; for even if you are not there it will undoubtedly reach you through forwarding.

With every good wish, I remain
Sincerely yours,
H. P. Lovecraft

Notes

1. Edna Hyde (formerly Edna von der Heide), editor of the *Inspiration.* Olive G. Owen, editor of *Just Me.*
2. When Winifred Virginia Jordan divorced her second husband, Horace W. Jordan, later in 1919, she retook her maiden name, Jackson.
3. HPL, "Helene Hoffman Cole: Litterateur." He also wrote the poem "Helene Hoffman Cole: 1893–1919."

[11]   [ALS]

Old 598
Feby. 23[, 1923]

My dear Cole:—
Ecce! The product of Providence pocketbook & North Attleboronian typography emergeth from primordial darkness & taketh its place among the ages! A small scrap of paper, but a big scrap for Michael Oscar White! May I ask you to criticise this epoch-making venture for the Natl. Amateur? Slam me all you like, but spare me chee-ild—little Frank Long the prose-poet.[1]

I am indeed sorry to hear of the malady which hath so sorely beset you, & trust you are now on a decided physical up-grade. Your household deserves a long respite from the shadow of ill-health!

Concerning that other dark shadow, whose bat-wings flapped so menacingly above the bright lights of that elegant dining saloon where I was so mercilessly grilled, I am half convinced that the fates have saved me by giving to Mrs. A.[2] an unalterable resolution to continue her candidacy. At least, I received from her an epistle wherein, besides a two-buck cheque for the O. O. fund,[3] was distinct mention of a campaign requiring money, & of a prospective Adams-and-Liberty journal to be intitul'd *The Campaigner.*

So, as Ya-know-me-Al would put it—that's that! If Mme. Eve[4] & Bro. Mortonius choose to alter their deep-laid designs, I suppose I can't help myself; but just now it looks as though they were sailing ahead in fine shape, so that Fortuna will spare a victim whose (semi-)willingness to mount the scaffold hath been so conclusively demonstrated. But even so, I hardly look for utter chaos. Something's been started, & if the ball is well rolling by the nones of Quintilis[5] it will surely have enough momentum to keep on a while. It'll take a full year to wipe Mike White off the map—& you can be sure Long & Galpin won't stop till that's done! Still—me woid is gave, & if the Adams-Morton move is changed, I stand ready for the axe. May Pegāna protect me if Olympus won't!

I'm glad that Wise Bozo Sandy[6] is so well disposed, but hope I won't be call'd upon to justify his confidence!

As to an editor—I haven't had a second to reflect on the problem or even to write Mortonius. Work—work—how I abhor the word!—hath ingulph'd me, & even at this moment I ought to be writing the preface to a book whose editing hath been jointly undertaken by James Ferdinand & myself. Martin[7] isn't perfect—but what I ask is, 'oo th' 'ell is? I can't think of a soul, but if you have confidence in Horatius Lausonius,[8] I've no gigantic kick coming! After all, if worst comes to worst & I can't dodge the blamed thing, I'll endorse any editor you recommend. That's me—passing the buck! Responsibility is the one word I won't tolerate in my vocabulary.

I hope to see you at Bro. Lynch's rough party at the Hemenway next month. On the day following that I shall visit *Newburyport,* next in the series of ancient towns. Truly, as our XX-minute egg would say, I've gone nuts over quaint old burgs & dumps! I really believe I'm getting fonder of Colonial architecture than of any other type of art. I don't t'ink of nuttin' nowadays but has-been Noo-England, & de ol' shacks what dey put up in de 17th & 18th centuries. You sure will be slippin' me some favour w'en you puts me next to Concord & Lexington in de spring!

And now I will conclude, reaffirming my readiness for conditional martyrdom with the greater eloquence, as the prospect of sacrifice becomes less & less imminent.

Wishing you a quick return to the most perfect strength
    I am ever
        Yr most h'ble & obt Servt
           H P L

P.S. The Olympians in my poffeffion are the following: June, '09, Sept. '09, Nov. '13, Jany. '14, March, '14, July, '14, Aug. '14, Sept.–Feby., '14–'15, Octr. '17. They certainly whet my appetite for perusal of the reft!

Notes

1. HPL refers to the publication of the penultimate issue of his *Conservative* (No. 12, March 1923), and alludes to Long's "An Amateur Humorist." See letter 13n10.
2. Hazel Pratt Adams (1888–1927), elected president of the NAPA for 1923–24.
3. The Official Organ Fund, a fund that solicited contributions from amateurs for the printing costs of the *National Amateur* and *United Amateur.*
4. Apparently a reference to Hazel Pratt Adams.
5. I.e., 7 July, the date of the NAPA convention (at which time the new president and other officers would be elected).
6. Albert A. Sandusky.
7. Harry E. Martin, Official Editor of the NAPA (1922–23).
8. Horace L. Lawson.

[12]   [ALS]

Old 598

Feby 24. [1923]

Ave!

Well, here we are again, but with bad news for your cause! Just heard from Morton, & will have to say—much as it hurts to deal out a cruel wallop—that this presidency stuff is *finally & irrevocably "off".*

I find that J. Ferd. is completely & finally committed to the Adams candidacy, & that any other move would *now* be a positive act of hostility toward him. He is too far committed to withdraw without seeming traitorous to the Adams cause; a cause which he embraced because he knew how abhorrent office-holding is to me. At the time he proposed my filling out Dowdell's term, the job seemed so repugnant that only the strongest personal friendship induced me to consider it a second; & in the end I really took it only on the understanding that Morton would help me next year in the United, if I decided to make an effort to wipe out the Woodbee[1] gang.* Thus my later willingness to consider conditionally a second term—as evoked by the spell of your chrysostomic & forceful logic—seems to Mortonius a species of vacillation . . . . as no doubt it is. Certainly, my dread of the burden became no less; but I found it hard to resist an appeal so poignantly put to me!

But I am sure you can see how it is. And even if I had found it honourably possible to take the nomination, I would have made a very poor executive; for the majority of my closest literary associates would have been pulling against the idea all the time. It was hard enough to reconcile people like Gal-

---

*We discussed a possible rapport or federation of all three amateur organisations, with each in its proper & amicable place—a thing which of course necessitates the preliminary extirpation of the Columbus morons.

pin, Campbell, Long, &c. to even the fragmentary term; & a re-seating would have caused a veritable explosion. Damn it all—but it sure is hard to be obliging when obligations tend in such diametrically opposite directions!!

However, as I said before, I believe that the Adams arrangement will agreeably surprise you. Mrs. A. is certainly a capable routine administrator, & Morton assures me that he stands firmly in the background as an inspiration & intellectual influence . . . . . not that he uses those words, which from him would be less becoming than from another! He will continue whatever policy is started this term—& Mrs. Adams is heartily ready to act as a sympathetic standard-bearer. Don't worry—there'll be enough provocative literary matter in the amateur press to keep things healthily moving, no matter who is president! It's the solid membership that really counts—watch the Victorians & Tennyson-hounds snap at my new *Conservative* editorial![2] And if Tracy will give me as good rates as he did this time, *Conservatives* won't be so damn rare. By the way—here's a go! I'll *promise*—as a private citizen—to publish *The Conservative* if *you* will publish a paper![3] Issue for issue—how's that?

Really, what amateurdom needs is to get away from the *official* idea—to ensure a spontaneous & diffused activity which shall render policies independent of the whims of the dumbbell majority of voters who install Tom, Dick, & Harry each year. It is absurd that a set of titled puppets should disturb a current of literary activity which ought to be above technicalities & red tape—we should try to depend less & less on the official board, lest we repeat such tragedies as that which overtook the United last July. If we looked, for our leadership, to *a few privately issued papers* instead of to an official organ whose policy is at the mercy of the politicians & the rabble, we should have a stability beyond the power of electoral whim to impair. If I had the money, I would assemble a group of clever men & try to make *The Conservative* such a fixed rallying-point. Indeed, I'm not sure but that some day I'll try to collect a gifted circle who can spare cash enough to ensure *a regular & voluminous coöperative paper of the highest quality, which shall gradually replace the United & National Amateurs* as a nucleus of literary activity. When I do try, you'll certainly hear of it—for such a thing wouldn't be complete without Olympian participation! We have no pineapples today[4] . . . . nice people!

So that's that. As I say, I certainly hate like hell to seem unaccomodating; but when I carefully survey the present situation, I become unswervingly certain that any attempt to introduce my candidacy this year would not only not help, but would actually cause irrevocable disaster by splitting the ranks of well-disposed amateurs & creating an opening for shrewd undesirables. So as our little classicist hath it—"Lay off, bimbo; lay off! Dey ain't nuttin' to it—see?" ¶ But I hope to apologise more eloquently when I see you—assuredly, I crave your most profound tolerance! // Yr most obt hble Servt H P L

Notes

1. The Woodbees, an amateur journalism group in Columbus, Ohio, which included Ida C. Haughton, Leo Fritter, and others. It published a paper called the *Woodbee*. This group had become hostile to HPL's "literary" circle in the UAPA.
2. See "Rudis Indigestaque Moles": "The average amateur paper . . . is unique in its allegiance to the accepted art and literature of the past; and in its happy oblivion regarding the menaces offered by the present and future. To read such a paper one would gather that Tennyson and Longfellow are still taken seriously as poets" (*CE* 2.63). HPL continued his attack on Victorian poetry and aesthetic standards in the "In the Editor's Study" column of July 1923.
3. HPL's *Conservative* for July 1923 was the last to be published.
4. HPL alludes to "Yes! We Have No Bananas," a novelty song by Frank Silver and Irving Cohn from the Broadway revue *Make It Snappy* (1922). It became a major hit in 1923 (number 1 for five weeks). See also EHC 14.

[13]   [ALS]

Home, James!

7th March[, 1923]

Your Double Ex-cellency: (how I envy you that first "ex"!)

        May all the exceptions of earth & Pegāna attend all res tonsilares, & ensure your august presence at the Donnybrook Fair av Maarch the Tinth![1] I'll be there—diis et via ferrea volentibus[2]—& (with exceptions aforemention'd) will avail myself unblushingly of the Roselandic hospitality so generously offered by your household. Yes—I shall hit the Hub rather early, & would be transported with joy at Colean companionship in the modest itinerary I have planned—an itinerary, by the way, which if successful will land you surprisingly near your own domestick hearth. In short, I design (an 't please your worship) to drag you first to the near-colonial abode of the Soc. for the Pres. of N. E. Antiquities—the Harrison Grey Otis house in Lynde St.—where, arm'd with kind words from (a) the old bimbo in charge of the Royall house at Medford, and (b) the well-disposed Salem spinster who makes placcques & has careless clerks, I hope to persuade the Big Cheese in charge (one Dowe, if memory plays no tricks) to issue me a passport to that highly exclusive Cooper-Austin dump (1654) in Linnaean St.[3] in your own Septentrional section of classick Cantabrigia.[4] Of course, I shall lap up whatever collection they sport around the H. G. O. joint, & may try to sandwich in an antique or two between then & the time we dive down into the elevated; but I mean to wind up at said Cooper-Austin, at whose exterior I so longingly gazed last Decr. And—sad thought—if they won't give me no passport— why, then I'll probably wreck the antique society's hangout & get sent to gaol, so that I'll be no further trouble to you as host.

But—if you know any better itinerary, don't hesitate to substitute it. This one of mine will keep—for Boston is a conservative burg.

[As to the time of arrival—I guess I'll try the 11:00 a.m., which gets to the S. Sta. (or is supposed to) at 12:27. The next one doesn't hit S. S. till 1:49. But no! That would bust up your dinner—so I'd better make it 1:49 after all.]⁵ Take your time at the Georgian cafeteria—pick your teeth 'n' everything—& blow into the Sou-Sta at *1:49*, ascertaining the correct track from the bulletin board in the waiting room. Then prepare for a long wait. Too bad you can't do Newburyport Sunday—I haven't yet had time to hear whether Kid Davis can.⁶ These old burgs certainly do captivate me. I'm even going to see a cinema thing called "Java Head" on the strength of the knowledge that it's from a novel of Old Salem.⁷ But in May we must do the thing more seasonably— vivat Concordia!

Now about this amachoor stuff—I'd hate to tell ya the unholy joy I feel at being let off from that second sentence of 365 days on top of the original one of half that extent!⁸ I could sing with the boidies of spring—if I hadn't a reputation for ponderous melancholy to live up to! But for Pete's sake, pray don't blame the Morton-Adams bunch for getting in the way, for their intentions are of the best. Even now they'd quit if they felt I really *wanted* the beastly job, but knowing how I abhor it, they feel (as I do) that their present course is best. Mrs. A. is dolefully afraid I have placed her in a position where you will blame her for obstructing progress—a fear of which I hope you will, for my sake, most cordially disabuse her!

Good work, them 3000 woids! I've held you up as a shining example of self-sacrificing industry & devotion in the March pres. message.⁹ I hope you chanced to include *The Brooklynite*, for I've been asked to see that a decent share of criticism falls to that worthy effort. Here's hoping your candour won't start a dozen new feuds—but at that, it's all right s'long as they're literary feuds. I've been coping with some bitternesses of less impersonal kind among others, so that I've let myself out quite savagely in the message against "pernicious personalities." If Martin prints my message uncensored, he'll print your report in like fashion! Something seems to tell me so.

But I hope you were not too hard on my poor little chee-ild Frank Belknap! Remember the title of his article—"An Amateur Humorist".¹⁰ It was meant primarily *not* as Lovemanic defence—S L needs no defenders—but as an attack on a dense & visionless critic who should be taught not to meddle in aesthetic realms beyond his own narrow, hard-fact, literal, prosaic, commonsense, feet-on-the-ground, unimaginative, obsolescent Victorian dog-kennel . . . . or I should say monkey-house in deference to Belknapian metaphor. Long revealed the natural disgust of a sensitive & widely read mind at the provincial pomposities & academic asperities of a conventional & bigoted Irishman bred in one narrow & now dying literary tradition. If you want to see what Long says when he really makes Loveman his theme, wait till you see his essay now in manuscript form![11] But never mind—criticism doesn't hurt Long as it does Loveman. The kid is 100% Anglo-Saxon, & Anglo-Saxons fight instead of faint! Later on you'll see Galpin's anti-White article, & I doubt if you can object to that. Alfredus is a hard little egg—the real 20-minute, don't givadam sort—& he withers our alabastine bog-trotter in a few well-chosen & scholarly words, without any purple paragraphs or simian tropes. That essay is coming out in the June *Oracle*[12]—yes, Michael Oscar sure did start something when he tried to measure Aonian art by bourgeois standards!

I certainly am sorry to hear of all the cumulative ills from which you have suffered, & sympathise most acutely regarding that pain. Last week I was myself all in—nervous exhaustion & continuous sick headache—so that for a long interval I could do nothing but loll around in easy chairs & take medicine.

A week ago Tuesday I had an amateur visitor in the form of one Vincent B. Haggerty, old-time politician. Tho' not a literary luminary, he impressed me as an amiable, pleasant, & altogether wholesome person. He spoke of visiting Boston Sunday—didst see him?

Preparatory to attending the Hub riot, I shall tomorrow witness Mr. Sheridan's excellent comedy, "The School for Scandal", as presented by a local stock company.[13] I last saw it in 1777, at the Drury-Lane Theatre. Having this January witness'd Mr. Gay's "Beggar's Opera", I consider my current share of 18th century drama not inadequate; tho' I cou'd well wish for more.

I appreciate all that you say concerning the cost of publishing activity— alas, most poignantly after contemplating a large *Conservative*. I'll confer later anent that co-operative journal—which reminds me—have I ever given you a copy of my last *United Coöperative?*

I hope Sister hasn't swallowed anything as tough as my last letter—that for her sake. For my sake I hope she didn't swallow the list of *Olympians* I so carefully made out! Enclosed is my Home Brew Horror—first instalment— together with a picture of our friend Kleiner from the same dignified periodical.[14] Needn't return—I have a raft of 'em! ¶ Hoping to see you Saturday, as soon after 1:49 as the ailing N Y N Y & H permits, I remain

                Yr most obt Servt

                    H P L

P.S. Can you get me a laureate judge of essay?

Notes

1. For the meeting of the Hub Club. HPL chronicled the event in "The Feast: (Hub Journalist Club, March 10, 1923)."
2. "The gods and the railroad [lit., 'iron road'] being willing."
3. Actually the Cooper–Frost–Austin House (1681) at 21 Linnaean Street in Cambridge.
4. I.e., the northern part of Cambridge, MA.
5. HPL has crossed out the section in brackets.

6. HPL visited Newburyport with Edgar J. Davis (age fifteen) of Haverhill, MA (see HPL to Samuel Loveman, 29 April [1923]; *MWM* 501–02).

7. *Java Head* (Famous Players/Paramount, 1923; silent), directed by George Melford; starring Leatrice Joy, Jacqueline Logan, and Frederick Strong. Based on the novel by Joseph Hergesheimer (New York: Alfred A. Knopf, 1919).

8. HPL refers to his decision not to run for president of the NAPA (as recounted in his letter to EHC of 23 February [1923]), after having served as interim president upon the resignation of William J. Dowdell.

9. HPL, "President's Message," *National Amateur* 45, No. 4 (March 1923): 4–5. HPL wrote: "The public work of the Bureau of Critics has been admirable and every member should honour the example set by Mr. Edward H. Cole, who contributed 3000 words while suffering from painful illness" (*CE* 1.327).

10. Frank Belknap Long, Jr., "An Amateur Humorist," *Conservative* No. 12 (March 1923): 2–5, a defense of Loveman's poetry against the attack made upon it by Michael White. EHC criticized Long in the "Bureau of Critics" column of the *National Amateur* for March 1923. HPL discusses the controversy in "In the Editor's Study," *Conservative* No. 13 (July 1923): 21–24.

11. Long's essay was intended to be a preface for a planned Loveman issue of the *United Amateur*. The issue was never published.

12. Alfred Galpin, "A Critic of Poetry." See Appendix.

13. HPL to Samuel Loveman, 24 March [1923]: "Thursday, March 8, seemed quite propitious—we made an 18th century day of it, seeing Mr. Sheridan's new comedy, 'The School for Scandal', eating in a restaurant in a building standing during George III's reign, & winding up by seeing the cinema of 'Java Head'" (*MWM* 489).

14. Referring to the first installment of "The Lurking Fear," titled "The Shadow on the Chimney." Rheinhart Kleiner's photograph appeared on p. [1].

[14]   [ALS]

The Eternal 598
9th June[, 1923]

Ave, Magne!

      Permit me, first of all, to make a modest addition to the list of journals whose dissection you are about to undertake! You are the only critic who can justly handle this bimbo, since I edited it, Samuelus heads it, & John Clinton Pryor is amateurically asleep. Into thy hands . . . . & for Pete's sake be at least moderately merciful! I note the rest of the list with interest, & hope you will also let Loveman know what you are doing, since he—instead of I— will tackle the residue. But stay—I'm a sport—I'll send the 2¢ stamp & tip him off myself!

      Now anent the trip . . . . omnia sunt OK. Gratefully do I anticipate the proffer'd Thurs–Fri hospitality & subsequent guidance, & vividly do I previsualise the r. b. which s. the f! Too damn bad you'll be held in Lynn Thursday aft., since Bozo Al had planned a triangular dinner for us before the meeting. Perhaps it'll yet be possible if not planned for too early an hour. Let Sandy know, & he'll let me know.

Yes—I guess the meeting sure will be hot dawg! We'll have to organise a Sanduskian party to battle the Lyncian despotism . . . . . . Aitch against Haitch; Saw against Seen!

I have—by some miracle—actually heard the new Sanduskese ballad anent the noble banana![1] It hath an appealing tune—which I recall virtually *in toto*—but sadly enow, the literary half escapes me. So unless Fate directs my steps in Woolworthian or Kresgian paths ere the meeting, my part in our musical trio will have to be exclusively instrumental . . . . . . whistling, or imitation of a jazz cow-bell. Yes—instrumental in making night hideous that we fools of nature may horridly shake our dispositions with shrieks beyond the reaches of our voices. Sweet Ad-ah-line[2]—we have no pineapples today!

Concerning Presidential burthens . . . whoopee! School's nearly out! Oh, baby, maybe I ain't weavin' some chaplet of funereal blossoms to adorn me joy-flush'd brow! And amidst my roseate visions I pause to raise a toilworn hand to Heav'n, as I murmur in sepulchral sincerity NVMQVAM. RVRSVS.! CREDE. MIHI![3] And then some.

Not an half hour ago I perform'd the last *rites* by shooting Martin ten pages of priceless bull—my July message[4]—and I'll enlighten the empyrean it sure was superheated Skye-terrier for giving hell to the apostles of the commonplace! Anticipating an Adamic administration of approximate acquiescence in the milder nugae of *la vie celebrale,* I gave the whole field of commonplace, matter-of-fact normalcy such a hyper-Menckenian razz that I'm half in doubt whether Henricus Edvinus will print it! I'm kinda ending up with a bang—getting violent & idiosyncratic again in my old age. And Oh, Boy, what I shot at White & his satellites in the section on criticism . . . . decorously camouflaged with the colours of impartiality, secured by giving an equal roast to an imaginary modern who attacks the conventional as stupidly as Michael Oscar attacks the imaginative! It's a great life . . . . & thank the crystalline spheres it's almost over. Ya kin tell it is by the sprightly way I'm cavorting around despite my increasing years & girth.

Some time this coming summer you will behold your pious fellow-preceptor Maurice Winter Moe, who is to take a pedagogical course in the aestival department of King's College, in New-York, & plans to make a lateral excursion to Boston, in the Province of the Massachusetts-Bay, if he can find a week-end host to save him a tavern reckoning. I shall be exceedingly pleased to inspect in person this veteran correspondent, whom I have known so well yet so invisibly since the fateful year of 1914.

But the hour advances, & the taper burns low. I must save tallow against my coming trip to town! Be it my good fortune, then, to see thee at the young Donnybrook fair next Thursday—or slightly anterior to that event if you &

Albertus can arrange for a vespertine coenatic session.
Until that blessed day—pax vobiscum!
Thine oblig'd & obt Servt
H P L

Notes

1. Sandusky's "new ballad" is unidentified. About Sandusky, HPL wrote "Bless the child. He wields a curious influence over me, for who else could have taught me to chant with jocose abandon, 'the contemporary shortage of the noble banana'," referring to the song "Yes We Have No Bananas." Quoted in Edna Hyde, *Oracle* 4, No. 3 (May 1924).
2. "Sweet Adeline" (1904), a song by Henry W. Armstrong (1879–1951), with words by Richard H. Gerard (1876–1948).
3. "Never again! Believe me!"
4. "President's Message," *National Amateur* 45, No. 6 (July 1923): 4–6.

[15]   [ALS]

598—
30 Septr [1923]

Ornatissime et doctissime:—
I will resist, Sir, that tendency toward the hackney'd playfulness of the petty wit, which might impel me to address this epistle to Mifs Margery Louise Cole; a kind of insipid humoursomeness which I fell into (I think) upon the advent of Edward Sherman.[1] Instead, I will extend the unaffected congratulations of unfeign'd benignity; & exprefs the hope that all three are doing well: mother & child, & the father upon his own cooking. It is ever the part of the exemplary citizen to sustain with equanimity his share in the production of the coming native generation; a responsibility so reprehensibly shirkt by some, that the foreigners are like to ingulph us in but a few years unless checkt by legislation & the Ku Klux Klan. And as Juvenal of old remarkt:

"..... Non possum fere, Quirites,
Graecam urbam; quamvis quota partis precis Achaei?
Jampridem Syrus in Tiberum defluxit Orontes,
Et linguam et mores et cum tibicine chordas
Obliquas nec non gentilia tympana secum
Vexit ...."[2]

Therefore, I approve & rejoice at the news of this latest jewel in your crown: and assure you, that you will be amply repay'd for all the asperities of your present month of isolation by the consciousness of having upheld the dignity of your race, & deserved well of your country.

Regarding the matter of pedestrianism, I wou'd put you in mind, Sir, that my touch of fatigue during our ambulation toward the Wollaston coach was but transient: that it pafs'd away upon my taking a glafs of toddy at the tavern, & that at its worst 'twas not half so great as the oft-exprest exhaustion of our brother Moe. Moreover, the next day had nothing to do with the case; since the point at issue is merely that of stoical fortitude upon a particular occasion. I will own, that last week after the departure of Mortonius I slept 4 stretches of 21, 11, 13, & 12 hours each, before feeling wholly my self again; but I defy you to discover any mark of weariness before the end, or any evidence of it betray'd to my learned companion. For the nonce I had put physical nature behind me, & was resolv'd to enjoy the diversities of pedestrian adventure without the limitations of corporeal fatiguescence; the which I accomplisht by falling into an aetherial condition of objective insensibility. But, Sir, I will absolve you from the imputation of fragility, upon attending your explanation of last month's excessive exertion; & will take upon my self that culpability, which belongs to myopick & unreflective adjudication.[3] I will furthermore put the invincible Mortonius in mind of your great atchievements of four years gone; at whose recollection I am confident he will amend that hasty calumny, which superficial appearances lately led him into.

I need not affirm the gratification I shall experience, when Fortune will permit you to visit Rhode-Island & engage with me in a trial of locomotive endurance amongst its manifold antiquities. I am conscious that the archaick effects in these regions are not always obvious to the indifferent passenger, & that to discover & absorb the best of them 'tis needful to employ a guide. On that account I am studious of conducting you hither my self; for I am closely familiar with most of the colonial reliquiae, & can shew you whole streets & vistas of Georgian edifices; the which can not be found in any part of Boston, save Beacon-Hill & Louisburg-Square, as introduc'd to my grateful vision by your self. I regret that the intervention of expansive territory forbids us to partake of joint expeditions in these your days of partial leisure; for truly, I shou'd relish the task of compleating your fashionable education by taking you on the Grand Tour of departed aeras. For mine own part, I have a new tour in mind when next I visit the Massachusetts-Bay; an inspection of certain antient mansions in Jamaica-Plain, as reported to me by my new grandson Victor Bacon, late of the Hub Club, but now about to depart for St Lewis, in New-France. This child hath just sent me, as a gift, a most marvellous book about those towns of Old England, from which the towns of New-England were nam'd.[4]

I am not astonisht that you, like my small grandchild Belknap as exprest in his prose-poem "Ingenue",[5] "prefer the pathetick cry of the penguin at dawn, to the cinema". In truth, it wou'd be remarkable if that popular form of exhibition were in any manner less absurd than it is, since for commercial reasons (the extream cost of hiring players & constructing scenes of great elaboratene∫s) it must be suited to the grovelling taste of the mindless & promiscuous rabble. There would be, Sir, scarce any advantage in making a picture with any intelligence in it; because such wou'd forfeit the patronage of the general, whilst failing to attract a like number of rational beings: & all men are equal at the box-office. It is of course remotely po∫sible, that some compromise cou'd be created; for tho' the herd reject the depiction of life, they may scarce be thought to demand those particularly absurd & clamorously un-idea'd distortions & contradictions of it, which the playhouses obtrude upon our vision. But we here encounter another consideration which dispels alike perplexity at the present, & hope for a future, condition. I mean the need for a large number of plays, which if they are to have as much as an idea apiece, wou'd demand a considerable company of skill'd writers, whose monetary remuneration cou'd not be other than substantial. Now, Sir, since the only business value of such full-brain'd persons wou'd be to preserve the patronage of the intelligent, & since the intelligent form so slight a part of the paying publick; is it not the part of greater astutene∫s to rest content with the indolent imbecilities of the Grub-Street & puppet-show train; confident that what audience they lose, is but a slight drain as compar'd with the sums that wou'd have to be payd real authors & clever showmen? The tragedy you so vividly report, is indeed a conspicuous improvement over the insipidities of the Grecian drama; where even amidst the excitations of the Aeschylus, no murther cou'd be done in the people's sight, but must be sav'd for the moving dithyrambs of choragic eloquence.

And now, Sir, I rise to the defence of my illegible hand, which I take to be a true mark of that genius which despises the trivialities of meer perspicuousness. Are you not, Sir, sensible that the peerless Galpinius possesses a script scarce more decipherable? I will go to the length of inclosing one of his communications (to be return'd) in proof of my statement, & as a specimen of that lordly contempt for the obvious, which hath ever been the mark of superior parts. Had my waste-basket not recently been empty'd, I cou'd shew you a writing above any you have ever seen in chaotick obscurity; that of amateurdom's most unique & irascible upholder, the Rt. Hon. Robert L. Roosma-Le-Cocq, (pro tem) departed presidential candidate in the B.A.L.A.[6] However, I shall some day surprize you with an epistle you can peruse; for a new ribband hath lately gone on my typewriter, (it is inanimate, but natheless fond of ribbands) which so excites it that it speaks very blackly & emphatically indeed. I last night dedicated it in the writing of an anonymous puff for my Belknap-grandchild, to be publisht in Mr. Lawson's "Zoilus" department.[7] Of my accuracy upon the writing machine it is not my place to boast. That I will leave to your own judgment when I address you in that medium.

With a grandsire's blessing on all your house—old & new—I am, Sir, Ever
Yr most obt hble Servt
H P L

Notes

1. Margery Louise Cole was EHC's daughter by his second wife. HPL also refers to the letters he wrote to Cole's son, E. Sherman Cole, in 1919.

2. Juvenal (D. Junius Juvenalis, 60?–140? C.E.), *Satires* 3.60–65: "I cannot abide, Quirites, a Rome of Greeks; and yet what fraction of our dregs comes from Greece? The Syrian Orontes has long since poured into the Tiber, bringing with it its lingo and its manners, its flutes and its slanting harp-strings: bringing too the timbrels of the breed" (tr. G. G. Ramsay).

3. See EHC, "Ave atque Vale!" (1940): "To this day I recall vividly the Saturday afternoon in July, 1923, wen Lovecraft, Maurice W. Moe, Albert Sandusky, and I went to Old Marblehead to visit the numerous colonial houses and other places of interest with which Howard was thoroughly familiar. He was so insistent that our friend from the West [i.e., Moe] should not miss a single relic or point of view over lovely town and harbor that he walked us relentlessly for miles, impelled solely by his inexhaustible enthusiasm until our bodies rebelled and, against his protests, we dragged ourselves to the train. Lovecraft was still buoyant" (*LR* 101).

4. See Bibliography under [State Street Trust Company, Boston].

5. Frank Belknap Long, Jr., "Ingenue," *National Amateur* 45, No. 5 (May 1923): 7.

6. Robert L. Roosma-Le Cocq, British amateur journalist, editor of *Le Cocq's Comment*, and candidate for the British Amateur Literary Association.

7. HPL wrote most of the six columns of "The Vivisector," published in Horace L. Lawson's amateur journal the *Wolverine* between June 1921 and Spring 1923. No further columns are known to have been published. HPL may be referring to his anonymously published article "The Work of Frank Belknap Long, Jr."

[16]   [ALS]

259 Parkſide Ave.,

Brooklyn, N.Y.,[1]

July 21, 1724.

Dear E H C:—

       I apprehend, Sir, how great a churl you will adjudge me by reason of the uncourteous silence I have observ'd since receiving your welcome congratulations; that, or else you will have conceiv'd me to have been compleatly undone by that state of matrimony, to which I have hitherto been so great a stranger. But, Sir, I wou'd have you know, that I have had neither the indifference of a boor nor the oppressions of a martyr; having instead been sunk in such a plethora of labour, that the agreeable offices of fraternal amity have perforce languisht in neglect.

       Well, Sir, you behold me at last in the sober & conservative state of a settled householder; as Georgian as ever, & as resign'd to the pleasing chains of wedlock as was ever any elderly & rotund country-gentleman. I am reduc'd to a state of the most compleat obedience; & never respond to a connubial admonition but by saying, in the most domestick manner imaginable, "Yes, My Dear!"

That I am so far remov'd from the Province of the Maſsachusetts-Bay is in truth a source of regret to me; & I hope that I may before long share with you & Bimbo Sandy some of those pedestrian *feats,* (paronomasia not intended) for which you & he last year shew'd so phenomenal an aptitude.

But you must not fancy me by any means sever'd from that Colonial antiquity which is so considerable a part of my vital essence. On t'other hand, I dwell in the midst of a venerable New-Amsterdam whose elder & labyrinthine streets each day reveal to me some new relick of better ages. With doorways as old as any in Salem, I am in continual contact; & you wou'd perceive how much in mine element I am, cou'd you but observe me threading my way about Georgian alleys in Greenwich-Village, or in the now squalid hill districts nigh the piers of the great bridge to Brookland-Parish. Flatbush, where I dwell, is a very old village founded by the Dutch; & I have but to walk a few steps from my door, to behold a 1796 steeple rising above the very quaintest of churchyards.

When I was in Philadelphia, I took a very great delight in the old edifices there; doting in particular upon that cluster of which Independence-Hall (as the rebels say) is one. The interior of this harbour of Yankee treason is one of the finest I have ever seen, whilst the whole region is admirably fitted for the contemplative enjoyment of such a mellow old gentleman as I.

Whenever you plan a coach or sailing trip to New-York, pray let me know, that my wife & I may pay you our respects. Shou'd you be here on a Thursday evening, you wou'd be made highly welcome by that little hebdomedal club of humoursome gentlemen call'd The Boys, which consists of such congenial souls as James F. Morton, Jun., Everett McNeil, Gent., Rheinhart Kleiner, Esq., Frank Belknap Long, Jun., Arthur Leeds, Esq., & yr obt servt. Our discussions are truly classick—at least in heat & verboseness.

With the sincerest compliments of Lady Theobald & myself to you, Lady Cole, Viscount Sherman, & the Hon. Sister & Marjorie, I am, Sir,

     Ever yr moſt oblig'd obt Servt—

          H P L

[*On envelope:*] P.S. Ill news! Just after sealing this epistle I learn that our Aonian friend R. Kleiner, Gent., hath been knockt down by an horseless chaise, & quite seriously tho' not dangerously injur'd.[2] He yet keeps to his bed, & I am certain he wou'd appreciate a consolatory line from you if you have time thus to alleviate the monotony of his accidental distemper. He hath had three stitches taken in his forehead—stitches in time, we are happily assur'd by the most ingenious & respectable doctors of physick.

Notes

1. At the time, following HPL's marriage to Sonia H. Greene, the Lovecraft's were living at what had been Sonia's residence.
2. See HPL's "[On Rheinhart Kleiner Being Hit by an Automobile]."

[17]　　[ALS]

nota optime　　　169 Clinton St.,
Brooklyn, N.Y.,[1]
Feby. 24, 1925

Theobaldus Carboni S.D.

　　　　　　　　　　　　I am not, Sir, deaf to those pricks of conscience* which apprise me how flagrant is my delay in answering yours of August last; but being of a cheerful & sanguine temper, I venture to entertain an hope of your forgiveness; in view of the plenitude of distracting circumstances which have lately ingulph'd me. In fine, the times have drawn heavily upon both my leisure & my energy; so that betwixt the tumult of household migration & the infelicity of my wife's illnesses—which have twice driven her to an hospital, tho' she is now better—my correspondence hath suffer'd a decline from which I am now stoutly endeavouring to extricate it.

　　My removal hath brought me to the venerable district of Brooklyn-Heights, the original village of Brooklyn, where stately rows of mellow brick & brownstone crown a steep bluff overlooking the harbour, & produce scenick effects not unlike those of Beacon-Hill or the Back-Bay. Our quarters are on the second floor of a plain brownstone edifice three squares up & back from the water—& on the floor above dwells another of the sacred circle—George Willard Kirk, Esq., bosom friend of Loveman, who migrated hither last summer. Loveman himself came in September, & has also secured lodgings in Brooklyn-Heights; taking a magnificent chamber in Columbia-Heights, whose bow-window commands the entire harbour panorama, & the faery skyline of lower Manhattan.

　　Your remarks on contemporary amateurdom are distinguisht by an uniform justness & acuteness, & I wish I might be able to do more than correct the prevailing inertia. It was a disappointment to me last summer when I could not follow up that May *United Amateur* with the requisite activity, & I am even now planning an issue in which the chief matter will be a particular appeal for the carrying on of the work whose prime burthen I can no longer sustain.[2] Alas for the days of yore! There was no convention, & in default of a replacement I suppose the old board is still in office—if there be still either

---

*I don't mix drinks, but metaphors are something else again

office or association. With which statement I will quit a subject so potent in the arousing of painful reflections.

When am I going to Virginia? Well, Sir, unless Fate conspires to make brokeness more broke, I shall set foot in that commonwealth on the 12th of April next, when several of our circle—Kleiner, Kirk, Loveman, Long, & perhaps Morton—plan an inexpensive one-day excursion to Washington, D.C.[3] I shall dispose of the city proper in those dull dawn hours betwixt the arrival of the train & the opening of the day's business, saving the best of the soujourn for the Colonial shades of Alexandria, & the story'd corridors of Gen. Washington's seat, Mt. Vernon. I am sensible how considerably the Georgian architecture of the South differs from that of New-England on the one hand, & from that of the Middle Colonies on the other; & am anxious to behold in person those particular features which I have hitherto seen only in portraitures. Since writing you, I have made several explorations in the regions adjoining New-York, & have found many striking reliquiae of the elder time. The towns of New-Jersey are all replete with pleasing specimens—Newark, Perth-Amboy, Somerville, & Elizabethtown, the latter being almost as colonial as Salem, & having still standing the brick mansion of His Majesty's Governor, Jonathan Belcher, Esq., a native of your Province of the Maſschusetts-Bay who likewise govern'd that colony (tho' with much unpopularity) before his advent to New-Jersey. I likewise spent, last November, many delectable days in Philadelphia & environs, putting up at the Y M C A & dividing my explorations systematically into towns of the various sections. In the area of the original urban Philadelphia—from the Delaware river to 7th or 8th st (or 15th st., if we allow for the later 18th century & early 19th) & from Christian St. on the south to Poplar on the north—there is still standing an amazing array of Georgian architecture; including not only many churches & publick buildings, but vast reaches of intersecting alleys just as they were in Dr. Franklin's day. Most of the latter are now negro slums, but one section has been restored in the Greenwich Village fashion, housing art shops, tea-rooms, & studios, & presenting a fair idea of what the town used to be. In this district—which centres in the confluence of Camac St with Chancellor & St James Sts.— stands the shop of the Centaur Press, which is publishing Loveman's critical volume on the late Edgar Saltus.[4] Another sort of Philadelphian exploration deals with the sumptuous colonial country-seats in the suburbs. I visited the mansion of the eccentric Dr. Bartram (1731) & other scattered estates, & made a complete round of the splendid manors in what is now Fairmount Park—these lordly piles being situate on high bluffs overlooking the crystal bends of the winding Schuylkill. One day I arose before dawn, & watched the sunrise from the terraces of Belmont, a house built in 1750. Below me were the bends of the river, & far off to the east rose the towers & steeples of Philadelphia. As the heavens paled, the town stood out in ethereal silhouette across the gorges of the river; & finally the red disc appeared, gilding the scene with a charm whose potency is hard for any save the poet to describe. The latter part of my sojourn I devoted to the ancient suburb of Germantown, founded late in the 17th century by Dunkards & Moravians at what was then a vast distance from Philadelphia, & (tho' now within the city limits) having absolutely nothing in common with that town in atmosphere or architecture. The place suggests New England—gambrel roofs, houses at odd angles with the streets, &c.—& but for the prevalence of *stone* construction might easily be taken for some thriving village on the Massachusetts North Shore. Naturally, I spent much time at its historical society—or "Site & Relick Society", as 'tis call'd—as indeed I did at the corresponding society in Philadelphia proper. Both museums are fill'd with marvellous reminders of other & better days. The sojourn was all too short—& I mean to go again when circumstances permit. Especially do I long to explore the supernally lovely valley of the Wissahickon, a wooded gorge surpassing in scenick value anything I have ever beheld elsewhere, not excepting Quinsnicket-Park in Rhode-Island or the Middlesex Fells in Maſsachusetts. I obtain'd but a taste of it, and am resolv'd to see it all on some future occasion. As to the relative value of the colonial architecture of Philadelphia & New-England, I may say that I deem the mansions of Philadelphia best in the broad arrangement & proportioning of the general mass, but markedly inferior to New-England houses in fineness of detail, especially as to doorways. I can still say that Chestnut St., Salem, presents the most splendid aggregation of doorways which I have ever seen.

Speaking of travel—Bozo Al did not wholly forget his Grandpa Theobald on his late-summer peregrinations; but furnisht welcome comment on the quaint architecture of New-France, & a pictorial representation of a worthy if not quaint structure in His Majesty's Province of New-Hampshire. I've just answered the child—& I hope that he, as well as you, can forgive an old gentleman for a delinquency caused only by adverse Fate.

And speaking of adverse Fate—commiserations on the tonsil siege! Though I can't speak from experience, my wife can—& her sympathy is enhanced by the shadow of a future trial—modification of nasal septum—to occur when the weather gets warmer. Oh, yes—& Kleiner! The boy lived . . . . . & so far as we can see, he is very much the same as before. The gent whose motor hit him gave him a consolatory purse of gold—which the rapacious bookstalls infesting this metropolis quickly ingulf'd.

Our Thursday meetings—now changed to Wednesday to accomodate an evening college class attended by our juvenile member Long—flourish as of yore. George Kirk, rare book expert from Cleveland, now shines in our midst; & there frequently twinkles among us the dainty Wheeler Dryden— dear boy—who can't yet understand the difference betwixt free-will & determinism, & who punctuates every philosophical argument with the repeated asseveration that, 'of course, y'know, he doesn't think Gawd is a nice old gentleman with long w'iskers!'

And good ol' Mortonius! Note that I give him a separate paragraph—for his latest achievement deserves it. Out in Paterson, New-Jersey, (to make a rambling beginning) there is a publick library owning a certain number of oddities which it wants to display in proper fashion. Last summer it decided that it ought to form a *museum*—to be the municipal museum of the town & eventually to rise to greatness in a separate building of its own beside the library building. To think was to act—& a date was set for a civil-service examination wherein aspirants might contend for the honour of being first curator & growing up with an infant industry. Of this exam our Jamie heard through the lady (sister of the librarian) from whom the B.P.C. Hikewaukas rent their cottage for their annual Labour-Day outing—& steeling his sensitive nerves, he took the test. Well—god bless his omniscience—he passed, & now he is a real, live museum head![5] The work is hard, but his spirit is strong; & we are all confident of his ultimate success. His first job is to arrange the exhibits in the stable of a place next the library, which place was purchased with a proviso that the seller—an antique citizen of about 85—be allowed to finish his earthly span undisturbed in the house. When the old gink croaks, the museum will overflow from the barn to the residence; & in later years the trustees hope to tear down both house & barn & erect a modern museum building. But anyhow, Little Ferdy is a regular curator, & our circle all regard him with awe, & tell one another about how 'we knew him when . . . .' Yes—one museum is surely going to be conducted with parliamentary precision!

With which climax—appropriate if not staled by previous relation from other sources—I will lay down my pen, transmitting as I do so my sincerest compliments to you, Lady Cole, & all the smaller if not less effulgent sparks. I regretted not reaching Boston last summer, & hope the future will be kinder to me, even to the extent of permitting me to end my days on the soil of my native Novanglia.

> Believe me, Sir,
> Yr most hble obt Servt
> H P L

Notes

1. HPL moved into this apartment on the last day of 1924 and stayed there until he returned to Providence in April 1926.
2. HPL refers to the *United Amateur* for July 1925, the only issue published during the 1924–25 term. It contained HPL's "Editorial" (*CE* 1.354–55), pleading for a revival of amateur activity.
3. Only George Kirk and HPL made the trip.
4. Loveman had written a critical study of the work of American novelist Edgar Saltus (1855–1921) in 1924, but the publisher abandoned plans to publish the book after the manuscript had already been prepared.

5. HPL refers to Morton's curatorship of the Paterson (NJ) Museum. See "The Call of Cthulhu" (1926): "I had largely given over my inquiries into what Professor Angell called the 'Cthulhu Cult', and was visiting a learned friend in Paterson, New Jersey; the curator of a local museum and a mineralogist of note" (*CF* 2.44).

[18]   [ALS]

10 Barnes St.,
Providence, R.I.,
Dec. 24, 1931.

Dear E H C:—

The good Lord will reward yuh, Mister! Your appreciated iron man brings the regiment up to 21—attributable as follows:

Tilden ----------------- 5.00[1]
Wylie ------------------ 5.00
Morton---------------- 5.00
E H C ----------------- 1.00
W P C ----------------- 1.00
H P L----------------- 1.00
Moe-------------------- 1.00
Murphy --------------- 1.00
Spink ------------------ 1.00

Many outlying districts are yet to be heard from, & I have no doubt but that by New Year's we shall be able to make the magnificent gesture. Smithy's independence—which was extended to almost brusque refusals of type donations in the past—is now reliably reported to be tempered with reason.[2] The spirit of the times, as it were. However, I shall not fail to employ my small maximum of tact & easy nonchalance in passing on the fruits of the campaign. I shall, of course, make it clear that the gift constitutes no attempt to bias his editorial policy—none of the contributors, so far as I know, being a candidate for political support! Assuredly I shall try to turn your cheque to gold before the granite of Quincy crumbles. Paper is damnably flimsy in these days, & even gold itself is getting dubious. I think that, at bottom, good old-fashioned barter is the only sure thing. Next time I shall ask all gifts to be expressed in basic commodities—salt, steel ingots, coal, petroleum, &c. &c. &c. But I shall request a colleague to attend to the minor details of transportation, exchange, &c. Perhaps you, as a Quincyite, might pay in blocks of granite.

You have certainly had your share of indisposition, & I trust the jinx will begin a long layoff in or before 1932. I've been rather more flourishing than usual during the autumn, owing to the singularly benign temperatures. No doubt the next few months will be cold enough to reduce me to my customary hiemal lassitude.

Boston seems to agree with good old Culinarius, for he continues in better health than I have ever known him to enjoy over a corresponding period. Have you seen his new quarters at 7 Hancock?[3] Same landlord, & not very far from the former dump; but a vast improvement both structurally & environmentally. Harrison Grey Otis house in sight from his front steps—which, by the way, bear a genuine foot-scraper.

Again calling the blessings of heaven down upon your head, & extending the customary felicities of the festive solstitial season,

I have the honour to subscribe myself

Yr most oblig'd, moſt obt Servt

H P L

Notes

1. Leonard E. Tilden (1861–1937), veteran amateur journalist of New Hampshire, and later Washington, DC.

2. HPL and his colleagues were taking up a collection to give money to Charles W. "Tryout" Smith so that he could buy badly needed new type for his press.

3. I.e., 7 Hancock St., Boston.

[19]   [ANS postcard][1] [HPL and W. Paul Cook to EHC]

[Postmarked Boston, Mass.,
2 January 1932]

Behold what a miracle a warm & rainy week-end hath wrought! Grandpa dragged out of hibernation, & embarked upon a gay round of museum-absorbing with the observant & appreciative Culinarius. Today—just to get warmed up—we cleaned out the Cantabrigian group . . . . . Germanic, Semitic, Peabody, Agassiz, & Fogg . . . . & tomorrow we dispose of the Gardner palazzo & the good old Fine Arts. Are we getting cultivated? We'll tip off the dysoptic empyrean! ¶ Fund is safely off to Smithy—hope he won't shoot it haughtily back & make me disperse the donations again! ¶ Trust your health is keeping improved. Best wishes for MDLCCCXXXII—H P L

Sorry you could not be with us.

W. Paul Cook

Notes

1. *Front:* Lowell House, Harvard University, Cambridge, Mass.

[20]   [ALS]

Woden's-Daeg
[27 July 1932?]

All-Highest:—

Caramba! Why couldn't E. Harold's available week-end be one week farther along—August 13–14th? Because James Ferdinand's stay in antient Providentium will extend from Tuesday the 2nd to Saturday the 6th, & I'd hate like the devil to walk out on him! That also virtually invalidates the earlier week-end of July 30–31, for if Grandpa is broke when the curl-crown'd Sage arrives, who'll pay the fare to Warren, Newport, & other regional goals on the tentative programme of the entertainment committee? It certainly is royally good of Carbo Sapiens to propose a Marblehead trip—for I *must* see that time-mellow'd port somehow this year if it busts me—& I trust you will convey to him my unlimited appreciation. And if he *could* make it the 13th instead of the 6th I'd be profoundly overjoy'd—because the 6th will have to find me on the Fox Point wharf at 7 p.m., waving adieu to the departing great.

Incidentally—is the 13–14th all right for you? You might, too, let me know before that time whether you have *all day* Saturn's Day or not. Tip me off what part of the week-end—Fri. aft. or Sat. noon—would be the best to come. Or if in a mood of determin'd œconomy, I might save an hotel bill by getting up for an early morning stage-coach Saturday . . . . . or, more calculatively, I might put some other Bostonian items before instead of after our session, & come Friday morning, meeting you (in case you *do* have all Sat.) as soon as you're at liberty. I've got to call on that Somerville client,[1] & also want to look up the weird writer Hugh B. Cave—I think I told you he is a Pawtucket man spending the summer in Bostonium.[2]

You no doubt receiv'd my card from antient Newport. Well—since that time (last Friday) I have been *twice more!* How come, you query? I reply—look at the enclosed advertisement. Can you beat it? The result of a steamboat rate war plus the depression. The old Mount Hope goes down to 75¢, whereupon the little old Sagamore—a former Bristol ferryboat now remodelled for all-year-round Block Island service—horns in & touches bottom at 50¢. This is too damn good to resist, so that Newport is likely to see a lot of the old gent this summer! The Sagamore has rather cramped quarters, & the lower deck is sometimes clutter'd with freight & cattle; but it gets you there—& that's the main point with Grandpa! Besides—it gives the traveller a half-hour longer in Newport—returning at 5:45 instead of 5:15. You've got to get down here & take advantage of the bargain before it cracks. How about the 6th & having a day with J. Ferd? We could make Newport Sunday the 7th. Think it over & lemme know. I'm getting the start of a tan as good as the one Florida gave me last year.

And so it goes. Young Spink is going to issue a pamphlet containing my final critical report for this year—one that was too long for the N.A.[3] After its publication—for some parts are not without candour—I shall be looking for bombs in the mail. Maybe amateurdom will see an assassination & a suicide in the same year—robust Elizabethan vitality!

Thanks effusively for the architectural shots. Some series! I never saw a better picture of the old feather store. There's a mistake in the Dutch one, though, as Talman could tell you. Actually, not a single *stepped gable* is left in the U.S. // Well—behave!—Grandpa

Notes

1. I.e., Hazel Heald, a client for whom HPL ghostwrote five stories.
2. Hugh B[arnett] Cave (1910–2004), prolific author of stories for the pulp magazines. He lived for a time near HPL in Pawtucket, RI. They corresponded briefly but never met.
3. "Notes on Verse Technique." Published as *Further Criticism of Poetry*.

[21]   [ANS postcard][1] [HPL and James F. Morton to EHC]
[Postmarked Providence, R.I.,
1? August 1933]
An appeal, O friend of learning, & of a literate amateurdom! Wilt help an old man civilise the renascent National? Have had Critical Bureau Chairmanship shoved on me, & can't find anyone of the new generation to serve as a prose colleague—that is, can't find anyone I deem qualified. Conscious of your distinguish'd services in the past, I make bold to ask if you will repeat them during the coming twelvemonth—I'll guarantee that all papers to be criticised reach you in time. ¶ Probably you know of my move to a real Georgian house—remember the new address—66 COLLEGE ST. ¶ Hoping you'll agree to attempt the prose criticism, I am, Sir, ever yr most oblig'd, most obt Servt
    H P L

Space left but for bare greeting. Best wishes. James.

Notes

1. *Front:* Van Wickel Gates, Brown University, Providence, R. I.

[22]   [ALS]

66 College St.,
Providence, R.I.,
August 9, 1933
Benefactor . . . Salvator . . . Σωτήρ[1]
                I bend my age-stiffen'd & silver-buckled knees in true Georgian gratitude! The absence of critical talent among the

current & regnant generation of Boys with Printing-Presses left me in despair regarding the completion of an adequate choir of carping chirpers, & I hated to impose upon veterans whose days are tryingly filled outside the amateur world. However, render'd bold & callous by the stimulus of James Ferdinand Morton's companionship, I finally decided to address my mendicancy to high places—& now, suffused with thankfulness, I can only murmur in appropriate accents, "God bless you!" I don't believe any reports will be wanted till early in October—in time for the December N.A. (the identity of whose official editor I have yet to learn.)[2] At that time, after making a bluff of eloquent wisdom concerning current doggerel, I'll forward to Wollaston the select prose fruits of the season—confident that they will evoke a review brilliantly outshining the residue of the quarter's oracularisings. Again, tibi mille gratias.

It was certainly a keen disappointment for me to have to forego the N.Y. convention—& all that I hear of that event's success adds sharpness to my pangs. My aunt's plaster cast was removed last Thursday;[3] but she is still in bed by the doctor's orders, & will later have to pass through an indefinite crutch period. I am naturally very closely tied down—having to be on duty each afternoon while the nurse goes out—& will continue to be so (as sole doorbell-answerer & link with the ground floor & outside world) long after the departure of the nurse. A whole summer has been excised from the programme of this household!

I am sorry your own poor health was so long protracted, & hope that you have now completely shaken it off. Amateurdom will wish you a prosperous & unworried winter both for your sake & its own! The news of bozo Sandy's illness was a complete & painful surprise to me—but I am glad he is better now. I hope he will maintain due precautions against any cardiac weakness resulting from his siege. That general get-together at Wollaston must have been a festive & delightful event, & I trust that the coming Belmont reunion may be no less notable.

My only outings this year have been brief & arduously snatched. Early in July the weird writer E. Hoffmann Price visited me in his car & participated in some rural antiquarian exploration, & later in the same month I spent 2½ days around Cape Cod with Frank B. Long & his parents, who were rusticating at Onset. Then last week I had the pleasure of entertaining our august friend James Ferdinand—with whom I took several antiquarian walks (on one of which we came across a splendid old-time well-sweep), plus a boat trip to archaic Newport. He is now headed for the snow-clad peaks of Vermont & New Hampshire.

Doubtless Culinarius told you something about the *genuine Georgian* retreat into which (with kindly & delicious irony) poverty has delivered my aunt & myself. The house—yellow & wooden—lies on the crest of Providence's ancient hill in a quaint grassy court just off College st.—behind & next to the marble John Hay Library of Brown University, about half a mile south of where I dwelt before. The fine colonial doorway is like my bookplate (which I once shew'd you, did I not?) come to life, tho' of a slightly later period (circa 1800), with side lights & fan carving instead of a fanlight. In the rear & on the western side are picturesque, village-like gardens—those behind being at a higher level than the front of the house. In front there are some flower-beds, an hedge, & a row of old-fashion'd posts to keep off vehicles. The upper flat we have taken consists of 5 rooms besides bath & kitchenette nook on the main (2nd) floor, plus 2 attic storerooms—one of which is so attractive that I wish I could have it for an extra den! My own quarters—a large study & a small adjoining bedroom—are on the S. side, with my working table under a west window affording a splendid view of the lower town's outspread roofs & of the mystical sunsets that flame behind them. In general, the interior is fully as fascinating as the exterior—with colonial fireplaces, mantels, & chimney-cupboards, curving Georgian staircase (sightly, even if ankle-breaking!), wide floor-boards, old-fashion'd latches, small-paned windows, six-panel doors, rear wing with floor at a different level (3 steps down—some problem for my aunt when she gets to the crutch stage!), quaint attic stairs, &c. &c.— just like the antique dwellings open as museums. After admiring such all my life, I find something magical & dreamlike in the experience of actually *living in one* for the first time. To come *home* through a carved Georgian doorway & sit by a white colonial mantel gazing out through small-paned windows over a sea of centuried roofs & dense verdure . . . . . . I keep fearing that some museum guard will come around & boot me out at 5 o'clock closing-time! The house is owned by Brown University, & has steam heat & hot water piped in from the adjacent John Hay Library . . . . . erudition in the very faucets & radiators, as it were! Now I can only hope fortune will permit me to hang on to this prize. Hope you can get around to see it in the course of time.

In conclusion, permit me to reiterate the thanks which forms the theme song of this epistle. I ought to add, that the post of typographical critic has been accepted by young Spink—who I am convinced will fill it faithfully & effectively.

With patriarchal blessings, & regards to Culinarius, Bimbo Sandy, & any other appropriate objects you may encounter, I have yᵉ Honour to ſubſcribe my ſelf, Sir,

Yr moſt oblig'd, moſt obᵗ Servt

H P L

Notes

1. "Deliverer!"

2. At the NAPA convention of July 1933, F. Earl Bonnell (1894–1988) was elected Official Editor, but Chester P. Bradley took over the office some time in the 1933–34 term.

3. Annie Gamwell broke her ankle, shortly after she and HPL moved into 66 College.

[23]   [ALS]

66 College St.,
Providence, R.I.,
All-Hallows'
[31 October 1933]

Salvator Diei:—

Mille Gratias! A car is no less caught because one just grabs
its retreating rear vestibule. Yesternoon the precious document began its
southwest journey to North East, & if editor Bonnell doesn't get it by All-
Saints' Day, it will be because Jim Farley[1] or some other postal guy is layin'
down on the job. The report itself strikes me as splendid & adequate—
pointed yet kindly, tactful yet specific. It gives the prevailing fad of triviality
the admonition called for, & furnishes constructive suggestions which all
might profitably heed. I have urged Bonnell to publish it intact if he possibly
can, doing all his major cutting on the verse report—since in recent years
there has been so much criticism of verse, & so little of prose. In case some
cutting has to be done, I've echoed your suggestion that the introduction be
the first thing to go—& repeated the request that each individual criticism be
published intact or not at all. That's really the only way to ensure the accuracy
of the various dicta, for nothing can be more misleading than a garbled text.
The association ought to be darned glad of that report, for it's a long while
since there has been a really well-balanced critical bureau.

I know you'd appreciate such a haven as 66 College, & trust that time &
grey hairs may eventually bring you such. Incidentally—I hope to high
Pegāna that the gods of luck, literary markets, economics, & the like may enable me to hang on to this one! It represents just about my ideal for a permanent anchorage—& I would add to my aspirations (in place of your aestival
Vermont) only a modest hermitage in ancient St. Augustine for the months
betwixt October & June [with perhaps a sub-retreat in Key West or the West
Indies for January & February]. One of the main assets of the place for me is
the *rus in urbe*[2] effect resulting from its situation at the back of a half-hidden
lane. The house & its old-fashioned gardens are altogether out of the bustling
world—in a way that scarce any sizeable city but Providence could provide.
Almost peculiar to this town is the vast amount of centrally situated terrain
remaining in an unchanged physical state since the semi-rural & village periods. Within a stone's throw of the downtown skyscraper district—guarded by
the steep precipice which discouraged commercial expansion in the pre-
zoning years—are fragments of grassy country lane; bits of farmyard overtak-
en, hemmed in, & passed by in the march of the urban frontier; streets &
lanes with the old houses, bank walls, generous gardens, brick sidewalks,
hitching-posts, & horse-blocks of village days; unpaved, grass-grown alleys &
cobblestoned courts; & numerous other marks of an unmechanised past
which virtually all other cities of this size have long ago lost. When I first

shewed Providence to the appreciative James Ferdinand Morton I was constrained to pause every now & then & point out something of this sort, in each case exclaiming—"And where, within an equal distance of the centre of any other large town, can you find a rural scene like this?" So many times did I repeat the formula that I began to abbreviate it by merely crying, "And *where* . . . . .?"—until at last the phrase *"andwhere"* became a standard compound noun in our personal vocabulary, signifying some anomalously surviving agrestic or village landscape effect at or near the centre of a large city. To this day one of the essential elements of a Mortonian visit is a leisurely & appreciative round of Providence's endless *andwheres*.[3]

The recent Culinary jump certainly left me a trifle breathless—especially since I had just been assured that he would be glad to act as Bostonese pilot to a young friend of mine whose labours have taken him to the Hub for a year. The youth knocked at #7 in vain—& about that time my card of notification arrived. But of course I knew that Culinarius was getting rather fed up on Boston, both climatically & psychologically; so that probably his present move is a wise one. His newly-acquired standard of success is rather a surprise to me—not less so because of the bitterly socialistic bits of divided prose or "free verse" which he is publishing in *Driftwind* under his "Crossman" pseudonym! I have been aware, however, that many of his standards have undergone singular & inexplicable alterations—he now repudiates all critical values except immediate surface pleasure (favouring cheap magazines & tales of wholesale combat), & announces that he means to "vegetate intellectually" (his own phrase to Long last July!) for the rest of his life! Well—I hope that his vegetation in the North Mount-polar[4] regions may give rise to a generous flowering & fruitage! He reported 12 inches of snow & a temperature of 12° the other day . . . . . & any guy who can stand that has a lot in him!

I—& the Kappa Alpha Tau[5]—learn with the keenest interest of Wollaston's exclusive feline circle. Napoleon's accomplishments remind me of those of the local clubmen—especially the Vice-President, who is not averse to nourishment at sundry postern gates betwixt naps. Wellington, I trust, exercises at least a modicum of moderation in his continued use of the engines of warfare. Bozo somehow appeals to me in his stark primitiveness—& I am sure that Nap the napper's ochraceous victim has his appealing points. The battles betwixt the two surely have an epic quality, & were I present at one I fear I could not be relied on to remind you of any cooling & neglected repast! You are fortunate to dwell in a richly feline neighbourhood. Barnes St. was lacking in that respect, but this present *andwhere* is well blessed with Lords of the Housetops. Another great ailouric centre is the Tryout office at Haverhill, now blessed with at least four specimens of diverse excellences. Dummy, Killer, Killer Jr., & the kitten. Killer Jr., a product of last spring, is developing into what his genial master considers the finest* cat he has had in all his 81 years.

I'll have to come up some day & see these furry warriors—& incidentally any human sages who may hang out near them. T'anks fer de invite! And fer de report.

Yr most oblig'd ob^t Servt

H P L

Notes

1. James Aloysius Farley (1888–1973), postmaster general of the U.S. (1933–40).

2. I.e., countryside in the city.

3. See W. Paul Cook, *In Memoriam: Howard Phillips Lovecraft* (1941), who notes that "and where" was "one of Howard's favorite phrases when showing visitors around the city. He would stop at a spot where the view would be comparable to that of a country village. 'Where, except in Providence,' he would ask, 'in the midst of a large city, will you find a view like that?' The next view would be a sylvan scene. 'Where save in Providence, in the midst of a large city . . .' he would say. The next step it would be, 'Where, save in Providence. . . .' And after that the single word 'Where . . . ,' with an expressive gesture embracing the scene before him" (*LR* 137).

4. HPL's pun for *Montpelier.*

5. Because 66 College Street was on Brown University's fraternity row, HPL devised the Greek name Kappa Alpha Tau, or K.A.T. (standing for Κομπσῶν Αἰλουρῶν Τάξις or "band of elegant [or well-dressed] cats") for the array of cats at the boarding house.

[24]   [ALS]

66 College St.,

Providence, R.I.,

Jany. 20, 1934

Honour'd Carbo:—

Once again (how dizzily the months whirl by!) it is my painful duty to pass along a prodding just received from Official Editor Bonnell, & remind you that a prose critical report is supposed to be in that drastic potentate's hands by *Feby. 1 sharp.* Enclosed is a list of the recent papers—& I'll gladly send you any you lack. I haven't cooked up my own verse report as yet, but mean to do so at once.[1] Hope this isn't too short notice—at least *I've* lost no time in shooting on the word! Bonnell urges brevity in reports, but I trust you won't take him too literally. I want this to be the year when prose gets a break—hence will let most of the compressing be exerted on the Aonian department. Last time I had my report whittled down to a minimum, too—so much so that my remarks on the general low quality of current stuff didn't get included. I was glad to see your report printed as sent—it has elicit-

---

*and considering Sir Thomas Tryout (1909–1921), that's a strong achievement!

ed many favourable comments. This time you can use your own judgment about sending to me or to Bonnell direct—perhaps the chronological rush will impel you to the latter course. I trust that you will not find the assignment a major inconvenience at this period.

I had hoped to get around to Boston before this, but one thing or another prevented. For a fortnight beginning Christmas I visited Frank B. Long in New York—incidentally seeing most of the local amateur high lights .... Loveman, Kleiner, & Morton after he returned from his own wanderings. I saw the old year out at Loveman's—where my kind host quite overwhelmed me by presenting me with several items for my modest private museum— including an Egyptian *ushabti* some 4000 years old, of bitumen-coated wood & nearly a foot long, & a small Mayan image of stone. His own collection is really marvellous—now including a genuine Greek head (of a maiden) of Parian marble, cleverly set in an electrically lighted niche prepared by his versatile roommate McGrath. Later I called on Mortonius in Paterson—seeing the new fluorescent minerals which form such a high-light of his institution. Off & on I managed to cover my favourite museums of larger scope—enjoying especially the striking new Assyrian, Etruscan, & Greek material at the Metropolitan. I picked up several book bargains—chief among which was the late Arthur Weigall's "Wanderings in Roman Britain", a thing I've wanted for years, & which is marvellously reminiscent of our old controversy of 1914. (*Twenty years* ago ..... *how* those damned years race imperceptibly past one!) I may wickedly add that Weigall vociferously supports my side of that debate— shewing pretty clearly how thoroughly Romanised the Province of Britannia was. But my chief Manhattan triumph was getting a fountain pen point & feed which will *really* work .... something I haven't had before since I lost my 1906 Waterman on the sands of Marblehead in good old 1923. I pestered the central Waterman office at Broadway & Dey Sts day after day, & at last got an adjustment which looks like the real thing! Naturally the cold spell of Christmas week was a frightful obstacle—but the protection of the subway system helped me to get around. All told, not a bad trip. Among the new weird-writing acquaintances I made was *A. Merritt* of "Moon-Pool" fame.

I kept up my autumnal walks till quite late—& celebrated the warm Thanksgiving by doing something I've wanted to do all my life—eating my feast on the historick soil of antient *Plymouth* itself—where the whole thing started 312 years ago. Christmas was festive—greens around the colonial sitting-room fireplace, & a furry clubman borrowed from the Kappa Alpha Tau to lend domestick atmosphere. The K.A.T., by the way, sends its collective greetings to Napoleon, Wellington, Bozo, & any other congenial souls in Wollaston.

And so it goes. I hope the report-request won't form an intolerable burthen! With advance thanks & heartfelt commiserations—

Yr obt Servt—

HPL

Notes

1. HPL did not publish another "Bureau of Critics" report until the June 1934 issue.

[25]   [ALS]

66 College St.,
Providence, R.I.,
Jany. 31, 1934
Temperature slightly amending.

Carboni Theobaldus Salutem donet:—

Saved! If Bonnell doesn't get the papers by the Kalends, it'll be the fault of the post-riders. Incidentally—I've saved a day by straightening out the address. That Philadelphia address is Segal's[1]—kept at the masthead to avoid the costly transfer of 2nd class rates. The real private inside address of the current sanctum is 32 Robinson St., North East, Pa.

Thanks vastly for the pre-view—& I hope fervently that Œ will make no excisions. Your text is a boon & a delight—exactly what is needed at this juncture. When I look over the current papers I am exasperated by the preponderance of material by chronic juveniles—hopeful perpetual beginners up to 75 years of age. I chuckled appreciatively over your deflation of the flatulent Floyds—Dean & Stentel. When I came upon their crap I wished that I could be prose critic for about 15 minutes—but I see that the wish was unnecessary. What I would have said has been said—& more effectively. And your citation from the Teleschovian tale is a sermon in itself. In short—& without any desire to flatter—I must say that I don't see how the current grist could have been covered in any more effective a way. I appreciated your introductory remarks on polemicks—a theme reminiscent of my own scrapping days . . . circa 1914–25. [In the present Smith–Heuman fight[2] I am all on Smith's side, for I don't think any place could be more appropriate for the Fossil Library than the Franklin Memorial. Tryout favours the central location of N Y—but to me the historical associations of Phila[da.], plus the infinitely superior display conditions of the Institute, are wholly overbalancing considerations. I haven't seen either *Tuesday Night* or *The Union Lance*, but hope to borrow them. A new *Boys' Herald* came yesterday.] The tone of your criticisms isn't a bit too drastic—& will be pretty well matched by that of the verse department. I've again sent Bonnell the fairly pointed general remarks which he cut out in December, & have told him to give them precedence over the individual criticisms—since the recent metrical crop is even less significant than usual. I'm glad you've recommended a good manual for the struggling prosists. Marks taught at Brown when he wrote "The Plastic Age"—that volume being the reason for his retirement by request from our staid hilltop academy.[3] As an illustration of the old "great minds run &c" gag—I've also

recommended a manual in my verse colyum . . . . George E. Teter's "An Introduction to Some Elements of Poetry." Teter is a colleague of our friend Moe in
Milwaukee, & this brochure of his is just what some of the National's poetasters need. But I wish some publisher had the nerve to issue Moe's own text-
book—"Doorways to Poetry."[4] I helped whip the MS. of this into shape, & can
trut[h]fully & confidently say that I never saw a finer & clearer presentation of
the rules, details, & basic principles of versification & poetic depiction. Moe has
a notable gift for definition & illustration, & his treatise is so lucid & ample that
almost anybody with even half a brain could slough off his major crudities after
a close & repeated study of it. No one can equal Moe in anticipating all the typical weaknesses & difficulties of the imperfect bard—a result, no doubt, of long
& observant years in amateurdom & in pedagogy.

So you have #6 of the Crossman limited edition. I have #4. I'll tell Culinarius of your impressive oneireious reaction to his Voltairean masterpiece—
perhaps it will inspire him to prepare a sequel! Both dream & original are well
worthy of analysis & reflection.[5]

You are ahead of me in the matter of the ponderous Antonius Adver-
sus[6]—the volume has been lent to me (by a gent in no hurry about its return),
but I've had no chance to get at it so far. My aunt is reading it now, & I'll
probably begin it before she finishes it—fortunately my major reading hours
are nocturnal whilst hers are diurnal. Don't know how well I'll like it—but
anything evocative of yesterdays always gets me. I believe the tale ends in old
Nouvelle-Orleans—a favourite town of mine ever since my more than a fortnight's exploration of it in 1932. I own the Poe biography by the same author—"Israfel". I must read "Rabble in Arms",[7] since anything touching
Quebec is of interest to me. However—I lack familiarity with the territory
covered in the slow retreat. My only travel west of Quebec was a nocturnal
train ride from Montreal.

As for temperature . . . . . well, I haven't been out of the house for three
days, although within doors I manage to keep alive by crouching over a radia-
tor in a thick woollen dressing-gown. Monday morning it was down to zero—which wasn't, of course, as bad as the worst of Christmas week. Just now
there seems to be some hope of improvement—though it's a question
whether or not this epistle will be mailed in person by its inditer. Ah, well—
the vernal aequinox is cross'd in 49 days . . . . one may live in hope if not in
present comfort! Guess I'll light my oil stove, which would admirably sup-
plement the radiators.

Again exprefsing my profound Gratitude for your acute & witty Contribution, I have the Honour to fubfcribe my felf, Sir,

　　　Yr moft oblig'd, moft obᵗ Servᵗ
　　　　　　　H P L

Notes

1. Harold Segal (1915–2009), editor/publisher of *Good Timers' Club News, The Sea Gull,* and *Campane.* Official Editor of the NAPA (1932–33).

2. Referring to a dispute between Edwin Hadley Smith and Charles C. Heuman (former editor of the *Fossil*) as to the location of the Fossil Library.

3. HPL refers to Percy Marks (1891–1956), author of several novels, including *The Plastic Age* (New York: Century Co., 1924), and the treatise *The Craft of Writing* (New York: Harcourt, Brace, 1932). He was teaching at Brown when *The Plastic Age*—a novel dealing with sexual and other irregularities at a fictitious college—was published. The university administration believed the college was based on Brown and asked him to leave.

4. *Doorways to Poetry* was a book on poetic appreciation on which Moe had been working for years, with some assistance from HPL. Although it was at one time scheduled to be published, it never appeared and the ms. is apparently nonextant.

5. Possibly *A Day in the Life of Willis T. Crossman* [North Montpelier, VT: Driftwind Press, n.d.]; rpt. in *W. Paul Cook: The Wandering Life of a Yankee Printer,* ed. Sean Donnelly (New York: Hippocampus Press, 2007), 173–88.

6. I.e., the bestselling historical novel *Anthony Adverse* by Hervey Allen.

7. A novel by Kenneth Lewis Roberts (1885–1957), and a sequel to his *Arundel* (1929), concerning the American Revolution through the Battle of Quebec.

[26]   [ALS]

Wednesday
[February 1934?]

Dear E H C:—

    It surely gave me a painful shock to learn of the sad event which prompts your extremely thoughtful note—just received. I recall your speaking of Sandy's serious cardiac illness last winter, but had hoped the trouble was becoming less acute & menacing.[1] I dropped him cards from my principal travel points during the year, & laid his non-acknowledgment to business pressure rather than failing health. At Christmas the usual card came. Though it is quite a period since the breezy, inspiriting bulletins in "Sanduskese" have arrived in large numbers, it nevertheless requires a sharp effort to realise that their unique & loveable writer is not still somewhere in the offing. The blow to his wife must be immense—& even Albert Jr. must be old enough by now to know him & vaguely if not acutely sense the loss.

    At present it seems very unlikely that I can be in the Boston area tomorrow; but if any circumstance enables me to be, I shall assuredly be most profoundly grateful for the guidance & hospitality you offer. Let me thank you sincerely for these timely & generous suggestions, even though I shall probably be unable to take advantage of them.

    My aunt is likewise shocked by the news, since in the old Cambridge days her son (my cousin Phillips Gamwell, who died in 1916)[2] slightly knew A A S in the Latin School. I think they also exchanged a word or two over amateur matters (in which I was getting my cousin interested just before his death at the age of 18) during the last year of my cousin's life. Please convey the sympathy of both of us to the Sandusky family.

Thanking you again—& regretting it if (as I fear) I can't get to Boston.—

Yrs in extreme haste,

H P L

Notes

1. Albert A. Sandusky died on 13 February 1934 in West Roxbury, MA.
2. HPL's "An Elegy on Phillips Gamwell, Esq.," an elegy to his cousin (23 April 1898–31 December 1916), appeared in the *Cambridge Chronicle,* the Providence *Evening News,* and the *Cambridge Tribune.*

[27]   [ANS postcard][1]

[Postmarked De Land, Fla.,

4 June 1934]

Hail! I keep staying on & on in De Land, & dread to head for the arctic regions. Barlow is a great kid—writer, painter, sculptor, pianist, printer, landscape gardener, book collector, & countless other things . . . . but handicapped by bad eyesight. ¶ Hopes of getting to Havana reduced to a minimum, but I'll spend a week in St. Augustine if it breaks me. Shall return north by slow stages—very possibly visiting honest John Samples (of Silver Clarion fame) in Macon. ¶ Did you see Culinarius when he was in Boston recently?

Blessings—

H P L

Notes

1. *Front:* A Cocoanut Tree, Florida.

[28]   [ANS postcard][1]

[Postmarked Saint Augustine, Fla.,

23 June 1934]

Ave, Carbo Doctissime! On the road again—& back in the past—at last! Ended a 7-week visit last Thor's-Daeg, when the Barlovii brought me up to ancient San Agustin in their car. It is surely a relief to be amongst old houses again . . . & America has none older than those before my eyes! Dwellings 2 generations old when the first timbers of the Fairbanks house in Dedham were laid are common. Am staying a week—at the same joint I patronised in MDCCCXXXI.[2] Have a fine tower room with running water—& a magnificent view—for only IV hebdomedal bucks. Absorbing antiquities at top speed—more old houses open as museums than in 1931. ¶ A fortnight ago I visited a marvellous place—Silver Springs, 60 m. N.W. of De Land. There's a chain of placid lagoons there, whose floor is riddled with vast pits 30 to 80 feet deep, & covered with strange marine vegetation. In some of the pits are the huge bones of prehistoric animals—& in one is a weed-crusted ship's boat which local tradition (don't ask me my opinion!) associates with the early Spanish explorers. I saw these things from a glass-bottomed boat. Out of the lagoons flows the Silver River—as typical a tropic stream as the Congo or Amazon. It was here that the cinema of "Tarzan" was made.[3] Palms, cypresses, & trailing vines & moss on the banks, & alligators, turtles, & snakes here & there. I took a 10-mile launch trip on it. ¶ Nearly broke, & will have to cut out most of the intended stops on the way north. Trust all is flourishing in the Bay Province.

> Yr ob[t] h[ble] Serv[t]
> H P L

Notes

1. *Front:* Oldest Frame House in U.S.A., St. George Street, City Gates in Distance, St. Augustine, Florida.
2. I.e., the Rio Vista Hotel in St. Augustine.
3. Six of the original Tarzan movies, starring Johnny Weissmuller, were filmed on location at Silver Springs between 1932 and 1942, including *Tarzan the Ape Man* (1932) and *Tarzan and His Mate* (1934).

[29]   [ANS postcard][1]

> [Postmarked Providence, R.I.,
> 14 July 1934]

Home at last—but the northern landscape still seems strange to me! Stopped in St. Augustine, Charleston, Richmond, Fredericksburg, Washington, & Philadelphia. Saw the Fossil Library in its new home, & visited Poe cottage in 7th St., Phila., newly opened as a museum & shrine. In N.Y. found Long & his family about to visit Ocean Grove, N.J. for the week-end, & went along with them. ¶ Grieved to learn of the death of Mrs. Miniter last month.[2] The familiar figures are passing! ¶ Young Bradley wants me to ask you if you'll help out his *Perspective Review* by acting as prose judge & editing a page of prose of high quality. I hope you can. The kid is bent on improving the quality of amateurdom, & deserves all the coöperation he can get. ¶ Recent election seems to have been quite satisfactory, & I hope a fruitful year will result. ¶ Trust all is well in the Merry Mount region.

> Blessings—
> H P L

Notes

1. *Front:* Moonlight on Highland Lake, Daytona Highlands. Daytona Beach, Florida.
2. Edith Miniter died 4 June.

[30]   [ANS postcard][1]

[Postmarked Providence, R.I.,
1 August 1934]

Ave, Carbo Magne! Our new executive Mr. Babcock has persuaded me to indite at least *one* more critical report, to be hustled into the *September* N.A., & I am relaying the summons to see if you can & will parallel my performance as usual. The new board are determined to revise Bonnell's policy of skimping the criticism. I've asked Babcock to try to find another critical chairman for the balance of the year, but have said I'll serve if he can't. How about you? Would you take the chairmanship? Or repeat your present function? I'm pinning a bit of faint hope on *Moe,* who is making something of a comeback. ¶ But for the present, the primary concern is for a hurry-up report to be sent at the earliest possible moment to Editor Bradley—215 E. Knight St., Eaton Rapids, Mich.—for the Sept. issue. Can you do it? If so, you'll deserve well of the association! I'm going to try my damnedest! ¶ Got home July 10. Great time in St. Augustine—then Charleston again, Richmond, Fredericksburg, Washington, Philadelphia (saw Fossil Library & newly opened Poe house), & N.Y. In N.Y. I found Long & his parents about to depart for a week-end in Asbury Park, so went along with them. Since getting home I've been paralysed with accumulated work, but diverted by a congenial black kitten at the boarding house across the back garden. And now (Aug. 2–3–4) I am about to welcome a visit of our sterling colleague James Ferdinand Morton. ¶ Well— do your best for the cause! Blessings from a fellow-martyr!
H P L

Notes

1. *Front:* First Baptist Church, Providence, R. I. Founded by Roger Williams, 1638.

[31]   [ALS]

Quinsnicket Woods—N. of
Providence. Aug. 7, 1934

Hail, Carbo!

Though having no fault to find with the current local temperatures except as regards the disconcerting coldness of the evenings, I none the less envy you—for scenic reasons—the trip in which you are indulging. Vermont is a glorious place when warm enough to be habitable, & I shall never forget the crowded green hills & omnipresent murmuring brooks amidst which I spent more than a fortnight in 1928. I was in the southern part of the state—the more northerly regions being still a terra incognita to me, save for window-glimpses from railway carriages bound to & from the still-loyal provinces of our Sovereign's empire. I trust your journey was uniformly enjoyable—as it must have been if all the scenes resembled the one on the card. The Coolidge exercises must have been highly impressive, even if productive of political oratory of a rather tragically reactionary cast. So the amiable Davenport was the invoker of supernatural approval![1] Truly, it was a time for amateurs to feel at home; & I wish I might have been present!

I wish, too, that I might have shared in the Culinario–Coatesian call at N. Montpelier. I didn't know that W P's ambitions extended as far as Manhattan—but I hope he can find some adequate professional opening either there or elsewhere. I have been urging him to make a side-trip to Providence from Boston. Now he can perhaps stop off here on his way to the seething cosmopolis on the Hudson.

Meanwhile let me express my most grateful appreciation of your suggestion that I participate in the Boston Culinary session from a Wollastonian base. If all goes well, I shall be extremely delighted to do so—& shall await further particulars as to when to be where on the 23d or thereabouts. I shall certainly have no difficulty—with Essex County at my disposal—in keeping amused during the hours when stern duty will hold my genial host in durance. In fact, I had meant to make a trip to Salem & Marblehead anyhow—it being absolutely impossible to let more than a year elapse without sight of these havens of the past. Another & more ambitious project of mine—though it may not be realised this year—is to see ancient *Nantucket* for the first time. I trust that nothing may interfere with Cook's presence during the season of Merrymount hospitality. James Ferdinand Morton may be darting through the Hub around that period, though so briefly that a get-together would scarcely be likely. Again, thanks for the invitation, which I hereby accept with the utmost pleasure!

Assuming that the bulk of my travel-cards reached you, I need not detail the sights I have seen since April last. Since my return home I have been inundated with tasks, but have (as per usual custom) taken my work or reading to some rural or semi-rural spot each pleasant afternoon. I am in such a spot today—after pulling the typical damn fool stunt of leaving my writing-paper behind. Hence the present ruled substitute—the best thing I could pick up at the one roadside emporium of the region.

James Ferdinand was here August 2–3–4, & we had the felicitous & verbally pugnacious sessions characteristic of such convocations. Our programme included visits to many spots of interest—including ancient Newport, where we saw the assembled men-o'-war in the harbour, explored the centuried byways, & made a complete circuit of the rugged ocean cliffs. I damn near froze on the boat ride back.

I wonder if you received my S.O.S. card of about a week ago, calling for a hurry-up critical report for the September N.A.? Babcock & Bradley want to put the preceding administration to shame by having a report in *every* issue. I managed to get mine in on time—but of course it's quite excusable if you didn't. I want if possible to dodge service this year, but have said I'll take either the chairmanship or some other post if there's a hopeless dearth of the simultaneously willing & literate. How about you? Would you accept a chairmanship—or a less ornate berth? If I have to repeat, I hope to have the same good company I have previously enjoyed! I am certainly anxious to see amateurdom's qualitative renaissance become a reality.

I trust that Napoleon, Wellington, & other local Kappa Alpha Tau brothers are flourishing. There is a microscopic coal-black kitten at the boarding-house across the back garden here that positively keeps my mind off my work. I borrow him on every possible occasion—he is a dynamo of kinetic sportiveness, & has just begun to purr.[2]

The old-timer George W. Macauley[3] writes of a plan to plant a grove of trees in his native Michigan, each one dedicated to the president of the N.A.P.A. Well, there's immortality of a sort for me! I never thought anybody would rear a column—whether vegetable, brazen, or marmoreal—in my honour!

And so it goes. I surely hope to see you on the 23[d] or not far from then, & will await particulars concerning the conjuration in question.

        Blessings—

           H P L

Notes

1. Walter Rice Davenport (1855–1942), clergyman and editor from Vermont.

2. Presumably "little Sam Perkins," who would die in September (see letter 34).

3. George W. Macauley (1884?–1969), amateur journalist of Grand Rapids, MI, editor of the *O-Wash-Ta-Nong* and father of Robie Macauley, editor of *Pine Needles*. He corresponded with HPL in the 1910s.

[32]   [ALS]

                     Home—just before starting for
                     the Tall Timber—Aug. 9, 1934

Ave, Salvator!

        Blessings on thee for the favourable response to my long-term plea! And the short-term plan was dispos'd of by the gods. Regarding the former—it is of course problematical whether I'll have any colleague-appointing to do. I told Babcock I'd take the chairmanship only in case no other goat could be found—& if any caprid victim[1] *can* be seized elsewhere, the responsibility is his'n. But even in such a case I hope your coöperation can be counted on. Good critics are so rare that the formation of each year's board is a major problem of selection & persuasion; & my successor—whoe'er he may be—will need a top-notch colleague as badly as I would under the same conditions. I had a sort of floating hope that Moe—who is coming back in a way which I hope will ultimately deserve the popular designation of "big"—would take care of the verse whilst you continued to exercise a salutary restraint over the plebeianisms of the Telschows & the flatulencies of the Stentels. You could settle the technicality of "chairmanship" (that imposing-sounding Kentucky colonelcy) with a flip of a cent. But all this remains to be seen. The eagle eye of the Babcock is ranging o'er the horizon, & if no other prey can be found, it will realight on Grandpa. And in such a case your coöperation will form an occasion for grateful obeisances.

Bradley was extremely grateful for your obituary of Mrs. Miniter, but rather grieved because you didn't accept his entreaty to serve as one of the prose editors of *The Perspective Review*. He wants a staff of qualified old-timers to serve in rotation as editors of his "literary page"—contributing helpful material themselves, or selecting stuff by others which they really deem good. Moe has consented—in fact, as you see, has already furnished one page. I, too, am on the list of acceptees, though I haven't yet come across with the goods. And if you want to make a most worthy youth happy, you'll hop on the band-wagon yourself. It isn't likely that anything arduous will be demanded of you—if I'd thought there were any heavy toil in the job I wouldn't have taken it myself. All the kids are strong on improvement this year, & anxious to secure the benedictions of the elders. Another downy editorlet—one John D. Adams of Oklahoma—has established a grey-bearded "Advisory Board" upon which, among others, Moe & I will sit drowsing idly in the sun.

I surely hope that nothing may mar the Wollastonian convocation of two weeks hence. It would be rather impracticable to try to surprise Culinarius with my presence, or anything like that, so I guess I'll write him all about it & see if he & I can get together before the 23d has become too mature. Then we—or I, if he can't be available—can meet you around 5:30 at whatever stage-coach terminal my valise may chance to be checked at . . . . or anywhere else that may be more convenient for you. Plenty of time for you to write suggestions & emendations. I'll leave this document unsealed until I find out what terminal I'm likely to pull into. Haven't been to Boston for a year, & the damn things are always shifting around. Being thrifty by necessity (rather than nature) in latter years, I choose the cheapest line; & in '33 was quite a patron of a pale-blue fleet of coaches called the "Independent" or "Interstate" or something like that, which soaked you only 75¢ for the complete run & had its Bostonese lair in lower Boylston St. not far from Washington. If this is still in existence, I presume I'll patronise it . . . . though the fare may have gone up. I'll let you know at the bottom of this sheet. However, if there's any difference in convenience you don't have to pick me up at any particular terminal. My valise is very light, & 5:30 can find me at any point of reasonable accessibility which you may designate.

Well—we'll see. And meanwhile I am full of pleasing & grateful anticipations of the event.

Sir, yʳ moſt oblig'd, moſt obᵈᵗ Servᵗ

H P L

Well—here we are! The I.R.T. is up to a dollar again, but I guess I'll patronise it for old times' sake . . . . if not for the 20¢ off on the round trip! Therefore I'll nominate their terminal—*30 Boylston St.*—as first choice for a meeting point, though any other place will be all right for me.

See you later!

H P L

Notes

1. *Caprid:* Of or pertaining to the tribe of ruminants of which the goat, or genus *Capra,* is the type. Thus, a *scapegoat.*

[33]   [ALS]

Home (actually so)
August 11, 1934

Dear E H C:—

You have my sympathy regarding the surgical ordeal you were forced to witness under such trying conditions! Despite my taste for warmth, the particular sort you underwent isn't exactly the variety I'd name as first choice—hence I am not obliged to be altogether objective in sharing your emotions. Let us hope that both you & the patient emerged in reasonably effective shape!

I dropped Cook a card, & hope that all plans may dovetail brilliantly on the 23d. Regarding stage-coach terminals—behold a coincidence! I was going to suggest a shift myself—though for a different reason. In looking over the time-table of the old reliable New England system I discovered that *they also* offer a round trip for $1.80—so, says I to myself, why the hell should I pack into one of those bobtailed ultramarine sedan-chairs & get whizzed over the perniciously modern & distressingly unpicturesque new highway, when for the same amount of jack I might take the regular coach & traverse the good old-fashion'd post-road that generations of my ancestors have known . . . . . past the lordly elms & ancient white steeples of Wrentham, & through the village squares of venerable Walpole & Norwood & Dedham? Thus I was about to revise my earlier tentative itinerary & advise you that—whatever might be the preferred rendezvous—the place I'll be pulling into will be the regular New England terminal which forms (or form'd when last I beheld it) a link betwixt Boylston St. & Park Square . . . . . Yup, still in the same place if I interpret the address in the time-table aright.

However, I'll leave all details of assemblage to you, since I will have all the free mobility ensured by a featherweight valise. Any part of Park Square or elsewhere will be quite oke by Grandpa . . . . . or the lea of Mr. Otis's town-house over-against Beacon-Hill if anything in the Culinary schedule makes that desirable.

Your philosophick accomodatingness concerning service on the Bureau of Critics reflects an amateur patriotism deserving of the highest commendation! Therefore permit me to commend, with the utmost gratitude & appreciation. As yet I have had no word from Babcock regarding other victims, so do not know just what my own responsibilities will be during the ensuing elevenmonth.

Young Bradley will be delighted to learn of your willingness to coöperate in the maintenance of *Perspective Review* standards, & I have taken the liberty of dropping him a card—which may possibly antedate your own document of acceptance—with the good news.

Speaking of favours—some day I am going to be boorish enough to renew a demand which I made in 1923 or thereabouts, & which was then rewarded by a tentative promise of fulfilment—namely, that you assist me in completing my file of *The Olympian,* which calculation tells me lacks six issues—one (Vol. II No. 3) betwixt March & July 1908, & the other five betwixt July '08 & June '09. I believe you said the desiderate issues were buried in the nether crypts beneath 36 Tower St., & I take occasion to suggest as delicately as possible that you keep Grandpa in mind the next time you chance to be burrowing amidst these archives. I'll remind you again after another eleven years!

By the way, I'm glad I've commented (at least I hope I have) on all the points in your recent missive, since a guest of mine shews a marked inclination to transfer the sheets in question to his small interior after some preliminary claw-shredding. Whether it is the piquancy of the prose style or the odour of the ink I can't say—but I can only state that my colleague seems to be tremendously appreciative! The gentleman in question is one whom I believe I have mention'd in a previous communication—a coal-black novice of the Kappa Alpha Tau who has developed extremely neighbourly qualities since his advent to the planet 1½ months ago. He is *Samuel* just beginning to purr. Incidentally, I'll let him add his signature to my own. ¶ Expectant of the auspicious 23d—   *his*   *mark*

Yr most obᵗ hᵇˡᵉ Servᵗ

H P L

Perkins

[34]   [ALS]

Out on Prospect Terrace
—Aug. 18, 1934

Dear E H C:—

Pray accept my sincerest & profoundest commiserations anent the added burthen of labour beneath which you are bending! The one redeeming feature is that it takes you frequently to antient Marblehead—a circumstance which I trust you can appreciate when there are wheels under you. Amidst such a turmoil of activity it is really a crime for you to be saddled with the additional responsibility of acting as host—& if I didn't think a shift of plan might be still more complicating at this late date, I'd insist on cancelling the sojourn out of common humanity! As it is, however, I fancy the simplest thing is to let the original design stand—though I shall try to make myself as little of a nuisance as possible, & will endorse any modification of the schedule which may help toward that end. Again, my keen & unaffected sympathy!

At 7 Hancock St., then, on Thursday, August 23ᵈ, at 5:45 p.m. Eastern Daylight-Saving Time, I shall hope to greet you in person . . . . a pleasure I have not had since 1931. I trust I may still be recognisable despite rapidly greying & thinning locks, & other stigmata of the passing years . . . . anyhow, the guy with Cook'll be me! The designated meeting-place will be ideal from my standpoint, insomuch as it will save another dime which the N.E. Terminal's parcel locker would otherwise soak me for portmanteau-storage. I've had a note from Culinarius acquiescing in the contemplated arrangement, & hope to get in touch with him in the morning for a day of congenial confabulation.

I shall be delighted to participate at the Saturday gathering at the Maison Myers[1]—a scene highly reminiscent of good old 1923 & the Moe visit. Now that I reflect upon it, I realise that I have not beheld any member of the Myers household in over a decade—so swiftly does time race by in these days of advancing age! It will likewise delight me to behold the almost fabulous Timothy Burr Thrift, Esq., of whom, & of whose works, I have heard so much from my amateurical (rather than chronological) elders. I once saw a few numbers of his renowned *Lucky Dog*—lent me by Campbell in 1916—& could not but admire the ambitiousness & enthusiasm of the venture, even though my taste does not incline toward the early-20ᵗʰ-century Elbert-Hubbard[2] preciocity which seemed undeniably present in prose style & format alike. I recall that *The Olympian* professed a certain discipleship to *The Lucky Dog*, yet (contrary to that Canine's 'disgustedness', which you suspect) must confess that my own preference has always inclined toward the alleged derivative rather than toward the original inspiration . . . . a preference which, in view of my well-known tastes, & of the relative style & aspect of the two publications, I believe you will recognise as genuine rather than an aspect of flattery. Nevertheless, I do admire the redoubtable Thrift & his enterprise most heartily, & shall feel quite impressed if this opportunity to meet him in person materialises . . . . . a sentiment which I feel sure that Culinarius will share. As for his recent exploits in the domain of advertising & big business—I always admire intrinsic ability in any field from art to piracy, & will endeavour to maintain a tactful & amiable silence regarding my opinion of what Mr. James Trunslow Adams so euphemistically & paradoxically terms "our business 'civilisation'"![3] I can well imagine that the years may have mellowed Thrift since his 1906 days of hauteur & arrogance. Time has its kindly as well as its destructive aspects, & the evolution of Mortonius is a process from which other amateurs are not likely to be exempted. Another good example is Ernest A. Edkins, the enfant terrible of the '80's, who is today the kindliest & most genial of mortals—& for the past two years one of my best correspondents. He, incidentally, is just back from a European tour.

Allow me to express my grateful appreciation of your plan to deposit me on the heights above Narragansett Bay next Sunday—an appreciation which reconciles me even to the untraditional aridity of the new synthetick highway. It will give me the greatest pleasure to display the idyllic Georgian shades amidst which I now vegetate, & my aunt will take delight in extending a welcome. If there are any local sights & antiquities which I can assist in exhibiting, pray consider me at your service as a guide. I assume that the journey will be timed sufficiently early to include at least a few vistas beyond the meagre modicum afforded by the new highway. If this expedition is a customary one with you, I trust that you will henceforward combine with it a call at 66-on-the-Hill!

Incidentally—my own sojourn at 66 Sunday night may be no more than a transient stop, since I have about decided to attempt a Nantucket trip whilst my valise is pack'd. Mortonius' descriptions of this remnant of early-America have been too much for me to resist, & I am resolv'd to see it if it breaks me. My original intention—in case I attempted the trip at all—was to go directly from Bostonium to Woods' Hole, which (despite the absence of coach service & the resultant expense of railway fare) would have been the most economical procedure in the absence of gratuitous Providence transportation. With such transportation, however, it will be cheapest to go from Providence via the New Bedford coach. I have never been to Nantucket, but from all I hear it must outdo even Marblehead & Fredericksburg & Annapolis as a repository of the past. Up to the present week I didn't think I could make it this year, but a combination of senile recklessness & a small revision cheque have given rise to a quasi-sudden determination. Unless James Ferdinand is a darned bum reporter, Nantucket is one of those places which simply must be seen by any wistful survivor of the 18th century.

In view of your strenuous programme, the delay in allaying young Bradley's grief is readily to be pardoned—especially in view of his notification from other sources. Equally pardonable is the slight hiatus in the donation of those *Olympian* issues. I shall come duly armed with an exact list of the numbers I have & of those I presumably haven't—& hope that the around-the-house stock may include all of the latter. In view of my seniority, I fear the plan of making me your heir wouldn't quite work out to my advantage—tho' I appreciate its generous intent! One never can tell—Mortonius, tho' not exactly my junior, has his eye on my hereditary copy of Cotton Mather's "Magnalia", & is very anxious for me to name him as its recipient in my will![4]

Your mention of the youthful angora fills me with pleasurable anticipation! Too bad you couldn't keep both him & his brother . . . . for I'm sure the elder feline generation could have become reconciled in the course of time. Meanwhile little Sam Perkins continues to be my almost daily guest—growing more sportive & dynamic as the weeks fly by. I seem to get all the benefit of him without the responsibility of feeding & housing!

Well—it's getting too dark to write out here, so I guess I'll subside. Don't get smashed up on the road before I can meet you at #7! ¶ Renewed sympathy, & pleasant anticipations of a congenial sojourn.

Yr oblig'd & ob^t Servt

H P L

Notes

1. The home of Mr. and Mrs. Denys P. Myers, whom HPL described as "old-time amateurs," and their son Peter.
2. Elbert Hubbard (1856–1915) was an American writer, artist, and publisher whose Roycroft Press specialized in handmade paper and elegant typography.
3. James Truslow Adams (1878–1949), *Our Business Civilization: Some Aspects of American Culture* (New York: Albert & Charles Boni, 1929).
4. HPL owned a first edition of Cotton Mather's *Magnalia Christi Americana* (1702). In his "Instructions in Case of Decease" he did leave the book to Morton (see *CE* 5.237).

[35]   [ANS]

[Postmarked Nantucket, Mass.,
29 August 1934]

[["Souvenir Folder of Nantucket, Mass." containing nine postcards: [1] [Map of] Nantucket Mass.; [2] Sankaty Head Lighthouse, Nantucket, Mass.; [3] White Elephant, Nantucket, Mass.; [4] Old Mill, Nantucket Island, Mass.; [5] Ash Lane, Nantucket Island, Mass.; [6] Stone Alley, Showing South Tower [Unitarian Church] and Town Clock / Nantucket Mass.]; [7] Quince Street, Nantucket, Mass.; [8] The [Jethro] Coffin House, Oldest on the Island, built 1686, Nantucket, Mass.; [9] Main Street Business Section, Nantucket, Mass.; [envelope verso] Harbor View, Nantucket, Mass. Other images show Atheneum Public Library; Bathing Scene and Jetty; Waterfront; The Old Ivy Cottage on Liberty Street; Dover Street; Ocean House; Cliff Beach Bath House; Steamer Martha's Vineyard; Stone Alley; The Lone South Shore, The Chopping Bowl

Tea Garden; Martin's Lane; Brant Point Light; Sunset in the Harbor; Monument Square; St. Mary's Church (Catholic).]]
From HPL

[36]   [Two ANS postcards]¹

> [No postmark; included in envelope?
> c. 29 August 1934]

[1] Hail, Carbo Magne! Look at the valuable gifts you left behind . . . . . . & at the marvel that is NANTUCKET! Words are wanting to convey the impression of living, breathing antiquity everywhere present. It is *not* a disappointment! ¶ Still basking in pleasant memories of the recent visit, & glad you all were able to get to Providence even briefly. Try it again when you have more time, & I can shew you sights more worth seeing than Warren! ¶ Had a good day for the Nantucket trip, & was not uncomfortably chilled on the boat . . . . because I went inside & sat near the door of some place whence a kind of genial warmth radiated—galley or engine room or something of the sort. The skyline of Nantucket is dominated by the Congregational Tower, the Baptist steeple, & the South Church belfry, & the waterfront is lined with ancient wharves. Inland everything is *exactly* as it was about 1820—brick sidewalks, old rounded cobblestones, hitching posts, ancient lanes, great Georgian mansions, quaint cottages, &c. &c. &c. Special features are the railed platforms for marine observation on nearly all the roofs—called "The Captain's Walk". This is a place about the physical size of Portsmouth or Newburyport, but without *any* of the modern touches of those places. It is *exactly* as they were about 1930. Trade is almost extinct except for summer visitors, & nothing changes. The town rises gradually from the waterfront, & picturesque hill streets are common. The main business section is cobblestoned, & forms a sort of long square (consisting of the wide part of Main St) with the [2] old Rotch counting-house (1772) at one end & the Pacific Bank bldg. (circa 1815) at the other. Great elms & other trees shade the town, though the rest of the island is treeless, owing to the cutting down of the original forest.

I've taken a coach trip of the entire island, & strolled around the ancient lanes of Siasconset. The island as a whole consists of low rolling hills.

Also visited the Jethro Coffin house (1686—oldest on island), old mill (1746), Elihu Coleman house (1722), Hist. Soc. & Quaker Meeting House, Whaling Museum, & Maria Mitchell Observatory. Saw Saturn through a telescope at the latter place. Haven't even begun to do the ancient streets thoroughly—noting all the vistas, &c. There are so many of them that one could hardly explore them in less than a week.

Only flaw is a slight trace of artificiality—showmanship—resortishness. No parks with benches to write in, but benches line certain shady streets, & there is a park of unadorned nature atop Mill Hill.

Am staying a week at The Overlook—a rambling old hostelry in Step

Lane, which rises from N. Water to Centre St. with the Congregational Church at the top. My room is on the 3d floor, & commands a splendid view of town & harbour & sea. I shall hate to leave when the time comes!

¶ Best regards to you & Mrs. Cole & Sister & Petrov Ivanovitch Kholevski & Napoleon & Arthur Wellesley—
Grandpa H P L

Notes

1. *Front: 1:* Colonial Homes, Nantucket, Mass. *2:* First Baptist Church, Nantucket, Mass.

[37]   [ALS]
The Ancient Hill
—Septr 17, 1934

Carboni Olympiano Theobaldus S.D.

Glad the Nantucketiana proved so timely—& I hope you were able to carry it off like an old Sherburnite before your insular kinsfolk! Believing so good a start to be worthy of further development, I enclose herewith some added odds & ends anent what Daniel Webster called—with his customary floridity (whilst trying some cases there a century ago)—"The Unknown City in the Sea".[1] My stay—except for the cold weather around its central portion—was certainly everything that could be expressed as the cat's whiskers, the aepyornis's wrist-watch, or any other of those quaint old phrases of good old 1923. I believe I absorbed about all there was lying around loose to absorb—& toward the end of my sojourn covered the environs of the town on a hired bicycle . . . . the first time in 20 years I had been on a wheel. Riding proved just as easy & familiar as if I had last dismounted only the day before—& it brought back my lost youth so vividly that I felt as if I ought to hurry home for the opening of Hope St. High School! I wish it were not conspicuous for sedate old gents to ride a bike around Providence! Well—Nantucket is certainly about the last word for surviving archaism! It shews in the little things—the cobblestones, the horse-blocks, the hitching-posts, the great silver doorplates, the box pews & galleries of the churches, & the virtual absence of all obtrusive modern defacements. It is probably more like Salem than Marblehead—for whaling brought wealth & stateliness & Georgian mansions. For that reason it has not quite the rambling, haphazard quaintness of old Flood Ireson's home port . . . . hence I fancy I may report my loyalty to the latter as basically unchanged. It has Marblehead's weak side—the art-colony & gift-'shoppy' stuff—in an even more marked degree, having been a summer resort & nothing else but since the early 1870's. There is not much of a trading district, & the prices of everything are atrociously above the "off-island" level. On the second day of my visit I beheld a spectacle which would have pleased our young friend Peter Myers—a neighbourhood festival on one of the wharves, with a large assemblage drest in the manner of a century ago. Even more effective was a device used to advertise this spectacle—an old Nantucket chaise driven by a gentleman in beaver hat & stock, & holding also a gentlewoman & two children in corresponding costumes. This equipage, circulating through the venerable cobblestoned streets past the fanlighted doorways & stone hitching-posts, imparted a sensation of surviving antiquity which few other devices could have parallell'd.

I reach'd home on the evening of Septr 3^d, & on the following morning my aunt departed for Ogunquit, Maine, whence she will return tomorrow. My fortnight of solitary dictatorship has been signalised by a distressing plethora of work, a picturesque siege of indigestion which had me in bed two days (I'm hardly out of it now), & a sorrow of unfeigned poignancy . . . . . the passing of my little black friend across the garden, of whom I spoke so frequently last month, & whom I vainly tried to find when you were here. Poor Little Sam Perkins! And he seemed to be getting along so well—even making his peace with the old Toms of the shed roof & becoming a member of the Kappa Alpha Tau! On the 7th he was here nearly all day—climbing over Grandpa, rustling the papers on the old gentleman's desk, & signing a letter to my aunt with a tiny footprint. But on the 10th he was found lifeless— from no apparent cause—in the garden, & was interr'd amidst universal mourning. Blessed little Piece of the Night—he lived but from June to September, & was spared the knowledge of what savage winter is like! The Kappa Alpha Tau chaunt his requiem o'nights, & I trust that Napoleon, His Grace, & Peter Ivanovitch may institute similar funerary observances.

> The ancient garden seems tonight
>   A deeper gloom to bear,
> As if some silent shadow's blight
>   Were hov'ring in the air.
>
> With hidden griefs the grasses sway,
>   Unable quite to word them—
> Remembering from yesterday
>   The little paws that stirr'd them.[2]

My aunt was especially delighted to meet you & your household, & I surely trust that the felicitous events of last month may be repeated. Rhode Island will still hold much of loveliness for several weeks to come—& I trust this autumnal splendour may not pass unperceived by the Olympian family & Chevrolet . . . . of which Grandfather Theobald will be at any time the most delighted of antiquarian guides. A word in advance will ensure the old gentleman's readiness at any designated hour. I doubt if local lawlessness will interfere with any of the best scenic routes. In the first place, it has now vastly subsided; & in the second place, I can't think of any affected factory zone on the best route of all—the way to the Gilbert Stuart house & mill, the Row-land Robinson mansion, the Hannah Robinson rock (with a legend[3]—plus the finest rural landscape vista in the United States), the marvellous old sea-port of Wickford, the drowsing colonial county-seat of Kingston, & other high-spots of Rhode-Island's famous "South County".

My sole post-visit communication from Cook is a newspaper cutting en-closed without further message in an envelope. I trust he is getting his equi-librium again, & hope his next Boston sojourn will be less disrupted. I dropped him a line from Nantucket. The cutting, by the way, told of a most lamentable tragedy . . . . the father of our weird-fictionist friend H. Warner Munn of Athol having been killed by a hit-&-run motorist.

Enclosed is a copy of the Miniter elegy which I finally produced in re-sponse to Smithy's urging.[4] It is wretchedly stereotyped & platitudinous—but if the old boy insists on verse, what can a basically unpoetic guy do? If Tryout hadn't hurried me so markedly, I could possibly have done better—but he wanted my copy early in order to allow for repeated proofreadings. I also of-fered to read proof on other elegiack tributes . . . . for I think it does a *little* good in the long run. Please return this carbon eventually—though there is not the slightest hurry. Later on I shall want to lend it to those who will have read the lines in print—in order to shew them what I wrote. I trust that by this time your own tribute is safely in Haverhill. You're getting called upon rather heavily—an obituary for the N.A., a tribute for Tryout, & later perhaps some appropriate remarks for Cook's memorial brochure.[5] I suppose Cook will want me also to prepare another tribute for that enterprise. Well—it's all deserved, in view of Mrs. Miniter's remarkable attainments & services to amateurdom.

Glad that young Peter the Archaist remembers Grandpa kindly! Pray give him & his mother my regards, & tell him I'll be glad to hear from him when-ever he feels like dropping a line.

My regards likewise flow forth to all the Carbones Olympiani . . . . & may Bast, Sekhmet, & all other feline deities watch over little Peter Ivanovitch & bring him to a safe (if not quite placid) maturity! My aunt's regards may be assum'd, tho' she be not here to utter them.

Sir, yr moſt oblig'd, moſt ob[t] Serv[t]

Theobaldus Senex

P.S. I duly appreciate the Salem touch in your epistle, & wish I had been there to circulate around old Federal St., Salem Common, Chestnut St., the Turner-Ingersoll house, & other familiar vestiges of the past.

Notes

1. The quotation is found in William Francis Macy (1867–?), ed., *The Nantucket Scrap Basket: Being a Collection of Characteristic Stories and Sayings of the People of the Town and Is-land of Nantucket, Massachusetts* (Nantucket: The Inquirer and Mirror, 1916), 79 (*LL*

631). The actual quotation says "ocean" rather than "sea." HPL's own essay on Nantucket is titled "The Unknown City in the Ocean."

2. EHC published the line beginning "My fortnight . . ." through the last verse of the poem in his *Olympian* (Autumn 1940). HPL's untitled verses have been published as "[Little Sam Perkins]."

3. Hannah Robinson (1746–1773) liked to gaze out at Narragansett Bay from a large boulder at Tower Hill Road in South Kingston, RI. She had eloped with her teacher, Peter Simon, whom her father had forbidden her to see, and they reconciled over the matter only after Hannah had become deathly ill.

4. HPL refers to the poem "Edith Miniter." He also wrote the essay "Mrs. Miniter—Estimates and Recollections" (1934; *CE* 1.378–86).

5. Neither Cook nor Tryout Smith published the Miniter memorial volume, but some of the material intended for it ultimately appeared in Hyman Bradofsky's *Californian* 5, No. 4 (Spring 1938). Smith did manage to publish a special issue of *Tryout* containing some Miniter material (see letter 38n2).

[38]   [ALS]

66 College St.,
Providence, R.I.,
Septr 29, 1934.

Ave, Olympiane!

          Your condolences on the passing of Little Sam Perkins are deeply appreciated by this household, by the grave, whiskered elders of the Kappa Alpha Tau, & by the bereaved Mrs. Spotty Perkins across the garden, who stalks mice & chases grasshoppers childless & alone. We envy you the sprightly grace & dynamic presence of Peter Ivanovitch—& trust that he may, through good luck & abstinence from chewing 110-volt electric toaster cords, grow to a ripe maturity & play an honour'd & patriarchal part in the generations to come.

          Glad you find recent verses not too conspicuously inept—& I surely hope that Smithy will leave at least a key to what I wrote as a Miniterian tribute. According to his latest plan, the Memorial will be a separate booklet like the Robbins memorial of 1914[1]—though it will doubtless be mailed as a supplement to *Tryout*. I am sure that, in view of your ample & inspired *National Amateur* sketch, your non-participation in this booklet can be fully excused. Forced writing is always to be discouraged—indeed, I regret that I had to grind out my mechanical quatrains before I had time to formulate anything spontaneous. Smithy prodded me with especial insistence because he was badly short of verse & wanted an evenly balanced issue. So great was his need of poetick numbers that he's taken some old elegiack lines of honest Doc Kuntz's, cut out an inapplicable stanza, & thrust them in as a Miniter tribute![2]

          As you will see by the enclosed epistle—my first personal word from Culinarius Augustus since his hurried return to Vermont—the major Miniter memorial is not likely to take form very rapidly. I've offered to solicit contributions if that will do any good—indeed, I'm at present engaged in digging one out of Edkins. Edkins knew relatively little of Mrs. Miniter's work, & did not appreciate the early specimens he saw. I've lent him "Our Natupski Neighbours" & the Dowe memorial,[3] & believe his eyes will be opened regarding the maturer merits of the brilliant amateur who joined the fraternity in the same year that he did (1883), & whom he met at one of the early Boston conventions.

Incidentally—you will see from Cook's letter that the country has not been as powerful an emollient for his jangled nerves as I had hoped it would be. When he's in the city he needs the country, & when he's in the country he needs the city! I wish he could strike, in one way or another, a fairly stable equilibrating compromise. About the last thing I'd ever recommend would be two years in the stink-hole of New York 'among the radicals below 14th St.'! Most of the specimens of subquartodecimal radicalism that I've seen can be endured just about two *minutes* without a violent combination of nausea & ennui. Still—de gustibus & all that. And he *could* cut those two years short!

Sorry your semi-Nantucket relatives-in-law encountered such forbidding weather on the Novanglian mainland! So far as *Providence* is concerned, & using a continuous Brooklyn residence of 2 years, 1 month, & 15 days (1924–6) as a basis of comparison, I'd be inclined to dispute violently any claim that the Noveboracense climate holds substantial advantages over that of *southern* New England. The annual mean temperature of New York City is precisely that of Newport, R.I., & only 2° above that of Providence. To anything short of a weather-bureau instrument set the meteorological differences are absolutely imperceptible. Seeing New York at every season, I ran into just about the same variety of good & rotten days that I encounter at home. Spring cheer & autumn chill came at the same calendar dates, & the winters were just as hellish. Indeed, the greatest suffering from cold that I ever endured was in Brooklyn in 1924–5. God! Will I ever forget that eclipse expedition to Yonkers with Jim Morton, Arthur Leeds, George Kirk, & Ernest A. Dench in January '25? We saw the eclipse & corona & all that—but I was just about all in for the rest of the winter by the time I staggered back to the protecting rays of my oil heater! No—when I move south to a better climate, it will be considerably beyond even the southernmost tip of Staten Island! However, I do think the climate of *Boston* is a bit rawer than that of Narragansett Bay—&, of course, N.Y. as well. You get a chill east wind from the ocean which somehow becomes tempered by the balmy influences of Dedham, Norwood, Walpole, Wrentham, & the Attleboroughs before its relatively innocuous residue whirls the vanes of these Plantations. Nantucket is distinctly milder in winter than either Boston or Providence—owing to the equalising effect of its insular situation. Last winter, for example, its perennial shrubs & hedges did not perish from the unprecedented cold; though their "off-island" kin shared one universal death.

So far the present autumn has been far from bad hereabouts. The present week has brought a number of delightful days, & last Wednesday I spent the entire afternoon in my favourite countryside north of Providence—doing my writing partly on a stone wall at a bend of the Breakneck Hill Road overlooking a magnificent sweep of verdant valley & distant steepled hillside, & partly on a rocky cliff beetling over a silent, glassy tarn in the midst of deep woods. Though the leaves had begun to turn, the general effect of the landscape was still quite aestival.

I rejoice that a respite from your dual labours is in sight, & shall welcome the Rhodinsular trips made possible by your relative leisure. While a postal heralding of such expeditions is always advantageous, I am sure that a more immediate telephonic message would be amply adequate—hence let me urge you to omit no opportunity to come, however impromptu the voyage may have to be. Even amidst the greatest haste, I fancy I could recall enough points of interest to keep you pleasantly busy as long as daylight lasts. And incidentally, damn the short-sighted legislators who—in both of our commonwealths—have decreed that daylight-saving time shall end now instead of a month hence! To my mind, there is no month in the year in which daylight-saving would be more useful & pleasant than October. As an initial trip, I believe the South County—with Gilbert Stuart birthplace, Hannah Robinson rock, &c—would include the most points of genuine interest. I'll exhume from my files the set of notes on roads & turnings—useful in getting expeditiously from place to place—which I jotted down last year when blazing trails on the trial & error system with the ever-tolerant E. Hoffmann Price.

Enclosed is a modest specimen[4] (one of 3 advance copies kindly sent me by Editor Adams) of what amateurdom's qualitative renaissance is beginning to turn out. I think you'll agree that, despite its admittedly incipient nature, it represents quite an advance beyond the usual juvenile congeries of "newsy notes" & personal paragraphs. Despite the presence of our names as members of the "Advisory Board", Moe & I had no hand in the choice & emendation of its Pierian contributions. I also have an advance copy of young Bradley's *Perspective Review,* which likewise shews signs of the upward struggle. The new N.A. seems to me excellent. It is possible that I am responsible for the restoration of the traditional black-letter heading, for I strongly urged this step as soon as I ascertained who the new editor was. Your Miniter obituary appears to advantage despite a few obvious misprints. Still more literary vitality is indicated by a poetical contest within the so-called Hodge-Podge Group, of which old Doc Kuntz, Charles A. A. Parker, & myself form the judicial triumvirate.

Well—I shall keep eyes & ears alert for harbingers of the Carbonaceous expedition. Meanwhile regards to all from myself, my aunt, & the surviving members of the Kappa Alpha Tau!

Yr obt hble Servt

HPL

Notes

1. *In Memory of Susan Brown Robbins, a Co-worker in Amateur Journalism, 1891–1898,* ed. Edith Miniter and C. W. Smith (Haverhill, MA: C. W. Smith, [1910?]).
2. Eugene B. Kuntz, "Not Dead But Living," *Tryout* 16, No. 9 (September 1934): [6] (unsigned). The issue was titled *In Memory of Edith May [sic] Miniter, a Co-worker in Amateur Journalism, 1884–1934,* ed. Laurie A Sawyer and C. W. Smith. The poem was reprinted from the *Clovis* [NM] *News-Journal* (29 October 1932): 4, where it was published as "In Memory of Mrs. J. L. Stevenson."
3. *Our Natupski Neighbors* (1916) was a professionally published novel by Miniter. *In Memoriam: Jennie E. T. Dowe,* ed. Michael White (Dorchester, MA: [W Paul Cook,] September 1921), was a book of tributes to Miniter's mother.
4. Presumably Adams's *Literati.*

[39]   [ALS]

Oct. 11, 1934

Ave, Olympiane!

Sorry the Chev expedition couldn't get here last Sunday amidst the solar refulgence & autumnal foliage. We shall hope for better luck on coming week-ends.

No doubt the appeal for critical copy duly arrived. No hurry as long as Editor Bradley has it by the 25th. I got my section off last Monday, & Spink says he'll be well on the sunny side of the deadline. It looks as if we'd have to stick the year out for lack of other victims.

But the purpose of this bulletin is to forward the enclosed epistle from the Wilbraham matron who is winding up the Miniter estate—which Culinarius has just sent me, & which he wishes me to relay to you. I will send, also, his own communication. The alleged wholesale mailing of Mrs. Miniter's last days certainly sounds bizarre in the extreme—although a failing of faculties might account for it. Cook, as you see, professes scepticism; but it seems to me that the deliberate invention of such a tale would be even more unlikely than the actual occurrence of the thing. The only object of the survivors in misrepresenting the facts would be to conceal some loss or destruction of valuable papers. An active imagination might connect the matter with the local hostility to the Natupski novel—fancying some plot to destroy the unpublished sequel—but that sounds rather extravagant in the cold light of day. I am suggesting to Cook that he see whether the claim about Mrs. M's failing mind tallies with the letters received from her. If he had lucid & capable-sounding letters during the period allegedly covered by the irresponsible mailing, then one may well suspect unreliability in the present report. Otherwise, the report itself sounds less extravagant than any alternative theory.

It will certainly be tragic & disastrous if nothing remains from the wealth of literary material in Mrs. Miniter's possession. A complete loss at Wilbraham would be an even greater calamity than the Allston mishap—& would surely suggest the makings of a peculiarly malign fatality![1] I am suggesting to Cook that he get in touch with the dead-letter office regarding packages with a N. Wilbraham postmark. Incidentally, the loss of his own material in the present chaos is surely regrettable enough.

Meanwhile Edkins has contributed a really brilliant reminiscent essay to the coming memorial,[2] & young Spink has promised one. An anonymous gift of $25.00 has given the financing a hopeful start. I have offered to help in soliciting contributions—& wrote the other day to Rev. F. S. C. Winks of Indianapolis, who knew Mrs. M. well during the 80's. Mesdams Avery & Dennis, as you'll see from Cook's letter, are hard to locate. But there's really no hurry about the matter—the Dowe memorial did not appear till two years after its subject's decease. I hope that Cook can manage to take the desiderate trip to N. Wilbraham & see what's what there.

Some pretty good exploring weather this week—I took rural tramps Monday & Tuesday, though it wasn't warm enough to sit around & write according to my aestival custom. Foliage hasn't quite reached its maximum vividness yet, although certain trees, shrubs, & vines are furnishing some bright touches around the Lincoln Woods. Hope to see you before the pageantry is over. Today only the (tiger) Vice-President is visible at the Kappa Alpha Tau. Black & white Pres. Randall (wonder if his folks are kin of Ex-Speaker Randall of 'noblest pursuit of American youth' fame?)[3] shares my own tastes as to temperatures. The V.P. sends salutations to Napoleon, Wellington, & Peter Ivanovitch.

Benedictions to all
—Theobaldus Senex.

Notes

1. See HPL to Helm C. Spink, 26 September 1935 (ms., JHL): "The relatives tell a fantastic tale of Mrs. Miniter's having partly lost her mind & having mailed away all her MSS. to indistinct addresses—but the evidence does not sustain this. All that does survive is material which Cook salvaged from the Kennedy home in Allston—just as Mrs. K. was about to give it to the junk man!"
2. Ernest A. Edkins, "Memories and Impressions," *Californian* 5, No. 4 (Spring 1938): 56–60; rpt. in Miniter's *Dead Houses and Other Works*, ed. Kenneth W. Faig, Jr., and Sean Donnelly (New York: Hippocampus Press, 2008), 70–75.
3. HPL apparently refers to Samuel J. Randall (1828–1890), a Democratic politician from Pennsylvania and Speaker of the House of Representatives (1876–81), who reportedly said that amateur journalism was "the noblest pursuit the youth of the land ever engaged in" (quoted in the *Leavenworth* [KS] *Times*, 15 August 1889).

[40]   [ANS postcard]¹

[Postmarked Providence, R.I.,
13 October 1934]

All Hail! Or rather, *snow*—of which we've had a liberal sample this morning! Hope you didn't run into any impassable drifts up Rutland way—or perhaps they keep the roads as well heated as the municipal pool! Just now I'm over-flowingly grateful for the steam that's keeping this room at 85°! ¶ No doubt you found my epistle of yesterday upon your return. The Miniter estate surely presents a variety of problems worthy of a more plutocratic hereditament! ¶ Glad you'll have the prose criticism by the 25th. ¶ Thanks immensely for the invitation next Friday—which it looks as if I could accept, with pleasure & appreciation! Let me know when & where to shew up Friday afternoon. In view of my always-light luggage, I could be in front of Chauncey Hall at any designated hour. How about it? Hope the skies & temperature will be favour-able—especially Sunday, when I want R.I. antiquities to appear at their best! The leaves ought to be near their maximum brilliancy unless blasted by some malign meteorological disaster. ¶ Hoping, then, to see you next Friday—& to hear of the time & place before that—I have yᵉ Honour to ſubſcribe myſelf
Yr oblig'd obᵗ Servt
H P L

Notes

1. *Front:* Southern Magnolia Flowers.

[41]   [ALS]

Dies Mercurii
[17 October 1934]

Ave!

My mourning today is only partial, since the surrender was only *proposed* on the 17th. The really heavy lamentation comes Friday, the 19th, when your Genˡ Washington received the sword of Maj-Gen O'Hara & our band was forc'd to play "The World Upside Down."¹ Watch for heavy tears when you greet me in Mr. Copley's Square. He, like me, was loyal to our rightful Sover-eign, & sail'd for the home land from Marblehead in 1775 . . . his son, Lord Lyndhurst, later becoming Lord Chancellor of England. God Save the King!

De re Miniteria—I certainly agree that the account in Mrs. Calkins's [for such is the name] letter contains no inherent improbabilities, & is (barring ev-idence whereof we know nothing) far less difficult to credit than any alterna-tive theory could be. The matter is distasteful enough in any event, but it seems to me that an attempt to dispose of MSS. by mail to supposedly suita-ble persons would be a far from unnatural procedure for one with failing fac-ulties & dark apprehensions, who had in palmier days been so dependent on the posts for contact with congenial colleagues. However, I await Culinarius's own explanation of his scepticism. He has meanwhile asked me to write to Chiles & Brubaker[2] for literary tributes—& wants me to ask you to ask Mrs. Myers for one. Nay, carrying the relaying process a step further, he wants me to ask you to ask Mrs. Myers to ask Thrift for a tribute. And so down the line! To me also has been entrusted the task of getting a tribute out of Tryout Smith. Distracted by the metropolitan clamours of North Montpelier—where he says he can't write letters—Culinarius intends to spend some time at his sister's in Sunapee, N.H. next month, preparing the bulk of his tribute-appeals. His long list of intended victims surely is of formidable aspect! I hope that idea of a collective trip to North Wilbraham can materialise during his Boston sojourn . . . . . that is, assuming that Chevvy has adequate heating facilities. Otherwise, the Ballad of Chevy Chase might have an ending as disastrous to me, in a frigid way, as to the brave Erla Douglas! Incidentally—I've cooked up a prose tribute to Mrs. Miniter covering 16 of these Georgiocircense pages,[3] & laying stress on the ancient Wilbra'm background. It is probably too long for use, so before I type it I shall send it to Cook for suggestions as to pruning. I may lug it along Friday for you to see—although, considering the quality of the pencil scrawl, I doubt if you'll get much out of it save through frequent oral elucidations from the author! Cook's remark about the funds, hinting at a change of editorship, reveals as little to me as to you. But the job will certainly be a tough one, & if he can find a suitable goat to supplant him in the burthen-bearing he has my sincere congratulations!

Coming now to the subject of the impending conclave—Chauncy Hall at 3:03 p.m. Eastern Standard on Friday will be ideal from my point of view. As a specific meeting-point I guess I'll choose Mr. Metcalf's chemist-shop . . . . especially since you allude so favourably to its temperature. Why climb up only to come down again? Assuming, of course, that the worthy chemist *is* on the terrestrial level. Anyhow, I'll nominate the pharmaceutical headquarters this time! May the gods grant a day as relatively civilised as this one—though Sunday is the one I'm really most anxious about. I have my list of South County directions all ready to grab from the table when we pass through here en route for the Gilbert Stuart country. [& Mr. Stuart, like his great contemporary limner, was loyal to our Sovereign even if he did return to the seceded colonies to paint Genl. Washington later on!] Copley & Stuart—quite an aesthetic itinerary for young Chevvy!

Until 3:03 Friday, then . . . . & afterward, so far as that goes . . . . . I have yᵉ Honour to remain, Sir, yr moſt oblig'd, moſt obt Servt—Theobaldus Senex

P.S. Here's something dedicated to the Old Gentleman—that may amuse you![4]

Notes

1. An English ballad, first published on a broadside in the middle of the 1640s as a protest against the policies of Parliament relating to the celebration of Christmas. Tradition has it that the British band played this tune when Cornwallis surrendered at the Siege of Yorktown (1781).

2. Walter C. Chiles, president of the Philadelphia Amateur Journalists Association, Official Editor of NAPA (1891–92 and again in 1897–98, upon the resignation of Edward A. Hering), and publisher of the prestigious journal, the *Rising Age*. Alson Brubaker (1872–?) of Fargo, N.D., president of NAPA (1893–94) and editor of *Ink Drops*.

3. I.e., long sheets of paper provided by HPL's friend George W. Kirk when he was living in Brooklyn.

4. Possibly Clark Ashton Smith's "The Epiphany of Death" (*Fantasy Fan*, July 1934), dedicated to HPL.

[42]   [ALS]

Tryout's Birthday
[24 October 1934]

Noblest of Olympians:—

        While still illumined by the glow of my idyllic weekend I received your timely report—sending it on without censorship [even the Edw. F. Suhre[1] stands—let the reader glean what he may!] to Bradley in time for his inflexible deadline. It strikes me as highly adequate, & I hope the amateur public may profit by the instructional suggestions. Let us also hope that this time the word *Themes* will take no more alien form than THEBES or THAMES or THERMOS! It surely was considerate of you to make a long journey to Neponset for the sake of timely mailing. I, in my turn, have been conscientious in getting the MS. into an early-evening collection on the day of receipt.

        Yes—my De Land host of last spring surely did manage to slip a macabre thrill or two into his *Perspective Review* effort![2] This fragment comes from his long picaresque attempt, "The Book of Garoth", & is rather tame as compared with some of the really horrible episodes. Barlow has a good many years to grow in, & I think he'll amount to something in the end. Pictorial art, though, is his principal field . . . . did I shew you those two paintings of his on my bedroom wall last August . . . . the nameless Dweller & the breaking waves? As for "Edward P. Lovecraft" . . . I shall continue to assume that it's a misprint unless Bradley tells me that he's fired me from his advisory board & appointed a hitherto unknown cousin! So far as I know, I'm the only Lovecraft in America. My progenitor in that line did not leave his native Devonshire till 1827—when, having been financially & territorially cleaned out on the ancestral sod, he sought a new fortune in a new land . . . migrating to Rochester, N.Y. with five sons & a daughter. Of these sons my grandfather

George Lovecraft was the 4th, & I am his only surviving male descendant. The others are wholly without living male-line representatives with one possible exception—Joseph Jr. having had one grandson who proved quite a roving character, went through a modest competence of 75,000 bucks, & drifted out of sight in the west. His whereabouts were unknown in 1921, when I was last in correspondence with such paternal relatives as survive. Thus, except for myself, he alone (or children of his) could have inherited the name Lovecraft in America today—& it is very doubtful whether he is alive or has descendants. Nor do I know of any further ingress of Lovecrafts from England. Last spring a letter appeared in the readers' department of *Weird Tales* signed "Edgar Lovecraft, Martinsburg, W. Va.",[3] but a letter of mine addressed to this potential cousin was returned by the P.O. Probably it was a fake—some boob using a convenient pseudonym picked from the magazine's table of contents. But for a moment I thought that this might be a son of the one possibly non-existent (though lost) line. Rather glad he isn't—for the letter displayed an execrably mediocre taste!

Well—here's some more Culinary light on the Miniter matter . . . & rather pessimistic light at that. It appears from Mrs. Calkins' second letter that Mrs. M. did considerable paper-burning; while, as you see, Cook still thinks that the natives (in the person of the Tupper cousins) disposed of such documents as they thought injurious to them. I had not realised that any work of Mrs. M's so ruthlessly reproduced the decadent ways of Wilbraham's insidiously retrograding Yankees. It certainly makes one see red to think of two or three novels—& hades knows how many short stories—as deliberately destroyed . . . . but the situation speaks for itself, take it or leave it! I am again urging Cook to make enquiries at the dead letter office. By the way—he wants Golden's address. I forgot to take it down for him when you mentioned it.

Glad you all reached home safely Sunday night—& trust that Sister had a pleasant time to report. Monday certainly was dismal & pluvial—but I thank the weather authorities for postponing the downpour that long! Yesterday was so warm that black & white Pres. Randall of the Kappa Alpha Tau appeared on the clubhouse roof. He & Vice-Pres. Osterberg (the tiger you saw Sunday) send regards to Naps, Duke, & the inimitable Peter Ivanovitch, as do I. With appropriately inclusive benedictions—

H P L

Notes

1. Edward F. Suhre (1879–1939), editor of the *Missourian* and *Occasional Press,* and president of the NAPA (1910–11).
2. R. H. Barlow, "The Inhospitable Tavern," *Perspective Review* (Autumn 1934): 3, 12.
3. *WT* 23, No. 6 (June 1934): 783.

[43]   [ANS postcard][1]

[Postmarked Providence, R.I.,
20 November 1934]

Ave! Shall be confabulating with Culinarius at 7 Hancock Friday & Saturday, & hope very much that you can get in on some of the sessions. Saturday, I believe, holds chances of liberty on your part at least in the afternoon. Cook himself will probably notify you, but I thought I'd take no chances. Let *him* know by postcard to 7 HANCOCK when you can be available [if, as we both strongly hope, you can be], so that he can arrange his crowded programme accordingly. He wants to see dozens of people around Boston about the Miniter memorial, & has only a week to do it in. If *Sunday* is your only free day, I could stay over that long. Cook has some Miniter MSS. with him, which he wants to discuss with you & me. I'll try to guarantee that he *really* shows up at the scheduled convocation! ¶ Hope the warm weather holds! ¶ Trust your armistice day N Y trip came off all right. ¶ Regards to all—& hope Peter Ivanovitch is flourishing!
Yr obt Servt
    H P L

Notes

1. *Front:* Campus, Brown University, Providence, R.I.

[44]   [ANS postcard][1] [HPL and W. Paul Cook to EHC]

[Postmarked Boston, Mass.,
25 November 1934]

Appreciative greetings on the morning after! We sure did have a swell time, & can glow with augmented gratitude for the taxi service as we jointly shiver & weep after a brief exposure to today's devastating frigor. But they *have* got some heat at 7 Hancock today . . . . as my ability to pen these lines proves. Have my luggage check'd at the stage coach terminal, & expect to be once more on Providence's ancient hill by midnight. ¶ Regards to all—& forgiveness for Peter Ivanovitch for not purring last night. ¶ With grandpaternal benedictions—H P L

We didn't have a post card session last night, so it has to be done today, and you will have one more of Lovecraft's cards to help fill that desk drawer. I suppose when it is really full you will move to another house (like Swinburne or someone)* to escape cleaning it out.
Cook

*[HPL's note:] It was De Quincey—but not de Massachusetts Quincy.

Notes

1. *Front:* New Parker House and King's Chapel, Boston, Mass. *HPL's note:* Culinarius' home after the Revolution.

[45]　　[ALS]

> Idibus Decembris
> MDCCCCXXXIV.
> [15 December 1934]

Ave!

The eminent Culinarius has asked me to forward to you a pair of notes from one Frank Roe Batchelder, Esq.,[1] illustrating a peculiar form of special-ised amnesia & slight partial recovery. I take great pleasure in complying—& in adding, albeit uninstructed, several more documents relayed from Sunapee & pertinent to the Miniter memorial project. These, in the main, speak for themselves. Stinson[2] contributed an excellent sonnet—marred only by a queer confusion of tenses in the sestette which I think I have straightened out very unobtrusively. To Miss Noyes—whose files, I understand, were con-sumed in a tragic holocaust a decade or so ago—I have sent my one *duplicate* copy of Cook's great July 1919 N.A. (with her article on Mrs. Miniter);[3] telling her that she may retain it if it is of any permanent use to her. I am especially sorry to hear of Murphy's poor health, & hope that the task of preparing an article may not be too great a burthen to him. The epistolette from the faith-ful & prayerful Mr. Riale[4] is a rather colourful document in its brief way. I wish I could think that one of my juvenile ventures was the First & Best School of Journalism in the United States . . . . a realistic habit of mind has its penalties! But the best news for the Miniter memorialites came from good old Tryout Smithy in the form of an address for which—as you are keenly aware—all hands have been frantically seeking. I here transcribe it for your benefit: *Mrs. Harriet Cox Dennis, Central St., Abington, Mass.* We were scouring the wrong side of Boston in our conjectures—all the while she was back on your own South Shore (or its hinterland) in the town whence (I believe) she originally sprang!

Well—the thermometer hasn't been any too kind since I was so mercifully delivered at the door of my Boston town house! As I think we told you on our joint card, we spent the following day shivering at 7 Hancock, in a room to which the thrice-accurst Polish landlord (may Russia, Prussia, & Austria re-partition him with every form of sadistic torture!) had not supplied a particle of heat. I wore my overcoat, but it didn't help much. That night I returned home, & the climb up the hill at 28° (above my usual deadline, but not so pleasant, either!) nearly laid me flat. Culinarius returned to Sunapee the next morning, & the infamous, dastardly B. & M. (no doubt abetted by the equally infamous &

dastardly laxity of the legislative assembly of His Majesty's Province of New-Hampshire) *turned off the heat in the stage-coach* at the Province line!! Mehercule! Culinarius—hardy tho' he is in comparison with Grandpa Theobald—was nearly paralysed by the time he reached Concord; & his sister, who met him, had to drag him into a restaurant for an hour's thawing out. The drive to Sunapee in her car was unheated, too—but he was bundled up this time. In health he continues so-so. He has consulted a new doctor, who tells him his blood-pressure is dangerously high & commands him to relax as utterly as possible physically & mentally. Poor chap—& now the icy horror of -15° .... with a busted heating-plant! (cf. his commentary on the 2nd Batchelder note.)

As for me—I've been a prisoner of the frost-daemon for the last 6 days, though a caloric upturn today—to the tune of a wet snow-flurry & a temperature of 30°—will now liberate me. It was repeatedly as bad as +10° here—the minimum being 8°. Young Long is urging me to visit him in N Y after Yule—but if spells like the recent one get frequent, I don't know. Yet here in the house it never fell below 82° or 83°, thanks to the marvellous 24-hour steam supply piped in from the college engineering building.

Just before the icy hell broke loose I enjoyed the concentrated session of lectures & cognate features provided by Providence's so-called Art Week. On one occasion two eminent local artists painted pictures in full view of the audience[5]—& another drawing card was the exhibition of some of the 717 important Japanese prints just acquired by the local art museum. I enclose a catalogue of the latter. We're getting in the running with your Museum of Fine Arts, which I understand claims to have the finest collection of Japanese prints outside Nippon itself! Still another of the many features was a display of the new aesthetic form—the correlation of shifting colour with music—but, alas, that came after the cold snap had made me a close prisoner of 66!

I trust all flourishes at Norfolk Downs & Copley Square! Regards to all—& tell Peter Ivanovitch that Tryout has a couple of new little tigers at 408. ¶ Blessings—H P L

P.S. None of the enclosed need be returned. ¶ I looked up the ancestral stuff in the Dowe memorial, & found we guessed wrong in placing the two Shields's, David & son Hector. They were Edwin Tupper's maternal grandfather & uncle, respectively. His wife—Catherine Orpha—was a *Moore*. And Cook has found that the young heir he is seeking is a Moore—not a "Barnes" as he had thought. Probably the livery-stable in Athol suggested "Barnes"!

Notes

1. Frank Roe Batchelder (1869–1947), editor of the *Go-Ahead*.
2. Samuel Scott Stinson (1868–1935), sixteenth NAPA president.

3. Mabel F[rances] Noyes (1867–1941), who, with Edith Miniter and Ella M. Frye, edited the *Quartette*. HPL refers to her article "Edith Miniter—A Character Sketch," *Prairie Breezes* 7, No. 6 (March 1898): 6; rpt. *National Amateur* 41, No. 6 (July 1919): 303–4; rpt. in Miniter's *Going Home and Other Amateur Writings*, ed. Kenneth W. Faig, Jr. (Glenview, IL: Moshassuck Press, 1995), 846–48.

4. Evan Reed Riale, one of the founders of the NAPA in February 1876.

5. Hezekiah Anthony Dyer (1872–1943) and John Robinson Frazier (1889–1966).

[46]   [ALS]

Ancient 66—
—Tiw's-Daeg
[15 January 1935]

Dear E H C:—

Commiserations on the super-crowded programme! Why in hades' name can't these damn'd politicians keep their squabbles under control? The same old story—N.A.P.A. in 1935 repeats the trouble of the U.A.P.A. in 1915. Incompetence . . . removals . . . challenges . . . . human natur'! I had hoped that the present year might be one of literary revival, with straightforward young chaps like Babcock & Bradley in charge—but alas! From all I had heard of the trouble I was somewhat inclined to side with Babcock . . . though possibly he may have shewn a slight lack of tact & flexibility. I give it up—& am dash'd glad I'm not an executive judge!

You are certainly to be excused if you can't grind out a prose report amidst the turmoil of other activities—& anyhow, the gap can be filled in the June issue. But let us hope for the best . . . perhaps the present belligerents can be persuaded to compose their trivial differences without setting all the judicial machinery in motion.

Had a very enjoyable near-convention in N.Y., as I probably mentioned on my card. Talman has just sent a set of the photographs which he took at the meeting when the subjects weren't looking [he has a small but costly German camera which will take clear views in ordinary electric light], & after an inspection of the various facial expressions I feel sure he could do a thriving blackmail business by snapping wealthy victims & threatening to publish the results! My own mug is probably the prize horror of the collection—may lightning blast the negative! Since my return to these Plantations I've been draggin' along tol'able—though just now I am a prisoner of the cold. Hellish yesterday—& nothing to tempt one forth even now. Let us hope that spring will not be far behind!

Regards from my aunt & myself to all the household . . . . I suppose Peter Ivanovitch is a colossal mountain of fur by this time! Only brief bulletins from Culinarius so far in 1935—though he sent the enclosed lately, which distinctly merits reading. Some of these brief & bitter fragments like "Rootless" have a genuine poignancy.[1] You might return the yaller sheets some time—no hurry.

      Benedictions—

         H P L

Notes

1. W. Paul Cook (as Willis T. Crossman), "Rootless," *Driftwind*, 9, No. 8 (February 1935): 242–43. In *Contradictions* ([North Montpelier, VT]: Driftwind Press, n.d.), 3–4; rpt. in *W. Paul Cook: The Wandering Life of a Yankee Printer*, ed. Sean Donnelly (New York: Hippocampus Press, 2007), 231–32.

[47]   [ALS]

                               Old 66

                           —Jany. 22. [1935]

Hail, Olympian!

        Grateful obeisances to a valiant spirit whom not even the extremes of oppressive care can crush into a non-performance of duty! Your communication arrived just as I was mailing my own brief verse report, & a longer article for *The Perspective Review*, to Editor Bradley.[1] Now ⅔ of the Bureau has met the literary & calendar requirements .... & let us hope that young Spink is following our noble example. Your critique is admirable in every respect—inclusive, incisive, & spirited. It won't be the fault of the Bureau if the amateur press continues in its state of triviality.

    I feel sure that your analysis of my writ-to-order Poe information will prove helpful to the struggling author—although I could myself have given those paragraphs an even more drastic lacing beforehand![2] The case is a typical example of (a) non-spontaneity, (b) haste, & (c) restricted space. I didn't want to write anything in the first place, but Hymie esk me I shood mek it ah article too-t'ousand voidts longk en ah hurry ... & you behold the dire result. Ordinarily I never write anything unless I have something to say. This time, without anything to say, but wishing to encourage Brother Hymie's long-prose policy, I allowed myself to sink to the level of the schoolboy essayist or emybronic amateur who simply sits down with a resolution to 'write something.' What the hell could I compress into 2000 words? (The man before Hymie got really reckless, with air-mail & everything!) Not a story .... & what sort of an "article" could be cooked up without being either artificial & unmotivated pedantry, or mere empty sententiousness like the placid anilities of Mary Morgan Ware?[3] Obviously, I'd better tell about something simple & concrete (though what I finally *did* tell of was largely *brick*)—something I knew well enough to describe, & of sufficient interest & freshness to forestall the obvious query as to why I bothered to compose & publish it. [Philosophy of Composition stuff][4] Well—the first thing that occurred to me was the newly opened Poe house in Philly, which I'd seen on my trip, & whose dedication (with speeches by the bland William Lyon Phelps[5] & others) I had heard over the radio the preceding January. So I described that. But hell—that wouldn't make 2000 words without padding, & I wanted to encourage Hymie in his ample-space policy! So I thought I'd better briefly list Ed's other hangouts & tie them all together into a single article. Hence a ransacking of memory, bookshelves, & files. But now a new problem—how in thunder to pack so damn *much* into as *few* as 2000 words! Oy, vot ah beezness! I began writing with the spatial millstone around my neck, noting the number of words at the end of each paragraph—& sink me if I didn't nearly use up the double-grand before getting Eddie safely fired from West Point! Obviously, this would never do! I must substitute streamlined cottage architecture for flamboyant Gothic! And so the boiling-down, adjective-lopping process began . . . & with an eye on the calendar, at that. Beard of Moses! You esk I shood sparkle, & how iss ah men goingk to sparkle when Brudder Hymie sess he shen't over too-t'ousandt voids go a'ready? Some off de colyum fellers, dey ken scintillate by der inch & neffer lap ofer de limit—but me, ah lot off elbow-room I gotta hcff! Yeh ken't tell me I shell sparkle in jest so many voids end no more . . . dey ain'dt no room to radiate in! And so I decided I'd have to be pedestrian & statistical & reasonably accurate & let it go at that! But ah, if you could only see the priceless wit & personality which my own regretful blue pencil had to kill!

You surely have my profoundest sympathies regarding your labours on the judiciary! My patience with people who stir up time-&-energy-consuming rows over absolutely nothing, & squander valuable thought on empty questions of technical convention, political expediency, & personal status—& this in an organisation supposed to exist for the literary development of its members—is so slight as to make my opinion of such folk almost unprintable! I still stick to the basic ideal that plunged me into so many fights in the old United days—that the idea of office-holding & administration in amateur journalism ought to be subordinated to the small minimum compatible with the financing & structural maintenance of the literary, publishing, critical, & letter-writing (with emphasis on literary, philosophic, & other significant discussion) fabric. Office-holding should not be exalted as a distinction, but simply accepted as a duty. The real titans of amateurdom—the effective writers & publishers—should receive primary honours instead of the false titans . . . the clever publicity-hounds, wire-pullers, convention-organisers, &c. It *matters* whether or not an association encourages high standards of writing—but it makes not a damn's worth of difference whether this or that person receives a certain technical trifle simply because he has rounded up an especially vast herd of dumbbell recruits or printed an especially vast poundage of vapid personal tripe. The "ideology" of amateurdom ought to be swerved away from the political toward the literary as far & as thoroughly as is in any manner possible. No doubt the task is hopeless—but it's a goal worth keeping in mind. It may be slightly approximated, even if never even nearly reached. And meanwhile may all the Black Entities of the Abyss blast the misbegotten spawn of Abaddon responsible for stirring up puerile technicalities in a year dedicated to qualitiative improvement! However—in view of the parallel showers of Hibernian confetti in both the Fossil & pseudo-United organisations, it can scarcely be said that the National forms an especially dire example. The whole damn'd amateur cosmos is dire!

There's surely no need of haste in anything connected with the Miniter memorial. All material comes in very slowly—& there'll be a lot of it now that Stinson is printing an appeal in his pseudo-Fossil paper. Cook has lately sent me articles by Joseph Dana Miller & Edwin B. Swift—both astonishingly badly written considering their authors' celebrity.[6] I've had to do a heap of straightening-out in each. Odd how these old geezers seem to have no idea of coherent syntax, rhetorical symmetry, or even clear statement. Doc Swift writes that "Mrs. M. possessed a personal charm amounting almost to *infatuation*"! And Miller says "now that she is gone, amateur journalism is enriched for her presence"! Does he consider her services posthumous, or does he believe in ghosts as well as the single tax? Ah, me—the reviser's life is not a 'appy one! Well—let us hope that one or two good Marblehead or Nahant jaunts may inspire you to eclipse them all! Culinarius himself can write—& write well—when he has a mind to. Some of his dry Vermont sketches deserve book publication—involving as they do myriad subtle arcana of Viridimontane folklore, idiom, & nomenclature. I never realised before the utter separateness of the North-Vermont local culture, which certainly has a life & thought & traditions all its own. A valuable monograph could be written on the subject of Vermont given names (cf. *Dubartes*) alone!

Benedictions—H P L

P.S. When you next behold my study, you'll see a long-needed addition in the form of two dark-walnut sets of drawers for filing purposes. Bought 'em yesterday & expect their arrival at any moment. I may superimpose one on the other & have one lofty composite file. Each cabinet contains 5 drawers. Got 'em at a bargain—fire sale—tho' they certainly look all right.

Notes

1. HPL refers to the "Bureau of Critics" article in the March 1935 *National Amateur* and "What Belongs in Verse."
2. HPL refers to the article "Homes and Shrines of Poe," commissioned by Hyman Bradofsky for the *Californian*.
3. Possibly a reference to Mary Alice Morgan Ware (1872–1957), who may have been an amateur journalist of the period.

4. HPL refers to Poe's essay "The Philosophy of Composition" (1846), in which he purported to explain the inspiration and composition of "The Raven."

5. William Lyon Phelps (1865–1943), professor of English at Columbia University and a leading critic of the period.

6. Joseph Dana Miller (1864–1939), Fossil librarian, proponent of Henry George's single tax, and author of several books of poetry. Edwin B. Swift (1859–?), editor of *Hyperion, Swift's Weekly Amateur* (1905–06), and later *Swift's Weekly* (1906–07), and twenty-first president of NAPA (1891–92).

[48]　　[ALS]

Feby. 11[, 1935]

Ave, Olympiane!

　　　　　　The enclosed material explains itself. So after all, there *isn't* any unpaid bill in connexion with the Dowe ashes! This being so, their neglect for 16 years defies my explanatory powers!

　　Now as to what to do—it seems to me there's hardly any question. Get the ashes, keep them safely until somebody gets a chance to go to Wilbraham, & then carry out Mrs. Dowe's original wish. Any objection from members of the Beebe clan is virtually unthinkable. Regarding the logical person to visit the libitinarius[1] & secure the cinerary reliques—I don't see why Mrs. Sawyer[2] is so necessarily such. She has (vide suam epist.) merely notified amateurdom of a condition, & left it up to others what to do about it. The only thing necessary in connexion with her is to thank her (which Culinarius can do) & assure her that something *will* be done. That would constitute no slight—in fact, I fancy she'd even prefer it, since she has plainly stated her inability to get about much now in cold weather (& *how* I sympathise!). Of course, if some sort of credentials were required to claim the urn, she could be called up or written—but that might not be needed. As the one really competent & justified person on the spot, I fancy that *you* might well pay Mr. Briggs the fateful visit—if the matter involves no prohibitive inconvenience. Later we can discuss ways of getting out to Wilbraham at an appropriate season & performing the long-belated rites. In all these matters I fancy you'll agree with me. From the tone of Mrs. Sawyer's letter I see no ground for Cook's fear that she will obtrusively butt in. You might drop W P C a line with your views. In any event, I do not think the destruction of the ashes ought to be permitted. Something, very clearly, should be done within the specified time limits.

　　Curse this circumambient continuity of hyemal rigours! However, there have been a few days warm enough to let Grandpa totter out of the house. Heard a delightful poetry reading by Archibald MacLeish at the college yesterday. On one or two occasions the tiger Vice-President of the Kappa Alpha Tau has appeared on his accustomed fence. He & I send joint regards to Nap, His Grace, & Peter Ivanovitch!

　　　　　　Benedictions——H P L

Notes

1. *Libitinarius:* Latin for "undertaker."
2. Laurie A. Sawyer, an amateur journalist in the Boston area.

[49]　　[ALS] [W. Paul Cook to HPL; HPL to EHC]

Sunapee, Feb. 19

Dear H. P. L.:

I fear I am more bother than I am worth around this old world! You must hate to see my name on an envelope.

I enclose a letter received today from Laurie Sawyer. She acts very fine about the matter,—willing to help but no obtrusiveness. In fact, her idea is the same as yours and mine. If Cole will do this it will be a magnificent thing.

Hastily

Cook

You will note the time is short, and I have asked Mrs. Sawyer to telephone Briggs to hold the ashes.

C

Buck-Passing Circuit
—Station III.

All this matter explains itself—I'm sending it along because of the altered aspect of the *time limit.* Incidentally—if that trip out to the columbarium seems a nuisance, just drop a card to Culinarius or me, & some other goat can be elected. The important thing, of course—as Mrs. Sawyer says—is to get the task performed . . . . no matter how or by whom! The only reason your name was so ruthlessly suggested at the outset, was that your combined reliability & on-the-spotness seemed to put the suggestion in our mouths—or Watermans.

¶ Tell Peter Ivanovitch there are 4 coal-black kittens (born Feby. 14— true Lupercalian scions!) at the boarding-house across the garden.

¶ Had a letter last week from Loring & Mussey of N Y asking to see some of my tales with a view to possible book publication.[1] Since this is the 5th time such a request has been made (W T 1926—Putnam's 1931— Vanguard 1932—Knopf 1933), without tangible results to date, I'm not as naively excited about the matter as I might otherwise be.

¶ You may see Culinarius before long—he plans a return to Bostonium to ease his financial stress. Hope he gets a job & sticks this time! He informs me he is now writing a vampire-werewolf story in my own characteristic vein—which I shall be exceedingly glad to survey upon its completion.

Blessings & all that—& drop a card if it ain't practicable to act de re mortuaria.

H P L

Notes

1. August Derleth had asked his publisher to consider publishing HPL's work.

[50]   [ANS postcard][1]

[Postmarked Providence, R.I.,
26 February 1935]

Ave! I'm surely relieved to hear that the cinerary matter has been safely attended to. Thanks a thousand times on behalf of amateurdom! I'm notifying Culinarius at once. All your suggestions concerning the final expedition seem excellent & generous—& I feel certain that Mrs. S. will not insist on inclusion. This matter, of course, lies considerably in the future. The important thing—thanks to you—has been accomplished. ¶ Did I tell you in one of my notes that young Robert Moe (whom you'll recall as a little towhead of 12 in 1923 when his pa was foregathering with us in Wollaston & Marblehead) has come to Bridgeport, Conn.? I am tentatively expecting a week-end visit from him next Sat. & Sun. I shan't know the young rascal by sight as a man of 24! You ought to see him some time—I assume his assignment to N.E. soil by the Gen. Elec. Co. is quasi-permanent. ¶ Considerable telephoning hereabouts in an attempt to find good homes for the new feline arrivals at the boarding-house. There'll be no infanticides if the local ailurophiles can help it! ¶ No word from Cook since the note I forwarded, so I don't know when he'll hit Bostonium. ¶ Well—thanks again for the patriotick services!

Yr obt Servt
H P L

Notes

1. *Front:* Looking down Niagara Street, Buffalo, N. Y. *HPL's note:* (Mere thrift—they didn't 'put me off at Buffalo'!)

[51]   [ANS postcard][1] [HPL and Robert E. Moe to EHC]

[Postmarked Warren, R.I.,
4 March 1935]

Ave, Olympiane Carbo! An echo of good old '23! Dost recall the day when we foregathered with good old Mocrates, Mrs. Moe, & the two little towheads Bob & Don? Well—here's towhead #1 eleven years later, a rising young U. of Wis. graduate & electrical wizard. Now at Bridgeport, but I hope he can get to Bostonium to renew old memories during the summer. Have been walking him all around the antiquities of Providence, & *he* hasn't squatted on a stone wall & balked as his pater (& *others*) did in Marblehead once upon a time! ¶ Yesterday a letter I got a'ready by *air mail* from Meester Bradofsky, & he vants I should remind you to send it by him ah contribution to The Kelifornian before the Ides of Aprilis. Ah story by me he vants also— I suppose I ought to fix up one to encourage the kid.[2] ¶ Blessings—H P L

Greetings to one whom I do not remember (sorry):—The irrepressible letter-writer (my host) has reminded me that I should pay a call on you, as long as I am in this neighborhood. I shall be delighted to meet you again, and "Grandpa Lo" assures me we will both be in for some more hiking. More power to you! R. E. Moe

Notes

1. *Front:* Benedict Temple of Music, Roger Williams Park, Providence, R. I.
2. HPL published no fiction in the *Californian,* but he did submit several essays.

[52]   [ALS]

66 College St.,
Providence, R.I.,
April 9, 1935

Rever'd Olympian:—

Glad to hear that your palaeographical researches have reached such a point as to permit of a reply to sundry Viacollegian bulletins. You, I fancy, are in a position to appreciate the nasty crack which one of the amateurs—young Aaron Baker of *Literati*—recently made in a pass-around letter of poetic comment. Baker, in the course of attacking a poem which good old Moe had praised, delivered this beautiful dual shot at the turrets of Milwaukee & Providence: "The poem, *like Lovecraft's handwriting,* is very beautiful, but doesn't convey much meaning"!!!![1] Well—at least, nobody ever called my rooster-clawings "beautiful" before! But I fear Aaron's rod carries a barb nowadays instead of the traditional almond-blossoms of Semitick mythology!

The envelope of much-passed buck duly arrived . . . . many thanks . . . . now I must shoot it back to Culinarius! Of the various items, the Stinson letter gains a melancholy interest in view of its writer's recent death. Probably the sonnet for the Memorial is the last thing he ever wrote for publication. As for Culinarius—predicting his motions is beyond me! He spoke months ago of an immediate move to Boston, but still nothing is doing. He has suffered quite a spell of illness—both nervous collapse & blood-pressure trouble (& I guess his old malaria, too)—but seemed to be pulling out of it the last I heard—which was March 22. He says that the climate of Sunapee seems definitely to disagree with him. I shall urge him to get in touch with you regarding the Wilbraham pilgrimage—an event which would really be incomplete without him. I don't think you need hurry unduly about the memorial article, for the copy will be very slow in getting into shape. Mrs. Dennis—who has had a nervous breakdown—asked for plenty of time, & Miss Noyes of Methuen likewise demanded latitude. No word can be extracted from Frank Morton of Sudbury—though one wishes all the Mortonii could be represented. Cook will endeavour to get something from Fanny Kemble Johnson, whose continued existence & activity are attested by an excellent story under her signature in the February *Weird Tales*.[2] The Huntington Ave. Miss Noyes sent an extremely fine article, in which a piece of original verse was incorporated. Well—in general, you can see that there is no hurry . . . so you might as well let the memorial have the benefit of a full crystallisation of your ideas. Better read the stories before writing anything—they will probably broaden (though they will scarcely change) your perspective regarding Miniterian fiction.

Concerning critical matters—by a species of coincidence, your enquiry about the June deadline arrived in the selfsame post with a card from Bradley proclaiming *April 26* as such. I trust you may, as before, have a brilliant & penetrating (.44 calibre!) report on hand at the demanded date. I was glad to see the previous report in type—& haven't yet had the heart to scan it for tryoutisms. I'm not sure whether I'll write a verse report myself or try to make Moe do it.[3] He promised to handle *one* during the course of the year—but his last letter indicated such a rush of overwork that I may not have the nerve to exact that long-pledged pound of flesh. Well—I have a couple of weeks in which to reflect on the matter.

Sorry you can't reward Mr. Bradofsky for the compliment paid by that air mail appeal & 5000-word allotment! Well—I myself couldn't do justice to his 7500-word (7500—count 'em—7500!) offer. Everything I have on hand was either a damn sight longer or a damn sight shorter—so in the end I chucked him a 3500-word attack on aesthetic modernism—really an introduction to a larger article on Roman architecture & its influence, but quite complete in itself.[4] Recently I received a card from the old-timer Burger[5] urging support of Bradofsky for president. I acquiesced—hell! I'm for any guy who would stand for 7500 words of my junk!

As indicated by the joint card, I had a delightful visit from young Bob Moe . . . & believe me, the brilliant young electrician of '35 represents some evolution from the 11-year-old towhead of '23! His devotion is to physical science rather than big business . . . . give him plenty of vacuum tubes, spark coils, & such-like, & he doesn't bother greatly about who runs the show! He seems to me headed notably for substantial achievement—& he is so enamoured of his work that he regrets the short hours & swift passage of time. Lucky bird! He came in "Skippy"—his 1928 Ford runabout—& I found him a permanent parking-place a block north on the ancient hill. We then proceeded to give Old Providence a thorough pedestrian once-over—including museum stops—without any balking or rebellion on the part of the guest. The evening was spent in discussion, & during the small hours the distinguished visitor occupied a camp cot set up in the living-room. The next day explorations were performed in "Skippy"—first some circling around urban streets, & then a sightseeing jaunt down the east shore of the bay . . . to ancient Warren (which you beheld last August) & historick Bristol. In going to Bristol we detoured through the Colt estate (generously open to the publick) & traversed a seashore road of greater attractiveness than the main highway. Finally—after a return to Providence—I saw the traveller off down the West Shore, accompanying him as far as East Greenwich & giving him careful directions for seeing venerable Wickford. That he nobly availed himself of this advice, two fascinating snap-shots from his kodak amply attest. I certainly enjoyed the occasion, & hope to see Young Mocrates again. I'm also advising him to look up the gang in N.Y.—of whom he has so far seen only one member . . . his fellow-electrician Koenig.[6] You'll certainly enjoy meeting him when he gets around to the repetition of his 1923 itinerary in the Province of the Massachusetts-Bay. Meanwhile his 20-year-old brother Donald (the other little towhead whom you saw) has got a job in the U. of Wash. library at Seattle, & expects to finish his education at that remote seat of learning. This leaves Pater Mocrates et ux. in a state of local childlessness—so that they plan to move to smaller quarters. Moe thinks he'll take a microscopic apartment for the main household, & hire a room near the high-school as a wholly independent study & retreat—where he can reign amidst his books in solitary state whenever he chooses. A damn good idea, I tell him! A further link betwixt Wisconsin & ancient New-England may be established next July, when Alfred Galpin—infant wonder of the 1917–23 period in the United, & now a musical composer & instructor of French at Lawrence College in his native Appleton—plans to make his first visit to these venerable shores . . . . by motor, accompanied by his wife & probably by an academic colleague.

Well—the Mocratick visit formed a sort of break in my hibernation. Several decently warm days (65° to 71°) ensued, so that I had quite a number of phenomenally early outings—including a 12-mile suburban walk on March 6. More recently, however, chilly days have supervened—& I wish to hades I could get down to Charleston or St. Augustine!

Sorry I couldn't have welcomed Old Chev during some of those mild March days—but still milder days stretch ahead! In a couple of weeks or so the enviable nature of your sub-profession—as regards its theatre of operation—will once more take on its prime conspicuousness! To your thoughtful invitation that I participate in some of this mellow North Shore glamour, I respond with gratitude that I'm certainly with you unless something damned unforeseen assails my programme! Don't twist your plans into anything unusual on my account—but if all is convenient at your end I'll surely be delighted to shew up at some designated point (presumably the north side of Mr.

John Singleton Copley's clearing) at some designated hour (not far from 3:03, I imagine) on Friday, May 3ᵈ .... or such other date as later developments may dictate. I shall await further particulars .... & again, thanks! Meanwhile Culinarius' programme will doubtless have much to do with the date of the Wilbraham expedition. Glad Mrs. Myers will participate. I suppose the person in charge at Maplehurst ought to be notified in advance as a matter of form—though the purely exterior nature of the pensive rites removes such notification from the sphere of necessity.

Your multifarious activities surely excuse any epistolary shortcomings you may have display'd! Speaking of desk-cleanings & cognate matters—behold Grandpa's achievements in the direction of order! I mention'd, I believe, the two chests of drawers obtain'd on Jany. 21. On March 23 I augmented this outfit with *6* small 4-drawer cabinets purchas'd at a bargain sale for a dollar each. These modest devices—made of papier-maché with wood frame—were probably meant to be *shoe-boxes;* but I have no prejudices against the lowliness of their motivation. They have a neat imitation-grain'd-wood finish, & their size (only 22 × 13 × 9½″ each) enables them to be tuck'd into odd corners without disturbing the general furnishing scheme. Two of them (plus 1 drawer of the larger cabinets to hold material over 7 × 10″) take care of my entire amateur collection, two more hold old correspondence, a fifth harbours early-Americana, whilst the sixth is a catch-all for odds & ends. The large cabinets take classify'd antiquarian material & family photographs. The combined layout of *34 drawers* has worked wonders in reducing my chaos of pamphlets, cuttings, pictures, &c. &c. to some semblance of order. I spent 48 virtually continuous hours transferring material, & as a result my things are in the neatest condition they've been in for a quarter of a century. Yet even so, a vast lot of stuff remains stack'd on open shelves or chucked in perishable cardboard boxes .... & a vast pile of cuttings remain unclassify'd.

Added an exceedingly useful item to my library the other day—the new 1-volume Modern Encyclopaedia, now issued by Grosset & Dunlap for only $1.95. I've been needing such a thing badly—my latest other encyclopaedia being of 1914. The original $3.50 edition of this work strongly tempted me in 1933, but now I'm glad I waited. This edition includes information as recent as *last November* .... fancy a general encyclopaedia with all the dope on neutrons, Nazis, & N.R.A.!

Am hearing some good 18th century stuff at the current Colver Lectures at the college—Prof. Verner W. Crane of the U. of Mich. (formerly of Brown) on Dr. Benjamin Franklin—his education, his social philosophy, his political ideas, & his effect on the unfortunate revolt against His Majesty's lawful authority.[7] The first one was last night. Nothing I didn't know before—but the later lectures will undoubtedly include original interpretations & inferences.

Hope to see that full-grown bush of dynamick grey fur next month. Of the four little niggers whose birth at the trans-hortensic taberna[8] I chronicled in mid-February, one remains as a permanent fixture—& Ædepol! what a diminutive ball of black lightning he is! His name is John Perkins, & his resemblance to his lamented brother Samuel (whom I vainly try'd to shew you last August, & who departed this life Septr. 10) is downright uncanny! He is now strong, active, playful, & belligerent—& is just beginning to purr. (His purring is now *almost* as good as mine!) He is entirely black except for a microscopic white shirt-stud—& his eyes still have the wide-pupill'd violet hue of infancy. A great boy—&, I trust, a future pillar of the Kappa Alpha Tau fraternity. I urge him to guard his diet & general health better than his late brother did. He is beginning to be a frequent & welcome guest at 66, & I hope you may see him next month if you decide to continue your first-hand education in Rhodinsular topography & scenery. Meanwhile the elders of the K.A.T. are beginning to appear on the clubhouse roof after their season of hibernation. Vice-Pres. Osterberg (tiger) is even now visible as I glance out the window, & day before yesterday I had a long & interesting conversation with (black-&-white) Pres. Randall.

Just landed a new recruit for the National—my first in about a year. Duane W. Rimel, Box 100, Asotin, Wash. Bright chap of 20—devoted to weird literature, & groping toward a coherent style in both prose & verse. Think I'll send him some of those duplicate *Olympians* which you so kindly let me have . . . . I've already given several to deserving recipients . . . . including Edwin Hadley Smith, who lacked the Oct. 1917 issue as well as the 1918 *Bema*. His copy, of course, goes to immortality in the Fossil Library. By the way—I believe the warfare in the National has let up a bit . . . at least, I hear less of it. Too bad young Bradley—who has done so well as editor—won't run for president. Bradofsky also expresses a reluctance to run—but this may be merely the conventional "nolo episcopari" gesture . . . indeed, Charles R. Burger seems to assume that The Californian's modest scruples can be overcome. Of much greater real importance is the identity of the new official editor—as to which I've heard no predictions or suggestions at all.

Buds on some of the shrubs—though the trees still claw barren-branch'd at the leaden sky. What a climate! With the greater part of the year well-nigh intolerable in its arctick rigours! Well—I'll let you know anything I ascertain about present or prospective Culinary motions, & will await details of any Norfolk-Downing & Marbleheading that the ensuing month may make practicable. Regards to all the Carbones—including the grey bush—& hope to get a direct glimpse thereof ere long.

   I am, Sir,
      Yr most oblig'd, most ob^t Servt
         H P L

P.S. Apropos of Handwriting—I was reading lately of the attempts of Raymond Weaver to decipher Herman Melville's unpublished MS.—Journal up the Straits. Quite a struggle. What at first seemed like "St. Catherine's massy dome" resolved itself into "St. Catherine's martyrdom." "Knights in green breeches" became "Knights in grey niches." But the prize of all was something which absolutely stumped Weaver. "Rosamund of Glinglos"? "Rosalind of Guinos"? No sense. Finally someone else, carefully studying both text & context (it referred to the fallen drums of an ancient column in Athens) hit the right interpretation. It was comparing the fragments of a column to a ROULEAU OF GUINEAS . . . a roll of coins!

Notes

1. HPL refers to the "Coryciani" round-robin letter cycle, begun in December 1934: "Mr. Baker, one sees, is very literal in his interpretations of poetry—revealing his predominant inclination toward prose. It is obvious that he misses the point altogether in considering the appeal of 'The Grapes of Eshcol'—mistaking a really original allusiveness for unoriginality merely because the background of allusion involves stable racial traditions." *Lovecraft Annual* No. 11 (2017): 139.
2. "The Dinner Set" (*WT*, February 1935). The work of Fanny Kemble Johnson Costello (1868–1950) appeared in the early 20th century's leading literary magazines, such as *Atlantic Monthly, Harper's,* and *Century.*
3. HPL submitted a column, published as "Lovecraft Offers Verse Criticism."
4. The full article (long thought to be lost) was "A Living Heritage: Roman Architecture in Today's America" (published in full in *CE* 5.119–39). The first part of it was published in the *Californian* as "Heritage or Modernism: Common Sense in Art Forms."
5. Charles R[obert] Burger (1865–1939), editor of the journal *Progress.*
6. H[erman] C[harles] Koenig (1893–1959), late associate of HPL who spearheaded the rediscovery of the work of William Hope Hodgson. He published HPL's *Charleston* (1936).
7. The lecturer was Verner Winslow Crane (1889–1974), author of *Benjamin Franklin, Englishman and American* (1936).
8. Roughly, "the hotel across the garden," referring to the Arsdale, the boarding house on the other side of the garden behind 66 College.

[53]   [ALS]

Pridie Kal. Maii
[30 April 1935]

Ave, Olympiane!

So be it—Friday the 3d, 2:20 p.m. Eastern Daylight Time—at the chemist's shop to which the rigid gesture of the reverend gentleman across the way will direct me! And may the gods send warmth & golden solar rays to bless the hebdomedal termination!

Congrats on attending the Fossil Banquet & becoming one of the boys! It sounds like a great occasion, & I hope to hear more of it orally. I'll have to apply for admission to that bunch before long . . . . when younger people than I begin to get in, it's time that I exercised the fullest prerogatives of senescence!

Well—Culinarius is once more very articulate, but a proposition now in the air makes it an open question whether he can participate in any vernal or aestival Wilbraham pilgrimage. All Boston job prospects blew up—when lo! out of the west came a glittering offer from our dashing & eternally optimistic old promoter-friend Paul Jonas Campbell (vide enc.). Knowing P J's wildcat commercial characteristics, Culinarius didn't get very excited about the idea of chasing westward after the golden apples of the Hesperides. His reply to the first approach was merely courteous & perfunctory. But it seems that for once P J really means business—for he says he is trying to arrange to have W P C's fare paid to East St. Louis! (& back if the deal doesn't go through). Lacking any other job, & being absolutely dead broke, Cook says he thinks he'll take a chance if Campbell really sends the cash or 'bus ticket. Therefore he may be many a long league away when the cinerary cortege winds westward along the ancient Bay Path.

If, on the other hand, the Campbell proposition falls through & evaporates, Culinarius will join the procession in his sister's car—motoring down from Sunapee & joining Old Chev at some designated point in Wilbraham. In this eventuality (now none too likely) his plan calls for my own transference to the borrowed Culinary chariot after the obsequies—to be followed by a week of touring in Vermont, with calls on Goodenough, Coates, & various other Viridimontane acquaintances[1] of ours. I was quite excited about this prospect till the Campbell proposition placed it outside the circle of likelihood. Meanwhile I await further bulletins. Much as New England would hate to lose Cook, it would be splendid if he could really land a remunerative job. The one thing I hope is that Campbell won't get him out to Illinois on a wild goose chase & then be unable to fork over the return fare . . telling him 'to put it down to profit & loss'!

Incidentally—Culinarius has a suggestion regarding the mortuary expedition. He thinks that, since the Maplehurst estate is soon to be in the hands of strangers, Mrs. Dowe would really prefer to have her earthly reliquiae scattered in the Dell cemetery—over the graves of her ancestors & of her daughter—rather than among the rush-bushes 'back o' the maountain.' When requesting the latter disposition, she did not envisage the changing order of things at Maplehurst—hence Cook feels that a Dell ceremony would be more in accord with the *spirit* of her wishes as distinguished from the mere *letter*. There is logic in this attitude, & I shall be interested to hear how it strikes you. But of course there is plenty of time for all such decisions.

Eheu, eheu! And so that prose report didn't make the Apr. 26 deadline! Well—let us hope that young Bradley isn't drawing that line too strictly. I sent a report quite early—& added a second section when some more papers arrived. Toil, toil, toil! Meestah Bradofsky—who is almost certain to be the next president—says he vants ve should soive it anoder toim right alunk a'ready . . . . but I've told him, as I told Babcock last year (though it didn't do any good) that I don't want to serve unless no other victim can be found. I'm suggesting a board with you (if willing) as chairman, & with young Richard Thomas or Ray H. Zorn (or both) on the verse end.[2] Indeed, in my final (I hope) report I'm urging a larger critical board with ampler & more detailed service.

Meanwhile young Bradley is anxious for some amateur historical material to use in his *Perspective Review*. He knew absolutely nothing of amateurdom's past till I gave a few hints & sent him a few of those duplicate *Olympians*—& when he had seen the latter he realised how defective his amateur perspective was. Knowing that all the rest of the present generation is equally ignorant, he now wishes to publish enough information about the past to reëstablish the National's continuous tradition . . . so that names like *Olympian, Vagrant, Monadnock, Stylus, Investigator* &c.[3] will mean something to the youngsters as well as to the veterans. He has asked me to write a reminiscent sketch of the Golden Age (1885–1895), but since my knowledge of that period is so fragmentary I shall not do so if any better historian can be found. I'm suggesting that a genuine survivor like Edkins or a trained historian like yourself be chosen as chronicler. Would you undertake the job if it can't be shoved on E A E? If I am forced to do it, I can do little more than repeat my old 1920 performance—that sketch I wrote for Tryout after he had lent me a bunch of ancient journals.[4]

By the way—speaking of the Golden Age—Edkins has just given me his copy of Fanny Kemble Johnson's book of poems, "Silver Wings". I had no idea that she was such a uniformly good poet. It would seem that she belongs to the Edkins–Emery–Loveman qualitative group. Probably I told you that a story of hers appeared in the Feby. 1935 *Weird Tales*, proving that she is still alive & active. E. H. Smith is going to get in touch with her, he says. Another thing Edkins sent was a sort of amateur association item—a de luxe, vellum-bound copy of Andrew Lang's edition of Poe's poems, presented to him in 1888 by his co-editor of *The Stylus*, Edwin B. Hill.[5] Hill & Edkins parted in a sort of feud (what a feud-factory amateurdom is!), & have never become reconciled.

I note that your postcard has a Bridgeport postmark. Well—not so long after you mailed it you must have passed, on the road, a battered 1928 Ford runabout driven by a lightish, prepossessing young fellow & bearing a N.Y. license plate. That Ford was bound for the burg where you mailed the card, & it had come from 66 College St. And its occupant was Robert Ellis Moe, son of good old M W M! You ought to meet young Bob sooner or later. Enclosed are some snaps (which please return) taken during his previous visit. Before the summer is over we may have a pleasant echo of 1923 in the form of an-other Novanglian visit from Pater Mocrates after 12 years! He hopes to get to see his son in Bridgeport—& if so, he'll have the latter drive him still farther east. I surely will be glad of another first-hand glimpse of good ol' Mocrates! We'll have to stage a general Marblehead reunion . . . . what a pity that Sandy can't be on hand to complete the 1923 personnel!

Well—the recent week-end with young Bob was pretty well packed with events. He came, as before, in "Skippy"—the '28 Ford—& we surely kept the old rattletrap busy! Saturday we visited old Newport—seeing 2 ancient windmills; a flock of sheep with small lambkins; the home of Dean (later Bishop) Berkeley (1729); the Hanging Rocks where this worthy composed his famous Alciphron; or, the Minute Philosopher; the lofty cliffs; a rock cleft called Purgatory; the house where the rebels captured Genl Prescott in 1778; & the venerable town itself . . . . with 1726 church, 1739 colony-house, 1749 library, 1760 market-house, 1763 Jews' synagogue, & private dwellings as old as 1675. Glorious hot day—82° in Providence, tho' not so good in Newport. I understand you had quite a bit of warmth in the Boston zone. Sunday we went to ancient New Bedford & thence to the Round Hills estate of Col. Green where the old whaling brig Charles W. Morgan (built 1841) is preserved at a wharf—solidly embedded in concrete as a permanent exhibit. We went all over the vessel—which is tremendously fascinating. On the estate is also an ancient windmill which Green moved from R.I. We then explored a region—where S. Mass. adjoins S.E. R.I.—which I had never seen before in my life. Splendid unspoiled countryside with idyllic villages of the old New England type . . . . . Adamsville & Little Compton Commons, the best ones, are both in R.I. Then back home via Tiverton, Fall River, & *Warren*—at which latter place we stopped at Maxfield's for a solid ice-cream dinner . . . a pint & a half each. Finally back to 66—after which I guided the guest out of town toward Danielson & Willimantic & took a 4-mile rural walk before returning home. Quite a session!

John Perkins sends regards to Peter Ivanovitch—& I add regards for all the Carbones. Hope to see you Friday at 2:20 D.S.T. ¶ Yr oblig'd ob^t Servt H P L

Notes

1. Associates living across the green hills of Vermont.
2. Richard A. Thomas, Jr. (1916?–2011), author of *The Star in the Dusk* (1933), a volume of poetry about life on the Mississippi near Memphis. Ray H. Zorn (1910–1997), military postal worker in the 33rd Infantry Division in World War II, until he retired as postmaster of Troy Grove, IL, in the early 1970s. He wrote poetry and music and published a literary magazine (*Nix Nem Quarterly Review*) and other small press items, including the *Lovecraft Collector.*
3. Published by, respectively, Edwin Hadley Smith, W. Paul Cook, W. Paul Cook, Edwin A. Edkins, and Truman Spencer.
4. HPL refers to the essay "Looking Backward," *Tryout* (February–June 1920); later published as a booklet.
5. Edwin B[liss] Hill (1866–1949), an employee of the U.S. Bureau of Reclamation, first in Mesa, AZ, later in El Paso, TX. Printer of limited editions with attention to the quality of typography. He owned the longest running private printing press in American history.

[54]　　[ALS]

The Afternoon After
[4 May 1935?]

Ave, Olympiane!

Hell! Glorious sunny day—temperature *66°* in the shade on
the N. side of the house. And it *would* have to be the day *after* our chill-
haunted explorations! Kin ya beat it? One is almost convinced of the lurking
presence of a malevolent intelligence behind the cosmic mechanism! And *today* little Johnny Perkins has shewed up (he's asleep in the semicircular chair
beside me), & both President (black & white) & Vice President (tiger) of the
Kappa Alpha Tau are drowsing in the sun on the clubhouse roof!

Well—in spite of all external handicaps I had a darned good time in the
Massachusetts-Bay, thanks to the graciousness of my hosts. Wish your call at
the Georgian Citadel could have been longer—& hope the return journey was
at least tolerable. Trust that Peter & the Duke were still there upon your arrival—rather than having imitated their brethren of Kilkenny.

Before I forget it, let me enclose one of those ancient stamps from the
Miniter papers, of which I believe you have an appreciative young recipient in
mind. Again I shudder as I think of the dozens of such which must have
passed to the junk man in the barbarous wilds of Allston!

Another enclosure—which you might pass along eventually to the youthful champion of the XIXth century in Cantabrigia—is the picture I mentioned
as bearing a possible resemblance to that pleasing exemplar of aesthetick atavism. You may think the fancied similarity somewhat remote—but I never
was much for recalling physiognomical details, anyhow.

Think I'll beat it for the tall timber now—with work in the inevitable
black bag. Benedictions & appreciations to all—

Yr oblig'd ob[t] Serv[t]

H P L

[P.S.] Hope the prose report burthen isn't harassing you!

[55]　　[ALS][1]

May 20, 1935

Great Olympian:—

Here are some bulletins which may be of interest. The very
Tuesday after I saw you, I received Haggerty's circular advocating Babcock's
squashing . . . a document which would have puzzled me but for the data previously obtained from you. Later—when I suggested to Bradley that he run
again—that promising youth stated positively that he could not . . . on account
of the burthen of scholastic work of his own. He had not, he declared, been
subjected to any external pressure. And now Bradofsky gives the opinion here

(over) recorded. Tryout is also supporting Babcock. Well—I guess it won't kill amateurdom even if he is elected. He is surely energetic enough—& he can be fired if he gets fresh. What he did to others may yet be done to him![2]

Qualitative renaissance plans go apace. Edkins is getting interested, & has sent in 2 articles—one on Golden Age for P.R., the other on defects & needs of contemporary amateurdom for *Californian*.[3] I'm going to see if he can be landed as a critick. As you may see on t'other side of this sheet, Leedle Hymie is gettink ent'oosiastick about that bigger & better critical bureau I suggested. Hope he doesn't insist too strongly on my serving as chairman!

In the course of correspondence I discovered *that Edkins had never seen The Olympian*. What a state of things—when the leaders of one generation know nothing of those of another! I at once sent him all the different duplicates I had, & he was utterly delighted with them. Says he spent a whole day reading them & recapturing the amateur spirit. Have you any more copies left for distribution to exceptional amateurs? If so, I beg leave to propose 2 worthy recipients—both recruits of mine, & one just landed:

R. H. BARLOW, BOX 88, DE LAND, FLORIDA
DUANE W. RIMEL, BOX 100, ASOTIN, WASH.

Neither has ever seen a copy of the O.—although I'm now sending Barlow one number (Vol. I No. 5—March 1907) which Cook has just passed on to me. I am now absolutely cleaned out of duplicates.

Well—that day after the trip wasn't as ironically fair & warm as I thought before I went out! It turned chilly & grey, & I had to cut short the contemplated trip. No outings since, either. What a "spring"!

Which reminds me—that Wilbraham pilgrimage personnel may get a jolt from another angle. Bob Barlow, who returns to Florida from Washington June 3, is urging Grandpa to come down & repeat the 1934 visit . . . a strong temptation if I can swing it financially. I'm wavering—for there isn't *any* time of year when I don't prefer the Florida climate to this. ¶ Culinary possibilities indicated in the enclosed note. ¶ Prospects of Moe's getting east this summer increase.

¶ Universal regards—
Yr ob^t hble Servt
H P L

[P.S.] Hon. John Perkins, now visiting me & busily engaged in subdividing a wad of paper, & strewing it about the room for his Grandpa to pick up, sends his most purring regards to Peter Ivanovitch!

Notes

1. On verso of letter from Hyman Bradofsky.

2. HPL refers to the upcoming NAPA election, which saw Hyman Bradofsky elected President. O. W. Hinrichs was elected Official Editor, but he later resigned (see letter 66) and Helm C. Spink replaced him.

3. "The Time Has Come." *Californian* 3, No. 2 (Fall 1935): 10–11, 15–16.

[56]   [ALS]

66 College St.,
Providence, R.I.,
June 1, 1935

Venerated Olympian:—

Alas that the chronological allocation of potential pleasures should involve a troublesome simultaneousness! As the Parcae *would* have it, I am scheduled to be in no higher latitude than 29° N. on the 14–15th inst., so that it looks disconcertingly unlikely that I can take advantage of your alluring & appreciated invitation for those dates! Palmettos & live-oaks & dependable over-80° temperatures form a species of bait to which I am peculiarly susceptible, & young Barlow applied such bait with ultra-hospitable insistence. I found I could just make it without such treasury raids as would excite auntly criticism & remonstrance—hence responded with an acquiescence which virtually casts the die. I'll keep you posted with bulletins . . . which may come from Charleston or Savannah. I can't afford to make any real stops on the down trip, but will linger a day each in the places above named. On my return (hades knows when) I hope to pause less briefly in St. Augustine & Charleston. No hope of getting south of De Land—though I'll make Cuba some day if I have to bum my way on a freighter!

Pray accept my sympathy on the indifferent health—which I have shared. Rotten digestion—though the open-air programme of De Land ought to set me on my feet as in '34. In view of all circumstances, I'm sure the omission of a critical report will be understandingly pardoned . . . . especially during a term when so many officials are, for other reasons, so much more gravely in need of pardon! Bless me, what a fight the boys are having! Here's a screed which our courteous young Fuehrer just sent Culinarius—in an evident attempt to marshal all the vindictive anti-Hadleyites of the past 40 years for purposes of his own. I enclose also a pro-Rooster[1] campaign card which you've probably received yourself. It surely is an exasperating situation—with no other well-qualified candidate to vote for. One is tempted to leave the editorial line a blank on one's ballot. And so Kempner[2] is in the fray, circulating "withdrawn" propaganda which the Rooster has nobly sought to suppress because of a policy (cf. the Canine Association invitation) of "ignoring" Smith! Boys, boys! How similar are first & second childhood! The quest for critical material—to fill out the enlarged bureau—does not prosper except negatively. (Zorn, he of the ladder-climbing tenors, wouldn't accept!)

Loveman, McDonald, & Culinarius have given definite turndowns, & I haven't heard from anybody else. I still harbour certain hopes anent Moe & Edkins. Others approached are Morton, Spencer, Detrick,[3] Jones, Harry E. Martin, & Richard Thomas. It has just occurred to me that Nelson G. Morton would be worth trying. We certainly gotta get a gang to use up them 8000 words per department allotted by Leedle Hymie! Did I mention that Edkins has furnished two brilliant articles, one on the Golden Age (for Persp. Rev.) & the other (for the Cal.) on the limitations & needs of the present?

Culinarius's deal with Orton is off after a week in Weston, Vt. The Campbell venture hangs fire. Meanwhile Coates says he wishes W P C would return to N. Montpelier.

I was sorry to learn—simultaneously from Cook & Tryout—that Goodenough's wife died May 15, rather suddenly, as the result of a shock. I've dropped the bard a note of condolence. Cook says that the blow will bear heavily on him. Mrs. G. was an extremely pleasant, capable, & likeable person, & probably did much to sustain the poet's spirits amidst poverty & adversity of every sort. If I remember correctly, Goodenough's daughter-in-law is also dead—leaving a wholly stag household of three generations . . . Arthur, Rupert, & little Malcolm. Culinarius intends to pay Goodenough a cheering-up visit before long, & I fancy a note of sympathy from you—& all the amateur leaders—would help in the task of sustaining his spirits.

I shall be grateful (& others will ultimately be grateful) for any further *Olympian* duplicates which you can spare. Barlow & Rimel—both my recruits—are the recipients I have most in mind. All those to whom I have given copies have been tremendously appreciative—especially Bradley (did you observe his note in the new P.R.?) & Edkins. I had not realised till recently how little is known of the achievements of amateurdom's middle period by either the real old-timers or the newest active generation. Something certainly ought to be done to ensure a greater continuity of tradition.

Recent climatic developments have surely been agreeable to me—save that the turning-off of the steam has brought out the old oil heater on several occasions. The cool nights are just what I *don't* like—hence my eagerness to shoot down to Lat. 29°. Heat has upon me an effect opposite to that which you—& most others—experience. The hotter it is, the *more* mental & physical energy, & general desire to be active, I have. In the north I seem to be a rather sluggish, inert specimen—but in Florida I am constantly up & around & doing. You ought to have seen me last year toting bricks, digging up & transplanting trees, carrying pails of water for young orange groves, &c. &c. &c.! No doubt I'll be doing the same thing—& assisting in the construction of a cabin across the lake from the Barlow place—during the weeks to come. Then when I hit the north . . . & the chill of autumn hits me . . . . I shall be my usual cloddish, lassitudinous self again. Hell, but why wasn't I born in Charleston or St. Augustine or somewhere?

Transmit my vicarious reproofs to Peter Ivanovitch! Still, youth will be wild. My young black friend John Perkins is getting to be quite a rough guy, & will probably clean up the entire Kappa Alpha Tau when he is of sufficient size. He's over here a good part of the time, & I have come to understand his language quite well—differentiating betwixt the squeaky "eeew" which is merely a bid for attention, & the fuller "eww" which indicates a wish for exit or nourishment. He plays like mad, & then becomes an immobile onyx paperweight atop Webster's Unabridged or on the magazines on the centre-table. He has the long legs, pointed muzzle, & wide ears of the ancient Ægyptian felidae, & I am sure he forms a reincarnation of some favourite of Bast who lived not later than the 18th Dynasty in Thebes or Bubastis. A very fine boy, taken as a whole . . . may his career be long, valiant, & prosperous! Hope Peter will soon shake off the coryzic effects of his late dissipation, & continue to maintain his dignity against all Wellingtonian aggressions. And I hope, too, that his divagations may not be frequently repeated!

Melancholy note: the row of quaint colonial buildings on the lower slope of College St. (far below 66) is about to fall to the vandals. I knew it was doomed—but the fresh realisation is no less a blow. Included in the cataclysm will be the house of Brown's first president (1771), a fine 1750 specimen, & one of those rare old archways leading under parts of a building to inner courtyards . . . of which the only *perfect* survivors in America are those on Providence's ancient hill. [There's a bricked-up specimen in Richmond & a boarded-up one in Philadelphia.] On this site will arise the new main building of the R.I. School of Design—which has long held the property. Two palliating features exist: (a) The preservation, restoration, & incorporation into the new building of the bottom (& only brick) house of the ancient row . . . . the old Franklin Hotel, with its quaint inn-yard archway. Thus the survival of *one* of the archways is assured. And (b) the choice of a splendid Providence-Georgian design for the new edifice. The structure's lower units will harmonise with the surviving Franklin House, while the upper units will blend in pattern with the residential buildings higher up on the hill. One part will even have a "monitor roof" like #66—a form especially  typical of Providence in the 1790–1820 period. The change is regrettable, yet it is fortunate that the character of the new building will be the same. Obviously—& despite the aberrant freaks of Louis K. Liggett & the Lerner chain down town[4]—Providence is remaining dominantly true to its traditional heritage of Georgian architecture, & avoiding the modernistic epidemic from which other parts of the world are so regrettably suffering.

Have had a few afternoon outings lately, thanks to the reasonably civilised weather. Darned sorry this Wollaston–North Shore–Wilbraham event has eluded me—& thanks for the participation which would have been mine!

Pray convey my congratulations to the other head of the household upon her coming alumnae presidency.

With inclusive regards from my aunt & myself,

I am ever

Yr most oblig'd, most ob^t Servt

H P L

Notes

1. A reference to Ralph E. Babcock, editor of the *Red Rooster.*
2. Louis Kempner (1863–1944), NAPA president in 1889, Fossils librarian.
3. Charles L. Detrick (1914–1969), editor of *Spare Time,* secretary of the NAPA (1934–35).
4. Louis Kroh Liggett (1875–1946) was an American drug store magnate who founded Rexall. Samuel Lerner, a New York manufacturer, founded the Lerner Shops, which became a chain of more than 450 popular-price clothing stores.

[57]   [ALS]

% R. H. Barlow,

Box 88, De Land, Fla.

July 3, 1935

Invincible Olympian:—

Trust you duly received cards from ancient Fredericksburg & incomparable CHARLESTON. I stay'd two days in the latter place, foregoing any pause at Savannah. Reach'd De Land June 9, & slipp'd back very naturally into the routine of last year. Things are much the same, except that Bob's father—a retired army colonel—is now at home. Another welcome addition to the group was Bob's brother Wayne—a 2nd Lt. from Ft. Sam Houston, Tex.—who was here on a furlough, but who has now returned to the stern task of the nation's defence. The season's chief novelty has been the building of a cabin by my young host in a quercine copse across the lake—wherein he conducts typographical & other intellectual activities. I have contributed unskilled labour to this project, & have single-handed (canst imagine Grandpa actually *at work?*) cut a roadway (good old Roman stuff) through the palmetto wilderness from the landing to the previous cabinward cart-path. Within this cabin projects of vast moment to amateur journalism— including a paper adhering to real golden-age standards—may yet be born. Of this more anon.

The felidae hereabouts would prove good company for Peter Ivanovitch Romanov—though none of them can equal him in size or in decibels of purring energy. Jack (tiger), Henry Clay (yellow), & Alfred A. Knopf (diminutive tiger with a sort of leopard-spot effect) are the outdoor roughnecks who correspond to Napoleon & Wellington. Within doors are the two sumptuous yellow Persians—Cyrus & Darius—which Barlow brought down from Washington. Cyrus is Peter's one remote rival in the field of purring—he can purr almost as loudly as I can. Darius is more austere & aloof. These two bushy sphinxes are full brothers & highly pedigreed—valued at 30 bucks each.

Well—as I said, Mr. Robert Hayward Barlow is planning a paper whose quality will leave all contemporary rivals ignominiously in the shade. He has an article & poem by Ernest A. Edkins (who is starting up as a prolific come-backer despite his technical scorn of active membership), & aspires to make the rest of the contents (& the format) of corresponding quality.[1] To this end I am asking you a dual favour on his behalf—since circumstances have placed two key matters in your hands:

> (a) Could you manage to send Barlow's quota of *Olympians* down here before I get home & to Wollaston? He really ought to have a model to go by, & the *Olympian* around 1914–16 is absolutely the best thing of its kind in existence. The only issue he has is an early one of '07—before the paper's real heyday.
>
> (b) Could you read one or two of the Miniter MSS. (especially "Dead Houses") & let Barlow have it . . or them . . . for consideration as part of his contents? He is anxious to have Mrs. M. represented by some of her best work.[2]

The kid really has limitless enthusiasm, & if he gets the right kind of stuff will issue a paper that will knock all competitors cold. Like Bradley, he distinctly deserves all the encouragement his elders can give. No hurry—for he is doing a preliminary job as printing practice—but he'll probably want to see this material before I leave. The duration of my visit is being prolonged outrageously through the insistent—almost fanatical—hospitality of my delightful hosts. I've tried a dozen times to break away to see Moe during his eastern trip, but both Bob & the colonel seem to take it as a personal slight if I ever try to set a getaway date before August! And the bracing effect of the southern climate on my health makes me a very easy subject to persuade. Down here I am alert & active to a degree incredible to anyone who has seen me only in the north. I have unsuspected reserves of energy, & sleep actually *rests* me as it never does above the 30th parallel.

By the way—hell seems to be popping for fair in the National. I voted for O. W. Hinrichs as official editor—& of course for Leedle Hymie as president. To me the eleventh-hour turning of Haggerty & others against poor Hymie seems absolutely inexcusable—trying to put over a coup by using the sure-fire name of Spink—who doesn't want to be president & probably knows nothing about his alleged candidacy. Honest Hymie has given amateurdom all he has—lookit a'ready by the new Cellifornian . . . soch ah paper!—& certainly deserves something more than a sock on the bean! For **that** he shood go into debt & publish ah first-cless magazine! Don't know how the election is turning out, but Ol' Doc Kuntz is doubtless on the spot, fighting with true Presbyterian valour for the Champeen of Israel! By the way . . . the quest for eminent critical material has borne surprising fruit . . . a prize un-hoped-for by anyone save the unquenchable Hymie. Guess who will consent to serve if appointed for 1935–6? TRUMAN JOSEPH SPENCER, no less! We are in eminent company!

And so it goes. On June 17 we visited a fascinating place—Black Water Creek, a tropical river whose lush scenery suggests the Congo, Amazon, & other exotic streams famed in history & legend. It winds through a steaming jungle of tall, moss-draped cypresses, whose grotesque, twisted roots writhe curiously at the water's edge. Palms lean precariously over the brink, & vines & creepers strow the black dank earth of the nearby forest aisles. Sinister sunken logs loom up at various points, & in the forest pallid flowers & leprous fungi gleam whitely through an endless twilight. It is much like the river at Silver Springs (Fla.) which I doubtless described to you last year—though I enjoyed it even more because of the more leisurely observing conditions. At the Springs I was whizzed ahead in a launch; this time we proceeded slowly in a rowboat. Each bend of the tortuous stream brought to light some unexpected vista of tropical luxuriance, & we absorbed the spectacle to the full. Snakes & alligators were somewhat in evidence—though none came near our boat. I hope for more trips of this kind—for I am especially sensitive to sub-tropical scenery.

All good wishes & thanks in advance for favours—
  Yr obt Servt
   H P L

P.S. Cook is virtually resolved to go to St. Louis & tackle P J C's venture. ¶ Has the Dowe pilgrimage been made?

Notes

1. R. H. Barlow's *Dragon-Fly* No. 1 (15 October 1935) contained "Fragment of a Letter to a Young Poet" (11–26) and "Bizarres" (32) by E. A. Edkins.
2. "Dead Houses," *Leaves* No. 1 (Summer 1937): 35–48; rpt. *Dead Houses and Other Works*, ed. Kenneth W. Faig, Jr., and Sean Donnelly (New York: Hippocampus Press, 2008), 343–68. The presentation of the story to R. H. Barlow was a source of consternation to W. Paul Cook, for he had intended to publish it himself.

[58]   [ALS]

To   Peter Ivanovich Romanov
            Arthur Wellesley, 1st Duke of Wellington,   ℅ Barlow,
            Napoleon Bonaparte, Imp. Gall.   Box 88,
Greetings from   Cyrus   De Land, Fla.,
                 Darius   July 15, 1935.
                 Jack
                 High
                 Alfred A Knopf
                 Henry Clay

Mighty Olympian:—

Observe my attempt to correct the slight imperfections & irregularities in my script—suggested by this convenient device in the front of a new pad! If I were younger, it might change the course of my entire visible literary life . . . . as it is . . . one may continue to hope.

90° temperatures? Lud, Sir, but I envy you! 88° is so far the highest we've had down here. However—I'm all right, since it rarely gets below 80°. Really, I feel so much better than I ever do in the north that I can scarce believe myself the same person! Maine . . . . brrrr! Who would *voluntarily* go any farther *north* than Marblehead (or at most Newburyport or Portsmouth) unless one were going to antient Quebeck?

My aunt was in Marblehead last week . . . but since I'll be passing through both *St. Augustine* & CHARLESTON next month, I don't need to lay the envy on too thickly. Hope there'll be some decent autumn weather for the Wilbraham trip. Cook is still hesitating on the brink of his great plunge into the western wilderness.

Thanks for "Dead Houses"—which impresses Bobby Barlow as much as it did Culinarius & me—& yourself, I trust. Bob is also ecstatically grateful for the *Olympians* . . . which will serve him as chief model for his forthcoming *Leaves*. The 1913 issues sent embody the full evolution of your *interior* typography, although your *covers* did not reach a maximum of tastefulness till 1914. Barlow is slowly improving his typography—& incidentally, I am setting type for the first time since my own sportive infancy. How it all comes back! *Leaves* ought to be quite a performance—with Edkiniana, Miniteriana, &c, & with Ol' Lympy as a chief model. Edkins is emerging valiantly from his long sleep—with many poems & a whole stream of critical essays. Shall distribute these (since I'm his lit'ry agent) among Hymie, Bobby, & young Bradley.

Election came out well . . . Hymie Pres.; Hinrichs Œ; Grand Rapids Conv Seat. They shew'd Babcock where to alight! I'm an execut. iudex . . . gawd save me from the trials which have been besetting you whilst sustaining a kindred burthen! The convention is slow in broadcasting its results—my info was relay'd by Edwin Hadley.

Moe is in the east, but it looks as if I were missing him. He attended the convention of the Erford pseudo-United in N Y July 4,[1] & introduced his son Bob to the crowd, but the youngster doesn't seem to think much of ams as a species. Probably he didn't see the most brilliant specimens . . . save for Jacobus Ferdinandus.

Had a note from J. Bernardus yesterday—he was coming to Prov. & wanted to know when I'd be in. Had to tell him that I was a few miles away from the old home hearth! ¶ Blessings—& thanks for the material sent.

Yr obt & subtropical grandsire—

H P L

Notes

1. J. F. Roy Erford, based in Seattle, was a leading figure in the United Amateur Press Association of America, a rival of HPL's UAPA.

[59]   [ANS postcard][1]

[Postmarked Saint Augustine, Fla.,
20 August 1935]

Hail, Olympianus Carbo! Have broken away at last, & am on the slow road north . . . after accompanying the Barlows to Daytona & helping them settle in the flat they've taken for a fortnight. It sure is great to see the antiquities of venerable San Agustin after spending 2 months & 9 days amidst rural modernity. Am lapping up centuried gables & facades at a great rate—& spending much of my time atop the old fort—where I've found the most fascinating grey kitten imaginable. Here for a week at the old Rio Vista where I stopped before. Basement room (bath & kitchenette) only $3.50. Eating on 20¢ per diem . . . with beans as a major base. Shall light out Aug. 25. 5 hrs in Savannah, & as much time as I can get in Charleston. Probably too broke to make any stop north of there. ¶ Barlow is slowly printing a paper called *The Dragon Fly,* modelled obviously after *The Olympian.* Leading article is by Edkins. ¶ Trust you'll serve again as prose critic—under Truman J. Spencer as Chairman. I've agreed to do the verse again. ¶ Suhre has been trying to persuade directors to resign in order that Babcock be appointed. I refused to accomodate! ¶ Hope you've had a goodly number of pleasant trips during the summer. How I dread the coming cold! Regards to Peter & everybody—

H P L

Notes

1. *Front:* Charlotte Street, St. Augustine, Florida.

[60]   [ALS] [W. Paul Cook to HPL; HPL to EHC]

[Sunapee, N. H.,
Sept. 21, 1935]

Dear H. P. L.:—

As usual, everything happens at once when anything happens! I did not go to the postoffice until 11:00 this morning. If I had received your note last night I *could* have gone to Wilbraham today. Very sorry not to be in on the ceremony.

Also an air-mail letter this morning from Campbell, and if I can get hold of the insurance agent from whom I am to get the money (turning in my last insurance!) I shall leave for St. Louis Monday morning. I do not think I shall stop this side of New York. Shall spend a night in New York, then complete trip at one leap.

Tell Cole I think it was a very fine thing for him to see about Jane Dowe's ashes.

More from somewhere.

Cook]

Woden's-Daeg
[25 September 1935]

Behold, Sir! If only we'd been one day earlier in deciding & dropping a line! And to think we missed a chance to say bon voyage before the big plunge! I've acknowledged this note—adding further details anent Saturday's pilgrimage. Now I shall await with interest whatever bulletins may come from future stations along the Culinary route. I think the St. Louis plunge is a damn rash move—but I wish the plunger well. Going out to grow up with a new country, like the 49-ers of old . . . . right in the footsteps of George W. Tupper![1]

¶ Had a good trip home—coach well heated. And today . . . glory hallelujah! we have *steam heat!* ¶ Still revolving pleasant memories of my delightful sojourn in the Province of the Maſsachusetts-Bay under the aegis of Carbonaceous hospitality. Once more I extend grateful acknowledgments to you & your household! ¶ Here's a cutting—most opportunely printed in Sunday's *Journal*—which sheds light on that burned boat we saw along the waterfront . . . "Sir Thomas Lipton's Pleasure Yacht". So it was an old Rhode Island fixture! One more (like the Comet) to add to the list of home things which I see for the first time away from home. Another cutting suggests a good way to take Peter Ivanovitch along on excursions.

Note from Ernie Edkins tells of his continued illness. Infection spread to jaw, & a slight touch of permanent paralysis (possibly affecting facial expression) *may* result. Has day & night nurses, but writes & reads considerably & is now allowed out of bed for an hour at a time. Plans to go to Florida around Nov. 1—a wise decision, for that's the place to set him on his feet if anything can!

Found a paralysing stack of mail—including a story to revise—when I got home. Worked solidly all day yesterday without going out. Among the heap was a badly mussed copy of that pictorial *Red Rooster* . . . shewing that the young folks haven't quite forgotten Grandpa.[2] Barlow reports 9 pages of *The Dragon-Fly* printed, but finds conditions so hard that he is a bit appalled at the prospect of a second issue. Don't forget to send him more *Olympians* when you can . . . . he needs example & encouragement!

Well—acknowledgments & benedictions!
  Yr ob^t h^{ble} Servt
     H P L

[On envelope (postmarked Providence, R.I., 26 September 1935):]

Wednesday Morning:—
    Yr note just recd. Damnation, what irony! To think that Culinarius was in Boston at the very time that we were tanking up at Huntt's & saying our adieux at the N.E. terminal! Well—that's fate! His St. Louis address for the present is, I suppose, % *Campbell, 5720 Westmoreland Place, East St. Louis, Illinois.* That is, he can be reached there. I am thus re-addressing the envelope I had addressed to Sunapee. Well—I hope he makes a go of it. Anyhow, he has his return fare guaranteed! I'll tell him about the circumstances in Boston, & how keenly you regret not having received his call. Yes—the whole thing was typically Culinary—I suppose he merely used the Crawford as a sort of head-quarters, as most people use the Touraine . . . but in that case, how did he fancy a telephone call could reach him (except through haphazard paging), & why did he say he was "staying" there? Maybe he *would* have stayed had he been able to get in touch with you. I give it up! But I'll relate all the circumstances to the gent concerned. ¶ Sorry the opening lecture of your course was dull—but I suppose that's true of all introductory discourses. Trust the eloquence will improve with time. ¶ Good luck with the venerable Chauncey—& may the cheques hold their own despite waning duties! ¶ No official assignment from Spencer as yet, so Lincoln's Cabinet is still unopened! I shall be on the lookout for Cole's Crisp Cracks in the prose colyum—& am confident that Segal & Babcock will at once be relegated to the also-ran class! Haven't yet had a chance to give any piled-up amateur papers an even cursory once-over. ¶ Just got a letter from Hymie stating that he intends to cease amateur activity after his term is over . . . his delicate soul is grieved at the activities of an element which he says he feels to be working against him. I think I'll reply: "You will snap out of it & use common sense—realising that every official has to take the knocks!"

Notes

1. George Washington Tupper was Edith Miniter's great-uncle.
2. *The Red Rooster and the New Times* 3, No. 1 (May 1935), published by Ralph A. Babcock. The thick issue included two photographs of HPL from the 1920s, and numerous photographs of other amateur journalists.

[61]   [ALS] [W. Paul Cook to HPL; HPL to EHC]

[Your treatment of Mrs. Dowe's ashes I would consider almost ideal. Distribution in the two places was very happy.

I am writing this sitting outdoors with the pad in my lap.

Item—one very small tom-tiger kitten, complaining because I do not hold it.

C

The Campbells send the best.]

Octr. 3[, 1935]

Well—here's the latest! Damme if I know of any Crawford *Chambers* as distinguished from *House!* Glad Culinarius likes E. St. Louis, & hope his venture prospers. Wish I could see that tiger kitten!

¶ Aunt & I may get a ride to New Haven next Tuesday. Hope the route will pass through picturesque Plainfield, Norwich, New London, & Guilford! I shall explore New Haven with much interest—have never been off the 'bus or train there so far. There are some fine old churches, a special sort of local late-Georgian residential architecture, & many colonial college buildings despite Yale's present Gothick predilections.

¶ Apropos of nothing—here are a couple of those old stamps—& envelopes—from the Miniter papers, which I believe a youthful nephew of yours would appreciate. We mentioned the matter last May, & I said I'd send one or two specimens—but I only just remembered it. That's the way with an old geezer's memory—pardon the delay!

¶ Took a long walk in the countryside Tuesday. Yesterday Mr. John Perkins was my guest all day—alternately playing, drowsing, purring, & rolling in catnip.

¶ Bundle of amateur stuff arrived yesterday. If Spencer doesn't get busy with the critical bureau, we'll have to go ahead & concoct our respective reviews in the accustomed way. I'm getting in touch with Kleiner.

Benedictions—H P L

[P.S.] ¶ Edkins is distinctly better—up & out riding the other day. Infection in face & neck at least provisionally checked. He hopes to get to Florida next month.

[62]   [ALS]

Uktubber 10[, 1935]

Dear Meestah Kul:—

    You vill ess soon like you ken mek it ah kreetiker report by der *Neshunul Emmachure*—shoost ess lunk like you veesh, & geefing der prose wriders hell like vhat dey need a'ready. You shood ged id by der eddidor, Meestah Hinrichs, shoost ess qveek ess pussible—so you shoodent fall by der wrunk side uff der December deadline . . . vhich I dun't know vhen iss, but vhich prob'ly iss soon a'ready.

In other words, Hymie is so steamed up about the venerable Truman's delay in organising the new & better bureau, that I'm taking pity on him & preparing to stir up the necessary reports in the good old way, as if the 1934–5 bureau were still in power.[1] Forget about any new frills, & just dish up a few well-chosen words in the usual manner—anything to stop the gap until the Sage of Hamden gets going. It would be hellishly awkward to have two issues of the N.A.—half the whole damn year—without critical material, especially in view of all that has been said about enlarging the functions & general usefulness of the bureau. I think it would be best—unless something new develops—to send all reports straight to Hinrichs . . . whose Dec. deadline can't be far off now. Of course I'm telling Spencer as a matter of courtesy that we'll send our stuff to him first *if he wishes*—but I scarcely fancy he'll wish! In choosing material to survey, I imagine it would be wise to give the preference to *recent* effusions . . . . but you can use your judgment on that.

Meanwhile I shall try to cook up some sort of verse review—though I'm assigning half the material (including "Lincoln's Cabinet"!) to Kleiner.[2] Hades only knows whether all the articles—yours, Kleiner's, Spink's, & mine—will get to Hinrichs in time for the Dec. issue, but even one or two would save the day after a fashion. Later I hope Trumie will get to going & shew the astigmatic world something vhat is something! Anyhow, thanks in advance—on behalf of Hymie, Trumie, the association in general, or what have you—for such timely prose comment as you can furnish.

I was rather close to Trumie geographically last Tuesday—indeed, I visited two museums on the very thoroughfare (Whitney Ave.) which he inhabits—but didn't get time to look him up. The musaea were about 2400 numbers south of our venerable chairman's abode . . . . in New-Haven proper, whereas the Investigator dwells in the septentrional suburb of Hamden.

The trip to New Haven was in every way a success—& I had 7½ hours for exploration whilst my aunt visited a friend. The day was ideally sunny (though I could have wished it warmer), & the ride through rural Connecticut scenery delightful. New Haven is not as rich in colonial antiquities as Providence, but has a peculiar charm of its own. Streets are broad & well-kept, & in the residential sections (some of which involve hills & fine views) there are endless stately mansions a century old, with ample grounds & gardens, & an almost continuous overarching canopy of great elms. I visited ancient Connecticut Hall (1752—the oldest Yale edifice, where the rebel Nathan Hale of the class of 1773 roomed), old Centre Church (1812—with an interesting crypt containing the grave of Benedict Arnold's first wife), the Pierpont house (1767—now Yale Faculty Club), the historical, art, & natural history museums, the Farnam & Marsh botanic gardens, & various other points of interest—crowding as much as possible into the limited time available.

Most impressive of all, perhaps, were the great *new* quadrangles of Yale University—each an absolutely faithful reproduction of old-time architecture & atmosphere, & forming a self-contained little world in itself. The Gothic courtyards transport one in fancy to mediaeval Oxford or Cambridge— spires, oriels, pointed arches, mullioned windows, arcades with groined roofs, climbing ivy, sundials, law[ns,] gardens, vine-clad walls & flagstoned walks— everything to give the young occupants that massed impression of their ac- cumulated cultural heritage which they might obtain in Old England itself. To stroll through these quadrangles in the golden light of afternoon; at dusk, when the candles behind the diamond-paned casements flicker up one by one; or in the beams of a mellow Hunter's Moon, is to walk bodily into an enchanting re- gion of dream. It is the past & the ancient mother land brought magically to the present time & place. The choicest of these quadrangles is Calhoun College— named for the great Carolinian (whose grave in St. Philip's churchyard, Charles- ton, I visited less than 2 months ago), who was a graduate of Yale. Nor are the Georgian quadrangles less glamourous—each being a magical summoning-up of the world of two centuries ago. Many different styles of Georgian architec- ture are represented, & the buildings & landscaping alike reflect the finest & maturest taste which European civilisation has yet evolved or is ever likely to evolve. Lucky (though doubtless, in most cases, unappreciative!) is the youth whose formative years are spent amid such scenes! I wandered for hours through this limitless labyrinth of unexpected elder microcosms, & mourned the lack of further time. Certainly, I must visit New-Haven again, since many of its treasures would require weeks for proper inspection & appreciation.

And so it goes. Hope the request for criticism won't cause you any major inconvenience. If it goes in the way of your private tutoring at Chauncy Hall, or your Swampscott & Marblehead sightseeing, just ignore it & feel confident that Trumie & Hymie & Grandpa & everybody will comprehend & sympa- thise!

No further bulletins from Culinarius.

Johnny Perkins—stretched at full length like an ebony club on the neighbouring rug—sends his regards to Peter Ivanovicth, as I do to all!

Pax vobiscum—

H P L

P.S. The aged sexton at Centre Church was a mine of historical infor- mation. He informed me, among other similar things, that the construction of the edifice was delayed in 1812 because of the outbreak of the Revolution. Also, that Benedict Arnold was *ostracised after the Battle of Ft. Griswold.* And that Wren's "si monumentum" inscription is in *St. Martin's-in-the-Fields.*[3]

Notes

1. HPL refers to Truman J. Spencer, the latter of whom was presumably chairman of the Bureau of Critics.
2. A "Bureau of Critics" column by HPL did appear in the December 1935 issue.
3. The inscription reads: "SUBTUS CONDITUR HUIUS ECCLESIÆ ET VRBIS CONDITOR CHRISTOPHORUS WREN, QUI VIXIT ANNOS ULTRA NONAGINTA, NON SIBI SED BONO PUBLICO. LECTOR SI MONUMENTUM REQUIRIS CIRCUMSPICE Obijt XXV Feb: Anº: MDCCXXIII Æt: XCI." In English: "Here in its foundations lies the architect of this church and city, Christopher Wren, who lived beyond ninety years, not for his own profit but for the public good. Reader, if you seek his monument—look around you. Died 25 February 1723, age 91."

[63]   [ANS postcard][1]

[No postmark; not mailed?
c. mid-October 1935]

Ave, Olympiane! Lookit where I've been! Hoped till the last to be able to give you at least a ring on the wire, but adverse fate intervened. *Loveman* blew into Prov. at 6 a.m. Wednesday, en route for book business in Boston. I accompanied him as guide, & we thought we'd have considerable time for sightseeing & chatting; but the programme couldn't be modelled as expected. However, Loveman may be in Boston again within a month or so. He's doing considerable business with an ex-professor in Walker Terrace, Cambridge—one Hugh Palmer. ¶ Hope you're fixing up a prose report. Spencer approves my act of stirring up the criticks, but asks that we *tell him what we are criticising,* in order that no review of his own may cover ground already covered by others. I've sent him a carbon of my report—which wouldn't be a bad idea to follow. Hope something will get to Hinrichs before the December forces close! ¶ The Lord be with you!

Yr obt Servt
H P L

Notes

1. *Front:* Faneuil Hall and Custom House Tower, Boston, Mass. Postage was removed from the card, which is not postmarked. Possibly an inclusion to letter 64.

[64]   [ALS]

Octr. 19, 1935

Theobaldis Carboni S.D.

Coincidence! Behold what I was about to despatch Wollastonward just as your note & admirable review arrived! With typical Caledonian thrift I have removed the ha'penny postal passport.

Well—I'll amend only one proviso. Since I've just written Spencer & enclosed a list of the items covered in your report, you needn't bother about notifying him yourself. Glad the main copy has gone to Hinrichs. From what I hear, I believe it ought to make the deadline. I sent my report[1] in last Saturday, & Spink & Kleiner say they are about to follow suit. So in spite of all the delay I guess the association will have some official criticism about as early as it ever does!

I assume that, as in my case, Barlow's *Dragon-Fly* (a kind of spiritual descendant of *The Olympian*) reached you too late for reviewing. Certainly, you would not otherwise have left it unreviewed! The typography is, of course, frankly beginner's work—but I think you can plainly recognise the taste & ambition lurking behind the venture. Edkins clearly dominates the issue—& I believe it will help to renew his interest in amateur matters. The illustration is Barlow's own handiwork.

Cook lately sent me the neighbourhood paper he & Campbell are editing. Not at all bad for a thing of its kind—I can see the improvement since the coming of Culinary aid.

Glad to hear that the solo, duet, & quartette classes at Old Chauncey are expanding a bit! The end of the Lynning & Swampscotting will surely relieve your programme considerably. Shall be interested to hear whether the Mohawking becomes possible. Even in November a stout heart & heavy overcoat ought (with the aid of a heated Chev) to make scenick mountaineering distinctly worth the attempt! I enjoyed the rides to & from Bostonium this week. On the return trip we traversed the Old Highway, whose beauty so vastly eclipses the landscape effects of its modern rival. Wrentham is a village hard to beat!

Congratulations to Peter Ivanovitch on his burglarious triumphs! Before long he'll be coming & going at will—& you'll be lucky if he doesn't run off with Chevvy! Mr. Perkins & the K.A.T. in general applaud in envy.

Well—now to work! I was damn sorry we couldn't arrange a Lovemanick get-together Wednesday or Thursday, but the poor chap was so laden with arduous tasks that not a moment was left for civilised relaxation. That independent business of his is about as bad as the old Dauber & Pine job! ¶ Salaam aleikum—& general regards to all—

—Yr obt Servt—

H P L

[P.S.] Your review just hits the spot!

Notes

1. Published as "Some Current Amateur Verse."

[65]   [ALS, leaf II only]

[19 November 1935]

[. . .] May 1st, sent to a reasonable number of members, & containing the given essay & story. I think Smith is trying to dodge this question. My letter to Mrs. Plaiser was sent to Haggerty for reading & forwarding on Nov. 2;[1] but he seems to have been slow in attending to the matter, since I've just had a note from Mrs. P. dated Nov. 6 & containing no sign of his having received my commiseration. Fortunately I had an extra carbon of my letter, which I've now sent her. I don't really see why Haggerty shouldn't save in formulating a decision, since the legality of his own laureate-judgeship is not under attack. I am recommending that he act with the other executive judges. Smith's position is an extremely destructive one. A liberal attitude toward red-tape regulations is all that has kept the National—or any organisation—a living institution—indeed, if this quibbling ultra-constitutionalism were retroactive, it would illegalise half our existing laureate awards & wipe out of technical existence the administration of some of our most useful & counterfeit officers! Rigidity is death to progress. I have fought legalism in amateur journalism for 20 years, & certainly don't want to see it employed today for the gratification of a private grudge! Not but what EHS *has* a legitimate grudge against Babcock. The young sauce box has exceeded all bounds of taste in his taunts & quips against the staunch old warhorse. But there is a limit to fighting the devil with fire, & it's pretty extreme to crack down on an opponent by invoking fossilised regulations which have not in years been invoked against anyone else.

Please return the enclosures at your leisure . . . I'm chucking in everything on hand connected with the mess. In the end, I'm afraid this will develop into a voluminous free-for-all comparable to that which engulfed you last year . . . the records whereof I perused into the small hours one night last May at #53![2] As a sheer waste of energy, this business of political machination takes all prizes! And if, on top of this, *Hymie* starts anything in the complaint or resignation line . . . Oy! You will egsept it *my* ressickneshion for der Egsecketiff Shudge!

Yes—this certainly has been a swell autumn! All through October I was out in the woods & fields with reading & writing nearly every afternoon. Not that the foliage was so hot, but that the thermometer surely did do its stuff nobly & generously. It was *80°* here Oct. 29, & on several occasions I wore summer weight clothing. I recall very few equally mild autumns—1920 & 1928 being those which most readily come to mind. These conditions must have been quite a boon to you in the course of your Swampscotting, & I fancy you will miss them as winter gradually asserts into malevolent power. Glad you improved the warming season with some longer trips—Cape Cod & the White Mountains surely run the gamut of New England scenery! The contrast in scenery on the two sides of the cape is surely curious. One would expect a divergence between south coastal & interior scenery, but to find a difference so strongly marked within so restricted an area is indeed far from what one would ordinarily presuppose. In Rhode Island the leaves were slow in going—indeed, some vivid greenery still adheres to a shrub or two in the garden beneath my window . . . not evergreen, either.

I assume, from your silence in that respect, that you have not yet received young Barlow's *Dragon-Fly*. When it comes—& it surely will come before long—I think you will hail it as something more completely within the best old amateur tradition than any other recent N. A. P. A publication. You cannot fail to recognise the subtle influence of *The Olympian,* & despite the occasionally fumbling typography (Barlow is new at printing) the taste of the enterprise is unmistakable. Edkins dominates the issue; & although not everything quite reaches his level, there is surprisingly little crudity of the sort that creeps into the *Californian, Perspective Review,* & other ambitious contemporaries. Which reminds me—as soon as you can exhume some more *Olympian* duplicates that you don't need, I can steer them into appreciative & perhaps fruit-bearing channels. Young Rimel (Box 100, Asotin, Wash.—very promising recruit) is eager to see copies, as is also the indefatigable Bobby Barlow. Barlow, by the way, recently gave Long a shock of surprise by presenting him with a published edition of the latter's own collected later poems! We printed it in De Land last summer, but lack of apparatus prevented its binding until October. It is called "The Goblin Tower" after one of its constitutional verses.

Edkins is slowly recovering from his illness, & on Nov. 4 departed for Coral Gables, Florida, where the genial clime will complete the healing begun by pharmaceutical art. Sadder news from Florida concerns the death of Long's aunt—instantly killed in a motor accident near Miami.[3]

Apropos of nothing—I wonder where I could get a copy of the *National Amateur* for May, 1923? It contained my tale "Hypnos", as well as reports & other junk connected with my presidential term. Just as a personal historical document, I want my file of the 1922–3 volume complete—but now some damned scatterbrain (to whom it was lent) seems to have lost this printed issue!

My caller Mr. Perkins has now definitely awaked, & is staging a purring parade between my chair & the outspread newspaper on which I sprinkled some catnip for him three hours ago. Is it possible that the young gentleman is hinting for a repetition of the courtesy? Mr. Purr-kins amply lives up to his name, being the third loudest vocalist in this line (he studied under me) that I have every encountered—the first being Peter Ivanovitch & the second Bobby Barlow's Cyrus. Johnny has three new brothers (or sisters, or both) over at the boarding-house where he lives—for all of whom good homes have been found. One is coal-black, & two are black-&-white. But they'll have to go some to beat their big brother!

Well—no hurry about returning the enclosed, but I thought it would amuse you to see how others have inherited the judicial burthens under which you staggered last year . . . . not, however, that the trouble so far is anything more than a mere warming-up! ¶ Regards to all, & hope to see you in course of time.

Yr oblig'd & obt Servt—Theobaldus Senex

Notes

1. Vincent B. Haggerty, HPL, and Jennie K. Plaisier (1882–1962) were the Executive Judges of the NAPA for 1935–36. Together they wrote "Report of the Executive Judges," *National Amateur* 58, No. 4 (June 1936): 2–3; rpt. *CE* 1.396–98.
2. I.e., EHC's residence at 53 Freeman Street, Wollaston, MA.
3. Mrs. William B. (Cassie) Symmes (1872–1935) was the author of *Old World Footprints,* which had a preface ghostwritten for Long by HPL. She financed Long's *A Man from Genoa.*

[66]   [ANS postcard][1]

[Postmarked Providence, R.I.,
22 November 1935]

Ave! Not that any new report is due, but I am asked to form part of a chain of notifications (Hymie to Spencer to Grandpa to Olympianus Carbo) whereby it is made known to the entire personnel of the bureau that we have a new official editor chosen from among our number! In other words— Hinrichs is out, & his successor is that genial & distinguished young magister typographiae *Helm C. Spink* of 513 Belgravia Court, Louisville, Kentucky! ¶ It certainly was about time that something was done to avert an organless year. Spink will make an ideal editor, I'm sure—as he did during his former term. Hope he'll feel able to take the presidency afterward, as he felt able to do after the earlier editorship. ¶ Wonder if there's any hope of a Sept. N.A. soon— & if so, whose it will be? ¶ Heard a darned good lecture last night—Prof. William Savery of U. of Wash on modern American philosophers. His general position on philosophic questions seemed to coincide very largely with my own. ¶ Regards to P. Ivanovitch
—Yr obt Servt
H P L

P.S. [on front] Hymie's note to Spencer said "Please (*not* you vill!!) forward all reports to Spink." Do you suppose he means that those sent to Hinrichs must be duplicated? Spencer fears it may—but I *don't* think so. Am asking Spink.

Notes

1. *Front:* New Providence County Court House, Providence, R. I.

[67]   [ALS]

Jany. 28, 1936

August Olympian (not chronologically meant):—

Here is something which I received from Wylie, & which according to the accompanying circulation list is to be forwarded to you . . . for shipment, in turn, to Iudex Vincentius, & ultimate return to its ex-presidential source. Willard Otis suggests that the author would probably appreciate comment on the document—which I shall try to give. There are undoubtedly points of merit in it—such as the combining of certain offices, the legal establishment of the mailing bureau, the creation of what might be called an "Assimilation Secretary", &c.—though on the other hand the whole thing seems a bit clumsy in arrangement, & contains many needless changes & points of doubtful advisability (such as demanding 4 consecutive years' membership for pres. & ex. iudices). One wishes that such a thing could be voted on in sections instead of as a whole. As it is, the bad will probably defeat the good. So much is merely a *transposition* of the existing constitution that the real changes could surely be isolated as separate amendments.

And curse the day that I didn't resign that damn'd exec. judgeship!! Now I can sympathise with you in full anent last year! Not merely the cursed Smith-Babcock row, but a whole raft of silly stuff from California to consider. Oakland kids want Hymie censured for omitting official data from his endless reports—Hymie himself vants ve should tell him vhat to do a'ready about a dozen different amendments (including the enclosed) submitted to him—oy! vhat ah life! In any case the matter is aggravated by (a) the absence of my N.A. file, which is lent to Kleiner, (b) an appalling & record-breaking pile of other insistent work which has disorganised my whole programme, & (c) an attack of grippe—or some damn thing producing headaches, nausea, weakness, & bum digestion—which has for a week prevented me from being up long at a time or eating anything in particular. I've had to pass up the writing of a March critical report—how about you? Kleiner is taking care of the verse.

Hope you got Barlow's *Dragon-Fly.* Be on the watch for Edkins' *Causerie*—great stuff, gentlemen! And of course you've seen Hymie's monumental *Californian.* Vhat ah men! Vhat ah men! That ought to silence his tormentors (cf. Babcock's performance in *The Enterprise*—at which I must admit I chuckled appreciatively despite my disapprobation of the ethics of this non-constructive & really non-*critical* attack) for a while!

I visited Long a week around New Year's, & saw most of the local gang—Mortonius, Kleiner, Loveman, Kirk, the weird writers, &c. Loveman's new book is out, & makes a fine appearance. Here's a circular describing it. Visited his new Bodley Book Shop at 104 Fifth Ave.—on the 17th floor of an office building. Also saw the new Hayden Planetarium at the Am. Museum. Tremendously interesting—don't miss it on your next metropolitan visit.

Regards to P. Ivanovitch. Local chapter of Kappa Alpha Tau sadly depleted through removal to another neighbourhood of black & white President & tiger Vice-President (brothers)—together with their human family. But black John Perkins sticks around—& the people at the boarding house have decided to keep his little brother, Gilbert John Murray Kynymond Elliot, 4th Earl of Minto.[1] Lord Minto is black & white—the former predominating in his northern hemisphere, & the latter in his southern. He is about half-grown now, & a dynamo of playfulness. I've just been watching him out the window. Snowdrifts & arctic temperatures seem to mean nothing to a young Scottish peer!

Well—don't waste too much energy reading the enclosed. I doubt if the whole thing will be submitted—indeed, as exec. judge. [*sic*] I shall vote for the separate re-submission of its really new parts.

Regards & all that—

Grandpa Theobald

Notes

1. The cat was named for Gilbert John Elliot-Murray-Kynynmond, 4th Earl of Minto (1845–1914), Governor-General of Canada (1898–1904) and Viceroy of India (1905–10).

[68]   [ALS]

The Antient Hill
—March 25, 1936.

Invincible Olympian:—

This delay in acknowledging yours of the 3d is *not* a piece of revenge for similar—but eminently excusable—tardinesses at the other end. Rather is it the result of a prevailing chaos which threatens to stigmatise MDCCCCXXXVI as one of my worst years . . . a time when unmerciful disaster follows fast & follows faster,[1] & when my programme of activities seems destined to explode amidst the confusion of multitudinous & conflicting duties. Letters remain unanswered & even unopened—one revision job refused & another probably fated for return unperformed . . . . In short, general hell! First came the mild grippe attack which laid me out for a week in late January. Then—before anything was straightened out—my aunt came down with an infinitely worse attack which at once tied me up as a sort of combined nurse, secretary, market-man, butler, & errand-boy.[2] This finally revealed complications necessitating my aunt's removal to the hospital—where she now is, albeit progressing nicely. And you can imagine about where I stand amidst the responsibilities imposed by these cumulative ills. Can I comprehend your inability to produce a critical report in time for the deadline? I'll say I can!

Well—the Babcock constitution seems safely shelved for the time being (vide March N.A.), but the woes of the Iudices will end only with the official year. The original E. H. Smith complaint still hangs over—& now comes another anti-Babcock complaint from the same source . . . albeit one less calculated to result in disagreement. It seems that the old fox has spotted the young rooster in a piece of really grave negligence—which will have to result in a verdict of censure. Babcock received 15 bucks in 1934 for the printing of some laureateship certificates—but has neither produced the certificates nor returned the cash! Obviously, he must be called to account—though of course he must have a chance to present any extenuating circumstances. I get more & more impatient with these sloppy officials who take their obligations lightly. If he couldn't print the certificates, then why the hell didn't he turn back the dough & let the association get somebody who could? My sympathy for Babcock is not at all increased by a perusal of the incredibly insulting & absolutely unmotivated attack which he has just sent poor Hymie—with the intimation that he may shortly use it as an editorial. Boys, boys!

You certainly have my utmost sympathy amidst the exacting inflictions of your arduous parallel jobs! The pace must really be nerve-shattering—& I surely hope that some lucky break may advance the fortunes of Chauncey Hall during the period in which your obligations will be heaviest. At least, let us hope that no turn for the worse may occur! Strains & disasters of kindred kind are numberless in ages of sharp transition—but that makes things none the easier for those actually involved. Meanwhile I trust you have not been shadowed by the added spectre of the prevailing grippe—& that the complications in your nephew-in-law's case did not prove as serious as was for a while feared. My aunt's grippe was also of the intestinal sort.

With *Causerie, The Dragon-Fly, The Californian,* & *The National Amateur* on hand, no one can complain that the present year is amateurically unfruitful! E A E is really back in the fray, & it gives me a tremendous sense of pride to have been instrumental in dragging the good old *Stylus* down from Valhalla to take up arms once more against the dunces of the mortal world. I've told Edkins that I think the Executive Judges ought to vote me a medal inscribed with a variant of the motto on the late Dr. Franklin's—ERIPVIT. C'LO. STYLUM. SCEPTRVMQVE. ASINIS![3] Ernie is certainly shewing the present decadent generation what the real old Ætas Aurea was like! Meanwhile Bobby Barlow is on his way up—whilst Hymie surely has given a lot of other folks' high-grade matter to the world. Hymie's presidential messages are classics of aërial expansiveness—though I don't know whether I endorse Spink's literal-rendition policy when it transmits such rare Bradofscisms as "Victor A. Moitoret was immediately notified of the decision, & was kindly explained to him the reasons therefor." Hymie seems to sling English *by ear,* like a nigger preacher . . . scorning the precisions of syntax & the ordeal of parsing! Spink, though, has put out a splendid N.A.—& Kleiner's criticism is the best verse reviewing we've had in years. Too bad you couldn't get a report in . . . how about next time? The deadline for June must be sometime in April.

Regards to Peter Ivanovitch. I still have occasional calls from John Perkins, & from his younger black & white brother Gilbert John Murray Kynymond Elliot, 4ᵗʰ Earl of Minto. Both appreciate the catnip Grandpa gives them!

Well—I hope the Neponset hasn't risen & drowned you! I'm really worried about Tryout, for the other night the *Bulletin* shewed pictures of Haverhill's business section under 15 feet of water. 408 Groveland is out toward the country, but not far from a bend of the river. I've dropped Smithy a card of enquiry. ¶ Hoping for better times—

Yr obt hble Servt

H P L

Notes

1. Poe, "The Raven," l. 64.
2. In fact, Annie Gamwell was hospitalized for breast cancer and underwent a mastectomy.
3. HPL alludes to a line (itself an adaptation of one from Manilius) inscribed by the French minister Jacques Turgot on a medal struck in honor of Benjamin Franklin: "Eripuit coelo fulmen sceptrumque tyrannis" ("He snatched lightning from heaven and the scepter from tyrants"). The allusion is to Franklin's discovery that lightning is produced by electricity, and also to the support he gave to his country in the asserting its independence from the British crown. HPL's satirical version means "He snatched the pen from heaven and the scepter from asses."

[69]   [ALS]

66 College St.,
Providence, R.I.
August 15, 1936.

Noble Olympian:—

Glad to hear you are still alive & active, even tho' harassed by some of the multifarious ills which are making 1936 a sort of nightmare for so many of the old gang. Congratulations on the well-earned Cape Cod vacation! Not that an "escape" from *heat* registers very impressively in my sub-tropical imagination, but that an escape from the madding crowd of insistent labours is a life-saver which even the most salamandrine of would-be West-Indians can profoundly appreciate!

Well—I'm glad your college marks followed the mercury into the 90's. Felicitations & admiration! But *what* a devastating programme you are swinging! Mine is bad enough, but yours would put Grandpa in Swan Point Cemetery in a week! I don't wonder at your stripping all activities down to essentials. That's what I'll have to do within my smaller-scale cosmos. Amateurdom is surely your debtor for the splendid reports you have turned out, & it thanks you amidst its tears at your inability to keep in harness. Your Murphy obituary was apt, dignified, sympathetic, & well received. Alas that such a thing had to be written!

News of the younger generation is always welcome. Congrats to E. Sherman on high-school editorship—& best wishes for his next bout with collegiate obstacles! Glad that the young aesthete-antiquary of Cantabrigia cleared the hurdles & won his five-spot . . . . once in a while these fledglings spring a surprise which makes us old folks sit up & take notice! The other Peter, too, seems to be making progress—as judged by his debut in the field of travel. I trust he enjoyed Cape Cod as keenly as did his bipedal companions!

Hope another year will send an ample crop of less-dense-than-usual specimens to Chauncey Hall, provide improved arrangements at dear old Burdett, & ease the Brookline burthens now oppressing Mrs. Cole . . . . a large order, one or two items of which might very conceivably be realised in part. In the interim, I presume, one may only grin, bear it, & snatch such rest as one can get.

Amateurdom simmers on with its usual ups & downs. Hymie sent out his usual temperamental S.O.S. to all the criticks—& then proceeded to resign "on physicians' orders" because of a "lack of coöperation". Townsend of Michigan has been appointed in his place—& promises a good N.A., though a less ample one than that which the Pomona Prune would have provided.[1] It's just as well that Hymie is out, for his lachrymose touchiness really unfits him for office-holding. Hope he doesn't abandon *The Californian*. According to all reports the convention gave young Babcock rather a trouncing—& almost convinced him that it pays to be a good boy. Boston is the next convention seat—& I can but hope that the youngsters of the N.E.A.P.C. will rise to the occasion & make the gathering more visible than their own regional assemblage of May 30. Spencer is the critical chairman once more, & is trying to round up another band of martyrs. Moe & Kleiner can be counted on, & I've promised to do at least a little. Your absence will form a bitter blow to prose—so that I believe the line betwixt prose & verse criticism ought to be made a bit less absolute. Some of the doggerel-dissecters ought to be detached for prose duty once in a while! There will, I fancy, be no such demand for copy as Hymie would have created—yet for all that the bureau ought to be larger than has been the custom in recent years. The work of each member is at present decidedly too heavy.

Glad you were able to attend the Fossil Dinner, & that so many of the traditional dignitaries were present. I surely hope the apparent decline in the organisation is not permanent, since of all the various alumni societies this one—with its continuous history since '04—is obviously most deserving of survival. Thanks immensely for the application blank—which I hope to use as soon as I am less financially denuded than at present. I believe I am fully eligible to fossildom—for although I didn't learn of *organised* amateur journalism until late in life . . . 1914 . . . I issued a hectographed paper independently (*The R.I. Journal of Astronomy*) as early as 1903. This is the date of amateur standing with which I am credited on the rolls of Smith's Alumni Association.

When I spoke of 1936 as a year of disaster all around I had plenty of cases to back me up—in addition to the heavy amateur necrology. Edkins has been in continual torment with a kidney complaint—one operation in early June & another now at hand. Wylie hurt in a motor crash, but now recovering. Barlow's home involved in some legal tangle with complete loss a possibility. Kleiner out of a job & in a frightful economic situation. My own health rotten, & my programme of activities in utter chaos . . . &c. &c. &c. And in the weird-fiction circle outside amateurdom the suicide of Robert E. Howard is just a sample of the day's news![2] Cook is dismally hanging on with Campbell in E. St. Louis, although their neighbourhood newspaper venture is in the shakiest possible condition. A great world!

As for local news—my aunt has been slowly recovering since last I wrote. Out of the hospital & into a convalescent home April 7, back at 66 April 21. She has not been away so far, & may stick around hereabouts the balance of the summer. Her daily programme is quite back to normal, though she has to be rather careful in avoiding fatigue. She extends to your entire household her sincerest regards & good wishes.

The stresses of the year threw my own schedule into such chaos that untangling is yet remote. May 4 I gratified my historical sense by attending a mock-session of the Rhode-Island legislature of 160 years before, at which session the rebel deputies adopted their seditious resolution separating this colony from our lawful King. In this mock-session each of the old-time deputies was represented by a lineal descendant in costume—the scene being the same room in the ancient colony-house (built 1761) where the original session took place. The costumes, pageantry, & speeches were surprisingly convincing—& I groaned as with fresh pain when the traitors had their way. God Save the King!

Later in May I took a trip to see the ancient Clemence house (1654), now recognised as the oldest edifice in Rhode-Island. Since its builder—Thomas Clemence, a friend of Roger Williams—is a lineal ancestor of mine in the 8th generation [he must also be a forbear of the amateur W. J. Clemence, although the latter can't trace his descent], I have more than a superficial interest in it. It lies just beyond the village of Manton (past Olneyville) on the western fringe of Providence's suburbs. Clemence purchased the land—8 acres—from an Indian named Wissawyamake, & proceeded to construct a typical stone-chimneyed dwelling of the period. It is much changed today—but the accompanying rough sketch shews it as it originally was. The

changes are all *excrescences*—dormers, lean-to, porch, &c.—so that it could easily be restored if purchased by an historical society as I hope it may be some
day. The present owner & occupant is an antient gentlewoman in destitute
circumstances. In the yard the old well-sweep still remains—one of the relatively few left in this colony.

I've also explored a triad of old urban houses—that of Stephen Hopkins
(1742) near #66, now filled with a notable loan-exhibit of furniture, plus two
spacious Georgian mansions farther south on the hill, recently thrown open
as publick museums.

Had a gigantick file-cleaning June 1st—but am all cluttered up again now.
Cold weather hung on accursedly in May & June, so that I was just about all
in by July—nervously & digestively. Then—on the 8th of July—the blessed
heat came . . . . & in two days the old man was on his feet again! Exhaustion
vanished, nerves relaxed, & digestion rapidly cleared up. In mid-July I took a
boat trip to ancient Newport—rambling as usual around the venerable town
& doing considerable writing on the high rocky cliffs—with nothing but a
saline solution betwixt me & the strife-torn Iberian peninsula.

July 18–19 I had a delightful visit from good old Moe, who made a tri-
umphal tour of the East after the convention—addressing the Poets' Congress in N.Y. & renewing all sorts of amateur contacts. It reminded me of old
'23 days, & I wished it had been possible to get in touch with you & reënact
our bygone Marbleheading—minus, alas, the slangy junior member of the old
trio. 1923 . . . Yes, We Have no Bananas . . . . Coolidge taking the oath by
lamplight . . . Mah-Jongg[3] . . . . eheu, fugaces! I hadn't seen ol' Mocrates since
that dim-remember'd primal age, & fancy he found me more changed than I
found him. His elder son Robert (the little imp of '23 whom I carried on my
knee in the car taking us from the South Station to the Myers mansion at 17
Clinton) brought him in the 1928 Ford, & we covered quite a bit of scenick &
historick ground in the all-too-brief span of 2 days. We finally took in ancient
Warren—down the bay's east shore—& had an all-ice-cream dinner at
Maxfield's [that place of many varieties which I shew'd you in '34 . . . a great
rendezvous of Cook, Morton, &c. when visiting hereabouts]—mine consisting of grape, pineapple, peach, raspberry, banana, & chocolate chip. Moe had
to call a halt after 2½ pints, but Bob downed 3 pints—with difficulty. As for
the Old Gent—I surrounded 3 pints with ease & avidity, & would have been
good for 3 more! Weather favoured us greatly, for we had warmth & sun
throughout—whereas the very next day was cold & rainy, with Grandpa
Theobald heavily blanketed & shivering over an oil heater!

Had an interesting view of Peltier's Comet on July 22 at the Ladd Observatory (which I used to haunt in youth) through [a] 12″ telescope. The object
shewed a small disc with a hazy, fanlike tail. I could have seen it through my own
small glass (3″) were the northern sky less cut off from the neighbourhood of 66.

On July 28 came an unexpected social event—the arrival in Providence for an indefinite stay of my one-time Florida host, young Robert Hayward Barlow of De Land. Some property adjustments about the De Land place are occurring, & R H B thought this would be a good time to pay Grandpa a visit & make his headquarters in antient New-England for a while. I surely was glad to see him—& forgave him the fierce-looking moustache & side-whiskers he has grown! He has taken a room at the boarding-house across the garden from 66, & certainly forms a most congenial neighbour. He's full of literary plans—including the establishment of a high-grade mimeographed magazine of distinctive material—& is rapidly squandering his patrimony on the alluring bookstalls of this ancient town. Occasionally he delves into genealogy— looking up his New-England lines at various local bibliothecae—& has established himself as my *6th cousin* by virtue of a common descent in the 7th generation from one John Rathbone of Block Island, born (in Roxbury) in 1658.

Last week—just to make the social season more feverish—there was a *second* visitor here—old Adolphe de Castro (friend of Ambrose Bierce & later a revision client of mine), who paused for 5 days en route from Boston to his home in N.Y. I shew'd him the sights—museums &c.—& on one occasion he, Barlow, & I sat on a tomb in a hidden hillside churchyard just north of here & composed rhym'd acrosticks on the name of *Edgar Allan Poe*—who 90 years ago used to wander in that selfsame necropolis when on visits to century'd Providentium.

Before Barlow leaves I hope to shew him such places as Newport, Salem, & Marblehead. Meanwhile he has elected himself a sort of successor to Cook & me as literary executor for Mrs. Miniter, & is busily going over the huge bale of unclassified Miniteriana which Cook sent here last year. Amongst this material is the long-lost novelette of 1923 (about a literary club with figures taken from the Hub organisation—I am recognisably depicted!) called "The Village Green", but no sign of the Natupski sequel.[4] Bob wants to get all possible material straight, & wishes you'd sub-lend him the 2 or 3 MSS. still in your custody. Would this be possible? He'd be vastly grateful.

My pile of unread borrowed books does not diminish as fast as it ought. Have just read lives of Roger Williams by Emily M. Easton & James Ernst— the latter of whom (despite a lousy & even ungrammatical style) adds importantly to our knowledge of R. W.'s emphatick influence on the revolution in England in the 1640's. Also finish'd Santayana's much-prais'd "Last Puritan"—a truly remarkable dissection of the sterile genteel culture now in its death-throes.

Well—pax vobiscum. Regards to all the household including Peter Ivanovitch!
    Yr obt Servt
        H P L

Notes

1. Clyde G. Townsend (1898–1966), editor of the *Oracle,* president of the NAPA for 1924–25 and 1925–26, and official editor of NAPA (1936–37), replacing Bradofsky.

2. C. L. Moore had notified HPL 16 June 1936 of the suicide of the pulp writer Robert E. Howard (b. 1906).

3. Vice President Calvin Coolidge became the 30th president of the U.S. when he took the oath of office at 2:47 A.M. on 3 August 1923 in the sitting room of a modest farmhouse. (President Harding had died only a few hours before.) Coolidge's father, a notary public, administered the oath by the light of a kerosene lamp, because he refused to install such modern conveniences as electricity. The tile-based game mahjong originated in China during the Qing dynasty, and became popular in the U.S. in the 1920s.

4. See Edith Miniter, *The Village Green and Other Pieces* (New York: Hippocampus Press, 2013). The sequel to *Our Natupski Neighbors* is apparently nonextant.

John T. Dunn

Letters to John T. Dunn

[1]   [TLS, JHL]

598 Angell St., Providence, R.I.,
July 20., 1915.

My dear Mr. Dunn:—

I received your letter this morning, containing Weckstein's *Common Sense*.[1] I am herewith returning the latter with thanks. While I am doubtful about the *sense*, I can easily see that its tone is lamentably *common*. Why doesn't the child wait till he is old enough to write before trying to publish?

As to the perennial German argument, I must say in the first place that if *any* nation has spent money subsidizing the American press, it is certainly *Germany*. The Germans are working through the cheap syndicates that serve the third-rate papers, and have succeeded in poisoning the Providence News pretty thoroughly.[2] I also certainly believe that it is Prussian influence which is causing the labour troubles in Connecticut. If I read correctly, The American Federation of Labour has not sanctioned the strike at the Remington Arms Co.[3] Can you name one *first class* paper in America (outside the Middle West, of course) that supports the German side? The standard papers of this country need no inducement to espouse the cause of the Allies; every real American's heart is with Old England. As a matter of fact, I am able truthfully to state that with only one exception, you are the only person with whom I have ever conversed that is not heart and soul against Germany. You trace your attitude to your dislike of England, but is that any good reason to endorse all of England's enemies? Turkey is at war with England, but do you approve of the Turks? Even though England were as bad as you evidently believe, Germany would be no more excusable. Look at the war from the *French* point of view, and see if you can find any excuse for the Prussians! But your whole prejudice against England is a misconception. You take a stand as an Irishman by descent, and enumerate all the past mistakes of England in the government of Ireland. Can you not see that experience has mellowed the judgment of England in these matters? Can you not see that every effort is being made to give justice to the Irish? That the land is being transferred from absentee landlords to the Irish people? That effective Home Rule will be in force before long? I believe that you are more hostile to England than the Irish still in Ireland, for the latter can perceive the coming changes in their favour. Can you not grasp the ultimate ideal of a unified British Empire, with Ireland as an integral, ruling part, not as a subject state? Perhaps with the Prime Minister of England an Irishman, and an immense Irish representation in the Imperial parliament at London? The British Isles are logically a geographical and national unit, and nothing but prejudice of the worst sort can prevent Ireland from being fused into the future solid British state, a state wherein the identities of England, Ireland, Scotland and Wales shall be lost politically, and local loyalty changed to that peaceful, sentimental sort which we see in this country as love of the several states by their inhabitants. Thus the Irish would love Ireland as we love Rhode Island, as their native sod, but recognising all the time that they are equal parts of a great country. Why do some Irishmen hold out bitterly against England, when most American Southerners, who have suffered horribly from the power of the Federal government, are practically reconciled today. Two years ago the veterans of the north and south fraternized on the old battlefield of Gettysburg.[4] Why may not English and Irish some day meet thus in peace to bury their ancient differences? England feels kindly toward Ireland at present, but if that kindness be repulsed with haughty scorn, who can say what will not follow? When I hear an Irishman crying "Delenda est Britannia"[5] I feel that the day may come when the Imperial government may be forced to drastic extremes hitherto undreamt of. If the Irish continue to talk of the "thrice accursed British Empire", I shall lend my sanction to the deportation of every man from Ireland who will not take an oath of allegiance to the Crown. If it comes to the question of either England or Ireland perishing, I would not hesitate to help clear Ireland of its rebels, and give the land to loyal British subjects. But as I said before, I am sure that all the Irish are not as anti-English as you assume. I believe that if the rebels were all to be transported to Australia or New Zealand, there would still be enough loyal Irishmen left to maintain the Green Isle in full splendour, as one of the most beautiful spots on earth, and one of the most patriotic parts of the British Empire. The dignity of England is a just one. The English were once but a few tribes occupying an area less than that of Ireland. By their own prowess and virility they have today become the foremost nation of the civilized world, and their sons have founded these great United States beyond the seas. Who could with reason wish to be other than a British subject? Will the Irish throw away the opportunity of an equal share in the supremacy of the world? I hope not, and I believe that time will eventually dissipate their rebellious sentiments toward the Mistress of the Seas. When comparing yourself to Hannibal, remember his fate and the fate of Carthage. Beware the tread of revengeful legions from Dublin to Galway and from Londonderry to Cork. As a poet once said; "England, with all thy faults I love thee well".[6] London is the future capital of the world, and her sons in all parts of the world will not fail her. Once Prussia is defeated, then let the world beware! Rule, Britannia!!

Returning to amateur matters, I am sorry that you admit even the possibility of the local club's being National in name.[7] The United, in order to build up as the leading association of the world, needs loyal members and clubs who will waste none of their money or energy on a rival association. Mrs. Renshaw has repeatedly been asked to join the National, but Daas writes that he has hitherto been able to dissuade her from joining. We hope to retain exclusively all our best recruits. I have great hopes for the Pawtucket Club which Mr. Wright[8] hopes to form in the fall. This, I understand, will be strictly United, and I hope to be able to aid it in a small way as long as it keeps clear of the National. Since I am so wholly a United man, I could not continue to support THE PROVIDENCE AMATEUR if it should affiliate itself with the National. The N.A.P.A. is dead. Even when it had life it was merely a means for individuals to show off their little accomplishments. There never was any really systematic educational ideal. When I see the influence of National conventions as displayed in Basinet's case, I am inclined to make up my mind not to attend the Boston convention next year, even though it be at my very door. Concentration of energy is what we need, and one association is enough for any man. Nationalism is an insidious thing, and I fear they will win you all over. In the May, 1914, UNITED AMATEUR mine was the only Providence name. Will this again be the case in May, 1916? I have no control over your club, but I do have a separate individuality, and am bound to the United by direct ties of loyalty. My first & strongest bonds are with the present association, so club or no club, I am a United fixture.

It was a good idea sending U.A.P.A. news to the local press. I have not seen your item either in the Bulletin or the humble News, but if it should appear in any paper, I wish you would reserve a copy for my scrap-book.

I have received THE TRYOUT by C. W. Smith (National) which contains references to Basinet at the National convention. It seems he was a von der Heide man, but could not stem the Houtain tide.[9] Daas says that Houtain is just the right man to ruin the National, so he is glad he is elected. I hope that Basinet issues his REBEL under the auspices of the National, so that the United may not have to endure any more red-flag anarchy. Shufelt[10] is bad enough for one association! He, by the way is an exclusively United man.

Daas may decline the official editorship, since it will interfere with his issuing THE LAKE BREEZE. He says the United must choose between his taking the office or having the Lake Breeze. He lacks time for both.

In conclusion, I must ask pardon for the frank and somewhat heated manner in which I have stated my political convictions. No ill is meant, but I am constitutionally unable to hear anything against the land of my fathers without making a rather decided answer. I wish all possible good to both Britannia and Hibernia, but when it comes to a choice—my colour is red!

  Sincerely,

   H P Lovecraft

Notes

1. *Common Sense* 1, No. 1 [1915], ed. Herman B. J. Weckstein, 142 Howard Street, Newark, NJ. Much of the issue was devoted to "consolidation" (i.e., union between

the UAPA and NAPA), which HPL at the time opposed.

2. At the time, HPL was writing astronomy columns for the [Providence] *Evening News*.

3. The strike at the Remington Arms and Ammunition Co. in Bridgeport, CT, involved issues of an eight-hour work day and minimum wage. Although Major Walter J. Penfield attributed the strike to German sympathisers, labor denied the charge and the accusation seems extremely unlikely.

4. The meeting took place on 1–4 July 1913, the fiftieth anniversary of the battle.

5. "Britain must be destroyed," an adaptation of the dictum attributed to Cato the Elder, "Delenda est Carthago" ("Carthage must be destroyed").

6. HPL quotes "Summer Morning" by Thomas Miller (1807–1874), although the text actually reads "England! 'with all thy faults I love thee well'" (30.4). Miller himself is quoting William Cowper. See letter 8n5.

7. Dunn's "Editorial" (June 1915), had, however, emphatically declared that the club "will give its first allegiance to the real U.A.P.A., the association of which Miss [Dora M.] Hepner is now President."

8. Herbert A. Wright of 301 Prospect Street in Pawtucket, RI. It does not appear that he ever formed the club.

9. Edna von der Heide (later Hyde, later McDonald; 1893–1962), an important figure in the NAPA and editor of the *Inspiration*. George Julian Houtain was editor of the *Zenith* (a NAPA paper); later co-editor, with W. Paul Cook, of *Epgephi*. He founded the professional humor magazine *Home Brew*, to which HPL contributed "Herbert West—Reanimator" and "The Lurking Fear."

10. Rev. Joseph Ernest Shufelt (1888–1966), RFD 1, Ghent, NY. HPL's outburst may have been a reaction to Shufelt's "The Cause of the Present War and Its Probable Outcome," *Badger* 2 (June 1915): 14–16. In commenting on that issue of the *Badger,* HPL wrote "Joseph E. Shufelt's article on the European war is an amazing outburst of socialism in its worst form. The idea that this shocking carnage is the result of a deliberate plot of the ruling classes of all the belligerents to destroy their labouring element is wonderfully ludicrous in its extravagance. We are let to infer that those best of friends, der Kaiser and his cousins George and Nicholas, are merely pretending hostility in order to rid themselves of a troublesome peasantry" (*United Amateur* 15, No. 2 [September 1915]: 19).

[2]   [TLS, JHL]

598 Angell St., Providence, R.I.,
October 25, 1915.

My dear Mr. Dunn:—

I received your letter of the 18th, and am glad to learn that all goes well with the local club. I completely agree with you regarding Charles D. Israelite's[1] overestimation of the importance of our card to him, and am rather amused at the manner in which he has followed the matter up. He answered my letter in which I assumed the credit or blame, and had many nasty things to say about the United. He said that Mrs. Renshaw had sent for all his recruiting or rather advertising matter merely for the purpose of steal-

ing his methods and using them in the United! Now as a matter of fact, he
was simply trying to divert her into the National, and she, acting on Daas' advice, refused to be alienated from the United. She has never used a single one
of Isaacson's methods, nor would any other United member. He made the
same slur against Dowdell, who is equally free from any such suspicion. That
Jew ought to be chained and muzzled.[2] Such things ought not to be running
loose. His second MINOR KEY, yellow of paper and yellow in contents, is
out, and he and James F. Morton Jr., make a joint attack on my CON-
SERVATIVE which covers about three and three quarters pages.[3] It sounds
fairly offensive at first reading, but there is so little really to it that it will not
take much time, space, or trouble for me to answer it in the January CON-
SERVATIVE.[4] Isaacson also attacks Mr. Alfred Hutchinson, who had not
even criticised him, more viciously than he attacks me. The fellow is absolutely rabid. Some one ought to put him out of his misery.

With the MINOR KEY came the rest of the Blue Pencil Bundle, the only decent part of which was Kleiner's PIPER. Kleiner sent me so many extra
copies that I am enclosing one. You said you had received no papers lately.
Houtain's mediocre paper, THE ZENITH promises a cessation of raids on
the United, and I certainly hope the promise will be kept.[5] Perhaps my letter
to Isaacstein did some good after all.

In order to be sure that you are receiving all the United papers I wish you
would tell me if any of the following have failed to reach you lately:

> The United Amateur (September)
> The United Official Quarterly (October)
> The Crazyquilt (July)

THE CONSERVATIVE was promised to me today, but it has not arrived.[6] I
hope Sandusky will have it soon enough for me to send out during the month
for which it is dated. Sandusky is disgusted with the National and the Houtain
administration, hence is going to put his best energies into the United. The
Boston side of the National has given way to the undisputed and disreputable
rule of New York and Brooklyn. The rupture with The Fossils seems to have
created quite a stir in National circles, for Houtain's ZENITH and A. M. Adams' DOPE SHEET both give the feud as much prominence as THE NA-
TIONAL AMATEUR did. Fortunately, the United has never relied on a
connection with The Fossils; our association is able to take care of itself and
stand alone.

Dowdell, after a long postponement, has begun planning the improved
BEARCAT with me, and between us I hope for a fine issue. He is going to
print the United's year-book absolutely free, including the picture of me
which occurs on the cover of the current UNITED AMATEUR. One of the
Wood-Bees, Mr. Melvin Ryder, has just had a book published, the circular

having reached me today. It is about college life, and the author, being editor of the LANTERN, Ohio State University's paper, is well qualified to write it.

Did you notice my temperance article in THE UNITED OFFICIAL QUARTERLY?[7] I think I shall send a copy to the Journal, though I scarcely can hope that they will heed it sufficiently to stop their beer advertising.

With best wishes for yourself and the club, and trusting that you will let me know if you have not received the papers above mentioned,

I remain

Very sincerely yours,

H P Lovecraft

P.S. I enclose my parody on Kleiner's "Mary of the Movies", which you will find in The Piper. I have sent it to the magazine which originally printed Kleiner's verse.[8]

[Enclosure: TMs of "To Charlie of the Comics."]

Notes

1. Charles D. Isaacson (1891–1936), editor of the amateur paper *In a Minor Key*, which HPL had attacked in "In a Major Key" and in "Gems from 'In a Minor Key.'"

2. Casual and open anti-Semitism was not unusual in early 20th-century American society. In a letter to Rheinhart Kleiner (6 December 1915), HPL acknowledged the prejudice of his youth: "I hardly wonder that my racial ideas seem bigoted to one born & reared in the vicinity of cosmopolitan New York, but you may better understand my repulsion to the Jew when I tell you that until I was fourteen years old I do not believe I ever spoke to one or saw one knowingly. . . . I never denied the mental capacity of the Jew; in fact I admire the race & its early history at a distance; but association with them was intolerable. . . . Then, all apart from this instinctive feeling, I very soon formed a conviction that the Oriental mind is but ill adapted to mingle with the Aryan mind—that the glory of Israel is by itself. Oil & water are both desirable, but they will not mix" (*Letters to Rheinhart Kleiner* 27).

3. Charles D. Isaacson, "Concerning the Conservative," *In a Minor Key* No. 2 [1915]: [10–11], and James F. Morton, Jr., "'Conservatism' Gone Mad," *In a Minor Key* No. 2 [1915]: [15–16].

4. HPL only response to the articles by Isaacson and Morton appears to be the poem "The Isaacsonio-Mortoniad," but he did not publish it.

5. Cf. George Julian Houtain in the *Zenith* (September 1915): 1: "The National Amateur Press Association is officially at peace with all organizations devoted to Amateur Journalism."

6. The issue for October 1915 (1, No. 3).

7. "More 'Chain Lightning.'" The article, on the temperance efforts of Andrew F. Lockhart, criticizes some newspapers, including the *Providence Journal,* for running a certain type of advertisement for beer.

8. Kleiner's poem "To Mary of the Movies" appeared in *Motion Picture Magazine* (May

1915): 121; rpt. *The Piper* No. 3 (September 1915): 12. HPL's response, "To Charlie of the Comics," appeared in the *Providence Amateur* 1, No. 2 (February 1916): 13–14.

[3]   [ALS, JHL]

598 Angell St.,
Providence, R.I.
June 10, 1916

My dear Mr Dunn:—

          I received yours of the 22nd ult., and noted your design of replying to McGavack's article.[1] But I fear another shock is awaiting you in the enclosed *Conservative,* lately off the press, where I have felt impelled to retaliate upon those who call my race "murderers" when seeking only to quell sedition.[2] Anglo-Americans cannot stand idly by whilst Irish-Americans seek to stir up feeling against England, and to use the United States as a catspaw in attacking the British Government; wherefore it becomes a duty for every son of Britannia to use every power in his possession in defense of the Mother Empire. The enclosed verses, "An American to Mother England" (already published in England, & soon to be reprinted & entered for U.A.P.A. Laureateship) illustrate the attitude which forces me to stand by the King and Country of my ancestors. I am preparing more material for use if any anti-English matter shall appear; it is time for England's side of the controversy to be presented in full, in order that real Americans may not be influenced by those zealots who would forfeit the right, if not the name, of Americanism through their hatred of the parent land. When the *Mayor* of an *American* city attends an un-neutral, anti-English meeting, and delivers an anti-British address there, (as Gainer[3] lately did) it is time for England's American friends to be un-neutral as well, in order to counteract the previous departure from neutrality.

      All of which I am stating to explain the manner in which I shall hereafter be devoted to the cause of Old England, and opposed to all her enemies. May the death of Lord Kitchener soon be avenged in German blood![4] I sincerely hope you will take no personal offense at the "Ballade of Patrick von Flynn"; in fact, I would not have thrust it before you if I did not think you ought to have an opportunity to read it and answer it if you are so disposed. I enclose copies for the other local members, but if you think they would be hurt by the lines, pray do not shew the paper to them. Remember, however, that stuff of this sort is by no means unprovoked—it is the result of hearing too much anti-English propaganda, and seeing too many references to loyal British authorities as "murderers". England is in the right, and not all the foes and rebels in purgatory & inferno combined can long becloud her fair fame. The Irish people will not listen forever to the fevered enemies of the Imperial Government, and some day there will be a loyal and happy Ireland, with Ulster a part of Great Britain, and the Southern provinces enjoying the privileges of Home Rule. As to the situation in America, I enclose a clipping which shews the sentiments of a prominent Irishman who refuses to sanction the antics of the England-hating element.

As to the term "Orangeman",[5] I am sure I had no idea of its being used as a term of reproach by any faction; I thought it simply applied to the Unionist element, the loyal supporters of the Empire, & the descendants of those who had supported William of Orange in the days of the Boyne.[6] I know that the Dublin rioters used the emblem of the Orange element, but I scarcely think they represented the public opinion of Belfast or Londonderry. This late revolt seems to have been the product of scholarly dreamers on the one hand,[7] and of discontented socialists or followers of the agitator Larkin[8] on the other, both acting under the hope of German connivance. The punishment of the leaders may seem severe, but such things must happen when law and order are to be maintained. It is significant that the execution of one rebel, Skeffington, is being investigated with a view to punishing the executioners if the act be found premature and illegal.[9]

The U.A.P.A. is experiencing no little difficulty in finding a suitable official board. I was offered the official editorship, but was forced to decline on account of ill health. Schilling can probably be persuaded, after all, to accept the post again.[10]

I am now struggling with reams of crude MSS. for the forthcoming paper of credentials; in fact, I have before me the entire contents of both MSS. Bureaus for revision. It is a monstrous task, and I fear I shall delay the appearance of the paper with my tardiness in completing work. I am also rushed with the July *Conservative*, which must go immediately to Sandusky if it is to appear before the convention. Sandusky is still working on Harrington's April *Coyote*,[11] but Harrington became so disgusted that he placed the July order elsewhere, so that it is now printed *before* the *April* number!

I am glad you enjoyed Kelso's song.[12] I do not think I shall use it in the credential paper, since the author has left the United. I recently composed a "take off" on James L. Crowley's silly songs and "poems", which I enclose. That fellow is a veritable "dedication fiend", in fact Lockhart declares that the only way he can get a piece published is by dedicating it to the publisher! You will notice the bad grammar and clumsy and trite language in my burlesque. I may publish the thing—it would certainly create some amusement![13]

Perhaps you noticed "To Flavia", by C. P. Munroe, a former Providence man, in the latest United Amateur. There is a bad misprint in the copy—the first word of line seventeen should be *"Small"* instead of *"Swell"*.[14]

But I fear I must return to my task of revision.

With best wishes, I remain

Very Sincerely yrs.

H P Lovecraft

[Enclosures: TMss. of "My Lost Love" and "An American to Mother England."]

Notes

1. It is not clear what work by Henry Clapham McGavack is being referred to. It may have been "Dr. Burgess, Propagandist," *United Amateur* 15, No. 9 (April 1916): 118–20. In the "Department of Public Criticism," HPL highly praised the work: "*The United Amateur* for April is made brilliant by the presence of Henry Clapham McGavack's terse and lucid exposure of hyphenated hypocrisy, entitled 'Dr. Burgess, Propagandist'. Mr. McGavack's phenomenally virile and convincing style is supported by a remarkable fund of historical and diplomatic knowledge, and the feeble fallacies of the pro-German embargo advocates collapse in speedy fashion before the polished but vigorous onslaughts of his animated pen" (*United Amateur* 15, No. 11 [June 1916]: 148).

2. See "Ye Ballade of Patrick von Flynn." "Murderers" refers to the suppression of the Easter Rebellion in April 1916, in which 103 British soldiers and 450 rebels and civilians were killed; later, the leaders of the rebellion were executed.

3. Joseph Henry Gainer (1871–1945), seven-term Mayor of Providence (1913–27) who developed the local Democratic Party ward organizations as an effective power base in RI state politics.

4. Horatio Herbert, first Earl Kitchener of Khartoum and of Broome (1850–1916), one of the most distinguished military and political figures in late 19th-century England, who died on board the H.M.S. *Hampshire* when it sank off the Orkney Islands on 5 June 1916 on the way to Russia.

5. A term originally designating Protestant small farmers in northern Ireland loyal to England in the late 18th century, later referring to quasi-military groups of Unionists in the north opposing Home Rule.

6. The forces of the Protestant William of Orange, later William III of England, defeated the forces of the Catholic James II at the Battle of the Boyne on 1 July 1690.

7. Referring to the poets Padraic Pearse (1879–1916) and Thomas MacDonagh (1878–1916), central figures in the rebellion of 1916, both of whom were executed.

8. James Larkin (1876–1947), a socialist who organized trade unions in Ireland in the early decades of the 20th century.

9. Francis Sheehy-Skeffington, shot during the Easter Rebellion by a British officer later found to be insane.

10. George S. Schilling did indeed become Official Editor of the UAPA for the period March–June 1916, taking over for Edward F. Daas.

11. William Thomas Harrington, editor of the *Coyote*.

12. Guy H. Kelso (1878–1950), a member of the Providence Amateur Press Club.

13. James Lawrence Crowley (1885–1962) (HPL's pseudonym "Ames Dorrance Rowley" is a parody of Crowley's name), whose verse HPL graciously revised at no charge. Earlier that month, in the "Department of Public Criticism," HPL had written: "'There's None like Mine at Home', by James Lawrence Crowley [*United Amateur* 15, No. 2 (May 1916), 141], is a characteristic bit of Crowleian sentimentality which requires revision and condensation. There is not enough thought to last out three stan-

zas of eight lines each . . . Mr. Crowley needs a long session with the late Mr. Walker's well-known Rhyming Dictionary! . . . Of the general phraseology and imagery we may remark that Mr. Crowley has much to forget, as well as to learn . . . So energetic and prolific a writer as Mr. Crowley owes it alike to himself and to his readers to develop as best he can the talent which rests latent within him." (*United Amateur* 15, No. 11 [June 1916]: 149). He later relented, and on a page from *Tryout* 6, No. 1 (January 1920): [11], beneath the poem "Scorned," HPL wrote: "This thing is really by Crowley—a dull effeminate fellow with a copper-plate handwriting—but I revised it beyond recognition, simplifying double rhymes, etc. Back in 1916 I used to spoof poor Crowley until I saw I really hurt him. Then I sought to make amends by helping him all I could" (A.Ms, JHL). HPL's "My Lost Love" was not published in his lifetime.
14. Chester Pierce Munroe (1889–1943) was a boyhood friend of HPL. "To Flavia" appeared in *United Amateur* 15, No. 10 (May 1916): 136. The line printed in error reads: "Swell maid, beneath whose hat of red . . ."

[4]   [ALS, JHL]

598 Angell St.,

Providence, R.I.

June 28, 1916.

My dear Mr Dunn:—

I received your letter of the 26th inst., and am scarcely surprised that the "von Flynn" ballad proved less than pleasing. It is, of course, a very broad caricature, nor would the average reader for a moment imagine it a serious delineation of the better element of the "Sinn Feiners". But it attempts to illustrate the fundamentally illogical sort of reasoning used against England; a reasoning which lacks proportion in considering events of history or estimating present political conditions. I certainly treated the Sinn Feiners no worse than they habitually treat and misrepresent England! As to its merit—I did not pretend to call it "poetry", as you may see from the fact that I used my old *nom de plume*[1] instead of my own name. But it is now McGavack's turn to exhibit some facts. The next *Conservative* will be devoted to his long & serious essay entitled "The American Proletariat versus England",[2] wherein he explains away many anti-British fallacies, including phases of the Irish question. This will be followed in October by an essay of my own: "Old England and the Hyphen".[3] I am pleased to state that neither of these pieces contains any sarcasm or ridicule.

Your estimate of the character of the Sinn Feiners is just, so far as those actually living in Ireland are concerned. They seem to me more like your friend Basinet than anything else I can think of. But some of their sympathizers in this country are rather more materialistic. I can find far more compassion for real Irishmen who rebel, than for Irish-Americans who abuse the hospitality of the United States in seeking to injure Old England. But I fancy that conditions on the Mexican border will cause a separation of the real

Americans of Irish descent, from the Sinn Fein hyphenates.[4] Those who are truly loyal to America will forget their pastime of England-hating for a while, and exhibit their allegiance to this country.

And speaking of Mexico, I enclose a piece which was published in the Providence News last night. It is an answer to a peace-advocate named Henry F. Thomas, who published a very unpatriotic "poem" a few days ago,[5] wherein he called it a "shame" for America to prepare for defence against the Mexican bandits. He said that "Arbitration were more sense". The execrable bad taste which Thomas showed in writing this piece at a time like the present, when all the nation is patriotically astir for action, was too much for me, and I forthwith composed the enclosed reply, entitled "The Beauties of Peace", which is probably the most caustic satire I have ever written. I may detest the enemies of England, but that feeling is mild compared to the unutterable contempt I have for the peace-at-any-price fanatics. *The News* evidently shared my sentiments, for they gave me an immense space, setting my verse in large 10-point type with heavy heading, and placing it on the editorial page. I send the MS., since I have not yet had a chance to obtain extra copies of the paper. If Thomas chooses to commence a controversy, I am ready for him! He has had some drivel in *The News* before, but though it was nearly as bad as Kelso's or Crowley's, it was never before so offensive and inopportune.

So you have beheld the rising of the *Cleveland Sun!* That paper is absolutely the most disgusting mess of slang, sportiness, and yellow journalism which has disgraced the United since the old days of stormy politics. That child Dowdell ought to secure a position on *The Police Gazette!* I hope you will pay no attention to Moitoret's editorial advice not to vote for Campbell's constitutional amendment.[6] He is working against the best literary interests of the association. Campbell[7] used a great deal of thought in preparing his measure, and I firmly believe it meets the requirements of the United as nothing else could at present.[8] Campbell is an extremely capable man, and in the interests of harmony he and all his ticket should be elected without opposition.

Schilling, as a member of the Ohio National Guard has been summoned for Mexican duty, and is therefore torn away from the United. There may be no July *United Amateur*, but I think Lockhart[9] should be elected for the coming year as official editor. Campbell offered me the nomination a month ago, but I knew that my ill health would prevent me from serving the association well, so I reluctantly declined. I was sorely tempted to accept, since there are so many reforms I should like to make in the official organ; but if I tried, I should be as complete a failure as M. W. Hart last year. Schilling is the first American amateur to respond to the call of martial duty, and he deserves the highest possible admiration of every United member. I wish I were strong enough to follow his example!

The United Convention will be held July 20–21–22, but Fritter privately informs me that it will not be a notable one. The Cleveland amateurs are mainly a group of young "sports" like Dowdell, who do not represent amateurdom nearly as well as the Columbus members. The National Convention is close at hand—July 1–2–3. I have been invited to attend, but have doubts about doing so. I am very much a *United* man. Yesterday I received the announcement of the long expected Cole–Hoffman wedding, which occurred Monday.[10] The former Miss Hoffman is fortunate in securing so gifted and scholarly a life companion.

I shall certainly *not* run for the Vice-Presidency or any other office.[11] I am physically & nervously unable to bear the strain, and have indeed been rather a failure this term. I have selected my favourite candidate for the position I am leaving—David Whittier of Boston[12]—and trust that your vote may help elect him. He will be more than a worthy successor—he will eclipse me entirely through his greater youth and vigour. But I shall never give up my place on the Department of Public Criticism till some future President refuses to reappoint me.[13]

I have finished revising the contents of the credential paper which Mrs. Whitehead[14] intends to issue, and expect to see it published before the convention. Dowdell is late with the ballots, as he is with everything else!

   With best wishes,
     Sincerely,
      H P Lovecraft

[Enclosures: TLS of "The Beauties of Peace."]

Notes

1. I.e., "Lewis Theobald, Jun."

2. Henry Clapham McGavack, "The American Proletariat versus England," *Conservative* 2, No. 2 (July 1916): 1–4.

3. See also HPL's later essay, "Lucubrations Lovecraftian" (1921).

4. Referring to the discovery in late 1915 of a plot by German-Americans to provoke an American war with Mexico, so as to keep the U.S. from supporting the Allies in World War I.

5. Henry F. Thomas, "A Prayer for Peace and Justice," [Providence] *Evening News* 49, No. 120 (23 June 1916).

6. See HPL's "Department of Public Criticism" (September 1916): "His [Anthony F. Moitoret] editorial hostility toward the Campbell amendment is, we believe, mistaken; yet is none the less founded on a praiseworthy desire to serve what he deems the best interests of the Association. Were Mr. Moitoret more in touch with the rising ideals of the newer United, he would realise the essential childishness of our 'official business' as contrasted with the substantial solidity of our developing literature" (*CE* 1.129).

7. Paul J. Campbell was president of the UAPA (July 1916–July 1917). See letter 10 regarding Campbell's earlier amateur career.

8. Regarding Campbell's amendment, see HPL's "Finale": "He would transform the

United Amateur into a monthly magazine of from forty to fifty pages, literary as well as official, and having a circulation not only within our ranks, but extending to the high-schools and public libraries as well, thus spreading abroad the all too restricted information which would bring us recruits in immense numbers" (*CE* 1.45).

9. Andrew F. Lockhart served as Official Editor of the UAPA (July 1916–July 1917).

10. I.e., Edward H. Cole and Helene E. Hoffman.

11. HPL had served as First Vice-President for the 1915–16 term. He was in fact on the ballot for the UAPA elections of July 1916. He lost to Paul J. Campbell for President by a vote of 38–2 and to Andrew F. Lockhart for Official Editor by a vote of 28–1.

12. For Whittier see HPL's essay "The Youth of Today." Whittier was elected First Vice-President of the UAPA in July 1917, but served only until September, at which time he was succeeded by Ira A. Cole.

13. HPL had been appointed Chairman of the Department of Public Criticism in November 1914 by President Dora M. Hepner, and was reappointed by President Leo Fritter for the 1915–16 term and by Paul J. Campbell for the 1916–17 term. In the election for September 1917 HPL himself was elected President, and he appointed Rheinhart Kleiner as Chairman of the Department of Public Criticism. For the 1918–19 term President Rheinhart Kleiner appointed HPL as Chairman; this was HPL's last term in the office, although he continued to contribute random pieces.

14. Daisy Crump Whitehead. HPL was assistant editor of an amateur journal called the *Credential* (1, No. 1 [April 1919]), but Whitehead was not associated with it. The editor of that journal was Anne Tillery Renshaw.

[5]   [ALS, JHL]

598 Angell St.,
7 / 4 / 16

My dear Mʳ Dunn:—

In response to your inquiry of 30ᵗʰ ult., I herewith sub-join an exact copy of the ballot which I have mailed to Cleveland:

President—Paul J. Campbell
1st V.P.—David H. Whittier
2nd V.P.—Florence Shepphird
Off. Ed.—Andrew F. Lockhart
Treas.—Leo Fritter
Laureate Rec.—Jonathan E. Hoag
E. MSS Mgr.—John Russell
W. MSS. Mgr.—Ira A. Cole
Historian—Chester P. Munroe
        —Mrs. J. W. Renshaw
Directors—Henry Clapham McGavack
        —Mrs. W. V. Jordan[1]
Convention Seat—Tallahassee, Fla.

"Yes" to both constitutional amendments

Schilling's departure with the Ohio National Guard places Lockhart as the best candidate for official editor.

Much to my surprise, I was called on the telephone at 7 a.m. Saturday by *Charles D. Isaacson,* who headed a party of Brooklynites on their way to the National Convention. Among those who stopped off in this city were *Kleiner,* Goodwin, and Dench.[2] I was able to get to the station at 7:45, & had an interesting conversation with these amateurs, particularly Kleiner. Goodwin may join the United in the near future. They invited me to attend the Boston Convention, but I was unable to go.

There is no particular hurry about mailing United ballots to Cleveland, since our convention is so late in the month, but I trust you may persuade Messrs. Shehan and McManus to forward their votes as soon as possible, thereby being on the safe side. The really important candidates are the first five on the list.

Hoping, as the political ward bosses say, that you will vote *early* and *often,*
I remain
Most Sincerely yrs.
H P Lovecraft

Notes

1. Mrs. Joseph W. Renshaw is the same person as Anne Tillery Renshaw. W. V. Jordan is the same as Winifred Virginia Jackson, who resumed her maiden name after divorcing Horace W. Jordan.
2. William Harry Goodwin, of Manhattan, was associated with Isaacson in the publication of *In a Minor Key.* Ernest A. Dench, a former British amateur then living in Brooklyn, was editor of the *Reflector.* All four men were members of the Blue Pencil Club of Brooklyn.

[6]   [ALS, JHL]

598 Angell St.,
Providence, R.I.
Aug 15, 1916.

My dear Mr. Dunn:—

Had I known that you were uninformed about the United Convention and its results, I should have sent you information before, but I supposed Dowdell had issued some sort of notice long ago. However, his failure to do so is only characteristic of him! He attempted some very cheap "politics" last month by withholding proxy ballot forms from those likely to vote against his policies.

I am pleased to state that the election was unexpectedly favourable to the United's best interests; due, no doubt, to the large delegation of Woodbees from Columbus, whose influence counteracted that of the local Cleveland element. Dowdell did not run for office at all, since he was shown rather clearly that his candidacy would not be acceptable to the majority. The following are the complete results:

```
Pres --------------------------------- Paul J. Campbell
1 V P -------------------------------- David H Whittier
2 V P -------------------------------- Elizabeth M. Ballou
Treas ------------------------------- Leo Fritter
Off. Ed. ---------------------------- Andrew F. Lockhart
Laur. Rec. -------------------------- Eleanor Barnhart
Historian --------------------------- Samuel S. Steinor
E MS. Mgr -------------------------- Albert A. Sandusky
W. "      " -------------------------- Freda S. de Larot
                 ---------------------- Anthony F. Moitoret
Directors -------------------------- Mʳˢ· J. W. Renshaw
                 ---------------------- Wesley H Porter
Convention Seat 1917 ------------- St. Louis, Mo.
Houghton Amendment ----------- Carried
```

Campbell Amendment Lost by 2 votes, but will be placed *on trial* for one year. Secretary not yet appointed

All things considered, the Campbell Expansionist Ticket may be said to have achieved a substantial victory. The only official likely to cause trouble is Moitoret, whose ideas are not in harmony with those of the more liberal element. He is strongly in league with Dowdell, and has the additional advantage of being a fairly fluent writer. His forthcoming issue of *The Cleveland Sun* may be rather a blow to the peace of the amateur world, since it will have a set of cartoons of amateurs, &c. I think I succeeded in frightening Dowdell a little about the matter of the *Official Quarterly,* which he failed to issue after soliciting and receiving monetary contributions. Mrs. Renshaw says she believes he would be really liable to punishment from the U.S. Postal authorities for this piece of work. At any rate, he seems much disposed to behave since the stinging defeat suffered by his so-called "Independent Party".

The Laureateships are not yet announced, but I have lost my chance for an award in any case, since Dowdell failed to print the verses I had entered.

As you surmised, my greetings to the Brooklyn scribes were extended to *individuals* and *amateurs,* nothing else being considered. As a matter of fact, Kleiner was the point of interest for me. His personality as revealed face to face exactly sustained my previous impression of him, proving that correspondence is not always deceptive in representing a person's characteristics. Isaacson interested rather than appealed to me. He is fat, flabby, and unmistakably Semitic, though neater and cleaner in appearance and more refined in manner than the average Jew. Ernest A. Dench is rather more coarse looking than I expected.

W. Harry Goodwin, the celebrated wit, is a handsome, slender young fellow of pleasing manner. He intends to join the United through Kleiner.

I am glad to hear that Basinet is about to revisit Providence,[1] and hope that you and he may be able to evolve something in the way of activity betwixt the two of you. I fear that he has not been very active in either association during the past year.

Speaking of activity, I hope that the United in general may be less quiescent in the months to come, yet fear that the rapidly advancing cost of paper and of linotype work may hinder the renaissance of publishing which is so much to be desired. Sandusky cannot print *The Conservative* any more, so I am now in quest of a suitable typographical artist.[2] The July number, sadly overdue, has been expressed to me, but is delayed in transit. If I do not receive it soon, I shall have to ask Sandusky to have the package traced. I will send you a copy as soon as I receive the edition.

Lockhart is in poor health, and on a vacation in the extreme eastern part of South Dakota, hence there may be no August official organ; but I am sure the subsequent numbers will compensate for the possible omission. He has promised me unlimited space for the Dept. of Public Criticism.

With best wishes for you & your fellow-amateurs,

I remain

Very Sincerely yrs

H P Lovecraft

Notes

1. Victor L. Basinet apparently had moved to Brooklyn, where he was receiving his mail care of Bellevue Hospital (*United Amateur* 15, No. 10 [May 1916]: 139).
2. The printer for the first *Conservative* was not specified. Albert A. Sandusky's Lincoln Press printed four issues, but those following do not indicate the printers. The next four issues must have been printed locally. W. Paul Cook printed the *Conservative* beginning with the issue for July 1918 (see *Letters to Rheinhart Kleiner* 115–16).

[7]   [Envelope only, postmarked Providence, R.I., 16 August 1916]

[8]   [TLS, JHL]

598 Angell St., Providence, R.I.,
October 14, 1916.

My dear Mr. Dunn:—

I received your letter of yesterday, and note your attitude toward my remarks on the Sinn Fein agitating element. I very sincerely hope that your estimate of the sentiment of the entire Irish people is erroneous; for while I have hitherto held no animosity against Ireland as a whole, a belief in your statements would force me into a vigorously anti-Irish position. My regard for Ireland is founded on its connexion with the British Empire; otherwise, I can but think of it as an outlaw province, which must be brought to its senses by the strictest measures possible. I fancy the question of conscription will settle the point in question.[1] If the natives are loyal to the Empire they will not resist a measure designed for its general good. England has been consolidated with Ireland too long for either to think of itself as apart from the other. Geographically, the British Isles are a unit, and a separation would only render both sections more open to the attacks of a foreign power. Combined, the Empire can and will resist the world.

As to the early civilisation of Ireland, it is needless to say that it was not superior to that which the Anglo-Normans introduced, else it would have survived. When two civilisations come in contact, it is the higher which remains, no matter which represents the conquering stock. Thus the Goths who conquered the Roman Empire became Romanised, though they were themselves the victors. The primitive Celtic culture of Ireland was no match for the strength of the Normans and Saxons, since these invaders represented the dominant world-culture of the period. However, the Irish need feel no shame at the fact that their culture did not survive; it is better that they should rejoice at the advent of a superior civilisation. England had experienced the same phenomenon herself, when the Saxon was overridden by the Norman. But the Englishman, with greater sense, did not resist the advance of a culture so much better than his own. He recognised at once the higher rank of the Norman culture, and proceeded within two centuries to adopt the Norman as his brother, so that today the advent of the Norman really is regarded as the opening of true English history. It was the union of Saxon and Norman elements which produced what is really the British nation. Thus with Ireland, it is quite erroneous for her present inhabitants to regard the primitive Celts as their only cultural forefathers; they owe as much to the Anglo-Normans who founded their present and more stable civilisation. Despite the gilded phrases of Hibernian panegyrists, the native Celts were little better than barbarians; in fact, they could at no period unite amongst themselves sufficiently to preserve their rudimentary culture. They lacked the indomitable Empire-building power of the Saxon blood. The superiority of the Saxon is racial as well as cultural. Today, the best Irish families are practically Saxonised through intermarriage with English settlers, so that they compare well with the English people; but they must not forget that it is England which gave them this better blood. Really, all the British Isles are of one racial admixture in varying proportions; that of a Celtic native stock overlaid with Saxon blood. In England the Saxon element is strongest, yet Cornwall and Devon are practically Celtic counties. In Scotland, the Celtic blood is predominant in the north, while the south has Saxon blood dating back to the original Teutonic invasion of 450 A.D. In Ireland the Saxon blood came later, but all these divisions of the British Isles owe much to both races. Every part of England, Scotland, and Ireland owes something to both, and ought not to adopt one in hostility to the other. If the Englishman should single out the Saxon antecedents as the Irishman singles out his Celtic origin, he would have to call himself a German, for it is from the forests of Germany that the conquering Saxon came. But the Englishman does not do this. He recognises the various influences which shaped him as he is, and is content to identify himself with the land itself; often poetically calling himself a "Briton", after the Celtic race which preceded him in the possession of Britain. It is by far the most rational plan for the British People; English, Irish, Scotch and Welsh alike, to forget the racial and linguistic differences which preceded the formation of the present United Kingdom, and to accept their lot as a combined Teutonic-Celtic race, no matter what the exact proportion of Teutonic to Celtic blood may exist in particular parts of the Empire. Time will bring an even greater homogeneity of racial elements if hostility can be removed. Ireland never can and never will become separate from England. All the irresistible might of the world's greatest organised power will prevent such an occurrence. If the Irish will cast aside their prejudices, they can share equally with the rest of Britain in the glory of England. The past relations of England and Ireland have undoubtedly been characterised by treachery on both sides, but in this age it would require only a little forbearance on the part of each section to create a lasting union and perpetual peace. Just now the Irish have difficulty in appreciating the increasing justice of the British government on account of the past. Conversely, the English fail to understand why Ireland should be so continually rebellious, hence are reluctant to give Ireland a large measure of power all at once. But if ever the two sections can arrive at a real understanding of each other, I have not the slightest doubt in the world but that Ireland will joyfully cast her destinies into the magnificent coalition which England and Scotland already share, and that England will accord to it a recognition and respect due its place as an equal and homogeneous part of the Kingdom. The case of Scotland is a perpetual reminder of the benefits of union. I have often wished that Ireland might have had an opportunity to join England in the same way—for if an Irish King had ever succeeded to the throne of England as the Scotch King did,[2] the whole Irish people would undoubtedly have followed his fortunes in the united nations. It would have touched their local pride in the right place, as with the Scotch in King James's time.

I do not suppose your early imbibed sentiments and your preferred courses of reading will ever permit you to feel truly the supernal glory of Britannia. It is almost a spiritual thing—almost a religion—which throbs in the Anglo-Saxon breast until death, its only conqueror, stills it. It is the glory of just and conscious power—a kind of fine exaltation at the thought of a divine Motherland which has spread its influence all over the globe, conquered the wilderness of America, and reared the loftiest structure of governmental equity which the world has known since the days of Rome. Saxon blood has never been conquered except by Saxon blood—and that is a thought which raises the embattled Briton to a pitch which can keep him unswervingly to his purpose through countless temporary defeats and over well-nigh insuperable obstacles toward ultimate and inevitable victory. England is absolutely unconquerable. We will win this war if it lasts a thousand years. We will win if we have to burn every Irish traitor at the stake and deport the remainder to the Australian deserts. Nothing under Heaven can withstand the power of Britannia. All that concentrated fixity of purpose and relentless determination of which we see today in the German, is still deeper ingrained in the Englishman, for he, too, is a Teuton. But he has more than the Germanic Teuton. He has the fire of the Celt whose blood is in his veins, and the Roman ideals of the Norman, whose culture is in his brains. Eight hundred and fifty years of proud, invincible national existence have made of the Englishman the dominant figure of the world; the ultimate master of all the nations. Englishmen know how to die, but not how to surrender. When I think of the vast, enormous power which the Sinn Fein Irishmen are trying to antagonise, as a mosquito or fox terrier tries to annoy a giant, I smile sadly at the sublime pathos of the pitiful farce. The sting of the mosquito or the snap of the terrier may cause pains and raise blisters, but the hand of the giant will soon crush the mosquito, or his foot drive away the terrier. Have you so little vision of greatness that you can hear unmoved those lines of the world's supreme singer:

"This ENGLAND never did—nor never shall—
Lie at the proud foot of a conqueror,

COME THE THREE CORNERS OF THE WORLD IN ARMS,
AND WE SHALL SHOCK THEM. NOUGHT SHALL MAKE US
RUE, IF ENGLAND TO ITSELF DO REST BUT TRUE!"[3]

As to the loyalty of Irish agitators to America, I believe that some possess it, while others lack it. Pres. Wilson, himself practically a pro-German, was man enough to send a pretty stinging telegram to the creature O'Leary, whom even the majority of England-hating Irish seem to repudiate.[4] Viewing the United States as a theoretically neutral nation, it is not disloyal for individuals to express dislike for England, provided they keep the United States out of the discussion; but the extreme Sinn-Feiners fail to do this. They seek deliberately to employ the United States as a tool against England, a power with which the United States is at peace. The enclosed cutting is a good example of this sort of thing. These swine (I will not call them Irishmen, out of respect to the Irish people) are the same animals who snort with rage whenever a severance of diplomatic relations with Germany is proposed; yet they would embroil the United States with England, which has not committed a millionth the outrages against America which Germany has committed. They obviously have no respect or regard for the United States as a nation. They cannot by the broadest stretch of the imagination be called Americans—not even "hyphenated" Americans—for America is to them nothing but a convenient weapon for use in carrying out their traitorous infamy against England. It is not "America First" with them; it is "Sinn Fein First", and America only incidentally. So far as loyalty is concerned, many Jewish nondescripts and Italian organ-grinders are better "Americans". However, the Jews have also offended in this direction, when their "American" money barons hired the government to abrogate the Russian treaty a few years ago.

I deny flatly that American civilisation is composite, or in any way otherwise than Anglo-Saxon. This land was a bleak, Indian-haunted wilderness when England found it. England made it what it is. It is the power of England which provided a series of colonies to which persons from other nations could emigrate. The Dutch tried it, but they failed. England alone could do it. Every individual, other than an Indian, who breathes the air of America today, is here because of the original efforts of England to carve an Empire from the forest. The language, laws, institutions, and moral excellencies of America are without exception English. It is because this country is English, that it is great. The second-rate nations of South America are the best that non-Saxon blood can create. The continued greatness of America depends upon the maintenance of the Anglo-Saxon ideal. If this nation ever becomes really composite; if the polyglot lower elements ever rise to the surface and direct the destinies of the whole people, then the United States will have undergone intellectual and moral death, and must be content to take its inferior place beside Argentina, Brazil, Chile, and other decidedly immigrant nations. For the glory of the world is the glory of England. This is Rhode Island—a State founded by Englishmen, and given its charter by His Majesty Charles II. If other nationalities are now represented here, it is only on sufferance. They are charity boarders, as it were. For this is an Englishman's country. Let the foreigners rejoice that they are permitted to stay here. They did not build the State, and would never have crossed the ocean if Englishmen had not made it easy for them. When America formally ceases to be English, then I shall formally declare myself a British subject. This may be poor "Americanism", but it is at least as good as that of the Sinn Feiners. My life and pen are forever dedicated to the race to which I belong, and I am prepared to stand by England in life or death, victory or defeat. The most poignant sorrow of my existence is that my physical health does not permit me to serve the King against his enemies on the field of battle. I stand by England against any foe which threatens and troubles—German or Irish. The blood of England flows in my veins without a drop of dilution, and I am prepared to defend that blood in whatsoever manner I am capable of doing. England is not perfect—Rome was not perfect—no nation ever has been or ever will be perfect—but I come of England's stock, and will uphold that which is my own. As William Cowper wrote over an hundred years ago:

"ENGLAND! With all thy faults I love thee still!"[5]

And when I say "England", I make no exception of her daughter. Rhode Island, my native state, is part of that vast domain which England rescued from the savage, and as such demands a share of all loyalty which is given to the parent island. The Revolution which separated Rhode Island from the King was not of my making, nor would I have participated in it had I been living in 1775. I shall further present my views in an essay in the October CONSERVATIVE, entitled "Old England and the 'Hyphen'".

Turning to amateur matters, I hope you will renew your membership in the United, and that you will be able in time to rehabilitate the Providence Amateur Press Club. Perhaps the lack of publishing activity this year has caused the members almost to forget that there is such a thing as amateur journalism. Many of my present duties are outside the association, in connection with the Symphony Literary Service,[6] which is now handling a goodly amount of verse. Pres. Campbell lately requested me to remind Messrs. Kelso and Wright of this State that their membership has expired; but judging from your club's attitude toward Kelso, and the rather hopeless nature of his verse, I think I will confine my persuasions to Mr. Wright, who never became really active.

With best of wishes for yourself and club,

I remain

Very sincerely yours,

H P Lovecraft

Notes

1. Compulsory military service for Irishmen did not occur until April 1918.

2. I.e., when James VI of Scotland became James I in England in 1603 upon the death of Queen Elizabeth I.

3. Shakespeare, *King John* 5.7.112–16.

4. Jeremiah A. O'Leary, President of the American Truth Society (a pro-German organization), labelled by the *New York Times* (6 March 1916, p. 4) as "the pro-German agitator and sympathizer," and a vehemently anti-British supporter of Irish independence. On 29 September 1916 O'Leary sent President Wilson a telegram criticizing Wilson's "pro-British policies" and threatening to vote against him in the upcoming election. Wilson replied with a telegram stating: "I feel deeply mortified to have you or anybody like you vote for me. Since you have access to many disloyal Americans and I have not, I will ask you to convey this message to them."

5. William Cowper (1731–1800), *The Task* (1783), Book 2, l. 206.

6. Anne Tillery Renshaw operated the Symphony Literary Service out of her rooms at The Randolph in Richmond, VA. Its letterhead listed her as Manager, Mrs. J. G.

Smith of Coffeeville, MS, as Prose Critic, and HPL as Verse Critic. The service was the source of revisions clients, such as David Van Bush, for HPL (see Renshaw to HPL, 28 February 1917; ALS, JHL).

[9]   [ALS, JHL]

> 598 Angell St.,
> Providence, R.I.
> Novr 13, 1916

My dear Mr Dunn:—

Your recent letter contains some vigorous arguments, but for all their vigour they fail to convince me. I think the real point of our difference lies in our conception of the right of conquest. You maintain, evidently, that no people may ever be conquered by another; and that even when such conquest is actually made, the conquered people have a latent right of rebellion, indefinitely extensible and demanding the sympathy of outside nations. Now to me, this theory is utterly fallacious, for if every bit of European and American territory were to be re-apportioned according to primitive boundary lines, annulling every effect of mutual conquest, a chaos beyond description would be the result. If the English authority over Ireland be morally unjustifiable, then what can be said of our own position in America; where we have slaughtered Indians by the million, and practically exterminated one of the racial divisions of mankind? As I view the matter, the conquest of Ireland is of such an early date, that no native claims are admissible. It is essentially part & parcel of the United Kingdom, and a rebellious Irishman is no more excusable than would be a rebellious Scotchman or Englishman. Much nonsense has been uttered about the '[']poor Irish martyrs" who were very justly executed for their treason of last April; but they were not a whit less culpable than seditious Englishmen would have been. What their *motives* were, is of no concern to the law. As conspirators and rebels against constituted authority they merited and received death. There was no discrimination against Ireland in this case. After the usurpation of Cromwell came to an end, a much greater number of his treasonable English followers were put to death by Charles II, without any particular storm of complaint from the public. The Empire must live, and all who oppose it must die—be they Irish, English, Jews, or negroes! The contemptible Dublin rebels shot down innocent soldiers without mercy, and personally I think it a pity that a greater number of Sinn Feiners were not hanged. As to the increase of the Sinn Fein, which you mention, this is well known to the Government, and the world may rest assured that England will not again be caught unprepared. Ireland was never a nation in the truest sense. The aboriginal Celts were too fickle, erratic, improvident, and quarrelsome to found and maintain one real government of their own. They possessed the same traits which Caesar detected in their continental kindred, the Gauls, and which made the latter easy prey for the Romans. The Celts always feel the necessity of fighting—if no external foe appears, they fight each other. They are turbulent & unruly, and were divided up into a score of hostile factions when England stepped in to produce a semblance of order. Alone, Ireland would go to pieces, but if ever its fiery sons will honestly accept their rightful lot as British subjects, the island will feel some of those benefits which have made its sister-island the centre of the world's greatness. You cannot introduce Ireland into a discussion of England's protection of small nations; Ireland is not and never has been a nation. It *is* a part of the British Empire, and *was* a seat of hostile tribes. It is, or was, a "nation" in about the same sense that the Iroquois were a "nation"—or the "Five Nations" as they called themselves.

In speaking of the English blood in Irish veins, I did not refer to the more recent cases, such as that of the traitor Pearce.[1] English and Norman—even *Danish* blood, has given most parts of Ireland a modicum of Teutonic character. There is no question at all about the inferiority of the Celt to the Teuton—but this does not imply inferiority of the *Irish,* for they *have* Teutonic blood, despite the claims of Gaelic enthusiasts. It is mainly for the idea of Teutonic superiority that Germany is fighting today. German friendship for Ireland is a jest. The Prussians, in their hearts, despise the Celtic race; indeed, their assumption of their own superiority over the English rests upon the notion that Englishmen are more Celts than Teutons (as in some cases they undoubtedly are.)

But as before, I deny any material line of racial cleavage between the various British elements. English, Irish, Scotch, & Welsh are all Teutono-Celtic in varying proportions; though in some individuals & localities one blood or the other may be most pronounced. Celts are nimble, quick-witted, fluent, voluble, excitable & imaginative. They are of a naturally artistic temperament, and seldom stupid. Their peasant classes, taken apart from their entire social order, are brighter than English peasantry of corresponding grade. They have, in France, contributed much to the formation of the national character. But on the other hand they are superficial, quarrelsome, bombastic, and unstable. They are not adapted either to self-government or Empire-building. As for the Teutons—they are heavy, thoughtful, deliberate, cold of demeanour, and slightly lacking in facility of imagination. They are probably somewhat more cruel, though more loyal, than Celts. Their peasant classes sink to stupidity, but their upper & middle classes possess a mental force and determination which have won them the supremacy of the world (a supremacy to be maintained however the war may turn out.) They are thorough and deep in whatever they do and produce the greatest philosophers since the days of Greece. In sustained courage nothing can compare with the Teuton. He inherits the valour of his Northern tribal forefathers, and fights with bull-dog tenacity. Celts can lead a gallant charge, but it takes the Teuton to *hold* the ground thus gained. Caesar found the Gallic Celts formidable at the first attack, but was easily able to rout them by continued pressure. The Teuton is also incomparably the better hand at government. No Celtic nation could possibly spread throughout the globe as England has done and as Germany almost did. Even a small nation like Holland has established vast colonial possessions. (Dutch & Flemish races are nearest the English in blood.)

An admixture of Celts & Teutons, such as that which is taking place in the British Isles, may well be expected to evolve a stock generally better than either component unmixed. The Teutono-Celt will be stronger and more rational than the pure Celt, and brighter and more artistic than the pure Teuton. Let us hope that such a race will not forever be divided against itself!

As to Wilson's pro-Germanism—you must admit that he gave birthday congratulations last year to the Berlin butcher,[2] and has shown unusual tolerance toward that rascal von Bernstorff,[3] who is certainly behind most of the illegal Prussian propaganda in this country. You make me smile a little when you speak of his favouring England, for he has shown almost as much hostility to the British government for its perfectly justifiable mail inspection, as he has shown to the Huns for their innumerable insults and outrages against humanity. But in strict truth, I think he is what few red-blooded men can be—absolutely and frigidly neutral. He has favoured no side in allowing the shipment of supplies—he permits our merchants to supply any customer who comes to them, and has said nothing against the shipment of Canadian nickel to Germany on the Deutschland, though this act really violates an agreement with Canada. Personally, I think Wilson is a weakling who will bow to the strongest master and do anything rather than stand up for either his own or his country's rights. I have no use at all for him, and was terribly disappointed when I learned of his reëlection. He is a mere straw who goes with the wind.

As to a "foreign country ruling America"—I am sure England is not really foreign. England made America, & ought to be ruling it today—but that is past. I would fight for England if I were physically able, for I consider it my country despite the Revolution, just as your *first* enthusiasm is *really* for Ireland. If I were you, I would not sneer at the "decadent British aristocracy", as you describe it. No nobler race of men ever lived than the gentry & nobility of Old England, and they have bled side by side with the humblest during the present struggle. The alarming rapidity with which titles are changing hands, ought to show you how well the wearers of coronets are working and dying for their country. There is nothing in the human race so generous, spirited, chivalrous, and patriotic as the true English gentleman. And England will win. It may be five years, & it may be five hundred—but England has a habit of winning.

The Conservative for October is in the hands of a local printer, and has been promised for delivery today. The issue has cost $30.00, and will be the largest ever published, though the small type may make it appear less bulky than the issue of a year ago. Its contents will be varied in nature, some of the articles being possibly more pleasing to you than that on England, which heads the prose contents. A weird, Poe-like short story by David H. Whittier[4] ought to interest you, while you may enjoy many of the poems as well.

Smith's *Tryout* comes to me regularly, though I am not a member of the National. Next month I shall have two pieces of verse in it—one under my own name, & the other signed "Lewis Theobald, Jun."[5] Smith does not know that I am "Theobald". I fancy you have had a *Woodbee* recently—albeit a very small and coverless one. The *National Amateur* has stopped coming to me; hence I suppose it has also ceased to reach you. The same is true of the rebel "United Amateur". This pseudo-United lately declared a sort of embargo on its products, forbidding members to have anything to do with our United.[6] However, I still receive *The Vagrant* from W. Paul Cook of Athol, Mass.

I have been appointed Chairman of the Year Book Committee, and am collecting material for a biographical directory of United members.[7] If I cannot find your old notes on yourself & other local members, I may have to ask you for a new set—particularly concerning yourself.

But I will close before I become wearisome with my extended epistle.

    With best wishes,
       I remain
           Very Sincerely Yours,
             H P Lovecraft

Notes

1. See letter 3n7.
2. President Wilson sent a birthday greeting to Kaiser Wilhelm on 27 January 1915.
3. Count Johann Heinrich von Bernstorff (1862–1939), the German ambassador to the U.S., who as early as 1914 had discussed the possibility of supporting a rebellion in Ireland. Early in 1917 Bernstorff was discovered to be involved in a plot to encourage a Mexican attack on the U.S., an action that indirectly led to U.S. involvement in World War I.
4. David H. Whittier, "The Bond Invincible," *Conservative* 2, No. 3 (October 1916): [5–6].
5. "Brumalia" and "Brotherhood."
6. For this "other" United, see HPL's essays "The Pseudo-United" and "A Matter of Uniteds." The UAPA had broken into two factions over a contested election in 1912.
7. The volume never appeared. HPL's essay "A Request" discusses the matter.

[10]   [ALS, JHL]

                    598 Angell St.,
                 December 17[, 1916]

My dear M[r.] Dunn:—

            I was rather interested in the novel point of view which you displayed in your last letter concerning several phases of British imperial rule. So far, I fancy you stand alone in believing that Canada & Australia will ever desire separate existence; for the dominant tendency in both of these colonies is to foster a closer union with the parent land. It is true that conscription is not generally desired in Australia, but I am sure a different sentiment would prevail if the safety or existence of England were threatened. As to England itself, it surprises me to note your evident hostility toward the nobility and Royalty. Many decades have elapsed since the King has been more than a nominal figure, while any power that the nobility might abuse has disappeared with the comparatively recent removal of the vetoing privilege from the House of Lords.[1] In short, England is today the most democratic of all nations in government, the United States not excepted. Personally, I believe that almost an excess of democracy has been attained, since the populace are permitted to interfere in many matters of state which they cannot direct to advantage. Lloyd-George[2] is a demagogue of demagogues, though he may in the present crisis forget internal politics whilst bending every energy toward the good of England as a whole.

In referring to the rebel Pearce as a traitor, I have no intention of depreciating the basic morality of his motives; he is a traitor because he conspired and revolted against the authorised government of the Empire of which he was a subject. It is not difficult to conceive that he meant well, for considering the distorted and prejudice-warped code of the Sinn Fein element amongst whom he was reared, his acts were what one might expect from a pure-minded zealot. He was the same sort of "patriot" that you or I would be, if we sought to "liberate" Rhode Island from the "tyranny" of the United States. The comparison to Gen. Washington which you make, is not at all erroneous, save in the matter of common sense. Washington had no right to rebel against his lawful sovereign, but he foresaw that the chances of success were not at all remote. Pearce, with criminal folly, caused bloodshed without the slightest hope of achieving his purpose. Only a fool or a fanatic—or an Irishman—could imagine for a moment that England would relinquish her hold on any part of her present domain. What these Hibernian "patriots" forget, is that Englishmen are just as devoted as they to the welfare of the cause they represent. What a wealth of loyalty is conjured up by

> "This royal throne of Kings, this sceptred isle,
> This earth of majesty, this seat of Mars,
> This other Eden, demi-paradise,
> This fortress built by Nature for herself
> Against infection and the hand of war,
> This happy breed of men, this little world,
> This precious stone set in the silver sea.
> Which serves it in the office of a wall
> Or as a moat defensive to a house,

Against the envy of less happier lands—
This blessed plot, this earth, this realm, this ENGLAND!"[3]
(Shakespeare—"King Richard II")

Reverting to amateur matters—I suppose you have received the recent *Bearcat* and noted the unjustifiable attack made upon Pres. Campbell & Mr Fritter by Dowdell. This irresponsible youth should be evicted from the association if he cannot better conform to the requirements of civil speech and dignified conduct. All the objections he urges against Campbell are either trivial or imaginary, while his hostility to Fritter arises merely from the neat manner in which the latter helped expose the fraudulent handling of ballots at the Cleveland convention. Dowdell enjoys a brisk quarrel, but he should be made to understand that amateur journalism is not a suitable field for the indulgence of his boorish tastes.

Pres. Campbell recently favoured me with the loan of many books & papers touching upon the older days of amateur journalism, and I was surprised at the extent to which this branch of endeavour once flourished.[4] The first generation of amateurs were mostly youths with printing presses, whose literary development was not remarkable; but during the decade of 1885–1895 a number of very highly cultured persons were active in the National, giving rise to the much-vaunted "Halcyon Days". These persons represented the intellectual plane which Edward H. Cole has typified in the era just closing, and most of them were infinitely brighter and more varied in their talents. In 1891 an amateur named Truman J. Spencer, a Shakespearian scholar and lecturer, issued a large cloth-bound volume of 512 pages, entitled "A Cyclopedia of the Literature of Amateur Journalism", whose contents would do credit to most professional magazines of today. It was compiled from selections from the works of the best amateur writers. Another matter of interest in the collection lent me, is the career of Pres. Campbell himself, as exhibited by a complete file of his various publications. He joined both associations in 1902, at the age of 17, and commenced issuing a miserable sheet called *The Ideal Politician*. The first number contained a "poem" entitled "You Can't Convince a Scotchman", which is one of the most wretched metrical misfits ever inflicted upon amateurdom. Quite naturally, this crude paper excited much ridicule and sarcasm from the older members, and Campbell began to attack his critics with great vigour. This controversial practice improved his bad English; and his second paper, *The Scottish Highlander*, reveals very plainly that mental keenness which was later to distinguish Campbell's work. At one time this enterprising amateur published *two papers* at a time; *The Scottish Highlander* for the National, and *The Prairie State Journal* for the United; meanwhile acting as associate editor of *The Reflector*, which was issued by L. M. Starring of Tennessee. In 1905 he commenced his most famous enterprise, *The Scotchman;* and by that time he had educated himself from complete crudity to a condition of enviable distinction as an essayist. His controversy of 1907–08 with the Gotham Club was exceedingly bitter, and enabled him to exhibit some of the sharpest and cleverest personal satire ever known to the amateur world. That was a rather undesirable period in the history of the associations; abuse and invective reigning everywhere, and scurrilous anonymous papers being sadly in vogue. Dowdell would have enjoyed himself in those days!

    With kindest Christmas regards,
        I remain
                Very Sincerely yrs
                    H P Lovecraft

Notes

1. In 1911 the House of Lords was pressured into renouncing its veto power over legislation initiated in the House of Commons.
2. David Lloyd George (1863–1945), Prime Minister of England from 1916 to 1922.
3. Shakespeare, *Richard II* 2.1.40–50.
4. HPL later wrote an essay on amateur journalism between 1885 and 1895 (*Looking Backward* [1920]), although the materials for that essay were provided by C. W. Smith.

[11]   [TLS, JHL]

                            598 Angell St., Providence, R.I.,
                                   January 13, 1917.

My dear Mr. Dunn:—

                I received your letter of 31st ult., and am wholly willing to declare a truce, armistice, or permanent peace regarding the questions whose discussion has occupied so prominent a place in our recent correspondence. Let me assure you that so far as personalities are concerned, I have not allowed the matter to transcend the purely academic state; being cognizant of the free right of every person to his own opinions. My desire that Ireland remain within the circle of British government goes hand in hand with an equal desire that it enjoy the height of prosperity and the most amicable relations with the rest of the Empire and the rest of the world.

    Regarding the amateur world, I share your wish that the activity and grade of scholarship which marked the 1885–1896 period, may return; yet I fear that such a renaissance is not likely to occur in the very near future. At present just the wrong persons are active; in fact, the best cultured wing of amateurdom is hardly represented at all in the publishing field. When a competent person does write, his work generally appears side by side with such unutterable rot that its effect is ruined by its inferior setting. What we need is a number of papers whose editorial grade shall measure up to the best of their contributions. It is toward this goal that I am striving with THE CONSERVATIVE; though my paper is still vastly below some of those which marked the "Halcyon Days". My next issue[1] will be small—only four pages—yet I think you will be inclined to like it, since it contains no matter to which you can take exception.

In conformity with your request for a piece of verse to be used at your sister's graduation, I have prepared the enclosed effusion of 62 lines. You suggested something of from 6 to 12 lines, but the nature of the subject prohibited anything so short. Class poems are a definite type in literature, requiring substantial length, and a certain classic atmosphere and versification. I am sure that the length of time required to recite it will not be excessive; in fact, it is only half or a third the length of many class poems. I think I have included the various points you mentioned, and have also thought it appropriate to pay a tribute to the noble character of the nurses' profession, a nobility which makes it a very suitable and inspiring subject for treatment in verse. I hope that the enclosed may prove satisfactory to you, your sister, and the ultimate audience.

      With best wishes, I remain
          Sincerely yours,
          H P Lovecraft

[Enclosure: TMs of "Lines on Graduation from the Rhode Island Hospital's School of Nurses."]

Notes

1. I.e., January 1917 (2, No. 4).

[12]   [Envelope only, postmarked Providence, R.I., 21 January 1917]

[13]   [ALS, JHL]

                          598 Angell St.
                          2 / 19 / 17

My Dear M^r. Dunn:—

      I am glad you enjoyed my brief verses on "Fact & Fancy", and that you sympathize with the point of view they express. Something of the modern practicality I decry is shown in the argument I am having with the editor of *The Literary Digest* anent deformed spelling. He does not care to use adverse arguments in the columns of the *Digest,* so answers my communications personally. All he can offer to sustain his advocacy of the destruction of historical & traditional forms of spelling, is that the change would benefit a few dull scholars, and *save money!* According to this line of reasoning, why use refined architecture in designing public buildings? Build square block monstrosities—it is *cheaper!* I have just sent him a copy of my old verses—"The Simple Speller's Tale", slightly altered so that its application is general, and not confined to amateur journalists.

It interests me to know that Bulfinch is an old acquaintance of yours. This was always a favourite of mine, and had its share in developing my predilection for the classics.[1] Its natural sequels in a course of reading are Pope's Homer, Dryden's Virgil & Garth's Ovid[2]—from whose pages I possibly formed my early taste for the heroic couplet.

Your opinion of current motion pictures is quite just. Save for a few Triangle, Paramount & Vitagraph pictures, everything I have seen is absolute trash—though some are quite harmless & amusing. Worst of all are the *serials*—whose authors are probably the same poor creatures that wrote the "dime novels" of yesterday. I have yet to see a serial film worth the time wasted in looking at it—or dozing over it. The technique could be surpassed by most ten year old children. However, the companies above named have occasionally released fairly creditable things; and would do better if they were not forced to produce such an immense *quantity* of film. My taste may not be a criterion; but I prefer viewing *travel* pictures like those of Burton Holmes[3] at the Strand, to being bored by tenth-rate "canned drama".

I am glad you like Fritter's article on "Personal Liberty" in *The Woodbee*, for I have a certain amount of personal pride in it. Fritter tells me that my arguments are the cause of his recent espousal of the prohibition cause. However—he was always a total abstainer himself. In my opinion, there is much more hope for nation-wide prohibition than there was a decade or two ago. I should not be surprised if I live to witness its enactment—duly exulting therein.

I have sent the R.I. Hospital verses to C. W. Smith's *Tryout*, where they will be printed *under your name*. I thought Providence deserved a little more representation in amateurdom; and you were really the inspirer of the piece. I shall see that you receive a sufficient number of copies.

I have just received an amusing letter from a very scholarly recruit of mine—Louis E. Boutwell of Scottsville, N.Y., who is an English teacher in the Rochester high-school. While admitting he has enjoyed the correspondence & publications of the United, Mr. Boutwell does not think, on sober judgment, that he has received *a dollar's worth* of enjoyment, hence he expresses his intention not to renew. All things considered, I believe the Association can survive the loss!

With best wishes for all your affairs & endeavours,

　　　I remain

　　　　　　　Very sincerely,

　　　　　　　H P Lovecraft

Notes

1. Thomas Bulfinch, *The Age of Fable.*
2. HPL owned all these volumes.
3. Elias Burton Holmes (1870–1958), American traveler and filmmaker.

[14]   [ALS, JHL]

598 Angell St.,
Providence, R.I.,
May 16, 1917

My dear Mr Dunn:—

I perused with interest your letter of 30th ult. The "events of world wide importance"[1] to which you allude, have not been unperceived by me; in fact, I lately tried to assume my share of the present responsibility by applying, despite my invalid condition, for enlistment in the National Guard. My attempt met with ultimate failure, for I am really too feeble for military service; but I have at least done my best to prove that my consistent opposition to pacifism is not a matter of words only.[2]

I am familiar with the "Austrian army" alliterative poem[3]—and even tried once to compose one of similar sort, hence can appreciate the ingenuity involved. There is another piece of this kind in existence, describing the dedication of the Bunker Hill Monument, but I cannot now recall even a line of it. My own effort had to do with Belgium's heroic defence at the beginning of the present war, and began something like this:

Armed against an arrogant attack,
Bold BELGIUM beats barbaric braggarts back.[4]

This was written before the fall of Liége;[5] when, in my unmilitary ignorance, I fancied the puny forts of Flanders had stemmed the Hunnish tide!

Your reference to my Lockhart verses[6] reminds me of the sad fact that our brave and gifted fellow-amateur has at last suffered defeat at the hands of his enemies—the vice & liquor interests of South Dakota—and has been sent to the Federal Prison at Ft. Leavenworth, Kansas, after a farcically unfair trial at Aberdeen, S.D. The press & public are unanimous in their regret at this flagrant legal injustice, and it is to be hoped that their indignation may serve to banish the political corruption which made possible the infamous indictment and contemptible conviction. Lockhart will appeal.

As to a good text-book on grammar & rhetoric, for which you inquire, I find it hard to be definite in my recommendations on account of the antiquity of the books from which I studied. Most of my elementary guides were printed before the year 1800, and are not now obtainable.[7] Perhaps it is to these old books that I owe my dislike for things modern. At high-school we used Lockwood & Emerson; but since I was already quite familiar with literature & composition, I gave it but scanty attention. I am sure, though, that it is an excellent treatise. Its continued use in our schools is a potent argument in its favour. One very good treatise is Kellogg's,[8] which I recommended to the United when the Department of Instruction was proposed. Mr. Daas obtained a copy and agreed with me regarding its merit.

I believe your membership expired some time ago, hence you may not have received recent issues of *The United Amateur*. Campbell has been very generous with duplicates, so I can supply you with any numbers you may lack. The monthly plan has been abandoned, since experience well demonstrated its unfeasibility. It is hoped that the magazine will be more regular, now that bi-monthly issuance has been restored. In the latest copy there is an interesting revelation of a plagiarist just brought to justice.

    With best of wishes for your success in literature and all other affairs,

        I remain

                Very sincerely yours

                H P Lovecraft

Notes

1. Referring, presumably, to President Wilson's signing a proclamation on 6 April that "a state of war exists between the United States and the Imperial German Government" (the Senate and House had passed the war resolution on 4 April and 6 April, respectively).

2. See *Letters to Rheinhart Kleiner and Others* 82–84.

3. HPL refers here to an anonymous verse, "The Siege of Belgrade," which begins: "An Austrian army, awfully array'd, / Boldly by battery besiege Belgrade: / Cossack commanders cannonading come, / Deal devastations dire destructive doom"; in *The Book of Humorous Verse*, ed. Carolyn Wells (New York: George H. Doran Co., 1920), 813–14.

4. From "The Bunker Hill Monument Celebration" by Sarah G. Hammersleigh. Each line is alliterative, although the poet omits lines for the letters J and Z.

5. The Belgian fortress at Liège fell to the Germans on 17 August 1914.

6. "To Mr. Lockhart, on His Poetry."

7. Such as Abner Alden's *The Reader* (1797; *LL* 25).

8. Brainerd Kellogg (1840?–1920) wrote several textbooks on English grammar and composition. HPL is probably referring to *Composition and Rhetoric* (1899), but Kellogg also wrote *A Text-book on Rhetoric* (1880), *A Text-book on English Literature* (1882), and *English Composition* (1906).

[15]   [TLS, JHL]

                        598 Angell St., Providence, R.I.,

                                  July 6, 1917.

Mr. John T. Dunn,

Providence, R.I.,

My dear Mr. Dunn:—

                I received your letter yesterday morning, and am sorry to state that I have used up all my back numbers of THE UNITED AMATEUR in recruiting work, save the last two. These I am sending under separate cover. I have been appointed Official Editor upon the resignation of Mr. Lockhart, and will edit the July number myself. I am planning an issue which will be long remembered in amateurdom,[1] though I am not certain that I shall succeed.

I enclose also some of the newer papers of the Association, besides a sheet from the current TRYOUT containing my answer to a particularly vicious anti-United article by Rev. Graeme Davis.[2]

I find it rather difficult to comprehend your present war attitude, for no matter how much you may personally dislike the government's policy, you are certainly bound as an American citizen to abide by the judgment and desires of those with whom the American people have entrusted their destinies. You may rest assured that the Nation did not enter hostilities without a grave consideration of the issues at stake,[3] and a conscientious weighing of moral values. The long aloofness of America from the world's supreme ordeal showed clearly the earnest wish of the country to maintain peace so long as it might be consistent with honour and common humanity, but it would be the summit of base hypocrisy to skulk any longer behind the protecting skirts of Great Britain and France. America has long known that the cause of the Allied powers is her own; and it is to her credit that she has at last assumed the responsibilities which are hers. It is better to suffer and die with a consciousness of duty, than to live out long ignoble years in shame for obligations evaded and needful acts unperformed.

It is my honest opinion that your opinions have been perverted by a long devotion to a biased and partisan press. Your allegiance to the Sinn Fein cause, and your consequent affiliation with societies and periodicals who place the interests of Ireland above those of the United States, has probably placed before your eyes a mass of inflammatory literature of scant reliability and no patriotism at all. It is well known that the so-called "Irish" papers published in this country are utterly unreliable, pandering to the crudest prejudices of irreconcilable Fenians and containing no more real truth than a Hearst organ. They belong to a low grade of flashy journalism that causes the genuine Irishman of culture and discernment to blush with vexation. One of the prominent amateurs of the United has as next-door neighbours a splendid Irish family with a splendid Irish name. One member is a Major in the British army and another is a Captain in the Canadian expeditionary force, whilst relatives are serving gladly as privates and non-commissioned men in the forces of the Empire. They are indeed bitter toward the blatantly plebeian press which is misrepresenting loyal Ireland to the world, and can keenly appreciate the distorted and mendacious nature of the appeal which cheap "Irish" and "Gaelic" papers are making to the discontented masses who are unable to appreciate the larger world issues at stake. If the readers of the alleged "Irish" press would pause to analyse what they are reading, they would see that the appeal is directed to the emotion and not to the reason, and that nine-tenths of the "news" given is either directly manufactured or artfully twisted in a misleading way. The fact that no propagandist paper of this type has ever occupied a place of dignity in modern journalism ought to be proof of their utterly flimsy character and want of authoritativeness. No mind fed on this rubbish can appreciate world issues or adequately grasp the present system of international relations. What I have seen of the "Irish" press generally conveys the notion that Ireland lies at the centre of the universe; that England is the territorial incarnation of Satan, and that America is a good-natured, gullible tool to be used by Ireland in twisting the British bulldog's tail. The world as seen through Fenian spectacles is a false, artificial world, with values confounded and proportions ignored. It is a fairy world—a world of Irish fairies, British ogres, and pliant American gnomes and elves, who must do the bidding of the Irish fairies! The Sinn Fein press is in exactly the position of the socialist or anarchist press, artificially working up cheap sentiment on a basis of cleverly selected and one-sided news and partisan penny-a-line editorials. It is on the order of THE MENACE, a paper which works thousands of simple-minded persons into a frenzy over the "evils" of the Catholic Church through a campaign of selected news items and filthy editorial sensationalism.[4] If you would form a just estimate of world conditions and world values, read the really representative press of the United States—THE OUTLOOK, THE NORTH AMERICAN REVIEW, THE ATLANTIC MONTHLY— magazines that owe allegiance only to their own editorial conscience. You have been seeing the world from a misleading angle, and in these stirring and active times you owe it to yourself to rectify your perspective. I had vowed not to bore you with these matters in future, but since you have allowed your doctrines to pass beyond the academic stage, I feel it a duty to do what I can to remove the false impressions which are so strongly grounded within you. I know that your convictions are sincere, which makes matters all the worse. I know how difficult it is to alter a settled and honest opinion! Your picture of the world today is, figuratively speaking, a cheap chromo obtained from a vicious partisan press. You must turn to a different grade of periodicals in order to gain the true photographic conception of affairs. Reflect how virtually unanimous is the sentiment of men of intellect and responsibility. Surely you cannot say that all the world is at fault and that only your "Irish" press is in the right! I am assuming that Ireland is the basis of your disaffection. If I am mistaken, and if Germany is the object of your loyalty—I have nothing to say. Not one thing which can be said in behalf of Ireland can be said for Germany; for she is frankly an outlaw power, guilty of every injustice which the Irish attribute to England. No person in his senses could possibly have anything to say for Germany now. Germany sums up all the tyranny and force which Ireland traditionally detests.

I am not suggesting that you heed my own words as a basis for changing your views. Frankly, I am an Englishman in spirit, with the integrity of the

Empire always in view. But I do urge that you adopt a more representative course of current reading, and gain a broader view of American public opinion. You are not asked to fight for America because she is on the Empire's side—though that would be reason enough for me—but because she stands arrayed for the defence of the enlightened European ideal against the peculiar revival of mediaeval notions which Prussia threatens to impose upon the world. You deem the draft an arbitrary and autocratic procedure, no doubt; but reflect upon the multitude of autocratic restrictions which would result from the Germanisation of modern life. As a descendant of true-born Englishmen I am proud of America's adherence to and defence of the Anglo-Saxon ideal; but that ideal is Anglo-Saxon only in the sense that England has best developed it. In the broadest sense it is the European ideal—the Western ideal—the democratic ideal—and even more inclusively, the white man's ideal. Germany, in rejecting this ideal, has really almost renounced the white man's heritage and retreated into the darkness of Asiatic despotism. She has betrayed her splendid Teutonic race in this mad defiance of liberal Europe and America. Never was there a cause in which a thinking man could more gladly and gloriously fight than in this culminating test of Liberty against barbarism. In the widest sense, the world today is in the position of the Roman world when threatened by the Cymbri and Teutones. It is the last and greatest of the many barbarian invasions which began when Brennus and the Gauls sacked Rome. By this test civilisation will stand or fall. If hate blinds you to the glory of Britannia, look upon France—"bled white", as they say, in the cause of humanity.

Why any true Irishman or lover of the Irish tradition could remain unsympathetic, is more than I can see. I should think that the whole thing in perspective would heat every drop of Irish blood in Christendom to a fighting fervour, and that no son of Erin would lay down his arms till Prussianism shall have been eradicated. It is a new crusade, and one upon which far more depends than the old Crusades for the Holy Sepulchre. Real representatives of Irish valour like the Mayor of New York[5] are quick to sense the inner spirit and cast aside their Anglophobia for the world's common cause. When I went to the Cranston Street Armory a couple of months ago, at a time when I thought I might be able to serve the Nation actively, I discovered that a large proportion of the recruits were of Irish descent. Perhaps the most admirable and intelligent young man in the company to which I would have been assigned, was Irish in name and features. But not a word of dissent did he have for the cause of America and the right. Instead, he embodied that manly ideal of the Irish soldier which Kipling has given us in so many of his poems and tales. And too, the first American to carry the Stars and Stripes into action at Vimy Ridge was of Irish extraction. Can you not surely see how isolated your position is becoming? Soon the only Irishmen on your side will be creatures of the Jeremiah O'Leary type, in the pay of the Kaiser. But I hope that you will not be long on that side! Men like T. P. O'Connor and Mr. Redmond[6] are pointing the way which every genuine Hibernian must traverse sooner or later.

It is, as you say, hard to get away from the war nowadays; for it meets one in print and in conversation, wherever he may turn. But if you could come to view it in its true light, I am sure that you would not dread reference to it so much. It is the prime business of the world today, and to obstruct it is as useless as it is criminal.

However, amateur journalism has been making so many demands upon me of late, that I have hardly had time to think of the conflict. The issuing of the Year Book is a monstrous task, involving the compilation of data from amateur papers ten or more years old. And besides this, I have now the added burden of Official Editorship—to say nothing of the increasing amount of professional work I am doing for writers outside the Association. I am named as candidate for the Presidency next year, and Campbell informs me that my election is very probable.[7] I shall stand for a purely literary programme, and shall endeavour to reduce political activity to a minimum.

I do not know how I can best serve the nation in time of war. Having been rejected by the National Guard, I registered on June 5th, giving my occupation as "Writer". I am told that it is possible I may be used even though I fail to pass the physical test for active military service. At least it is believed by some that many drafted men unfit for the trenches will be employed in capacities for which they are best suited. I hope that my name will come up in the drafting, for I should like to be placed intelligently where I can accomplish the most good. Unguided, it is rather difficult for me to determine how I can best help; for my feeble health makes me very unreliable where steady work is concerned.

Amateurdom is producing some excellent papers this year, such as EX-CELSIOR, THE INSPIRATION, INVICTUS, THE COYOTE, THE VA-GRANT, and THE WOODBEE;[8] but I fear if you should rejoin the United you would find matters much too martial and British to suit your taste. The amateur press shows a decided tendency to stand behind the government.

Hoping that you will seriously consider my suggestion of adopting a broader and more representative course of periodical reading, and trusting that affairs are all going well with you,

    I remain

              Sincerely yours,

                H P Lovecraft

Notes

1. This was the *United Amateur* for July 1917.
2. "A Reply to *The Lingerer.*"

3. In addition to publications from Belfast, Cork, Dublin, and London, the following American "Irish" and "Gaelic" papers probably were available in Providence during 1916–1917: *Hibernian* (Boston), *Ireland* (New York), *National Hibernian* (Camden, NJ), and the *Irish Press* (Philadelphia).

4. The *Menace,* an anti-Catholic weekly, was published by the Free Press Defense League in Aurora, MO, from April 1911 to December 1919.

5. John Mitchel (1879–1918) was Mayor of New York City from 1914 to 1917. On 4 May 1917 he spoke at a meeting of loyal Americans of Irish birth or descent.

6. T. P. O'Connor (1848–1929), journalist and politician who supported Home Rule and, as M.P. of the Scotland Division of Liverpool (1880–1929), was the only member of the Irish party to sit for an English constituency. John Redmond (1856–1918), politician who supported Parnell's Home Rule movement in the late 19th century and helped to introduce the Home Rule Bill in 1912, although passage of the bill was delayed by the war. He urged Irishmen to join the British Army in the war effort and denounced the Easter Rebellion as a "German intrigue."

7. HPL was in fact elected president of the UAPA for 1917–18.

8. Edited, respectively, by Clement C. Chase, Edna Hyde, Edward H. Cole, William Thomas Harrington, W. Paul Cook, and Ida C. Haughton.

Alfred Galpin

Letters to Alfred Galpin

[1]   [ALS]

598 Angell St.,
Providence, R.I.,
Jany 26, 1918

Dear Hasting:—[1]

This is just a note to display to you the latest feat of my slow-moving wit, regarding the name of the book you recommended to me: *Etidorpha*.[2]

This name, obviously Hellenic, puzzled me; since I assumed it to be a compound of ἔτι. Then I saw light, and perceived that the *e* as easily be an *eta* as an *epsilon*—thus: ΕΤΙΔΟΡΦΑ. Now what is this, unless it be *Aphrodite* (Ἀφροδίτε) *written backwards?* Thus you see, my dear Niplag, that I have made a discovery! At least, it appears to be a discovery; though I cannot for the life of me conceive why a reversed Aphrodite should have anything to do with metaphysics and the philosophy of the ultimate. I should like to see this curious Ἐτιδορφα. Of course, I *may* be all at sea about this name—*but* if it be a coincidence, 'tis one of the most singular coincidences I ever encountered. I spent full half an hour looking up an hypothetical word δορφα in Liddell & Scotts Greek Lexicon, to match the supposed ἔτι, before the analogy dawned upon me!

Trusting you are not completely prostrated by that massive letter of a few days ago, I remain

Most humbly & respectfully yours,
        L. P. Drawoh

Notes

1. In his autobiographical notes, Galpin explains that his pseudonym "Consul Hasting" is derived from the etymology of *Alfred* (*Elf-Red* = wise in counsel; hence *Consul*), and a play on his surname (*gallopin'* = hasty).
2. By John Uri Lloyd. The novel, dealing with a journey to the hollow center of the earth, may have influenced *The Dream-Quest of Unknown Kadath* (1926–27).

[2]   [TLS/ALS]

Nowhere, May 27, [1918] 10 p.m.

O thou of microscopic years but telescopic mind:

My reason for replying before waiting for an inspiration is this: Through a singular combination of circumstances I have disposed of *all* the accumulated correspondence which has so long vexed me, including even the dreaded letters to possible laureate judges, so that tonight there await me only your much appreciated treatise and a brief and unimportant note from a mediocre recruit named Thalheimer.[1] Tomorrow I may be "swamped" with a burden of portentious [*sic*] mail, hence find it best to write whilst I have the leisure, even though my thoughts are likely to prove the very reverse of scintillant. I wonder if I am wise in doing this? I note that in my last communication, fatigue led me to perpetrate a puerility which attracted your immediate notice— i.e., the silly comparison of instinct and *knowledge*. I am glad that you cannot know the deadly fatigue and lethargy which accompany a state of health such as that under which I have been staggering for ten years and more. At times the very effort of sitting up is insupportable, and the least added exertion brings on a sort of dull tiredness which soon shews itself in the lagging brilliancy and occasional incoherence of my literary and epistolary productions. I fear you will find me disappointing as a fellow-philosopher—if, indeed, my current contributions to the world's fund of mediocrity have not already removed any illusions you may have entertained in this direction.

Buckling down to business, I see the fatuity of my statement regarding *knowledge*, but strangely enough, do not withdraw my original contention! I concede an error of expression, but do not yet see the error in deduction. (how dense!!!) My amended statement is this: instinct is born in the young animal *in full working order*—all the major instincts are at once capable of expression, and require absolutely no *instruction* for development. The young animal or human (pardon the distinction—I do not make it scientifically) would develop the same instincts if utterly isolated and without external impressions. Young lions do not have to be taught their fierceness, nor human beings their greedy treacherousness. The qualities are innate and unconnected with the genuine intellectual faculty. Turning to reason, we see that it is only a *capacity*—not an automatically working function—which may or may not be developed according to environment. You refer to the *instinctive* use of very simple reasoning processes—the addition of 2 and 3 to obtain 5, as you express it. Now I believe that this is not *inborn,* but that it is the result of elementary observation. Only the *capacity* is inborn. On the other hand, the cry of a child for food *is* instinctive and inborn, as is its automatic flinching if approached by a seemingly menacing object, or its fear of the dark—or any of those things which develop without so much as a glance at surroundings or hint of instruction. Let me elaborate: I maintain, rightly or not, I leave it for you to judge—that a human being born without the five senses and utterly isolated from intercourse with the world, would *never* develop the slightest trace of manifested rationality, even though endowed with a mind of high grade and perfect soundness. That same man, if trained by particular methods, might become a genius. BUT—the *instinctive* processes of that man would develop exactly the same in either case! Do you perceive my trend? Reason requires something to work with—instinct does not. My error lay in calling *reason itself* acquired. I meant to say, and should have, had I been less fatigued, that the *manifestations* of reason are acquired, whilst those of instinct are innate. The distinction which I draw satisfies me of the essential difference of the two attributes, though I should be the last to assert dogmatically that reason is not a product of evolution from instinct. As to the matter of *aphorisms,* or seemingly innate displays of the reason, I will not try to be too precise in arguing with so great an opponent as yourself. So little is known of the true inwardness of psychology, that I would hesitate to deny the existence of some borderland betwixt reason and instinct. But I will say that in my opinion, even the simplest reasonings are the result of observation and experience— conscious or subconscious. Instinct is otherwise.

N.B.—Do not mistake me—beasts have an appreciable share of reason, and many of their seemingly instinctive acts are doubtless compounded of instinct and reason, just as many of man's seemingly rational acts have in reality a liberal share of instinct in them. If I have revealed any new fallacies and absurdities this time, pray do not hesitate to let me know about them. I am very humble at heart, despite my forbidding and dogmatical exterior.

Concerning the correct personnel of the staff of an average 8-page city daily, I cannot even guess, for dailies hereabouts are inclined to run over that size to a considerable extent. The *Evening Bulletin* has never published less than 18 pages within my recollection, whilst it frequently runs up to 48. 30 is the average number. The late *Evening News* was not a paper—it was a joke.[2] And I am not much interested in its successor, since the request of its editor for me to make my articles "so simple that a child might understand them" caused me to withdraw from the field. He did not use "child" in the sense which the word conveys at 779 Kimball St. He meant the grade of mentality prevailing in the ranks of the Democratic party—of which the reconstructed *News* is an organ and exponent. But as to the *Crescent*[3]—it is easy to see that the paper is sadly undermanned—reminding one of the late *News.* I never thought I could take much interest in Sporting Editors—but circumstances alter cases! If you wish to develop a sporting vocabulary, read Thomas Moore's comic piece, "Tom Crib's Memorial to Congress", published about an hundred years ago, with very learned notes, and beginning:

> "Most Holy and High, and Legitimate *squad,*
> First *swells* of the world, since *Boney's in quod,*
> Who have everything now, as Bill Gibbons would say,
> Like the bull in the china-shop, all your own way—
> Whatsoever employs your magnificent *nobs,*
> Whether *diddling* your subjects, and *gutting* their *fobs,*"—etc[4]

And now for the puzzle—*Dreams*—which may be destined to reveal to you in all its hideous reality my unutterably and infinitely Boeotian density and sluggishness of wit. Possibly the safest way to reply and not reveal the clumsiness of my guessing, is to be as enigmatical as you, and ask you to *guess* what my guess is!! I will oil the way with a compliment or two—the language and atmosphere of your piece are really quite captivating and haunting; nor is it in a spirit of unintelligent and obvious comment that one may compare the style to that of Mr. Poe. I shall send this to Cook, minus the N.B.'s, for though he was forced to return your "Two Loves",[5] he asked me for a piece of your *prose* if I had anything of the sort on hand. (Note my playing for time—I am trying to distract your attention whilst I neglect to try for a solution of the mystery!) But what is the use? You can penetrate all shams and pretences, so I might as well face the ordeal: I fancy you are—er—er—thinking of theories advanced in the Kleicomolo[6]—er—er—which I disputed to some extent, yet which I admired for their boldness of conception and so forth—(I hope I am indefinite enough to be able to make this sound like the right solution after I learn the truth from you. The gentle art of non-committal ambiguousness is a great asset to a would-be philosopher.) But again, wot's de use? I think you are hinting at your dream theory—that all entity is but an agitation in the ether, and that it is coexistent and identical with the pitiful unrest known as human consciousness. Now you know all. I stand revealed. Have pity!

Once more the fair—and otherwise. I appreciate your position, which is the average one, and am glad you are not to be classified as a "fusser"—a term not so new or local as you think, since it existed in full glory in my day, many, many, years ago. As to the Massachusetts monstrosity—you have my sympathy—a sympathy of comprehension rather than experience, since so far as I know, no feminine freak ever took the trouble to note or recognise my colossal and transcendent intellect. "It" must be an interesting caricature. Why not use It to excite the jealousy of your Hibernian Chloë, thereby awaking the interest of the latter? Such is the approved method of fiction. Or possibly Its utter ridiculousness precludes the course! [ALS begins here:] I paused a moment for a somewhat humorous poetical note—& find the hour too late to admit of Remingtonian clattering.[7] Pardon the relapse. The following may apply to your heart entanglements:

A PASTORAL TRAGEDY
of Appleton, Wisconsin
By
Kleinhart Reiner, Esq.[8]

Young Strephon for his Chloë sigh'd
    In accents warm but vain;
Th' Hibernian nymph his suit deny'd,
    Nor melted at his pain.

But one day from an Eastern scene
    Fair (?) Hecatissa came;
She eye'd the swain with fav'ring mien,
    And felt the Paphian flame.

No answ'ring flame the youth display'd;
 He scorn'd her doubtful charms,
And still implor'd th' Hibernian maid
 To seek his outstretch'd arms.

Thus Strephon, both unlov'd and lov'd,
 Both pleading and refusing,
Plann'd, that to passion might be mov'd
 The maiden of his choosing.

With seeming scorn he ceas'd his sighs,
 And careless turn'd away;
Then courted with dissembling eyes
 The maid from Boston Bay.

The willing fair (?) his wooing heard;
 With bliss his suit receiv'd;
Bright Chloë, list'ning, notes each word,
 With jealous longing griev'd.

At length the nymph for Strephon frets,
 And mourns the lonely lack;
In tears her frigid course regrets,
 And yearns to win him back.

One kindly glance the fair one sends,
 And Strephon's at her side;
In grief poor Hecatissa bends—
 Forsaken ere a bride!

And on that joyous nuptial morn
 When Strephon wed the fair,
A hooded figure, wan, forlorn,
 Stole thro' the dewy air.

Down to the dam the sad one went,
 Pray'd Heaven to forgive her,
Then leap'd with desperate intent
 Into the swift Fox River!

P.S. The river-god her face espy'd,
 And felt a sudden pain—
Declin'd to claim her as his bride,
 And cast her back again!

Your adaptability, to which you refer, is a very enviable characteristic; and one which I share to the extent of relaxing gravity & perpetrating things like that on the other side of this sheet. However, my own adaptability is very limited, and I lack interest in a vast number of things that others are deeply concerned about. As I said before—*games* form one of the provinces in which I am unable to take much interest. The reason for this is undoubtedly my feeble store of energy. I am only about half alive—a large part of my strength is consumed in sitting up or walking. My nervous system is a shattered wreck, and I am absolutely bored & listless save when I come upon something which peculiarly interests me. However—so many things *do* interest me, & interest me intensely, in science, history, philosophy, & literature; that I have never actually desired to die, or entertained any suicidal designs, as might be expected of one with so little kinship to the ordinary features of life.

Regarding your absorption of ideas in class—I always found that a *written* fact remained in my memory far better than a *spoken* one. I could, with the same amount of mental energy, obtain twice as much from a book as from a lecture. On the same principle, I am a much better writer than conversationalist. (Heavens! what a confession to make after the written trash I have revealed to the public!!)

As to *concentration*—I am a bit baffled as to the proper method of cultivating that gift, since my own "single track mind" (I borrow a phrase from a statesman of whom I am none too fond) is always so *stupidly* concentrated on whatever I am doing. I think lack of excess mental vitality is an aid to concentration—that is why I, and the statesman alluded to, are such d—n fools. Pardon, please!! My innate concentration is so complete that I cannot be diverted from a subject by any amount of digression on the part of those with whom I may be conversing. I am the direct antithesis of the person who says—"Yes, I wrote that last Friday; you know, the day we went down town and met John Smith who had just bought such a pretty cottage in Riverside, where the Joneses live—you know, the Joneses that are related to the Browns who used to live in Auburn—and by the way, isn't it too bad how the fare has been raised to 7¢ on the car line to Auburn; oh, I think these war prices are *terrible*—what a terrible war it is, anyhow! I wonder how this new German offensive will be met—and—dear me! What *was* I talking about?"

But *your* lack of concentration is *not* of this familiar type. Yours is obviously based on a mental vigour which calls for more exercise than the external aspects of one ordinary topic afford. You perceive obscure analogies—the *overtones* of your subject, as it were—and in an effort at following all the parallel lines of thought, find a lack of concentration on the dominant phase. In my abysmal ignorance of the subtleties of psychology, I can suggest nothing but a conscious comparison of relative values—a recognition of the ascendancy of some *one* phase of the subject before you—a phase to & from which the lesser phases must of necessity lead. Do not think of *concentration* in a concrete way. Simply think of the *main topic*—the *thing itself.* Probably this so-called "advice" is valueless & unintelligent. At least give me credit for suspecting its emptiness!

As to "Sherlock Holmes"—I used to be infatuated with him! I read every Sherlock Holmes story published,[9] and even organised a *detective agency* when I was thirteen, arrogating to myself the proud pseudonym of S.H. This P.D.A.*—whose members ranged between nine & fourteen in years, was a most wonderful thing—how many murders & robberies we unravelled! Our headquarters were in a deserted house just out of the thickly settled area, and we there enacted, and "solved", many a gruesome tragedy. I still remember my labours in producing artificial "bloodstains on the floor!!!" But in conformity with our settled policy of utter candour, I must admit to you that the entire venture was more dramatic than psychological in objects & essence; and that our "deductions" were generally pretty well provided for in advance.

As for deducing your habits & biography from the letters I have received—pray assign me an easier task! You & Sherlock are beyond me! But if you have any more discoveries about me to tell, let me hear them! Your conclusions about my typing are practically correct. I use forefingers only, & employ a Remington machine—though *not* #11. [Query—is this machine, or is it not, a visible writer?] As to your mode of deduction—did I *tell* you about my typing methods—as I may have mentioned to many—or did you judge from the *kind* of mistakes I am prone to make—or from the evident pressure I give the keys—or from the fact that I prefer to write by hand? About my *speed*— here is something to think over. I began this note at 10 p.m. When the household retired, I changed to handwriting—ergo, the two pages typed represent what I can do in the time between ten & the retiring time of the average household. But on the other hand, this was not copying but original argumentative composition. Obviously, I may have ceased work from time to time to frame a reply to some point, or think up a new line of defence.

About current detective stories—I have read only a few, which I happened to stumble upon in the ordinary course of human events. Most of them seem to me too artificial to be interesting. I read two or three of the Craig Kennedy[10] tales several years ago, but deemed them too *mechanical* to be really absorbing. It all comes from Poe, *via* Doyle. M. Dupin[11] is the prototype of Holmes, & Holmes is the prototype of every other detective of fiction, if we except Nick Carter and Old Sleuth,[12] dear to the small boys of other generations, and studied almost invariably without knowledge or consent of the reader's parents! There is, though, another sort of mystery story, in which the detective plays rather a minor part. This is the type of which "The Moonstone"[13] & the first tales of Anna Katherine Green[14] are the earliest examples. A few months ago I happened upon a new atrocity of this sort—"Faulkner's Folly"—by Carolyn Wells. I knew the outcome before I had read the thing a quarter through—and sure enough—I was right! But as you remark—it was not by genuine deduction based on the circumstances

---

*Providence Detective Agency

that I solved the murder mystery—it was merely by a familiarity with the conventions & technique of this sort of novel. So far as real evidence went, there were two persons more likely to be guilty than the real culprit—but I knew that owing to their *positions* in the narrative, they simply *could not*. If you have read this effort, I will speak of it more in detail.

Your analysis of the Sherlock Holmes technique is very acute, & coincides with my own views on it. (egotism) However—did you notice how, a few years ago, Mr. Doyle excited considerable newspaper attention by actually solving a simple case by methods akin to those with which he invested his hero? He succeeded in establishing the innocence of a man unjustly accused of the very singular crime of injuring live-stock on a farm by stabbing. I wish I could recall more of the case.[15]

About the word *"peruse"*—possibly I do employ it to excess, but Mr Addison was ever my model of style in prose. Owing to my devotion to many very un-Addisonian subjects, I have strayed far from the classic diction of the Spectator in many ways; but the original impress is ineradicable—at least, I *hope* it is. Addison hath never been surpassed in grace, and the most pleasing of American essayists, Mr. Washington Irving, obtains much of his charm & urbanity by a close adherence to the manner of the older and greater writer.

Your procedure in *apparently* curtailing the length of your St. Nicholas poems, is very ingenious—quite worthy of a master mind. "Nemesis"[16] metre readily lends itself to such condensation. I sincerely hope you win a prize. Concerning the *American Magazine* contest, I shall try to investigate the matter, though I have not been out lately & have not seen the magazine for uncounted aeons. I could compete with serene consciousness of injuring no chance of yours. My own entry could not begin to equal yours in merit, for I am little in touch with the present interests of people. I do not write for the public, but only for my own satisfaction. I wish you could win first prize and I second, if second there be.* But probably I shall never get around to accomplishing the labour.

I hope you can find a way to win renown in the Sankt Nikolai League before old age shall debar you.[17] Seventeen! What a weight of years for a tiny tot only 73 inches in height to sustain! You are well headed toward that celestial infinity which we love so well. My own altitude is 70.5 inches in ordinary shoes, hence we can both claim kinship with the lofty. Another old gentleman, Mr. Hoag, claims an even 72 inches—we of the United are not at all inclined to be lowly!

Concerning Alfred the Lesser[18]—I will not forbear to pay homage to his undoubted art and excellence. He had a remarkable command of smooth melody & imagery, and never fell below a high standard.† I respect him. But

---

*I see there is a second—and seven more—according to your later allusion.

†Someone has said T. is too artistic—that he is the slave of his style, & that sometimes he KEEPS ON WRITING after INSPIRATION has gone.

as a matter of personal preference, I select older & more vigorous bards. I never seem to turn of my own accord to A. T.—or to recall bits of his composition—as I do with my favourite Georgians & pre-Georgians. I hardly think Tennyson, or even Milton, can be compared to Shakespeare in excellence. I am slightly unappreciative of Shakespeare, but I can easily see that he is the leader of all. No other writer possessed so universal a genius, & so broad an understanding of mankind. All this notwithstanding a multiplicity of defects, including some positively puerile errors & anachronisms.

In my ultimate definition of poetry, I presume I am not so far from you and Mr. Poe. As you will see in a forthcoming article of mine,[19] I subscribe to a great extent to the dicta of the Baltimore Bard. Beauty is certainly the prime object; Truth is to be considered only when coincident with Beauty—which is not so often as the late J. Keats believed. I am aware that my favourite Georgians lacked much in the true spirit of poesy—but I do admire their *verse*, as *verse*. I have often felt that I possess but a slight grasp of the poetic principle, & but a fragmentary appreciation of genuine poetry. (See previous *Kleicomolos*) You will shudder with outraged poeticism when you read my latest effusion—a 48-line XVIIIth century pastoral in octosyllabic couplets!!!!![20]

Your poetical contrasts are illuminating—I appreciate their force—but I realised all this before. I entertained no notion of Mr. Pope's literalness or Grecian simplicity in his Iliad. Dr. Bentley, indeed, told M[r] Pope, 'that it is not Homer'.[21]

Your *retentiveness* is to be envied. Mine varies with my state of health—I am very dull when prostrated with a headache, or struggling with a less obvious tangle of refractory nerves—not that I am ever so *very* far from dulness!! (I have enough constitutional stupidity to keep on liking the Georgian atmosphere despite all evidence against it!) I sincerely trust you may receive your expected 100% in the Commercial Law examination—it will certainly constitute a varied testimonial of your genius.

The general reception of your "Two Loves" is most gratifying to me, both as an endorsement of my own opinion and otherwise. I cannot suggest just the professional magazine for it, but Mo's suggestion will undoubtedly be satisfactory. In amateurdom, I think you had best send it to the new recruit—James J. Moloney, 430 Main St., Athol, Mass. He will, I am sure, be delighted to print it in his coming paper—which according to all accounts will be a somewhat ambitious venture.[22] The Association must not be denied the privilege of seeing it, after having endured the original. Did I tell you that Miss Gidlow is President of the rival "United" Amateur Press Association which split off from ours in 1912? It is a puerile thing, with very easy literary standards. Some idea of its calibre may be gained by noting the opinion of the majority of its members regarding the weird & wondrous work of the Mills-Gidlow duet. They call it "very *highbrow*"!! At least, this is what Cook informs me, & his acquaintance with this circle is fairly representative.[23]

About your sonnet—pray do not think *I* consider it poor. In analysing it, I merely suggested why *you* might deem it below your usual standard. The experimental nature of its construction would never have impressed me, had you not revealed the secret voluntarily. It is, as I have remarked, an excellent production, with the one slight technical exception previously noted. I am sure Moloney will appreciate it. My own recent ode is akin in purpose & construction. It is a pure experiment, which I am never likely to repeat. Up to date I have written *one* sonnet and *one* ode—no more.[24] Couplets & quatrains are my specialty, with blank verse in rare homœpathic [*sic*] doses.

As to Klei—you will see a most touching eulogy of his recent poem "Ruth", by our friend Mo in the May Dept. of Public Criticism. Mo compares my "Astrophobos" to "Ruth", much to the disadvantage of the former.[25] This incident has impelled me to perpetrate a gentle parody on "Ruth"— which here behold:

GRAYCE

(With Unstinted Apologies to the Author of "Ruth")

by Kleinhart Reiner, Esq.

In the dim shade of the unrustled grove,
    Amidst the silence of approaching night,
I saw thee standing, as thro' boughs above
    Filter'd the pencils of the dying light.
Grayce! I had thought thou wert by far too proud,
    Too weary of the world and all its pain,
To pause so wistfully, with fair head bow'd,
    Forgetting all thy coldness and disdain.
But in that instant all my doubts and fears
    Were swept away, as on the evening breeze,
When I beheld thee, not indeed in tears,
    But rack'd and shaken with a mighty *sneeze!*

N.B. If you have not read "Ruth", you can find it in the February *Brooklynite.*[26]

Klei edits *The Brooklynite* now, & if he can surmount the difficulties of his task—the thankless task of recording social gossip—he will produce a paper worth a more careful reading than most *Brooklynites*. He has owed me a letter for ages—in fact, he has not yet acknowledged the *Kleicomolo* I sent him a month ago. I am still debating with myself whether or not to send Ἐπιδορφα around the circle. Would it, or would it not, be beyond Kleico.? I wonder! Co likes imaginative flights—but Lloyd brings in just a trifle too much science and pseudo-science for the absolutely wild & woolly reader. And as for Klei—I fear there is not enough soft Cyprian romalince for him!

I am trying to issue a July *Conservative*, as I think I told you before. I expect to produce some 8 pages, with your "Selenaio-Phantasma" as one of the leading contributions.[27] My Klei parody may be included, though this is amongst the items to be dropped if any space congestion occurs. I have already sent the MS. to Cook for printing, but on account of his pressure of work, hardly expect to be able to publish it for a month or two. I have usurped a vast deal of the space for myself, though there will be in all five other contributors.

I note your reference to the beauteous Miltonico-Shakespearian fellow-prodigy at A.H.S., & trust that you may succeed in arousing within her soul any possible 'dormant genius of authorship'! However—you prejudice me against her when you relate her naive estimate of my precious heroic measure! One thing, though, shews good sense—her apparent aversion to the much overrated peasant warbler R. Burns. This fellow fatigues me, though he succeeded in gaining the qualified approval of as great a poet as W. Cowper.

I have not yet purchased *Sankt Nikolai,* nor taken any steps toward League recruiting—in fact, I have not been out at all since last addressing you. After the Presidency is off my hands, I may be able to assist you a bit in the recruiting department; in fact, I will accept appointment as your subordinate on the committee. I could handle a very limited number of cases. You will make the best 1st Vice-President since the term of Chester L. Sharp—1913–1914—the year I joined. I never corresponded with him, but find glowing testimony of his ability on the official records. As you know—the Hon. Don Eduardo Daas "roped me in"—an utter stranger. He had seen some of my metrical heroic wails in the back of a mediocre magazine.[28]

Note the *envelope* in which this missive will reach you—unless it bursts or pines away & dies. It is home-made, an excellent example of Theobaldian craftsmanship. Wherefore, sayest thou? I reply! I am all out of envelopes, & not wishing to encroach on my mother's rather different supply, have utilised my matchless constructive skill in supplying my needs. This is an age of conservation, & I fancy I have made good use of waste paper.

Have I been too boresome? Pray let me hear from you when you have recovered.

> Yr. ob^t humble Servt
>
> L. Theobald Junr.

Notes

1. Joseph Thalheimer, Jr., a graduate of Stanford University (Palo Alto, CA).
2. HPL wrote monthly astronomy columns for the Providence *Evening News* from January 1914 to May 1918.
3. Presumably the *Appleton Crescent,* the major daily newspaper in Appleton.
4. Thomas Moore (1779–1852), *Tom Crib's Memorial to Congress* (1819), ll. 1–6.
5. The poem, as by "Consul Hasting," appeared in the *Conservative* (July 1918).

6. HPL refers the correspondence group the Kleicomolo, consisting of Rheinhart Kleiner, Ira A. Cole, Maurice W. Moe, and HPL. In "Memories of a Friendship," Galpin mentions "a monstrosity called the Kleicomogallo," which ultimately became the Gallomo, consisting of Galpin, HPL, and Moe. There supposedly was a Gremolo—presumably consisting of Sonia Greene, Moe, and HPL—but nothing is known of this cycle, and no letters from it are extant.

7. I.e., typing. HPL had a 1906 Remington typewriter.

8. A spoonerism of the name of HPL's friend Rheinhart Kleiner, who wrote many light love lyrics.

9. Later HPL confessed that he had read only the first three Sherlock Holmes collections (*The Adventures of Sherlock Holmes* [1892], *The Memoirs of Sherlock Holmes* [1894], and *The Return of Sherlock Holmes* [1905]), three novels (*A Study in Scarlet* [1888], *The Sign of the Four* [1890], and *The Hound of the Baskervilles* [1902]), and "an odd (& rather mediocre) pair or series of tales appearing about '08" (HPL to August Derleth, 26 March 1927; *Essential Solitude* 77).

10. Arthur B[enjamin] Reeve (1880–1936) created Craig Kennedy, scientific detective. His work appeared in *Hearst's Magazine, Cosmopolitan,* and *Nash's Pall Mall Magazine.* The tales were gathered in many collections, beginning with *The Silent Bullet: Adventures of Craig Kennedy, Scientific Detective* (1912). Reeve also wrote several novels featuring Kennedy.

11. Poe's detective, C. Auguste Dupin, featured in "The Murders in the Rue Morgue," "The Mystery of Marie Roget," and "The Purloined Letter."

12. Nick Carter was created by John R. Coryell (1848–1924). Old Sleuth was the dime novel detective created by Harlan Halsey (1839?–1898).

13. By Wilkie Collins.

14. Anna Katharine Green (1846–1935), the first American mystery writer to remain consistently on the bestseller lists.

15. Written up by Doyle in "The Case of Mr. George Edalji," serialized in the *Daily Telegraph* in 1907, and published in book form as *The Story of Mr. George Edalji* (1907).

16. HPL alludes to his poem "Nemesis," the meter of which is derived from Swinburne's *Hertha.* Galpin's "Selenaio-Phantasma" uses the same form.

17. *St. Nicholas* (1873–1940, 1943) was a popular monthly American children's magazine. The "St. Nicholas League" department of the magazine offered awards and cash prizes to juvenile readers for the best work submitted.

18. I.e., Alfred, Lord Tennyson.

19. "The Despised Pastoral."

20. "The Spirit of Summer."

21. Richard Bentley (1662–1742) was the leading classical scholar of his time. He made a celebrated comment upon the publication of Pope's translation of the *Iliad* (1715–20): ". . . it is a pretty poem, Mr. Pope; but you must not call it Homer" (quoted in G. Birkbeck Hill's notes to Samuel Johnson's essay on Pope in *Lives of the English Poets* [Oxford: Clarendon Press, 1905], 3:213).

22. Moloney edited *The Voice from the Mountains.* The issue for July 1918 contained Galpin's essay "Man and the Supernatural" and his poem, "Sonnet to Poetry." The latter presumably is the item discussed in the next paragraph.

23. For this split in the UAPA, see HPL's "A Matter of Uniteds." HPL addresses the amateur paper *Les Mouches Fantastiques,* ed. Elsa Gidlow and Roswell George Mills, in the essay "*Les Mouches Fantastiques.*"

24. The sonnet is "Sonnet on Myself," the ode "Ode for July Fourth, 1917."

25. "'Astrophobos,' by Ward Phillips, is another recipe poem; although his recipe is so much more intricate that it is not to be recommended for the Freshman. The critic would denominate a poem composed according to this recipe, a ulalumish poem, as it has so many earmarks of Poe. True to type, it is ulaluminated with gorgeous reds and crimsons, vistas of stupendous distances, coined phrases, unusual words, and general touches of either mysticism or purposeless obscurity. Such a poem is a feast for epicures who delight in intellectual caviar, but it is not half so satisfying to average poetic taste as Mr. Kleiner's 'Ruth.'" "Department of Public Criticism," *United Amateur* 17, No. 5 (May 1918): 95.

26. *Brooklynite* 9, No. 2 (February 1918): 5. HPL's "Grace" was published as part of the article "Ward Phillips Replies" (*Conservative,* July 1918).

27. Galpin's poem "Selenaio-Phantasma," "Dedicated to the Author of 'Nemesis,'" a pastiche of HPL's "Nemesis," was published in the *Conservative* (July 1918). A manuscript entitled "Luna-Phantasma" survives among HPL's papers at JHL.

28. I.e., the *Argosy.* See *H. P. Lovecraft in the* Argosy.

[3]   [TLS]

598 Angell St., Providence, R.I.,
August 21, 1918.

Theobaldus Tertius, Esq.,
Esteem'd Godson:—

I am overwhelmed! How can I possibly convey a suitable idea of the pleasure and gratitude I experienced, and am still experiencing, as a result of your communications of 18th inst.? I will begin with the verses, which are, if grossly flattering, excellent indeed; and which must represent a great aesthetic sacrifice on your part, considering the medium in which they are cast.[1] I am so used to the heroick atmosphere that your delightful tribute does not sound at all like doggerel to me. I think it most graceful. Should you desire Private Criticism, I will say that (1) In line 5 the word "questioners" might be shortened to "doubters" to get rid of a syllable, (2) The word you have as "e'er" should be "ere", (the two are different), (3) "I-*de*-als" has 3 syllables, and cannot rhyme with "feels". I have substituted

The Gods themselves thy high ideals guide;
They only know the passions that preside.

(4) The word "omnipresent" contains no "c". I felt like sending the lines somewhere for publication, but on second thought decided that I could not, good as they are, since to do so would savour of egotism. They are too complimentary to me! Therefore for once in my life I am going to let something

of yours languish in unpublished obscurity! But I will have revenge—and last night celebrated my birthday by scribbling a reply which I shall copy on the machine for your perusal. Theobald II can scarcely equal Theobald III, but the enclosed is the best I can do.

And now about the book—!!!² Words fail me in describing my pleasure at receiving this exquisite volume, whose appearance is as delightful as its contents—and that is saying much. I fancy it covers a great deal of ground with which we are familiar, and shall probably have a few words to say about it in my next epistle. I may have perused this among other Emersoniana in the dim past, but I recall it not, and shall read it with all the zest of first acquaintance. I generally neglected the more recent philosophers in favour of the ancients, and have never quite understood the habit of so many of my acquaintances in proclaiming their undivided allegiance to the Sage of Concord. Your timely gift has reawakened my interest in him, and it is not unlikely that I shall in the near future give him a good share of my attention. I am like a great many others, who neglect the riches near at hand whilst searching in far fields. Whilst I have been roving through antient Hellas in the company of Democritus,³ I have slighted my fellow-New-Englander! You are helping me broaden my education! Again I will attempt to suggest all the abounding thanks which I cannot visibly frame, both for the delectable poem and the appropriate and artistic book. Your thoughtfulness is most highly appreciated!

I am hopelessly engulfed in your "hyperbolic oleaginity"! Pray do not slander yourself so! Your intellect is no more imitative than any other—you are seeking the truth, and therefore examining all men's thought and selecting what appeals to you. That is the only way to form ideas—and your genius for assimilation is all that is needed to stamp you as a remarkable thinker. The curiosity which leads you to consider philosophical questions, supported by your discriminating method of selecting and analysing opinions, is an ample testimonial of your genius. Others hear the same things you hear—but never stop to think about them—or if they do think they become confused and give it up. You have a plenitude of years in which to work out an original eclectic system of thought—and you certainly will work one out! As a disillusioning proof of my lack of super-intellect, I refer you to the Sonneberg article. Illness, withdrawing me from active duties, has relieved my mind of an infinite amount of concentration on details and left it free to wander at will through the realms of the abstract and unpractical. It is not likely that I expend any more actual brain activity in considering infinite space, than the average business man expends in attending to the innumerable trying details and responsibilities of his office work. It is merely a matter of direction—and so prone to fatigue am I, that I occasionally feel that my mind must be very mediocre. Mr. Pope, for one, triumphed over greater bodily illnesses than mine—yet I get nowhere.⁴ So you see that I have enough self-derogatory material to match the modest remarks you make at the head of your epistle. It is rather fortunate we ran across each other, since we are both dwellers in a rather singular region of thought, with few near at hand to share our views. My family are as delightful and kind as any family could be—my mother is a positive marvel of consideration—but none the less I am not thought any particular credit socially—I am awkward and unpleasing—much more so than you, I am certain. Comparing us, I find you most like me of anyone I know—yet with real impartiality I must concede the brighter mentality to you. Your rate of assimilation really surpasses mine by far. To trace, for instance, my philosophical views. I began to study astronomy late in 1902—age 12. My interest came through two sources—discovery of an old book of my grandmother's in the attic,[5] and a previous interest in physical geography. Within a year I was thinking of virtually nothing but astronomy, yet my keenest interest did not lie outside the solar system. I think I really ignored the abysses of space in my interest in the habitability of the various planets of the solar system. My observations (for I purchased a telescope early in 1903) were confined mostly to the moon and the planet Venus. You will ask, why the latter, since its markings are doubtful even in the largest instruments? I answer—this very MYSTERY was what attracted me. In boyish egotism I fancied I might light upon something with my poor little 2¼-inch telescope which had eluded the users of the 40-inch Yerkes telescope!! And to tell the truth, I think the moon interested me more than anything else—the very nearest object. I used to sit night after night absorbing the minutest details of the lunar surface, till today I can tell you of every peak and crater as though they were the topographical features of my own neighbourhood. I was highly angry at Nature for withholding from my gaze the other side of our satellite! It was not till 1904 that I dabbled much in philosophy, and even then I used to smile at extravagant speculation. I had always been an agnostic because I saw no proof of Deity, but I was not by any means a cosmic sage. My real philosophical interest began when I was just your age—1906. I then set about writing a book—a complete treatise on astronomy[6]—and in doing so I resolved to use all the best material at hand. I would not write till I had made myself absolute master of my subject. Wherefore I commenced a campaign of intensive reading, devouring everything I could find on astronomy. This perforce turned my attention to the structure of the universe, and to problems in cosmogony, and literally obtruded upon my attention the matters of infinity and eternity which have since interested me so keenly. Before 1907 I was deep in speculation, and have not been able to get out yet! When I look back, I can see that I always held the idea of the earth's insignificance—but it was in a passive way before 1906. I knew it, but it made no impression on my thought. I was a great reformer then—(in my own mind), and had high ideas about uplifting the masses. I came across a superficially bright Swedish boy[7] in the Public Library—he worked in the "stack" where the books are kept—and invited him to the house to broaden his mentality (I was fifteen and he was about the

same, though he was smaller and seemed younger.) I thought I had uncov-
ered a mute inglorious Milton[8] (he professed a great interest in my work), and
despite maternal protest entertained him frequently in my library. I believed
in equality then, and reproved him when he called my mother "Ma'am"—I
said that a future scientist should not talk like a servant! But ere long he un-
covered qualities which did not appeal to me, and I was forced to abandon
him to his plebeian fate. I think the experience educated me more than it educated him—I have been more of a cynic since that time! He left the library
(by request) and I never saw him more. Pardon the autobiographical reminiscences, but I seem to be in a retrospective mood—perhaps as a result of my
birthday, which is a natural time of recapitulation.

Mention of your heroic couplets, written in a lady's album, reminds me
of some correspondence I had with Klei last fall. At the 1917 convention of
the National he was called upon to perpetrate some album verse, and he retained a copy to send me. I thought it excellent, but believed I could equal
it—hence dashed off five specimens in this vein for Klei's approval. I will
copy them here if I can find them, and will leave it to your judgment whether
or not I succeed in the field of poetical gallantry. First Klei's effusion:

FOR THE ALBUM OF
MISTRESS MARJORIE OUTWATER[9]—JULY, 1917

> Sweet girl, be always good and kind,
> And you in each glad hour shall find
> Some fragrance ere the time is flown;
> Some beauty rising to your own.
> Give love, and hearts will ever bow
> Before your tender spell, as now;
> So you in other lives may shine—
> But not more brightly than in mine!
>
> RHEINHART KLEINER

Now behold the products of the Master Mind—sheer abstractions, written
coldly and without the inspiration of the fair:

TO THE INCOMPARABLE CLORINDA

> You ask for verse—yet who cou'd justly write
> When dazzled by your beauty's radiant light?
> What line so smooth, but 'twould seem harsh and weak
> Beside the velvet softness of your cheek?
> My ill-scrawl'd words can win no greater praise
> Than having drawn the glory of your gaze;
> And much I fear, 'twill seem too rash in me
> To rise from mere Olympian themes to thee!

(Very confidential P.S.)
With this, Clorinda, must thou rest content:
'Twou'd be no better, *even if 'twere meant!*

KLEINHART REINER

TO SACCHARISSA, FAIREST OF HER SEX

When Nature fix'd the lamps of space
    To gild the plain and light the blue,
She made three orbs of diff'ring grace—
    The silver Moon, the Sun, and You.
The lesser two she plac'd aloft
    As Guardians of the Night and Day;
But You she left, whose magick soft
    Rules *both* with sweet resistless sway!

EDVARDUS SOFTLEIUS[10]

TO RHODOCLIA—PEERLESS AMONG MAIDENS

Were the blue of the sea and the blue of the skies
Half as sweet and as pure as the blue of your eyes;
Were the scent of the fields, and the flow'r-laden air
Half as potent and rich as your dear ⎰ golden ⎱ hair
                     { nut-brown }
                     { raven }
                     { silver }
                     ⎱ crimson ⎰
Then the world were an Heaven, and mine were the bliss
To write verses forever as freely as this!

A. SAPHEAD

Note the adaptability of the above gem to all varieties of maidens. True, the [*sic*] is no alternative for *blue* eyes—but in poesy all eyes are blue.

TO BELINDA, FAVOURITE OF THE GRACES

    Nymph, whose glance demure and kind
        Turns the darkest hour to joy;
    In whose witching face are join'd
        Venus and the Paphian Boy;
    Take this tribute, tho' my hand
        Ne'er cou'd pen a tribute meet.
    Labour done at thy command,
        Howe'er fruitless, still is sweet!

TO HELIODORA—SISTER OF CYTHERAEA

When Paris made his fateful choice
    According to his duty,
To Venus with unfalt'ring voice
    He gave the prize of beauty;
Her godlike sisters, hard to please,
Grew piqued, and turn'd his enemies.

Now were that prize bestow'd today
    Poor Paris needs must tremble;
For greater ills wou'd haunt his way,
    Cou'd he not well dissemble:
For *ev'ry* god his foe wou'd be,
Since Beauty's prize belongs to Thee!
            ANACREON MICROCEPHALOS.[11]

You may use any or all of these specimens if occasion arises—I have given them to no one else but Klei, and his field of conquest is widely remote from yours—Brooklyn and Appleton are well separated! They ought to melt even the beautiful perverse Delia! You young gallants are a sad lot!

Ascending—or descending—to seriousness, I am flattered that you should think my idle comment on "Progress" worthy of publication in *The Open Court*.[12] I did not write it with an eye to the publick, and fear the rhetorick is somewhat lacking in elegance. Also—one or two plainly personal and epistolary comments may have crept in between the lines. But I will trust to your good sense to prepare a revised version should you find the magazine still flourishing and willing to print comment on so obsolete an article. Ye Gods! For 'Eaving's sake abstain from sending my "mission in life" letter to Mistress Durr.[13] I recall saying in it that I thought she was minding other people's business! I have given her a 22-page broadside, calculated to demolish any pragmatical notions which may still becloud her mentality, but have not gone into personal excuses for idleness beyond saying that my constitution does not permit of systematic endeavour, else (of course) I should be doing something the same as any other rational human being. What does she think I am—a corner loafer? She might know better—for if I were, the "work or fight" law would have "got" me long ago, and I should be toiling in some munition factory or shovelling sewers at some cantonment. I am not particularly anxious to discuss my affairs with relative strangers—my letter was for you, not for her. I wished to demonstrate to *you* why I am such an apparent parasite on society. And just to prove how anxious I am to labour—if the *Crescent* wants a New-England correspondent, and is willing to take a thorough anti-Hun, I speak fer de job!

I trust you are satisfied with your critical assignment—to which I will add one trifle—Glause's new venture, *The Pathfinder*.[14] Follow your own methods, and nothing essential will be changed—though I should like the privilege of going over the copy for details before publication. One thing—guard against the so-called "split infinitive", the use of which sometimes appears in your work. THE "TO" OF AN INFINITIVE MUST NEVER BE SEPARATED FROM THE MAIN VERB-FORM BY ANOTHER WORD. It is incorrect to say TO SLOWLY GLIDE. You must say either SLOWLY TO GLIDE or TO GLIDE SLOWLY. At all events keep TO GLIDE as an unbroken unit. This is one of the tests of mature scholarship, as Kleiner told me some time ago. In amateurdom and elsewhere there are many fearful offenders in this little nicety—but it pays to be on the side of perfection. Details count in the long run. I have to correct vast numbers of split infinitives in the U.A. Both Miss McG[15] and Cook are confirmed infinitive-splitters, though I have lectured both on the subject. As to the improved style of criticism which you suggest—by all means give it a trial. The main argument for detailed revision in print is that most of the faults corrected are universal faults of crude writers, and that correction is therefore of general benefit. The public see just what sort of errors need mending, and learn what verses to copy and what not to copy. This idea is not mine—Father Mo was doing the same thing before I ever heard of amateurdom—for proof, see your file of back U.A.'s. But I am no enemy to rational innovation, and bid you go as far as you like. I have much respect for your taste, despite the few years in which you have had an opportunity to exercise it. I may even alter mine own critical style if your idea meets with general approval. Write Klei and Father Mo about it—they will be interested. One thing about my criticism—it is liable at times to become hackneyed and unoriginal. I have been at the task so long, that I fall into ruts and mannerisms, repeating myself unconsciously. The United deserves a better critick, and I am expecting you to become the Young Sam Johnson of the Association in a few years.

I can see how the *Flatbush* may have failed to impress your sense of humour. Different persons react differently to Hasemann. Cook, for instance, feels only *disgust* when reading the F.A.P.[16] I feel amusement and pity—whilst another, such as you, may with equal naturalness feel nothing but boredom. To members of my amateur generation, Hasemann is something like a Ford car. If you hear his name, you think you must laugh.

As to Klei's silence—I will enclose a card from him which came today. As you see, he is with us in thought, e'en tho' the cares of commerce keep him occupied to the exclusion of all else. I think you are wise to exercise a certain amount of Vice-Presidential concentration on your home town. A local club, if active, is a vast incentive to general enthusiasm. See if you can interest former press club members, whose names you can glean from old *United Amateurs*. There were some very passable poets among them, I believe. The only two veterans that "stuck" are Schilling and Miss Merkel;[17]

the rest have evaporated into infinity. I am corresponding lately with a lady friend of yours—or your mother's—the would-be poetess Mrs. Agnes Richmond Arnold, who thinks you are a very bright child indeed. She seems to be a nice old lady, though she uses simplified spelling. She is very much interested in the Association, and if you can secure her aid you may be able to capture some adult recruits. Also—for Heaven's sake teach her how to use metre. She wants to be a poet very much, but must master many a technical rule first. I have amended one of her effusions and have offered to do more, for I have a very keen sympathy for the old folks who develop their ambitions too late in life to improve them. I judge Mrs. Arnold (though not from any real evidence) to be about 70—and if Mr. Hoag can succeed (with aid) at 87, there ought to be hope for her. I think she would appreciate your help, and in return might help your recruiting, as I said before. By the way—in her latest note, Mrs. Arnold says she hopes you have not "imbibed any of your father's Ingersollism."[18] I told her that while like all deep thinkers you could not be orthodox, you were not at all an anti-clerical, and had a keen respect for the church. She admires your mother's staunch Presbyterianism! Turning to the younger generation, I trust you can capture the Shakespeario-Miltonick person for the United, though if she has lived to high-school age without indulging in original composition I doubt if she is a really natural-born author. Most writers began about as soon as their hands were strong enough to hold a pencil. My poetical career started at the age of seven. (Pardon implication that I am a typical great author!) I shall endeavour to write the fair nymph, whom I hope you will choose as your new divinity in place of the cruel Delia. The French are patriots and worthy folk, whilst the Irish are slackerish and seditious. If I write, I shall allude to the 1st Vice-President in a way calculated to heighten her interest in that young gentleman! I am much interested in your allusion to "the town's most prominent poet", and hope you can "land" him for the Association. Any poet more prominent than Alfredus Aurelius Galpinus Secundus must be prominent indeed! If you will send me the names of all your prospects, I will supply them with *Conservatives* and application blanks, and possibly form letters. The latter I shall carbon in lots of six. Special recruits like Miss Shakespeare or the poet, I shall seek to write individually, though I cannot promise speed. I wonder who will finance the new application blanks? There is no constitutional provision for them, and it is usually left to the Secretary, though for the past two years private individuals—Campbell and Miss McGeoch—have philanthropically come to the rescue. I would aid this time if I could, but my financial situation is not bright just now. You might suggest as diplomatically as possible to the Secretary that she could well use a bit of her *Crescent* salary in having some nice new blanks printed, with her name on them.

I am still struggling with the typing of *Hesperia*.[19] It is execrably boresome work, and I shall be lucky if I can finish it alive. I shall await with interest your opinion of my dime novel—the conclusion of the "Mystery of Murdon Grange".[20] A vast amount of the magazine is critical—confined to British amateur journals. Since but few American amateurs have seen these journals, I am thinking of omitting this section in the American edition—for the sake of paper conservation. (To say nothing of my readers' patience.) British amateurdom is relatively undeveloped, and confined to a not aristocratic section of the population. The only thoroughly cultured British amateur is Rev. W. F. Pelton, (Wilfrid Kemble), and he says he has not time to bother with his less erudite fellows. I induced him to revise a little of Sub-Lieut. M'Keag's verse, but he found the task uncongenial. But I must break off abruptly, else I shall never finish.

Sincerely, gratefully, and godparentally yours,
Ludovicus Theobaldus Secundus

Notes

1. The poem must have been a tribute to HPL; it does not appear to survive.

2. Evidently a de luxe edition of Emerson's *Culture* (cf. *SL* 1.73); perhaps the edition published by Barse & Hopkins (New York, 1910).

3. Greek philosopher (c. 460–370 B.C.E.), one of the founders of Atomism.

4. Pope suffered from curvature of the spine (he was only four and a half feet tall) and also from a tubercular condition.

5. Elijah Hinsdale Burritt's *The Geography of the Heavens, and Classbook of Astronomy.*

6. Presumably *A Brief Course in Astronomy* (1906), which HPL notes as having reached 150 pp. (*SL* 5.140–41). It does not survive.

7. Arthur Fredlund (1892–?), who was briefly made editor of his juvenile periodical the *Scientific Gazette* in 1905–06.

8. Thomas Gray (1716–1771), *Elegy Written in a Country Churchyard* (1751): "Some mute inglorious Milton here may rest . . ." (l. 59).

9. Marjorie Outwater (Roxbury, MA) was a member of the NAPA.

10. A Latinization of HPL's pseudonym "Edward Softly."

11 "Anacreon" refers to the Greek poet (6th century B.C.E.) known for his drinking songs. "Microcephalos" is HPL's coinage meaning "small-head."

12. The *Open Court* (1887–1936) was a magazine published by the Open Court Publishing Company, devoted to the critical study of religion, science, and philosophy.

13. Mary Faye Durr (1893–1979), who would be elected President of the UAPA for 1919–20.

14. The *Pathfinder,* ed. Edwin H. Glause (b. 1902) of Cleveland, reviewed by Galpin in "Department of Public Criticism," *United Amateur* 18, No. 2 (November 1918): 29–30.

15. Verna McGeoch.

16. *Flatbush Amateur Press,* ed. John H. Hasemann, Jr. (1894–1974), of Flatbush, NY. At least six issues were produced from January 1918 to April 1920.

17. George S. Schilling of Madison and Gertrude L. Merkel of Appleton, WI.

18. Robert G. Ingersoll (1833–1899), renowned agnostic lecturer and writer.

19. "'Hesperia' is a manuscript magazine which I circulate in Great Britain" (*SL* 1.136, 4 June 1921). HPL to Rheinhart Kleiner, 27 June 1918: "My *Hesperia* will be critical & educational in object, though I am 'sugar-coating' the first number by 'printing' a conclusion of the serial 'The Mystery of Murdon Grange'" (*Letters to Rheinhart Kleiner and Others* 119). No issue of *Hesperia* has been discovered.

20. "The Mystery of Murdon Grange" seems to have been a round-robin serial appearing in *Spindrift*, an amateur journal edited by Ernest Lionel McKeag (1896–1976) of Newcastle-upon-Tyne, England, who later wrote boys' fiction. One segment—published in *Spindrift* 5, No. 1 (Christmas 1917): 26–27, and signed "B. Winskill"—has been located, but no other segments have come to light. HPL, however, discusses several segments in his "Department of Criticism" columns of January, March, and May 1918.

[4]   [ALS]

598 Angell St.,
Providence, R.I.,
Aug. 29, 1848. [i.e., 1918]

Edgar A. Poe, Esq.,
Appleton, Wis.:—

My Dear Mr· Poe:—

I beg to acknowledge receipt of your favour of 25th inst., enclosing the story "Marsh-Mad",[1] written under the pseudonym of "Alfred Galpin, Jr." I deem the tale fully up to your usual standard, though in some respects surpassed by your former story "The Fall of the House of Usher". The ascription of sentient life to something not usually considered conscious reminds me of "Usher", but in detail your newer story is markedly original and splendidly developed. Atmosphere & vocabulary are alike remarkable, & I anticipate no trouble in placing this masterpiece in a prominent magazine.

Your development of the "living tree" idea will probably cause me to change a plot of my own, long conceived but never elaborated into literary form, which also involves such a thing. For your edification I will outline this plot:

Two close friends, either artists or authors, live near each other, and maintain their early intimacy & cordiality despite strong rivalry for fame. Finally the *more successful* man sickens and dies of a *mysterious malady*, causing the devoted friend to mourn long and unconsolably. The dead man is buried in a neighbouring meadow which he loved in life, and from his grave springs a tiny green shoot which grows into a tree. As long years pass, the other man works toward a celebrity almost equal to that of him who died. Finally he completes a masterpiece which, when shewn to the world, will bring him a fame *greater* than that of his departed friend. The tree had grown very rapidly—much more rapidly than is the wont of such a tree—and on the 25th anniversary of the buried man's death, it is of great size. On that night the surviving man, about to gain supreme laurels and earthly triumph, goes to his friend's grave and looks long at the grassy mound. And his lips twist strange-ly, even considering his great grief. There was no wind that night, but the next morning (just as the long-bereaved friend was to have enjoyed his new fame) the tree was found uprooted—as if the roots had voluntarily relinquished their hold upon the ground—and beneath the massive trunk lay the body of the faithful mourner—crushed to death, & with an expression of the most unutterable fear upon his countenance.[2]

———————

Such is the plot I was *going* to develop—but *now* it seems weak & futile in-deed! You have (in the language of the masses) "beaten me to it", & exhausted the possibilities of living trees. Likewise—my plot is pathetically ordinary & pro-saic beside yours. I congratulate you!! You are master in the regions of the dimly terrible and ineffably hideous. I need not be so anxious for you to see "Dagon" & "The Tomb".[3] They will appear tame to you, for you have outdone my best. Last night whilst vainly trying to sleep, some wildly sinister verses crept through my brain so insistently that I arose & set them down. After 2½ lines my inspira-tion gave out, but I think I shall some day concoct a suitable plot & conclusion to go with this promising (?) prelude. The following is what I wrote:

> 'Twas at a nameless hour of night
> When fancies in delirious flight
> About the silent sleeper reel,
> And thro' his mindless visions steal;
> When flesh upon its earthly bed
> Sprawls corpse-like and untenanted—
> Vacant of soul, which freely flies
> Thro' worlds unknown to waking eyes.
> The hornèd moon above the spire
> With ghastly grace was crawling high'r,
> And in the pallid struggling beams
> Grinn'd memories of ancient dreams.
> Aloft in heav'n each starry sign
> Flicker'd fantastic and malign,
> Whilst voices in the gaping deep
> Whisper'd to me, I must not sleep.
> (This scene, one night in chill November,
> I shall thro' many a year remember.)
> Beneath that selfsame moon I spied
> A bleak and barren countryside,
> Where spectral shadows darkly crept
> Across the moor————————[4]

This sounds like something I have heard before. I shall investigate in order to avoid subconscious plagiarism. Does it sound familiar to you?

P.S. I have just looked up in Poe where I *thought* I had read something like this, & find it is not so! Perhaps this is fairly original after all! But Mo, even if he would not call it "rubber-stamp" work, would dub it a "recipe poem"—so what's the use???

Perhaps, after reading this d—— foolishness, you will advise me not to complete it. Nor do I blame you for such advice!

As to our exchange of heroics—allow me to correct something in my own answer—line 22. For *become*, read *becom'st*. Archaism must be consistent. If you keep the verses, I wish you would make the change on the copy. If not, you are at least informed of the error, and aware that I am as alert in spying out mine own faults as those of other poets & poetasters. Goodenough's tribute, according to latest evidence, seems to have been absolutely serious.[5] He acknowledged my counter-tribute in a very kind note.[6] He is 47 years of age, & in October will celebrate the 30th anniversary of the publication of his first poem. His *serious* tribute sounded more comical than your semi-serious one—hence it is not remarkable that Miss McGeoch should fail to grasp the spirit at the bottom of your graceful lines. I agree that they are (considering the unworthy subject) scarce suitable for publication in the official organ. I am glad Miss McG speaks so well of me. It would be easy to say a great deal more in reciprocity, for I have seldom encountered her equal in kindly breadth of opinion, exalted ideals, high sense of duty, dependable efficiency, conscientious responsibility, & general nobility of character. This sounds like Theobaldian oleaginousness, but since nearly every other amateur can give a similar verdict, you may see that it has much foundation in fact. She is certainly one of the pillars of amateur journalism. You surprise me when you state that even other favourable references to me have reached you. I have always had a sort of sensation of unpopularity—knowing how odd and utterly boresome I am. I fear most of my correspondents would be sadly disappointed on meeting me—I hope Klei did not find me so uninteresting that he will lose his zest for further correspondence![7] In his case, I think I am safe, for his letters *since* calling me are just as cordial as those which he wrote *before*.

I am glad Father Mo found Miss D's epistle so interesting. She has a sort of pert, laconic humour or smartness, of which she is evidently fairly proud, & which she is not at all reluctant to employ. Anent the new and Gallic charmer—Mlle. Shakespeare—I am glad your *affaire du coeur* is progressing so well. Surely she is a much more worthy helpmate than the scornful Delia— whose attitude can be ascribed only to inherent cruelty of temperament & absence of good sense. In the evening of life, after youth & beauty are fled, you would find Delia a monstrous dull companion; since lacking intellectual interests, she would have naught in common with her transcendently gifted spouse. On the other hand, you will find Mlle. Shakespeare—or Mme. Shakespeare-Galpin—eternally congenial & delightful in literary discussion, so that down to your very graves you may be blessed with the most perfect mutual understanding and harmonious fellowship. Long live Lycë the fair—Down with Delia! Incidentally—I made it a point the other day to write your Lycë a full recruiting letter. Assuming that you had roughly outlined the United to her, I used the "second letter" text, which aims to set forth the especial ad-

vantages of amateurdom very vividly. In my Galpinian interpolations, I took
care to avoid any appearance of fulsomeness, but merely stated casually that
Mr. Galpin is indeed a very remarkable young man, who despite his few years
has come to be one of the leading workers in our cause, *& who has a great future before him.* Note this last item. By predicting a great future, I imply, of
course, that anyone who *shares* that future will be fortunate indeed! I gave her
to understand that her new gallant is esteemed & respected by all his elders—
which ought to count in your favour. I did not lay my praise on thickly—but
worked scientifically & psychologically! If she replies & thereby gives me a
chance for more scientific pro-Galpinism, I will have her proposing to you in
a month or two! All hail to Theobald the Matchmaker!! And by the way—in
excavating old papers to send her as samples, I came across one I am not sure
I sent you—*The Providence Amateur*—relic of my philanthropic club experiment of 1914–16. If you have not a copy, let me know; for I have two extra. I
also sent a letter to Secy. Kelly[8] as you suggested, seeking to arouse her interest in outside amateur journals. My plan was to describe at some length, & a
trifle humorously, each of the papers which are now receiving contributions;
urging her to submit stories already written if she had nothing new or was especially busy. Accompanying my letter I despatched a set of Chase's *Amateur
Journalist*[9] as a possible stimulus of interest. [Have I sent you a set—5 numbers? If not, I will] If all this does not make an amateur out of Misthress
O'Kelly, you had best secure a more potent persuader than I. My guess as to
M^rs. Arnold's age was based on her exceedingly tremulous & uncertain handwriting. Few persons as young as 55 have such an outwardly senile chirogra-
phy. She has just offered to pay me professional rates for verse revision, but I
shall not accept remuneration for anything designed for the *amateur* press.
However—if she has any large amount of work to be prepared for outside
publication, I shall be pleased to handle it as I handle Rev. David V. Bush's.[10]
It will not be such hard work, since Mrs. A. could not possibly perpetrate
such utter & unqualified asininity as Rev. D.V.B.

Concerning philosophy—it flatters me to learn that so much of your present system came from a perusal of mine own humble attempts & speculations. You place me in a position of grave responsibility—the pious & the
orthodox will revile me as a pernicious corrupter of youth!! And yet—since it
was MO who first shewed you my lucubrations, I cannot so deeply blame myself. Some day, when you have left me far behind & formulated a new system
of your own, I may return the compliment by borrowing ideas from you!

The science of chemistry, in which I am glad to find you interested, first
captivated me in the Year of Our Lord 1898—in a rather peculiar way. With
the insatiable curiosity of early childhood, I used to spend hours poring over
the pictures in the back of Webster's Unabridged Dictionary—absorbing a
miscellaneous variety of ideas. After familiarising myself with antiquities, mediaeval dress & armour, birds, animals, reptiles, fishes, flags of all nations,

heraldry, &c. &c., I lit upon the section devoted to "Philosophical & Scientific Instruments", & was veritably hypnotised with it. Chemical apparatus especially attracted me, & I resolved (before knowing a thing about the science!) to have a laboratory. Being a "spoiled child" I had but to ask, & it was mine. I was given a cellar room of good size, & provided by my elder aunt (who had studied chemistry at boarding school) with some simple apparatus & a copy of "The Young Chemist"—a beginner's manual by Prof. John Howard Appleton of Brown—a personal acquaintance. "The Young Chemist" was just the book for me—devoted to easy & instructive experiments— and I was soon deep in its pages. The laboratory "work"—or play—seemed delightful, and despite a few mishaps, explosions, & broken instruments, I got along splendidly. Soon I acquired other books, & began (March 4, 1899) to issue a chemical magazine called *The Scientific Gazette,* which I maintained for eight years. This was, I suppose, my entry to amateur journalism! By 1901 or thereabouts I had a fair knowledge of the principles of chemistry & the details of the inorganic part—about the equivalent of a high-school course, & not including analysis of any kind. Then my fickle fancy turned away to the intensive study of geography, geology, anthropology, & above all *astronomy,* after which came a revival of classicism, latinity, &c. Not until 1906 did chemistry come into my life again. In that year I encountered *physics* in high-school, which reawaked my dormant laboratory instincts, & led me back to the study of matter, its constitution and properties. I increased my chemical library by fully 20 volumes—to say naught of the physics text books I bought—& obtained a plenitude of new instruments. I was now in a smaller house, with a smaller laboratory, but the new room was ample for the purpose. In 1907 I took chemistry in high-school, but since I knew all the course before, had more fun than instruction in the class room. I left high school certified in physics & chemistry, & intended to specialise in those subjects at college; but just then my nervous system went to pieces, & I was forced to relinquish all thought of activity. Yet at home I continued my chemical studies, dabbling in a correspondence course which helped me in matters of *analysis & organic chemistry,* hitherto neglected by me. But in the mean time literature had been on the increase once more, & I found my interest centreing more & more in old-fashioned scribbling. By 1912 I had practically ceased to be active in chemistry, & have since partially dismantled my laboratory, owing to my mother's nervousness at having deadly poisons, corrosive acids, and potential explosives about the place. One tangible memorial of my hobby remains—a bulky manuscript entitled "A Brief Course in Inorganic Chemistry", by H. P. Lovecraft. 1910.[11] There is also a physical memorial—the third finger of my right hand—whose palm side is permanently scarred by a mighty phosphorus burn sustained in 1907. At the time, the loss of the finger seemed likely, but the skill of my uncle—a physician[12]—saved it. It is still a bit stiff, & aches in cold weather—as no doubt it always will. During the bandage & splint days I had to pick out my verses & articles with my left forefinger only on the type-writer. I am not at all regretful of the time I spent in chemical pursuits, for I have time & again found use for the information I imbibed. I should not feel competent to make philosophical conjectures, were I without at least a moderate knowledge of the laws & properties of matter & energy.

About the constitution of *common sand*—I should say it is mainly SiO_2 with perhaps a few intermixed silicates—i.e. salts of silicic acid. Probably—in fact positively—its exact constitution varies according to the geological nature of the locality. It is safe to say that the leading constituent is silicon dioxide. I should be interested to hear the details of the A.H.S. controversy which exposed the ignorance of the instructor. What book do you use? In Hope Street we had Hessler & Smith's, but I disliked the latter half, owing to the unscientific order in which it discusses the metals. It is out of harmony with the periodic system. I like Remsen's text-book much better. My earliest favourite—he whose name is even as your native town—is not so successful with non-elementary treatises, hence though I own all his works, I have found little inspiration in any save "The Young Chemist". I have some archaic text-books which my grandfather used in his youth, but they are quite obsolete. Chemistry has changed vastly in the past sixty or seventy years. At one time I was especially interested in the more minutely theoretical aspects of chemistry—atoms—ions—electrons—&c., but find all this has changed immensely since my day. Some articles which your father recommended to me showed how radically the science has progressed since I ceased greatest activity. One phase of chemistry in which I dabbled was spectrum-analysis, & I still have my spectroscope—a rather low-priced diffraction instrument costing $15.00. I have also a still cheaper *pocket* spectroscope,[13] which was the delight of my fellow students at H.S.H.S. It is unbelievably tiny—will go into a vest pocket without making much of a bulge—yet gives a neat, bright little spectrum, with clear Frauenhofer lines when directed at sunlight. Many are the times I have passed it around at school. Radio-activity interested me enough to cause me to obtain a spinthariscope—containing, of course, a minute quantity of radioactive matter. Speaking of science in general—I have an excellent *microscope,* which I have used for various purposes. I must again ask pardon for an autobiographical lapse. My boyhood, on account of my slightly better health & consequently more active life, is crowded with events as compared with my older years; hence its memories are still of utmost vividness. All these things seem as but yesterday—in fact, it would not be at all hard for me to forget the last decade altogether, & imagine myself not much older than you!

I am sorry that modesty caused you to refrain from telling your early experiences in "uplifting the public", for I am sure they must be interesting. My last attempt was in 1914–16, when I laboured with a "literary" club of Micks who dwelt in the dingy "North End" of the city. The brightest of them was an odd bigoted fellow named Dunn, two years older than I. He hated

England & was a violent pro-German—& I was foolish enough to waste time trying to convert him—as if an Irishman could reason!! Even after I gave up the club as hopeless, I continued corresponding with this fellow, for he was well-meaning & quite intelligent in his way. But in 1917 came events which caused me to drop him. He took the war very badly, & wrote treasonable letters by the score. When the draft came, he refused to register, & was arrested by government agents. In July he was drafted, but refused to respond to the summons—hence was court-martialled & sentenced to 20 years in the Atlanta Federal Prison—where he still languishes, I presume. I am done with Dunn!

Your repertorial work has assuredly been most exacting of late—yet it must be interesting in its way. To a recluse it seems very picturesque. I wish I lived in Appleton & could help you on some of the hard assignments—though I should probably be more of a hindrance than a help.

August 30.

Since adjourning yesterday the following self-explanatory post-card has come to hand:

8/27/18

My dear Lo:

  I have received a post-card from my local board advising me to "be ready to go between Sept. 3d & Sept 6th." I expect the final notification this wk. This will mean a change of plans in regard to the U.A.P.A.

  Sincerely,

  R. Kleiner

In other words, Klei hath been drafted at last, and the burden of the Presidency is likely to fall at once upon Consul Hasting, Esq. It is possible that if Klei is placed in some clerkship on this side of the sea, [he goes only for limited service as a clerk] he may be able to finish his term without nominally resigning—but in any case you will be the real leader, & will most probably be elevated to supreme office. I hope you may not find your new duties oppressive—count on me to give you all the assistance & coöperation in my power. Your promotion will automatically make M^rs. Jordan 1st V.P., leaving another 2nd V.P. to be appointed. (At least, this is what I think the Constitution says, though I have not a copy before me) But first let us see just how nearly total Klei's cessation of activity will have to be.

I have been re-reading "Marsh-Mad"—& the more I analyse it the better I like it! I shall make every effort to get this in the official organ—failing which I shall send it to Cook with positive instructions *not* to give it to Moloney but to use it himself. That is far too good to waste on any but a first-rate paper! Try it on the *Black Cat*[14] professionally. I have been thinking about how to modify my own living-tree plot, & I think I see a way to convey the central idea without resorting to ligneous consciousness. It will make the narrative somewhat more complex & elaborate, but that will [be] all the better.

August 31

Still another interval! Before I forget to mention it, let me express my appreciation of Emerson's "Culture", which is assuredly full of sensible precepts & acute observations. Measured by the Emersonian standard, I am certainly lacking in even culture, for many phases of life in its fuller sense have been, & are likely to continue, sealed pages to me. To be actually cultured, one must needs possess a multiplicity of exquisite tastes and social graces, and a range of mild interests, far beyond the sphere of a feeble & sequestered egotist. I have far too much impatience of disposition to become absorbed in many of the minor aspects of perfect beauty which are theoretically essential to absolute culture. I am not so sensitive to beauty that I require every nicety of perfection in stationery, bookbinding, and furnishing, as is the case with some persons I know. Many pictures on my wall, for example, are lacking in artistic perfection, yet are retained for various reasons, and do not outrage my aesthetic sense every time I contemplate them. In art also I show a lack of breadth and profundity. I used to think I was a devotee of classic art—but when I analysed my predilection I found it was not so much intrinsic & intelligent, as because classic art reminded me of the classic Graeco-Roman age which I so much admired as a whole. Still—I think I possess a distinct preference for the ideals & technique of the ancients. In modern art—painting—I am as one-sided as in most things. I have no appreciation of portraiture, but am captivated by landscapes—mostly quiet rural scenes in England. In this connexion—I have a curious fondness for *one particular type* of scene—a rustic panorama with much verdure & possibly a quiet river in the foreground, and in the background many low hills, with a steepled hamlet resting in their midst. In my own disastrous attempts at pictorial art, I have tried to reproduce innumerable modifications of this favourite subject. I am more acutely sensitive to *architecture* than to any other form of visual art—in fact, certain architectural combinations have the power of pleasing & repelling me very powerfully. I have never yet been able to understand how human beings *can live* in absolutely ugly localities. Just as you might surmise, I love 18ᵗʰ century architecture above all else for residences and gardens—though for other types of buildings Gothic & Graeco-Roman forms appeal to me. I do not care over much for the Italian Renaissance types now so prevalent in local public edifices. As a rule, I have the ancient classical preference for form as opposed to colour. I appreciate *contour* much more than harmonious blending of tints in a decorative scheme. This I take to be an Aryan, western trait. It is Asia & the East that are completely devoted to chromatic beauty. I dislike gaudy hues of every kind except occasionally *in nature*, as, for instance

> The bursting blossoms that bedeck the scene,
> And gaily pie the smooth enamell'd green.

Detached flowers charm me singularly little, & I find it nearly impossible to go into ecstasies over a bouquet. I demand the *natural environment*.

My Poe tastes make me fond of wild scenery and nocturnal landscapes, and I have a great liking for the weird creations of Doré.

But it is in *music* that my crude, uncultured, gothic, barbaric, unappreciative nature makes itself most manifest. Frankness impels me to confess that in this field I have the most execrable & altogether abominable & deficient taste conceivable. The musical classics not only fail to attract me, but actually repel me. An infantile fondness for simple tunes led my mother to start me on violin lessons when I was seven years old, and through the insistence of a teacher who said I had musical genius, the farce was kept up for two years. I played the exercises because I had to—but abhorred all the classics that came before me, and for *pleasure* would go back to whistling those utterly light & frothy tunes which I really enjoyed. In 1899 violin practice made me so nervous that it was stopped by doctor's orders—and thus closeth one branch of L. Theobald's culture. To this day I have not improved, & though I revel in absolutely frivolous light opera & musical comedy airs, I cannot bear serious Music with a capital M. However, I am not so narrow that I do not understand its aesthetic value, & I never laugh at it in the manner of Lord North[15] and other celebrated antimusical personages. So fond am I of *light* and catchy music, that I tried to write a comic opera when about ten years old! But pardon the relapse of autobiographical mania. My egotism is appalling in its thoroughness & persistency. In this case, though, I shall use my sad one-sidedness to point a moral. Let me urge you, in your own aesthetic development, to slight no phase of culture, however uninteresting it may seem to your young mind; lest you become subject to eccentricities & prejudices such as mine. I have sadly few points of contact with the majority of minds, and my mother deems me a rural barbarian indeed. Let thine own culture be more even. Probably you do not need this advice, since you seem to shew remarkable catholicity of interests; yet an old man ever feels it incumbent upon himself to advise his juniors.

I have been reading a great deal of Emerson's work since writing you last, & find him something of a Platonist. He is too humanocentric to furnish a model for such an infinity-roamer as I, yet his ideas are all of remarkable soundness & appeal. He is less annoyingly human than most writers; his poems in particular being almost esoteric. He deals with ψυχή unalloyed, yet never seems to reach out beyond the sphere of the familiar. He seems to forget that there may be such a thing as *mind* utterly unlike anything we know—whose only trait in common with human mind is the one eternal entity of *pure reason*. All in all, I think I can see how he became, as he did, the centre of a sort of cult in New-England. His qualities united profound insight with acute common sense. He was typical of the best thought of his era & locality. Comparing Emerson with Poe, my choice falls to the latter. The Baltimorean had the more genuine Pierian spark, and both in boldness of thought & beauty of art was the superior. Emerson is an excellent guide to practical living, but as a creative artist Edgar A. outruns him. Emerson's conception of poesy was as an exalted expression of philosophical truth—which is not correct. Poe hated the metaphysical bards, & vowed beauty to be the poet's goal. Both men were intellectual giants, & will forever add to the lustre of literature & the pride of their native land.

Speaking of Poe—I hope you received the letter I wrote you discussing his "Eureka".[16] In your last, I noticed no specific reference to it; & knowing the uncertain state of the mails, I take this occasion to enquire. It contained also the latest copy of *Les Mouches*.[17]

But I must conclude at last, since I have a fearsome amount of typing to do. I trust you will send me your critical report when it is complete.

I enclose a bit of Latinistic nonsense for your amusement. It need not be returned.

With customary expressions of esteem, and the hope that I may ere long be favoured with an epistle from your direction, I beg yᵉ honour, my dear Sir, to subscribe myself as

> Yr. most humble, most obedient Servt.
> Alexander Pope

Notes

1. Published in Galpin's amateur journal, the *Philosopher* (December 1920).

2. This is the plot of HPL's "The Tree" (1921).

3. HPL wrote both stories in the summer of 1917, after an eight-year hiatus in fiction writing.

4. An early version of HPL's "The Eidolon."

5. "Lovecraft—an Appreciation" (*Tryout* 4, No. 8 [August 1918]: 1–2; rpt. in Goodenough's "Further Recollections of Amateur Journalism," *Vagrant* [Spring 1927]: 101–2). HPL was taken aback by Goodenough's somewhat grotesque compliment: ". . . I make no doubt / Laurels from thy very temples sprout."

6. "To Arthur Goodenough, Esq."

7. Kleiner visited HPL in Providence in 1917 and 1918.

8. Muriel P. Kelly, Secretary of the UAPA.

9. Cf. HPL, "Report of First Vice-President" (*United Amateur*, November 1915): "A less spectacular but nevertheless considerable work is the gradual free distribution of files of The Amateur Journalist, Mr. James H. Chase's extremely valuable but now discontinued magazine, among the newer members of high grade. The complete file consists of five numbers, and will be sent on application to any person who has not already received it. The undersigned has at his disposal, through the generosity of Mr. Chase, the entire remaining stock of the magazine, approximately one hundred complete sets" (*CE* 1.81)

10. David Van Bush (1882–1959), "psychological lecturer," founder of *Mind Power Plus,* and longtime revision client of HPL. HPL proposed Van Bush's reinstatement in the UAPA in 1922 (he had joined originally in 1916).

11. Nonexistant.

12. Dr. Franklin Chase Clark (1847–1915).

13. The spectroscope is a key instrument employed in "The Colour out of Space."

14. An early magazine (1895–1922) devoted to horror and suspense.

15. Frederick North, Earl of Guilford (1732–1792), prime minister of England during the American Revolution.

16. *Eureka: A Prose Poem* (1848), a philosophical study of the mystical and material unity of the universe.

17. See letter 2n23.

[5]   [ALS]

ROMAE.

A.D. XIV. KAL. NOV. [1918][1]
M. RINARTIO CLINA.
A. GALPINIO. SECVNDO. COSS.[2]

L. METADIVS. CAELO. A. GALPINIO. SECVNDO. S.D.
SI. TV. VALES. BENE. EST. EGO. QVOQVO. VALEO.[3]

Let me open this document with a spirited defence of your colleague in the consulship, M. Rinartius Clina, who to you a pain administereth. It is not through negligence but through misfortune that our leader is so silent. His mother is gravely ill with Spanish influenza, & though he has assistance in the daytime, he has to act as her nurse throughout the night. He is utterly exhausted, & to cap the climax is now fighting a cold which may prove to be the same affliction from which his patient is suffering. This influenza is nothing light, & I certainly hope Appleton may escape. I fancy you will agree that under the circumstances we must admire Klei's fortitude & filial devotion, rather than criticise his unavoidable inactivity! Klei offers once more to resign, but I really think we should not accept his resignation. Care after care seems to beset him, & he deserves all the encouragement & displays of confidence which we can give him. Once he is "out of the woods", I am sure he can conduct a tolerably efficient administration. He now asks me to instruct the following officers in their duties—a task he would cheerfully discharge if able:

> 1st Vice-President
> Secretary
> Laureate Recorder.

Beginning with the 1st V.P., I find it hard to lay down any set programme; mainly because Vice-Presidents have hitherto been very independent (when not inactive) folk—working on their own initiative & according to their own ideas. When I was V.P.[4] my work was overshadowed by the 2nd V.P. department, then under the direction of that incredibly energetic recruiter Mrs. Renshaw; & I did little save follow up the multitudinous prospectives she unearthed. But in general, I fancy the following things should be done.

(a) Form your committee by securing definite acceptances from as many persons as you can. Tell them their duties—to write all persons whose names you may send for such a purpose—and make up some suitable form letters for their use. If the men I suggested on my postal card will not serve, try others. Try young Nixon of Florida, whose letter I enclose. Get Ingold to join & act if you can.[5] New members sometimes make the best recruiters, being enthusiastic & impressed with the novelty of amateurdom. If you cannot secure the full quota of seven, less will do. I never knew all the members of a committee to be faithful workers, anyway!

(b) Unearth as many prospectives as you can, & ask your subordinates to do the same. For young boys, an element we desire very strongly, cull the names of prize-winners from the B.K.B. department of *Browning's Magazine*.[6] For mature persons, look up the names of authors in *religious* (!) papers—who are never paid for their work, & are therefore potential amateurs. Also—scan the "readers' column" in various magazines; where the public express opinions & sometimes give bits of verse. Ask Mrs. Jordan to send you lists of *Boston Post* prize-winners. High-school & college publications ought to furnish many names, which you & the 4th V.P. can apportion betwixt yourselves. Rely not at all on the 3d. V.P., but write her anyway—see if you can accomplish the impossible by awaking her.[7] A new voice might arouse her dormant sense of responsibility. Prepare your lists of "prospects" for distribution amongst committee members, giving in addition to each name a brief description of the person in question, as judged from what you have read. Whenever you receive a reply, pass it around amongst your committee, so that each member can send "follow-up" matter. Tell your members to send their replies around in the same way. It is much easier to write a person whose letter you have seen. Finally—go ahead with the *St. Nicholas* idea you outlined a few months ago.

If there is nothing new or enlightening in these simple bits of advice, blame my stupidity & incompetency rather than question my intent or willingness to help. I desire to assist as much as I can, & will be glad to answer to the best of my limited ability any question you may ask. As to the critical question, my resignation has met with considerable disapproval, and Klei refuses to accept it; implying that I am deserting the United in time of need. In view of this, & in view of his own inability to be active just now, I have left the matter in his hands & am hanging on a while. But I shall make you do more work—July

Brooklynite, Pathfinder, & all the *Silver Clarions* which come your way, & anything else I can think of to burden you with. There is no hurry, though. Influenza is holding up the work at Athol, & there may be an amalgamation of Sept^r. & Novr numbers of the U.A. I hope Cook's family is better, & that Moloney lived through his attack after all. His life was despaired of at the time of Cook's last note.

As to Secretary's instructions—I will ask you to see that this official does the following things:

(a) Send Kleiner a large batch of blank certificates for Presidential signature.

(b) Record each application received; send the applicants their certificates, properly filled out, with suitable words of welcome; and send all credentials to one or both of the MS. Bureaux—preferably the *Eastern,* unless she can endure dealing with that utterly impossible Haughton creature.[8]

(c) Once in two months make out a report of all new members, reinstatements, & renewals, sending it in duplicate to Official Editor & President—or better still in *triplicate* to O.E., PRES., & 1st V.P. In this list should be included all changes of address.

(d) Once in two months send all money received to the Treasurer, specifying whether from new members, or for reinstatements or renewals. It is best to itemise it—thus:

```
From John Smith, membership fee --------------------------0.50
  "      Robert Jones,     "        "-------------------------0.50
  "      James Brown, reinstatement -------------------------1.00
  "      Joseph Addison, renewal ---------------------------1.00
  Total -----------------------------------------------------3.00
```

(e) Notify by postal card EVERY member whose dues lapse—telling him his membership has expired & urging him to renew. Acknowledge all voluntary renewals & re-instatements.

Let me furthermore ask you to initiate your 4th V.P. in any manner you deem wise. This official is legally your subordinate, & is of course to work as the 1st V.P.'s department sees fit. Of course, as you say, Mistress חושב[9] will not need such explicit guidance as a less bright & competent person might require; but her department is under yours according to the constitution, & the two must necessarily coöperate closely. No one knows yet, just how the 4th V.P. dept. ought to work out its details of administration. It was devised by the nebulous Miss Lehr, who was expected to supervise the development of her idea, but failed as usual to do so. As the only living ex-4th V.P., you ought to know more about the thing than anyone else. Miss A. is indeed a bright infant—she quoted Cicero & has decided opinions on many questions. Had I not encountered the young consul A. Galpinius Secundus first, I should consider her rather a prodigy—a species in which your town seems unusually rich. I have notified Klei of Miss Merkel's selection for the Reception Comm. Chairmanship, & presume he will endorse it as usual. It is very generous of Appleton to finance the blanks. I will help out if necessary, since so much of my peerless prose adorns their reverse side.

Daas complains of not hearing from you. He tells me *I* am Chairman of the Directors, & wants me to take the first steps in unearthing the true inwardness of the old official organ debt—conflicting statements concerning which emanate from Campbell & Cheney.[10] I expect to see him in December when he visits New England—& Cook also expects to see him. At present he is busy organising a local club in Washington, D.C., assisted by Mrs. Renshaw.[11] I hope it will be more literary than his Milwaukee *vereins.* Probably it will be, since Mrs. R. is a genuine litterateuse, & likely to be prominent in anything she is concerned with.

Turning to your epistle, I am impressed by your super-active life—which reminds me of our colleague Mo & his incessant whirl of duties. The *Crescent* near-scoop is very interesting. Our papers took no such trouble last Saturday, being content to issue the "big news" in the Sunday editions. But perchance the ☽ and ⚓ have no Sunday editions. Let me congratulate you on your success as a newsboy—I hope you shouted "Extry!" "Extree!" in approved style.

I have witnessed "Hearts of the World",[12] & agree with the approbation which your recommendation implies. It is certainly effective in the highest degree, histrionically, mechanically, & artistically in general. As presented in Providence, an appropriate orchestral accompaniment enhanced its vividness & appeal. If it is less striking than "The Birth of a Nation",[13] it is because of a necessary lack of quaintness, (which, however, Griffith does his best to supply) a certain remoteness of locale which contrasts with the immediate scene of the older picture, and a lack of traditionary background such as is afforded by Civil War problems, which have been discussed & portrayed for half a century by every fireside. Then too—the excellence & magnitude form less of a *surprise.* The "Birth" prepared us for something great, and we are *satisfied* rather than taken off our feet. Continuing in the dramatick line, but ascending the scale several degrees, I find "Hamlet" a most absorbing character, even as you do. It is hard for me to give an original estimate or opinion, since other commentators' opinions are so abundant; but I find in Hamlet a rare, delicate, & nearly poetical mind, filled with the highest ideals and pervaded by the delusion (common to all gentle & retired characters unless their temperament be scientific & predominantly rational—which is seldom the case with poets) that all humanity approximates such a standard as he conceives. All at once, however, man's inherent baseness becomes apparent to him under the most soul-trying circumstances; exhibiting itself not in the remote world, but in the person of his mother & his uncle, in such a manner as to convince him most suddenly & most vitally that there is no good in humanity. Well may he question life, when the perfidiousness of those whom he has reason to believe the best of mortals, is so cruelly obtruded on his notice. Having had his theories of life founded on mediaeval and pragmatical conceptions, he now loses that subtle something which impels persons to go on in the ordinary currents; specifically, he loses the conviction that the usual motives & pursuits of life are more than empty illusions or trifles. Now this is not *"madness"*—I am sick of hearing fools & superficial critics prate about "Hamlet's madness". It is really a distressing glimpse of *absolute truth*. But *in effect*, it approximates mental derangement. Reason is unimpaired, but Hamlet no longer sees any occasion for its use. He perceives the objects & events about him, & their relation to each other & to himself, as clearly as before; but his new estimate of their importance, and his lack of any aim or desire to pursue an ordinary course amongst them, impart to his point of view such a contemptuous, ironical singularity, that he may well be thought a madman by mistake. He sums up this position himself when he says:

> "How weary, stale, flat, & unprofitable
> Seem to me all the uses of this world!
> Fie on't! ah, fie! 'tis an unweeded garden
> That grows to seed. Things rank & gross in Nature
> Possess it merely."[14]

Now comes the ghost business—which (leaving out Marcello's, Bernardo's & Horatio's sight of the ghost) ought to be taken allegorically as the growth of a terrible *suspicion* in Hamlet's mind. He now hath an object in the world—Revenge!! Rrrevenge!!! His devotion to this object is necessarily enhanced by the absence of all other objects. He seizes it as his one guiding motive in a life devoid of all other motives; it sustains, energises, awakens, & perhaps even *comforts* him. In his assumption of madness, he gains verisimilitude from the lightness with which he regards life. Stolid critics fancy no man could think up such extraordinary grotesqueries & incoherencies as Hamlet's, were he not somewhat deranged; indeed, a very prosaic & dignified personage of strict sanity *would* have a hard time doing so. But we must remember that to Hamlet *all the world* & its pitifully inconsequential doings are just as grotesque as any fantastical babbling can be. Having so slight an estimate of human dignity, Hamlet delights in pseudo-idiotick satire, through which even ivory-skull'd old Polonius can glimpse enough light to mutter:

> "Tho' this be madness, yet there's method in't."[15]

As the Prince himself saith; 'when the wind is southerly, he knoweth an hawk from an hand-saw'![16] All this grim phantasy is intensified by Hamlet's intense temperament.

Throughout the action of the play the attitude of Hamlet is clearly shewn. In the artless grace & affection of Oleary—I mean Ophelia—he sees but delusive & superficial qualities. His killing of Polonious affords him merely an opportunity to vent more cynicism—"how a King may go a progress thro' the guts of a beggar."[17] In the churchyard scene Hamlet's contempt of man is the central theme. In skulls & rotting flesh he sees the end of all humanity. What is the use of life? Alas, poor Yorick!

> "Imperious Caesar, dead & turn'd to clay,
> Might stop a hole to keep the wind away;
> Oh, that that earth, which kept the world in awe,
> Should patch a wall t' expel the winter's flaw!"[18]

It is in consonance with this nature, that Hamlet always drifts. Not even his dire purpose causes him to do anything save when circumstance directs. His detachment from human motives destroys the correlation of will & action, & makes him dependent upon circumstance. Whatever he does actively, is brought about by causes or situations outside himself—a fact that makes "Hamlet" a true tragedy, wherein Fate is the impelling power. Hamlet's is the poetic, visionary, semi-irresolute mind. He recognises his limitations in the speech beginning "Oh, what a rogue & peasant slave am I".[19]

But let me bore you no longer with these disjointed & probably unoriginal observations. Probably a thousand writers have said the same thing—perhaps you have yourself, in the essay which prompted your interest in the unfortunate Prince. Let me see your theme when copied; it may not be too long for some amateur journal, after all. You will do well to study Shakespeare more detailedly than in school. He is certainly a splendid exemplification of genius, & the most natural reproducer of Nature & mankind in literary history. In variety & range he stands alone. However—I could never be such a Shakespearite as your Hypatia. The freedom, irregularity, & anachronisms of the great bard weary me when administered in too great doses. For purely pleasant reading, I seem to sink back into my favourite age of Pope. I can sympathise a trifle with Mr. Dryden, who writ of Shakespeare, albeit admiringly & sympathetically, that he was

> "Untaught, unpractis'd, in a barb'rous age."[20]

I shall be interested to see just what you substituted for the "nameless vagueosity" previously designed for the *Pippin*.[21] I am glad you are taking to *heroicks*. The editor informed me that you had contributed to the magazine "a poem which will give it the necessary high & abstract quality", but I know not whether she referred to the original effusion, or to the hastily substituted heroicks. I am sorry Father Mo was so iconoclastic—though I had an idea there was some room for improvement in the lines, despite your expressed conviction that you would never do better work. Unless you object, I think I shall send the piece, with a title & under an absolutely unrecognisable pseudonym such as "Cyril Fitz-James Grosvenor" or "Percival Byron Flanagan", to the *Tryout*[22]—just to see what comment it may elicit from the publick. Keep on with versification, and do not let any amount of criticism dampen the poetick feeling to which you allude. As your style grows increasingly clear, your work will become more & more manifestly meritorious.

Last Sabbath Day I mailed to you a couple of *Amateur Journalist* files—one for you and t'other for your Delia-Margarita. As I said before, you ought to have the opportunity of making the benefaction in person. I am surprised to hear that the wingèd Eleanora[23] takes second place in your young affections. Pray do not fracture the sweet Hypatia's heart, or drive her to suicide! The 4th V.P. saith that the Lady Eleanora is quite a pote-ess, & intendeth to become an English teacher. I advise you to wed her in preference to the Delia person. Never mind Delia's looks—they will soon fade! Probably she will make a hideous-appearing old woman fifty years from now, whilst Misses Hypatia and Eleanora will be distinguished old ladies, either or both of whom would do you credit as spouses. You interest me in Mr. John Ingold, Jr. Try to secure him for the United! I hope the additional man-power in the Press Club may not be quite so mediocre as you fancy—at least, I hope some of it may become interested enough to join the United. I fear, though, that the Hon. Silas Buchman, or to put it classically, C. Silius Bucmanus Saltator, would hardly be desirable. We are in no need of dancers or other frivolous folk. Was it not my old friend M. Tullius Cicero who said in some oration or other, "Nemo fere saltat sobrius, nisi forte insanit!"?[24] I trust Ericson[25] may issue your *Pippin* by 1919 or 1920. He will never acquire the cognomen or agnomen of *celer*[26]—though to do the man justice, I believe he hath reform'd enough of late to print the Hon. Jno. Milton Samples' *Silver Clarion* on an approximately monthly schedule.

I am astonished to hear that der *Staats-Zeitung*[27] iss allowedt in der ☽ office.[28] Ach! I thought Mr. Meyer vass giving avay Lipperty Loan posters mit der paper—dot he vass all conferted to Amerikanism yet alretty! At least, such was the semi-impression I received from your poetick friend Mrs. Arnold. By the way—that good lady recently sent two pieces for revision at professional rates, & one of them was a really splendid albeit simple lyric—better than anything from her pen which I had previously seen. The metre was all tangled up, but when unravelled, the result was surprisingly good.

Speaking of clients—you & Miss Durr will be satisfied at last. I am a real labouring man! In other words, I have undertaken to make a thorough & exhaustive revision of Rev. D. V. Bush's long prose book—now called "Pike's Peak or Bust", though part of my job is to find another name.[29] Rev. David is now Religious Director of the Central Y.M.C.A. of St Louis. I do not see how the fellow manages to get on so in the world. He is, literarily, such a complete d—— fool!

I have decided not to alter the name of *The Conservative*, though it does incense me to find the title preëmpted. Has your *National Amateur* arrived? I asked Cook to be sure to remember you regularly.

I hope Mo *is* working on the *Gallo'mo*. Otherwise I should fear he has dropped me altogether. Deep broods the silence o'er the templed hills of Madison!

> VALE.

> L. METADIVS. CAELO.

Notes

1. This letter was written 18 or 19 October.

2. "In the consulship of M. Rinartius Clina and A. Galpinius Secundus." Kleiner and Galpin were president and first vice-president of the UAPA for the 1918–19 term. In mid-September 1918, HPL wrote a mock drama about Galpin's high school romances, called *Alfredo* with Rheinhart Kleiner as King Rinarto and himself as Teobaldo.

3. The standard opening of a Latin letter: "L. Metadius Caelo sends greetings to A. Galpinius Secundus. If you are well, it is good; I am also well." Caelo is imaginary.

4. HPL was first vice-president in 1915–16, when he wrote the recruiting pamphlet *United Amateur Press Association: Exponent of Amateur Journalism* (1915).

5. Raymond B. Nixon of Tallahassee, whose paper was the *Capital City News;* John Ingold, Jr. of Appleton, WI.

6. *Browning's Magazine* (1890–1922) had a department called "Beta Kappa Beta," where boys eighteen and older could exchange views on sports and other interests.

7. The 4th vice-president of the UAPA in 1918 was Margaret Abraham (Appleton, WI); the 3rd vice-president in 1918–19 was Mary Henrietta Lehr (Redlands, CA).

8. Ida C. Haughton (1868–1935?), an amateur living in Columbus, OH, and editor of the *Woodbee*, was at this time western manuscript manager. She would later become involved in a bitter dispute with HPL over the administration of the UAPA; in response, HPL wrote the vicious satirical poem "Medusa: A Portrait" (1921).

9. I.e., Margaret Abraham (HPL's Hebrew is the masculine form of the word meaning "intelligent").

10. Fred W. Cheney of Georgetown, IL.

11. Anne Tillery Renshaw (1890?–1953?) of Washington, DC, later to become offical editor of the UAPA (1919–20).

12. *Hearts of the World* (Paramount, 1918), directed by D. W. Griffith; starring Lillian Gish, Dorothy Gish, Robert Harron, and Adolphe Lestina. A propaganda film about World War I.

13. *The Birth of a Nation* (David W. Griffith Corp., 1915), produced and directed by D. W. Griffith; starring Lillian Gish, Mae Marsh, and Henry B. Walthall. A celebrated film about Reconstruction.

14. *Hamlet* 1.2.133–37.

15. *Hamlet* 2.2.204.

16. *Hamlet* 2.2.374.

17. *Hamlet* 4.3.31.

18. *Hamlet* 5.1.203–6. HPL quotes the first two lines in "The Materialist Today" (1926).

19. *Hamlet* 2.2.538.

20. John Dryden (1631–1700), "Prologue" to *Troilus and Cressida,* l. 7.

21. A journal produced by the Appleton High School Press Club. See HPL's two poetic tributes to the *Pippin* (*AT* 346–47, 350–51).

22. HPL published numerous poems in *Tryout* under pseudonyms.

23. Presumably Eleanor Evans Wing of Appleton, WI.

24. Cf. *SL* 1.35. HPL there maintains that he said this ("Scarcely any sober person dances, unless by chance he is mad") to his mother at the age of 8 when she wished him to take dancing lessons. The sentence comes from Cicero's *Pro Mureno* 13 (not the Catilinarian orations, as HPL declared).

25. E. E. Ericson of Elroy, WI, for many years the official printer of the UAPA.

26. Swift. *Celer* is an actual Roman cognomen.

27. The *New York Staats-Zeitung* was one of the oldest German-language newspapers in the U.S.

28. Apparently a reference to the *Volkszeitung,* a German-language newspaper published in Appleton under the aegis of the *Crescent.* In his autobiographical notes, Galpin reports that it "soon disappeared as a war casualty."

29. The original edition was *"Pike's Peak or Bust"; or, The Possibilities of the Will* (Webster, SD: The Reporter & Farmer, 1916). There is no record of a revised edition.

[6]   [ALS, leaves III–IV only]

                                                                    30th June [1922]

[. . .]

Pray send the preceding two sheets, writ yesterday, to our Presbyterian pal Mocrates. He likes the travelogue stuff,[1] as I have before intimated. I now have your more recent cards & letter, & am infinitely delighted to learn with how great felicity the Galpinio-Lovemanick meeting was effected. I was quite certain that you wou'd be surpris'd with the scholastick attainments & engaging manners of S L, since I am so well aware alike of their vast extent & of S L's custom of systematically underrating & understating them. The modesty of the great one is almost incredible. Your coming will be a tremendous boon to one who is not only lonely & unappreciated, but singularly susceptible to the pangs caused by that condition. I had already gather'd that his family are out of sympathy with him—you must teach him to regard them as mere inconsequential parts of the landscape; beyond the radius of worriment, as it were. That so vast a scholar & genius shou'd regard me & my works with favour, is indeed a source of gratification to me. Dulce est, saith an old proverb, laudari a viro laudato![2] I hope he realises, in return, the vast esteem & admiration in which I hold him & everything connected with him. Certainly, there is no one of any degree of taste who knows him, but shares this high opinion.

Small Belknap hath just sent Mme. G.[3] an acknowledgment of the new *Rainbow*, & most of his text consists of an extended rhapsody on the arts & graces of the distinguish'd author of the "Letter to G. K." Pray tell this to S L in case Mme G. does not send him the epistle.

This reminds me that said Belknap is indeed a tantalisingly infrequent correspondent. I must limber the child up—at least to the extent of letting him know that he is on the particularly favour'd list. A great boy—I hope I can persuade him to stop off a day in Providence whilst on his way to the summer camp at Lebec Lake, Maine.

I wish that I might get to Cleveland—Aedepol! how I wish it! But apparently any serious attempt would rend #598 with a civil war of no mean proportions. Poverty—ugh! how I hate it! Ask Sam what it's like! My best hope of seeing you lies in a possible Lovemanic move to N.Y.—faintly shadow'd forth in a recent epistle of his to Mme. Greenevna. That might lure you thither to see him—& then Grandpa'd get there if he had to be a stowaway on the New-York Boat!

Monday—night before the Fourth

'Sh no ushe! Jesh shimply can't get zish letter done! One thing after another comesh up! This time it was a campaign matter. Campbell's sister-in-law, Miss Eliz. Barnhart, is planning an anti-Woodbee paper—a mock *United Amateur* as Fritter would edit it—& asked me to contribute the "credentials" in a hurry so that the thing can be hustled out before convention. I concocted three spoofs like your old *Clarion* wheeze—the Knutzenel prize-winning Ford essay—representing the sort of stuff Fritter would accept & publish. One is a "poem"—"The Wonderful Hills" by Hiram N. Good. Another is a social-amateur "essay"—"A Day in the Country" by Otto Nobetter. The third is a "story"—"Uncle John's Legacy",* by Bella Dumm. I don't know how funny they really are, but they were at least funny enough to convulse Mme. G. with mirth. I guess they'll give the Won't-Bes a reasonably *mauvais quart d'heure*. Miss Barnhart is going to print the thing herself on Campbell's press, with intentional misspellings & misprints.[4]

My aunt tells me that the Gallic stuff has safely arrived at #598. Thanks, O Tiny Hyacinth-Bud! Shall be damn glad to see it when I get home. All right about the amateur stuff—any time—no hurry—n'importe.

Thanks for the kind words anent that first attempt at Baudelairian translation.[5] It was merely a piece of luck, though, if it was any good. Perchance I'll try the second again, using your literal translation, when I get home & see the original again. Sure I'll do some more if they'll do ya any good, Kid! But don't expect anything worth anything.

---

*If it doesn't beat "Aunt Minerva's Ku Klux", I'm a damn liar!

This region is not as near the Haverhill section as I thought, so I shall not be able to drop in on the Davis kid.[6] When I get home I'll send you his 18-pager, so that you can judge him more fully even if you don't care to adopt him as a literary grandson. By the way—it looks as though the Galpinian cast-asides are going to found a scholastic salon of their own, for this a.m. there blew into the Magnolia P.O. two bulky duplicate letters for Mme. G. & myself, from good ol' Mocrates in Madisonium. He calls the new circle the *Gremolo,* & doubtless intends it as the standard refuge for rejected second-raters. Well, I'm glad something waked the old sport up—I like him.

About that Carlylean puff for the Old Gent's stories—t'anks, Sonny! Glad you can speak well of 'em! Shall read the completed work with interest. Mme. G. has just taken to this sort of composition—has written one & planned two more—& I'm damned if they don't look like good stuff! The first one, "Four O'Clock", has some images noxiously Poe-esque—I shall polish it up for use in the U.A. or something else.[7] The others pertain to the sea, attesting to the inspiring effect of the wild Magnolian coast & the colourful (& odourful) harbour of antique Gloucester.

The Glorious 4th—9 a.m.

Some day I guess I'll give the immortal Remy the once-over—he sounds interesting.[8] That crack about fire is a wise one—my uncle-in-law Dr. Clark once made a very detailed study of the "descent of fire" & legends appertaining thereto, even going so far as to make an excellent translation of an especially apposite article in your favourite lingo—an article in the *Revue des Deux Mondes.*[9]

About "Arcady"[10]—I'll follow your instructions when I get home & have the lines before me. It is a riotous intoxication of aesthetic magnificence—who gives a damn what it's about? But Sam's obscurity will, of course, always tend to baffle the academic mind. Mo gives a cruel anecdote in the new *Gremolo,* which you must not repeat to SL on pain of death. He had shew'd the "Letter to G. K." to an English professor at your delightful alma mater, & asked him what he thought of the line

"The red Lustration of a Soul that dies"[11]

—whereupon the literate one responded: "Sounds like a hemorrhage!" I hope the guy wasn't your friend Bill Ellery.[12]

Now that you & Sam are together, I trust you can synchronise the "Hermaphrodite" & the critique for inclusion in July U.A. copy.[13] The May issue is still in press, & there is no hurry. *I will omit Bingville Bugle Notes* from the Loveman issue. I hope you will change your mind about poem—it ought to appear, & it's too late for the (May) issue with the Saturnian critique.[14]

Well, I'd better shut up. Lemme hear from ya as often as ya care to sling the new quasi-Lovemanick violet ink or pound the newly beribboned Corona.

And give my most abundant regards to your illustrious companion; urging, encouraging, entreating him to drop a line to his aged grandfather!

Yr obt Servt

M. LOLLIUS

Notes

1. The first two leaves of this letter presumably contained an account of HPL's trip through New Hampshire in early June 1922 (cf. *SL* 1.183–85).
2. "It is sweet to be praised by a man who has been praised."
3. Sonia H. Greene, the second number of whose *Rainbow* was published in May 1922. Among other contributions, it contained Loveman's poem "Letter to G—— K——," addressed to George Kirk. See n. 11.
4. It is not clear whether this paper was ever published.
5. Evidently a reference to HPL's attempt at "translating" a poem of Baudelaire (presumably from *Les Fleurs du mal*) based upon a literal prose translation by Galpin.
6. Edgar J. Davis of Haverhill, MA, with whom HPL made a trip to Newburyport in April 1923.
7. There is no known publication of Sonia H. Greene's "Four O'Clock" prior to its appearance in *Something about Cats and Other Pieces* (1949). Greene maintained that she wrote it entirely herself at HPL's suggestion, but HPL here implies that he plans to revise the story.
8. Remy de Gourmont (1858–1915), author of *A Night in the Luxembourg* (1906; Eng. tr. 1912), read by HPL in the autumn of 1923 (*SL* 1.250).
9. The *Revue des Deux Mondes* is a leading French journal, founded in 1831, and is still published.
10. A poem by Samuel Loveman (*National Amateur*, March 1908).
11. Samuel Loveman, "A Letter to G—— K——," *Rainbow* No. 2 (May 1922): 15, l. 6.
12. William Ellery Leonard (1876–1944), poet, classical scholar, and professor at the University of Wisconsin.
13. A *United Amateur* for July 1922 did not appear.
14. Loveman's amateur magazine, the *Saturnian,* ran for three issues. Galpin addressed the third issue in "Department of Public Criticism" (May 1922).

[7]   [ANS][1]

[Postmarked Brooklyn, N.Y.,
8 October 1922]

Hey, Kid! Recd. your latest, & will answer presently. Am showing my aunt the big town. Glad as the deuce you're coming to Columbia—I'll sure manage to see you! ¶ What the _____ did you write Sommer[2] about Loveman? For Pegāna's sake take an old man's advice about considerateness unless you want to hurt the whole bally circle of your acquaintants! More anon.

Grandpa

Best regards from S. H. G.

Francois + TIBALDVS

James F. Morton, Jr.

A. E. P. Gamwell (aunt of Theobaldus)

Notes

1. *Front:* The Parthenon (model). The Metropolitan Museum of Art. Addressed to "Dr. Alfred Galpin, Jun." Signed by HPL, Sonia H. Greene, Frank Belknap Long, James F. Morton, and Annie E. P. Gamwell.

2. William Sommer (1867–1949), painter and member of Hart Crane's literary circle whom HPL had met in Cleveland.

[8]   [ANS][1]

[Postmarked Brooklyn, N.Y.,
12 October 1922]

Just read Belnape's epistle—for —'s sake chuck the free verse! Hope you got my letter all right. Have been tiring out my aunt—taking her to museums, Van Cortlandt mansion, & Columbia College. Tonight the gang dines at Belnape's—pipe de Jawn Hancocks;[2]

Grandpa Theobald & aunt A.E.P.G.

Mrs. F. B. Long

Francois

S.H.G.

T. S. Eliot

Edgar A. Poe

Notes

1. *Front:* The Dutch Room. Van Cortlandt House.

2. Signed by HPL, Annie E. P. Gamwell, Frank Belknap Long and his mother, and Sonia H. Green. The person(s) who signed as Eliot and Poe are not known.

[9]   [ANS][1]

[Postmarked Providence, R.I.,
21 November 1922]

Hey, Kid! Back from Boston—& have brung A. M. Adams, Esq. with me to shew him a *real* city. Pipe de art stuff! Yeh—we gotta museum just the same as Chi! Glad you saw Hecht, & hope he appreciated the honour. I'll write shortly—Grandpa

Just learning that even Providence has charms

A M Adams

Notes

1. *Front:* Rhode Island School of Design / Hagar and Ishmael, Francesco Collantes (1599–1656). Addressed to "Dr. Alfred Galpin, Jun."

[10]   [To Galpin and Frank Belknap Long] [AHT]

[early February 1923]

To my dear Grandsons, Alfredus and Belnapius;

Children:—

If you will gather close to Grandpa's knee, the Old Gentleman will tell you all about his late trip to Boston, and other parts of the Province of the Massachusetts-Bay.

I left these plantations on Thursday, the 14th of December, arriving at Boston late in the afternoon, where I was met by my genial and scholastick host, the Hon. Edward Cole, of Cambridge. Convey'd by him to his house, a pleasing domicile in the best part of town, near a church, I was regaled by an excellent meal. The better I know Mr. Cole, the more pleas'd I am with him; and the more I regret the lack of earlier acquaintance. His household consists of himself, his wife[1] (an excellent tho' unliterary person), his son by his first wife, (ag'd four and three-quarters) and a daughter by his present wife, ag'd one and three-quarters. The precociousness of both infants is extreamly amazing, and without doubt inherited from their illustrious common parent. The daughter, for example, can at her early age walk and run with perfect vigour, to say naught of playing continually, and talking with much fluency and intelligence. By these children I was greatly reminded of yourselves, who so far surpass all ordinary babes of your years.

After dinner, my host and I set out for Maplewood, in Malden, where I was bespoken to address the Hub Club upon my favourite author, Lord Dunsany.[2] The gathering was bright and numerous, most of the feuds of local writers having been tolerably compos'd; and my remarks were attended with flattering diligence and encomiums. I followed my address with a reading of Dunsany's work, and induc'd several auditors to pledge themselves to a future perusal of him. I am of an opinion, that Lord Dunsany's manner is the only artistick manner possible in this aera of decadence. Scientifick learning having rendered obsolete all the illusions of our youth, and realistick expression having become perforce a chaotick mess like Mr. Eliot's "Waste Land",[3] it behoves the lover of beauty to create an artificial pattern amidst the meaningless desert of Life; and what pattern can be more appropriate to his purposes than that body of mythical thought and fable which Time hath invested with so many priceless associations? After my reading, and the social period which follow'd, Cole and I return'd to his house, which we did not reach till 2 a.m. on account of the snowfall and wretched tram service.

On the following day, my host being occupy'd with the labours of scholastick instruction, I perform'd despite a head-ache a careful tour of the more antique parts of Boston. Chusing the North-End as my seat of travel, I walk'd up
Hanover-Street, view'd the home of Paul Revere, Esq. in North-Square, and
branched off thro' Prince and Salem Streets to Christ-Church, built 1723,
commonly call'd the Old North Church, tho' that edifice was really burnt for
firewood during our occupation of Boston at the time of the Yankee rebellion.
It was in the steeple of this church, that Mr. Revere display'd the traitorous
lanthorns which warn'd the rebels of our coming in 1775. At Christ-Church I
was confronted by a curious small boy, of Italian blood, who began without
looking directly at me to recite in a mechanical monotone the history of the region. The effect was highly comick, since the urchin scarce knew what he was
repeating. I believe he had learnt it by heart, and used it as a means of earning
stray pence from travellers. I was later told, that this region abounds in such
diminutive and acquisitive ciceroni. From Christ-Church I went to Sheafe-
Street, where was born the grandfather of our good friend and companion
Mortonius; the Rev. S. F. Smith, author of the Yankee version of "God Save
the King".[4] A tablet marks the house where he saw the light in 1808. Thence I
proceeded to Hull-Street, and up the steps to that fascinating necropolis which
thro' some singular fate I had never before seen—the Copp's Hill Burying
Ground.[5] Here are interr'd some of the most illustrious Colonial dead of the
Province, including the Mathers, who are interesting to me from my possession
of Cotton Mather's "Magnalia Christi Americana". But the chief charm of the
scene is in the entire broad effect; the bleak hilltop with its horizon of leaden
sky, harbour masts, and Colonial roofs. In sight are many houses of the early
18th century, to say nothing of the rebel frigate "Constitution", which defends
the harbour from attack. Over the sod was a thin coat of snow, thro' which the
slabs peer'd grimly whilst black leafless trees claw'd at a sinister lowering sky. In
fancy I could conjure up the Boston of the late 17th century with its narrow,
hilly, curving streets and quaint wooden and brick houses. At present this part
of the town is abominably squalid, and inhabited by peasant Italians of the filth-
iest description.

From Copp's Hill I proceeded to the corner of Park and Tremont
Streets, where I had agreed to meet my host; but my journey was interrupted
by a stop in Cornhill, where at an old shop I purchas'd the compleat works of
Ch: Lamb, Esq. for two shillings. This collection, in one thick volume, is precisely like the one at Eglin's, in Cleaveland, which was sold to Clarence
Wheeler, Esq. It is well to recall, that this Cornhill is not Boston's original
Cornhill, but meerly Hillier's-Lane renam'd. Cornhill was originally the name
of part of Boston's main street, other parts being call'd Newbury and Marlborough. After the lamented rebellion, the whole thoroughfare was joyn'd,
and invested with the patronymick of the illustrious Genl. Washington; whilst
the former individual names were elsewhere plac'd. Cornhill, as mention'd,

was apply'd to Hillier's-Lane; whilst Newbury and Marlborough were given to new streets later made when the Back-Bay was fill'd in; a circumstance reminding us that much of modern Boston stands on artificial land. The Old Boston of my day was but a slight peninsula, almost an island, containing the North End and Beacon Hill, and linkt to the mainland by a narrow isthmus. Amongst the streets named for illustrious men I was pleas'd to note a Belknap-Street, commemorating the Revd. Jeremy Belknap, minister of a church in Federal-Street, and founder of the Boston Historical Society. The name of this street hath since been chang'd to Joy-Street, and I am sure that no reader of my small Belknap's phantasies can deny that Belknaps invariably afford joy!

Having met Cole, I proceeded with him to the State-House, completed in 1798, whose golden dome was by a poet call'd "The Hub of the Universe".[6] I had often seen, but never enter'd, this distinguished edifice; hence I was glad of expert guidance on this occasion. The modern wings and additions I did not stop to observe. Cole next usher'd me from the rear door, and shew'd me the antique Beacon-Hill district, which also I had never before seen. Here I was mov'd to speechless admiration by the numerous memorials of better days; whole blocks of 18th century brick houses, magnificent Colonial doorways, and an unending succession of picturesque panoramas along the steep narrow streets leading down the hill. The climax was Louisburg-Square, nam'd from our glorious victory over the French in 1745 under Col. Pepperrell, later Sir W: Pepperrell, Bart.[7] This is a perfect Georgian Square in perfect preservation, still decent in population, and quaintly situated on the side of an antient hill. Many literary persons have dwelt therein, and I am sure their work hath gain'd thereby. The hour being now late, Cole and I threaded our way thro' many narrow thoroughfares and down many steep hills, till at last we reach'd the North-Station and travell'd to Cambridge (across the Charles River) by a steam route not often available. That evening was spent at the home of Denys Myers, Esq., an international lawyer of pleasing parts, tho' afflicted with idealistick delusions and a love of universal peace. Mrs. Miniter, the Coles, a colourless couple named Johnston, and myself were the guests; Mr. and Mrs. Myers doing honours in the traditional Boston manner.

On Saturday, the following day, Mrs. Miniter, Cole, and myself, made an exhaustive tour of historick sites. Cole and I, before meeting Mrs. Miniter, took lunch at an ordinary call'd the Georgian Cafeteria; which interested me as a perfect replica of the typical Cleveland cafeteria—a type not found in New-York nor in Providence. In fancy I was transported back to August days—to Mills', or Chapin's, or the Statler; and I was several times on the point of addressing my companion as "Sonny", fancying him that small boy with whom I sate on those earlier and Mid-Western occasions! I wish'd, indeed, that I might step out to 105th and Euclid and purchase fresh fruit salad sundaes for the company! At the Transcript office we stopt to obtain the small free guide there publisht; a copy of which I enclose for each of you children. Then we met Mrs. Miniter at

232 ❧ Letters to Alfred Galpin

the Old State House, and proceeded to explore that edifice. You, little Belknap, have no doubt seen this pleasing pile; but to you, small Alfredus, I must some day shew it. I remov'd my hat whilst gazing at the golden lion and unicorn symbolick of His Majesty's authority over the Province, (they were pull'd down by the rebels in 1776, but subsequently restor'd) and thereafter enter'd the building and noted the remarkable collection of antiquities. It was with a family pride that I noted some possessions of John Phillips, Esq., first Mayor of Boston, with whom genealogy remotely connects me. I am, by the way, told, that at Watertown there still stands the brick 17th century house occupy'd by my lineal ancestor, the Rev. George Phillips, who was among the settlers of that place in 1630. This fact I have not verify'd, but I design to do so at some future date. From the State-House we proceeded to Faneuil-Hall, and thence to the Paul Revere house built in 1676, one of the three remaining 17th century buildings in Boston proper. This house was much spoilt by modern change, but was restor'd in 1908 to the condition it had when inhabited by Mr. Revere the goldsmith from 1770 to 1800. How can I do justice to the ineffable charm of this hoary dwelling? Tho' my proper century is the 18th, I am peculiarly fascinated by memorials of the century before; and to me there is something alluringly sinister in these massive, low-pitch'd, heavy-beam'd, diamond-window'd remains of the first Puritan times. The odour of them is alone sufficient to awake dark speculations—I found it most pronounc'd in the antient Ward house in Haverhill, the oldest part of which was built in 1640. The cavernous fireplaces, too, add to the macabre grotesqueness. In this house were many relics, including old maps of Boston (1728) and papers containing Mr. Revere's advertisements. There were on sale replicas of the old 18th century lanthorns which Revere fashioned, as well as pewter spoons newly struck from his own well-preserv'd moulds. I obtain'd a lanthorn for myself, and a spoon apiece as Christmas presents for my aunts, who share my fondness for New-England antiquities. I am enclosing for each of you boys some printed matter which I obtain'd at Mr. Revere's; and hope it will interest you during your holiday vacations. From Revere's we went to Christ-Church (where I mounted the pulpit and gesticulated in ecclesiastick fashion unseen by the sexton) and Charter-Street, where I shew'd Mrs. Miniter the only two 17th century houses besides Revere's—structures of which despite her antiquarian erudition she was previously ignorant. They are ill-kept, and in frightful slums; some society shou'd reclaim them.

[*The rest of this letter has been lost.*]

Notes

1. Mildred Cole. Cole's first wife, Helene Hoffman Cole (b. 1893), died in 1919.

2. "Lord Dunsany and His Work."

3. T. S. Eliot (1888–1965), *The Waste Land,* first published in the U.S. in the *Dial,* November 1922 (*LL* 254).

4. Samuel French Smith (1808–1895) wrote the song "My country, 'tis of thee" in 1832. The tune is based upon "God Save the King."

5. Four years later HPL would incorporate this burying-ground in his tale, "Pickman's Model" (1926).

6. Boston is known as "The Hub" (hence the name of the local amateur journalism club, "The Hub Club"), short for "The Hub of the Universe" (or "of the Solar System"). The original "Hub" was the Massachusetts State House. See Oliver Wendell Holmes, *The Autocrat of the Breakfast-Table* (1859), ch. 6: "'[The] Boston State-House is the hub of the solar system. You couldn't pry that out of a Boston man, if you had the tire of all creation straightened out for a crowbar.'"

7. Sir William Pepperrell (1696–1759), colonial American merchant, politician, and soldier who in 1745 commanded land forces that, with a British fleet, captured the French fortress of Louisbourg (now in Nova Scotia).

[11]   [To Galpin and Frank Belknap Long] [AHT]

[mid-February 1923]

Alfredus and Belnapius:

[. . .]

Accordingly I embark'd upon the Medford coach, with the purpose of viewing the mansion of the late Col. Isaac Royall, which was built around the walls of an older house in the year 1737.

Grey thro' the trees I saw the old manor-house from afar; with its brick ends, tall chimneys, and extensive slave quarters. Its aspect was of the freshest, and I was hard put to it not to fancy Colonel Royall standing in the doorway, in his short full-bottom'd periwig, to extend me the welcome which in these days of Yankee sedition one loyal King's man owes another. My welcome, however, was given by a venerable person of the yeoman class: one George Fuller, who acts as curator of the estate. Upon admitting me, he shew'd me a vast hall with arches and pilasters of the finest classical carving; the work of such honest artisans, with a true eye for beauty, as cannot be found in these days of rabble degeneracy, trade guilds, and such like monstrosities of an evill aera. You, little Belknap, will comprehend the beauty of these decorations when I tell you that they surpass the finest carvings in the parlour of the Van Cortlandt Mansion;[1] but you, small Alfredus, must behold a Colonial dwelling before their merit can justly impress you. 'Tis sufficient to remark, that in the panelling of the walls, the arching of the windows, the framing of the doors, and the designing of the mantelpieces, our mansions of the eighteenth century surpass'd every other sort of edifice before or since for pure grace and loveliness of outline and proportion. The architects and decorators of that time, amongst whom Saml: McIntyre of Salem[2] takes a prominent place, had an eye for beauty which the uniform good taste of the eighteenth century marvellously develop'd; and I am truly of an opinion, that their creations and carvings are just as genuine poesy as anything ever writ in lines and rhymes. Their age had in it some subtle stimulant to their particular sort of genius, which subsequently vanish'd, and will not return till after another age of barbarism. If we wish to shine in the building and adornment of houses, we can but copy these predecessors with fidelity; the which I am well-pleas'd to see some of our architects doing. I was on this occasion shewn about by Goodman Fuller, who prov'd to possess a singular amount of intelligence and information. He permitted me to overlook nothing; and upon my displaying interest, stay'd an hour after the usual closing time to converse with me about the past. His age is above eighty, and his memory of Old Boston phenomenally distinct. He can recall, for instance, the best days of Louisburg-Square; when old gentlemen in white, bell-crown'd beaver hats and swallow-tail'd coats with brass buttons used to bow low to prim old ladies with large bonnets and hoop-skirts, who would courtesy profoundly in return. When I purchas'd the customary post-card pictures, (for I am collecting views of all the antique places I visit) my honest friend was so generously amicable as to give me a slightly aluminum card tray with a picture of the mansion thereon; an object which I shall treasure as a symbol of that antient good-will which ought to exist betwixt the yeomanry and the gentry. Of everything in the house, aside from the architecture and carving, I think I lik'd most the sign of an old tavern own'd by Col. Royall and once standing in the publick square of Medford-Village. It had finely painted upon it His Majesty's arms, but was marr'd by a wanton musket-ball shot into it by straggling rebels on the night of April 19, 1775, when the scoundrels defied the authority of our regulars. Next to this, I most liked the painting of the younger Col. Royall at the age of 22; a finely bred young fellow in scarlet coat and neat periwig of the fashion of 1741. Poor man, he liv'd to see foul treason stain these rural shades, and in 1775 went to the Mother Land; dying at Kensington in 1781. He was a man of unquestion'd virtue and extensive ability, serving the Province in many important military and political capacities. In 1763 he gave to Medford the first fire-engine it ever possess'd, and upon his death (notwithstanding the secession of the Province) bequeath'd a valuable tract of land to Harvard-College. He was born in Antigua, in the West-Indies, where his father was for some time a planter. In faith he was sincerely attach'd to the Establish'd Church, holding a pew in King's Chapel, Boston, (which I have seen) and being foremost in works of philanthropy and publick spirit. I shou'd have felt honour'd by his acquaintance; and indeed took pride in spending three hours under his hospitable roof.

Upon quitting the Royall House, which I did with much reluctance, I repair'd to an ordinary in Boston, where I procur'd a meal of the same sort which you and I, small Alfredus, used to obtain at Clark's Taverns in Cleaveland. Thereafter I call'd a chair and proceeded to the meeting of the club; which was held in Huntington-Chambers, near Copley-Square. I here found the usual numerous assemblage, including Mr. Cole, Mrs. Miniter, and

Mr. Nelson Morton (brother to my bosom friend in New-York), whom I vastly respect; Mr. Sandusky, whom I vastly like; and Mr. Michael White,[3] whom I essay'd to snub throughout the entire evening with no success—for truly, he seem'd dispos'd to take offence at nothing I cou'd do without causing a publick riot.[4] The speaker of the evening was one Osborne (not him who Sam: Johnson knock'd down) who edits the National Magazine,[5] and who told the company how to write salable short stories. Upon the matter of literature he touch'd not; doubtless recognising the taste of most of his auditors. All was over by midnight; at which time I accompanied the Parker-Miniter delegation[6] home, but not before promising to meet Mr. Cole for dinner the following night, at the Copley-Square Tavern. Arriv'd with my hosts at their Maplewood home, I sat up conversing with them till half past five in the morning; at which time all retired. I awaked at nine, was treated to an excellent breakfast, and after bidding suitable adieux to the six cats and numerous human beings, set out for my next important goal—the antique and daemon-haunted town of SALEM.

Arrived at Salem, I determin'd to spare no effort to learn the town from end to end; even better than I learnt New-York during my stay of many weeks. I therefore flouted fatigue, and proceeded to follow the long general itinerary prescrib'd in the excellent guide-book of the Essex Institute. This took me first to the Grimshawe House (where Mr. Hawthorne not only courted his wife but laid the scene of a weird tale),[7] and the antient Charter-Street Burying Ground adjacent. And what a scene delighted my eyes in that story'd and venerable necropolis! Picture, my children, an extensive undulating tract cover'd with snow; the blacken'd slabs peering thro' like the helmets of a crop of daemons got by sowing dragons' teeth.[8] On the north is Charter-Street, above which it broods over a bank wall. On the northwest the Grimshawe House (now sold to Jews, and the finely carv'd doorway remov'd to the museum) abuts; with its fence looking on the graves of Justice John Hawthorne, Dr. John Swinnerton, and young Nathaniel Mather, the Belknap or Galpin of his age, whose stone reads: "an aged person that had seen but nineteen winters in the world". Nathaniel died on the 17th of October, 1688, amidst universal mourning; and is accounted one of the most learned individuals in the Province; in theology, philosophy, Latin, Greek, and Hebrew alike. Farther from the fence is the simple but dignify'd sepulchre of the mighty SIMON BRADSTREET, twice Governour of the Colonie, and a man of magnificent parts; born at Horbling, in Lincolnshire, in the last yeare of our blessed sovereign ELIZABETH.

> Majestick here on ev'ry Hand arise
> BRITANNIA'S Glories, mounting to the Skyes![9]

236 ❋ *Letters to Alfred Galpin*

On the south is a bluff, which formerly overlookt an inlet from the harbour, but beneath which is now the made land of recent times, containing an extension of Derby-Street. Still lofty in position, the graveyard is swept by the winds of heaven by day and the winds of hell by night. Out of its terrible soil crawl vast funereal willows; one of gigantick size and curious convolutions occupying the exact centre. This tree hath so expanded, that its bole now infolds the greater part of an antient slate slab; growing solidly around it so that in time it will be wholly swallow'd up. The slab is one dating from the reign of Charles the Second, which is by no means old for a place whose earlier interments reach back to 1637. (I have, tho', seen older graves in Boston, where some reach back to 1630.)

From the graveyard I went down to Derby Street, observ'd the Custom-House where Mr. Hawthorne work'd, and once more inspected the House of the Seven Gables in Turner-Street on the harbour. This scene is one which no man but an artist cou'd rightly describe, hence I can meerly suggest the bolder parts of it—the narrow street with no house visible of later date than 1700, and with two of the antient Gothick houses in sight; houses of the peaked sort that preceded our familiar "Colonial" architecture, and whose diamond-paned lattice windows, exposed beams, and overhanging gables are of a school of construction extending back into the Dark Ages and seen on every towne streete in England when Richard the Lion-Hearted sate on our throne. Boston and Salem were once fully built up with this sort of houses, copy'd directly from those of London; but by 1690 they were largely replac'd by the gambrel-roof'd type out of which evolv'd the "Colonial" style. That style itself (tho' I have heard no one else remark it) is palpably the result of an anomalous fusion peculiar to New-England and later to the Colonies; namely, the superposition of *manor-house* architecture upon *town-house* architecture; the whole later embellish'd by that Greek and Roman classical influence which distinguisht the eighteenth century. To go back to the Gothick houses: I know not any which fully preserv'd its antique aspect thro' the centuries. All were to some degree modify'd by succeeding generations; so that such as we now see are largely the result of expert restoration. This restoration is one of the great works of the famous Essex Institute of Salem; an institution which of its kind is surpass'd by nothing in the United States. In Salem there are many of the Gothick houses; in Boston only one: that of the late Paul Revere, Esq. Overhanging gables are more common, having been used in the earlier gambrel-roof'd houses; though there is no record of one later than 1700. In Boston there are but three houses with such a feature, but in Salem and Marblehead innumerable specimens exist. This feature was the occasion of a dispute betwixt myself and Mrs. Miniter last December, when that learned lady insisted that the overhang was an American device for protection against the Indians. How so proficient an antiquarian cou'd fall into so great an error, I know not; unless it be that her erudition does not extend back across the ocean; for in truth, the overhanging gable was not meerly mediaeval, but existed in many of the ROMAN houses, even unto the early times of the republick. (Tho' in the GRECIAN houses, the upper storey not only did not overhang, but seldom cover'd so much space as that below it.) Amongst the Romans, the overhanging storey was called a *maenianum,* and many have been found in Pompeii. In later Imperial times they were forbidden because of the narrowness of the streets, an edict against them being pass'd in A.D. 368, tho' it soon fell into obsolescence. The ban was reviv'd by Imp. Honorius (he that abandon'd Britannia and play'd with poultry) and Imp. Theodosius II., tho' exemption was granted in case of an open space of 10 or 15 feet before the maenianum in question. When the Goths destroy'd the empire, all Roman customs slowly decay'd away; and we find the overhanging gable prominent in the new Gothick architecture, from whence it pass'd to the early towns of America.

But I digress. This scene, at the foot of Turner-Street, is one of the most impressive in existence. Landward we behold the seventeenth-century scene just describ'd; seaward we behold the deserted harbour, deep and nobly landlock'd, yet holding only the ghosts of the ships that once made known the name of Salem on distant shoars of Ind. It is a terrible sight, for as I lookt I saw a spectral train of galleons and frigates, barques and brigantines; sailing, sailing, sailing, with tatter'd sails distent by no breeze, and with seaweed and barnacles on the wormy hulls and high sterns.

I turn'd away and went inland, mourning to see the antient houses on Derby-Street fill'd with loathsome Polacks. Crossing to Essex-Street, I breath'd better; for here are the old Salem folk unchang'd, and lineally descended from the pioneers of Mr. Winthrop's colonies of 1626. After looking at the Narbonne-House (1671), I cross'd to the region of Washington-Square, or Salem-Common; where (God be devoutly thank'd) dwell some of Salem's old aristocracy in their fullest pristine splendour; inhabiting the houses in which their forbears entertain'd Sir William Pepperrell and Genl. Washington. I look'd at the stately rows of mansions with their sublime doorways and shining brass knockers; and cou'd not but remove my hat out of respect to the genius of our ENGLISH nation, which planted this colonie and rais'd it up to the summit of taste, dignity, and elegant simplicity. GOD SAVE THE KING! I now went to Mall-Street, where Mr. Hawthorne for some time dwelt; and doubling around venerable Bridge-Street, essay'd to return to the Common down Williams-Street. (So named from Rev. R. Williams, founder of the Providence-Plantations, who dwelt in Salem before 1636.) Here I was destin'd to encounter a very agreeable shiver of spectral horror, for I had not walkt far when I came upon a very antient house of unknown date, but certainly standing prior to the witchcraft of 1692. It was now abandon'd and condemn'd, and when I went up to one of the tiny, small-pan'd windows to peer into the black interior, I saw that the main floor had mostly fallen thro' into the cellar, whilst the second floor was sagg'd down nearly to where the main floor shou'd be. There were doors leading farther into the interior, and amidst the dusk I cou'd see fallen plaster, gaunt walls, empty doorways, and quantities of mould, discolouration, and water in stagnant pools. It was not a nice place to peer into late in the afternoon, for it is not good to look upon midnight and death when the sun shines. None the less I peer'd again and again; till at last I saw more than I had seen before, being aided by the eye of sinister fancy. From every door-frame hung a corpse in some state or other of decay; a few skeletons, and a few with purple putrescence left. They were all aged, and drest in rags, and were both men and women. And when I lookt down toward the floor I saw there was not any floor, but only a black unfathomable abyss, into which straggled vainly the lurid phosphorescence of the corpses. And I stared in fascination till a workman passing by on the sidewalk brush'd against me and reminded me of the proper dignity of an old gentleman, who shou'd not be standing in a publick street staring into bleary windows and subject to the passing contact of plebeians. And I saw a cat on that street. A tiger cat.

Thence I proceeded to Brown-Street, where I was determin'd to buy some marvellous bas-reliefs of antique Salem and Marblehead places, that I had two months before seen in an art shop window. In December I had been penniless but for coach fare; this time I was (for me) fairly well supply'd with money. The shop in question was that of one Sarah Symonds, a spinster of elderly years and unquestion'd genius; of the oldest Salem stock, and an artist of much local celebrity. Her sole specialty is the brown or tinted bas-relief of ancient and weird places; and in the shop windows all of Salem, Marblehead, and Old Boston stare at the passenger with curious magick. It was, indeed, the haunting placque of Marblehead there, which induc'd me to make those enquiries last December which resulted in my visiting that singular town. This placque I was resolv'd to buy, together with one of the Salem Witch House, brooding under its horrible overnourished oak tree. I can scarce convey in words the sentient terror or antiquity in those placques for it is too subtle for human expression.[10] It broods . . and leers . . I am convinc'd that no medium is equal to the bas-relief in expressing such peculiar gradations of fear and age as Salem and Marblehead possess; and believe that Mistress Symonds hath made a master stroke in its selection and exclusive use for the purpose. The execution is of the highest order; with just the proper balance betwixt impressionism and realism—and my judgment is confirm'd by the discriminating publick, whose purchases make of the shop a thriving institution. On this occasion I was tempted to buy all the contents of the shop, for truly, the spirit of antiquity was captur'd in all the objects hanging about; but I confin'd myself to the two I had originally wisht, together with two small witch placques (a shilling each) as souvenirs for my aunts. The artist was out, and I was waited on by a young nymph of much intelligence and loquacity anent Salem antiquities; who directed me to several places not in the guide book, but who finally did up the wrong placques thro' negligence, so that I was that night disappointed when I sought to shew them to Edw: Cole, Esq. From the shop, bearing (as I thought) my precious placques, I proceeded to East India Marine Hall, (which wou'd make you, little Belknap, think of the India-House in Hanover-Square, New-York) now the property of the Essex Institute and housing the Peabody Museum of Marine and Oriental antiquities. There I revell'd the time away; browsing amidst models, relics, and memorials of antient New-England shipping, till I feel I cou'd now write as good a sea story as Arthur Gordon Pym;[11] and afterward delving into the Japanese collection so deeply that time became a myth. There is no collection half so good elsewhere: even the New-York Metropolitan Museum is infinitely behind this special horde of Japanese curiosities; whose fulness is due to the long years of active trade betwixt Salem and the Orient. My New-England blood leapt at the thought of this former maritime glory; and I swell'd with the pride of a Nordick, a son of uncounted generations of blond-bearded men of power and adventure . . . . conquerors, ... slayers . . . . a master-race!

From Marine Hall I went to a shop and bought the cards which I sent you children. Then I started out, by a winding route, for Gallows Hill. Ascending St. Peter Street, I stopt at St. Peter's Church (a place for all the world like an old parish church in England) to view the graves. They are scatter'd about in all angles of the hoary edifice, even straggling in single file along the narrow plot of grass separating the north wall from the flagstone walk beside it. One stone, in a southwest angle of the church, contains a name used by Mr. Hawthorne in connexion with one of his novels: reading "Here lyes buried ye body of Jonathan Pue, Esq., Late surveyor and searcher of his Majesties' customs in Salem, New England".[12] He died in 1760. I was now at the corner of Federal Street, site of the town gaol of 1692 where the suspected witches were confin'd. One wall of the gaol is still standing, built into a house now number'd 4 Federal St. Being yet at liberty I paused not here, but walkt along Federal St. westward, following the route prescribed by the book and my later informant. I beheld some of the most famous mansions of the town, including the Pierce-Nichols House (1782), into which I could not get till the following day, tho' it is own'd by the Essex Institute. I several times paused to stroke cats, which abound in all parts of the town; whether or not left there by witches, none may say. At last I reached bleak Boston-Street on the western rim of the town, and walkt north toward Gallows-Hill. Here the houses were greyer and more uncommunicative, and the cold wind made sounds I had not before notic'd. A very old man told me where to find the approach to Gallows-Hill, and hobbled beside me a while as if knowing that I was, like himself, in some way strangely linkt to the spectral past. When the ascent became steep he left me, but not without hinting that Gallows-Hill is not a nice place to visit at night. On and on I climb'd, crunching under my heavy overshoes the crushed, malignant snow. The wind blew and the trees tossed leaf-less branches; and the old houses became thinner and thinner. Some were not over a century and a half old, but others had overhanging gables and latticed windows which told me that they had been standing there when the terrible carts rattled with their doomed load from the gaol in Federal Street. Up . . . . up . . . . up . . . . Damn that wind—why *can't* it sound less *articulate?* At last I was on the summit, where in the bed rock still lurk the iron clamps that held the witch gallows. It was getting on in the afternoon, and the light was red-dish that glow'd over all the outspread town. It was a weird town in that light, as seen from that hill where strange winds moaned over the untenanted wastes on the westward. And I was alone on that hill in that sepulchral place, where the allies of the devil had swung . . . and swing . . . and hurled out curs-es on their executioners and their descendants. I recall'd a witchcraft judge (Major Bartholomew Gedney) in mine own maternal ancestry, and thought of certain imprecations of the dead in fact and fiction. . . . . "God shall give them blood to drink."[13] And at that moment, as God is my judge, I heard faintly but distinctly the clanking of chains in the wind . . . . the chains of the gibbet which had not stood since 1693 . . . . and from that accursed wind came a shriek that was more than the shrieking of wind . . . . . a malignant, daemoniac sound that left in my ears the hideous echo of a syllable . . . "-ire" . . . . which in turn brought up as if in shocking memory a crude couplet I never heard before or since:

> "We swing higher,
> You feed the fire!"

And so I hung around Gallows Hill so long that Marblehead became out of the question for that day. Silently I descended past the leering houses with their centuried small-paned bleary windows, and as I did so my fancy brought vividly to my eyes a terrible procession going both up and down that hill be-side me—a terrible procession of black-cowled things bearing bodies swathed in burlap. And so ample were the cowls, that I could not see the face of any of the things . . . . or whether they had any faces. And as I neared the bottom of the hill they faded silently away, leaving me to pick my way back to Chest-nut Street, the most exclusive part of the town, where in palaces of Colonial architecture still reside the aristocratic descendants of the captains and mer-chants who planned so well. The street is a veritable boulevard with its rows of antient chestnuts and its stately and opulent mansions; it is the London West End of George the Third's time, transplanted to these colonies. The hour was now late, and I hasten'd past the Old Pickering House (built in 1660, the year of his Majesty's glorious restauration) to the Broad-Street Burying Hill, where I trod under cypresses on grave-snows which held no print but mine. It was cold on Burying Hill. Thence a tortuous walk to the station through slums of Greeks and Italians—slums that were standing when the usurper Cromwell spread treason through our Kingdom. In one filthy Greek alley I found the house where the father of the architect McIntyre liv'd, early in the 18th century, and where the artist John Singleton Copley[14] liv'd for a time . . . . a true loyalist, who went to England in 1775, and whose son became the Lord Chancellor Lyndhurst. After that the station, a coach-ride to Boston, and a meeting with the Hon. Edward Harold Cole.

Dinner at the Copley-Square Hotel . . . but a skeleton at the feast! Politics! To make a long story short, Cole pleaded, wept, and got down on his knees in an effort to make me run for the *National* presidency next July.[15] Sancta Pegāna! He said that if I had any friendship for him, or any solicitude for the amateur cause, I would not leave my work uncompleted; and lugubriously assur'd me, that if I shou'd retire in July all my former work wou'd be lost. It was a piteous spectacle—Cole was Morton with a quarter of a century knock'd off . . . . these Harvard men are frightful entreaters! I pacify'd him as best I cou'd, remain'd non-committal, bade him sleep well, and departed for the Brunswick. Meanwhile I had tried to shew him my new placques and found the wrong ones. Damn.

On the following day I started again for Salem and Marblehead; this time with a programme more carefully plann'd. I first visited the Essex Institute, view'd again the collection I had admir'd last December, including the scarlet-coated PEPPERRELL before the walls of Louisburg, and obtain'd a card of admission to the Pierce-Nichols house. Thence I visited the Symonds Shop in Brown-Street to exchange the placques, and by rare good fortune discover'd the artist herself in charge. Mistress Symonds is a plain, stoutish, elderly person who brilliantly refutes the fallacy of some little boys I know, that artists must be decadent, bohemian, hecktick, dissipated idiots; for to a genius of the most undoubted sort, she adds the homely and wholesome personality of an old New-England conservative aristocrat. She has dwelt always at Salem in the conventional manner of an old Salem gentlewoman, and lives in a house that knew the tread of an ancestor's buckled shoes. When I enter'd the shop she knew who I was, for her clerk had describ'd me as one who not only admir'd the bas-reliefs but loved all things old and weird. And thereupon I struck an ideal fountain of antique Salem lore, for Mistress Symonds has hunted up every ghost and ghoul in the town, and is on familiar terms with most of the daemons. In 1692 she wou'd have been hung as a witch, but in 1923 she is safe in expressing an undying devotion to Poe and all that is antient and sinister. From her I learnt of new sources of wild tales, and incidentally obtain'd a note of introduction to John Gauss, Esq., brother to the H. E. Gauss whose free-verse poem on Salem I quoted in my last joint letter to you children. The Gausses are old Salem stock. And I also receiv'd a card of introduction to Mr. Dowe of the Soc. for the Pres. of N. E. Antiquities, which will help me enter the old Cooper house (1654) in Cambridge. In turn I describ'd to Mistress Symonds many of the antiquities in Providence which she had not seen, and shew'd her pictures of the Royall House, which so imprest her that she decided to go at once and model certain parts of it. Mention of art led to mention of Clark Ashton Smith, Esq., and she was anxious to see his work—of which I regret I have not better specimens to shew her. Thence conversation inclin'd toward weird tales, and I mention'd that I had written some. Interested by this, she ask'd to hear some of the plots; and these having been related, she desired me to lend her the manuscripts as soon as I reach'd home—which I will do, subject to the usual temporal aberrations of confirm'd indolence. And as a final courtesy, the generous dame presented me free of charge with a most attractive placque of the Salem Town Pump—nor did she forget to exchange the placques I had bought. All now adorn my walls, and I gaze with a shudder at that Witch House glowering under its terrible oak—horror stalks there. And beside it rise the mad maze of gables, vanes, and chimney pots that form hoary Marblehead! Truly, my travels have come home with me, for the scenes live poignantly in those vividly fashion'd bas-reliefs.

I now crost over past the old church to Federal Street, and sought the Pierce-Nichols House. This is a poem in white wood and magic carving, the masterpiece of that SAMUEL MC INTYRE whose name shou'd live for ever in the annals of art. 'Tis still inhabited by descendants of the Salem Nicholses—two pitiful old maids nearing eighty, who a few years ago ran wholly out of money and were forc'd to put their house on the market. Salem, having a dignify'd and proper respect for its antient and honourable families, cou'd not suffer a NICHOLS to be in want, or even in penury; so that in the end the Essex Institute bought the house as a triumph of Colonial architecture, but gave it back to the poor old ladies with only one proviso: that on Wednesdays and Saturdays they admit to three rooms on the ground floor such visitors as have a card from the institute and desire to see the wonderful interior panelling and carving of the illustrious McIntyre. I struck thrice on the knocker (for no Salem aristocrat wou'd tolerate a doorbell—such things are unknown to the finer mansions) and was admitted by a serving-wench of plain but respectable appearance; who conveyed the sad information that one of the poor old ladies was ailing and like to expire. Naturally, I made to withdraw at once, but as I did so the other old lady call'd the wench from within and bade her ask me to view the rooms; for such is the pride of a true old aristocrat, that the shirking of a duty of honour, such as was imply'd by the Institute's purchase of the house, wou'd seem abhorrent. Accordingly I adopted that course prompted by tact, and went perfunctorily thro' the parlours and dining-room shewn by the wench; noting as I pass'd the breathless beauty of the carvings, panels, and cornices, and the shining brass latches and stately Colonial furniture. Then, having no doubt satisfy'd the poor old gentlewoman on the stairs that she had done her duty by the Institute, I departed in decent haste, saying (that the old lady might overhear) 'that I was grateful for having seen a dual monument of Salem's taste: a decoration that bespeaks a master designer, and a furnishing and atmosphere what bespeak a life of culture and nobility.' Today that stately mansion may be a house of death, where Salem ghosts in full-bottom'd wigs waft wistfully away with them the poor shrivell'd soul of their next the last daughter. But I hope that it is not, and that the antient sisters may float away together a long time hence, when the time comes, so that their dying will be scarce distinguishable from their living. Then there will be a funeral, and pompous people will say things they do not mean, and the house will become a museum under the efficient guidance of the Institute which is destroying one by one (to the vast disgust of Mistress Symonds) the more tenuous and nebulous myths of the antient town. Mayhap the shadowy Misses

[*The rest of this letter has been lost.*]

Notes

1. The Van Courtlandt House is located at Broadway and 242nd Street in the Bronx; it was built in 1748.

2. Samuel McIntire (1757–1811), a leading sculptor distinguished for his carving of portals and architectural decorations.

3. All are fellow amateur journalists: Edward H. Cole; Edith Miniter; Nelson G. Morton, brother of James Ferdinand Morton; Albert A. Sandusky; and Michael Oscar White.

4. HPL alludes to his dispute with White over the latter's attack on Samuel Loveman in the article "Poets of Amateur Journalism" (*Oracle*, December 1922). HPL responded to White in "Bureau of Critics" (March 1923) and "In the Editor's Study" (July 1923).

5. The *National Magazine* (1894–1933) was a professional periodical that years before had reprinted several of HPL's poems first published in amateur journals, and published for the first time "On Receiving a Picture of the Marshes at Ipswich" (January 1917). Its managing editor at this time was M. L. Osborne.

6. Charles A. A. Parker. At this time he and Edith Miniter were sharing quarters at 30 Waite Street in Malden, MA.

7. Nathaniel Hawthorne's *Doctor Grimshawe's Secret* (written 1861, published 1883) is set in a house next to the Charter Street Burying Ground in Salem.

8. HPL alludes to the myth of Cadmus.

9. The couplet appears to be by HPL.

10. See HPL to Elizabeth Toldridge (5 October 1933): "I have a very attractive bas-relief of the old Witch House hanging above my table—together with a companion piece depicting the ancient gambrel Roofs of Marblehead; both the work of the ingenious sculptor Sarah Symonds of Salem. . . ." (253).

11. A reference to Poe's tale of nautical adventure, *The Narrative of Arthur Gordon Pym of Nantucket* (1838).

12. Jonathan Pue is a surveyor who has preserved the tale of Hester Prynne, as related by Hawthorne in the preface (titled "The Custom House") to *The Scarlet Letter* (1850).

13. This is the curse uttered by Matthew Maule upon Col. Pynchon in *The House of the Seven Gables* (1851) ("him" for "them" in Hawthorne). HPL cites it in his discussion of the novel in "Supernatural Horror in Literature" (1927).

14. John Singleton Copley (1738–1815), American painter of portraits and historical

subjects; generally regarded the finest artist of colonial America.

15. HPL had become interim president of the NAPA in December 1922, taking over for William J. Dowdell, who had resigned. Although HPL served the remainder of the term (till July 1923), he did not run for re-election.

[12]   [To Galpin and Frank Belknap Long] [TLS]

598 Angell St., Providence, R.I.

May 1, 1923

To Belknap and Alfredus:

My dear Little Grandchildren:—

Tho' long delay'd by the vicissitudes of labours and distempers, I will at last take my pen in hand to tell you of my late travels in the Province of the Massachusetts-Bay.

I quitted Providence on a late afternoon coach Thursday, April 12, arriving in Boston shortly before the time of the Hub Club meeting to which I had been invited, and which form'd the excuse for the trip. This meeting lack'd the intellectual vigour which Edw: Cole, Esq., or Nelson Morton, Esq. wou'd have brought to it, but was amply enliven'd by the presence of my learned young friend Albert Sandusky, Esq., whose piquant additions to our English speech have earn'd him so just a celebrity in his native province. To employ his own diction, Bimbo Sandy[1] was there with bells on—you tell 'em, kid!—and ladled out enough spoonfuls of 190-proof syncopated socony to cop the fleece-lined electric fan for bulging brows. Sizzling sausage! but that egg sure did knock the other goofs west for a row of Aethiopian aeroplane hangars! We have no bananas today! Torrid atmosphere of less scholarly nature—but assaying a darned sight more C.P. egotism to the cubic centimetre—was provided by Al's bosom friend (they park their automatics outside when forc'd into the same room) Joseph Bernard Lynch, Esq., who seen his duty an' done it good, tipping off the empyrean at some length how he, and he alone, built up the new Hub personnel—and how the other guys has gotta come acrost wit' de kale if they expects he's gonna keep it up. Deep stuff, Joe—deep stuff! However, the principal speaker of the evening, George Brinton Beale, editor of the BOSTON SUNDAY POST MAGAZINE, was no flivver; and slung a pernicious line of gab on story writing and magazine requirements in general. Snappy stuff—except that he paus'd not to touch upon so trivial a concernment as artistick composition. He's one of them bozos what wants a spiel to be real uplifting and wholesome, and couldn't think of enough cuss words to lam at Eliott Paul, Esq.,[2] Boston's one realist, who from all accounts (I ain't read nothin' of his) is the Ben Hecht of New-England. Beale thinks Paul is just too awful and horrid for anything—an opinion which fossilised Boston shares, and which Paul recently reciprocated by telling Burton Rascoe, Esq. 'that he found it more interesting to live in

Boston than in a civilised community'. Well—the meeting rolled along so-so. Michael White, Esq. endeavour'd to prove a pleasing and sociable talker, and inform'd me, that he lik'd my criticism in the NATIONAL AMATEUR![3] My gawd—the smelling-salts—quick! The bally dumbbell *liked* it, after I spent an hour trying to make it as subtly stinging as possible! No use—ya gotta bean that bimbo wit' a sledge-hammer afore he'll get wise that ya ain't pattin' him! Good night!

The meeting dispers'd without overt violence at about 11 p.m., and I accompany'd the Parker-Miniter delegation to their modest abode. There, after a conversational session with my joint hosts which lasted nearly till morning, I retir'd early and slept soundly; dreaming mainly of "Victory", the six-weeks-old kitten who had sat, squirm'd, or scratch'd in my lap during the entire period. Victory was born March 1st, and is the most engaging mite I have beheld in years. He climb'd over the entire area of his aged and adipose Grandpa, and finally settled on the back of the Old Gentleman's neck as an ideal sleeping-porch. But I digress. In the morn I greeted the natives, consum'd a moderate breakfast, and set out for my favourite antique Salem region. This time I went on the electrick coaches, twice having to change (at Revere Beach and at Lynn) before attaining Salem. 'Tis a ride of extream attractiveness, and must have form'd a diversion of prime magnitude in the days when open cars ran direct from Boston to Salem. But all things decay, and nothing more so than the rural tramways of New-England. The country is not what it was when I was young, and only the gods know what we are all coming to!

Arriv'd in Salem, I stroll'd a while through the venerable streets, and finally embark'd for Danvers—call'd "Salem-Village" in the 17th century, and forming the seat of most of the witchcraft cases of 1692. The coach ride was delightful, giving frequent glimpses of ancient houses in a fashion to stimulate the antiquarian soul. Suddenly, at a graceful and shady village corner which the coach was about to turn, I beheld the tall chimneys and ivy'd walls of a splendid brick house of later Colonial design, and espy'd a sign which proclaim'd it open for publick inspection. Captivated by the sight, I signall'd the driver and alighted; determin'd to add an item to my Colonial itinerary. Inform'd by the sign that this was the Capt. Samuel Fowler house, built 1809, accessible for eightpence, and the property of the Society for the Preservation of New-England Antiquities, I loudly sounded the knocker and awaited developments. Nothing develop'd. I then knock'd at the side door, but with equal futility. Then I noted a door half open in a miserable "ell" at the back of the house; and believing the place tenanted, made a third trial there.

My summons was answer'd simultaneously by two of the most pitiful and decrepit-looking persons imaginable—hideous old women more sinister than the witches of 1692, and certainly not under 80. For a moment I believ'd them to be Salem witches in truth; for the peculiarly sardonick face of one of them, with furtive eyes, sneering lips, and a conspicuously undershot lower law, intensify'd the impression produc'd by their incredible age and gauntness, and the utterly nondescript bundles of brownish rags which form'd their attire. The "ell" in which they dwelt was in a state of indescribable squalor; with heaps of rags, books, cooking utensils, and the like on every hand. One meagre wood stove fail'd altogether to heat the barren room against the cold of that sharp afternoon. The smaller, and probably older, of the two spoke first—in a hoarse rattling voice that dimly suggested death, and that was occasionally halted by a curious guttural impediment. This was the crone who did not have the corpse-like sneer—but what a study they wou'd both have made for a Poe, a Baude-laire, or a Goya! If, however, their weird aspect and hideous squalor were sinis-ter; what can one say of the *contrast* involv'd when the guttural salutation of the speaker became intelligible? For despite the omnipresent evidences of a slat-ternly decadence beyond words, this ancient witch was mumbling forth a court-ly and aristocratick welcome in language and accents beyond question bespeaking the gentlest birth and proudest cultivation! The witch apologised for the unfavourable conditions prevailing, and lamented that she had not heard my knocking at the front door of the mansion proper. There was, she coughed in explanation, not enough fuel to heat the mansion; so she and her sister had to dwell in the wooden "ell" once used as a shed and storehouse. But in sum-mer, indeed, they dwelt in the mansion—for was it not their own by inher-itance, and had they not been born in one of its upper rooms? Yes—it was the old, old New-England story of family decay and aristocratick pauperism—a case like that of the poor Salem Nicholses, but infinitely worse. These tatter'd ancients were the Misses Fowler, own granddaughters of the proud seafarer and fighter who in his dashing prime had built that house for the comfort, dig-nity, and splendour of his descendants. Short-sighted man! Had he but foreseen the depths to which those descendants wou'd be driven! To think of their rags and kennel, and of his fastidious elegance in demanding the best French wall-paper, the finest brass latches, the choicest carved mantels, cornices, and wain-scoting, and the most delicate silver, china, and ornaments that both Europe and America cou'd furnish! 1809–1923—one hundred and fourteen years of slow, insidious decay. In the veins of those horrible wrecks—last of their line—flows the mingled blood of all that was proudest in the Salem region—Ende-cotts who boasted the first Colonial governor, Fowlers who were known the seven seas over, Pickmans who bowed only to those whom they thought wor-thy, Ropeses whose halls were portrait-galleries of great ancestors, Pages who live in history ...... the great-grandmother of these poor relics was that sprightly Mrs. Page who, at the time of the Colonial tea agitation, serv'd her guests with the beverage *on the roof* after her husband had forbidden her to serve it *under his roof.* Such is the dying New-England of today—a whole section's tragedy was epitomised when these unfortunate survivors paus'd beneath an oaken frame and amidst their tatters hoarsely call'd attention to the coat-of-arms which bespoke the haughty gentility of the Fowler blood. The house is finely preserv'd and restor'd, having been purchas'd from the aged sisters at their frantick request by the Society for the Preservation of New-England Antiquities. The Society hath given them the care of it for the pitiful remainder of their lives—as is the custom of such societies when dealing with such cases— but it has not money enough to keep them in food, fuel, and clothing. Still—it is better than the almshouse. The lives of the sisters is not wholly dull, for many intelligent persons come to see the house and its marvellous interior. The day before I was there, an architect from New-York had been over the place, and had copy'd many of the priceless Colonial designs for modern use. Fallen New-England! And yet how great were thine ancient glories! Who today cou'd create such things of beauty as the carvings of Salem craftsmen, the plate of Boston silversmiths, or the designs of classick architects all over the several provinces? Golden 18th century! It is not in jest that I hail thee as the age of universal taste and vigour! Led by the Sibylline wraiths of decay'd gentry, I explor'd the house from cellar to attick. Its decorations are of unrivall'd beauty, and its furniture, ornaments, china, and silver, are beyond description. Fine ancestral portraits, old garments of great richness, priceless laces and other Colonial remnants of domesticity—all these recall uncannily a bygone prosperity which the present mocks. I was allow'd to don a cap which Capt. Fowler wore in the War of 1812, and a civilian swallow-tail coat of the same period—a cream-colour'd dress garment which fitted me finely, and shew'd that the good captain was as stout an old gentleman as your grandpa. Finally I left—pressing upon my pathetick hostesses the admission fee which they sought to refuse in a last gesture of reminiscent aristocracy.

The afternoon was now well along, and I wish'd to visit two other places before leaving the region. Walking a mile to Danvers Square, I visited the old Page house (1754), where the great-grandmother of the Fowlers had once serv'd tea on the roof, and where now the Danvers Historical Society holds forth. The contents of the house did not prove of extream interest, but the building itself did. I examin'd the architecture with unaffected joy, and climb'd to the gambrel roof where the tea-party was held.

I now put the aera of Colonial refinement behind me, and hark'd back farther still to an age of darker and weirder appeal—the age of the dreaded witchcraft. Leaving Danvers, I struck out along the roads and across the fields toward the lone farmhouse built by Townsend Bishop in 1636, and in 1692 inhabited by the worthy and inoffensive old widow Rebekah Nurse, who was seventy years of age and wished no one harm. Accused by the superstitious West-Indian slave woman Tituba (who belong'd to the Rev. Samuel Parris and who caus'd the entire wave of delusion) of bewitching children, then denounc'd blindly by some of the hysterical children in question, Goodwife Nurse was arrested and brought to trial. Thirty-nine persons sign'd a paper attesting to her blameless conduct, and a jury render'd a verdict of "not guilty"; but popular clamour led the judges to reverse the verdict, (as was then possible) and on July 19, 1692 the poor old grandam was hang'd on Gallows Hill in Salem for a mythological crime. Her remains were brought back from Salem and interr'd in the family burying-ground—a ghoulish place shadow'd by huge pines and at some distance from the house. In 1886 a monument was erected to her memory, bearing an inscription by the poet Whittier.

As I approach'd the spot to which I had been directed, after passing thro' the hamlet of Tapleyville, the afternoon sun was very low. Soon the houses thinn'd out; so that on my right were only the hilly fields of stubble, and occasional crooked trees clawing at the sky. Beyond a low crest a thick group of spectral boughs bespoke some kind of grove or orchard—and in the midst of this group I suddenly descry'd the rising outline of a massive and ancient chimney. Presently, as I advanced, I saw the top of a grey, drear, sloping roof—sinister in its distant setting of bleak hillside and leafless grove, and unmistakably belonging to the haunted edifice I sought. Another turn—a gradual ascent—and I beheld in full view the sprawling, tree-shadow'd house which had for nearly 300 years brooded over those hills and held such secrets as men may only guess. Like all old farmhouses of the region, the Nurse cottage faces the warm south and slopes low toward the north. It fronts on an ancient garden, where in their season gay blossoms flaunt themselves against the grim, nail-studded door and the vertical sundial above it. That sundial was long concealed by the overlaid clapboards of gothick generations, but came to light when the house was restored to original form by the memorial society which owns it. Everything about the place is ancient—even to the tiny-paned lattice windows which open outward on hinges. The atmosphere of witch-craft days broods heavily upon that low hilltop.

My rap at the ancient door brought the caretaker's wife, an elderly unimaginative person with no appreciation of the dark glamour of the ancient scene. This family live in a lean-to west of the main structure—an addition probably 100 years less ancient than the parent edifice. I was the first visitor of the 1923 season, and took pride in signing my name at the top of the register. Entering, I found myself in a low, dark passage whose massive beams almost touched my head; and passing on, I travers'd the two immense rooms on the ground floor—sombre, barren, panell'd apartments with colossal fireplaces in the vast central chimney, and with occasional pieces of the plain, heavy furniture and primitive farm and domestick utensils of the ancient yeomanry. In these wide, low-pitch'd rooms a spectral menace broods—for to my imagination the 17th century is as full of macabre mystery, repression, and ghoulish adumbrations as the 18th century is full of taste, gayety, grace, and beauty. This was a typical Puritan abode; where amidst the bare, ugly necessities of life, and without learning, beauty, culture, freedom, or ornament, terrible stern-fac'd folk in conical hats or poke-bonnets dwelt 250 and more years ago—close to the soil and all its hideous whisperings; warp'd in mentality by isolation and unnatural thoughts, and shivering in fear of the devil on autumn nights when the wind howl'd through the twisted orchard trees or rustled the hideous corpse-nourish'd pines in the graveyard at the foot of the hill. There is eldritch fascination—horrible bury'd evil—in these archaick farmhouses. After seeing them, and smelling the odour of centuries in their walls, one hesitates to read certain passages in Cotton Mather's strange old "Magnalia" (which you, little Belknap, shall see when you come to visit your old grandpa) after dark.[4] After exploring the ground floor I crept up the black crooked stairs and examin'd the bleak chambers above. The furniture was as ugly as that below, and included a small trundle-bed in which infant Puritans (even as you, children) were lull'd to sleep with meaningless prayers and morbid hints of daemons riding the night-wind outside the small-paned lattice-windows. Poor little creatures! No wonder there were very few Alfredi or Belnapii amongst them—what artistick or intellectual mind cou'd survive so stultifying an environment? It was the somewhat more civilised class in the larger towns, and the newer colonists from Mother England, (GOD SAVE THE KING!) who in the next century burst forth into that sublimation of beauty which is Colonial architecture and decoration. That was New-England's one gift to the fine arts—and a magnificent gift it was. But still the old Rebekah Nurse house broods and leers on its ancient hill. I saw old Rebekah's favourite chair, where she used to sit and spin before the Salem magistrates dragged her to the gallows. And the sunset wind whistled in the colossal chimney, and ghouls rattled ghastly skeletons from unseen attic rafters overhead. Tho' it was not suppos'd to be open to the publick, I persuaded the caretaker to let me ascend to that hideous garret of century'd secrets. Thick dust cover'd everything, and unnatural shapes loom'd on every hand as the evening twilight oozed through the little blear'd panes of the ancient windows. I saw something hanging from the wormy ridge-pole—something that sway'd as if in unison with the vesper breeze outside, tho' that breeze had no access to this funereal and forgotten place—shadows . . . . . shadows . . . . . shadows . . . . . And I descended from that accursed garret of palaeogean arcana, and left that portentous abode of antiquity; left it and went down the hill to the graveyard under the shocking pines, where twilight shew'd sinister slabs and rusty bits of fallen iron fence, and where something squatted in shadow on a monument—something that made me climb the hill again, hurry shudderingly past the venerable house, and descend the opposite slope to Tapleyville as night came.

After that I rode uneventfully back to Danvers, (where I mail'd cards to you children) Salem, Boston, and Maplewood. Partaking of dinner with Victory on my lap chewing my watch-charm, I again participated in conversation till the small hours, and retir'd to await the dawn which wou'd usher in my Merrimack and Newburyport excursion. Victory was with me to the last—after he became tired of chewing his grandpa's fingers and watch-chain, he scrambled up to his favourite place behind the Old Gentleman's neck and there slumber'd peacefully whilst discussion wax'd high amongst the meer human beings present. Blest atom of happy life! Wou'd that all the world might be as thou! And yet are not thy cousins the subtle sphinx, and the insatiable lion of Libya and Numidia?

Dawn of Saturday! I was up betimes, and ate breakfast with Victory climbing sportively all over me. Near the close of the meal, my young friend essay'd a journey from the floor up my leg and chest to his chosen perch behind my neck; but as he near'd the summit he unwisely chose the lace ruffles of my shirt instead of my brocade waistcoat or velvet coat as a hand-hold. Unponderous as he was with his meer month and a half of terrestrial entity, the dubious fabrick of the too-often-launder'd garment was not enough to sustain him—and down he went, leaving an aching void in my aged bosom!! Not that he was hurt—bless my soul! . . . the mite was kicking and rolling about gleefully in my lap before I knew what had happen'd—but that aching void was in a place which neither suit nor cravat cou'd cover, and in my attempt to "travel light" I had provided no other shirt! Eheu! And when I sought to bunch the place and fix it with pins, my fingers made new rents! No use—the old rag had reach'd the end of its rope—and it had to choose a place like Malden for the grand finale! Well—the only solution was a new shirt, so after bidding my hosts adieu, and running off a page of the new HUB CLUB QUILL on Parker's press, (it took three trials to shew me the knack of feeding and pedalling the confounded thing) I beat it for Boston, where I stock'd up at a linen-draper's and threw the old outfit away. I could not find anything antient enough exactly to suit me—the new shirt hath cheviot fabrick and turn'd-back soft cuffs—but any port in a storm. So, duly garb'd, I took the coach for Haverhill and was there by mid-afternoon.

Transferring to the Merrimack coach, and speeding toward the abode of my great-grandchild Davis, whom I was to visit, I pass'd Whittier's birthplace (built 1688 by his ancestor Tho: Whittier, inhabited by the poet till 1837, and scene of "Snow-Bound") and beheld a region of delightful scenery. The trip was not long, and I soon alighted by the large early Victorian house in sleepy Main-Street which shelters the youthful near-Galba and his family. Edgar himself answer'd the door, and lo! I found him in his first suit with long trousers! How you children do grow! His 15th birthday occurr'd a week ago last Friday, and he is consuming the second year of high-school as a pure pleasure. When, recently, intelligence tests were apply'd to all the pupils in the Merrimack High-School, Edgar came out with a rating conspicuously highest! He has a reputation to live up to, and I predict that he will fulfil every expectation—even tho' you, small Alfredus, scorn to honour him with your epistolary communion. I trust that you, little Belknap, will be less haughty; and will take the time to give the infant a general stimulus in the direction of art and voluminous reading. Remember his abode—16 Main St., Merrimac, Mass. Name, Edgar Jacobs Davis.

After briefly greeting such of the family—mother and sister—as were present, I departed with Edgar for the ancient shades of Amesbury; it having been decided that Newburyport shou'd be saved for the morrow. The coach took us thro' some of the choicest scenery of New-England, for in this northerly region the hills are gentle and graceful, and unexpected vistas of old village roofs and spires are frequent. Commerce and manufactures have not destroy'd the Arcadian simplicity of the inhabitants, and they still dream the years away amidst scenes but little alter'd by the passing centuries. We alighted at the ancient graveyard where Whittier lies bury'd, and marvell'd in the sombre pines and willows, slabs and monuments. Edgar reveal'd an imagination of high quality, and upon one occasion call'd my attention to the inimitably *Babylonian* effect of a certain granite memorial of pyramidal outline, as glimps'd thro' distant trees against the iridescent sunset. The older part of this necropolis is on a hill, and as we wander'd among the hoary slate headstones we feasted our eyes on many a gigantick elm or incredibly antient house. As the sun sank, we rambled on past the "Captain's Well" mention'd in Whittier's poem, and finally attain'd the actual village of Amesbury, which holds much of its primitive quaintness despite a ridiculously metropolitan traffick sign at one of the central junction points. Strolling along Friend St., we sought the later home of Whittier; finally pausing to ask an aged man its whereabouts, and discovering to our chagrin that we had made the inquiry directly in front of it, so that the old villager had only to point to the conspicuous tablet which we had wholly overlook'd. One, so to speak, on us! Tarrying briefly, we sought the coach; and were soon whirling thro' the mystick loveliness of old New-England toward the Davis mansion.

That evening I met the entire family, including William, the aged and dignify'd cat who thereafter spent much of his time in Grandpa's lap. Another interesting object was Herman F. Davis, Esq., head of the house and father of the prodigy, who tho' of excellent ancestry was born in the district of Maine, and retains a rustick love of citizenly practicality which makes him lamentably unsympathetick with his civilised son. Despite his provincial and commonplace ideas, and dogmatick way of arguing, he is intelligent and hearty; and I took considerable pleasure in verbal warfare with him. I try'd to make him realise that his "lazy and dependent" child is not to be criticised too sharply; and that he shou'd be proud of being the parent of so superior an individual. Edgar's mother is sympathetick toward his aspirations, but distinctly Victorian in her own literary activities and appreciations. The sister—now in college—is a conscientious and undistinguish'd "grind"—learned but not gifted. On this occasion a college friend of the sister's was present—an unimaginative encyclopaedia of the same type; about to win a Phi Beta Kappa key, yet essentially provincial and commonplace. Amidst this dull-grey environment small Edgar hath sprung up and blossom'd like an exotick plant—dimly admir'd yet never understood. He is a true 12 o'clock feller in a 9 o'clock town—or I might say a 2 a.m. feller in an 8 o'clock town! Critical, cynical, iconoclastick, unsentimental, tolerant, civilised—he belongs around B'way and 116th St. rather than on Merrimack's Main Street.* But the future beckons him, and he is sufficiently independent to map out his own course . . . . even tho' his father complains that he's unpractical to the extent of sitting and shivering rather than fetching wood for the fire. His general type is just now perhaps a trifle more Galpinian than Belnapian; but he is by no means one-sided, and only an authentick prophet cou'd justly presume to define his course thro' the farce call'd life. The Davis home is of the solid type of two generations ago, opulently clutter'd with the hideous black-walnut of the 1850 period. I was assign'd an immense room—perhaps even larger than my old room at my birthplace—in which was running water . . . . . an archaick marble set-bowl just like those at good old 454 Angell! In these homely if rococo surroundings I dropt peacefully to sleep, to be awaken'd on the morrow by the gentle tap of my great-grandson.

Sunday morning was spent in general discussion, the entire household sitting like a Roman audience at the Amphitheatrum Flavianum whilst Davis' father and I good-naturedly tore each other to pieces. It was so spirited a fight, that Edgar and I were late in starting for Newburyport; but finally we contriv'd to board a coach at the village square. We had wish'd to take honest Tryout along with us, but he writ that he was nervously ill, and cou'd not bear even so much as a caller at his Plaistow hermitage. Poor, amiable old faun! Here's hoping the warm weather gives him new vigour and calls him forth to disport with Pan and the satyrs and dryades of his native groves! He's around 72 now, but still a gentle, unspoilt boy at heart. I wish I cou'd have seen him.

Changing electrick coaches twice—once because of a broken bridge and the other time just because—we sped along the old Colonial river country in delight. Crossing Chain Bridge over the Merrimack—the oldest suspension bridge in America—we approached the suburbs of Newburyport and began to get whiffs and glimpses of the neighbouring sea, and to descry the ancient houses and chimney-pots of the famous town which, tho' said a century and a quarter ago by John Quincy Adams to possess a social life more cultivated and brilliant than that of Washington, is today locally known as "The City of the Living Dead".

Up the narrow street we rattled—deciding to stick to the one-man coach for a preliminary panorama, and to defer the pedestrian exploring till later. Ineffably quaint and archaick are those Georgian streets which we saw from the windows—fascinating hills lin'd with venerable dwellings of every description, from 200-year-old hovels huddled together in nondescript groups with rambling extensions and lean-to's, to stately Colonial mansions with proud gables and magnificent doorways. One feature possess'd in common by nearly all the houses, great and humble alike, especially held our attention;

*He now lives in Boston.

this being the curious old-world abundance of *chimney-pots*, here more prevalent even than in mysterious Marblehead. All at once the coach reach'd a spacious square, lin'd on every side with the quaint brick mercantile buildings of
the Revolutionary period. It was a sight such as we had never seen before—a
city business section of the 18th century, preserv'd in every detail. As the
coach pass'd on, entering again a delicious maze of ancient streets and turning
almost every corner in sight, we wonder'd when we shou'd reach the modern
business section; but after a time the houses thinn'd out and we found ourselves speeding past the shanties (shantih shantih shantih)[5] of fishermen toward the salt marshes of the open country to the south, with the sand-
choak'd harbour on our left, and the long stretch of Plum Island in the distance beyond. Then we question'd the driver, and discover'd the truth of a
suspicion which had cross'd our minds but fleetingly before. It was really
so—that Georgian business section was in fact the business section of today
as well! You children have seen it on the cards Edgar and I sent—can you
imagine it? Fancy, little Belknap, the New-York of 1780 still surviving—with
Broad and Pearl Streets lin'd with the principal shops and counting-houses,
Wall Street distinctly northerly, the City Hall Park too far uptown to be a
good land investment save for dwellings. Grotesque? Yet the commercial
Newburyport of 1780 still stands . . . truly, a City of the Living Dead!

There are only three restaurants, two of which are Hellenick dumps frequented only by the peasantry, and the third of which is the cafe of the Adams House—an hostelry over a century old which keeps its original sign. This
eating-house wou'd (small Alfredus) make any Cleveland Clark's Lunch look
like the main dining-room of the Statler, or (little Belknap) any upper Broadway cafeteria look like the Plaza,—and yet it is Newburyport's only civilised
place of refection! But what prices! Cheap? Say! 65 cents bought a bigger dinner than I could eat; tho' Edgar managed to stow his away.

Upon alighting from the coach, at the end of its route, we stroll'd back
thro' the maze of picturesque streets; ecstatically drinking in the antique houses of wood, brick, and stone, with peaked, gambrel, or flat roofs, massive or
graceful chimneys, quaint chimney-pots, and artistick Colonial doorways. It
was the past brought to life—flashes of 18th century bye-streets, silhouettes of
Christopher Wren steeples, kaleidoscopick etchings of old-time skylines,
snatches of glistening harbour beyond delectably rambling and alluringly ante-
diluvian alleys that wind lazily down hill—a true paradise of the born antiquarian! Once we walk'd the whole length of a ramshackle alley without losing for
a second the illusion of the Colonial age of sea-power. Thro' a cross-alley we
saw the splendid facade and columns of a stone mansion in the distance—
engaging vista! Thoughts of the past well'd up—here were the lodgings of adventurous sailors who knew the far Indies and the perfum'd East, and there
dwelt a solid, periwigg'd captain whose skill had led many a sturdy barque
around the Horn, or thro' Magellan's tortuous strait, or past the Cape of Good

Hope. Then we went down to the rotting wharves and dream'd of old days, and in fancy saw the heaps of cordage and bales of strange Asian wares, and the forest of Yankee masts that reach'd half across to Plum Island. Ah, me— the days that were! After this we return'd to the business section, bought some cards at one of the two visible chemist shops, (the other was clos'd for Sunday!) and set out for famous and opulent High Street, where stands the old mansion of the celebrated eccentrick Timothy Dexter.

Timothy Dexter—or Lord Timothy Dexter, as he lov'd to be call'd— died 117 years ago, but is still the principal topick of interest in Newburyport. His fame, indeed, went far beyond his native shoars; and you children have probably heard of him as the man who was jested into buying warming-pans to export to tropical Cuba, yet who made a fortune with them because the Cubans eagerly bought them as molasses ladles; who was trick'd into buying some useless whalebone, yet who made another fortune with that because of the rise of a new fashion which put the commodity in demand; who stock'd his cellar with needless provisions in expectation of a visit from the heirs of the murder'd Louis XVI, whom he had spectacularly invited to live in his mansion; yet who sold those provisions at an handsome profit when the visit fail'd to materialise. "Lord" Timothy is a semi-legendary figure, and New-England will never forget him!

Timothy Dexter was a common and ignorant leather-dresser, born in Malden Jany. 22, 1747. Later moving to Charlestown, he made a very substantial fortune by marrying a rich widow and increasing her prosperity thro' shrewd investments such as "cornering" necessities in a small way, and buying up the depreciated continental currency which ascended spectacularly when Mr. Hamilton put the U.S. finances on a solid basis. The close of the 1780's found Dexter quite wealthy, but with a grotesque temperament which made that wealth the source of unprecedented vagaries. His first step was to try to gratify his extravagant social ambition, and to seek equality with the Hancocks and other rising mercantile families of Boston. This, quite naturally, was rather a joke; since he could not even speak or write grammatically; but his failure caus'd him to quit Boston for ancient Newburyport, whence his wife had come, and whose society he erroneously deem'd more accessible than Boston's. Settling in Newburyport, Dexter bought the finest mansion in the town, and proceeded to embellish it in what his ignorant mind conceiv'd to be the best European taste. Within a month he was a general laughing-stock; for aside from his clumsy social advances, he had begun to evolve around his house a bizarre chaos of absurdity and grotesqueness such as New-England had never seen before. Flamboyant carvings bedizen'd the mansion—carvings which violated every aesthetick principle—and ridiculously laid-out gardens offended the eye on every hand. Erecting a high fence with massive posts, and within it a variety of conspicuous arches and pedestals, Dexter topp'd each post, pillar, and arch with hideous wooden statues of celebrities, clumsily wrought by a young ship-carver named Joseph Wilson, whom he later underpaid and abused. The statues had no resemblance to their purported subjects, and when Dexter tired of one hero he wou'd have him alter'd to another . . . . thus Genl. Morgan soon became the rising soldier Buonaparte, whose future majesty the eccentrick shrewdly forecast. Other statues were of the American presidents, added one by one as they were elected; sundry Indian sachems; Benjamin Franklin; Horatio Nelson; the goddesses of Fame and Liberty; and chief of all, Timothy Dexter himself, with the self-assum'd title of Lord, and the following modest inscription—which Joseph Wilson spell'd out for him:

"I am the First in the East, the First in the West, and the Greatest Philosopher in the Western World."

Dexter, failing to enter Newburyport society, contented himself with perpetual drunkenness, dissipation, and ostentation. He liv'd in the utmost disorder, mussing and tearing the valuable books which an expert had purchas'd for him, (and in which he only try'd to spell out the obscene passages) and breaking half of his elegant French furniture. He had a splendid coach with a coat-of-arms (taken at random from a book) painted on it, and bought a country house in Chester, N.H., afterward styling himself "King of Chester". Sometimes he wou'd go afoot thro' the streets, drest in rich cloathes and well-powder'd periwig, carrying a gold-headed cane and follow'd by a curious little hairless dog. The more aristocratick children wou'd mock at him, but common boys wou'd follow him and hail him as "My Lord", which ever bought a shower of money from his capacious pockets. He affected to be a great lover of nobility, and had the church-bells toll'd when the French mob kill'd King Louis XVI, whose heirs he invited to share his mansion. He hired a sort of David V. Bush to be his poet-laureate—a miserable ex-fishmonger who produc'd stanzas like this:

"Lord Dexter like King Solomon
Hath gold and silver by the ton,
And bells to churches he hath giv'n
To worship the great King of Heav'n."

This "poet"—whose name was Jonathan Plummer[6]—he drest in a most gorgeous livery. Dexter had a magnificent coffin prepar'd for himself, and like the late Mde. Bernhardt sometimes slept in it.[7] Once he publickly rehears'd his funeral, and afterward beat his wife because she did not weep enough. His half-wit son Samuel, a debauch'd gamester, and his almost wholly idiotick daughter, he educated expensively; having special masters since they cou'd learn nothing in any school. Later he marry'd the daughter off to an Englishman of much refinement, who divorc'd her as soon as he perceiv'd the extent of her imbecility. But all the while Dexter kept his business shrewdness. He speculated wisely, and was interested in the building of Chain Bridge across the Merrimack. Some have even believ'd that part of his eccentricity was as-sum'd for advertising purposes. His wealth was probably overrated, however, for he left only $35,027.39 in his will. His superstition was extream, and he not only kept an aged negress as household soothsayer, but frequently con-sulted the celebrated Moll Pitcher of Marblehead; a "witch" then living in Lynn at an advanc'd age.

In 1796, stung by the ridicule of the publick, Dexter publish'd what was probably America's queerest book—Bush's "Peace Poems and Sausages" not excepted. This hilarious pamphlet, intitul'd "A Pickle for the Knowing Ones", consisted of odd scraps of Dexter's views on everything under the sun; together with some sharp rebukes of the inquisitive Newburyporters who gossip'd about how he made his money. It is here that he told the warming-pan and whalebone stories which are so famous, yet which are set down by modern criticks as meer fabrications of Dexter's odd ironick hu-mour. Among the subjects discuss'd by "Lord" Timothy are the folly of sepa-rating Newburyport from the town of Newbury, the value of bridges, the world situation, and such like. In one place he singularly anticipates that other fool Woodrow Wilson in the "League of Nations" matter—listen, children, to this specimen of his genius, copy'd *verbatim et literatim* from his "Pickle" as still preserv'd in the publick library at Haverhill:

> "I Command pease and the gratest brotherly Love and Not fade be Linked to gether with that best of troue Love so as to govern all nasions on the fass of the gloub not to tiranize over them but to put them to order if any Despout shall A Rise as to boundreys or Any maturs of Importance it is Left franse and grat britton and Amacarey to be setteled A Congress to be allways in france all Despouts is to be there settled and this maybe Dun this will balless power and then all wars Dun A way there-fore I have the Lam to Lay Don with the Lion Now this may be Dun if thos three powers would A geray to Lay what is called Devel one side and Not Carry the gentleman pack hors Any longer but shake him of as dust on your feet and Laff at him."

Is this not truly Woodrovian—aside from spelling and punctuation? By the way—people complain'd that Dexter's "Pickle" was unpunctuated, so when he issued a second edition he added a full page of assorted punctuation marks at the end—though again failing to punctuate the text—and explain'd himself in the following note:

> "mister printer the Nowing Ones complane of my book the fust edition had no stops I put in A Nuf here and thay may peper and solt it as they plese."

Of this book Dexter gave away thousands of copies, so that it is fairly obtain-able today by collectors with the requisite finances. Edgar says he feels akin to

Lord Timothy—but I have not yet seen the likeness.

Drunken, revelling, cursing—Timothy Dexter died on Octr. 26, 1806, and was cheated of interment in the garish mausoleum which he had built behind his house—since the Newburyport Board of Health forbade it! He rests obscurely in a churchyard—the yard of a church which refus'd the gifts he once offer'd on condition of having a statue set up to him in an alcove. Vain to the last—an object of ridicule—he is still the best known feature ever connected with the dead city whose people so thoroughly repudiated him. After his decease, the grotesque mansion was inhabited by his idiot daughter and her own small daughter—also an imbecile,—till the two died, about the same time. The son surviv'd his father only a year. Later, in the absence of any legitimate heirs, the place was sold by the town; and is now restor'd to sanity, nothing but some columns (which are hard to remove and not very conspicuous) and the gilt eagle on the cupola (which is not at all ugly) remaining today of all the gewgaws affix'd by the erratick "Lord". In our family there is an old print of the place as it look'd in 1810—four years after Dexter's death—and the scene is indeed grotesque!

Having found and gaz'd at the Dexter mansion, Edgar and I proceeded to explore other parts of stately High Street. It is a splendid thoroughfare, and remarkably alive considering the deadness of the business section; tho' it must be less gorgeous than when Talleyrand prais'd its beauty. I wou'd not think of comparing it to Chestnut St. in Salem. The reason for its vitality as compar'd with that of the anaemick "downtown", is that most of the residents are very wealthy, and keep in touch with Boston thro' their coaches. When they wish to buy or see anything, they make for Tremont St. rather than their own village square; thus being practically Bostonian & leaving Newburyport commerce to the small fry—or such of them as do not trade in Haverhill. High St. boasts even a traffick watchman!

The day was now advancing. As we stroll'd south from Dexter's mansion we notic'd the antient churchyard and the new church going up within it. That edifice will mark Newburyport's awakening to the great aesthetick truth which Salem hath always realis'd—namely, that every old town hath its fixt architectural atmosphere, to which all new buildings must conform. In the hideous Victorian age of tastelessness, nearly every old town but Salem was ruin'd by the construction of ugly nondescript buildings like New-York's Post-Office, Providence's City Hall and Butler Exchange, Boston's City Hall and Post Office, etc. Salem alone knew the need for harmonious congruity, and stuck to classical and Colonial models. But just now Newburyport is waking up, and is trying to reclaim its heritage. In this old churchyard, where once a Colonial belfry saluted the sky, an ugly neo-Gothick church was built some time in the 19th century when the original structure decay'd or burn'd. It was horribly out of place in Newburyport—but what cou'd be expected of Victorian times? Now—Pegāna be prais'd—taste hath reappear'd; and the

Gothick monstrosity hath been torn down to make way for a beautiful new stone edifice on the simple and classical lines of the original Georgian fane. Gloria in excelsis! Once more the ancient slabs will look up to noble walls in harmony with their atmosphere, and the quiet corner—where a venerable bye-street slopes shadily and beckoningly down from the travell'd way—will outdo the Church and Flatbush Ave. intersection where you and I, little Belknap, have often ponder'd on the faith and mortality of the New-Netherland burghers. In this churchyard Edgar found the graves of some of his ancestors of 200 years ago—Adamses and Jacobses. His great-great-great-grandfather once spent a night in gaol in Newburyport—arrested for travelling on Sunday! Who says the times are not improv'd? Here we were doing the selfsame thing, yet chatting amicably with the watchmen instead of shunning their gaze!

Still farther south we went, admiring the stately mansions of old captains, with the tall cupolas where they used to scan the sea with spy-glasses. Good old days! Providence has some of these cupola'd houses—on the old hill overlooking the bay, which I shall shew you children when I can lure you to this village. Salem has many, but Newburyport probably has the most of all. On a side street we found an old house whose lower floor was in process of conversion to a shop. The new shop-window, with its glassless frame and broad seat, invited us; and we sate down for a long rest, gazing at ancient houses—one fully 250 years old—and stately, gigantick elm-trees. But time was flying, and it was growing cold. We had now reach'd a point which involv'd a retracing of those quaint, narrow streets and alleys we had first explor'd; and delightedly we set about it, pausing now and then to admire some particularly picturesque scenick effect—whether of quaintness, magnificence, or antique decay. Reaching the central square, we partook of the meal before mention'd—veal, potato, peas—coffee—coffee jelly with whipt cream—all for 65¢ apiece! Finally fill'd, we took the coach back to Merrimack; spending the evening in heated tho' friendly discussion—with Davis Senior and myself as prime antagonists.

Monday dawn'd rainy, and I barely had time to greet and breakfast with Edgar before his departure for school. I had intended to leave soon after, visiting Marblehead (which haste had excised from my programme) if the weather improv'd; but Mr. and Mrs. Davis prov'd such interested arguers that I did not get away till after dinner, when Davis Sr. took me into Haverhill in the family Ford. He's a good chap, for all his dogged commercialism and opinionatedness; but I'm infernally sorry he doesn't appreciate his son more. If Edgar were my boy, I'd consider myself damn'd lucky; but Davis merely mourns the child's absence of practicality and business sense. It is a vague ambition of Edgar to be a lawyer, and thus employ his strong *analytical* sense; but Davis Sr. can't see anything but the hardware business. At that, though, I guess he's a good hardware man—the leading one of Haverhill. I had Davis drop me at the Publick Library, where I spent the rest of the afternoon reading up on Timothy Dexter, whose picturesque eccentricity awak'd the responsive chord of eccentricity within myself. Among other things, I swallow'd the entire "Pickle for the Knowing Ones"! Haverhill hath a live and excellent library, which publishes a regular bulletin—I enclose a copy to each of you children, touching upon a man who help'd to make the 18th century the most artistick in history.

The city itself is quite delightful in its way—extremely vigorous and prosperous, as strikingly contrasted with Newburyport. The one lack is *picturesqueness,* for although Haverhill is an old town—settled in 1640 and incorporated in 1645—its large size and prosperity date only from the dawn of the boot and shoe industry of the last century. Accordingly, whilst a few Colonial houses of the original village remain—including the delightful edifice of the Historical Society which I think I describ'd to you boys a year and a half ago—most of the present city was built up since 1870, and is correspondingly modern. There are no truly ancient districts, as in Providence and Boston, or even New-York, and no comparison whatsoever can be made with such places as Salem and Newburyport. What distinctive features there are, are of modern origin. Among these is Winnikenni Castle, a true replica of mediaevalism constructed some years ago by a wealthy man, and crowning a wooded hill whose slopes are a delightful publick park. I visited it last year. Another is the new country-club—the second in the town, and not yet finished—which reproduces perfectly a mediaeval Gothick abbey. Apparently Haverhill, lacking Georgianism, is determin'd to go back to the Dark Ages! The population of this place is nearly 54,000, and constantly growing. Tryout misses it in his Plaistovian retirement, and has half a mind to return next winter. In the evening I climb'd the gentle slope to the station, and took the Boston coach. Once more in the Hub, I dined at a classically Hellenick dump across the street from the North Station (have you seen it, Belknap Sonny? The proprietor is one of those few neo-Hellenes who are conscious of the past, and has actually covered the walls with fine ancient Greek designs!) and hit the trail south. Instead of rattling to the South Station on the elevated, I chose the subway, (I am exceedingly fond of all things dark and subterranean, and miss the rides up to 96th!) taking a train to Washington-Summer and there transferring to a S.S. train. The trip was uneventful, as was the later Providential trip, and midnight found me back at the old shebang.

It was a great trip, but fatigued me prodigiously. Since then a sort of modify'd grippe hath claim'd me, and I am at this moment nearly stone deaf! But my trust is in the Lord, and I am confident of better things to come. Your visit, small Belknap, will work wonders in bracing the Old Man up, and if you, little Galba, cou'd but join the conclave, I am certain I shou'd be cur'd forthwith!

Well, boys, the clock advanceth, and my aunt is reminding me that I must prepare to go to the matinee, after which I shall have a fitting of my new summer suit of sober grey. The outside world seems quaint to my deaf ears—

I was vastly amus'd a week ago, when I ventur'd forth with the novel deafness so stably fixt upon my aged head.

Well—be Grandpa's nice boys, and don't let your French novels corrupt your native English taste! Remember the honour and dignity demanded of a man of the world's master-race, and learn a lesson from the robust old captains of Newburyport, and the simple-hearted wood-carvers of ancient Salem, whose sincerity and devotion builded an art which shall outlive all the faddishness and indecency of modern, degenerating Gaul and Italy. Grandpa's getting old, childish, and rambling these days, but remember what he tells you and let it influence you sometimes after he is dead and buried in an old New-England churchyard. Be good children, and you will know a tranquillity which is better than all the hectick anticks of drunken Frenchmen.

Yr most aff: ancestor and obt: Servt:
GRANDPA THEOBALD

Notes

1. Sandusky regaled HPL with his use of contemporary slang. HPL dedicated his poem "The Feast" (1923) "To Wisecrack Sandusky, Esq., B.I., M.B.O. (Bachelor of Intelligence, Massachusetts Brotherhood of Owls)."
2. Elliot Paul (1891–1958), journalist whose early novels, *Indelible* (1922), *Impromptu* (1923), and *Imperturable* (1924), were hailed by highbrow critics as landmarks in realism.
3. See letter 11n4.
4. Long did not visit HPL in Providence until July 1927.
5. HPL mockingly repeats the final line of T. S. Eliot's *The Waste Land* (1922).
6. Jonathan Plummer (1761–1819), American poet whose work included *The Awful Malignant Fever at Newbury Port, in the Year 1796: An Elegiac Epistle to the Mourners, on the Death of Forty-four Persons Who Died of Malignant Fever . . . in the Summer and Autumn of the Year 1796*.
7. French stage actress Sarah Bernhardt (1844–1923) was said to have slept in a coffin.

[13]   [ANS][1]

[Postmarked Providence, R.I,.
17 July 1923]

See Grandpa's mug on t'other side! ¶ Taking in the sad sea waves to enhance my pessimism—they moan with a beautiful melancholy! ¶ It sure is hell without a fountain pen—I gotta get one soon.

Yr obt grandsire Theobaldus

Notes

1. *Front:* Old Man's Face, Point Judith, Narragansett Pier, R. I. Written in pencil.

[14]   [To Lillian M. Galpin]   [ALS]

169 Clinton St.,
Brooklyn, N.Y.,
August 16, 1925.

Dear Mrs. Galpin:—

Your gifted young husband having informed our local circle of aesthetic dilettanti of your impending arrival on the S.S. *Majestic*, & having delegated to us the agreeable responsibility of showing you such sights & salient points of interest as you may care to inspect here, I herewith take it upon myself to facilitate your location & identification of the circle in question. Mr. Galpin tells me that you will call me up by telephone, but it occurs to me that I may not have given him the number of this haven of remunerative guests; in which case you will look in vain through the book for a telephone in my name. Let me, therefore, here state that the correct number is *MAIN 1401*, at the Brooklynward end of which a proper sentry will be posted during the day of your arrival as estimated by the White Star offices—Tuesday, Aug. 18.

It furthermore occurs to me that, since you have met none of our local contingent in person, you may have trouble in identifying whomever of us may be first to meet you. To obviate this difficulty, I herewith enclose the rudiments of a portrait gallery in which the physiognomies of the two representatives likeliest to be on hand are rather explicitly treated. You will not, I think, find it hard to pick out either one or both of these individuals—Mr. Samuel Loveman & myself—when you observe them at any designated point in attitudes of expectancy. I must, by the way, request the return of these modest likenesses—each being the only one of its kind in my possession.

Pray consider our unassuming group most entirely at your service as guides & expositors—so far as those of us still in town are able to act adequately in that capacity. We all hold your spouse in the most abounding esteem as a favourite adopted grandson; & anything we can do to enhance the pleasure of his accomplished consort will afford us the keenest delight. We regret that our only youthful member—the meteoric Mr. Frank Belknap Long, Jr., of whom you must often have heard Mr. Galpin speak,—is now sojourning at the Thousand Islands; so that he will be unable to add the zest of modernity to the welcome which we antiques & fossils shall extend. On Wednesday evening, the 19th, our group holds its hebdomedal meeting at the abode of one of the members; & should you care to participate in the session you would not only do honour to the hostess, but confer distinction upon a coterie to whose lips the name of Galpin is no stranger.

And may I not add, as an individual, that my wife & I are both very anxious to meet the bride of our young prodigy-friend? Since my wife will be called imperatively West on business by Wednesday at the latest, she bids me ask you if you will not favour us with your company at dinner on Tuesday evening—at a restaurant, perforce, since we are this year existing in a rented room instead of housekeeping.

Such, then, are the essential features of the reception committee. Be assured that the telephone MAIN 1401 will be competently manned, & that the sentinel will be empowered to make whatever arrangements for meeting & guidance you will find most convenient. Meanwhile my wife & I trust that you may not have formulated any previous plans for Tuesday evening, when we should be so delighted to act as your hosts.

With renewed expressions of pleasure at your prospective arrival, & heartiest regards to yourself & your scintillant husband,

I have the honour to remain, Madam,

Yr. most ob^t humble Servt:

H. P. Lovecraft

[15]   [Postcard, nonextant][1]

[Postmarked 12 May 1930]

Notes

1. *Front:* Bruton Parish Church Williamsburg, VA.

[16]   [Postcard, nonextant][1]

[Postmarked 24 May 1930]

Notes

1. *Front:* Japanese Wave Screen from Metropolitan Museum New York.

[17]   [ALS, on brochure *Maymount on the James and The Dooley Museum*]

Thor's Day—May 15, 1930[1]

Son:—[2]

Gad, Sir, I swoon! I swoon with the conscious contemplation of compleat & culminant beauty! I can't begin to describe it—for I am without breath & without words—but just look at this folder & at the accompanying postcard. They may faintly suggest, tho' they can never fully reveal. For Pegāna's sake chuck Peterborough & come down here at once! This is something to see & dream about all the rest of one's life! I am sure I shall think of very little else during my few remaining days! It is Poe's "Domain of Arnheim" & "Island of the Fay" all rolled into one—with mine own Cathuria & Gardens of Yin[3] added for good measure. It *must* be a dream, after all. I stumbled on it yesterday afternoon, & have come out today to enjoy it from 11 a.m. to the closing hour of six, bringing some revising work with me. Ædepol! But it wholly eclipses the upheaved Wade Park of Birchdale days[4]—& my erstwhile favourite Japanese Garden beside the Brooklyn Museum is as nothing to it!

You are perhaps sensible, from many olden observations of mine, that to me the quality of *utter, perfect beauty* assumes *two* supreme incarnations or adumbrations: one, a mass of mystical city towers & roofs & spires outlined against a sunset & glimpsed from a fairly distant balustraded terrace; & the other, the experience of walking (or, as in most of my dreams, aërially floating) thro' ethereal & enchanted gardens of exotick delicacy & opulence, with carved stone bridges, labyrinthine paths, marble fountains, terraces, & staircases, strange pagodas, hillside grottos, curious statues, termini, sundials, benches, basins, & lanthorns, lily'd pools of swans & streams with tiers of waterfalls, spreading gingko-trees & drooping, feathery willows, & suntouch'd flowers of a bizarre, Klarkash-Tonick pattern never beheld on land or beneath the sea . . . . . .

Well, Son, call your Grandpa an aged liar or not—*I have at last actually found the garden of my earliest dreams*—& in no other city than antient Richmond, home of my beloved Poe! How I wish it cou'd have been here in his day! I doubt if there is another such realm of faery open to the publick in these American colonies! ¶ Shall probably have to begin my reluctant northward trek tomorrow. Eheu! ¶ Hope to see you in 3 weeks or so.

Yr obt Grandsire

Θεοβαλδος

P.S. "The Rivals" was great Tuesday night.[5]

Notes

1. Written from Maymont Park, Richmond, VA.

2. This is the earliest surviving letter of many using this appellation. Note that the son of the narrator Delapore of "The Rats in the Walls" (1923) is named Alfred.

3. Cathuria is featured in "The White Ship" (1919). "The Gardens of Yin" is sonnet XVIII of HPL's *Fungi from Yuggoth* (1929–30).

4. I.e., 1922, when HPL stayed with Galpin at 9231 Birchdale Avenue, Cleveland, during a visit with Samuel Loveman.

5. HPL saw a performance of Richard Brinsley Sheridan's *The Rivals* in Richmond at the Lyric Theatre on 13 May 1930.

[18]   [Postcard, nonextant][1]

[Postmarked 25 June 1930]

Notes

1. *Front:* The Old State House, Newport. Short greeting signed by HPL and James F. Morton.

[19]   [ALS]

Tuesday [c. September 1930]

Son:—

    Your pre-autumnal exodus caused you to miss my travel postcards—directed to Appleton—at the time your much-appreciated epistle was sent. By this time you doubtless have them, through forwarding, & are aware that the Old Gentleman has at last set foot on soil still loyal to our rightful Sovereign, to say nothing of inspecting the quaintest & most exquisite relique of antiquity in the western hemisphere—the venerable & beautiful fortress town of *Quebec*.

    Quebec! Can I ever get it out of my head long enough to think about anything else? Who cares for Paris or Antipolis now? Never have I beheld anything else like it, & never do I expect to! In due time you will see a travelogue on it[1]—but for the present I am wholly inarticulate. All my former standards of urban beauty are superseded & obsolete. I can scarcely believe that the place belongs to the waking world at all. A mighty headland rising out of a mile-broad river & topped by a mediaeval fortress—city walls of cyclopean masonry scaling vertical cliffs or towering above green table-lands—great arching *city gates* & frowning bastions—huddles of pointed red-tiled roofs & silver belfries & steeples—archaic lanes winding uphill or lurking in the beetling shadow of precipices—horse-drawn vehicles, & all the vestiges of a mature, leisurely civilisation—these things are only a fraction of the marvellous totality that is Quebec. The trip was amazingly unpremeditated. I was just back from Cape Cod with Belknap when I saw the advertisement of the $12.00 excursion from Boston. This, I decided at once, was an ideal last fling of summer—& what a fling it turn'd out to be! The weather favour'd me miraculously—& as for Quebec, it outdistanced my wildest expectations. I had only 3 days there, but my sightseeing was so continuous & assiduous that I really form'd a surprising acquaintance with the place. I threaded virtually all the antient streets of both upper & lower towns, made a compleat circuit of the old city wall,—in some places walking on top—[unlike the walls of your precious Paris, Quebec's wall is *all standing in good condition* except for 3 gates removed & 1 partly removed] ascended to the citadel & obtained various views therefrom, crossed the ferry to Levis & climbed the cliff there for a sunset view of the Quebec skyline, & in general assimilated the aspect & atmosphere of a region whose linkage with our age & continent is truly of the feeblest & most nominal sort. Quebec is really a part of old Bourbon France—a Norman hill town of the year 1700 or thereabouts. In retrospect the whole thing is a fantastick dream. On the way back—as you doubtless know by this time from a postcard—I stopped off at Boston for an all-day boat trip to Provincetown, at the tip of Cape Cod. This village (which I did not reach by land during my Belnapian journeyings) I found to be somewhat overrated, but the sail—my first experience on the *open sea*—was well worth the price of the excursion. To be on limitless water out of sight of land is (as the Atlantick hath doubtless taught you) to have the fantastick imagination stimulated in the most powerful way. The uniformly blank horizon evokes all sorts of speculations as to *what may lie beyond,* so that the sensations of Columbus, Madoc, Arthur Gordon Pym, the Ancient Mariner, & all the other voyagers of song & story are rolled into one & sharpen'd to expectant poignancy. Who can tell what strange port or temple of the sea will loom suddenly ahead? To approach Boston Harbour at sunset from open water is something one can never forget. Grey headlands—monolith-like lighthouses—low-lying, cryptical islets—what vespertine realm of mystery is this which rises mirage-like from vapour-shrouded vacancy? Phaeacia—Avalon—Tyre—Carthage—Alexandria—Atlantis—the City of Never—The net effect is some sort of mystical defeat of the intolerable limitations of time & space & natural law—some burst of escape (or hint of a possible burst of escape) from known conditions & dimensions, & passage through strange, inconceivable sunset gates to realms of beauty & wonder which one has formerly known of only darkly, in hints & touches of pseudo-memory that are strong in childhood but dead in adult years except among those few who have not forgotten how to live.

I rejoice to hear of the improved milieu you have achieved, & of the prospect of bringing it within the radius of financial safety through judicious management. I hope the new furniture is of 18th century design—at least, I hope it is not of that stiltedly artificial & irrelevantly unmotivated sort which laboriously pretends to express the present age & goes under the popular appellation of "modernistic". Ugh! Too bad you have to wait for the new paradise in such semi-squalid quarters—but after all, the interregnum is brief, & will give you all the keener zest for the ultimate haven. You seem very well situated as regards neighbours, & I trust you may be able to make the spot a fixed & permanent headquarters—punctuated, of course, by such excursions into the varied outside world as circumstances may permit.

No—you hadn't previously mentioned the relay'd greetings from the quondam Mme. Theobald;[2] an incident which prompts the usual platitude concerning the microscopic dimensions of this planetary spheroid. My messages from that direction during the past two years have been confin'd to Christmas & birthday cards, but if occasion arises to exchange more verbose greetings, I shall assuredly add your respects & compliments to my own.

I am glad that your youthful law-kinsmen enjoy'd my tales, even tho' it was but a renewed acquaintance in one case. Up to the present writing, the assortment has *not* been return'd to Rhode-Island waters—but there is not the least hurry so long as the MSS are safe. You might make diplomatick inquiries when next you converse with the sprightly twain—always taking care not to express an impatience which I wou'd be the last to transmit.

The cutting you enclosed was my first intimation—& so far as I know, active amateurdom's first intimation—of the passing of Alfred L. Hutchinson.[3] I am sending the news to Tryout & to young Spink—the National's official editor—in the belief that they will wish to make items of it. Poor old duffer—I didn't know he was ill, & it seems to me I recall his having written or telegraphed greetings to the recent Boston convention. An amateur to the last! He had his crude spots, from all accounts, (I hardly knew him myself, & doubt if I ever exchanged five letters with him) but I guess he meant well enough basically. An odd character; short on formal education & long on egotism, but gifted with a salty horse sense & general gregariousness which gave him a rather good time in the world, all told. His *Trail* was a naive & spicy addition to the amateurdom of its day,[4] & I doubt not but that his dearly cherish'd tome "The Limit of Wealth" (which I am urging the amateurs to mention in their obituary items) was much less silly than I imagined it to be in those days of my own relative youth & narrowness. I recall your meeting with him at the Dells convention[5]—indeed, I have more than one group photograph of that event which includes you both. He would scarcely have been a fount of congenial conversation for a young philosopher already far removed from mundane commonplaces—but it is to his credit that he recognised juvenile genius when he saw it. I am glad the local press gave him a final publicity commensurate with the ample exploitation he liked. Poor old Hutch—but after all, he probably got as much out of the empty mockery of existence as most do.

I am glad to hear that your magnum opus has attained something like a definitive shape, & hope its orchestral production will prove a conspicuous triumph. Too bad so much rearranging of "West Wind" is necessary—but I suppose one cannot begrudge pains expended in bringing a work of art to perfection & presentability. I can imagine the labour which must go into all this part copying—hence can fervently thank the Creator that inclination & ability did not combine to make me a musician! Still—when it comes time to reap rewards, the rewards of a successful & conscientious composer are undoubtedly very great.

I hear frequently from good old Moe, & am daily expecting to hear of the acceptance of his poetry-appreciation textbook[6] by some standard firm. This book—whose MS. I looked over last year, & for which I furnished many metrical exercises—is really a marvellously fine thing, & ought to do more than any other influence to teach mediocre minds to distinguish betwixt real poetry & hackneyed sentimentalism. Mocrates is the same amiably orthodox soul of yesteryear, & in time his faithful plodding ought to gain him the comfortable niche in paedagogical pantheon which probably forms the apex of his ambitions. By the way—he has just looked up our bizarre & piquant old pal Co—Ira A. Cole, the one-time Kansas poet & present Colorado theologist. Poor Co has never recovered from his 1917 attack of pentecostal religion, & throws forth impressive hints of having suffer'd strange martyrdoms for his faith; but for all that he sounds like a reasonably contented agrestick soul, whose messianick responsibilities neither bow his shoulders nor hamper his digestion.

I just had quite an echo of marine adventure in the form of a letter from the young New Zealand amateur Robert G. Barr. Stampless, watersoaked, & marked with a rubber stamp—

> Salvaged from S.S. Tahiti
> Lost at sea.

In its unspoken drama it makes me think of the letters I used to receive from the British amateurs during the war, with their stickers of government censorship & their occasional salty marks of oceanick mishaps.

Well—if I don't get to work I'll never clean up the pile of junk which my Quebec truancy allow'd to accumulate. Here's wishing you a speedy transfer to your new & palatial quarters, & a successful term of Gallicising a fresh generation of more or less Anglo-Saxon youth.

With customary expressions of grandparental esteem, & sincere regards uxori fratribusque, I have the honour to subscribe myself

Ever y^r most oblig'd, most ob^t Servt

Theobaldus Avus[7]

P.S. Our old fellow-amateur Paul J. Campbell is now living in Chicago. Address, 7528 Honore St.

Notes

1. HPL eventually wrote *A Description of the Town of Quebeck, in New-France* between October 1930 and January 1931.
2. Sonia H. Greene, formerly Mrs. Lovecraft.
3. Alfred L. Hutchinson (1859–1930) was the author of *The Limit of Wealth*.
4. HPL published "On a New-England Village Seen by Moonlight" in the *Trail* for Summer 1915; his "The Crime of the Century" and "A Rural Summer Eve" appeared in the January 1916 number.
5. The UAPA convention at the Wisconsin Dells occurred in July 1918.
6. *Doorways to Poetry* was never published.
7. "Theobald the grandfather."

[20]   [ALS]

Aug. 28, 1932

Son:—

Well, well, Sir! Grandpa is glad to welcome the wandering Consul Hasting back to regions of familiar impressions & more certain postal communication! Sorry the retrograde path was beset with costly obstacles—but all's well that ends well, & the roar of the Fox River dam again resounds on the ear of the return'd native. I hope you will not fail to bring Felix–Charles-Pierre Baudelaire[1] from Chicago—how has he thriven under the care of your quondam-Charlestonian acquaintance?

The card from antique Londinium duly came, & filled me with envy at your opportunity to behold civilisation's capital, if only for a single full day. If I were in Europe, I would devote not less than 2 or 3 weeks to London—& might not get outside of Britain at all. The British Museum card surely reveals one of my (or Klarkash-Ton's or Sonny Belknap's) extra-human monsters in disguise—indeed, I am positive that this entity reached Java as a relique of sunken Mu, or of the still more monstrous & fabulous R'lyeh! Thanks!

I don't envy you your semi-arctic voyage—except for the glimpse of whales, icebergs, aurorae, & other terrestrial marvels—but I would envy you your Quebec–Montreal vistas if it weren't that I expect to see both of those antient cities a week hence. You don't mention stopping in Quebec . . . . . is it possible that an inhuman steamship company denied you landing privileges in this, the most interesting & exquisite town on the North-American continent?

Sorry so many practical responsibilities awaited you on home soil, & hope all the various difficulties may presently be adjusted without too nerve-racking a series of ordeals. Before long, I dare say, your duties at the Methodist Seminary[2] will begin; & I trust that these may not prove irksome beyond endurance. Alas, that good old Mocrates is not on the job at A.H.S. to give your youthful charges some preliminary enlightenment before they tread the classick Laurentian shades!

I appreciate very much your expressions of sympathy concerning my recent bereavement—an event which indeed aggravates the barrenness of existence, despite one's recognition of its inevitability.[3] Shall be glad to get your post-Hispanick epistle if it turns up, & am eager to hear more of your impressions of London. Meanwhile the Majorcan travelogue, with its graphick map & pleasing rotogravure illustrations, afforded me the keenest delight—& will no doubt duplicate the performance with Little Belknap & Fra Samuelus.

I had no idea that the charm & quaintness of the Balearick Islands was so great, tho' in truth I suppose all the less frequented parts of Europe are full of such unchanged deposits from the past. Such richness in visible history is almost dizzying to a native of the western world, where 300 years forms the limit of architectural age. I must some day get at least a momentary glimpse of the old world with its piled-up accumulations of centuries & millennia, & its curious survivals not only of tangible edifices but of modes of life. The Baleares, I believe, have a civilis'd history extending back to the days of Carthage (as indeed your folder mentions), & were esteem'd for the skill of their inhabitants in the warlike use of the sling—Balearick slingers being valued in all the armies of antiquity. Besides the Punick settlements, there were less vigorous ones establish'd by the maritime Greeks. One of the present towns of Minorca—Mahon—

is of Punick origin & perpetuates the common Carthaginian name of *Mago*. It is my impression that the islands kept their Punick culture till after the fall of Carthage proper, being brought under the dominion of ROMA only in 121 B.C., when the piracies of their denizens induced our Senatus to despatch against them the younger Q. Caecilius Metellus. Q. Metellus, having subdued them, colonised them with 3000 settlers from Italia & Hispania, introduced the classick olive which so much impress'd you, (& which I wou'd give my eye-teeth to behold!) founded the towns of Palma and Pollentia on Balearis Major, & assum'd the title or agnomen of Balearicus in honour of his exploits. The isles became part of the province of Hispania Citerior—tho' toward the decline of the empire they form'd a separate administrative unit till overrun by the Vandals in A.D. 423. Tho' you have not mention'd any ROMAN remains, I am inform'd that such do indeed exist—notably an aqueduct at Pollentia—or Pollenza, as I believe the modern inhabitants call it. This, however, is in the northern part of the island, which you did not visit. The Moors took the Balearicks from the Vandals in A.D. 790, & in 1009 they split off from the Emirate of Cordova as a separate Saracen kingdom—notable (as in Punick days) for piratical exploits. These piracies made the islands the object of a crusade dictated by the Romish Pope; & in 1232 (or 1229 as your folder gives it) Don Jaime, El Rey de Aragon, conquer'd them & made of them a Spanish kingdom under one of his sons. In 1439 they were united to Aragon. In modern times, in the war of the Spanish Succession during the glorious reign of Her Majesty Queen ANNE, whom God save, our troops under Gen[l] STANHOPE took Minorca (1708) & temporarily added it (under the treaty of Utrecht in 1713) to the BRITANNICK Dominions; tho' the cursed French seiz'd it from 1756 to 1769. About 1770 Minorca's history joins to that of the American colonies by reason of the great number of peasant labourers exported thence to Florida (now gain'd by us in 1765) by Dr. Andrew Turnbull, to work his great plantations at New-Smyrna, below St. Augustine. Dr. Turnbull so mistreated his Minorcan bondmen that the indentures were cancelled by His Maj[ty's] Governor at St.-Augustine in 1776; whilst the Minorcans themselves settled around St. Augustine, where their descendants may be found to this day. Minorca was retaken by the Spaniards in 1782, temporarily restored to ENGLAND in 1798, & finally ceded back to Spain in 1803.

It is indeed difficult to imagine anything more fascinating than Majorca with its ancient towns, frowning castles, terraced hills, & rugged coast-line. Your long walk was assuredly a notable event, & I trow fatigue and footsoreness were none too great a price to pay for it. Bañalbufar sounds like a fragment of a dream, whilst all the scenick suggestions inspire one with a wish to emigrate thither. All this would have transported Little Belknap's Spanish soul in the pre-1932 days before he went Bolshevik. Incidentally—I am sending your travelogue to the child, with instructions for trans-shipment to

Samuelus. (who is now home visiting in Cleveland, tho' financial reverses have forced his family to leave the familiar shades of 1537)

I myself have taken advantage of phenomenally cheap boat rates (50¢ round trip) & have visited ancient Newport repeatedly this summer—thus not being wholly out of touch with either venerable streets or rugged cliffs. On Tuesday I start for Boston, & Wednesday W. Paul Cook & I will (weather permitting) view the eclipse from some point (either Newburyport or Portsmouth) north of there—incidentally stopping at Haverhill to see good old Tryout Smith, who will be 80 in October. On Friday, Sept. 2., I shall start from Boston on an incredibly cheap rail excursion to both Montreal & Quebec (whole thing *$12.00!*)—seeing Montreal for the first time. It won't give me much time in either city, but it's all I can afford—and a glimpse is better than nothing. I *could* make it all-Montreal & have more time—but it would break my aged heart not to see Quebec as well. You will receive postcard echoes of this brief & hurried Odyssey next week.

And so it goes. Hope home won't seem too tame after the picturesque antiquities of Europe. More later.

> Yr obt Servt
> Grandpa

Notes

1. Galpin's cat.
2. Galpin's term for Lawrence College in Appleton, founded in 1847 by two Methodist clergymen.
3. HPL's aunt Lillian D. Clark (b. 1856) had died 3 July 1932.

[21]   [ALS]

> Theobald Grange—
> Octr 27, 1932

Son:—

I am consum'd with appropriate envy upon hearing of your new sable charge. Bless my old bones, but what an elf of darkness the little Spinx (to use Sonny Belknap's pronunciation, which he insists is good Manhattanese) must be! But I mourn, simultaneously, at the unmistakable reference that M. Felix Baudelaire has evaporated into his native shadow. Rex mortuus est—vivat Rex! I am sure that there cou'd be no worthier heir of the departed than this sprightly emissary from the nighted gulphs of Dis. In matters of nomenclature I am sure you have observed the precepts of good sense, & I trust that mounting years may never cause the lively creature to belie the dual implications of his title. Your account of his ancestry I have perus'd with the utmost interest & attention, & I wish I might behold the singular household of decay'd gentry where so many of his kind are bred & harbour'd. I assume that the family of Grignon is descended from the earliest French pioneers of the region—trading posts & missions having existed there since the 1660's. It seems to represent the sort of picturesque & pathetick decline which so much appeals to the increasing realistick genius of another young Wisconsin friend of mine—August W. Derleth of Sauk City, whose work is now beginning to appear in magazines like *Pagany* & *The Midland*, & who was three-starr'd by O'Brien in this year's "Best Short Stories."[1] Cats & curiosities—what better accessories to attend the fading of a great house? Wou'd that my own last years were thus appropriately environ'd! The late founder of the feline dynasty assuredly had the right idea regarding the place of the cat in domestick œconomy, & I regret that his venerable relict does not echo his attentive devotion to the species. That nocturnal search for the future skipper must have been an event of pleasing & mystical weirdness, & I am glad that its result was so eminently fortunate. I trust that the later & undiscover'd brood turn'd out to be equally attractive. In the Dutch Nieuw Nederland this latter group wou'd have been call'd *stubbletje* cats because of their late summer birth at a time when the mown fields bristle with stubble. Such a brood was traditionally held to be of inferior quality, tho' I doubt if many kittens were banish'd because of birth-date alone. My friend Wilfred B. Talman—whom you may or may not have met during one of your Noveboracense[2] passages—is of the old Dutch stock & now lives again on his ancestral farm at Spring Valley. He last August inform'd me of the birth of some stubbletje kittens to the household Sphinx; but so far has tradition declin'd, that each of the young arrivals was carefully cherish'd—one for permanent retention at the Talman bouwerie, & the other two for affectionate placement with pious & respectable patroons elsewhere in the colony. I am glad that Skipper is maturing gracefully, & that he is not afflicted with the nervous irritability of the urban train. I have ever maintain'd, that large towns are not fit for gentlemen to live in, or for the young to be rear'd in; & rejoice that your charge will have an opportunity to grow up amidst the beechen groves that line the Vulpine stream. Happy the cat whose wish & care a few paternal acres bound! I hope that no rapid chariots course along the way where Skipper's nimble steps are like to stray; for perils lurk where ruthless haste attends, & furry wand'rers meet untimely ends.

"War & Peace", in two ample volumes, is among the paternally inherited section of my library;[3] & upon your enthusiastick endorsement I am almost tempted to consider its perusal. The fact that its text leaves are cut, plus the evidence supply'd by fly-leaves that they were originally uncut, leads me to the conclusion that my father must have surviv'd a voyage thro' it; tho' it is possible that he meerly amus'd himself of an evening by running a paper knife thro' it. What I have read of Count Lyof Nikolaievitch's work has not filled me with enthusiasm. Both in him, & in M. Dustyoffsky's efforts, I have seem'd to discern an exaggeration of neurotick traits which, however true they may be for the brachycephalick, moody, & mercurial Slav, have not much meaning or relevance in connexion with the Western part of mankind. I will not deny the greatness of these authors in reflecting the environment around them—but I understand too little of that environment to appreciate its close pourtrayal. But since "War & Peace" is actually in the house, it is not impossible that I may at least begin it some day. (N.B. Having just taken a look at the *size* of the volumes, I'm not so sure!)

Glad you've been working toward the greater permanence of your natal rooftree. My native edifice still stands[4]—being now used as an office-building by 12 physicians. The rear part of the grounds, with the stable, was sold separately; & last year the venerable barn (whose cupola had long been succumbing to worm & fungus, & which had for years been vacant) was razed to make way for a smug mock-Tudor residence. Eheu—thus pass the landmarks of my youth. In the early days of decline, after we had given up our horses & carriages, that stable was my exclusive personal playhouse—a whole echoing building with shadowy, mysterious loft, cavernous carriage room, empty stalls, & trim, office-like harness-room all at the disposal of one tenant of ten years' growth! Ah, me—in those days it was a police station, theatre, army headquarters, car barn, railway round house, outlaws' rendezvous, fire station, house to be robbed, & everything else that youthful imagination could make it! And now it is gone! It was not so very old in reality—being the second stable on its site. My grandfather built it in 1880, & my surviving aunt,[5] then a small girl, put a tin box of records into the unfinish'd walls, to be exhum'd & studied by the archaeologists of a fabulous posterity. Alas that she shou'd live to see its destruction & reclaim the records herself! Last summer, when the workmen had it partly razed, she went over & looked in the place where she had put the records 51 years before. They were still there—Harsford's Baking Powder box rusted but intact, & the contents only slightly touched by the mould of intervening aeons. My aunt's tintype, & that of a youthful friend (now dead) quite decipherable, & their messages to a future civilisation legible in every part. She still has the box—but alas, we have no hope of erecting another family castle in which to reincorporate it with a XX century postscript! By the way—it must be pleasant for you to have a sprightly & altitudinous young brother-in-law about the house.

Glad to hear that the Methodist Seminary is improving since the days when a young intellectual titan, wearied with the puerilities of one Farley & other upholders of obsolescent illusions, fled in desperation to the more congenial shoars of crystal-blue Mendota. I hope your position there, aided by the better element, will grow more & more favourable—& that in time the giggling Hadrianus & his inexperienc'd Antinoüs may be put compleatly to rout! Meanwhile you are undoubtedly accumulating much useful influence through your extra-collegiate labours in cosmopolitanising the local patricians—& are, I trust, so firmly reëstablishing yourself on hereditary soil that you will not wish to quit it again without some uncommonly great inducement. There is no place for a man like the rural acres or village lanes from whence he sprang; & in my opinion any lack of brilliant conversation (easily palliated by reading, travels, & correspondence) is more than aton'd for by the ineffable harmony resulting from the sight of familiar roofs & spires & gardens, & from the presence of a million imponderable influences connected with one's earliest & most valu'd memories. I am acutely sensible of the pleasures of travel, & none likes strange, far climes more than I; but all their delightfulness is really dependent upon my knowledge that Old Providence is awaiting my return with well-remember'd hills & steeples & winding lanes. After all, there is no real life except that which allows for the natural relationship of the individual to the soil which produc'd him. If a mechanis'd modernity is to make of our descendants a rootless & nomadick race, it will certainly impoverish our antient English civilisation by subtracting a vital element whose place can never be adequately fill'd.

Musical creation, I trust, will in course of time enliven your moments of leisure. As for study—I have not perus'd the second volume of Spengler, tho' I believe it hath long been put into English. The original (&, I conceive, the most general & inclusive) volume I read some years ago[6] with much attention & a great degree of acquiescence, tho' I think the philosopher errs when he draws too close a comparison betwixt the life of a culture & that of a single biological organism. In effect, the parallel may indeed be close; for it is certain no civilisation can last more than a limited length of time without going thro' various typical phases of decline. But when one considers the nature of the interdependence betwixt the parts of an organick unit, & compares this type of indivisible union & inevitable development with the looser bonds linking the elements of a culture, it becomes plain that the case is one of *resemblance* rather than of *identity*. Whilst the ultimate senescence & extinction of a culture are virtually unavoidable, the degree & conditions of its aging are certainly much more variable through chance & calculation than are those of a living organism's aging. Spengler is probably right in his prophecies concerning Western Europe's decline, but he is probably less so in his attempts to assign a precise initial cause. Another philosopher who deals with the decline of the west is one Egon Friedell;[7] whose ultimate conclusions are marr'd by a kind of mystical optimism unjustify'd by any evidence he produces. I hope you have been able to make contemporary international relations clearer to your clientele than they are to the average person—including most statesmen. Do you attempt to account for the magnitude of the present depression? In surveying the effects of mechanis'd industry upon society, I have been led to a certain change of political views. Formerly I favour'd the concentration of resources in a few hands, in the interest of a stable hereditary culture; but I now believe that this system will no longer operate. With the universal use & improvement of machinery, all the needed labour of the world can be perform'd by a relatively few persons, leaving vast numbers permanently unemployable, depression or no depression. If these people are not fed & amused, they will dangerously revolt; hence we must either institute a programme of steady pensioning—panem et circenses[8]—or else subject industry to a governmental supervision which will lessen its profits but spread its jobs amongst more men working less hours. For many reasons the latter course seems to me most reasonable—especially since the vast accumulations of the commercial oligarchs are not now used to any great extent for cultural purposes. Therefore (deeming both democracy & communism fallacious for western civilisation) I favour a kind of fascism which may, whilst helping the dangerous masses at the expense of the needlessly rich, nevertheless preserve the essentials of traditional civilisation & leave political power in the hands of a small & cultivated (tho' not over-rich) governing class largely hereditary but subject to gradual increase as other individuals rise to its cultural level. How practicable such a programme could be, only Pegāna can say; but it seems to me at least a more rational ultimate goal—in a very general sense—than any other. Its approximation could be facilitated by a gradual modelling of the publick mood & standards in its favour, to be accomplish'd through the coöperation of various agencies in control of instruction & expression. The ideal of a benevolent monarchy & wise aristocracy ought to be revis'd & justify'd in practice—confirming the judgment of Claudian of old, when he writ (amidst another aera of decay much like our own) "Nulla libertas gratior, quam sub rege pio."[9] God Save the King!

As for my travels of August & September, as I writ you on a card, the eclipse was a compleat success for Paullus Culinarius[10] & me. Having fixt upon antient Newburyport as our post of observation, we repair'd thither on the stage-coach by way of Haverhill; where he stopt to converse with honest Tryout Smith. (he turned 80 last Monday, but is still as spry as a boy) We cou'd not persuade him to go with us, but he had a very good sight of the eclipse (tho' the totality did not last so long) from his own dooryard. Once in Newburyport, we chose an hilltop meadow north of the compact section as our station. Some clouds in the sky made us anxious, but the sun came out every little while & gave us long glimpses of every stage of the phaenomenon. The landskip did not change in tone until the crescent of the fading sun was rather small, & then a kind of sunset vividness became apparent. When the crescent waned to extream thinness, the scene grew strange & spectral—an almost deathlike quality inhering in the sickly yellowish light. At last the outspread valleys sank into unnatural night—Jupiter came out in the deep-violet heavens—ghoulish shadow-bands raced along the winding white roads—the last beaded strip of glitter vanish'd—& the pale corona flicker'd into aureolar radiance around the black disc of the obscuring moon. The earth was darken'd more deeply than in the eclipse of 1925, tho' the corona was not so bright. We absorb'd the whole spectacle with the utmost impressedness &

appreciation—totality lasting a surprisingly long time (it seem'd nearly a minute) despite our distance from the central line of the eclipse. Finally the beaded crescent reëmerged, the valleys glow'd again in faint, eerie light, & the various partial phases were repeated in reverse order. The marvel was over, & accustomed things resum'd their wonted sway. I may never see another, but it is not everyone who has, like me, witness'd two solar eclipses.

My trip to New-France was also a decided success, tho' your own passage thro' the region will make my account seem less than novel. Montreal—which I saw for the first time—struck me very pleasantly; tho' of course it cannot compare with Quebec. I saw it with some thoroughness, taking several different motor tours (including Lachine Rapids) & exploring the antient waterfront sections on foot. The interiors I saw were the Cathedral, (1827) Chapel of Notre-Dame de Bonsecœurs (1771), & Chateau de Ramezay (1705)—aside from modern places. I don't need to tell you anything about the city & its suburbs, including the totally British *Westmount*. I had an excellent view of the whole region from Westmount Mountain. Montreal is much less French than Quebec—for as you have seen, the dominant language west of St. Lawrence Blvd. is uniformly English except for official bilingual signs like

DEFENSE DE STATIONNER
———
NO PARKING

(The *Quebec* idiom for this same sign is NE STATIONNEZ PAS, showing a distinct local difference in usage.) But I was glad to get to primaeval & mystical Quebec—of which you can have had but the most tantalising glimpse from the river. As in 1930 I revelled in the mass'd reliquiae of antiquity—the rugged cliff, frowning citadel, precipitous winding lanes & flights of steps, antient, crumbling facades & tiled roofs, magnificent scenick vistas, queerly robed priests & friars, centuried publick buildings of grey stone, beetling, cannon-lined ramparts, & the scenes of our glorious WOLFE'S victory over the Gallick foe. God Save the King! On this occasion I explor'd the neighbouring Isle d'Orleans (which you must have seen from the boat—& did you also see Montmorency Falls on the N. Mainland shore?), where the old French countryside remains in an unspoil'd state just as when WOLFE landed in 1759. There were endless brick farmhouses with curved eaves, wind & water mills, wayside shrines, & quaint white villages clustering around antient silver-steepled parish churches. Nothing but French is spoken, & the population—seigneurs & habitants—live where their ancestors have lived for 200 years & more. I hated to go home—& when passing thro' Bostonium eased the transition by making a side-trip to antient Marblehead. Since then I have been kept on the move by two successive visitors, after whose departure accumulated work compleatly ingulph'd me. I did play truant, however, on warm & sunny Octr 9, when I took a farewell auto trip to archaick Salem & Marblehead. And now hibernating time draws near—alas!

Best of wishes—

Yr most obt

Grandpa.

P.S. Samuelus—now moved around the corner from Col. Hts. to *17 Middagh St.*—may pay me a visit before winter closes down. ¶ As to being a weird-fictional celebrity—if so, I've receiv'd very few reports of it! On the contrary, magazines were never more hostile to my stuff. I've about stopped trying to contribute. ¶ Here's an echo of my recent work in amateurdom.[11] Needn't return it. Can't quite shake the old associations!

Notes

1. Derleth's "Five Alone" was on the Roll of Honor in O'Brien's *The Best Short Stories of 1933* (1933).

2. Adjectival form of *Novum Eboracum* (New York).

3. Probably a reprint of the first English translation of *War and Peace*, "translated into French by a Russian lady, and from the French by Clara Bell" (1886; rpt. New York: W. S. Gottsberger, 1887; 2 vols.; *LL* 974).

4. 194 (later 454) Angell Street; it was razed in 1961.

5. HPL's maternal grandfather, Whipple Van Buren Phillips (1833–1904), and his aunt Annie E. P. Gamwell (1866–1941).

6. HPL read the first volume of Oswald Spengler's *The Decline of the West* (Eng. tr. 1926–28) no later than February 1927. See *Dawnward Spire, Lonely Hill* 122.

7. HPL refers to *A Cultural History of the Modern Age* by Egon Friedell (1878–1938), his only work to be translated into English.

8. "Bread and circuses," the celebrated phrase from Juvenal, *Satires* 10.80.

9. "There is no liberty more welcome than under a pious king." Claudius Claudianus, *De Consulatu Stilichonis* (c. 400 C.E.), 3.114–15 ("Numquam libertas gratior extat / quam sub rege pio" in Claudian).

10. I.e., W. Paul Cook.

11. *Further Criticism of Poetry.* The ms. of the essay is titled "Notes on Verse Technique" (18 April 1932).

[22]   [ALS]

Tenbarnes—

Jany. 20, 1933.

Son:—

"En Route" is indeed delightful, & I surely hope you will set it to music as you suggest. It has a profound, fundamental beat not unlike that of the ocean it celebrates; & ought to give you great opportunities for aural effects. The "Deep Sea Meditation" is sprightly & appealing—& full of the true speculative feeling proper to a philosopher. Many thanks for both—I shall keep them, since they are not attached to any part of your epistle which demands the confidence-keeping processes of combustion.[1]

Concerning the matter of emotion—I fancy about 3 or 4 rounds of an old-time Kleicomolo discussion would remove more than one point of difficulty & possible misconception, but whether it would leave you on the side of gawd & Mocrates or on that of the devil & Grandpa Theobald I don't yet know—not having kept track of all your philosophick mutations since the Golden Age of unstinted dialectick. Possibly you're coming around to the "spirituality"-recognising position of the Methodists—so that you & Lawrence's founders will be in utter harmony. I may yet hear of your rolling around in the sawdust of a camp-meeting tent & begging the holy ghost's mercy for your sins! As for me—I don't see any reason for going beyond the possibilities indicated by the evidence around us. There is no ground for fancying the existence of other "spiritual" orders superimposed on the general order of which we perceive a fragment, & within this general order it is clear that all organick life, including human, is the merest temporary accident occurring now & then—that on any one planet being only a flash in galactick history, & leaving nothing behind to indicate that it has ever existed. Yesterday man did not exist; tomorrow there will be no trace of him, & the cosmos will be exactly as it would have been had he never existed. During the second that the race lives, it develops certain structural reactions to external conditions, which ramify & multiply as environment grows complex & as the organic substance becomes modified & specialised to meet various natural changes. The phenomenon of consciousness arises, & reactions become classified as they contribute to or detract from the sense of normal adjustment. Experience becomes complicated by the retention of impressions left on the tissue by former experience, & originally simple reflexes acquire distinctions & overtones depending upon memory, association, & suggestion. Sensations & judgments are built upon, & conceptions & feelings become more & more elaborate—both in directions leading to increased comprehension of relationship & environment, & in directions leading to fundamental misconceptions & fallacies. Whatever has been experienced is erroneously thought capable of isolation & intensified (even infinite) experiencing, whilst whatever exists is erroneously thought capable of existing on an intensified or even infinite scale. Analogously, the fulfilment of some desires (i.e., the production of normal adjustment after the perception of abnormal adjustment) is accepted erroneously as evidence that all desires can potentially be fulfilled, & that perfect states without any maladjustments whatsoever (impossible in view of the complex nature of the higher organisms & the consequent conflicts of impulse with impulse within a single organism—not to mention the instability & relative unmanageability of environment) are theoretically if not actually possible. Thus out of simple instinct plus experience, memory, association, & suggestion, there grows the tenuous yet powerful quality of *imagination*—which works both for & against the perception of reality. On the side of unreality we have the natural tendency toward illusion-formation & grandiose expansiveness which arises from the unreflective extension of principles & phenomena seen on a smaller scale, & from the application of false analogies in explaining the unknown. Gradually man comes to acquire a false & cosmically amusing sense of the supreme importance of certain things which may not exist at all, or which may be mere meaningless routine phenomena or fragments of phenomena that happen to suggest or symbolise (through steps of plausible though purely illusory linkage) non-existent but gigantic & impressive things or processes or conditions erroneously conceived through the misapplication of consciousness. Thus the impressive popular conceptions of "god", "righteousness", "sacredness", "love", "evil", "tragedy", "mystery", "humanity", & so on. All these things seem tremendously important to the organism which refrains (either through ignorance or through tradition) from analysing them—tied up as they are with certain real & elemental impulses, & inculcated as they are by facile illusions of reality & by countless generations of naive & often compulsory acceptance at face value. It is not remarkable that this is so, or that the force of these erroneous conceptions persists powerfully in the average organism's reflexes long after the conscious brain has grasped their actual unreality. But this does not alter the fact that the conceptions actually *are* unreal, & built up falsely through misleading associative processes. They may *seem* very real & potent in the history of the ignorant race, & their clutch on human sensations & actions may remain very strong despite the recognition of their nature by the thinking minority; but that is no evidence in favour of their actuality. And it follows that the minority who understand the *essential meaninglessness* of these grandiose fallacies, & of the emotions they have drawn into their service, will tend to be more independent of their capricious dominion than will the ignorant or wilfully unanalytical majority. The wise man will use the misconceptions decoratively & intelligently when he can get pleasure or stimulation thereby, but he will be able to *undermine their associated emotions* through reflection on their meaninglessness & triviality when such emotions tend to operate against his larger well-being . . . . i.e., either his physical welfare or his general emotional equilibrium. Thus Schopenhauer pointed out that the one way to circumvent the pain resulting from the will is to undermine the will through reflection on its actual place & function in the universe. When we grasp the fact that the emotions are nothing but tangled & misleading linkages of memory, association, symbolism, & suggestion with the eleven or twelve primary instinctive reflexes of protoplasm in the vertebrate stage, we shall find it less difficult to reconcile their elaborate imagery, ideology, subjective force & illusion of cosmic significance, & claims to importance & authority, with the actual physiological basis of glandular secretion & hormonic discharge under-lying them. Of course the elaborate structure would not exist if the immediate secretion & discharge were not joined to a confused jumble of left-overs from other organic reactions; but conversely, it would not exist if the left-overs were not tickled by a fresh secretion & discharge—which may proceed from one of many different causes, some psychological (perception of images suggesting situations calling on the given gland for coöperation in the œconomy of the au-tonomick nervous system) & some purely mechanical or physical, & altogether irrelevant to the grandiose chain of sensations & conceptions resulting from accidental combination with the left-overs. It is merely *convention,* ignorance, traditional inhibitions, or mental indolence which finds anything remarkable or incompatible in the contrast betwixt the pompous & grandiose pseudo-significance—& the intense poignancy—of certain emotions as *subjectively* ex-perienced, & the actual triviality & fortuitousness (for it is largely a matter of chance & caprice just what especial left-overs will happen to combine with any given hormonic impulse) of these emotions themselves, considered *objectively* in relation to the immediate environment & to the cosmos in general. There is no reason whatever to feel shocked or incredulous at Joseph McCabe's[2] assertion that the difference betwixt the cry of a dog & a symphony of Beethoven is purely one of *degree,* not of *kind.* It is of course understood that the more im-pressive & elaborately illusory conceptions & emotions are peculiar to the more complex organisms—since only complex organisms generate enough left-overs to supply the associative structure of such things . . . . but that does not make the things themselves any more really important or related to cosmic truth. They are very pretty as long as they can be used to advantage in embellishing our monotonous & accidental period of existence & conscious-ness (though Joseph Wood Krutch in "The Modern Temper" believes that their field of effective use in this direction is sharply narrowing); but when they begin to get in the way of one another, & of the less elaborated & less exag-gerated emotions concerned with more direct environmental adjustment, it is time to deflate & minimise the more intrusive & mischievous ones by expos-ing their real absence of cosmic significance & causing the independent part of the mind to withdraw its support from them. Of course, not everyone can profit by such an exposé. Even the most keenly intelligent persons are often so powerfully dominated by traditional inhibitions, primitive reflexes, & other anti-cerebral influences that their abstract intellection is locally retarded or nullified. But at least, everyone can try; & many may find themselves surprised by the degree to which they can win emancipation from troublesome emotional con-flicts. The most useful question in the world, as concerns the moulding & harmonisation of the human personality, is "Well, what the hell of it?"

Your discussion of this point does not impress me as being of quite the old Consul Hasting acuteness, but haste & possible bias account for that. You ask whether it is more probable that glandular discharge causes emotion, or that emotion causes glandular discharge. In reply to this, one might ask what causes emotion if glandular discharge doesn't? It has long been recognised that emotion is the result of perceptions of physical impacts on the nervous system—the relationship being too repeatedly verifiable for doubt. All that I have said of the part played by instinct, memory, association, suggestion, symbolisation, &c. has been well understood; it being certain that nothing ever gets into the emotions or consciousness which does not come through the five senses. All this matter of the "significance" of emotion & of intuitive impressions was carefully threshed out *long before* the discovery of the part played by the ductless glands—with the result that no sober & impartial thinker could for a moment credit the existence of anything save chance & caprice behind such parts of man's subjective feelings as are not the direct expression of primary instincts. Thus glands & hormones need not enter into the matter at all. Everything was settled except the *exact physiological way* in which perceptions or physical stimuli became translated into the sort of autonomic nervous impulse which manifests itself as an instinctive reflex & (in the case of complex organisms with associative left-overs) as a psychological emotion. Discovery of the role of the glands & their secretions merely supplied the gap & settled this question—but did not change any major conception of independent biologists & psychologists. The facts about the cosmic insignificance & fortuitousness of human emotions do not rest in any way upon endocrinology . . . . . . so that it was simply as a *symbol* that I happened to choose gland-secretion as typical of the kind of thing really lying behind pompous & pretentious emotions. Getting back to the *order* of gland-discharge & emotion, it is certain that discharge comes as a result of some direct impression, either physical or psychological, which acts on the gland. If the impression is purely physical or chemical, no *need* for the discharge may exist—yet some emotion will result if the organism is sufficiently complex & if certain associative left-overs happen to be in the right position for combination. Thus glandular injections, as well as the Steinach operation (which renders an external secretion internal by making gonads wholly ductless), often cause complete changes in emotional life. If the impression is psychological, it is almost never originally an *emotion*, but simply the *perception of a condition naturally tending to demand this particular gland-discharge*. The primary product is an instinctive reflex—which becomes an emotion only after taking on certain associative factors. Clearly, the action precedes the emotion in the first place, although of course the exercise of the resultant emotion renews the original gland-exciting perception in such a way as to increase & prolong the hormonic discharge. An instinctive reflex precedes each emotion, but the latter strikes back & renews the excitation of the instinct. All this has been determined by various types of actual experiment explained in some detail in books on endocrinology. In ordinary life, the question is complicated by the fact that what we commonly regard as single emotions are in most cases very far from that—being complex & sometimes capricious or even contradictory groups of totally unrelated emotions, which change irresponsibly & imperceptibly before we can reach anything like a genuine analysis. The interaction of the components of these groups, as they strike back & influence the underlying instincts, is of tremendous & hopeless complexity—& well illustrates the capriciousness & essential meaninglessness of everything in the emotional field.

What I said some time back regarding the non-remarkableness of the elaborate sensations which come from purely capricious & mechanical causes (top of sheet II, 1.) ought to dispose of your exaltation of "unfathomably rich emotional phenomena which alter characters, transform lives, & in the social realm occasion murders, marriages, procreation of the species, & incalculably more." Do not irrelevant trifles determine everything? Have not lives been changed by the missing of a morning train, or battles determined by what a general ate the night before? Many a man has married because he was drunk, & George Jean Nathan[3] once pointed out that most of the great philosophers probably thought or reasoned as they did because of such minor & overlooked factors as diet, digestion, wife's temper, debts, & so on. A stomachache may have just as much effect on the world, & almost as much on an individual's thought, as an ecstatic adoration of the Virgin Mary. What is more—you betray subjectiveness & conventionality in taking for granted the importance of such things as character, life, murder, marriage, procreation, & so on. What do these things really amount to in the cosmos? All things are merely incidents in a blind cyclic flux from nowhere to nowhere, so far as probability suggests. The fact that emotions cause great consequences in the lives of those not sufficiently strong or sufficiently on guard to resist them means absolutely nothing. A plain knock on the head or knife-thrust between the ribs can change a life to nothingness, while a bad tooth infection can completely alter a person's psychology, motivation, personality, social adaptability, & intelligence level. I don't see where your argument is. Even your climactic parallel fails to sustain it—for as a matter of fact even the greatest of the philosophers with his psychological problems **is** only the natural & inevitable result of two cells stuck together to form an egg. Of course there are many steps between the original egg-cell & the full-panoplied Galpinius or Democritus, but it is all a fixed mechanical process resulting from the structure of the universe. The full-blown & subjectively powerful & important-seeming emotion which moulds character is of course the product of a vast number of accidental association-processes superadded to a simple reflex—but that does not make it a whit more *truly* important or typical of cosmic design than is the itch of a flea-bitten hog. Such *virtual,* empirical, apparent, or relative importance as it may have is wholly artificial—to be gauged only by the thin & variable standard of effect on a certain variable personality under certain momentary conditions. Any really serious estimate of such pseudo-importance is a mockery. True, the emotion may operate powerfully on a given individual under a given set of conditions—but so may the kick of an army mule. There is nothing in all this to demand exaltation & bated breath. If the damn thing tickles pleasantly & doesn't do anybody any harm, let it alone. Certainly, some of our finest diversions & strongest non-primitive reasons for living come from *the intelligent manipulation* of such raw material. So also do fine things come from the intelligent manipulation of lumpish bronze, random bricks, aimless colours, & casual sounds. But if the damn thing tickles or grates *unpleasantly*, there's nothing "sacred" about it which needs to prevent our deflating & largely banishing it through a rational analysis of its purely biochemical irrelevance. Emotion is essentially *raw material*. It is a magnificent thing to harness & use, but a damned poor & inappropriate thing to obey as a master or worship as a god.

If you'll reflect on this you'll see a good many of your objections removed. No one wishes to dispute the value of *emotion well managed*, or to claim that as much aesthetic possibility resides in a dog's yelp as in a musician's symphony. One wishes merely to emphasise that the complexity of evolved emotion is nothing other *in kind* than the multiplication of simple biological reflexes, so that it has *no intrinsic cosmic value* whatever, & no relative value *except when it is used to advantage*. Grant that it is better *raw material* for something of subjective value than a hog's itch is—but that doesn't make it valuable *until* it is well used. The fact remains that it is merely a fortuitous result of bodily accidents, & that it does not mean in any way what it appears to mean in our illusion-blinded & unanalysing consciousness.

I don't think that a rational view of these matters is by any means peculiarly American, though it may be that certain Americans have used the basic facts as an excuse for depreciating aesthetically valuable imponderables. Actually, the fortuitous & meaningless nature of the emotions need not cause us to abandon their artistic use whenever they can be made to bolster up pleasing illusions of ego-expansion & liberation. Indeed, a vast number of exploded concepts are still capable of stimulating decorative use. Whatever is closely allied to basic animal instinct is imperishable, & the emotional & imaginative world grows so gradually out of the realm of instinct that the line will always be hazy. Despite what Krutch predicts, it is unlikely that the illusions of the fancy will be drained of their titillative value for some time to come—especially since all of us must live through a vividly impressionable childhood during which the fruits of disillusion are inoperative.

It is a mistake to try to isolate one form of truth-appraisal from another. When people talk of "science", "philosophy", & so on they are in danger of letting *nomenclature* interfere with genuine ideas. In looking over the universe it is possible to get many different sorts of perspective, & the separate investigations of the various sciences merge together in the correlative processes of philosophy. After all is said & done, there is really no trace of reason to consider organic life in general—or the human species in particular—as anything of importance or of more than momentary duration. All of the pseudo-importance felt by man himself before he surveys the wider field necessarily drops away—as does the illusion of a fly's giganticism when we remove the magnifying-glass through which we have been looking. It still remains a fact that man is the most complex organism in this immediate part of the universe—but *what of it?* Nobody tries to deny the obvious facts regarding man's consciousness & grasp on certain parts of the external world. His superiority to other immediate forms of matter is clear, & we can even get a hint at the precise structural reasons for that superiority. What the de-bunker attacks is merely the absurd & gratuitous (though natural enough as a result of early ignorance) assumption of the tradition-blinded part of mankind that the race is especially differentiated from the rest of molecular matter, especially endowed with ideas not coming through the senses, & especially important to the mythical consciousness governing the cosmos. And no de-bunking is too drastic for such puerility—into which I hope to Pegāna you are not falling! Don't join good old Mocrates & revive the defunct Biblical Alliance of 1918![4]

Life itself—the especial form of union betwixt carbon, hydrogen, nitrogen, & other elements in which certain unique processes & energy-forms develop—is probably a widely-scattered phenomenon; but there is no reason to think that its more complex forms of growth (dependent as these are upon environment) are even remotely similar in widely separated parts of the universe, or that the psychological attributes of any one highly complex branch are parallelled in any other. Such things as honour, beauty, love, &c. are by no means to be regarded as other than local to the momentary race of primates harbouring these conceptions. On the other hand, *hunger* is probably basic with all vital compounds. The number of bodies in the cosmos containing life-forms at any one time is probably vastly less than was commonly supposed prior to twenty years ago—since we now believe life-sustaining planets to be very rare accidents. However, even so, it is not likely that terrestrial man is the most complex of all things in the *totality* of the varied galaxies—or at least, it's only an even guess that he is. And in the endless history of time & space it would be foolish to fancy that he has not been vastly surpassed vigintillions of times.

As for your present perturbations—I think a year or so will find you much less agitated, since all amorous attractions are essentially transient. And of course, if you'd get outside yourself, take an objective & panoramick survey, & give some really serious thought to the fortuitous meaninglessness of all emotion, you would be greatly helped in the cooling-off process. That's the only process worth cultivating unless the other victim gets ashamed of accepting luxury from a deceived partner & coöperates toward putting the whole matter on an open & straight-forward basis. Meanwhile one may only advise that you "coast" as inconspicuously & indecisively as you can—with eyes open as to possible exits & solutions. Let us hope that your wife will have time in Chicago to think on the value of the prize that is slipping away, & that a renewed affection on her part may assist in toning down the new & capricious hormone-storm. But time & common sense will doubtless bring their own adjustments.

Little Belknap has had a bad spell of influenza since my visit, but is now adequately convalescing. ¶ Did I tell you in my last that Cook has presented me with a three-volume copy of "Melmoth, the Wanderer"?[5] Glad you're doing some congenial composing, & hope the folk-song comes out well. ¶ Heard a lecture on Schopenhauer Wednesday night[6] which made me think of many an old Gallomo discussion. ¶ There's a course of poetry readings in town which will bring hither our one-time debate-subject *T. S. Eliot*.[7] I expect to hear him . . . . Shantih, Shantih, Shantih! ¶ So you've had snow in your part of the world? None here—in fact, the winter has so far been as mild as last winter.

And so it goes. May Pegāna guide you in paths of only moderate feloni-ousness!

   —Yr obt hble Servt—

       Grandpa

Notes

1. A manuscript entitled "En Route (An American to Paris, 1931)" survives among HPL's papers at JHL. "Deep Sea Meditation" has not been found.
2. Joseph McCabe (1867–1955) was a well-known philosopher, historian, and free-thinker, author of such works as *The Evolution of Mind* (1910) and *The Story of Evolution* (1912). He also translated Ernst Haeckel's *The Riddle of the Universe* (1900).
3. George Jean Nathan (1882–1958), drama critic and essayist. The comment referred to probably derives from *The Autobiography of an Attitude* (New York: Knopf, 1925): "A man's philosophy, his attitude toward the world, is very seldom found to be the result of carefully reasoned reflection, meditation and deduction. It is, on the contrary, gen-erally the largely fortuitous end-product and sum-product of a hundred and one extra-subjective occurrences, adventures and phenomena that have figured in his life" (3).
4. See HPL to Adolphe de Castro, 14 October 1934 (ms., JHL): "For years he [Mau-rice W. Moe] was associated with the late William Jennings Bryan (supplying the brains, perhaps, while poor old Bill supplied the wind & braying!) in some sort of scheme called the 'Biblical Alliance', for giving bible courses to students in state uni-versities where such teaching is barred."
5. By Charles Robert Maturin.
6. I.e., on 18 January, by a Prof. Baylis.
7. Eliot's reading occurred the week of 24 February. See letter 23.

[23] [ALS]

          Tenbarnes—

          March 24, 1933

Son:—

  I am very glad to hear that, in spite of distracting influences, you have been improving & solidifying your collegiate position, & laying the foundations for better conditions next year. After all, security & tranquillity are the foundations of all things—as I am alarmingly reminded by my own financial instability, which may soon force me to quit #10 for cheaper & accordingly less congenial quarters. A firm & comfortable foothold on one's native sod is assuredly something to be adhered to with utmost sedulousness. Which reminds me that Cook (who has, alas, just lost his job through the closing of his firm) lately sent me a picture of an extremely quaint Gothick masterpiece on your local campus—whose medium of construction, however, speaks rather forbiddingly of the climate from my tropick-demanding point of view. Were you (whose critical knowledge of St-Etienne de Mont & other ecclesiastical landmarks of the Old World might well make you an expert in such matters) by any chance associated with its construction? I enclose the view in question. And incidentally—whilst upon the subject of architecture & its accessories—let me enclose another cutting to shew how well Rhode-Island has resisted the degenerate tendency toward building & decoration of the modernistick sort. You may have a set of epigoni in the West; but by God, Sir, the true & authentick civilisation of white Englishmen still survives in antient New-England! God Save the King.

As for those matters of emotion lately under discussion—whilst I certainly do believe that the purely human & derivative emotions are richer in permanent satisfactions than the more primitive impulses, & therefore to be preferr'd to the latter; I wou'd not be thought of as unduly minimising the raw material, or implying that it is *always* oppos'd to the most superior processes of the personality. Rather wou'd I say, that it is to be ruled against only when it demonstrably interferes with some process of the higher sort, & thereby tends to reduce the personality to a lower level than it might otherwise attain. That, I conceive, was the position of the celebrated Spinoza; a lecture upon whom I last December describ'd to you. But in general my point was not so much a championship of the evolv'd over the unevolv'd, as a championship of the *balanc'd whole* over *any* hypertrophick or disturbing ingredient, be it of the human or bestial sort. It was—& is—my position, that a man's entire, coördinated personality ought to be the unimpeded arbiter of his destinies; that no irrational caprice, or isolated overdevelopment of some single impulse, be it high or low, ought to enslave him by defeating that rational course of action which the bulk of his impulses & faculties dictates, & which therefore is essential to his tranquillity & good adjustment to life. Such a position does not necessarily look down upon any particular impulse or set of impulses as compar'd with others. It meerly looks askance at *any* impulse which, by growing out of its proper proportion, conflicts badly with the general emotional equilibrium & total welfare of the possessor. 'Tis a case of prescribing the sound classical maxim of *nihil nimium*,[1] as over against the feverish & irrational mediaeval attitude summ'd up in the title of Mr. Dryden: "All for Love; or, the World Well Lost."[2] Conceiving, therefore, that the reduction or deflation of certain isolated & disturbing emotions is often of value in the development of the whole personality, & the tranquil governance of existence; it is but natural that I shou'd bring up the purely mechanical & non-"sacred" character of all human feelings, in order to remove that superstition which allies them to the "divine" & resents any attack upon any of them. I claim, & I think not without reason, that the extream force of any emotion can very sensibly be blunted by a careful examination of all the trivial & fortuitous factors which go into its composition. More than one determin'd person has very successfully & advantageously modify'd his character by the rational & deliberate toning down of emotional predispositions which warr'd against balance, tranquillity, & social adjustment. This, indeed, I know from many concrete & verifiable cases—not excluding my own, wherein a tendency toward quick & violent anger, highly inimical to urbanity, has been vastly diminish'd since the hot-temper'd days of my youth. The important thing to fix in mind is *that no emotion is really worth anything in itself.* All that is of value is the pleasing *balance* brought about by the harmonious *correlation* of the various emotions. The emotions themselves are simply existing forces—not to be valued or worshipp'd in themselves, but simply to be accepted as natural phaenomena & manag'd to the greatest advantage of the whole personality. The *value* of a feeling depends altogether upon its adjustment to the fabrick compos'd of all the other feelings.

As to the emotional development of those persons distinguish'd in the arts—it is very possible that certain (but not all) types of creativeness are associated with a lack of balance otherwise unfortunate. That the keener sensitiveness demanded by art is often associated with uneven development & lack of rational control, can scarcely be deny'd—& did not the late Max Nordau[3] associate all genius with degeneracy? But that is no argument against every man's trying to be as well-balanced as he *can* be—& fortunately for society, not many of us are of the extream & irresponsible hyper-artistick type. Most persons, happily, are more or less capable of transferring a little of their artistick sense into the art of living itself; instead of pouring it all into specifick external enterprises & living with a loose & slovenly ugliness which they wou'd scorn to have associated with their professed work. I am an advocate of making life the chief of one's arts—of being a gentleman first & a specifick artist second if at all. All of which, I trust, even tho' it is not likely to accomplish any convincing or conversion, may at least remove a little of the aspect of error or inconsistency from my arguments.

Our enlivening discussions & diverting parodies of a decade ago were last month vividly recall'd to me by a poetick reading which I attended—the celebrity being none other than our old-time nucleus of debate, the eminent & incomprehensible Shantih S. (Waste Land) Eliot, now grown to be 45 & looking every year of it.[4] He hath pick'd up a strong Britannick accent thro' his long (& now naturalised) residence in London, & despite his love of symbolick chaos it is easy to picture him in his latterly announc'd role of 'royalist in politics, classicist in literature, & Anglo-Catholick in religion.'[5] His remarks were tinged with a pleasing infusion of humour, & it was perhaps not without an unobtrusive ocular scintillation that he asserted the essential *plainness* & *simplicity* of his poetical emanations. He read from "The Waste Land", "Ash Wednesday", & other products made famous by his criticks, & appear'd to hold his surprisingly vast audience in that state of tense awe which only a combination of reputation & incomprehension can produce. After the lecture he held a kind of court in a hall adjoining the auditorium; his starry-eyed admirers filing past & introducing themselves with a deferential handclasp—a naive ceremony in which I did not think it necessary to participate. I enclose some accounts of the event, & of a rather comical interruption of it, from the pen of the columnist Bertrand Kelton Hart, Esq., literary editor of the local *Journal*.[6] I would appreciate the return of these at some time—to preserve betwixt the pages of that now-tatter'd copy of the Nov. '22 *Dial* which contains "The Waste Land." Shantih, shantih, shantih!

Another thing I shall send when I can find it (my files being in the worst possible state of disorder) is a cartoon of the syndicated "Metropolitan Movies" series (drawn by one Wortman)[7] in which our old friend George Willard Kirk & his Chelsea Book Shop are very plainly delineated. G K is shewn leaning against the wall in a very characteristick posture, & even his face is distinctly suggested despite certain departures from line-for-line realism. The Chelsea seems to have grown into something of an institution on the borders of Greenwich-Village.

My programme has of late been exceedingly crowded with annoying tho' doubtfully remunerative revisory tasks—& the correction of an 80,000-word novel MS. looms formidably ahead.[8] A fortnight ago a job took me to Hartford, in His Maj[ty's] Province of Connecticut, to assist a client in some research[9] at the Athenaeum there, & I took advantage of my sojourn to survey many picturesque memorials of the past. As I doubtless writ you in 1931, when another job gave me my first sight of central Connecticut, Hartford itself is not a town of especial interest; most of its antiquities (save the late-Georgian Bulfinch state house, now superseded for that purpose) having succumb'd to the venom of the years. On this occasion, however, I had time to explore the antient suburbs of Farmington & Wethersfield, & found them abundantly rich in my favourite kind of material. Farmington is one of the most beautiful of all the villages of this continent, lying 9 miles S.W. of Hartford in an exquisitely rolling countryside replete with adventurous vistas of hills beyond hills. Its vast elms are of a highly impressive aspect, & the well-kept plenitude of colonial houses—a few of the antique 17th century mode, with peaked gables & second-story overhang—impart an induplicable charm. The inn at which I stopt was a rambling composite with a nucleus dating back to 1638 (the year of Farmington's foundation) & with no part newer than 1790. The village church, white & steepled, was built in 1771, & many picturesque burying-grounds are present. Restrictions on the sale of land have kept the place in a state of great selectness. Wethersfield, 4 miles due south of Hartford, is likewise an absorbing repository of tradition, tho' vastly different from Farmington in aspect. It lies in a flat region, & has a wide village common shaded by the greatest elms east of the Rocky Mountains. Its abundant array of 18th century houses display the distinctive marks of Connecticut Valley architecture, & include the Webb house, where in May 1781 Genls. Washington & Rochambeau, & other damn'd rebels & foreigners, plann'd the crucially disastrous battle which took place the following October in York Town, in Virginia. The brick church, with a well-design'd spire, was built in 1763, being then accounted the finest church in New-England outside Boston. The view from its belfry is prais'd in the letters & diaries of all the French officers who pass'd thro' Wethersfield in 1781. This region was, & probably still is, fam'd for the growing of onions. It was at Wethersfield that the Pequot war started in 1637.

The winter here has, on the whole, been mercifully mild; tho' I am none the less glad to hail the advent of spring. I fear that bad finances will debar me from any long trip this year, tho' I hope to make the most of short ones. Best wishes—& may good sense guide you in all the departments of life.

Yr most obt hble Servt—

Grandpa

Notes

1. "Nothing in excess."

2. Dryden's play is an adaptation of Shakespeare's *Antony and Cleopatra*.

3. Max Nordau (1849–1923), *Degeneration* (1895); translated from *Entartung* (1892–93).

4. HPL wrote a parody of Eliot's *The Waste Land*, entitled "Waste Paper: A Poem of Profound Insignificance."

5. The quotation comes from the preface to Eliot's *For Lancelot Andrewes* (1929).

6. Bertrand Kelton Hart (1892–1941), was literary editor of the *Providence Journal* and author of the column, "The Sideshow." He discussed Eliot's lecture—given on 19 February at Faunce House, on the Brown University campus—in several columns, including those of 20 and 22 February 1933. In the latter column, Hart noted an interruption in Eliot's lecture when a janitor handed Eliot a slip of paper, at which point Eliot stated: "I am requested to announce that Mr. Greenwich Black is wanted on the telephone."

7. Denys Wortman (1887–1954), whose work appeared at the Armory Show in New York in 1913, worked for Metropolitan Movies for 30 years.

8. This work has not been identified. HPL mentioned to correspondents that he would be paid only $100 for his work. The novel may not have been published.

9. Actually, he appears to have gone to Hartford at the urging of his ex-wife Sonia; see her *Private Life of H. P. Lovecraft* (West Warwick, RI: Necronomicon Press, 1992), 22: "I took a trip to beautiful Farmington, Conn. I was so enchanted with this beautiful Colonial city that I wrote to Howard at once to join me there which he did." It was their last meeting.

[24]   [ALS]

Note & record. The sincerest
form of flattery—though I
haven't gone so far as to ape the
"Ave." or the 536 (or 726 E.)!

66 College St.,
Providence, R.I.,
June 24, 1933.

Son:—

  Well, Sir, the Old Gentleman is indeed glad to hear from you after all these silent weeks! As you will note from the above, the period has not been a quiescent one for Grandpa—& knowing the settled habits of advanced years, you can picture to yourself the cataclysmic magnitude—material & psychological—of the upheaval. I think I told you that the alarming state of our family finances was making it necessary for my surviving aunt & myself to embark on a series of radical retrenchments, & that the chief œconomy ahead was a consolidation of households in one cheap flat. This has now come to pass—so that we are sharing a 5-room-&-attick apartment at a cost no greater than that of my *one* room & alcove at good old #10. Thus I am once more, as in the youthful & middle-aged days of 598 Angell, part of a private family household instead of a mere roomer. But none of this tells the whole story; for as felicitous fortuity would have it, the present move is no ordinary one. Poverty being the spur, I was all steeled up to brave a plunge into a less congenial neighbourhood—when a streak of pure luck put us in touch with something not only cheap, but so incredibly desirable that our move *down* has all the externals of a move *up*. But before I describe the prize secured, let me narrate the current bad news—news of that which has completely spoilt the summer for my aunt—& indirectly, for me.

  On June 14, before the complete settlement of our new abode, my aunt broke her ankle through a slip on the stairs while descending to answer the doorbell during my absence. Doctors . . . . ambulance to R.I. Hospital . . . . . x-ray . . . . . setting under aether . . . . . plaster cast . . . . . room in Ward K . . . . . prospect of being in bed six weeks & on crutches several more . . . . & a financial strain utterly ruinous to us at the present juncture! Such is life. Of course there is no danger or actual illness, but the restriction to bed is accursedly unpleasant & productive of backaches. After another week my aunt will probably be brought home with a nurse. She reads, writes notes, & eats fairly well—very well, in fact, today. I call at the hospital each afternoon. Naturally the disaster has kept me overwhelmingly busy—with the house in its unsettled state & everything in the air—& it is very unlikely that I can accompany W. Paul Cook to the N.A.P.A. Convention in New York (July 3–4–5) as originally planned. I was going to stay with Sonny Belknap—in fact, the Longs had postponed a contemplated trip to Asbury Park on my account—but I fancy I had better tell him not to expect the Old Man. The Convention promises to be one of more than average interest & activity.

But about 66 College St. The one overwhelming thing from my point of view—& you know what an architectural antiquarian & general 18th century relique your Grandpa is—is that the house *is a colonial one!*[1] All my long life I have been enthralled by the mellow old Georgian houses on Providence's ancient hill. Nothing else on earth has so deeply coloured my imagination or so persistently woven itself into my dreams. Never had I lived in one, yet always did I long to do so. And now, I *am* living in one! Pure luck. What we sought was cheapness plus practical convenience—yet through some fantastically fortunate miracle the cheapest & most practical thing *was colonial* . . . . the sort of place I'd pay any price for if I had the money. And, to complete the miracle, no sacrifice of neighbourhood quality was involv'd. The locality is predominantly collegiate, with the business district surprisingly close—yet far, far down the steep precipice which divides the city into two separate worlds. The main Brown campus with its great clock tower can be seen from our easterly windows, & a goodly quota of our neighbours are fraternity-houses.

The edifice itself—yellow & wooden—lies on the crest of the ancient hill in a quaint grassy court just off College St.—behind & next to the marble John Hay Library of Brown University (which contains the famous Harris Collection of American Poetry—greatest in the world), about half a mile south of 10 Barnes St. The fine colonial doorway is like my bookplate[2] come to life, though of a slightly later period (circa 1800) with side lights & fan carving instead of a fanlight. In the rear &
on the western side there are pictur-
esque, village-like gardens—those
behind being at a higher level than
the front of the house. In front
there are some flower-beds, an
hedge, & a row of old-fashion'd
posts to keep off vehicles. The upper flat we have taken contains 5
rooms besides bath & kitchen on
the main (2nd) floor, plus 2 attic
storerooms—one of which is so attractive that I wish I could have it for an

extra den! My quarters—a large study & a small bedroom—are on the south side, with my working desk under a west window affording a splendid view of the lower town's outspread roofs & of the mystical sunsets that flame behind them.[3] In general, the interior is fully as fascinating as the exterior—with colonial fireplaces, mantels, & chimney-cupboards, curving Georgian staircase, (would that no ankles had been broken thereon!) wide floorboards, old-fashion'd latches, small-paned windows (old style—innocent of cords & weights), six-panel doors, rear wing with floor at a different level (3 steps down), quaint attic stairs, &c.—just like the old houses open as museums. So

like a museum is it that I keep fearing a guard will turn up to chase me out at 5 o'clock closing time! The sensation of *actually living* in such a place is indescribably fascinating—to come *home* through a carved colonial doorway & sit beside a white Georgian mantel looking out through small-paned windows over a sea of ancient roofs & sun-golden foliage. The proximity of many belfries makes each hour the occasion for a symphony of chimes—which even a musician like you cou'd not but approve. Our old family furniture fits in marvellously well—& we have rescued from storage many items belonging to the old home broken up in 1904 . . . things for which we've had no space since then. Naturally we play up the least Victorian pieces—& the colonial mantels in my study & my aunt's living-room are perfect throwbacks to the 18th Century. I have on mine an old clock, vases, & candlesticks, & above it a marine painting by my mother, newly fram'd in the authentick Georgian manner. Bookshelves actually play a large part in my furnishing scheme—I've had to get 4 new cases to replace the built-in shelves in my alcove at #10. It remains

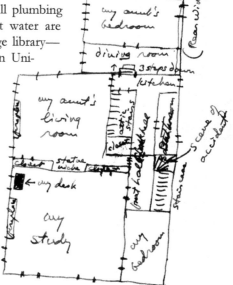

to be added, that the dominant antiquity in no way detracts from comfort & convenience in the most contemporary sense. All plumbing is modern, & steam heat & hot water are piped in from the adjacent college library— the house being own'd by Brown University. Appended is a plan of the Theobald–Gamwell flat—main (2nd) floor.[4] As you see, my quarters are perfectly distinct from my aunt's, so that each can have company without disturbing the other. The whole effect, though, is that of a single well-rounded household—my study answering to the family library, & my aunt's living-room to the parlour. I moved in May 15th—half a month ahead of her—& had my quarters (books & all) fully settled exactly one month ago to a day—May 24th. Right now my place looks as mellow & homelike as if six generations of the family had dwelt here! My aunt moved in June 1st, & had her living-room settled by the night of the 3rd. Her bedroom is partly settled, but the dining-room is still a chaos of piled-up crockery. We are going to hang over the fatal staircase a huge painting by my late elder aunt—the Rocks at Narragansett Pier. Something about the atmosphere of the place & its familiar furnishings reminds me curiously (in miniature) of my birthplace at 454 Angell St.—the old home

292 ❀ *Letters to Alfred Galpin*

broken up in 1904, & preceding #598. This quality does much to neutralise any homesickness I might otherwise feel for 10 Barnes. Now the desperate problem is how to hang on to it! My aunt has always been the family banker, but now that she is down I have charge of all papers & accounts, & can see in stark plainness the utter desperateness of our financial situation. With the bottom completely out of revision, & with no knack whatever for commercial fiction, I am certainly up against a stone wall as to how to get the cash to keep alive. No one ever had less instinctive aptitude or experience in the cryptic & devious ways of money-making . . . unless it be Little Belknap.

I am glad to learn of your debut as a gentleman-agriculturist, & trust that a rich harvest may crown your ploughing & sowing. The eternal soil & its immemorial ways have ever form'd for me a subject of the most intense attraction & admiration; indeed, I am convinc'd that those customs, perspectives, & imaginative reactions which do most to lend the illusions of direction, interest, significance, & purpose to the formless chaos of human existence, are those which spring most directly from man's primitive relationship to the earth, its bounties, its cultivation, & its vary'd phaenomena. When agriculture is totally left behind, there grows up about life a sense of instability, artificiality, & ultimate meaninglessness (born of a separation from the visibly aeternal & cyclick processes of Nature) which cannot but be destructive of the best qualities of civilisation. I agree largely with the eminent Spengler when he affirms, that an agrarian aristocracy is the best form of social organisation possible to mankind. Whilst I have not a personal aptitude for the operations of pastoral & agrestick life, I delight in the antient tradition of country squirearchy, & in my close ancestral connexion with it. You may be assur'd, that my colonial study mantel has swinging from it the undying Farmer's Almanack of Robert B. Thomas[5] (now in its 141st year) which has swung beside the kindred mantels of all my New-England forbears for near a century & a half: that almanack without which my grandfather wou'd never permit himself to be, & of which a family file extending unbrokenly back to 1836 & scatteringly to 1805 still reposes in the lower drawer of my library table . . . . which was likewise my grandfather's library table. A real civilisation, Sir, can never depart far from the state of a people's rootedness in the soil, & their adherence to the landskip & phaenomena & methods which from a primitive antiquity shap'd them to their particular set of manners & institutions & perspectives. God Save the King!

I am glad your domestick affairs maintain a certain quiescence, if not ideal adjustment; & trust that time may do its own salutary & imperceptible modelling toward a stabler & sounder equilibrium. You have no need, I am sure, to lament the absence of grandiose projects in musick; since this is clearly a period of incubation & acquisition in no way to be confounded with idleness. It is pleasant that your friend Wessel can visit you, since I presume you have not many chances to converse with persons whose interests & experiences are so closely parallel to your own.

You are, I think, correct in believing that the thirties will form a rich period for you, owing to the union of a lingering youthfulness with a ripening maturity. Indeed, I believe that the true secret of most creative genius lies in that prolongation of psychological youth which permits of such an union. Nearly all young folk have the sensitive emotions of artists, though without the experience & fund of ideas needed to transform meer feeling into art. Likewise, most persons have by middle life acquired a potentially rich supply of experience & ideas; which, however, remains artistically ineffective because of the loss of the fire & sensitive vision which cou'd advantageously employ it. It is when, in relatively rare cases, the fire & sensitiveness survive to join with the fruits of maturity, that creative work of depth & authenticity is produc'd. If I were you I wou'd indulge to the full any reviving penchant for literature & literary expression. It certainly will not detract from your musical capacity; but on the other hand, will probably prove a stimulus & auxiliary to that side of your personality. Your taste for ideas & their expression in youth was too great not to indicate a powerful & permanent element in your nature, which can never permanently disappear, no matter how many times it may suffer an Alpheus-like submersion. The new delight in physical phaenomena, which you say dates from your Majorcan sojourn, is probably a still further asset to your aesthetick capital. It cannot but add to the products of sensitiveness & experience a poignant touch of reality scarce to be duplicated by those who live with less gusto. This is something I am forc'd to imagine more or less objectively, tho' I suppose I have approximations to it in the pleasure I experience when extreme heat combines with glamourous sun[lit] scenery, bird-songs, floral perfumes, & objects whose tradit[ions] & associations are agreeable to my imagination. I th[en fe]el a kind of buoyancy & elation as much of the body as of [the sp]irit— tho' it fades as soon as the temperature drops [much] below 85 degrees. Obviously, I cou'd never know a life [of] physical gusto in any but a tropical environment. M[ost of] my nearly 43 years in New-England I have spent in [semi]-numbness & shivering from the rarely-interrupt[ed c]old . . . . . . as you can well appreciate from remembering [how] the poor old man shiver'd in Cleveland back in '22 when the 5 o'clock lake breeze began to rattle the library windows![6]

Ah me, good old 1922 . . . . . & what hath time done to the various oddly-assorted figures that knocked about 1537 E. 93th St., 9231 Birchdale, Wade Park, Clark's Lunch, Taylor's Arcade, Eglin's, & all the other half-fabulous landmarks! Despair & the black caves of the sea-bottom for one, for others mediocrity & merging with the crowd, for some progress & growth, for still others a sort of changeless crystallisation, & for a few a stagnation temper'd only by the loss of certain major crudities & inexperienced errors of judgment. How vary'd are the effects of time upon differing types & temperaments! Good old Samuelus is the premier Endymion of them all; he having chang'd less both in mind & aspect than any other of the period I can recall. On the whole, I don't think any one has better prospects for maturity than yourself. With a powerful, quick, & acquisitive intellect at all stages of development, & added to the sum a new physical gusto. What combination cou'd augur better? In truth, you ever had a tendency to join the advantages of different ages. I think it was upon your 17th birthday—in the tense, remote hours before the signing of the armistice in 1918—that I addrest to you some congratulatory lines containing such observations as:

> Is't true, indeed, that thou ſo ſhort a Time
> Haſt known the Air of our terreſtrial Clime?
> Art thou not rather some experienc'd Sage,
> Who haſt, like *Æſon,* loſt thy hoary Age?

> . . . . In this fair Train, that riſe on ev'ry Hand,
> Foremoſt of all can gifted GALPIN ſtand:
> Young as the youngeſt, brilliant as the beſt,
> Thy lightening Brain was made to lead the reſt.
> 'Tis thine to combat ev'ry ling'ring Wrong;
> To help the feeble, and ſubdue the ſtrong:
> Stand forth, bold Youth, within whoſe Boſom bright
> The Paſt's grave lore, and Future's Force, unite![7]

As for local events—aside from the [Great] Migration & the still more recent disaster, they are not many. D[uring] the hot spells I have been active & have taken long & pleasant [ram]bles in the countryside, whilst during the cool spells I have sh[iver'd.] On Sunday, June 11, my aunt & I attended a Musick Festival ([see pro]gramme &c. enclos'd) whose excellence you would doubtless ha[ve appre]ciated far more than I. Amusingly, my back is visible in the group [photogr]aph taken for the preſs—a copy of which I enclose, together with [some . . . . . .] timely humorous commentary on the whole art of getting into [group pho]tographs.

Fra Samuelus is rejoicing in the acquisition of a *real Grecian sculptur'd head,* which he pickt up with remarkable cheapness at an antique shop in 6th Ave. It is the first thing of its kind he has possesst, & he lately sent me photographs of it, which indicate an object of extream beauty & unmistakable Hellenism.

Klarkash-Ton the Atlantean, High-Priest of Tsathoggua, continues his triumphant course as a master of fiction. Enclos'd is a circular of his recent brochure[8]—containing six phantasies of the highest merit, rejected by commercial magazines because of their lack of rabble-appeal. If you still retain any of those qualities of fancy which produc'd "Marsh-Mad" in the good old days, I recommend this modest collection to you as a rare bargain you will not regret. I have a new tale coming out—with woeful misprints—in the next

Weird Tales—the one on the stands July 1st.⁹ Also—my "Shunned House" booklet may appear at last—finally issued by Walter J. Coates of Driftwind.¹⁰ ¶ Well—may the Muses continue to bless thee!

Yr obt h^ble Servt—

Grandpa

Notes

1. The Samuel Mumford House (1825) at 66 College (later moved to 65 Prospect).

2. HPL designed his bookplate to have a fanlighted doorway. The artwork was made by Wilfred B. Talman.

3. HPL's description here (as in other letters) was later adapted in "The Haunter of the Dark" (1935) to indicate the vista from Robert Blake's apartment in Providence.

4. Nonextant. But see another in *Marginalia* (Sauk City, WI: Arkham House, 1944), facing p. 215.

5. *The (Old) Farmer's Almanack* (1793f.).

6. The ms. is mutilated at this point. The text in brackets here and on subsequent pages is conjectural.

7. From "To Alfred Galpin, Esq.," ll. 21–24, 43–50. The poem was written for Galpin's nineteenth birthday.

8. Clark Ashton Smith, *The Double Shadow and Other Fantasies.*

9. "The Dreams in the Witch House." The misprints are indicated in HPL's letter to Farnsworth Wright of 18 June 1933 (*Lovecraft Annual* No. 8 (2014): 30.

10. *The Shunned House* was typeset and printed in 1928 by W. Paul Cook's Recluse Press, but the sheets were not bound. In 1933, Walter J. Coates's Driftwind Press was going to bind the sheets but never did so. R. H. Barlow acquired 115 copies in 1934 and 150 more in 1935 but bound only a few copies. Arkham House eventually bound and distributed the sheets Barlow obtained in 1959–61.

[25]   [Postcard, nonextant]¹

[c. 3 September 1933]

Notes

1. *Front:* Porte St. Louis, Quebec.

[26]   [ALS]

66 College St.,
Providence, R.I.,
Octr. 5, 1933

Son:—

Well, Sir, your Grandpa's glad to hear the news—even though such an annoying item as a salary reduction forms part of the current record. I was certainly interested in the compliment paid you by your noble Austrian friend—& can imagine how pleased you must have been to have your cherished continentalism recognised by a real sprig of the original continental-cosmopolitan culture! It reminds me of the state of ecstasy to which I have twice been raised by having strangers of obvious intelligence & cultivation (both times in Canada, as chance would have it) ask me if I am not of British birth & education. Your Freiherr Karl Tinty zu Schloss Schallaberg &c. would seem to be quite a boy, all told, & I am surely glad you happened to run across him. As for the *Roman* angle—I rather fear the baron had in mind not so much *my* Romans of the hardy age of P. Cornelius Scipio, T. Quinctius Flamininus, Q. Fabius Maximus, C. Laelius, L. Valerius Flaccus, M. Acilius Glabrio, L. Aemilius Paullus, & all the rest, as the *modern* Roman nobility whose origins are in the city-streets of the Middle Ages & of Little Belknap's once-beloved (before he acquired "social vision" & became a young bolshevik) Renaissance . . . . . no mean bunch, at that, though! Probably *you* would like such a comparison much better than one linking you to the Claudii, Julii, Pompeii, Licinii, & Caecilii. Not A. Galpinius Secundus, but Conte Alfredo delgi Galpini! Incidentally, did I ever tell you that you ate dinner with a real Italian nobleman as early as 1922? If not, I may mention that about a year ago I saw an item in the paper stating that our old Cleveland confrere Raoul S. Bonnanno,—the guy who taught me how to eat spaghetti at Luccione's—had fallen heir to 18 titles, several sulphur mines in Sicily, & sundry estates, through a decision of the Italian courts. He is still a member of the N.A.P.A. (there's the democracy of true rank for you!), though I haven't heard from him since the old Birchdale days. Whenever, nowadays, anyone criticises my way of gulping spaghetti, I am prepared to come back with the withering retort that *I* was instructed by a real dago of *title*—no mere peasant or tavern-keeper!

It is gratifying to learn—even tho' it implies no great change in your basick philosophy—that you have extinguish'd the altars of Astarte in favour of those of Urania & Hymenaeus. In your easy recovery from the aberration you might well read a confirmation of what I previously told you regarding the wholly capricious, cosmically un-grounded, & therefore essentially trivial nature of such seizures. They are simply temporary biological-psychological surface twists—& when one thoroughly realises the trivial mechanical character of such emotional phaenomena, he ought to be able to analyse them out of existence whenever they interfere with the well-harmonised & appropriate course of his life, or with the practice of that fairness, honesty, & open, aboveboard conduct which distinguishes artistic living from sloppy, messy living. In the course of time—when the shock of emancipation from religious delusion & ill-based celestial morality has had a chance to subside & reveal the essential squalor & ugliness of disorderly, uncoördinated existence—I fancy that rational aesthetick standards of conduct will be reared anew; replacing the present "lost generation" of anchorless epigoni with a generation once more having loyalties . . . . albeit perhaps loyalties to new & unfamiliar norms. As it is, an element of poignant & definite beauty has been lost from human character.

I trust that your plans for escorting the disorganised young millionaire—whose unfortunate emotional misdirection ought surely to have expert psychiatric attention—will mature successfully, & that the joint European session will not only benefit the patient but prove rewardingly interesting to his guides. You are certainly amply fitted to initiate any neophyte into the arcana of intellectual & artistick Paris! It would surely be providential if circumstances protracted your stay long enough to admit of a Sorbonne degree. Who knows, you might find a permanent berth in La Ville Lumière, become a French citizen, & end up as a Minister of Education or Fine Arts or something of the sort, with a town-house near the Parc Monceau & a villa on the Riviera! But at any rate I trust you'll begin your fuller Gallicisation at Quebec—which is extremely appropriate, since French Canada represents the traditional, pre-revolutionary France of the church & the Capets, logically preceding the liberalised & decadent France which has come into existence on the original ground.

My own Quebec trip of last month[1] was a glorious success—four days of hot & sunny weather in the ancient fortress of the north, beneath the Union Jack of my forefathers. God Save the King! I lingered in all the accustomed spots, absorbing the time-mellow'd sights so dear to my spirit—the frowning citadel, grim city walls & gates, beetling cliff & bristling ramparts, shining silver spires, tangles of centuried lanes, old grey convents, 18th century facades, red roofs, & chimney-pots, dizzying vistas of varied levels, glimpses of broad, blue river, verdant countryside, & far-off purple mountains at the ends of glamourous streets . . . . . & all the rest. I walked to Sillery—3 miles up the river, with its curious headland church—& took a trolley ride to the upper level of Montmorency Falls, where I saw the fine (but now defaced—made into an hotel) Georgian house built by Genl. Sir Frederick Holdimand & later occupy'd (in the 1790's) by H.R.H. the Duke of Kent, afterward father of her late Majesty Victoria. I also look'd up the exact place of Genl. Wolfe's ascent of the cliff—not an easy task, since the spot is not mark'd, nor do the local Frenchmen care to point out the route of their immortal conqueror.

One thing that impress'd me at Quebec was the singular & picturesque aspect of the *sky*—involving odd formations of cloud & mist never seen in more southerly latitudes. This begins, however, as far south as northern New-Hampshire & Vermont—the whole region about Lake Memphramagog having the most fantastick sort of vapours hanging over the peaks & vales each dawn. I do not wonder, in view of this mystical veil of mutation, illusion, & uncertainty hanging perpetually aloft, that the northern races of mankind excel those of the hard-outlined, sunbaked Mediterranean in richness & fertility of fantastick imagination. On this occasion I beheld several atmospherick spectacles of the highest interest, especially one at sunset on Labour-Day. This involv'd a predominantly clear sky & a strangely burning flood of ruddy vespertine light upon roofs, spires, ramparts, & the trans-fluvial cliffs of Levis—coupled with a dense funnel of churning nimbus cloud extending from the zenith to the southeastern horizon. From this interloping mass jagged streaks of lightning darted frequently down to the distant country side beyond Levis, whilst low rumbles of thunder follow'd tardily after. Then, to crown all, a pallid arc of rainbow sprang into view above the verdant Isle d'Orleans, its upper end lost in the forbidding black cloud. The total effect was indescribably stirring to the imagination, & was remark'd by not a few of the several spectators on the lofty citadel whence I witness'd it. My train-ride home was of unusual pleasantness; not only because of the absence of the swinish beer-guzzlers who used to frequent Canadian trains in the days of intensive prohibition, but because of the fine effects of sunset & full moonlight upon the rural landskip of Quebec province. Some of the isolated villages, each clustering in the lee of a quaint, silver-steepled church, are of the greatest imaginable charm; & it was with much pain that I learn'd a fortnight ago of the destruction by fire of one of the churches I saw—that at Valleyfield. Dawn arrived amidst a beautiful lake region in New Hampshire—the train not long afterward taking me within a few feet of the house (now an orphanage) where Daniel Webster grew up . . . at Franklin, formerly Salisbury Lower Village.

On both outbound & inbound trips I paused in Boston to see our good old friend Culinarius. In the outbound trip I also look'd up an extreamly antient house in the suburbs of Boston—the Deane Winthrop edifice, built in 1637 & having a secret room in the vast brick chimney-base. Inbound, I made a side-trip to my beloved old Salem & Marblehead—renewing my acquaintance with familiar antiquities & assimilating a few fresh points. Among the novelties at Salem was a perfect reconstruction of the original pioneer settlement of 1626–30, with the crude shelters, wigwams, huts, & cottages which preceded the building of actual houses of European size, pattern, & solidity. Of course no originals of these rude domiciles survive, but accurate scholarship has been able to fashion pretty definite fac-similes from detailed contemporary accounts. The restored village is situate in a park at the harbour's edge, amidst a landskip made to look as much as possible like the primal topography of Salem. Not only are the early huts represented, but typical industries like blacksmith-shops, salt works, fish-drying outfits, saw-pits, & the like are faithfully shewn. The whole forms the clearest & most vivid presentation I have ever seen of the very first stage of New-England life, & ought to help anyone to reëstablish the true ancestral orientation which these disorder'd times so gravely disturb.

My aunt is now much better, being all around the house on a cane, & each day getting out into the garden for a while. The nurse went nearly a month ago, & in order to emancipate me from door-tending we have install'd an electrical device (one of the few palliating boons of the machine age) which allows my aunt to open the front door from the upper hall. On several occasions I have taken her to walk in the adjacent college grounds, whilst last Saturday she had her first real outing in the form of a motor ride to antient Wickford (one of those quaint villages down the bay's west shoar, which my guest Price[2] & I visited last July) thro' the sunlit autumnal countryside. From now on I shall not be greatly tied up, hence it is possible that I may pay Sonny Belknap a visit in New-York before the month is out, or accompany friend Samuelus to Boston for a museum session if he decides to visit New-England after his return from Cleveland. But all such things are problematical. The approach of cold weather limits my outdoor activities, though I still work in a rural walk now & then, & shall seek to view the turning leaves amidst the mystical silences of the Quinsnicket woods.

Regarding writing affairs—just as I expected, the Knopf bubble duly burst in course of time . . . . differing from the Putnam fiasco only in that the readers praised the stories literarily whilst pronouncing them commercially unfeasible.[3] Since then a man in the state of Washington has broached the subject of issuing my "Colour Out of Space" as a separate brochure[4]—which I shall surely let him do if he wants to, though the project is scarcely likely to mature. I writ a new tale in August, but am very ill-satisfy'd with it.[5] Indeed, I am becoming so ill-satisfy'd with all my attempts, that I have begun a sort of analytical re-reading of the various weird classicks to see if I can discover means of improvement.[6]

Good luck with the painting of Old 536![7] I'll wager it never had such an artistick application of mural colour before! Trust the agriculture will prosper as well. How is Skipper these days? One of my present delights is the club of solemn old Toms which assembles on the roof of a shed across the garden, in plain sight of my study windows. There are sometimes as many as 6 or 7 members present, & I have dubb'd it (in view of the prevalence of fraternity houses in this neighbourhood) the Kappa Alpha Tau. (ΚΟΜΡΣΟΝ ΑΙΛΥΡΟΝ ΤΑΞΙΣ) The huge, sleek, black & white President is grown a great friend of mine, & rolls over & kicks & purrs like a kitten when I approach him. I see him now out the window! Asleep at full length. ¶ Well—be as good a boy as possible, & receive an old man's blessings

Yr ob[t] h[ble] Serv[t]

Grandpa

Notes

1. The third of HPL's trips to Quebec, the others being in 1930 and 1932.

2. E. Hoffmann Price visited HPL on 30 June–3 July 1933.

3. HPL submitted a total of 25 stories to Allan G. Ullman of Knopf on 3 and 16 August 1933, but the stories were rejected. G. P. Putnam's Sons had rejected a collection of HPL's tales in 1931.

4. F. Lee Baldwin of Asotin, WA, had hoped to publish "The Colour out of Space" as a booklet, but it never appeared.

5. "The Thing on the Doorstep," written 21–24 August 1933.

6. This reading resulted in "Weird Story Plots," "A List of Certain Basic Underlying Horrors Effectively Used in Weird Fiction," "List of Primary Ideas Motivating Possible Weird Tales," and "Suggestions for Writing Story" (later "Notes on Writing Weird Fiction").

7. I.e., 536 College Street, Appleton, WI—Galpin's former residence.

[27]   [ALS]

Octr. 25[, 1933]

Son:—

Am I still delighted in my colonial dwelling? Excellent example of needless enquiry! Not only does the charm not fade, but it actually *increases*. This is due in part to the greater degree of orderly settledness attained since the relative recovery of my aunt—who is now all around on a cane, taking strolls in the nearby college grounds & getting even farther afield with my assistance. The rooms are now in better order, the great oil painting is hung over the fatal staircase, & a console slab of veined, yellowish Siena marble (relique of departed glory) is about to go up in the front hall under the wall hatrack & mirror as soon as we can find the ornamental brackets amid our stored household goods. Here is a snap of the place which I took not long ago from the courtyard of the neighbouring college library. I'll ask the return of this. Later I'll send you a fuller, closer view of the house which you can keep if you have any permanent album of such material. I may also send a booklet lately issued by the school department, whose frontispiece exhibits this whole hill neighbourhood & plainly reveals #66 in its retired court.

Glad you had a good Chicago trip, but sorry you picked up a cold. Since I have one myself at the present moment, I can extend a peculiarly vivid message of sympathy, snuffle for snuffle! As for the philosophy & aestheticks of domestick organisation—I still don't agree with your essentially cloudy & ill-defined system of standards. The common emotions connected with primary instincts, & not extensively linked with imaginative associations & a sense of pattern, are undeniably largely mechanical matters which, while *powerful* in the sense that a rap on the head or a siege of typhoid is mechanically powerful in its effect on the system, are certainly not *important* in the artistic experience of complex conscious living. Assuredly, they are not important enough to justify their easy interference with the fulfilment of other emotions whose richness & coördination give them a really pivotal place in an harmonious life of widely-realised possibilities. I feel confident that the current fashionable endorsement of messy living will vastly diminish whenever a reacquired cultural stability gives our most active minds a renew'd chance for mature & leisurely reflection.

Wright seems to be re-using that list of author's friends for which he asked last June. Glad the new W.T. had points of interest for you.[1] My "Festival", written exactly a decade ago, seems somewhat crude & overcoloured upon re-reading. Quinn is a brilliant attorney turned author who could write splendid stuff if he would, but who prefers to cater to the popular market. Sonny Belknap's piece is fair, but not the best the child can do—the horror being somewhat diffuse & strung out. The Klarkash-Ton specimen is excellent, though not illustrating the creator's most imaginative side. If you want to know the contemporary CAS at his best, send to him for that brochure of 6 tales of which I gave you a descriptive circular. Robert E. Howard is an interesting Texas character; only 27 years old, yet as full of the reminiscent lore of the old Southwest as any grizzled cattleman of the 1870's. You ought to see the gigantic set of snake-rattles (12) he has just sent me! He has an odd, primitive philosophy—hating all civilisation (like Lord Monboddo[2] & other devotees of the "noble savage" in my own 18th century) & regarding the barbarism of the pre-Roman Gauls as the ideal form of life. He writes fiction purely for money, hence his more or less stereotyped caterings to popular trends. Once in a while, though, he unconsciously achieves a very genuine power in his depictions of ruins, catacombs, & cities redolent of unholy antiquity & blasphemous elder secrets. "The House of the Worm" is by a new writer wholly unknown to me, but I think it shows a real promise beneath obvious crudities. It has real atmosphere—& that is the big thing in spectral fiction. Yes—I thought I saw touches of my own style here & there.[3] It would amuse me if some writer were to build upon my work & achieve a fabric infinitely surpassing the original! Glad the magazine seems to be selling—for its survival is very precious to those who count on its cheques. Others appear & vanish. Just now *Astounding Stories* is revived—its editor, Desmond Hall, being in touch with Petit-Belnape & others of the gang in N.Y. I doubt if my work would fit this, however. Klarkash-Ton & I are just now unloading a great number of our early & rejected MSS. upon two new magazines (*The Fantasy Fan* & *Unusual Stories*[4]) which don't pay anything. Wright would be glad to see you if you ever called on him. He is probably a good deal more cultivated than his magazine indicates, & shares your devotion to music—being indeed a former critic of that art. He is a sufferer from that odd form of paralysis known as Parkinson's Disease—no longer able to write with a pen, & with a face purged of all flexibility or expression through the failure of the nerves to function.

I've heard of "Wolf Solent", though I haven't read it. Sooner or later I must absorb its contents. I don't think, though, that John Cowper Powys or any of his equally-famous brothers were born in America, though some of them now dwell here.[5] The literary editor of the Providence Journal became especially enthusiastic about Wolf Solent when it first appeared.

Hope your European trip develops successfully . . . I envy you all the time spent in England! Next month I may pay Kid Belknap a visit—though

his mamma is now ill from food-poisoning. I've made the most of an unusually mild & sunny October—taking long walks through remote & primitive
stretches of countryside. I generally proceed by coach out some main highway, then striking across country afoot till I reach another coach-bearing
highway along which I can return. In this way I have explored many regions
which I never saw before—some delectably-unspoiled, with narrow rutted
roads winding betwixt briar-twined stone walls, ancient gambrel-roofed farmhouses with their barns, byres, & gnarled orchards, primitive well-sweeps &
moss-grown water mills, belts of shadowy woodland, distant village spires &
glimpses of curving river-valley—all those traditional marks of long, continuous habitation which New England took over bodily from Old England &
marked with rich, distinctive touches of her own. Last week I came on a very
ancient house built by a lineal ancestor of my own—Thomas Clement [*sic*]—
in 1654. It has a great pilastered stone chimney & is still in excellent shape
despite its age. Other recent glimpses of the countryside have come through
participation in rides given the family convalescent by motor-owning friends.
But now the chill of winter is nigh, & desolation looms in the offing!

 Yr most obᵗ hᵇˡᵉ Servᵗ—

 Grandpa

P.S. Saw a demonstration of *television* last Saturday. Vague & flickering, like
the cinema of about 1898. ¶ I enclose the Holland Society's paper with an antiquarian outburst of mine.[6] Our former fellow-amateur Talman edits this
sheet. You might send it back if you have no permanent use for it.

Notes

1. HPL refers to the following stories from *WT* (October 1933): "The Festival" (orig.
January 1925); Seabury Quinn, "The Mansion of Unholy Magic"; Frank Belknap
Long, "The Black, Dead Thing" (later titled "Second Night Out"); Clark Ashton
Smith, "The Seed of the Sepulcher"; Robert E. Howard, "The Pool of the Black
One"; Mearle Prout, "The House of the Worm."
2. James Burnett, Lord Monboddo (1714–99) gained notoriety and ridicule when, in
the first volume of his *On the Origin and Progress of Language* (1773–92), he reported the
account of a Swedish sailor named Keoping that there were men with tails living in
the Nicobar Islands.
3. Prout's story clearly plagiarizes portions of HPL's "The Call of Cthulhu." See Will
Murray, "Mearle Prout and 'The House of the Worm,'" *Crypt of Cthulhu* No. 18
(Yuletide 1983): 29–30, 39.
4. Edited by Charles D. Hornig and William L. Crawford, respectively.
5. A complex social novel set in Dorset. Powys's brothers Llewellyn (1884–1939) and
T. F. Powys (1875–1953) also were noted authors.
6. "Some Dutch Footprints in New England."

[28]   [ALS]

Nov. 4, 1933

Son:—

Congratulations on the restoration of your creative activity! The words sound tremendously graceful, & accentuate the shivers of the season; & I feel somehow certain that the music is of equal beauty & aptness. There is a genuine originality in that image of the slate-blue sky crawling on the sun & freezing the wind. I wish to hades I had facilities for hearing music well-rendered—if I did, I'd demand a wide variety of your compositions as a loan in order to get an idea of how your genius works in its chosen main line. I shall, indeed, if I ever happen to strike an opportunity for interpretations. I can sympathise with your impatience regarding halts in your course of creation. Just now I am singularly unable to embody any ideas in tales at all satisfactory to me, so that I have devoted much time of late to experiments in new methods & perspectives. Thanks, by the way, for that news item—which surely may prove useful as a story nucleus. Another ocular idea which has long fascinated me pertains to the luminous shapes—geometrical & otherwise—seen against a background of blackness when the eyes are closed.[1] It would be rather good, in a story, to attribute these to scenes in other dimensions or spheres of entity, glimpsed obscurely & fragmentarily when the tri-dimensional world is shut out. One could delineate a person who has cultivated the art of seeing & understanding these alien vistas with especial clearness, & who ultimately learned terrible cosmic secrets from them. In the end the observer might learn of a way to cross bodily to an exotic cosmos, & thus vanish from the sight of man. One stage in this crossing to another plane ought to be just such an inxplicable blindness as that overtaking the Roumanian boy in the item.

Glad the snap of Grandpa's hillside abode proved of interest. Here are some others, which I'll also ask to have returned in the course of time. One shews the whole house at fairly close range. The window above the door is of my bedroom, those at its left being the south windows of my study. (The study also has 2 west windows, at one of which I am now sitting, gazing across the roofs of the ancient hill to a strip of far horizon & a distant steeple[2] on Federal Hill 2 miles away.) Another view is of the colonial doorway in detail (note the fan carving), with my aunt standing in it.[3] A third snap shews my aunt against ancient University Hall (1770) in the neighbouring college grounds. A fourth—of comic rather than serious intent—is of the old gent seated in a corner of the college gateway.[4] The please-help-the-blind effect is caused by the sun in Grandpa's eyes—which were closed when the camera was prematurely snapped. The blurring is due either to the perturbation of the ancient Brownie at its repulsive subject, or to a lack of steadiness in the grip of the photographer. These cheap Brownies have such slow shutter action that they have to be held very still even for allegedly instantaneous exposures. You'll note that Old Theobald isn't such a hippopotamus as he was in

Birchdale days—a 50-lb reducing in 1925 having achieved mercifully permanent results. But the old geezer certainly has aged!

By the way—I fear your colleague's Providentian geography is all wet. *Cushing St.* is a full quarter-mile north of here; & instead of going up the great hill, slopes gradually downward from near its summit over the eastward plateau on top. (Like Barnes St.—which is not far away) It is around this street that Pembroke College, the female department of Brown University, clusters[5]—whereas College St. (commonly called "College Hill") tops the main & exclusively masculine part of the institution. In colonial times College St. was known successively as Presbyterian Lane (from the meeting-house at Benefit St., where the great Court House now stands[6]), Rosemary Lane, & Hanover St.—but never as Cushing St. Your friend somehow has the main college mixed up with the women's college in his recollections. College St. has been the accepted name of this thoroughfare since 1771, when the university's classes were transferred here.

Glad prospects still look good for a well-balanced European sojourn. For the past year I have had such a knowledge of Paris that I've felt tempted to advertise my services as a guide without ever having seen the damn place—this erudition coming from a ghost-writing job[7] for a goof who wanted to be publicly eloquent about a trip from which he was apparently unable to extract any concrete first-hand impressions. I based my study on maps,[8] guide-books, travel folders, descriptive volumes, & (above all) pictures—the cards secured from you forming the cream of the latter. Fixing the layout of the city in my mind, & calculating what vistas ought to be visible from certain points (pictures seen under a magnifying-glass furnish a splendid substitute for first-hand vistas), I cooked up a travelogue which several Paris-wise readers have almost refused to believe was written by one never within 3000 miles of the place. If I ever get to your beloved burg I shall be able to start in sightseeing without any preliminary orientation-tour or rubberneck-wagon ride. In my article I took a vicious fling at the ugly Eiffel Tower, & ventured the suggestion that the Victorian Trocadero is an eyesore at close range, but glamourous when seen in the distance against a flaming sunset. Other parts of the text touched on Chartres, Rheims, Versailles, Barbizon, Fontainebleau, & other tourist high spots. I revelled in the *London* section (I studied Old London intensively years ago, & could ramble guideless around it from Hampstead Heath to the Elephant & Castle!), but was not able to do it justice because of the nominal author's hasty passage through it. Nothing but the Tower, the Abbey, & the Cheshire Cheese seemed to give him a first-class kick.

No further word from The Child—I hope his mamma isn't worse. Damn cold today—though Hallowmass, All-Saints', & All-Souls' were admirably sunny. On each of those days I took rural walks—& discovered still another region previously unknown to me. At a hilltop bend of a stone-walled road on the town's northwestern rim I encountered a sunset vista of surpassing loveliness—

meadows & orchards sloping down to a pond & river, wooded hills on the western horizon, a steepled village in a northward vale, & a great round moon climbing above the rocky eastward ridge. ¶ Well—try to behave yourself!

    Yr obt

        Grandpa

Notes

1. Cf. HPL's commonplace book, entry 157: "Vague lights, geometrical figures, &c., seen on retina when eyes are closed. Caus'd by rays from *other dimensions* acting on optick nerve? From *other planets?* Connected with a life or phase of being in which person could live if he only knew how to get there? *Man afraid to shut eyes*—he has been somewhere on a terrible pilgrimage & this fearsome seeing faculty remains."

2. St. John's Roman Catholic Church (1871), 352 Atwells Avenue, the edifice that became the Free-Will Church of the Starry Wisdom sect in "The Haunter of the Dark." The steeple fell in 1935, and the church was razed in 1992.

3. See *Marginalia,* photo facing p. 54.

4. See *SL* 3, photo facing p. 134, in HPL is seated outside the Van Wickle Gates, across from the John Hay Library; erroneously captioned "H. P. Lovecraft in Brooklyn."

5. The campus of Pembroke College occupies buildings at 182–222 Meeting Street. The land for the campus was assembled piecemeal early in the 20th century from lots in the area bounded by Meeting, Brown, Bowen, and Thayer streets. A block of Cushing Street between Brown and Thayer streets eventually was eliminated.

6. The Providence County Court House (1924–33), 250 Benefit Street.

7. Apparently a reference to "European Glimpses" (19 December 1932), a revision job for HPL's ex-wife Sonia H. Greene. It is possible that HPL did not wish to admit to Galpin that he was continuing to do work for Sonia. All the sites in Paris and London mentioned in this paragraph are in fact discussed in "European Glimpses."

8. HPL owned a map of Paris (*LL* 343).

[29]   [ALS]

                                     Charleston, S.C.,

                                      April 28, 1934

Son:—

    Well, of all coincidences! Look at what I had in my hand just ready to post as I stopped for my mail at the desk of the Charleston Y! Glad to hear from you! Sorry your winter was as bad as Providence's—as it seems to have been. Ours didn't begin so early—I took outdoor jaunts all through October—but when it did set in it sure laid the torture on thick! All the northeast had it just as bad. I almost refused Kid Belnape's holiday invitation—but finally accepted it . . . . using the subway to keep under cover. Feby. 9 was the coldest day ever recorded by any weather bureau in southern New England . . . . it being *17 below* in Providence. That is 5° below any previous known Prov. minimum, & over 10° below any minimum usually reached. What saved the situation for me was the magnificent *heat* at 66 College St.—steam being on in abundance 24 hours a day. But of course I was a virtual prisoner indoors, & as a result felt like a limp rag. I started on my present trip April 14–15, stopping a week at Sonny Belknap's & seeing everybody. One new figure of great interest is Howard Wandrei, brother of the Donald who has been compared to you in physique & iconoclastic genius. This youth is a pictorial artist of macabre & fantastic genius—miles ahead of any of the rest of the gang in his accomplishments, & certain to be heard from seriously in the future. His style is so original that it's difficult to say what its sources & analogues are. One thinks of Beardsley, Sime, Harry Clarke, Goya, & what not. Later on, if you're interested, I'll send you some photographs of his drawings, taken by his brother. Among other new people I met was the fairly famous fantastic magazine writer A. Merritt, whose "Moon Pool" I have admired ever since its appearance in 1918.[1]

Glad to hear you have embarked on an artistic renaissance, & hope it will prove fruitful & permanent. Your whole attitude toward the subject of aesthetic expression is such that I feel certain you have major material in you—& I feel equally confident that you will sooner or later find adequate channels for communicating that material. That's a lot more than I can say concerning many others whom I thought freighted with genius in the old days. All too often later years find these young Shelleys & Baudelaires with no particular message to give, & no sense of uneasiness at being unable to communicate the moods & impressions within them. I myself am still irked & oppressed by my inability to give form & expression to the reactions produced in me by certain phenomena of the external world—& certain combinations of ideas & images—but at my age I know that I shall never be able to utter what I wish to utter. The net result is a barrenness as great as that of the cooled-down young Keatses. I have something to say but can't say it; they could say something if they had it to say, but they haven't it! What a world! But you have more solid gifts, & need only time in order to utilise them. I'll wager this new quintette is an important thing—& surely hope the Chicago orchestra will present your older symphony next season, as hinted by its conductor. The emotional & external sources of your quintette are surely highly interesting to consider—especially the idea from our old friend of 1919 & 1920, the impassioned author of "Zarathustra".[2]

I haven't had much published under my own name recently, since W.T. has acquired a sort of prejudice against my work. In the June issue (I think) will appear a collaboration by E. Hoffmann Price & myself[3] which is virtually all my own. My stuff dissatisfies me so badly that I am repudiating a great many of my old tales, & experimenting with possible ways of eliminating certain characteristic flaws & weaknesses. Just now I have a new tale planned—but it seems puerile to me already—even before the start of the actual writing![4]

Today was cold & overcast—cold, that is, for Charleston at this season; though it would pass for a mild spring day in Providence. I've concentrated on interiors—giving the excellent Charleston museum a rather thorough inspection, & visiting the ancient 44-gun frigate *Constitution,* now very appropriately in the ancient harbour of Charleston. A good old tub—I visited its sister ship the *Constellation* (permanently stationed at Newport, R.I.) when it was in Philadelphia at the Sesquicentennial. The *Constitution*'s home port is Boston . . . . but I have a habit of visiting New England sites abroad! When at home I take them as a matter of course & neglect them!

Well—in four days I'll be down in Florida. Cold days like this will reconcile me to leaving Charleston, so long as that leaving can be southward!

Regards & benedictions—

Grandpa

Notes

1. A[braham] Merritt (1884–1943), "The Moon Pool," *All-Story Weekly* (22 June 1918); *LL* 26. HPL disdained the later revised version.
2. I.e., Friedrich Nietzsche. Galpin had published "Nietzsche as a Practical Prophet" in Sonia H. Greene's *Rainbow* (October 1921). The same issue contained HPL's "Nietzscheism and Realism," culled from HPL's letters to Greene.
3. "Through the Gates of the Silver Key." It actually appeared in the issue of July 1934.
4. Possibly a reference to the never-written tale described in a letter to F. Lee Baldwin (27 March 1934): "I'm not working on the actual text of any story just now, but am planning a novelette of the Arkham cycle—about what happened when somebody inherited a queer old house on the top of Frenchman's Hill & obeyed an irresistible urge to dig in a certain queer, abandoned graveyard on Hangman's Hill at the other edge of the town. This story will probably not involve the actual supernatural—being more of the 'Colour Out of Space' type . . . . . greatly-stretched 'scientifiction'" (*Letters to F. Lee Baldwin* 54).

[30]   [Postcard, nonextant][1]

De Land, Fla. 1 June 1934

Notes

1. *Front:* Old Mill at De Leon Springs.

[31]   [Postcard, nonextant][1]

[Postmarked St. Augustine, Fla.,
23 June 1934]

Notes

1. *Front:* Old Watch Tower, Fort Marion, Fla.

[32]   [ALS]

% Barlow, Box 88,
De Land, Fla.,
June 6, 1934.

Son:—

What you say of the possibility of adequate artistic expression on Grandpa's part is surely encouraging, & I wish indeed that I could look forward to such a prospect. Time will tell—though I have less fatuous optimism these days than I had in youth. It's been hard to tell whether or not my subsequent attempts will predominantly reek of New England soil—at any rate, they will be far removed from the pseudo-Dunsaniana of the early 1920's!

I rejoice to hear of your musical prospects in various directions, & hope that your symphony may eventually be played by the Chicago Orchestra.[1] A concert wholly composed of your own work would surely be a notable & helpful event, & I trust that the contemplated Evanston event may material-ise. Let us hope, too, that the present stirrings toward new compositions may bear rich fruit.

Your welcome epistle probably crossed the postcard which told of my continued sojourn in subtropical De Land. This is a great place, & the genial climate peps the old man up tremendously. My hosts[2] are so super-hospitable that all suggestions of moving along are violently ruled out—yet before long I simply must get started. Hopes of Havana about gone—but I'll have a week in antient St. Augustine if it breaks me! Shall return north as slowly as possi-ble—haven't yet decided about visiting honest Jawn Milton Samples in Macon. I want to see Charleston again if I possibly can. Expect to stop a week with Sonny Belknap on my way home, & I'll surely give the household your regards.

Glad that the household matters are recrystallising favourably, & hope the dual Appleton–Chicago arrangement may ensure you an ideal summer. You surely have enough prospects, projects, & activities to keep you pleasant-ly busy! Assuming that college is closed, I'll address this missive to your natal mansion, the erstwhile 536 . . . . meanwhile keeping your Chicago address in mind. If you're at the latter, you will doubtless receive the document through forwarding.

Enclosed is an item design'd to remind you of old amateur & Mocratick days—a paper containing an article by our good old Sage. I never thought Mocrates could be dragged into amateurdom again, but the persuasion of a bright boy editor turned the trick. By the way—Mocrates' elder son Robert, now graduated from the U. of Wis., has just gone to Erie, Pa. to fill an im-portant position with the Genl. Electric Co. He seems destined to become a technician of some note, & to reflect new lustre upon the already-honour'd name of Moe.

Speaking of old days—my brilliant young host (present story laureate of the N.A.P.A.)[3] is curious to collect certain papers of the past, especially your short-lived *Philosopher*.[4] Have you any residual copies of the latter tucked away in the attic? If so, pray send one to Barlow & make him your lifelong debtor! He surely is quite a kid—a veritable neo-Galpinius in many ways. If he had decent eyesight he'd be even more visibly brilliant than he is.

I guess I described my present temporary habitat on the postcard. De Land is a pleasant little village of modern origin, shaded by great live-oaks & possessing a college—Stetson University. The Barlow place, 14 miles to the west, is in a delightfully lone region of small lakelets, with no other human habitation in sight. I've been taken on various trips to neighbouring regions—including such antiquities as are to be found. No doubt I spoke of the old Spanish mission built in 1696 & demolished by an expedition from South Carolina in 1706. Many of the stone arches & walls are still in existence—thickly clad in vines, & forming by all odds the most picturesque ruin I have ever beheld. Near this mission—at New Smyrna—can also be found vestiges of Dr. Andrew Turnbull's famous indigo plantation of 1768–1783—where he had the Minorcans who later settled in St. Augustine. Turnbull himself ended up as an apothecary in Charleston—founding a shop still in existence, at which I've bought more than one dish of vanilla ice cream.

And so it goes. Let's hear any news that develops, & I'll keep you posted on my moves.

With customary blessings—
Yr obt hble Servt—
Grandpa

Notes

1. Galpin's *Berg-Symphonie* was performed by the Chicago Civic Orchestra.
2. The young R. H. Barlow and his family.
3. Barlow won the NAPA story laureateship for "Eyes of the God" (*Sea Gull*, May 1933).
4. There was only one issue (December 1920).

[33]   [ALS]

Home again—
July 17, 1934

Son:—

Permit me to congratulate a scion of wealth & leisure! I found your note of the 3d upon my arrival home the 10th; but was so ingulph'd by matters demanding instant attention, that no reply was possible till now. This unexpected œconomick boon is surely one of the pleasantest things I have heard of in many a year. True, plenty of young men encounter good fortune; but seldom does that blessing befall one so well-fitted to enjoy & properly utilise it. To the average tradesman-minded youth of America, an income of this sort wou'd mean meerly a nucleus for frantick efforts at senseless multi-plication; whereas to you it will serve as a key to the rational savouring & em-ployment of life itself. Again, my congratulations! For once a good thing hath come into the right hands!

You last heard from me, I conceive, in antient St. Augustine; where I spent a delighted week amidst the monuments of a past exceeding even New-England's. It is impossible to describe the fascination of streets & houses which were fifty years old when the first Pilgrim landed on Plymouth Rock—houses older than any *private* dwelling in London itself! And the crumbling city gates—& the massive stone fortress overlooking the tropical harbour—& the great sweep of deserted beach on neighbouring Anastasia Island! It cost me a great pang to quit so venerable a scene, but my reluctance was temper'd by the 2-day stop I was able to make in Charleston. Compar'd with the tropick scenes of Florida, in which I had been so long immers'd, Charleston seem'd relatively northern & barren of vegetation; yet it held a charm of authentick English mellowness & unbroken antique survival which nothing in Florida cou'd equal. It is, without doubt, the most fascinating spot in these colonies. My next stop was Richmond, where I spent a day amidst the boyhood scenes of Poe. Here I was doubly sensible of the northernness of the scenery, tho' I soon became re-concil'd to the traditional landskip which Europe & most of the colonies share in common. After all, this landskip doubtless hath more of artistick fineness in it, than hath the more opulent landskip of the tropicks & subtropicks. The graceful disposition of its parts, & the delicacy of the details, amply overbalance any lack of richness & profusion which it may have. An afternoon in antient Fredericksburg, following upon Richmond, confirm'd me in this opinion; & help'd to reaccustom me to the ordinary scenery of my youth.

I was two days in Washington, during which time I did several things I had never done before—namely, visited Rock Creek Park, explor'd the inte-rior of the Capitol, ascended the Washington Monument (from whose top can be had the finest prospect I have ever beheld—outspread hills & meads & reaches of blue river), & examin'd the furnish'd interior of Arlington, the Custis-Lee mansion on the heights across the Potowomack. This last hath lately been fitted up as it was during the tenancy of the Lees a century ago; & forms the best possible example of a Virginia manor-house.

It was with vast regret that I continu'd north to Philadelphia—but the weather was kind, & kept me surrounded with temperatures of 96° & 97°. In the old colonial metropolis I visited my favourite antiquities (tho' many have van-ish'd in recent years) & indulg'd in trips to antient Germantown & the splendid gorge of the Wissahickon. I likewise inspected the home of Poe (1842–44) at N. 7th & Spring Garden Sts., lately open'd as a publick museum. This small brick cottage is precisely as it was in Poe's day, & hath been appropriately fur-nish'd. In a building adjacent is an ample collection of reliques, including copies of most of the magazines containing the first appearance of the various tales &

poems. The effect of the place is extreamly lifelike, & it was not difficult to imagine the bard as present in person to welcome & guide the pilgrim.

Upon reaching New-York, I found Sonny Belknap & his parents about to depart for a 2-day sojourn in Asbury Park & Ocean-Grove, in New-Jersey; & upon their cordial invitation I went along with them. I had not cash enough to linger in Manhattan for any considerable time, hence did not look up any other acquaintances save Brother Samuelus. I came home on the midnight coach July 9–10th, & beheld the spires & domes of antient PROVIDENCE outspread in golden morning light. It was good to behold once more the rolling hills, stone walls, giant elms, & white village steeples of the venerable region of my birth.

Since then I have been struggling with the accumulation of letters, periodicals, & miscellaneous tasks which I found awaiting me. The cold nights are sometimes disconcerting; but the days are reasonable warm, & I take my work out to the countryside each sunny afternoon. I am now on the antient Seekonk river-bank which hath not chang'd a jot since my infancy. But there is a new attraction at home—a tiny coal-black kitten at the boarding-house across the back garden, born last month, & just beginning to be active & playful. He looks like a bear-cub of paperweight size, & promises to become a worthy congener of Felix Baudelaire & Skipper—to which latter gentleman he sends his sincerest compliments.

And so I will conclude, again extending those congratulations which are appropriate to the occasion.

> Yr obt Servt—
> Grandpa

P.S. An occasion for universal regret amongst the amateurs is the death of the venerable Mrs. Miniter on June 6.[1] ¶ Mocrates attended the amateur convention in Chicago, & appears to have enjoy'd the occasion with extream gusto.

Notes

1. Edith Miniter. See HPL's "Mrs. Miniter—Estimates and Recollections" (*Californian*, Spring 1938). In his poem "Edith Miniter" (*Tryout*, August 1934) he gives her date of death as 8 June.

[34]   [ALS]

Home—July 25[, 1934]

Son:—

Indoors today—too damn cold & dismal for my favourite rural spots. Yet it hasn't rained yet. In fact, except for a couple of very transient showers in Richmond July 1st. I haven't seen a trace of rain since the end of the deluge in De Land June 15th.

Yes—I fancy it's just as well not to advertise your recent good fortune over town. The use so far made of it seems eminently sensible—I recall your having mentioned years ago what a nuisance the Delta Gamma was. It seems to me certainly wise to stick to home soil, where you are already rooted. A modest competence will go farther there than anywhere else; & there is a sense of quiet harmony in an adjustment to native & hereditary lands, which nothing else in the world can supply. My keenest envy is of the man who can die in the house he was born in.

Your "yarb"[1] garden is surely full of interesting potentialities, & I shall delight in seeing samples of its produce. When you have exhausted the gastronomic possibilities of your crops, you can turn to the Æsculapian side & experiment with the many herb remedies which generations of rural New England folklore have extolled. You might even devise a popular patent medicine—Dr. Galpin's Carminative Bitters, or something of the sort. The lore of "yarbs" is a definite element in the colour of early America, & one of the salient features of the reproduced pioneer village in Salem is a garden where all the traditional species are cultivated, so that the visitor may see them both growing, & hung up on walls & rafters to dry.

I trust that the music-copying may not prove unduly arduous. If it affects you as prose-copying does me, you have my sympathy! To me, nothing is more utterly enervating, exhausting, & soporific than the mechanical process of writing (especially on a machine) when unaccompanied by the zest of original creation. In music it may be even worse, since so many complex details have to be kept in mind. At any rate, I feel sure you will have amply earned your vacation when the session of pure recreation comes around—& trust that season may prove restful & diverting enough to reconcile you to the coming grind in Main Hall 23 at the Methodist Seminary.

Concerning political matters—I trust you won't allow them to engulf your whole personality, as they have with poor little Belnape. That child can scarcely think or talk of anything but his beloved bolshevism these days . . . . . where we used to hear about Baudelaire, Rimbaud, & the virtues of the "sensitive artist", we now hear only of the "infamous American ideology", the "monstrous, sadistic horrors of capitalism", & the need for a sanguinary overturn of all existing values in favour of the Golden Age as now flourishing in Muscovy.

For my part, I believe I am both a fascist & what I would have contemptuously called a "damn socialist" in my younger & middle-aged days. It has become clear to me that, with intensive mechanisation, there will never—even in the most "prosperous" times—be sufficient work to go around amongst the population under a traditional regime of laissez-faire economics. Economy in production will make it possible to supply all human needs with a minimum of labour, so that more & more persons will be *permanently* unemployed. The myth that new needs always arise to take care of the increasing body of the unemployed is now thoroughly exploded. As it is, we know that the effect of "rugged individualism" is to deprive growing numbers of people of any chance whatever to earn food, shelter, & clothing; to reduce still greater numbers to a degrading form of peonage; to increase the prodigious bulk of resources privately owned & withheld from any useful function; & to confirm the vicious enthronement of rapacious acquisitive ability (as distinguished from cultural capacity) as a criterion of human worth. Such a system has nothing whatever to recommend it, & its continuance is now definitely impossible unless it doles out immense sums to provide bread & circuses for the unemployed throngs it creates. Heretofore, general unemployment has been merely temporary. It cannot exist as a permanent condition because an actually starved population will revolt. No state can survive where millions are dying of cold & hunger; for when these millions feel they have nothing to lose, they are certain to strike out desperately in the forlorn hope of keeping alive somehow. The number of desperate unemployed, plus that of those whose insecurity & enslavement make them sympathetic toward any desperate step, is certainly enough to unseat any government or economic order if sufficiently aroused. The question is not an ethical one, as the old-time socialists insisted, but a very practical & material affair. It might be quite all right to 'let the bastards starve' in the approved Hoover way if one could be sure they *would* starve instead of revolting. But one can't be sure. In fact, one can be pretty damn sure of the opposite! And the resistance of the old order is vastly weakened by the fact that nobody under 50 years old really believes in it any more. The concentration of useless resources in the hands of a pushing, parvenu handful of grasping boors while millions starve & the cultivated classes experience varying degrees of hardship is so grotesque a state of things that it cannot be taken seriously. In the past, when resources were scarce, they had to be withheld from the many in order that anyone might have enough to found a tasteful way of life on. Now that machinery has created a plethora of resources, this condition no longer exists. There are enough resources for everyone, & their present useless concentration while millions starve becomes ridiculous through lack of motivation. Thus the capitalists will have to do one of three things: lull the unemployed into quiescence with a dole, accept the destruction & chaos which a revolution will bring, or submit to a governmental supervision which will cut down their profits by distributing work artificially (short hours—more employed) & providing for old-age pensions & unemployment insurance. Of these three courses, it hardly needs to be said that the third is the only sensible one; & we may hope that (in spite of contemporary howlings) capitalists will have the brains to realise it before it is too late. Laissez-faire economics is dead—killed by the machine. No workable distribution of the resources of a group can ever be achieved in future except through a purely artificial allocation—performed by governmental agencies. It is of no use now to drag up archaic & meaningless whines against "the interference of government in business". The welfare of private business is a secondary concern as compared with the primary need of maintaining an orderly society, feeding the population, & creating & distributing the articles necessary to civilisation. Private business, if it cannot fulfil these functions, is no longer worthy of toleration. If it can't justify itself it will have to give place to something which will really work. But of course all change should be gradual. The thing to do now is not to start a general upheaval, but merely to see whether the existing system can be modified enough to work. Give capitalism a chance to see whether it can stand the reduced profits effected by the spread work, pensions, & insurance which governmental supervision will make compulsory. If it can, well & good . . . at least, for a while. If it can't, then the government will have to take over the larger industries & operate them for service & production alone—on a non-profit basis. Actually, there is no reason why anyone should receive resources except in exchange for services performed—it being understood that everyone will be guaranteed a chance to perform services. *Profits* as distinguished from *salary* are fundamentally an absurdity amidst the new conditions of the machine age. However— all this is a far longer way from Petit-Belnape's communism than it is from old-time capitalism. If capitalism is absurd, then so—in tenfold measure—is the Marxian jumble of nonsense about the superiority of manual labour, the ethical need of absolute equalisation, the economic basis of culture, & the need of overthrowing all the aesthetic & intellectual habits of the past. If capitalism is a suicidal ride toward chaos, bolshevism is virtually that chaos toward which capitalism is riding—a wanton & hideous destruction of three-quarters of the imponderable values which create the illusion that life is worth enduring. There is no endurable life for high-grade people save one which has its roots in the past—which has fixed aesthetic points of reference to give the illusion of placement, direction, significance, & interest to the meaningless round of phenomena which bombards our consciousness. And these roots & reference-points bolshevism tends in very great measure to destroy. Therefore I am unalterably against it, let Sonny shriek what he will. Rational adaptation of our economic life to existing conditions need involve no such wholesale holocaust as this. The general cultural values of the past are still valid, & all that we must have is a new way of applying them to the new conditions. Suppose the government *does* own all large industry? It can, as always, reward those who operate the processes according to the quality of the services they perform—with high pay to the brain-workers whose contributions are great & whose scale of life is highly evolved, & with correspondingly lower pay to the labourers whose contributions & needs are less. Pensions & insurance, of course, to be similarly graded. What is eliminated is merely the waste of *profit*—resources foolishly & criminally diverted to those who do not *work*, but who merely "own" . . . . a word describing an artificial condition without basic meaning. And of course all this public ownership would apply only to amounts of resources so large as to form serious economic factors. There is no reason in the world why it should prevent individuals from "owning" homes & all the other accessories of reasonably comfortable living. To those who complain that governmental supervision or ownership of industries would "destroy the hardy initiative of the American character", I have only a thumb upon my nose. In the first place, no quality is worth preserving if it must be preserved at the cost of wholesale starvation & misery. Secondly, it is childish & asinine to measure the qualities of a people by the one standard of material acquisitive ability.

Now as to governmental *methods* as distinguished from *aims,* as I told you, I am an unreserved fascist. A democracy of universal suffrage is today mainly a joke—or a tragedy. More than that, it is a paradox—for it does not & cannot exist. All we can have is something or other masquerading as a democracy. It ought to be plain to all, that in nations of the size & complexity of ours, every problem & issue of national policy is infinitely beyond the comprehension of any but trained specialists. To imagine that the masses are capable of grasping or deciding any measure, or of judging which of many courses is best adapted to the achievement of a given end, is simply infantile in view of the complex technicality of all measures & courses. A vote in the hands of a layman is ridiculous, & a legislature of laymen prescribing acts which they do not even begin to understand is both ridiculous & dangerous. Even when a few people in a democracy understand what is best, the cumbrous processes of legislation generally postpone or defeat the needed measures. Of course, it has to be the bulk of a people who decree roughly what ultimate ends to pursue. If a minority try to depart too far from the collective will, they are unseated by revolution. But, ultimate ends being agreed upon, it will certainly be necessary in future to devise a more intelligent way of effecting these ends. There must be a way to seat governments which not only know how to do what needs doing, but are able to put that knowledge, without hindrance, into effect. And what is that way? Well, so far as I can see, the thing is to simplify government, eliminate needless debate, & place things in the hands of experts in the various subjects involved—all being accountable to some central authority (either one man or a very few men) with power to appoint, depose, & decide without appeal. As to the way to set up such a central authority—I fancy that a very restricted system of voting would be best. Let the qualifications for popular voting be very high—involving examinations in economics & civics, as well as in general cultural subjects. Of course the voters, even so trained, will not be able to grasp all the measures that will be enacted; but they will at least—through general mental discipline—be able to judge of the general worthiness of proposed objectives, & of the general sincerity & competence of the executives to whom they will grant—& from whom they will sometimes take—such absolute & far-reaching quotas of power. This high scholarship requirement for voting will immeasurably raise the intelligence-level of the electorate—thus making its native judgment as well as its fund of knowledge vastly superior to what is now available. Naturally, it will be the duty of the government to see that every citizen has a chance to receive the education necessary for suffrage; but this will not make for rabble rule, since only the superior can master the necessary material & quality for the ballot. If it be complained that no provision is made for a potentially creative leisure class, two replies can be given. First, that any mature government must necessarily regard major aesthetic & intellectual work as a legitimate occupation, & see that first-rate artists & thinkers are duly rewarded for their creative or scholastic efforts. Second, that under a regime of properly spread work virtually everyone will have leisure in sufficient quantities to admit of a rich mental & artistic life, whether or not this life be definitely creative enough to win a governmental subsidy.

As for existing fascist regimes—I fancy Italy's is immeasurably the best so far. Of course, it has many drawbacks, & it does not go far enough in the direction of rational resource-allocation; but it has shown a stability as yet unrivalled. Its worst trouble is the extent to which it meddles in cultural affairs. While a government may well *encourage* trends which it deems sound & *discourage* those it deems unsound, it ought never to carry its preferences to such a length as to imperil perfect aesthetic & intellectual freedom. If the present American regime were evolved enough to be termed true fascism, I'd be inclined to place that above all others; for its efforts to control economic life are wholly free from any corresponding effort to control personal & cultural life. Indeed, I think it is the best possible thing for America at the present time. Intelligent experimentation is all that can be expected at this juncture; & in view of the deadly backward pull of howling, senile reactionaries we need not wonder that unemployment has been only imperfectly palliated. Allowing for all the inevitable mistakes of a pioneering policy, I believe that the much-maligned "Brain Trust"[2] is headed in precisely the right direction . . . . although, ironically enough, I believe that the length to which that direction must be followed is far greater than any which even the boldest Brain-Truster would be willing to endorse at this stage of the game. As for Herr Hitler—I think he undoubtedly means well, & that the Nazi regime is about all that could have saved Germany from collapse last year. At the same time I regret the extent to which the Nazis have interfered with cultural matters—suppressing honest literature & substituting certain arbitrary & often erroneous scientific concepts for actual truth. That is what, in another direction, the bolsheviki have done. Regarding Der Schön Adolf's much-advertised anti-Semitism—the whole question is so damn'd complex that I can only say I'm both for & against him! There is no question but that the Nazis are perfectly right in *two* of their views on the subject: (a) that no minority culture-group ought to be allowed to modify—much less to direct or represent—the main stream of a nation's culture; & (b) that Jewish culture is basically antipathetic to ours—permanently hostile, & incapable of admixture or compromise. It is, therefore, extremely advisable to emulate Nazism in any nation to the extent of restricting influential or "key" positions in cultural life (high executives, judges, large-scale publishers & theatrical producers, educators, attorneys, book reviewers &c) to persons thoroughly belonging to the racial culture-stream of the bulk of the population . . . . . in our case, to Nordic Aryans. It might even be advisable, in the case of an evolved fascistic commonwealth with a small, educationally selected electorate, to make racial-cultural homogeneity an additional voting-qualification. Where the Nazis indubitably go too far is (a) in the extension of alien disqualification to economic matters affecting merely a daily livelihood, & (b) in the adoption of a ridiculously rigid & biologically unsound definition of membership in the dominant Aryan fabric. Point (a) is easiest to excuse, since *at present* private economic resources can prove such a dangerously powerful force in national life that their possession by aliens is potentially dangerous. However, under a fascistic regime of governmental supervision or ownership of resources, no private fortune could attain influential proportions; so that aliens might safely be allowed to share equally with others in the economic as distinguished from the cultural field. Conceivably, though, it might be well to give preference to members of the dominant group when any distribution of opportunities is involved. Regarding point (b)—since the major differences between the Aryan & Semite groups, so-called (actually, each is infinitely varied & lacking in biological homogeneity), is *cultural* rather than *biological*, it is absurd & unwise to carry discrimination to the point of disqualifying thousands of cultural Aryans who may happen to possess a stray drop of Semitic blood. Biology & ethnology reveal the so-called Jewish "race" of modern times as a collection of various mixtures; some totally unrelated to any of the others, & containing every sort of blood from Mongoloid to Mediterranean, Alpine to Nordic, Sumerian to Punic. Its sole claim to homogeneity is a certain persistent *culture*—just as the sole claim to homogeneity of the swart mongrel Sicilian, the erratic, satyr-nosed Slav, the lean, Oriental Spaniard, the mixed, volatile Frenchman, the grave or beefy Englishman, & the stolid, flaxen Icelander is a certain *culture* called Aryan. Now of the various blood-stocks embraced within the Jewish culture-radius, just as of the various blood-stocks embraced within our Aryan culture-radius, some are undeniably lousy & decadent. Of that, a visit to Manhattan's East Side will amply convince one. But on the other hand, the Jewish radius contains many elements biologically equal—& perhaps superior—to anything we can boast. Spinoza—Einstein—Disraeli—Mendelssohn—Maimonides, & so on. Now any biologist knows that innate racial identity plays a damn small part in the moulding of cultural details. The culture a man has is not what his blood has determined, but what the massed impressions & traditions he has received have given him. Jewish culture is not a product of blood, but of historic accident. So is ours. Bring a Jew up in Aryan culture, & he will in the main be a real Aryan unless Jewish ancestral influences get at him . . . & a good or bad Aryan according to his intrinsic biological status. Conversely, any of us could be a Jew if brought up among Jews & severed wholly from our own inheritance. It is, therefore, not at all important to maintain rigid barriers against every trace of Jewish *blood* when our real & legitimate object is merely to exclude Jewish *cultural* influences (which *are* hostile & unassimilable) from our national life. So long as a man has been brought up in our tradition & no other, & retains no vestiges of alien perspective & thought-habits, it does not make a particle of difference whether or not his ancestry contains a trace of blood from any of the other *superior* races—be it Jewish, Chinese, Polynesian, Japanese, Hindu, or American Indian. [The negro & australoid, of course, are another story.] That is, provided his blood-alienage does not involve any marked physiognomical aberrancy of such a sort as to set him apart & drive him back upon his lost alien heritage. It is easy to establish a practical, common-sense classification of persons as to culture-affiliation, even when their blood is not precisely homogeneous. Einstein *is* Jewish—in heritage & loyalties—but what sensible standard would also class as "Jewish" (as outside the Aryan pole) such well-assimilated persons as, for instance, Walter Damrosch, or the publicist Walter Lippmann?[3] These latter men undeniably *think* as Aryans—& therefore any sensible committee on classification (to which, under a rational regime of Aryan fascism, all debatable cases would of course be carried) would group them as Aryans. It is amusing to think of the thoroughly Aryan people who would be placed outside as aliens if the strict Nazi test were made worldwide. Palgrave, compiler of the Golden Treasury[4] (whose sire was born Cohen), the present Lord Rosebery (whose mother was a Rothschild), the aristocratic Belmont family of America (whose forbear changed his name from Schönberg), the Hamiltons of Philadelphia (Andrew Hamilton, the lawyer famous in the Zenger freedom-of-the-press case of 1735 & the designer of Independence Hall, married a Jewess named Franks) & so on! Indeed—since the Nazi ban is not merely on Jews but on all *non-Aryans,* it would come down heavily upon all who bear a trace of *Indian* blood—such as the descendants of Pocahontas, famous throughout Virginia & including men as eminent as John Randolph of Roanoke! Plainly, then, the present attitude of the Nazis on this point is an extreme & unscientific one . . . . . although, as I have said, I certainly believe that actual members of the Jewish culture-group ought to be kept from securing a grip on the legal, educational, artistic, & intellectual life of any Aryan nation. They had gone too far in Germany, & they have gone too far in America—where so much literary & critical material is either of Semitic origin or (through Jew-owned publishing houses) Semitic selection. It is certainly time that the Aryan people everywhere made sure that they are not being led by fundamentally antipathetic aliens, & that they are not permitting such aliens to serve as their mouthpieces of opinion.

Regarding communists & their possible danger in America, it is hard to know what to think. Certainly, the flood of bolshevistic pap that pours out of the ghettoes & Greenwich-Villages of the large mongrel cities is enough to make one see the guillotine's shadow on the next month's calendar page— but after all, the bulk of the natives throughout the country are tremendously against such things. Foreigners, low-grade itinerant workers, & self-conscious parlour intellectuals like Sonny Belknap are the backbone of bolshevism in America. They sound formidable in view of the glib organs of opinion they control—but how much do they amount to when scaled against the solid people, from farmers to merchants & from mechanics to professional men, who still preponderate except in the mongrelised industrial centres? The South is especially firm against radical extremes, & many sections (like the northwest) favouring flexible economic experimentation would come out valiantly against a jump into the ideological excesses of Leninism. I did fear a spread of bolshevism fifteen years ago, but today I really don't think the American people want it. Certainly, they are not satisfied with the present moribund reign of thieving individualism, & might conceivably stage a revolution if Republican obstructionists succeed in slowing up or wrecking the New Deal. But their revolution would never have bolshevism as its object. It would be toward a far milder form of control & collectivism—& if it got out of hand & went bolshevik it would be because of the disproportionate influence of foreigners trained in the technique of revolt. That, of course, is the ever-present peril inherent in all well-meant revolutions . . . . the peril of their going far beyond their original objects. And because of that peril I am devoutly hopeful that a revolution may be avoided through the success & speeding up of the New Deal, with its unmistakable promise of an evolution toward a more rational economic order when conditions are ripe for it. Depend upon it—Grandpa & Little Belknap-Trotsky have many a stirring fight nowadays on the social-political-economic question! You ought to get the little bolshevik going yourself & hear him squeak & sputter!

And so it goes. I'm expecting Morton here next week—August 2–3–4— hence am all primed for three days of continuous oral debate on an interesting variety of themes. Amateur journalism is perking up—& good old Mocrates is beginning to make his comeback even more thorough than I had hoped. He is rejoining both National & [pseudo] United, & has promised to interest his classes at school. First thing we know, there'll be a revival of the *Pippin* . . . . & perhaps the discovery of another Galpinius, if they breed 'em in this puny & decadent generation!

The black kitten isn't visible today, but my older friends of the Kappa Alpha Tau are sedately perched on the shed roof across the garden. As seen from my window, they are marvellous company!

Yrs for the blackshirt march on Washington—

—Grandpa

Notes

1. Dialectical variant of herb.
2. Originally a reference to three professors at Columbia University—Raymond Moley, Rexford G. Tugwell, and Adolph A. Berle, Jr.—who advised President Franklin D. Roosevelt on public policy issues before and after his election, and later used to denote the large group of intellectuals who joined his administration.
3. Walter Damrosch (1862–1950), German-born composer and conductor and longtime conductor of the New York Symphony Orchestra (1885f.). Walter Lippmann (1889–1974), widely published journalist and political commentator, and author of *Public Opinion* (1922), *A Preface to Morals* (1929), and other volumes.
4. Francis T. Palgrave (1824–1897), edited *The Golden Treasury*. His father, William Gifford Palgrave (1836–1888), was a famous traveler.

[35]   [Postcard, nonextant][1]

[Postmarked Buttonwood, R.I.,
4 August 1934]

[Signed also by Mortonius.]

Notes

1. *Front:* New Providence County Court House, Providence.

[36]   [Postcard, nonextant][1]

[Postmarked 3[0 August] 1934]

Notes

1. *Front:* Upper Main Street, Nantucket, Mass.

[37]   [ALS]

66 College St.,
Providence, R.I.,
Septr 24, 1934.

Son:—

    Well—Grandpa certainly had a great time on Nantucket,[1] & a new set of colonial images hath duly taken up its abode in the Old Gentleman's imaginative background! Of the length of my stay & the type of scenes I encounter'd, I believe my card from the antient town itself sufficiently inform'd you. Toward the end of my sojourn I cover'd suburban points on a hired *bicycle*— the first time in 20 years I had been on a wheel! Riding was just as easy & familiar as if I had last dismounted the day before—& it brought back my youth so vividly that I almost felt as if I ought to hasten back home for the opening of Hope St. High School! I think I told you of the earlier coast trip around the island, during which I saw the antient fishing village of Siasconset (locally pronounced *S'conset*).

Nantucket is an island about 15 miles long & 7 wide, situate 30 miles out at sea. The town (call'd Sherburne prior to 1795) lies on a capacious land-lock'd harbour on the northern side. It was first seen by Bartholomew Gos-nold in 1603, but was not settled till 1659, when some Massachusetts men purchas'd it as a residence to better their condition & escape the savage & illogical Puritan laws of the Bay Colony. At first outside the bounds of any formal colony, it was in 1664 made part of the Province of New-York, then being form'd from the conquer'd New-Netherland colony. In 1692, upon the reorganisation of the colonies after the accession of William & Mary, it was transferr'd to the Province of the Massachusetts-Bay, within which it hath ev-er since remain'd. The great industry of Nantucket was whaling; first practic'd in 1672, & originally conducted in small boats near the shoar. When, after 1700, whales grew scarce in New-England waters, the practice of equipping large whaling-vessels for distant cruises arose. By 1730 Nantucket whalers cover'd the whole Atlantick, & after 1791 they rounded Cape Horn & made the Pacifick their own. Tho' much set back by the wars of 1775–83 & 1812–14, the industry reach'd its climax around 1842, after which it declin'd. The lessen'd demand for whale oil was primarily responsible for this falling-off; tho' scarcity of spermaceti whales (which yielded the choicest product) accel-erated the process. Nantucket whaling ceas'd in 1870, tho' New-Bedford kept the industry alive half a century more—devoting itself to the pursuit of the inferior tho' more common "right whale". After the cessation of whaling, Nantucket came to depend on its summer visitors for a livelihood. The per-manent population—some 3800—all descend from the original settlers—Macys, Coffins, Starbucks, Folgers*, Rays, Gardners, Pinkhams, Wyers, Hus-seys, Colemans, &c.—& when not in the summer real-estate business con-duct a rather slim & precarious shell-fishing industry. No other place—except perhaps parts of the South—is so free from foreigners. There are some nig-gers, but no Jews. At one time Quakerism was dominant on the island, but it is now extinct there. The islanders have a sturdy & distinctive character of their own, & use several idioms peculiar to their domain. The surface of the island consists of treeless, undulating moorlands. Rocks are very rare, & the only groves are of small pines planted around 1845. The town, however, has rich vegetation & fine old trees. Fresh water ponds abound, & their supply is so copious that physiographers are vastly puzzled about the matter. The exact contour of the sandy coast is constantly changed by the sea, which washes soil away in one place & deposits it in another. There was once a sizeable In-

---

*Dr. Franklin's mother was a Nantucket Folger.

dian population; which was well-treated by the whites, but which disappear'd altogether not long after 1800. The first village was about a mile west of the present town; the site shifting in 1722, when the earlier harbour was clos'd by a sand bar. Many houses were moved bodily to the new location. Nantucket architecture resembles that of Salem more than that of Marblehead, & possesses many features peculiar to itself. A typical attribute is the rail'd platform on the roof—call'd the "walk", & used for marine observation.

Well—I am glad to hear all the news, & hope you will not find the transition to class work too sudden & arduous. How are the "yarbs" coming along? I enclose something about a similar enterprise. These old cloisters are very familiar to me—indeed, Belnape, Mortonius, & I visited them for the first time not long after our memorable Cleveland sessions of '22.[2] Too bad that discord developed in Mme. Hasting's work, but trust that her retirement to domesticity will not be any grave financial blow. Hope the desiderate touring may materialise when summer comes. As for sites for permanent settlement—I suppose Maine has its attractions . . . . indeed, my aunt has just been spending a fortnight there . . . . . but I wou'd consider it far too cold for hyemal habitation. Florida is the place for year-round residence if I am any judge. But not many would care to leave all trace of home soil behind, so that Madison no doubt has strong claims. For that matter, what's wrong with Appleton? To my mind, the ideal life is that of the man who can live & die in the house he was born in. Your recent enquiring into ancestral pursuits is interesting—& I hope you will eventually get hold of that first bank-note of your father's. Surely you of all persons ought to have it! My grandfather's cousin Gilbert Phillips also followed the banking profession, being president of the Prov. Inst. for Savings at the time of his death.

I don't worry much about politicks, for I think things may naturally drift in the safest possible way. The trend toward the New Deal . . . . toward the policies so long represented by your own La Follette[3] (the "Bearfox" of your allegory of years agone!) . . . . will form a safety valve against any bolshevistic eruption. Sonny Belknap has sold quite a few stories of late, & is getting so interested in money-making that he doesn't remember to cry down the infamous, barbarous, obscene, sadistic capitalistic system quite as continuously as formerly—tho' he is still explicit in outlining his burning, undying hatred of it.

I wish you would look up good old Mocrates in Zythopolis.[4] His address is 1034 N. 23rd St. He still feels rather sore about that tart epistle from 9231 Birchdale 12 years ago, but a cordial word or two ought to annul anything like that in a second. He's a fine, solid old boy, & certainly does know his profession. And that unpublished poetry manual of his actually is a wonder!

Nearly swamped with tasks since my return from Nantucket, especially since a cursed indigestion attack took a clear week out of my programme. I enjoyed the Boston visits with amateurs which preceded the Nantucket trip. Possibly I mentioned that Cook & I went to Haverhill & called on Tryout

Smith, who hasn't changed a bit in the 13 years I've seen him—though he'll be 82 next month.

All good wishes, & hopes for a not too strenuous winter.

Yr most ob^t h^ble Servt—

Grandpa

Notes

1. HPL visited Nantucket on 31 August–6 September 1934. See "The Unknown City in the Ocean."
2. HPL refers to the George Gray Barnard Cloisters (now a branch of the Metropolitan Museum of Art) in upper Manhattan. It has an extensive herb garden.
3. Robert M. La Follette (1855–1925), governor (1900–05) and U.S. Senator (1905–25) of Wisconsin. He ran for president as a third-party candiate in 1924.
4. Zythopolis is HPL's coined name for Milwaukee; i.e., "Beer-town" (from the Greek ζυθος). Cf. "An Epistle to the Rt. Honble Maurice Winter Moe, Esq. of Zythopolis, in the Northwest Territory of HIS MAJESTY'S American Dominion" (1929).

[38]   [ALS]

66 College St.,
Providence, R.I.,
Octr. 19, 1934.

Son:—

Glad to receive your bulletin of the 9th, & trust that by this time the ennui amidst which it was written is fully banished. Too bad someone else got the appointment for which your wife was aiming—but I fancy some sort of substitute activity will develop in time. And your improved status at the quondam Methodist seminary ought to form a strong compensating factor. Glad the faculty replacements have brought you some congenial colleagues. Some of the old-timers must have been rather hard cases. I recall your descriptions of one Farley—who I believe presided over the philosophical department.

I surely hope you will get in touch with old Mocrates during the autumn or winter. In case you've lost my earlier epistle with his address, I'll repeat the latter: *1034 N. 23^d St., Milwaukee, Wis.* After a bit of ice-breaking you both ought to get a real kick out of archaic reminiscence. Every now & then he speaks of his pleasure at running up against some old Appletonian.

No—I haven't had any new stories for over a year. *Weird Tales* rejected some of my best, & I have become dissatisfied with virtually all of my past performances. I am having a sort of intermission, as I did between 1908 & 1917—meanwhile reading the best things I can find in my own line, & pondering on ways to obviate some of the recognised defects in my former methods. Possibly I'll start up writing a whole series of things before long—& possibly not. I certainly can't until I get some of the circumambient revi-

sion out of the way. I'm now debating whether or not to tackle a [. . . . . . .]
by old Adolphe de Castro (the friend of [Ambrose] Bierce) which will bring
no advance pay,[1] [. . . . .] because of influential sponsoring—
[. . . . .] successfully.[2]

Autumn is now here with all its chill, & my outdoor excursions are getting fewer & briefer. I have, however, managed to take enough rural jaunts to
see the best of the turning foliage. Fortunately an ideal steam-heating system
makes my seat of hibernation safe until April.

All good wishes—
Your ob^t h^{ble} Servt
—Grandpa

Notes

1. See HPL to F. Lee Baldwin (23 December 1934): "The MS. [by De Castro] is a full-
length book of miscellaneous social, political, & historical essays rather vaguely entitled 'The New Way', & has very little internal coherence. It appears to endorse the
philosophy of Lenin & the bolsheviks, & in certain parts tries to give new & sensational interpretations of accepted history" (*Letters to F. Lee Baldwin* 116).
2. The ms. is mutilated here.

[39]   [ALS]

Jany. 17, 1936

Son:—

Your welcome bulletin of 28th ult. was duly forwarded to Castle Belknap, where the old gentleman was paying another grandchild a New Year's
visit. Sonny was as glad as I to hear the news, & you may be having a word
from the Child ere long—though since his highly remunerative absorption in
the cheap fiction business he has been nearly as bad a correspondent as most
of the younger generation!

Needless to say, I perused the current Appletonian chronicle with customary interest, & absorbed with delight the account of Messrs. Skipper &
Brokaw. I had been wondering how our inky friend was faring down the
years—& I now learn with satisfaction of his continued prosperity & his acquisition of a suitably mettlesome sparring partner. Mr. Brokaw is obviously a
personage of distinction, & I heartily congratulate the household upon his
affiliation. I can picture him vividly through your admirably graphic description, & can well imagine what a beautiful & fascinating object he must be. His
linguistic powers, & his dauntless combative mettle, elicit admiration & respect. Not often is a blooded & pampered patrician of the hearth so definitely
a "regular guy"! I can understand his devotion to warmth, & fancy he would
appreciate the abundant 24-hour steam piped into this venerable domicile.
But for all of Mr. Brokaw I shan't go back on good old Skipper. In some

ways the ordinary short-haired feline cannot be surpassed—& surely none of the choice, new-fangled breeds is even half so closely associated with traditional domesticity. Regards to them both—& may they eventually compose their differences & become united in true bonds of fraternal esteem.

While I do not own a cat, I am very frequently a host to the young black gentleman, Mr. John Perkins (b. Feby. 14, 1935), who dwells at the boarding-house across the back garden. He is an elfin creature, with the long legs, large ears, & pointed nose typical of antique Ægyptus' sacred felines. His spirit is exceptionally valiant, & his courtesy to enemies sometimes limited. He has the curiously canine habit of keeping his tail in restless motion—when pleased more than when angered. Indeed, it is a truly eloquent appendage. Mr. Perkins's eyes are large & yellow, & his conversation holds much variety. For minor requests he retains the hesitant, apologetic little "..eew" of his infancy—a characteristic almost amusing in so large a beast. For John has waxed mighty in size, & bids fair to form the leader of the local Kappa Alpha Tau fraternity. The K.A.T., by the way, has fared badly of late. First (last spring) its dauntless fighting champion & Vice-President—the tiger Count Magnus Osterberg—was slain in battle with a vile crawling canine. R.I.P . . . . he never feared any living thing, & is now doubtless dismembering dragons in Valhalla . . . yet he never attacked any adversary first. I weep as I think of his passing. And now—just this month—a further but less tragic loss has occurred—through the removal of the black & white President Peter Randall, Esq., & his tiger brother Stephen (Count Magnus's successor in the Vice-Presidency), from the neighbourhood in conjunction with their human family. Verily, I feel desolated—& the adjacent shed roof seems bleak & barren without the familiar furry forms sprawling in the sun! I must find out where the Messrs. Randall live, & pay them a call.

Some of my friends & correspondents have marvellous felines. Out in California Clark Ashton Smith's coal-black Simaetha has attained an astonishing age & matriarchal dignity—so that her wizard-master can scarcely recall a day when she did not exist. Not far away the weird writer E. Hoffmann Price has 2 cats, including old pure-white Nimrod, the most intrepid battler & fabulous eater who ever slew & devoured a million gophers in a single night. Down in Florida young Barlow has a teeming feline menagerie whose high spots are two Yellow Persians, Cyrus & Darius; whilst in the Boston zone the amateur E. H. Cole boasts a truly royal tiger-angora companion—Peter Ivanovitch Romanoff—whose purr surpasses in volume any other recorded in history or zoölogy.

Descending to merely human matters—I trust that financial asperities will soon be smoothed out, & that domestic life in general will be clarified by a resigned realisation of the irreconcilability of romantic glamour with middle age. Meanwhile I hope the Ph.D. deal will go through without a hitch . . . for *Dr.* Consul Hasting is a very appropriate designation for a philosopher. Congratulations on your new musical production—& upon the increasingly civilised & contemporary nature of the faculty at the ol' Methodist Seminary. After all, there are several endurable elements in the dragged-out process of human existence!

As for your Grandpa's recent annals—I fancy a postcard hath appris'd you of my second long Florida visit. After pauses in Fredericksburg & CHARLESTON, I reached De Land on June 9th, & remained a guest of my young friend Barlow till August 18. During a part of the time his brother—a fine young fellow, 1st. Lt. of Infantry at Ft. Sam Houston, Texas—was home on a furlough. I had several side-trips to picturesque tropical scenes, & helped my host build a cabin across the lake from his home. In that cabin a printing-press was set up; & there we prepared—as a complete surprise for Petit-Belnape—a 32-page collection of the Child's later poetry . . . all, in fact, since the issuance of "A Man from Genoa" a decade ago. The title of the new volume is "The Goblin Tower"—after one of the constituent poems. Barlow couldn't assemble his binding apparatus till after my departure, but by October he began binding copies one by one. Sonny was prodigiously surprised & pleased—& even forgave us for straightening out the consciously irregular metre in one or two of his sonnets. The typography is nothing to brag about—being a first job for all hands—but there are at least no gross misprints. If you'd like a copy of this collection—which includes, I can assure you, some damned good stuff—just send a dollar to the publisher—R. H. BARLOW, BOX 88, DE LAND, FLORIDA—& he'll bind one up & send it as soon as possible.

On my way back I paused in ancient St. Augustine, magical CHARLES-TON, Poe-remembering Richmond, pleasant Washington, & brooding Philadelphia—finally tarrying a fortnight in N.Y. among the gang . . . staying with Donald Wandrei & having meals up at Belnape's. As usual, I saw everybody—Mortonius, Kleiner, &c. &c.

After my return to 66 I read up 3 months of old papers & magazines—taking a vacation long enough to visit E. H. Cole in the Boston zone & make some pilgrimages in his car . . . to Marblehead, to Cape Cod, & to the wild hills of Wilbraham, where the old-time amateur Mrs. Miniter first saw the light of day in 1867 & breathed her last in 1934. This latter pilgrimage was a sort of funereal mission—its purpose being to scatter on the ancestral soil of Wilbraham (in accordance with the deceased's wishes) the ashes of Mrs. Miniter's mother, Mrs. Dowe,[1] who died in Boston in 1919. Mrs. M. had neglected to carry out this maternal request, & now, after her own death, the duty seemed to devolve upon New England amateurdom in general. It was melancholy to revisit, after the death of those who had been my hosts, the remote & picturesque scenes where I was the guest of Mrs. M. & her cousin Miss Beebe in 1928.[2] A spectral aura seemed to hang over the immemorial hills—though there were no outward evidences of change since I was there before. Cole & I placed half the ashes in the ancient burying-ground, & half in the deserted garden which Mrs. D. had loved in youth.

On Octr. 8 my aunt & I had a trip to ancient *New-Haven* in a friend's coach—which gave me 7½ hrs. for exploration (I had never before been off a moving vehicle in the town) whilst my aunt did some visiting. The day was ideally sunny (tho' I could have wish'd it warmer), & the ride thro' autumnal Connecticut scenery (100 m = 2½ hrs) delightful. New-Haven is not as rich in colonial antiquities as Providence, but has a peculiar charm of its own. Streets are broad & well-kept, & in the residential sections (some of which involve hills & fine views) there are endless stately mansions a century old, with generous grounds & gardens, & an almost continuous overarching canopy of great elms.

I visited ancient Connecticut-Hall (1752—oldest Yale College building, where the rebel Nathan Hale of the class of 1773 room'd), old Centre Church on the enormous green (1812—with an interesting crypt containing the grave of Benedict Arnold's first wife), the Pierpont house (1767—now Yale Faculty Club), the historical, art, & natural history museums, the Farnam & Marsh botanick gardens, & various other points of interest—crowding as much as possible into the limited time available.

Most impressive of all the sights, perhaps, were the great *new* quadrangles of Yale University—each an absolutely faithful reproduction of old-time architecture & atmosphere, & forming a self-contained little world in itself. The Gothick courtyards transport one in fancy to mediaeval Oxford or Cambridge—spires, oriels, pointed arches, mullion'd windows, arcades with groin'd roofs, climbing ivy, sundials, lawns, gardens, vine-clad walls & flagstoned walks—everything to give the young occupants that mass'd impression of their accumulated cultural heritage which they might obtain in OLD ENGLAND itself. To stroll thro' these cloister'd quadrangles, in the golden light of late afternoon; at dusk, when the candles behind the diamond-paned casements flicker up one by one; or in the beams of a mellow Hunter's Moon; is to walk bodily into an enchanted region of dream. It is the past & the antient Mother Land brought magically to the present time & place. God Save the King! The choicest of the Gothick quadrangles is Calhoun-College—name'd for the great Carolinian[3] (whose grave in St. Philip's churchyard, Charleston, I had visited scarce two months ago), who was a graduate of Yale.

Nor are the Georgian quadrangles less glamourous—each being a magical summoning-up of the world of two centuries ago. Many distinct types of Georgian architecture are represented, & the buildings & landscaping alike reflect the finest taste which European civilisation has yet developed or is ever likely to develop. Lucky (tho' no doubt unappreciative at the time) is the youth whose formative years are spent amid such scenes! I wander'd for hours thro' this limitless labyrinth of unexpected elder microcosms, & mourn'd the lack of further time. Certainly, I must visit New-Haven again, since many of its treasures wou'd require weeks for proper inspection & appreciation.

Oct. 16–18 I had a pleasing visit from our friend Saml. Loveman, Esq.— spent partly in Boston, where we visited the Mus. of Fine Arts & brows'd among the bookstalls. Samuelus hath now left Dauber & Pine, & is the proprietor of an independent establishment call'd the Bodley Book Shop, which holds forth at 104 Fifth Ave., on the 17th floor of an office-building. Also (vide enclosed circular), he is at last the author of a regularly publish'd book.[4] This volume makes a very neat appearance, & is (I hope, since I read the proofs thrice) reasonably accurate as to text.

The autumn was a mild one hereabouts, & I continued to haunt the agrestick meads & groves throughout October. After that something more like hibernation set in, tho' I attended many local lectures of interest. At Christmas we again had a tree, & the air of traditional festivity was considerable.

Dec. 30 I arriv'd at Sonny Belknap's for a week of sociability with the old gang, & succeeded in exchanging greetings with most of the veterans—Morton, Kleiner, Kirk, Loveman, Talman, Leeds, Wandrei, &c. &c. &c. I attended several gatherings, including a dinner of the Am. Fiction Guild, & saw a good many of the cheap magazine hacks whose names are familiar to the reading proletariat. Petit-Belnape & Wandrei are getting deep into hack fiction-writing—to the great financial advantage, tho' to their aesthetick detriment. Sonny sent you his most cordial regards—&, as I have said, express'd a design to write you. By the way—on Oct. 20 Belknap's aunt Mrs. Symmes, the one who financed "A Man from Genoa", was instantly killed in a motor accident near Miami. A bit of tragick irony—even at that moment Barlow was binding a complimentary copy of "The Goblin Tower" for her.

On two occasions—once with Sonny & once with Sonny & Wandrei—I visited the new Hayden Planetarium of the Am. Museum, & found it a highly impressive device. It consists of a round domed building of 2 storeys. On the lower floor is a circular hall whose ceiling is a gigantick orrery—shewing the planets revolving around the sun at their proper relative speeds. Above it is another circular hall whose roof is the great dome, & whose edge is made to represent the horizon of N.Y. as seen from Central Park. In the centre of this upper hall is a curious projector which casts on the concave dome a perfect image of the sky—capable of duplicating the natural apparent motions of the celestial vault, & of depicting the heavens as seen at any hour, in any season, from any latitude, & at any period of history. Other parts of the projector can cast suitably moveable images of the sun, moon, & planets, & diagrammatick arrows & circles for explanatory purposes. The effect is infinitely lifelike—as if one were outdoors beneath the sky. Lectures—different each month (I heard both Dec. & Jan. ones)—are given in connexion with this apparatus. In the corridors on each floor are niches containing typical astronomical instruments of all ages—telescopes, transits, celestial globes, armillary spheres, &c.—& cases to display books, meteorites, & other miscellany. Astronomical pictures line the walls, & at the desk may be obtained useful pamphlets, books, planispheres, &c. The institution holds classes in elementary astronomy, & sponsors clubs of amateur observers. Altogether, it is the most complete & active popular astronomical centre imaginable. It seems to be crowded at all hours—attracting a publick interest in astronomy which did not exist when I was young.

I visited Morton in Paterson on Jan. 6, & that midnight took the coach for home—being delay'd an hour in the sightly colonial village of Hampton, Conn., to await the sanding of a slippery hill. Since my arrival, I have been ingulph'd by an almost unprecedented vortex of tasks—so hopeless that I have had to give over the design of writing a N.A.P.A. critical report. Amateurdom is having a kind of renew'd life—including the usual political warfare.

Clark Ashton Smith's mother died on Sept. 9—an event imposing a severe strain on his nerves. He has now taken up a new artistick pursuit, at which he is succeeding to a remarkable degree—viz. *sculpture or carving* in the soft minerals of his native region. Within the past month or two an unexpected *professional* demand for the products of his chisel has arisen—so that for the moment his writing is quite eclipsed. Most of his statues are miniature grotesque heads or figurines (he has given me two—each representing a monster in some tale of mine), tho' he hath prepar'd several statuettes & bas-reliefs of a more common sort to order.

I surely hope that I can see the cinema "Mad Love"—which several have recommended to me. I was never able to witness "Dr. Caligari", about which I heard so much 13 or 14 years ago. I attend the cinema but seldom—the best production I have lately seen being a highly impressive Irish tragedy intitul'd "The Informer." I also saw "Ah, Wilderness",[5] which made me homesick for the vanish'd world of 1906!

With usual benedictions, & compliments to Skipper, Mr. Brokaw, & everybody, I remain

      Yr ob[t] h[ble] Serv[t]

        Grandpa

P.S. You can find a 3-part story of mine—"At the Mountains of Madness"— in *Astounding Stories,* beginning with the February issue. The W.T. now on the stands reprints my old "Dagon." ¶ You can find stories of Belnape's in many of the current science-fiction & detective magazines.

Notes

1. Jennie E. T. Dowe. See HPL's "In Memoriam: J. E. T. D."

2. HPL's visit influenced "The Dunwich Horror."

3. John C. Calhoun (1782–1850).

4. *The Hermaphrodite and Other Poems.*

5. *Mad Love* (MGM, 1935), directed by Karl Freund; starring Peter Lorre, Frances Drake, and Colin Clive. *The Cabinet of Dr. Caligari* (Decla-Bioscop/Goldwyn, 1920), directed by Robert Wiene; starring Werner Kraus, Conrad Veidt, and Friedrich Feher. *The Informer* (RKO, 1935), directed by John Ford; starring Victor McLaglen, Heather Angel, and Preston Foster. *Ah, Wilderness!* (MGM, 1935), directed by Clarence Brown; starring Wallace Beery, Lionel Barrymore, and Mickey Rooney.

[40]   [ALS]

66 College St.,
Providence, R.I.,
June 20, 1936.

Son:—

Your recent bulletin proved very welcome indeed, & helped to mitigate the woes of a season of considerable asperity. For 1936 has proved a
very bad year for the old man—forming, virtually ever since my return from
the New Year visit to young Belnape, a continuous chronicle of disaster. First
a congestion of thankless & unprofitable tasks which threw my whole schedule awry. Then an attack of grippe which had me flat for a week & multiplied
the prevailing chaos a thousandfold. And *then*—before I was well over the
grippe—the *real* trouble began! My aunt came down with a grippe attack infinitely worse than mine,[1] so that I was at once reduced to the composite status
of nurse, butler, secretary, market-man, & errand-boy. All my own affairs
went to hell—revision jobs returned, letters unanswered, borrowed books
piled up unread . . . .

> "With ruin upon ruin, rout on rout,
> Confusion worse confounded."[2]

Complications setting in, my aunt had to go to the hospital in mid-March—
which altered without materially diminishing my added responsibilities. And
the financial aspect can be imagined! Very luckily, my aunt soon began to improve—being promoted to a convalescent home on April 7, & returning to
#66 on the 21st. She is now fully ¾ back to normal, having resumed a great
part of her usual activities & spending most of her time outdoors in the garden. But my programme remained all shot to hell, & at present I feel just
about on the edge of a nervous breakdown. My energy & power of concentration are sunk to a minimum, & my eyesight is not what it was when I was
young. The lingering cold of a late spring has helped to keep me down—& I
have found it impossible to embark on any trips, notwithstanding a cordial &
tempting invitation from Barlow to repeat my Florida visits of '34 & '35.
However, the tardy approach of vernal mildness has been of some benefit, &
I have been able to keep out of doors to some extent. Would that 98° weather might set in!

Well—congratulations on the new—& first—detective novel, which I
know must be good, & which I surely hope to peruse sooner or later! Here's
hoping it wins the prize—or, failing that, that it lands advantageously with
some publisher in the regular way. Regarding the best markets—I am scarcely
an expert in detective-novel placement, but recall that the most prolific author of such material whom I know—your brilliant young fellow-
Wisconsinian August W. Derleth of Sauk City—began most successfully with
the relatively new firm of Loring & Mussey (now, I believe, called Barrows

Mussey, Inc.), 66 Fifth Ave., New York, N.Y. (in the same building with Dauber & Pine, where Samuelus once held forth.) Whether he'd advise that same firm today, I can't tell—but I am asking him about the matter. As the author of half a dozen successful detective novels (the "Judge Peck" mysteries)[3] & of one serious book ("Place of Hawks"—1935—a group of regional tales with convincing Wis. background), he ought to know a lot more about the game than I do. I have requested him either to write you directly, or to give me all the necessary information for purposes of relaying. I rather hope he'll write you, for you'd find him an interesting cuss. Here is a cutting about him & his work—which I'll ask you to return some time. Regarding the way to fasten a thick MS.—if (as 225 pages probably are) it's too thick to go neatly in a large envelope, I fancy a common elastic band is all that could be demanded. *Permanent* fasteners—i.e., things like the long brass specimens which punch through the top or side of all the sheets to make a sort of quasi-book—are usually not desired by publishers, since they like to be able to separate the MS. into parts if necessary. *Clips* for thin MSS., elastic bands or nothing at all (i.e., just the large envelope in which the MS. is mailed flat) for medium MSS., & elastic bands for very thick MSS. would seem to be the ordinary custom. However, I've asked Derleth if there's any new-fangled professional custom which ought to be followed. As to the date of first financial returns in case of acceptance—I'm inclined to doubt the wisdom of expecting anything this summer. Arrangements differ, of course, & E. P. Dutton Co. used to make good old Everett McNeil small advances upon accepting his various juvenile volumes; but whether this system would hold good in the case of a first novel I can't be sure. Here again I'll seek the latest & most authoritative data from young Derleth. The bulk of remuneration usually comes through "royalties"—a certain percentage of the receipts from sales forwarded at stated intervals when there's anything to forward.

Well—you'll hear again before long, either from Derleth or from me. The outline which you give suggests something of marked power & interest, & the realistic, first-hand nature of the setting ought to remove it considerably from the usual rut. The generous allotment of tragic & violent events is in the best detective tradition (in one of his novels Derleth kills damn near everybody off!), while the dialogue medium surely reflects the prevailing taste. Your chosen title & pseudonym also appear to me to be definite assets. So here's to a bright future for "Marsh-Mad's" first successor! "Strive blindly toward the light that kills, for the eternal hills & valleys will preserve!"*

Any recent story of mine in W T must have been a reprint. My last two published efforts (the first-named of which was frightfully mangled) are "At the Mountains of Madness" (antarctic serial) & "The Shadow Out of Time"

---

*From "Mystery", an essay by Consul Hasting, Esq. in *United Amateur* for January 1918.

332 ❀ *Letters to Alfred Galpin*

(novelette), in *Astounding Stories* for Feb.–Mar–April & June, respectively. Both of these received cover designs,[4] which rather tickled my aged ego.

The few reviews of the Herm which I have seen have been rather discouragingly lukewarm. It is evident that a new generation of modernistic youngsters has seized the critical thrones in most of the papers, & has begun to spread its analytical & subjective doctrines. The tendency is to regard Lovemaniana as something derived from obsolete sources—as a musical echo of images & sentiments no longer fraught with meaning, but merely repeating the emotions of the elder bards. That I thoroughly disagree with such dicta goes without saying—but there's no stopping a pack of young upstarts once they get going! It is this same tendency which has worked to the advantage of poor Crane & made him such a symbol of the poetic present. I can agree with Mr. Untermeyer regarding Crane's unintelligibility,[5] & am myself convinced of the unsoundness of any symbolism whose key rests with the author alone. You may have seen an article—largely based on Crane, & including an image-by-image interpretation (furnished by the poet on request) of one of his shorter verses—on this subject some few years ago in *Harpers* . . . "Poets talking to Themselves", by Max Eastman.[6] He conceded that Crane's obscure allusions are not capricious or irresponsible, but expressed strong doubts of the value of associative processes so purely dependent on the contents & workings of one person's mind.

Amateurdom has had a slight revival this year—owing largely to the return of the old-timer Ernest A. Edkins (now in the Evanston Hospital, alas, with a kidney operation) to the fold. I've sent you a copy of his paper—which contains among other things a not too sympathetic review of Sonny Belknap's new volume of verse.[7] Belnape, by the way, has been having rather a hard time—pushed to the wall with hack-writing, & with both parents recently down with grippe. Samuelus' bookshop seems to keep him amply busy—which is equally true of Kirk's. Good ol' Mocrates expects to get east again this summer—attending the celebrated Bread Loaf Writers' Conference in Vermont. I hope to see him here—for the first time since 1923. In the intervening 13 yrs Grandpa has changed a lot more than he has! His elder son is still doing brilliantly in Bridgeport, whilst the younger is still at college in Seattle.

I hope to see those snapshots of you before long, but trust you'll get rid of the lip-fuzz as soon as the novel is complete! Congratulations on your pleasant spring—bright contrast to the chill & lagging season hereabouts! The landscaping sounds highly interesting, & I trust I may see some photographic evidence thereof. I certainly envy you your ability to dwell down the years in your birthplace! How are the felidae getting along? Sooner or later I want to see your novel—& meanwhile I wish it luck in the contest. I'll shoot along additional market hints at the earliest possible date.

Ever y^r most ob^t h^ble Servt—

Grandpa

P.S. Last moment. I've just recd. the 2nd issue of *Causerie*, & will try to get a copy for you. The criticism of S L is in the main acute & fair, tho' Edkins blames the bard unduly for what he calls his "defeatist" attitude toward life.[8] Actually, a poet's attitude toward life doesn't matter one god damn—so long as he crystallises & transmutes with suitable grace & power, whatever mood or attitude he *does* happen to have.

Notes

1. Actually, Annie Gamwell underwent surgery for breast cancer.
2. John Milton, *Paradise Lost* 2.995–96.
3. *The Man on All Fours* (1934), *Sign of Fear* (1935), and *Three Who Died* (1935). Derleth published ten Judge Peck novels in all. HPL owned and read the three mentioned.
4. "The Shadow out of Time" and *At the Mountains of Madness*, both illustrated by Howard V. Brown (1878–1945).
5. Louis Untermeyer, *Modern American Poetry: A Critical Anthology,* 5th rev. ed. (New York: Harcourt, Brace, 1936), 588: "There will be those who will find Crane's poetry not merely tangential but cryptic. The difficulty is caused by his combination of allusiveness and allegory, especially since the allusions are often remote and the allegorical symbols personal to the point of privacy."
6. Max Eastman, "Poets Talking to Themselves," *Harper's Magazine* 163, No. 5 (October 1931): 563–74.
7. [Ernest A. Edkins], *"The Goblin Tower,"* *Causerie* (February 1936): 2–4.
8. Edkins reviewed Loveman's *Hermaphrodite and Other Poems* in *Causerie* (June 1936): 2–4.

[41]   [ALS]

66 College St.,
Providence, R.I.,
July 31, 1936.

Son:—

Glad indeed that my recommendation of young Auguste-Guillaume, Comte d'Erlette, proved a good one. I thought he had the skill & experience needed to make his fictional advice of value, & it seems I was not wrong. He is really a great chap—with a driving energy that perpetually astonishes the rest of the gang. Slowly & steadily he is climbing out of the cheap fiction class into the domain of serious writing, & within a decade I believe he will be recognised as a substantial regional novelist. His productivity is almost fabulous—including everything from pulp junk up to Scribner stories & published books. It is impossible to pick up one of the better-grade "little magazines" without coming across his name. Among readers of detective fiction his "Judge Peck" novels are classics of a sort. His enthusiasm in helping & advising fellow-craftsmen is prodigious—& is perhaps one result of his superabundance of energy. I hope you'll have a chance to meet him before long, &

believe he'll prove as congenial in conversation as in correspondence. His acute musical appreciation will surely form a link in common.

As to his personality—while I've never met him face to face (though my friends the Wandrei brothers have), & have never formed an intimate picture of his daily life & amusements, I fancy you would find in him a kind of blend of the convivial & aesthetic. He probably changes somewhat as he develops. A few years ago he was an almost amusing egotist who deliberately cultivated egocentricity in order to irritate the complacent bourgeoisie of his somewhat smug & provincial village. He wore a monocle & a flaring-tailed overcoat that almost touched the ground, went outdoors (& once to a social gathering) in a dressing-gown, & had himself snapshotted in all sorts of asinine poses. Now he is maturing & getting over the kid stuff—his ego cropping out in nothing more bizarre than his de luxe letter-heads with different woodcuts for every season. He likes to be thought important, but has a saving sense of humour. I think he enjoys the modest pleasures of society—in fact, he is an avowed enemy to the puritanic attitude—though on the other hand he despises the decadent hedonism of urban & sophisticated circles. He spent a year in Minneapolis as assistant editor of a cheap magazine,[1] & left it in disgust at the affectation, bohemianism, triviality, & laboured "smartness" of the local literary & aesthetic groups. After all, he is essentially a villager with his roots deep in Wisconsin soil. He understands the importance of fixity & of profound geographic traditions, & never writes without a sharp consciousness of the long stream of events, folkways, & personalities behind the "Sac Prairie" of today. To him, basic & permanent human emotions seem to be embodied far more truly & visibly in rural or semi-rural life, than in the rootless, restless, pointless & kaleidoscopic life of a mongrel metropolis. He has never been east or in Europe, nor would he care to live & work anywhere save in his native town. Sauk City appears to be rather an unusual place—a prairie town peopled about 1830 by a small group of Germans of the haute-bourgeoisie & lesser nobility, & sharply differentiated both from such Yankee towns as good ol' Appleton, & from the *peasant*-German areas. Small & self-contained, it has cherished a sometimes enjoyable & sometimes exasperating clannishness. Its old families furnish the curious brooding characters so frequent in Derleth's serious fiction—proud, grim old gentlewomen harbouring various secrets; decadent scions with relentless hereditary taints; patriarchal or matriarchal tyrants dominating individual children or entire households; haughty, destitute aristocrats recalling past glories amidst present squalor, &c. &c. &c. In former years I fancy Derleth was locally disliked for his incessant inquisitiveness regarding the lives & pasts of his fellow-villagers; but he persisted in his "nosey" pestiferousness in order to gain the knowledge of human affairs, emotions, relationships, thought-patterns, & inheritances which he needed for his realistic fiction. Now the natives seem inclined to forgive & respect him—for (having pumped them dry of family secrets) he probably pesters them less with questions, while his growing literary reputation presumably impresses them. In time he will doubtless grow into something like a local oracle—& the outside world may know Sauk City chiefly because of his birth & residence there. No—Derleth isn't a farm boy in any sense of the word. He lives in the village*, & has a really cosmopolitan outlook. His financial circumstances seem to be moderate; so that he has plenty of time in which to develop his professional writing skill, while he has not been forced to pander to the cheapest editors in order to keep afloat. He is now, moreover, making quite a bit with his stories—so that he paid an income tax for the first time this year. But he is no rich man's son, either—indeed, he used to piece out his spending-money in summer by taking a part-time job in the local canning factory. His tastes would be rather fastidious & sybaritic if he had the means to indulge them, but he is too devoted to literature to attempt commercial enterprises. On the other hand he is a very shrewd business man in the domain of literary marketing, & will probably be financially secure within the next few years. Altogether, Little Augie is quite a boy—amply sustaining the reputation of Old Wisconsin as a nursery of precocious genius. You'll like him.

Sorry the novel needs so much reconstruction—though I suppose the process really forms an invaluable lesson in fictional technique. You can be counted on to use any sound hint to the best possible advantage in the shortest possible order! In the end I hope success will result—favourable professional placement, if not the winning of the coveted Dodd-Mead prize.

As for the Old Gent—my touristic programme is so far (& is likely to remain) an approximate zero—for reasons which are now (in view of my aunt's recovery) wholly financial. Yuggoth, if I could only get down to Charleston for some life-giving *continuous* heat amidst this chilly summer! I've felt like hell most of the time, though two hot spells helped to brace me up. In mid-July—when a week of 90° weather put me on my feet—I took a boat trip to Newport—rambling as usual around the ancient town & doing considerable writing atop the high, hilly sea-cliffs.

July 18–19 I had an enjoyable visit from our good old colleague Mocrates the Sage, now on a visit to various eastern points after a sojourn at the Grand Rapids N.A.P.A. Convention. It was my first sight of the old boy in 13 years, & I fancy he found Grandpa a damn sight more changed than I found him. He came with his son Robert (now of Bridgeport, Conn.—he visited me twice last year) in the latter's car, & we covered quite a bit of scenic & historic ground in the all-too-brief span of 2 days. Weather favoured us greatly, for we had warmth & sun throughout—whereas the very next day was cold & rainy, with the Old Gent heavily blanketed & shivering over an oil heater. Good ol' Mocrates! We recalled the Kleicomolo & Gallomo days of 20 years ago, dug up issues of *The Pippin* from my amateur files, & in general acted the

---

*pop. 2000 or 3000

part of grey, reminiscent elders to the life. I fear young Bob was quite bored to death by the senile gabbling of Pater et Avus!

Had an interesting view of Peltier's Comet on July 22 at the Ladd Observatory[2]—through the 12″ refractor. The object shewed a small disc with a hazy, fan-like tail. I could have seen it through my own small glass but for the obstructed nature of the northern sky in the neighbourhood of 66.

Just at present I have the pleasure of being a sort of long-term semi-host—as Loveman was to us in the good old 9231 Birchdale days of '22—since my young friend Robert Hayward Barlow (my host in De Land, Fla. in '34 & '35) has come to Providence for a sojourn of indefinite length. Some property adjustments about the De Land place are occurring, & Barlow thought this would be a good time to pay the Old Gent a visit & make his temporary headquarters in ancient New-England for a while. I surely am glad to see him—& I forgive him the fierce-looking moustache & side-whiskers he has grown. He has taken a room at the boarding-house across the garden from 66, & will certainly be a most congenial neighbour while he stays. He is full of literary plans—including a realistic novel & the establishment of a high-grade mimeographed magazine of distinctive material.[3] My aunt fears he will go broke because of his ferocious raids upon the local bookstalls!

Well—here's hoping you have a pleasant visit with M. le Comte d'Erlette ere long—& that his critical suggestions may help you to put "Death in D-Minor" across big. Best wishes for the plantation at 726!

　　　Yr obt Servt—
　　　　　Grandpa

P.S. Loan exhibit of Clark Ashton Smith's grotesque miniature sculpture has reached me at last. Great stuff! Some of the items shew a genius of the most distinctive kind.

Notes

1. *Mystic Magazine,* a magazine devoted to the occult.
2. 451 Hope Street in Providence.
3. Barlow published two large issues of the mimeographed magazine *Leaves* (1937, 1938).

[42]　　[ALS]

　　　　　　　　　　66 College St.,
　　　　　　　　　　Providence, R.I.,
　　　　　　　　　　August 9, 1936.

Son:—

Glad to hear of progress on the reconceived "Murder in Montparnasse". You surely have made a radical change in approach & method, & I fancy the present course is much more likely to produce a definitely marketable result. It pleases me to learn that Derleth has been such a help, & I hope you two can meet before long.[1] He refers to you in the most admiring terms in a recent letter, & I have no doubt but that the get-together will be a congenial one when it comes to pass. By the way—if you'd like to see some of Comte d'Erlette's work, I'd be glad to lend you his book "Place of Hawks", or some of his detective novels. Let me know if you wish them. Glad some of your verse is going into M. le Comte's anthology, & hope to see "November" before long.[2] Little Augie is also asking Pater Mocrates for some metrical material—which I imagine the good old boy will be able to furnish, since he's getting rather poetical in his declining years.

Glad you've been somewhat active in music, & hope you'll turn out some memorable compositions before long. Glad also that you've received both *The Dragon-Fly*[3] & *Causerie*. Edkins certainly hit off Samuelus' work finely—so justly that S L is genuinely pleased with the review & has asked for copies.

Sorry to hear of the Appleton drought. Lawns are rather scorched here, but the dessication is on the whole less uninterrupted. I envy you your over-100° temperatures, though a few 90° days have helped to keep me in trim.

Barlow is still here, & last Wednesday the party was further swelled by the arrival of old Adolphe de Castro (erstwhile Gustav Adolf Danziger), onetime friend of Ambrose Bierce & co-translator of the fairly well-known "Monk & the Hangman's Daughter".[4] He was, as you may recall, a revision client of mine in 1928–9[5]—& Belknap wrote the preface for his life of Bierce published in '29.[6] Old 'Dolph is 77 now, & quite down & out—on public relief in N.Y. His wife died last year, & he is now en route back from Boston, where he carried out her ante-mortem request that her ashes be scattered over the ocean off the coast. As usual, the old boy is trying to saddle me with half a dozen speculative (& undoubtedly unprofitable) revision jobs, but so far I've succeeded in refusing without offending him. Meanwhile I'm shewing him the sights of the town, & listening to his tales about all the bygone celebrities (Swinburne, Anatole France, Bierce, Theodore Roosevelt, &c. &c. &c.) he used to know . . . . how he helped Warren G. Harding become President, & how his advice also won the presidency for Taft . . . . . . Friday we were all in the hidden hillside churchyard somewhat north of #66—where Poe used to wander during his courtship of Sarah Helen Whitman—& each of us (at Barlow's suggestion) composed a rhymed acrostic on the letters of Poe's name.[7] Here is mine—the mechanical & inspirationless product of a single half-hour, writ as I sate upon an ancient tomb:

IN A SEQUESTER'D CHURCHYARD WHERE
POE ONCE WALK'D

Eternal brood the Shadows on this Ground,
Dreaming of Centuries that have gone before;

Great Elms rife folemnly by Slab and Mound,
Arching above a hidden World of Yore.
Round all the Scene a Light of Mem'ry plays,
And dead Leaves whifper of departed Days,
Longing for Sights and Sounds that are no more.
Lonely and fad, a Spectre glides along
Aifles where long paft his living Footfteps fell;
No common Glance difcerns him, tho' his Song
Peals down thro' Time with a myfterious Spell:
Only the Few who Sorcery's Secret know
Espy amidft thefe Tombs the Shade of POE.

Old 'Dolph's & Barlow's efforts are (pardon the egotism) even worse! Most emphatically, poetry cannot be written to order.

Today I shall meet Barlow & de Castro at noon, & we shall do the art museum[8] (only a block down the hill from 66)—which R H B has seen only in part, & which will be wholly new to Old 'Dolph. There's some pretty good stuff in it, even if it isn't a rival of the Metropolitan in N.Y. Attached to the museum proper is a perfect reproduction of a colonial mansion, containing the finest collection of American colonial furniture in the world.

Well—good luck with the novel, & with all your other ventures. Hope you'll meet the scintillant Comte d'Erlette ere long, & that he will not prove disappointing.

Sir, yr most h[ble] & ob[t] Serv[t]—

—Grandpa

Notes

1. Derleth met Galpin only after HPL died in 1937, when he and Donald Wandrei went to Appleton to retrieve Galpin's HPL manuscripts.

2. August Derleth and Raymond E. F. Larsson, eds., *Poetry out of Wisconsin.*

3. Edited by R. H. Barlow.

4. Ambrose Bierce (1842–1914?) and Gustav Adolph Danziger (1859–1959), *The Monk and the Hangman's Daughter* (serialized 1891; book publication 1892; translated from the German of Richard Voss). HPL owned a later edition.

5. HPL revised "The Last Test," "The Electric Executioner," and "In the Confessional" for de Castro from his book *In the Confessional and the Following* (New York: Western Authors Publishing Association, 1893). The last revision is nonextant.

6. *Portrait of Ambrose Bierce* (New York: Century Co., 1929). The preface is signed "Belknap Long."

7. The three acrostic poems and others by M. W. Moe and Henry Kuttner were published in David E. Schultz, "In a Sequester'd Churchyard," *Crypt of Cthulhu* No. 57 (St. John's Eve 1988): 26–29.

8. Museum of Art, Rhode Island School of Design, 224 Benefit Street.

Adolphe Danziger.

Letters: H. P. Lovecraft and Adolphe de Castro

[1]   [TLS, JHL]

[Adolphe de Castro]

113 West 88,
New York City,
November
Twentieth,
1 9 2 7 .

Howard P. Lovecraft Esq.,
10 Barnes Street,
Providence, R.I.

Dear Sir,

My friend, Mr. Samuel Loveman, was kind enough to mention that you might be inclined to aid me in bringing out one or the other of my labors which sadly need revision.

If you can, please let me know and under what conditions we can co-operate.

Yours sincerely,
Adolphe de Castro.

[2]   [TLS, JHL]

[Adolphe de Castro]

113 West 88th Str.,
New York City,
November
Twenty-fifth,
1 9 2 7 .

H. P. Lovecraft Esq.,
10 Barnes Street,
Providence, R.I.

Dear Sir,

In receipt of your letter of the 23rd instant, I beg to thank you for the information you were kind enough to impart and to assure you that from the very composition of your letter I am quite certain that you can do all you say where revision is concerned and a manuscript needs the touch to pass in-to Allah's Paradise, alias, the editorial doorway.

What appears to me to be a bit too formidable for my delicate financial condition is the array of fees for revisionary work. Not that work such as you may lend will not merit a thousandfold more than you ask, but there are times——

I am at present "property poor", if I may allow myself such a high sounding adjectival application. What I am trying to do with the unexpected sunshine that has come my way through the publicity given me by my dear friend Bob Davis of the Sun,[1] is to make a bit of literary hay. But I dread the straw that is mixed with it and is likely to make it unavailable to the oversensitive and highly di[s]criminating editorial autocrat—or other rat—but which is always sufficient to cloud the author's landscape.

Now fortunately a publishing firm has sent for me and the head and shoulders of the concern pumpt me so dry that I had to look up a disused bootlegger to get on my feet again. The long and the short of the matter is that if I had anything worth while, in a volume of some sort, I might just manage to put it over.

I happen to be one writer who knows his limitations. I am always unsure of my English; I always think some one will laugh at my form of expression—not that I care a damn, but that I would rather laugh at the other fellow, particularly when his best girl smiles at me. The only thing I am fairly sure of are the thoughts—for I have translated from at least sixteen languages, and have a current notion of what the line is.

Years and years ago I published a volume of short stories (now not to be had at any price, and Uncle Sam and myself are the only ones who have copies of the same) and if these stories could be licked into shape, I am certain they would be published. It all depends upon my literary godfather. Suppose I send you part of one of these stories just for a passing judgment whether you would be inclined to consider the matter, if all things become equal?

Please, let me know and meanwhile be assured of the pleasure I have in knowing a man who knows that he can do something, I shall do all in my power to bring you to the attention of my friends and particularly of Dr. Moore who has a book he wants revised and who has the money to spend on it—and then some.

Sincerely yours,
Adolphe de Castro.

[Enclosure: clipping][2]

Bob Davis Recalls:
New Light on the Disappearance of Ambrose Bierce.

In the history of American literature the name of Ambrose Bierce shines with unusual brilliance. His output, which includes poetry, fiction, cynical essays, dictionaries, fables and text books, stands quite apart from the works of his contemporaries and manifests genius.

Bierce was born in Ohio in 1842, enlisted in the civil war at its outbreak, was brevetted major for distinguished service and went in 1866 to California, where he plunged into the romance of that new land. London received him in 1872 and in 1874 the English critics hailed a new book which purported to be translations from Zambri, the Parsee, published under the title "Cobwebs From an Empty Skull." In 1874 Bierce returned to the Pacific Coast and took up literature as a means of livelihood. In 1886 he formed the acquaintance of Dr. Adolphe Danziger de Castro, in collaboration with whom he published, in 1892, "The Monk and the Hangman's Daughter," a novel of soot and fire. In rapid succession followed "Black Beetles in Amber," "Can Such Things Be?" "In the Midst of Life," "Fantastic Fables," "Shapes of Clay," "The Cynic's Word Book," "The Shadow on the Dial and Other Essays" and "Write It Wright." [*sic*] He also contributed through all the years a column headed "Prattle" in the San Francisco *Examiner*.

In the year 1909 Adolphe Danziger brought out a novel all his own, "Helen Polska's Lover," which, contrary to custom, Alfonso of Spain acknowledged, read and approved.

In 1913 Bierce, now internationally celebrated, suddenly left the Army and Navy Club in Washington, D. C., and set his steps toward Mexico, where Carranza and the picturesque Francisco Villa were engaged in a death struggle for mastery. Shortly thereafter all traces of Bierce faded to thin air. Rumor, ever vigilant, took charge of his affairs and whispered that he died at the battle of Chihuahua under Villa; that he emerged from Mexico and was confined in a California asylum; that he was in hiding and at work upon a biography which would startle the nation; that he had fled to parts unknown and had become a hermit.

There now reenters into the chronicle Dr. Adolphe Danziger de Castro, with whom Bierce wrote in collaboration thirty-five years ago "The Monk and the Hangman's Daughter." Yesterday, here in New York over a thick portfolio of material documents, Dr. de Castro gave me his own version of the last hours of Ambrose Bierce. All that follows is from the doctor's lips:

"From 1922 to 1925 I conducted in the City of Mexico, under the authority of the Government, a publication called *The Week in Mexico*. It contained a summary of events and carried a series of special articles dealing with the lives of that country's leaders. I had written of Calles and Obregon and wanted to include Villa, who had gone into retirement at Canutillo, Durango. I wrote and asked for an appointment. I hand you Villa's reply. "

What follows is a literal translation from the original Spanish, written on a sheet of paper containing in the upper left-hand corner a figure of Justice blindfolded and holding the scales:

CANUTILLO, March 15, 1923.
Dear Sir—I have received your letter of the 8th of March and I note the particulars you mention. In reply I would like to tell you that my life at present is dedicated to labor and the development of this property, which is also my domicile. . . . I do not care at present to break the resolve to which I have set myself. I thank you just the same sincerely for the distinction of which you desire to make me the object. . . . Once you grasp my reflections I dare say you will find it unnecessary to visit me as you desire to do. I remain with great thanks yours very truly,

FRANCISCO VILLA.

To Dr. Adolphe de Castro.

"Ignoring the suggestion that the journey would be useless, I sent a telegram announcing my approach and took the train for Canutillo forthwith. Villa, wearing two six-shooters in ammunition belts and accompanied by his aids, was at the station when I detrained. I said in the Mexican manner, 'My General.' Not knowing me by sight he replied, 'With whom do I speak?' I answered, 'De Castro.' He held out his hand. 'You are daring; come to my domicile.' Through armed men I went to his home and to his table. Hipolito Villa, a brother of Francisco, executed by Calles's government in 1926, and General Reyes, executed two weeks ago, were at the table with us.

"The conversation dealt with general subjects until I asked the question: 'Were there many Americans in your army? Do you recall at Chihuahua a man named Bierce—Ambrose Bierce?' An ugly gleam came in Villa's eyes. 'Si, si, senor! The cursed Ambrozio! He was a traitor.' General Reyes and Hipolito at mention of Bierce exchanged glances of distress. 'Traitor?' I questioned. 'Impossible. He was a soldier in our own civil war under General Thomas.' Villa's face clouded. 'Caramba! He criticized my campaign. He dared to find fault with my leadership. Ambrozio pointed out to me what he called my mistakes. I do not tolerate advice from others. Villa needs no instruction.'

"'What became of him?' I asked. 'Lo hemos hecho fuera!' (We threw him out) snarled Villa. 'He had a peon servant with him. They drank too much tequila and talked to some of my men about Carranza's greatness. Is that not enough? If he wished to join Carranza—well? Ambrozio left at night with his peon secretary, bag and baggage. Lo hemos hecho fuera.' Villa shrugged his shoulders and made a negative sign 'Quien sabe?' (Who knows?) There the conversation concerning Ambrose Bierce ended."

"Did you investigate?" I asked.

"It is unwise in Mexico to pursue inquiries," answered Dr. de Castro, buckling his portfolio.

"Was Bierce seen anywhere later?"

"Yes. That night, about a mile out of town. Never again—neither Bierce nor his peon. And, besides, after the battle of Chihuahua the vultures came. I understood that some clothing was found. It is difficult, however, to identify bones on a field covered with them. I returned to Mexico City with my own convictions. In 1924 it was pretty well established that the peace of Mexico was imperiled by Villa's existence. He also fell to the bullets of his enemies."

Notes

1. Robert H[obart] Davis (1869–1942), editor of *Munsey's Magazine* from 1904 to 1925, columnist for the *New York Sun* from 1925 to 1942. As editor of *Argosy*, he rejected HPL's "The Rats in the Walls."
2. *New York Sun* (17 November 1927).

[3]   [TLS, JHL]

[Adolphe de Castro]

113 West 88,
New York City,
Dec. 5th 1927.

Dear Mr. Lovecraft,

I have your letter—had it, in fact, several days, but was too ill to send you word. I am now sending you a story, to get your judgment whether it could be made "fit for publication", shortened or what. If you can gage by this, which is about the average of my other manuscripts, you might tell me what it would cost me to get one or two medium sized books read for the publisher.

Hoping to hear from you at your earliest convenience, I beg to remain,

Yours sincerely,
Adolphe de Castro

[*Notes written on letter by HPL:*]

10,000   10 stories to a book
                                        MS. 10,560 wds

0.50 per p. untyped   32
0.65 typed   .65
                             160
This story 16.00 untyped   192
        20.00 typed   20.80

(10 st.)
Book—$160.00 untyped
        200.00 typed

(higher) Reconsidered rate
    1.00 per page untyped
    1.15 "   "   typed

[4]   [TLS, JHL]

[Adolphe de Castro]

Dec. 8, 1927.

My dear Mr. Lovecraft,

Your revelative letter is read in part—for I read it again and yet again. Everything Loveman said about you, you yourself have bettered a thousand times, and as I am not in the habit of "slabberation"— new word this—I will only say, I thank you.

What you say about modern transmission of thought, once called "literature", is absolutely true. Deflation is the idea and the realization. That it bespeaks a shrinkage in mental abilities, in that *otium cum dignitate*[1] which characterized formerly literary activity, particularly fiction, is another and, who knows, perhaps a better story. Bulfinch in his introduction to his "Age of Fable", holds that literature ought to amuse. The question is only the tempo. We are living in faster tempo, therefore even our music has no longer the mood the Germans call *getragen*. We have jazz and we must live up to it if we do not want to die of starvation, lolling in regret of the days beyond recall.

This reminds me that since my return from Mexico I have been waiting—very watchful waiting—for the realization of something I have a knowledge of in that rather disturbed land. This means that I am not very flush. But flush or not I would not narrow down a man like you who has my affection even without personal contact. I have "served" at the feet of Ambrose G. Bierce for a quarter century only to acquire a smattering of the English language, and I know how to appreciate persons of your stamp. In view of this I naturally accept your terms—and will pay you what you mention is the best you can do as a fee. I am not a very pious man, but I wish to all the gods that I could do for you what is in my heart to do. You give me the best evidence that you can help me.

Now, to something else. You probably have seen the flush of publicity I have received lately with regard to Bierce. I have written the first part of a book, BIERCE AND I. It is the part relating to the west. I lost over two thousand letters of B. in the San Francisco fire. But the letters, 14 in all, he wrote me since 1900 I have and with these I am going to build the second part. Bob Davis assures me that he will get me a publisher at once. This means that I would be able to realize some money from the work. In this work, however, no revision as you suggest for the story is possible, for the reason that it [is] my "I" that enters in the work and my style, with the exception of some expression here and there, is fairly well known. As these are purely reminiscences, even the aesthetic arrangement could not be changed. As the matter of the story is virtually settled—and it would please me if I could get it next week—what idea can you suggest about BIERCE AND I?

I am so completely worn out that it came to me a ride on the Omnibus from here to Providence would be a healthy diversion. On this jaunt I could fetch my *B & I* with me and let you look at it. What say you?

See, how we differ. To you writing longhand comes "handy", whereas I cannot write anything in longhand. I have become so used to the machine that it yields me a certain inspiration by the staccato it produces.

Permit me to return for a moment to the Bierce book. In this I want nothing or very little autobiographical. It is all about Bierce and how he "shows up" during a close intimacy of more than twenty years. Incidentally my own efforts in writing the—then—vernacular take up some space. I speak of the invitation to write an article about the Jews of San Francisco, the preliminary investigations I made, the funny incidents connected with this etc. The question arises in my mind whether the article itself (I mean about the Jews of San Francisco) would be in place with B & I? Or should I leave this for another book which I wrote entitled THE EMPIRE OF THE GHETTO?

A little candle light on the subject would be keenly appreciated.

Hoping this incoherent letter will find you in good health and spirits— you must have them if you can write as you do—I am,

> Yours sincerely,
> Adolphe de Castro.

Notes

1. "Leisure with dignity."

[5]   [ANS]

> Jan. 4—1928

Dear Mr. Lovecraft,

             I am barely out of the "shadow". It caught me pretty hard and laid me up when I was prepared to take the "bus" for Providence. But hope to do so the weather gets a bit milder.

> With best wishes,
> Sincerely yours
> Adolphe de Castro.

[6]   [TLS, JHL]

> [Adolphe de Castro]

> 113 West 88
> New York,
> Feb. 4th, 1928.

Dear Mr. Lovecraft,

             Your very writing and your manner betoken the gentleman and I cannot possibly imagine that you'd deliberately hurt my feelings.

The return of the cheque etc. has just done this. If my suggestion has offended you I am sorry. I do not as a rule try to hurt any person directly or indirectly—no matter what my own circumstances may be, and I think you do not.[1]

You have done pretty hard work on this story and should not lose money on the matter in any event. I beg you to accept the cheque. I am not very strong at this moment, owing to the persistent work I have done on the Bierce book. I am trying to get into it all those blessed memories that come to me and which delighted my life for twenty-five years in a friendship of which few persons were even aware. He was so jealous in this respect. . . . . . It is for this reason and the terrible cold that I have not been able to go to Providence; but another few days will see the crude work of the manuscript done, and then I'll be free to die or to go to Providence to see you.

> Sincerely yours,
> Adolphe de Castro.

Notes

1. See HPL to Frank Belknap Long, "Thursday" [c. January 1928]: "And I *am* calling in your aid right now in the case of old 'Dolph! He's too gordam fussy to make his work a paying propositon for me—for his fiction is *unspeakable,* his paying ability meagre, & his demands for revision—after his first version—extensive. I about exploded over the dragging monotony of a silly thing which I renamed 'Clarendon's Last Test'; & after I wearily sent in the result of a whole month's brain-fog, (incurred for a deplorable pittance!) the old reprobate shot it back with requests for extensive changes (based wholly on the new ideas I had injected!) which would have involved just as much work again, & without any additional fee. That was too much. I hurled the whole Hastur-hateful thing back at him—together with his measly cheque & a dollar bill to cover the postage he'd expended—but he took it all in good part, & returned the cheque & dollar with a laudably generous gesture! Now—after thinking it over—he decided to use the tale just at I fixed it up. Vaya con Dios, Don Adolfo—here's one reviser who won't raise any controversy by claiming authorship of the beastly mess! But I can't tackle any more of his fiction. It raises a choking kind of mental "complex" preclusive of effort. I'll consider his straight prose memoirs, but nothing where constructive art is concern'd" (*SL* 2.207–8). AdC's original title for the story was "A Sacrifice to Science." It was published as "The Last Test."

[7]   [TLS, JHL]

> [Adolphe de Castro]
> 113 West 88
> New York City,
> February 7, 1928.

Dear Mr. Lovecraft,

Thank you for your letter and its contents, but you disillusioned me terribly. I thought you were an old man, and now I see that you are disgracefully young—I wish somebody would say this of me—with some decree of truth. However, I have the best of you; for you have not my photograph. What sort of picture you have I am unable to tell, as my papers these days are in a hopeless mess, owing to my concentration on the Bierce book, which, laudamus deum, is finished, even to the table of contents, which I enclose and from which you will see that Bierce is in considerable evidence. But this is exactly what I wanted. To lay a stone on which better builders can rear a fine structure is also glory and to have reared a foundation for such a work on Ambrose is enough for me.

No, Mr. Lovecraft I am not connected with any petagogical [*sic*] institution. Fate keeps me on the waiting list. If I had your youth I would not stay in the cold North. There is nothing to compensate for warmth and sunshine. Humanity, gardens, landscape, all these, plus the expedition by aeroplane of anything one desires, is now no bar to living anywhere. Why, there are persons living in San Diego, California who do revision for persons living in New Hampshire, I happen to know.

Many years ago, I met Nordhoff the great writer of his day who actually edited a Magazine in St. Louis, while living at Coronado, and he had to rely then on the slow expedition of the railroads.[1] Yesterday I got a letter written by my brother Saturday at San Francisco—incredible almost.

I'm sending you a copy of the pirated edition of the "Monk", and a letter clipped from the SUN. I almost fainted when old Dr. Glaser came to see me. But he is the same, short of breath, miopic, very learned and proud to have done me a favor—he thinks, not knowing that Bierce himself confessed that I wrote the book. Glaser has gone to Germany to close his days in a republic for the ideals of which he was once driven from Germany.

I haven't as yet had the time to look up Mr. Long. And mentioning Mr. Long recalls that I have never asked you if, in your opinion "Clarendon's Last Test" is likely to have a market. I shall not make any changes in the story, but when it is typewritten I shall send it on its rounds, and le bon Dieu peut savoir if it will find some one to take it. The horror story isn't much in demand now, I fancy.

Hoping this will find you well and I soon also, I am,

Sincerely yours

Adolphe de Castro.

[Enclosure: clipping]

"The Monk and the Hangman's Daughter."

To the editor of the SUN—*Sir:* I was delighted to read the article on Ambrose Bierce by your Mr. Davis. I knew Mr. Bierce in California, having been editor of the *News Letter* for a time,[2] and I had reason to respect the trenchant criticism of that literary giant. But I also knew intimately Dr. de Castro, who then wrote and was known under the name of Danziger, which was the ancient name of the doctor's family. More than all do I happen to know the history of the book mentioned by Mr. Davis, "The Monk and the Hangman's Daughter," which Dr. de Castro had given me to revise. I later read the story in the San Francisco *Examiner*, and declare that with the exception of a word here and there, and perhaps the turn of a phrase, Mr. Bierce had not added a single phrase to that story. I felt no ill will against Dr. de Castro for having given Bierce the position of collaborator. Certainly Bierce's name was better known than mine. But I did feel that the $200 which the doctor paid Bierce to revise the story would have been enough without giving the man the big slice of fame "The Monk" brought Bierce.

As I read Mr. Davis's admirable article I felt that this correction, or rather this fact among the many it contained, ought to be published.

GUSTAVE GLASER.

New York, November 21.

[Enclosure, TMs]

BIERCE AND I

TABLE OF CONTENTS:

Notes

1. Apparently Charles Nordhoff (1830–1901), American journalist and author of *Politics for Young Americans* (1875) and books about California. The magazine he edited is unknown.

2. A "G. Glaser" is listed as a member of the "Staff" of the *San Francisco News Letter and California Advertiser* in 1892, a year after *The Monk and the Hangman's Daughter* was serialized there. No other information on this person has been found.

[8]   [TLS, JHL]

[Adolphe de Castro]

113 West 88
New York City,
February
twenty-fifth,
1928

My dear Mr. Lovecraft,

I'm a-thrill with the article you wrote in the RE-CLUSE.[1] It is comprehensive and masterfully presented. While I do not treat the life of Bierce altogether in reference to the quality of his literary productions, I might have been tempted to do so, had I read your monograph before.

However, since I wrote you I added about fifty thousand words to the Bierce book, original matter written by Bierce and bearing on certain reminiscences I note.

The title of the book will not be BIERCE AND I but simple AMBROSE BIERCE. As I appear in the book a great deal as the teller of the story I deemed the former title over-descriptive.

What pains me, I frankly confess, is that there are probably many literary blemishes of which a book of this sort ought to be absolutely free. But I have written more than 115,000 words and have grown very tired. It is equally obvious that I cannot have the work done—as correctors might prove correctioners—spoiling the personal tone for an assumed form. It is not every one, my friend, who has your sure touch and is so sympathetic to the subject under discussion.

Albert & Charles Boni have the matter under consideration (this is in confidence, of course) but they are a number of publishers quite desirous of bringing out the book.

After I had written "finis" to the Bierce book, I was under the impression that I'd put a tooth brush and a collar in my grip and go away. Unfortunately I found the badly scratcht-up manuscript of THE EMPIRE OF THE GHETTO staring me in the face and I took it up. I am at it now; but as this is only a small matter—somewhere about sixty thousand words and jocularity rather than accuracy involved, I hope to get through with this soon.[2]

Hope this will find you in a less freezing condition than I am here at present and that I may yet see you some time soon, I beg to remain,

Sincerely yours,

Adolphe de Castro

Notes

1. "Supernatural Horror in Literature."
2. The book was apparently never published.

[9]   [TLS, JHL]

113 West 88
New York,
Feb. 27, 1928.

Dear Mr. Lovecraft,

In the several notes I wrote you lately I always meant to—but never did—ask you whether your antiquarian enthusiasm extends to "opera latinae" [*sic*][1] of the early 16th century, particularly referring to works printed then in Spain, and more particularly in Alcalá where the famous columnar Bible was printed by the great Eguia.

I have an Erasmus—"De Copia Verborum" with the dedication to John Colet, Dean of St. Paul, London, written 1518 and printed 1529 at Alcalá.

However, this is not the only bit of rarity about this book. It is evidently a "censored" copy, and contains on the title page the ominous legend "auctore damnatus", with many parts of the text Xed out in ink, with the episcopal sigilium in writing after every condemned passage. I picked it up during my consular term in Madrid, and not being a collector, have no idea whether I was done out of twenty dollars or I have a reasonable hope of ever getting my money back. If you know anything about the matter, please let me know. It is in very good condition.

Sincerely yours,

Adolphe de Castro.

Notes

1. "Works in Latin" (properly *opera latina*).

[10]   [TLS, JHL]

[Adolphe de Castro]
Note address: 55 West 88th Street
New York City,
April ist, 1928.

Dear Mr. Lovecraft,
      With my own suffering fingers I finished last night the copying on the typewriter of THE LAST TEST, and I don't know whether to send you an *abrazo*—a brotherly embrace—or, you being so much younger than I, to give you my fatherly blessing for what you did for me; for the more I read the story the more I find that it has "workmanship" and a masterly touch.

For a moment I wanted to send you the story *as I copied it,* thinking you might perhaps elect to change a word here and there, as your own judgment should direct, and then I said to myself "Lovecraft's eye has missed little as he went over it 'scratching' " and I sent the story on to "Weird Tales" at Indianapolis.

You will notice that I underscored the words "as I copied it", meaning thereby that I took the liberty to write a phrase or use a word as I had been taught by Ambrose Bierce. These are: the word 'persons' for people. The latter referring to the people of a city, county, state or nation, the former referring to individuals,—"there were a number of persons" and not "people"; or many people for many persons. The second is a Biercean doctrine that a sentence ought never to begin with a negative assertion of something denoting a positive, and *vice versa,* such as: "I don't believe Jim cares for it"; whereas it should be "I believe Jim doesn't care for it", which is really the essence of the assumption or belief. In other words; we believe a thing is or is not, it is our attitude in the matter, but if we say we don't believe, we establish a non-attitude (although it might equally be a non-believing attitude) in the case where a positive is concerned.

I am very eager to hear your opinion in the matter, comprehending, of course, that idiomatic form or usage is excepted.

I confess that your entire review of the matter relative to the story is correct, although I do not regret to have written you as I did, since it brought forth your most illuminative letter. And what is more, Egad! I really like the story.

Now to something else. Belknap Long wrote a nice bit of preface to my Bierce book; but I'll be this, that and t'other, if I like the book as I wrote it; although Belknap thinks it very good. There is something missing in it, something I could do if I were away from harassing conditions and disturbing elements. It has been read by three publishers and rejected on a certain *expressed criticism* and the adulti stulti seem not to comprehend that I know better than they what is the trouble. The book is written by the person who for more than twenty-five years was in closest touch with Ambrose Bierce with little confidences that no other human being knew or heard. Naturally it is written in the first person singular—how else could it have the personal touch? However, this makes it "reminiscent" rather than biographical, and they want a pure unadulterated biography—*although not quite true,* as one publisher expressed it; and this publisher actually offered a big advance royalty—what do you think of that? No wonder I am bewildered and don't know how, where, and to whom to turn. Nor have I put any great criticism of Bierce's works in my book, but I have left out oceans of matter of a most interesting personal character—not wishing to make the book too long.

Here is the situation: a work that will not only live but will afford sources for a dozen books when I am with Clarendon's bacilli, and no means of getting it into print for want of something—what? Then there is the other aspect. At least fifty thousand Bierce lovers will buy a copy of the book at two-fifty or three dollars, meaning that at the highest expenditure in cost of production fifty-thousand dollars can be made, not to speak of the translations and the foreign English readers in the British dominions.

I would take the omnibus today and go over to Providence, but for the fact that I have a number of engagements to meet to-morrow and Tuesday.

If Mencken (who at first wrote me in a gentle then in an offensive manner) were not such a bore I would consult him. After all, it is not de Castro but Bierce who counts; and it is well worth to put him right before the American public.

Hoping to hear from you, I am, dear Mr. Lovecraft,
        Sincerely yours,
                Adolphe de Castro.

[11]   [ALS, JHL]
                     10 Barnes St.,
                     Providence, R.I.,
                     Novr. 15, 1925 [i.e., 1928]

My dear Dr. de Castro:—
                Your letter & the book arrived safely, & I shall give the latter a survey & revisory estimate the very first moment I can snatch an opportunity. Just now I am utterly engulfed by insistent tasks involving rigorous time-limits, but meanwhile I can assure you of the volume's absolute safety. I realise its uniqueness, as well as the natural fragility & brittleness of a paper-bound book which has weathered 35 winters; hence am keeping it very carefully in an undisturbed place & in its original wrappings.[1]

When I do get around to quoting rates & making suggestions I shall try to guard against exorbitance—for surely no one is better able to understand straitened finances than I! I have no doubt but that many of the tales would be professionally acceptable in a new dress, & will give close attention to the possibilities of each as I view it. I hope I can render some sort of a report within two or three weeks—if my present batch of work permits me to survive that long!

Let me congratulate—or commiserate, if you prefer it!—you upon your recent natal anniversary; & express the not unhackneyed hope that you may experience a multiplicity of felicitous returns of it. Such days tend to form a season of quizzical recollection & sententious reflection, as my own mood of last August 20th illustrates; but in the end there is not much to decide except that all is as it is. It might have been just as monotonous not to have been born as to be born!

I note the nature of Belknap's researches, & think the idea of having such "high spots" is a good one. I believe I said last spring that I thought an accentuation of Bierce's literary work would be an excellent thing for the book—indeed, I think a rounded appraisal of Bierce's major writings, including both your own views & the quoted views of other critics, would form a most acceptable feature.

Your verses—"She Knows"—impress me as delightful, & I am sorry you did not include the two additional stanzas. Verse, I really think, is your natural medium of expression. When looking over your MSS. it struck me that your poetry would need far less revision than your prose. That characteristic of thinking naturally in metrical rhythms is one I rather envy, for in my younger days I dabbled sedulously in prosodic attempts without producing anything which my later judgment could call successful. I went in for 18th century effects—long pastoral or didactic pieces in the heroic couplet—with characteristic passages like this:

> Yon tiny torrent, fed by swollen springs,
> Leaps in the sun, & o'er the mountain sings;
> Thro' meads below the streamlet flows along
> With greater amplitude, & less of song—
> At length the force of thankless toil to feel,
> And strain incessant at the whirling wheel.
> Thus with mankind—the sweetest days are first;
> From youthful lips the songs spontaneous burst;
> Maturer years a graver aspect give,
> And men become more wretched as they live.[2]

Hoping to report on your tales before very long, & meanwhile extending my very best wishes for the Bierce enterprise, I remain—with kindest regards from all—

Yr most obt Servt
H P Lovecraft

356 ❦ *Letters: H. P. Lovecraft and Adolphe de Castro*

Notes

1. De Castro had sent HPL a copy of *In the Confessional and the Following* (1893).
2. "Quinsnicket Park" (1913), ll. 19–28.

[12]   [ALS]
                    [The Bellevue-Stratford / Philadelphia . . .]
My dear Lovecraft,
                    Got material and am returning same for typing. Please do
it as a good fellow. I am in the throes of trying to arrange certain matters and
have to have the little intelligence that has not gone hung with me—so that I
have not had time to read anything and could not—even if you did not put
Sanscrit on paper God bless you.
                    With affection of the sincerest sort
                    Yours
                                   Adolphe de Castro.
Jan. 8 / 30

[13]   [AHT]
                                   66 College St.,
                                   Providence, R.I.,
                                   Septr. 21, 1934
Dear Dr. De Castro:—
                    Now regarding rewriting or collaborative jobs—as I
have said before, they are really the hardest type of work to handle, so that it
does not really pay to undertake them unless the remuneration is certain, and
of an amount which seems savagely exorbitant to the client. If the venture is
merely speculative—with the reviser as well as author taking chances of acceptance or rejection—it always works against the reviser; for even if the result is accepted he receives only a *part* of the proceeds, whereas he would
probably have had equal chances of acceptance with *all* the proceeds his, if he
had put the same amount of time and energy into an *original* work of the same
length. The only exception to this condition, of course, is the case of some
special idea of phenomenal uniqueness—some highly important and utterly distinctive conception or item of information which would give a piece of writing containing it a marketing-chance radically greater than that of anything
which the reviser could turn out alone. For these reasons, I have found it imperative virtually to eliminate all but paid-in-advance collaboration from my
programme—indeed, I have refused three propositions of the speculative
sort within the last month.

However, though Long has said that you could not deal except on a speculative basis—I would like to be of assistance in any way that is practicable. While—with my desperately crowded schedule and in my present state of poor health—I could not guarantee to add any fresh responsibility to my already nerve-shattering load, I would be glad to look over whatever you have to be done, give a sincere estimate of its possibilities, and perhaps furnish bits of constructive coöperation here & there as conditions determine—anything, in fact, short of the arduous and prolonged creative modelling involved in actual re-writing. & of course, I wouldn't want to say dogmatically that I wouldn't *ever* undertake even the latter extreme task. If the subject matter justified it in some phenomenal way, or if I were given unlimited time—a matter of indefinite months—in which to produce results, it is within possibility that I might be able to participate to such an extent. But of that I could not tell without seeing the job in question.

With every good wish—

Yrs most cordially,

H P Lovecraft

[14]   [ALS, JHL]

66 College St.

Providence, R.I.

Oct. 14, 1934

My dear Dr. de Castro:—

I am surely sorry to hear that recent years have dealt you so many blows, & hope most profoundly that Mrs. de Castro's health may presently take a turn for the better. It is easy to understand the anxiety you must feel—& with your own ocular troubles the burden is further aggravated. Your writing activities in the face of such handicaps are surely remarkable—& I hope they may all result in ultimate advantage. I envy you the energy which permits of such productivity. Of late, under the increasing strain of revisory tasks, my nerves have almost reached the breaking-point, & I have been unable to produce much of my own.

The new—or newly completed—works which you describe all sound exceedingly substantial & interesting. It is unfortunate that you could not get to Washington in connexion with "The New Way"—though I dare say the value of the book is quite independent of any such conference.[1] I assume that the essence of this volume—the thread connecting the three apparently dissimilar parts—is a discussion of the deep & far-reaching changes now taking place in many aspects of civilisation. This would tend to give it a certain timeliness much in its favour. Possibly its publication chances might be enhanced if you could get a preface—or at least a brief preliminary word—from some influential government personage. The interest expressed by Pres. Roosevelt & Mr. Bates would suggest that such a thing might be attainable.

That this & the other books contain live material, no one could well doubt. Naturally much would be controversial—but that is all good advertising! Incidentally, I imagine that your genealogy of Jesus would draw challenges from many diverse sources—since the authenticity of all known ancient references to this shadowy figure is so doubtful. I believe it is firmly established that all allusions to Christ in Josephus & Tacitus are spurious interpolations, so that only the carefully & far from impartially edited gospels of the New Testament remain as even roughly contemporary accounts. And even they probably do not antedate in final form the latter part of the 1st century. It has always seemed doubtful to me whether any one person answering to the traditional Jesus ever existed in fact. In many respects the forms of Christianity closely follow those of the popular mystery-cults of the period— Dionysiac, Apollinian, Pythagorean, etc.—which joined Oriental & Hellenistic concepts in a variety of ways. With this cult-background (wherein the idea of sacrifice & atonement was so marked) to start with, & with the age-old Jewish idea of a Messiah super-added, it would be easy to build up a religious & heroic myth around any one of the sporadic evangelists of the East—or around several of them, fusing their various personalities into one idealised hero or demigod. This, it seems to me, is what must have happened. The tissue of miracles & too-neatly-dramatic episodes undoubtedly represents the purely mythic element; but certain touches of verisimilitude now & then suggest a substratum of fact. Incidents in the lives of several rustic preachers may be involved—though possibly one figures more extensively than others. Just who this one was, & to what extent the padded & myth-decked gospel narrative relates his actual history, it seems to me can never quite be settled except through the discovery of hitherto unknown source-material. Parts of the popular tale—sacrifice, resurrection, &c.—are obviously derived from the nature-myth of Linus, Dionysos, or Zagreus. Other parts—trial, &c.—might be tested by certain comparisons with contemporary accounts. But the lack of *really reliable* sources is almost fatal. That is, so far as general scholarship knows. The new sources you mention certainly sound exciting—although of course their authority in representing events which must vastly antedate them would have to be defended. *Germanic* lore would necessarily be purely *oral* as far back as the time of Christ—& anthropologists would see many opportunities for interpolation before it reached the written stage. Semitic lore, on the other hand, has been so carefully examined that any new interpretation would doubtless evoke a flood of criticism from traditional academic quarters. Jewish allusions, I believe, are scattered, hostile, & fantastic—either reflecting the myths of the gospels or enlarging upon them with matter equally improbable. And Islamic references are all uncertain & derivative—merely echoes from already myth-strown Christian & Jewish sources . . . & oral sources, at that.

Of Pontius Pilatus singularly little is known from reliable accounts. Even his supposed suicide, I believe, has no better or earlier authority than the late Christian writer Eusebius[2]—a contemporary of Constantius. And of course the so-called "Acta, Epistola, Paradosis, & Mors Pilati"[3] are all late concoctions—none of them antedating the 2nd century. Amidst this labyrinth of myth & forgery, the discovery of any really dependable source—a source that could *prove* its dependability both through internal evidence & through correlation with external evidence—would be a triumph indeed! So, as before mentioned, you certainly have a prize topic on your hands—& one which will bring plenty of debate. *Tyrus of Mayence,* I must admit, is a new figure to me.[4] In the time of any grandfather of Christ, Mayence could have been no more than a crude wattled village of the Celts, for it was not till B.C. 13 that the Roman camp forming the nucleus of the classical & modern town was established by Drusus Claudius Nero. I know that lines between the Celts & the Near East existed in & after the 3d century B.C., but I hardly thought any relations with the homeland were maintained by the expatriate Galatians. I knew, though, that they retained their Gallic speech—even far into the Byzantine period. In any case your mention of a Tyrus of or from the Vangionian capital of Magontiacum on the Rhine excites my profoundest curiosity!

But pardon the digression. As to the matter of revision—at the present moment the pressure of preëxisting tasks is so great that I really would not dare assume any further substantial responsibility. My nerves are so close to the breaking point—involving spells of insomnia, mental & physical exhaustion, &c—that I only last week refused a novel-revision job with certain pay . . . simply because I knew I could not do it. For the present I am, perforce, staging a sort of one-man revolution against responsibilities . . . . which is just as well for my clients, since if I tried to do work under pressure it would probably be of poor quality & full of slips & oversights.

In relation to the tasks you have ready for tackling—the only way in which I could be of any help would be to take one of the books for *very gradual* revision—with a virtually unlimited time-allowance. Even on this basis anything of full book length makes me shiver & pause at the moment—but if I made no promises as to delivery, the strain would of course be somewhat mitigated. I don't believe, on mature reflection, that I could very well attempt anything in the *fictional* line just now. Fictional revision is the most exhausting of all so far as I am concerned—for the re-casting & management of narrative elements in another's story involves all the labour of original creation without any of the zest. Besides, the market for fiction is very doubtful. One never can tell what will & what will not be accepted—Wright has turned down two of my best stories. Even the novel for which consideration is assured could not be accepted definitely unless the story value were up to a certain level—& I could not at the present time guarantee to bring it up. So I fancy that one of the works of pure scholarship or philosophy would be rather better to start with.

I am really tremendously sorry that my nervous & overburdened state prevents me from being of more immediate assistance—but there is of course the rather dismally consoling fact that even my instant collaboration might not be of any financial value. In this period all questions of book-acceptance are necessarily a precarious gamble—even when a MS. has apparent chances above the average, as a goodly number of yours seem to have. I have been made acutely aware of this through the experience of several friends who have recently tried to place book MSS.—some of them highly distinctive & valuable works. It is a stern but inescapable fact that anyone who prepares a book MS. today—whether through original writing or collaboration—does so with at least a more than even chance of having all his work go for nothing so far as profitable publication is concerned. In the case of an original author with a creative message which he wants to record for sheer art's or scholarship's sake, this circumstance does not really count. He would probably want to get his concepts down on paper even if he knew there were no chance of publication. When, however, it comes to a question of revision, the case is somewhat altered. Work performed under difficulties & bringing no tangible return is certainly a just cause for exasperation—& conversely, when the work cannot be done there is at least a trace of *wry-faced* consolation in the thought that if it could be, there would be more than an even chance of its being wasted. So it need not be thought that every piece of unperformed revision necessarily represents a real loss. The chances are that *with* revision only a small number of any average assortment of book MSS. could find early placement. Things are sadly altered since the easy-going days of 1929!

However, as I have said, if a very leisurely, long-term siege of tinkering on a non-fiction MS. would prove valuable to you, I wouldn't want to refuse that much coöperation. I fancy you can see, in view of the present state of pressing tasks & nervous tension, why I could not safely promise more at present, as I'd like to do. If you wished to follow such an arrangement, I'd leave the choice of the MS. to you. I wouldn't be too exacting in my demands for royalty-shares unless the amount of needed revision were almost equivalent to original composition. If the work required were only moderate, I certainly wouldn't want to claim as much as half the proceeds in case of success. I might venture to hope that typing (a peculiarly exhausting process for me) would not be required. *Light* revision, I presume, could be made on the original MS. itself—in pencil, if you wished to reserve the right of annulling any revisory touches. In such a venture I wouldn't want to claim any public credit unless I actually contributed something to the thought & content of the work—which would scarcely be likely in a non-fictional venture. I'm past the age when publicity has any charms for me. Indeed—what I wish I could do is to get some life-sustaining job wholly unconnected with writing, & then use my spare time in writing what I wish to write—without a thought of publication.

But just the same, I do wish that you could get more of your books in shape, so that they might be ready for publication when chance opportunities turn up. Too bad Long can't handle anything just now. Did I mention another possible reviewer with whom you might get in touch? You might try *Maurice W. Moe, 1034 N. 23d St., Milwaukee, Wisconsin.* He is a high-school English teacher & a graduate of the U. of Wis. ('04). Anything involving Biblical scholarship would be especially in his line, for he is almost a fanatic in that direction. He specialised in Semitics at the U. of Wis., & can even read Assyrian cuneiform a bit. For years he was associated with the late William Jennings Bryan (supplying the brains, perhaps, while poor old Bill supplied the wind & braying!) in some sort of scheme called the "Biblical Alliance", for giving bible courses to students in state universities where such teaching is barred. It was only recently that he began to take on revision jobs. It is he who has taken that recent novel-revision job off my hands. This will be finished on or before Jany 1st.—& after that he might be open for further work . . . that is, if you could convince him that the chances of profitable publication are reasonably good. At any rate, I think it would pay you to write him. Another thing occurs to me—if you have any especially distinctive ideas in the *weird fictional line,* you might very possibly interest at least two capable exponents of that art to the extent of collaboration. The most likely prospect is *E. Hoffmann Price, 5314 East 12ᵗʰ St., Oakland, California*—a gifted ex-Army officer (West Point '23) whose fantastic Orientales in W.T. you've probably read. He is a devoted student of Arabic & everything connected with the Islamic culture—& is also an absolute wizard with plots. He has collaborated in the past with persons as widely different as Otis Adelbert Kline & myself, & is now doing over a story of Long's.[5] If you had an idea that suited him, I think he might jump at it. At all events write him. I'll urge him to consider a proposition when I write him next. The other & less likely prospect is *Clark Ashton Smith, Box 385, Auburn, California.* He has done collaboration, though he does not accept it at all times. It is needless to call attention to his superlative skill in the line of weird-fictional construction.

And so it goes. I certainly hope that everything will turn out for the best all along the line, & regret profoundly that the state of my nerves will permit of no greater assistance than that previously outlined. Regarding such a gradual revisory plan—I will leave choices & details to your own judgment. If any actual nervous collapse like that of 1916 should threaten, I would of course see that the MS. was safely restored, in whatever stage of partial revision it might be. I can't tell at the moment just what the effect of any added responsibility on me would be. The tension now is greater than last month because of a new job I couldn't possibly pass up. That is now under control, so I may in time feel less close to the brink of explosion. But all revision is woefully nerve-racking work—at least to me. When I gave out in 1916 I had to send all sorts of jobs back unfinished.

Hoping for the best, & again expressing my sincerest sympathy concerning both your wife's illness & your own eye troubles,

I remain

Yrs most cordially,

H P Lovecraft

Notes

1. The book was never published.

2. Eusebius of Caesarea (260?–339?), author of the *Historia Ecclesiastica* (Ecclesiastical History), in which he states that Pilate killed himself on the order of the Emperor Caligula in 39 C.E. (*Hist. Eccl.* 2.7).

3. The *Acta Pilati* (Acts of Pilate, also called the Gospel of Nicodemus) is an apocryphal gospel probably written in the 4th century C.E. Included in the *Acta* are other legendary writings: *Epistola Pilati ad Claudium* (Pilate's Epistle to Claudius), *Paradosis Pilati* (The Surrender of Pilate), and *Mors Pilati* (The Death of Pilate).

4. Tyrus of Mayence was a legendary figure of whom, in some traditions, Pontius Pilate was the illegitimate son.

5. Price collaborated with Kline on "Volunteers from Venus." The collaboration with Long is unknown and may not have been written.

[15]   [ALS]

66 College St.,

Providence, R.I.

Oct. 22, 1934

My dear Dr. de Castro:—

I am sorry to note that you hold such a skeptical & critical opinion concerning my present predicament of excessive work & nerve strain, since the misconception places me in an undeservedly unfavourable light.

The facts are simply these: That I have, for the past year or more, undertaken more literary obligations than can possibly be discharged in the 16 hours per day which form the maximum normal schedule of work. To imagine that the given amount of labour can be compressed into a shorter time is to err. There is no way to do that except by lowering the quality of the work, & this I will not do. Therefore I have tried to overcome the difficulty by taking hours from my sleep period—sometimes cutting out a night's rest (& in some cases 2 continuous nights) in order to clean up a crowded programme. But this will no longer serve. It diminishes my power of concentration, causes me to do poor work, induces spells of unconquerable drowsiness, weakness, & inability to think, & even upsets my digestion. I have had these spells before when similarly overworked—either in school or in connexion with revision—especially in 1906, 1908, & 1916. Common sense ought to show that, when in such a dilemma, I cannot very well "forget my nervousness" & take on **more** work!!! Would it *help* to stop sleeping altogether (as I would naturally have to do in order to handle *more* work when my programme already contains far more than I can do in 16 hours per day!) & assume fresh obligations which I could not possibly perform? Is that unwise & suicidal procedure necessary to the realisation of the motto "never say die"? I, myself, think it is a good deal more laudable to try to finish what I have started, than to take on new burdens which I know I could not possibly finish. The only effect of adding *another* burden would be to ruin the whole programme by making me incapable of any mental concentration or continuous work whatever.

There are only so many hours that I can work; & when all of these are crowded to the limit—with much still undone—it is plainly absurd to suppose that I could take on *more* tasks. When could I perform them? I often have to stay in a week or more at a time, working virtually night & day, in order to keep abreast of my schedule. On every one of my trips I have had to take along so much work that time for sightseeing & relaxation has been reduced to a meagre minimum. Now my work is getting poor & full of mistakes—the mistakes due to sheer exhaustion. I cannot do more. Instead, I must do less. *Rest at any cost* is, from sheer necessity, my present motto. I am conducting a sort of revolution, with its concomitant declaration of independence, in sheer self-defence. That is how I pulled out of similar semi-collapses in '06 & '08, & '16. To call such collapses mere illusions of 'auto-hypnosis' or trivial results of smoking [I don't smoke] is simply to miss the point.

Well, as I said last time, I was sorry to hear that other revisers were so hard to get—hence suggested that I might try to handle at least one of your MSS. little by little, if no time limit whatever were imposed. I certainly could not have started *now*, since jobs already contracted for will take all my time & more for 2 or 3 months. That is why I had to transfer the recent novel job to Moe. I left it to you whether you could derive any benefit from any arrangement that I conceivably *could* make—i.e., some plan not involving much work till next spring or summer, & without a specified time of delivery. Otherwise, I would of course have to admit that I am not able to consider any new work of substantial magnitude. And it might indeed be the wisest policy not to undertake anything—for whatever fragmentary schedule I *could* promise would seem messy & dilatory to you, & would hang over me as a sort of impending burden . . . . perhaps impairing the value of my imperative & immediate work. It might be far better for me to assume no fresh obligation until my present schedule is under control—& then to notify you of my ability to consider matters, unless you by that time find another suitable reviser. At any rate, I must first finish what is already started—& that can't be done by crowding my overfilled programme still more, & making my mind less & less capable of continuous concentration or effective results. What I must do is to cut out everything which possibly *can* be cut out, so that I can finish—with the proper quality attainable only through a decently rested mind—those things which *cannot* under any circumstances be cut out. I'd *like* to help—but the best I could do just now, even at the cost of mental torture & dangerous nerve-strain, would not be of very substantial assistance.

I judge from your letter that you would choose, as the first piece of revision, the section of your new book which treats of the possible parentage of Christ—plus perhaps the section on Moses; this text to be made self-sufficient & independent enough for separate publication if current opportunities dictate that as the most feasible policy. That choice, I imagine, is eminently sensible—particularly if you know of some publishing house especially receptive toward material of this kind. I surely hope that the project can go through—either with the coöperation of some other reviser at the present time, or with my revision later on when I can handle more work. Of the possibilities of profit, I am of course too poor a business-man to judge. It is well, however, not to be unduly optimistic; since even in case of publication a lucrative sale can by no means be counted on. Still, that would not form any good reason against the undertaking of the project if it were feasible; since the presentation of a powerful argument, & indeed any enrichment of scholarship, is a primary end in itself. So, as indicated above, I'll surely let you know whenever I can tackle any new task of the sort—unless previously notified that you have secured another collaborator. In any event, I hope the ultimate outcome will be favourable.

Regarding the subject-matter of the book—I of course made no pretension to any sort of scholarship in stating what my vague & inconclusive guesses are. All that I have picked up are the odds & ends of common knowledge everywhere easily available. Perforce, I have to rely on the statements of others regarding the authenticity of this or that historical source. It is years since I have given this field any attention; & even in the past my attention was merely that of a superficial reader driven into occasional shallow delvings in order to justify my complete absence of all religious belief. Personally, I have not the slightest interest in any religion or its history; for I approach the whole problem of cosmic organisation from a totally opposite angle—that of objective scientific analysis based on the evidence of the visible universe. Nothing seems more certain to me than that nature altogether lacks any indication of conscious governance. On the other hand, psychology & anthropology clearly explain why people in pre-scientific ages felt the so-called religious emotions & invented the various systems of poetic mythology to account for those emotions & to explain the then unknown phenomena of the earth & sea & sky around them. Although no technical disproof of a "cosmic mind" exists, there are two almost invincible reasons for not believing in such: first, the fact that it is the most awkward & least evidentially justified of all possible explanations of things; & second, that it is so obviously a human invention . . . . a product of the animistic attribution of human qualities to the non-human & abstract. Thus to me all *traditional* consideration of religion seems essentially *irrelevant*, & even *trivial* except in connexion with historical & anthropological research. We can see too plainly behind all religions to take any of them seriously, or to prefer any one of them to any other except in terms of social, intellectual, & ethical effects. So far as truth or justification is concerned, they are all alike—hence I can look upon their tales & characters . . . . Zeus, Brahma, Odin, Jesus, Gautama, Yahwe, Mohammad, Ahura-Mazda, Moses, Gitchie Manitou, Quetzalcoatl, Mary Baker Eddy, Damballah, the angel Maroni, & all the rest . . . . only with such objective & analytical detachment as one finds in Frazer's "Golden Bough". What interest I have in the well-known religions of the ancient & modern world is purely *historical*—measured by their effect on the stream . . . . or varied streams . . . . of civilisation. Thus Jesus & Yahwe—& all the folklore behind them—mean no more to me than Apollo or Thor or Mavors or Tanit or Huitzilopotchli; & do not command any more of my study & attention than do these fellow-objects of deific regard. Hence my lack of special scholarship in their direction. What interests me is the whole human pageant, & not any especial corner of it—except so far as environment & caprice have given me a particular concern for Anglo-Saxon civilisation in the modern world & Roman civilisation in the ancient world . . . . a concern not exclusive enough to destroy the scope & objectivity of my larger general perspective.

It is, then, only as an incident of history that the question of Christ's personality, origin, existence, or non-existence interests me. I have not explored the subject in detail, & do not pretend to have any but casual, second-hand knowledge. When I gave a guess, it was only a rough tentative one—based on what data are commonly floating around. In saying that a new theory would be hard to establish, I meant that there must be scholars who *have* minutely gone over *all* the available evidence many times before, & who would therefore challenge any interpretation of that evidence which might differ from their own interpretations . . . . or from the interpretations of earlier scholars. In the case of obscure Jewish records, it is natural to assume that these must have been minutely explored by the vast number of profound Jewish scholars who have lived since the period of Christ. These scholars would have no motive for concealing any facts they might have discovered, or conclusions they might have reached, concerning the existence & parentage of Jesus. Standing outside the religion which seeks to make this figure a demigod or god, they would naturally be perfectly frank in setting down what they knew of him—just as they would be in describing any figure whose significance is purely historical to them. Nay, more—they would probably be eager to bring forward any facts about Christ which would overthrow the claims of those who make a god-begotten Heracles or Theseus or Castor or Pollux of him. That the erudite Jewish scholars of nineteen centuries have not done this, despite their

366 ❋ *Letters: H. P. Lovecraft and Adolphe de Castro*

access to vast reservoirs of Hebraic tradition & records, would seem to indicate that the evidence on which any estimate of Christ's parentage could be based is either newly discovered or else subject to controversy regarding interpretation. That is what I meant when I said a book containing a theory of this sort would have to withstand a general fusilade of debate. But of course you realise this yourself, & are doubtless prepared to welcome the discussion. If it turned out that your interpretation of Talmudic & other records could successfully establish itself against the negative interpretations of antecedent scholarship, your position would become one of vast importance indeed! My own opinion, as I have said, is in a state of flux—as all laymen's opinions must necessarily be. All I can do is to judge at third or fourth hand—relying on the extent to which real scholars agree or disagree—of the validity of the sources on which various historians base their arguments. I must endeavour to see a copy of your "Jewish Forerunners of Christianity"—which must be an extremely interesting & historically revealing book all apart from its bearing on the present topic. Too bad it is now out of print—or perhaps that is not so unfortunate after all, since you say that its method of approach to its theme is not what you would prefer to use today. I'll see if any of the local libraries have a copy.

Regarding Moses—here again is a figure which I have often felt must be at least partly mythical . . . . a typical tribal hero around whom have clustered numberless legends, & to whom are perhaps attributed the deeds of many other heroes of many ages. I believe that some of the anecdotes related of him are clearly from Babylonian sources. But of course all my impressions are fragmentary & unsystematic. I shall be interested in seeing what your views on this shadowy figure are.

Yes—there surely is a curious irony in the series of accidents which have imposed upon the Western World a dominant faith of Semitic origin. Nietzsche, I believe, was the first of the moderns to point this out with emphasis. The general effect of this faith has been in part good—in that it has inculcated certain ethical factors more strongly than another faith might have done—& in part unfortunate, since it has raised certain demands & expectations impossible of fulfilment by men inheriting the Western culture-streams. Itself springing out of the racial experience of a people vastly different from our own cultural forerunners, it naturally fails to embody & express those deeply-grounded feelings & aspirations which are really ours. Embodying other feelings & aspirations which we cannot share except in a superficial & artificial way, it leads to a curious duality between *formal ideals* on the one hand, & *real ideals & actual conduct* on the other hand . . . . a duality leading to wholesale & systematic hypocrisy. We pretend to follow a philosophy of justice, meekness, & brotherhood, while actually continuing to base our secret working standards on strength, personal inviolateness & unbrokenness, & the struggle for domination. We go to church on Sunday—yet continue to fight, grab, & exploit in the most approved pagan fashion. And the deep springs of action which really move us are never based on the meek Christian concept of *virtue*, but always on the strength-prideful Teutonic concept of *honour*. We can laugh good-naturedly when anyone tells us we are *unjust*, *vicious*, or *impious* (i.e., delinquent in our relations to the governing forces of the universe), but are aroused to the fighting point when anyone dares question our *honour* (i.e., the straightforwardness of a man so strong that he has no need for subterfuge) or *independence* or *courage*. The difference in our instinctive emotions when confronted by these two different types of ethical attack is tremendously significant as regards the placement of our *real & profound loyalties*. Thus in spite of all the centuries of ostensible Christian belief we are not Christians except in name. It would have been more honest & less hypocritical if we had continued to adhere to the polytheistic pantheism which is our culture's natural heritage, & which therefore more truly embodies & expresses what we really think & feel. A system synthesising the best of Epicureanism & Stoicism would have served us much better than our accidental importation has done. It is, however, rather late in the day to change back—especially since the part played by *any* religion in the life of our civilisation is rapidly waning. Forces & feelings far removed from the ecclesiastical are the things which really count in the crisis of transition around & ahead of us.

I'm glad to hear that your eyes are better, & hope you may keep them so through a careful avoidance of overstrain. I hope, too, that you can arrange for the revision & publication of some of the fascinating mss. which you have in reserve. Better write my friend Price about the fiction. My regret that I can't help at present is really most sincere—& as I've said, if you don't find someone else in the interim, I'll notify you when I can begin some very gradual work on a MS. ¶ And now I must get to work—the pile of stuff ahead of me being virtually appalling! ¶ All good wishes—Yrs most cordially,
H P Lovecraft

P.S. Enclosed is a little magazine with some of my stuff—which you may find momentarily amusing.

[16]   [ALS, JHL]
66 College St.,
Providence, R.I.,
Novr. 6, 1934
Dear Dr. de Castro:—
          I am tremendously sorry to hear that Mrs. de Castro's illness is necessitating an hospital sojourn—but hope that observation & treatment there may afford decidedly favourable results. Sometimes the expert care & continuous medical attention in such a place produces unexpected upturns in cases which seemed very discouraging at home.

Price mentioned hearing from you—& if he is able to undertake any collaboration (as I think he may be) you will undoubtedly find him very pleasant & satisfactory to deal with. He is an extremely brilliant & interesting personality—with a superabundance of energy which is my constant envy. Born in California in 1898, he served in the World War & afterward secured a West Point appointment. He graduated in 1923, & served for a time as a cavalry officer both in the U.S. & in the Philippines; but later resigned & went into private business—as head of a branch of the Prestolite Co. in New Orleans. All this time he had been an amateur Orientalist & author of occasional fantasies. In 1932 his job blew up as a result of the depression, & he turned to commercial writing—at which he has succeeded remarkably. His interests & accomplishments are so varied as to bewilder one—he is a distinguished mathematician, a master of languages, an expert fencer, a connoisseur of Oriental rugs, a pianist, an artist in metal-work, a mechanical genius, a keen traveller, a wizard at exotic cookery, an explorer of odd phases of life, & above all a writer of infinite fluency & vividness. He has been a *Weird Tales* standby since 1925, & knows the spirit, technique, & dramatic values of fiction from the ground up. In short, you couldn't get hold of a better man for the purposes of effective collaboration.

I am greatly interested in your mention of early work & writings in the direction of religious rationalism, & your founding of a prototype of the Ethical Culture Society. Organisations of this sort have often seemed to me the logical goal toward which the present Protestant churches should develop. While Catholicism represents the emotional, non-rational, and decorative side of religion, Protestantism represents essentially the efforts of more consistent & less emotional thinkers to carry out the obvious ethical objects of the general type of religion from which Christianity is derived. It thus has a goal & substance independent of the mystical & the supernatural, & does not need to perish as a continuous tradition when the idea of supernaturalism perishes. Ethics, after the death of supernaturalism, naturally divides once more into two actual components—the element of utilitarian policy & the element of aesthetic taste; but in practice it is perhaps still inculcated as a unit, since the *external* bearings of both of its elements are so similar. That the inculcation of harmonious attitudes & conduct—a task so difficult in view of the essential primitiveness & natural lawlessness of the human animal—will require more than a casual effort after the backing of religion is withdrawn, would seem to be more than likely. It will not be enough to let ordinary sociology take care of the utilitarian side while ordinary art instruction takes care of the aesthetic side. Mankind is neither rational nor aesthetically sensitive enough to respond to such abstract & dissociated precepts. Obviously, centralised ethical inculcation must still continue—backed up as before with a certain amount of emotional (though no longer supernatural-invoking) force. In Europe this function is beginning to be mixed up with politics—as exemplified by the concept of the "totalitarian state". Thus Russia has a sort of compulsory state worship of the personality of Lenin & of the abstract idea of manual labour, whilst Nazi Germany whips up devotion to a vaguely unified cause including intensive nationalism, made-to-order biology, & a special local version of the traditional older religion. However, this method appears to me to have grave disadvantages; being not only potentially antagonistic to the development of free culture, but absolutely repugnant to the basic temper of many peoples— especially the Anglo-Saxon. Far superior, it seems to me, is a system of organised but non-political ethical instruction & inculcation which shall involve no special nationalistic concepts but simply take over the general heritage & tradition of the dying religion .... perhaps even the old church buildings & the historically cherished charters of the ancient congregations. Such an element of *continuity* would help to supply that factor of *convincing emotional authority* which all *new* systems find it so hard to achieve, & which the bolsheviks & Nazis have sought to supply by linking general ethics with the special political goals at which they are aiming. It would be ideal if the old white-steepled church on the village green could still form (albeit without the ancient supernaturalism) the same constructive influence in the community that it did a century ago. An evolution of this sort is indeed slowly under way—as witness the birth of Unitarianism, & the development of many Protestant churches (such as the Riverside in N.Y.) away from orgiastic supernaturalism toward the ideal of human character-moulding. So also the popular "humanism" movement of 3 or 4 years ago. As yet these tentative developments are lacking in authority & popular support—but that is no indication of what they would be if given the best efforts of a majority of social thinkers. Another generation away from the supernatural-believing past may make a vast difference. To be vital, an ethical institution must serve *real* & not fictitious or merely traditional needs, & must represent what people *actually* think & feel. The successors of the churches have a chance to recapture this long-forfeited vitality by revising their precepts to fit the social, economic, & intellectual conditions of the present—& there is no insuperable obstacle to such a revision. Catholicism, however, would seem to be excluded because of its utter dependence on dogma & sheer emotionalism.

But pardon the digression. I am certain that your "New Way" must have an immense amount of vital material, & I surely hope that it can be published sooner or later. The endorsement of the basic aims of Lenin & Stalin will no doubt give many cautious readers a jolt—though perhaps you do not extend your approval to the sudden & autocratic methods whereby those aims are sought in Russia's particular case. My own views on the subject are really in a state of flux. Though formerly a political conservative, I have in recent years come to realise the impracticability of unsupervised capitalism in a thoroughly mechanised industrial civilisation—but just how far toward utter collectivism it will be necessary to go I am still frankly uncertain. Each nation, no doubt, can best follow a separate course based on its own cultural heritage & inclinations. It seems certain to me that the glib "economic determinism" of the "Marxian Dialectic", whereby the bolsheviks pretend to predict the whole course of society in the future, is just as fallacious as the older orthodoxies whereby capitalism seeks to justify itself. All orthodoxies in sociology are necessarily false, since human nature & human needs are too varied & complex ever to be fully understood or reduced to a system. The present Russian system is quite intolerable because of its interference with personal matters apart from economic necessities, & because of its wasteful & destructive break with the cultural heritage of the past. Yet many of its assumptions & details are of immense value—forming important sociological discoveries in the truest sense, & capable of useful adoption by other nations after such modifications as the differing character & conditions of those nations may demand. Of *internationalism* in any extensive sense I am profoundly sceptical, since each distinct culture-group harbours profoundly-seated subconscious ideas, values, & emotions peculiar to itself & often directly antagonistic to those of other groups. These cannot be abolished at will—even through the most frantic efforts. Thus even amidst the synthetic "ideologies" of the bolsheviks, with their violent repudiations of the past, we may still discern all the essential traits of the old Russian character—its mystical faith (now transferred from ikons to machines & political catchwords), its natural ruthlessness & absolutism, its disregard for the individual as distinguished from the mass, its lack of certain factors of *proportion* found in older cultures, its keen sensitivity & creativeness in certain directions, & so on. So far as I can see, fusions of culture can be accomplished only through the forcible conquest of one group by another, & the persistent imposition of the conquerors' mores upon the conquered—as when the heritage of the Celts in Gaul was replaced by that of the Romans. But even this sort of fusion is impossible when the defeated culture is of long standing, high intrinsic development, & perfect adaptation to its possessors. Thus no part of the world which had become Greek ever ceased to be Greek—despite the dominance of Rome—until the utterly devastating sweep of the Moslems uprooted all sources of continuous inheritance; while in modern times the cases of still-French Quebec, of Poland, of the Balkan states, & of many other regions prove the enormous difficulty encountered by a conqueror in extirpating a culture deeply seated in a soil or a people. To fancy, as the Marxians do, that any sense of economic *class* can ever replace this dominant & ineradicable sense of *inherited group folkways,* is to my mind naive & absurd in the extreme. Therefore I attach very little importance to internationalism as a whole—though hoping that various compromises & non-encroachment agreements may some day lessen the frequency of armed conflict . . . . whose rapidly increasing disastrousness in an age of mechanical invention is obvious to all.

But to return to "The New Way"—the table of contents surely looks interesting, & I presume your introduction supplies a link of logical connexion betwixt the somewhat separate divisions. Although, as I have pointed out, I cannot promise early reports or results in this matter, I would surely be glad to read the volume & see whether the amount to be done to it is within the limits of feasibility. Regarding the manner of sending—if I am able to revise it, I would certainly want all the text before me at once, since the length & tone of any one section of a book is always more or less subtly conditioned by every other section. It never does to trust fragments in the absence of the other parts of a manuscript. On the other hand, since any revision I could make would have to extend over a considerable period, you might prefer to see some of the early part before the whole is done—although I'd want them back for reference in doing the later parts. (Unless, of course, the dissociation of the three main sections is complete). Thus it might be well to send the MS.—though complete—in *unbound* form. In this way individual parts could be sent back & forth for discussion. But I'd certainly want *all* the text before tackling any part. You might let me know how much you'll be willing to have the manuscript physically defaced with revisions—for I am hoping this will be a job of only *light* revision, performable without the preparation of a new script. In any case I fancy I shall work in pencil, so that unwelcome changes can be easily removed.

By the way—I recall the infinitely clever bindings which you give your book MSS. That certainly is an admirable way to keep unpublished material— allowing it to be handled & lent with a minimum of wear & tear. I am less methodical & efficient—& as a result I fancy a good deal of my stuff will be scattered or worn to powder without ever seeing the light of print. Not, however, that the loss will be anything important!

Well—by midnight tonight we shall know, roughly, what the nation's voters think on our more or less 'new ways'! To my mind the present administration forms a very fair start toward gradual evolution in the needed direction, & I hope to see it receive a heavy endorsement. Of course, not many voters really know what they are voting about—but that is a basic fault of free-&-easy democracy. I'd like to see the franchise restricted to persons able to pass a really stiff examination in history, psychology, economics, sociology, & other relevant subjects. That's the only way we shall ever have a really intelligent government. Other necessary measures cluster around the artificial spreading of work to counteract technological unemployment. Something like the N.R.A.[1] is indispensable, no matter how inadequately the present measure seems to work. Old-age pensions & unemployment insurance are likewise absolute necessities in a highly industrialised machine civilisation. If all this makes necessary the public ownership of the larger utilities & industries, then such must come—whether the business man & financiers like it or not!

Again expressing the hope that Mrs. de Castro's health will soon respond favourably to treatment—

I remain

Yrs most sincerely

H P Lovecraft

Notes

1. The National Recovery Administration, a major New Deal program.

[17]   [ALS, JHL]

66 College St.,

Providence, R.I.,

Novr. 14, 1934

Dear Dr. de Castro:—

Let me hasten to acknowledge yours of the 11th, & to report safe receipt of "The New Way". I shall read the latter with keen interest & close attention at the earliest opportunity, & will then comment at length upon all the disputed phases before beginning to mark up the text. At that time I will try to give my sincere opinion regarding the style, chapter-headings, &c. But first to get a general impression of the whole. I don't believe such an encyclopaedic battery of quotations & acknowledgments will be demanded—especially if the book is meant, as you state, for popular reading. However, it might be just as well to have all authorities listed where important controversial matters are touched upon. A cursory glance at the text seems to indicate a work of much interest & timeliness, & I am sure that I shall enjoy its perusal. The original version, with 956 pages & classical notes, must surely have been a formidable tome! I trust you have not discarded the excised material, for it might serve usefully in case the volume is published & becomes a subject of discussion.

It was certainly thoughtful of you to try to get me a copy of "Jewish Forerunners", but I fancy I can find it in a library sooner or later. Evidently it is quite a mine of interesting & little-known material. I hope you will eventually prepare the life of Christ as once planned—it ought to have a wide appeal, & any points contrary to the orthodox myths would excite less opposition than they would have a few decades ago.

So you have yourself achieved distinction in swordsmanship & written a book on the subject! I'll mention that to Price, for it will interest him. You & he seem to be rivals in versatility! I trust that our correspondence with him will result in some mutually profitable collaborations. You may see him next summer, for he plans to transfer his headquarters to Chicago & do considerable touring in the east.

Interesting that my previous letter formed a birthday card! Permit me to wish you, with much sincerity, the traditional many happy returns. For most persons I imagine that being born is neither a calamity nor a boon—it is just an event. They are about as well off alive as dead—it doesn't make much difference. A smaller number are definitely worse off alive than they would be had they never been born. And a still smaller number are perhaps actual gainers in pleasure by being alive. To the universe it makes no difference whether or not organic life happens to exist on any of its planets. The incident is too trivial to be of importance—& indeed, life cannot exist for more than the briefest fraction of a planet's total existence. It is a mistake to regard the cosmos as either favourable to life or unfavourable to it. It is simply indifferent & unconscious. However, that forms no occasion for sorrow on man's part. Whether he has a fairly good time or a wretched time being alive depends greatly on his own skill & good sense in adapting himself to the environment within which accident has thrown him. Barring unusual eternal misfortunes, a man of sense can generally gain enough contentment to make existence at least no worse than non-existence. There is always pleasure in artistic expression, the acquisition of ideas, & the trace of vague expectancy inherent in any experience whose future stages are beyond fathoming.

Am in the middle of a troublesome job, but hope to read & make preliminary comments on "The New Way" before long. The manuscript certainly is in admirably neat shape!

Damnably cold today—I surely dread the prospect of winter, though this place is blessed with ideal steam heat.

With every good wish, & best regards to you & Mrs. de Castro, I remain
Yrs most sincerely,
H. P. Lovecraft

[18]   [TLS, JHL]
66 College St., Providence, R.I.
January 26, 1935.
Dear Mr. de Castro:—
                    Let me thank you sincerely for the gracefully written & tastefully printed acrostic received yesterday. It forms, to my mind, an extremely well-merited tribute to one who is performing invaluable work in bridging the gap between the dying order of unsupervised capitalism and the probable future order of semi-collectivism and widespread social control. I have no patience with the blind reactionaries on the one hand, and radical extremists on the other hand, who sneer at the experimental middle course followed by the present administration. So far as laissez-faire plutocracy is concerned, no case at all remains. That era is as dead as Nineveh & Tyre. And while it is probable that the permanent future order will have to lie much fur-

ther toward the left than the present New Deal, the fact remains that the New Deal is the leftmost course which could, at the moment, stand any chance of peaceable adoption through popular acclaim. The coming transition must be gradual—step-by-step—and it would be hard to find any entering wedge more really useful than that which the President is now inserting in the custom-and-prejudice-bound national fabric. Your acrostic ought to be very popular—& I am sorry that you are deriving no material return from it.

Let me express my sincerest sympathy regarding your recent illness— which I trust may not soon be repeated. Considering the nervous strain you must be under, I can hardly wonder at the attack—but the rest obtained through the collapse will probably help to ward off another. I hope that, upon reflection, you will not take the tactless pessimism of that nun too seriously. A mere nurse is not a physician, and the lesser fry around an hospital sometimes acquire a casual outlook greatly subversive of accuracy. It does not do to give up hope prematurely in anything as potentially controllable as tuberculosis. As I have mentioned, there are thousands of persons living with lungs impaired to a vast degree—for once the spread of the trouble is checked, a surprisingly small fraction of the pulmonary apparatus can serve to carry on the vital processes.

So if I were you I wouldn't be totally discouraged. A spirit as indomitable as that of Mrs. de Castro is itself a great bulwark against disease—you may recall that in vast epidemics the psychology of the patients is so influential that the most hopeful and determined are usually the ones to pull through. It is certainly tremendously lamentable that this affliction has had to come—but at the same time it is far too early to conclude that it will not safely pass over and lead to a pleasanter outcome. Don't believe all the croakers—they've had many a person mentally in the tomb, who is today hale and hearty again!

It is enormously generous of you to think of letting me have that copy of Baudelaire's "Lettres"—but you must not spare from your own library anything which is of use and pleasure to yourself. I can keenly appreciate what a prize this volume must be—for Baudelaire has always been a favourite of mine. Let me thank you most profoundly for your thoughtful idea—but don't carry it out if you have the least bit of further use for the volume!

I continue to struggle with accumulated tasks, and doubt if I can make Manhattan again till April at the earliest. My last visit was very hurried, with scarcely any time for the scheduled events. I'll note your changed address, and trust the new quarters may be more comfortable than those you are now occupying. At the first possible moment I hope to read further in "The New Way", making minor suggestions about verbal usage etc. as I go.

With renewed thanks for the acrostic, and with every good & hopeful wish for you & Mrs. de Castro, I remain

Yours most cordially,

H P Lovecraft

[19]   [ALS, JHL]

66 College St.,
Providence, R.I.,
April 11, 1935.

Dear Dr. de Castro:—

Let me thank you most sincerely for the volume of Baudelaire letters which arrived yesterday afternoon. It forms a fascinating inner glimpse of a personality whose brilliance I have always admired at a distance—& whose biography I read some 13 years ago.[1] The eminence of some of the recipients—Gautier, Gerard de Nerval, Sainte-Beuve, Barbey d'Aurevilly, Flaubert, Houssaye, de Vigny, Manet, Rops, &c.—gives one a sense of peculiar proximity to one of the greatest ages of French art & literature; while the occasionally-mentioned name of *Poe* links this world to one still closer from my point of view. (Some ultra-fastidious stylists have claimed that they can enjoy Poe's tales only in Baudelaire's translation!) Around 1857 one notes echoes of the legal furore over the "Fleurs du Mal"—& in general the long vanished age & scene come vividly to view. I shall assuredly enjoy going through these time-dissolving pages—dictionary at my right-hand for guidance in emergencies.

Once more let me express my sympathy concerning your bereavement.[2] Activity, as you say, is certainly the best weapon for combating such an emotional blow—& I am glad you have occupied yourself with the anthology. Much of your verse which I have seen strikes me as exceedingly brilliant & graceful, & I hope that some publishing arrangement can eventually be made. However, in any case it is an advantage to have the choicest specimens neatly assembled. Books do not get into print easily these days. Last February Loring & Mussey of N.Y. asked to see some of my stuff with a view to book publication—but since this is the *fifth* time I have had such a request, without tangible results to date, I am not as naively excited over the matter as I otherwise might be. However, I sent a few stories along—merely on the general principle of never leaving any stone unturned. I have heard nothing from them, but do not expect any favourable action. My only hope is that the MSS., upon return, will not shew as many signs of ill-treatment as those which came back from Putnam's in 1931.

If you make your contemplated Boston pilgrimage, I surely hope that you will stop off in ancient Providence. At almost any date specified in advance (except May 3–4–5, when I shall myself be in Boston) I can meet you at any designated transportation terminal—boat, 'bus or train—& pilot you up the hill to #66 . . . or to any historic, scenic, & antiquarian sights which would be likely to appeal to you. Don't fail to let me know ahead, so that I can surely have my programme open. Incidentally—in case of some hitch on arrival—the telephone of this establishment (in the name of my one surviving aunt, Mrs. Phillips-Gamwell) is *PLantations 2044.*

I had hoped the spring would be an early one—indeed, early in March the mild weather (65°, 71°, etc.) lured me forth on several outings, including a 12-mile rural walk. Since then, however, some beastly chilly weather has supervened. But the shrubs in the garden are budded, so that the atmosphere is not altogether without hope. I wish I had the cash to get down to Charleston or St. Augustine!

Picked up a rather useful item the other day—the new 1-volume Modern Encyclopaedia, now issued by Grosset & Dunlap for only $1.95. I really needed this badly, since my latest other encyclopaedia is one of 1914. I was strongly tempted by the original edition in 1933, but now I'm glad I waited. This edition mentions events as recent as *last November*.

Tasks have piled upon me in prostrating profusion, but I still hope to go through the "New Way" MS. in a light fashion—improving the flow of the prose in spots, though not attempting any thorough revision. I'll also give an opinion as to subsequent re-casting—though a lot of consideration & a better scholar than I are needed for that job.

Again thanking you profusely for the Baudelaire—& with renewed sympathy concerning the ordeal through which you have passed—I remain

Yrs most cordially & sincerely,
H P Lovecraft

P.S. I've recently done something toward putting my chaotic files of papers & pamphlets in order—by purchasing 8 small cabinets with drawers, which fit into my study without disturbing the existing furnishing scheme. As a result, my things are in better shape than they've been since 1910—though much still remains in cardboard boxes or on open shelves.

Notes

1. Possibly Théophile Gautier's *Charles Baudelaire: His Life* (1915) or Arthur Symons's *Charles Baudelaire: A Study* (1920).
2. De Castro's wife Georgina Sterling McClellan de Castro-Danziger (1880–1935) died on 23 January.

[20]   [TLS, JHL]

[Adolphe de Castro]
268 West 91,
New York

June 26, 1935.

Dear Friend,

Recovered from a serious wrangle with *Mr. Mort;* and even then it has taken me days to return to a bit of normal.

How are you and how is the NEW WAY getting on? If I improve as I have so far, I may take the Bus for a ride in your direction, as my dear brother-in-law wants me to visit him.

Hoping this finds you in the best of health, I am as ever,

Sincerely and faithfully,
Adolphe de Castro

[21]   [ALS]

℅ R. H. Barlow,
Box 88, De Land, Florida
July 11, 1935.

Dear Dr. de Castro:—

I was very glad to receive your letter of the 7th, & hope I can see you when I re-pass through New York on my way home next month. Later I trust you can make the New England trip, stopping off in Providence. So you have been having warm weather in the north? Down here the temperature exactly suits me—always in the 80's. I am never comfortable under 80°, & really do not know what it is to be too warm.

I was interested to hear of your presidential correspondence regarding the penal system, & am sorry you could not arrange a trip to Washington at the right time. Eventually I hope that you can arrange for the publication of all the vital material in "The New Way" in an adequate fashion—though, as you realise, considerable selection & re-formulation will be necessary.

Regarding the problem of revision & editing—as I have said before, the feverishly crowded nature of my programme makes it really impossible for me to undertake the full procedure which the volume needs. The pressure of existing duties on my time is so maddeningly heavy, that no major added responsibility could possibly be undertaken. Even as things are, various duties are preventing my doing any writing of my own. To assume any additional burden would be practically sealing the doom of my own writing career. My present sojourn in Florida is by no means a vacation, since all my activities continue in full force. Among other projects I am assisting my host in establishing a small publishing venture.

Therefore it seems really imperative—much as I regret it—that another *first* editor & reviser be found for this volume. What I said I would try to do if I possibly can, & if unlimited time be available—is to give the text a careful reading & improve the sentence-structure in places, & to furnish suggestions & criticisms of possible aid to you & to the final reviser. This all depends upon the virtual absence of any time limit—& of course rests with you. Meanwhile the question of the historical material toward the end remains a paramount issue. As you must certainly see from my explicit letter of last autumn, this matter will have to be attended to before the corresponding section of the volume is offered for publication. There cannot be some slip regarding the Teutonic sources mentioned, since the existing account presents the widest possible discrepancies with authentic Roman history. Re-examination of source material, & a checking-up of the various points by some recognised historical expert, form an absolute pre-requisite to the offering of such novel material *as history*. If, on the other hand, the material were to be offered *as fiction* (& the theme would make a very promising novel or tale on the order of Anatole France's "Procurator of Judea"),[1] it would be necessary only to alter the early parts of the narrative in such a way as to conform to known facts. That is—rewrite the story from the start, recognising that Germany was not occupied by the Romans till 12 B.C., that *Poncius* is an old Samnite family name, that the Etruscans were peacefully assimilated members of the Roman fabric in the Augustan age, &c. &c. &c. Even so, some expert on Roman (or general ancient) history ought to check it up. It would, if properly remodelled, make a fine story—even though the element of sheer *coincidence* seems overworked a trifle as judged by the canons of realism. But I leave all this to you. First of all, re-read my long letter of last autumn as thoroughly as possible & see just what needs attention. Then look sharply to the sources whence the non-historical dates & statements were derived.

Thanks for the interesting cutting of Mithridates the Great—who has surely become quite a figure of legend. He was the last of the Kings of Pontus, & his wars with the Romans (ending with his death in B.C. 64) are famous because of the eminent generals involved—L. Cornelius Sulla, L. Licinius Lucullus, Cn. Pompeius, &c. His kingdom (later a Roman province) was the *real* Pontus—in Asia Minor on the Black Sea—of which I spoke in my letter of last autumn. There never was any "Pontus" *in Italy*. Incidentally, there is not the least connexion between the pseudo-Hellenic name of *Pontus* (derived from the *Pontus Euxinus* or Black Sea on which it bordered . . . . the original name being Καππαδόκια πρὸς τῷ Πόντω [*sic*] or "Cappadocia toward the Pontus (Euxinus)") & the aboriginal Italic root whence the Samnite family name of *Pontius* (a name which figures in the earliest history of Italy—cf. the victor of Caudine Forks, &c.) was derived. That is—there is no connexion this side of the prehistoric period when some "Pelasgian" language ancestral to both Italian & Hellenic tongues probably contained some widely inclusive *Pont*-root pertaining to water or the sea. Anyhow—the main point is that the Samnite (& later Roman) name *Pontius* had nothing to do with any place called *Pontus*. It was an ancient family *nomen* or gens-name existing in Italy from the earliest times. The *agnomen* or honorary title which would be awarded to any hero of the Mithridatic Wars in *Pontus* would be *Ponticus* (like ASIATICUS & GERMANICUS).

When I get home this autumn & have a chance to read "The New Way" I will further discuss this & other historical & scientific points which seem to me to need discussion. This, I hope, will form a service atoning in a small way for my inability to handle the exhaustive remodeling & editing as a speculative professional job. I may add that this discussion will not be anything in any sense professional—it will be purely a matter of good will without any obligations. In such cases I shall speak purely as a layman—having no *expert* knowledge of my own—but will refer you to authorities in cases where I feel sure some reconsideration is necessary. For example, I am absolutely certain that modern biology calls for a modification of your theory of the predetermination of the sex of offspring—a theory which figures (to an extent which might be seriously criticized as naive & over-confident) in your account of Christ's parentage. I likewise feel certain that comparative mythology calls for a modification of the treatment of the Moses-legend . . . . the incident of the cradle in the bulrushes being plainly borrowed from earlier sources (Babylonian if I remember correctly). Moses is obviously a culture-hero around whom a wide variety of borrowed tales has come to cluster. All this, however, in good time—since I have neither your MS. nor any reference-sources in my own working library—whose resources are doubly valuable to me because of my lifelong familiarity with them. If I ever move permanently to Florida I shall have to bring all my things with me.

Speaking of libraries—it is infinitely generous of you to think of giving me the books you mention, but you must not think of parting with anything of continued usefulness or pleasure to yourself. I recall some of your material in *The American Parade,* & would be infinitely grateful for the copies in question—though I could not let you give away your only file copies. I hang on to my own volumes most tenaciously, & certainly don't intend to break up my library as long as I can find any place whatsoever in which to house it.

My presence in Florida continues to help my health enormously—I am infinitely stronger than when I reached here June 9th. To my mind there is no other climate equal to this—at least in the U.S. Probably I'd like some of the West Indies even more. It is clear that a subtropical or tropical milieu is the proper one for me—since my energy in the north is always at a low ebb. I shall probably be returning to Providence some time in August—I won't want to wait here until the north gets chilly, or else my return will involve an unpleasant climatic plunge. If—as I hope—my finances allow me to pause a few days in New York, I shall certainly try to get around to 268 W. 91.

I trust that your various ventures are all going reasonably well, & that you & Price will eventually be able to collaborate to advantage in some fictional experiment. Regarding "The New Way"—while I don't see how I can undertake the elaborate final revision, I hope I can later (if the time-element does not count) offer some remarks at least slightly useful.

With every good wish, & hoping to see you in person next month, I remain
Yours most cordially & sincerely,
H. P. Lovecraft

Notes

1. France's "The Procurator of Judea" ("Le Procurateur de Judée," 1891), included in an English translation by Henri Pène Du Bois in the volume *Tales from a Mother-of-Pearl Casket* (New York: George H. Richmond, 1896), is a story that shows the elderly Pontius Pilate reminiscing about his life and failing utterly to remember his crucifixion of Jesus Christ. The story is also in *Golden Tales of Anatole France* (1909).

[22]   [TLS, JHL]

ADOLPHE de CASTRO
803 West 180
NEW YORK

September 24, 1935.

Dear Mr. Lovecraft,

Thank you for sending the script, which I received this morning. There is evidently some mistake, owing to something I wrote you. I do not know the publisher. My agent does, and he has not told me. But from what I told him of the subject matter, he was exceedingly anxious to submit it to a publisher who, he thinks, is eager for just such material.*

If he is not successful the script will be sent back to you, as you are the only man I know and the only friend I have able to handle this book to make it look acceptable from the standpoint of construction and thought. And as you agreed to take "potluck" with me in this work, it is only right that you should see it at least to your satisfaction literarily.†

The diverse losses I suffered, the grief that attacked me has not left my mind unscathed. I cannot for the moment lay my hands—or my memory—on the authorities I read (in German, Mommsen, Niebuhr, Ranke and others)[1] not to mention Gibbon and others relative to my assertions. But there is a vast literature in ancient and modern Hebrew (I mean during the 8th century A.C.) that have a variety of suggestions—for you may believe me that I did not concoct this statement just to be "smart," or sensational. If the suggestion is taken up at all, it will bring forth the originals. These are not from some unknown author, but, as I recall, by the great classical historians, whether in German, French, Spanish or other of the languages I read for research purposes, I cannot at the moment tell.‡

I sent Price a short story for collaboration, but he seems either disinclined or he is so busy making money from the "Pulps" that he has no time. He is, by his own statement to me, by the way of becoming a bloated plutocrat, with cars and estates and the like.

Hoping this finds you well, I am as ever,

Adolph de Castro

Notes

1. Theodor Mommsen (1817–1903), author of a pioneering history of Rome (*Römische*

---

*[The side notes on this letter are HPL's:] He asked for his MS.—saying a publisher had expressed a wish to see it.

†Damn!

‡See how old Dolph tries to bluff out the hilarious historical boners in his "parentage of Jesus" fake?

Geschichte, 1854–56); Bartold Georg Niebuhr (1776–1831), who also wrote an important history of Rome (*Römische Geschichte,* 1811–32); Leopold von Ranke (1795–1886), author of a history of the Roman republic (*Weltgeschichte: Die Römische Republik und ihre Weltherrschaft,* 1886) and other historical works.

[23]   [ALS, JHL]

66 College St.
Providence, R.I.
Septr. 26, 1935

Dear Dr. de Castro:—

Glad the MS. safely arrived, & hope it will fare well with the publisher whom your agent has in mind. Even if it does not land now, it may not be long before it will do so.

Regarding further revision in case it is not placed at present—as I said this summer, I don't see how it would be possible for me to give it a *thorough* or *final* overhauling in the limited time at my disposal. That would require immense funds of time & energy, & a devastating amount of historical research. What I *would* be able & glad to do, would be to read it through carefully, & polish up the prose style of the whole in the same way that I have already polished up that of the first chapter or two. This would not be a *final* revision, but it would make the final revision cheaper & easier when the time might come for that. And I would certainly make no charge for such a polishing—given unlimited time for the process. But let us hope that the present publisher may make such procedure unnecessary.

Regarding the historical points—I did not mean to imply that the account was concocted for purposes of sensationalism. I simply pointed out that, in present form, it might "go over" best if given the *semblance* of an historical novel. Just how the material could be given in any other way—lacking correction & verification from original authorities—I really can't see. As you may readily perceive, this account states & implies dozens of things at direct variance with well-known historic facts—such as the presence of Roman rule in Germany before B.C. 13, the use of "Tyrus" as a Roman name, the location of provincial rule at Magontiacum at too early a date, the identification of *Pontus* as an *Italian city,* the idea of Etruscans in revolt after their full absorption into the Roman people, the false derivation of the common Samnite gens-name *Pontius,* the existence of the *duel* in pre-medieval times, & other points which could not pass inspection for a moment. No matter what original source supplied the general thesis, these specific points (& others like them) would cause it to be attacked at once—hence *it is absolutely necessary to remove these obvious errors* (however they may have crept in) before the text can go before the public. With these absolute & unmistakable errors, the thesis could never be judged on its own merits. It would *seem* to rest on overt & flagrant contradictions of common fact. It is not fair to the thesis to offer it under such an insurmountable handicap—nor do I think that any publisher would be willing so to offer it. Thus it seems *imperative* at this stage to get the mistakes cleared up, so that the message will be in deliverable form.

I realise of course the difficulty of reassembling authorities when no notes have been kept—but how else is the original account to be rediscovered? The existing mistakes *could* not have been in any of the solid sources . . . so *what was it* that the solid sources *really said?* I can assure you that Mommsen, Niebuhr, & Gibbon do not sustain any contentions contrary to accepted history, for I have in my day read them (M. & N. in English translation). In view of the bold & revolutionary nature of the assertions, it ought not be difficult to narrow down the search for their origin by eliminating many of the standard authorities. In any case, you can see how impossible it is to present revolutionary claims without any visible sources—especially when linked with dozens of palpable errors.

Of course, the most important thing is to eliminate the flagrant *errors*. If *that* were done, the lack of accessible authorities would be a less *immediate* handicap—especially if the quasi-fictional style were adopted. But in the end, of course, the lack of visible originals would weigh heavily.

So it is clear that the one thing which *must* be done now is to *clear up the errors*. This might not need a consultation of the original sources—but could perhaps be done at once by yourself with the actual historic facts in mind. Remember that there was no Roman rule along the Rhine till the time of Drusus Nero—B.C. 13–12, & that the region did not have a *civil* governor anyhow till *A.D. 17,* when the provinces of Germania Superior & Germania Inferior were formed. Remember also that *Pontius* was a common Samnite nomen—& that *Pontus* was a Black Sea province pacified long before & joined administratively with Bithynia . . . . nothing to do with Italy or the Etruscans—the latter element being, by the way, fully absorbed by the Roman people. Surely the narrative could be re-cast in harmony with these absolutely certain & widely known historic truths.

I am sure you realise that all these suggestions of mine are made without hyper-critical intent, & simply to aid the success of the book. It obviously cannot be published until the errors are straightened out—hence the one important thing is to *get* them straightened as soon as possible. And that is something which only you can do, unless your original authorities become accessible to others.

Of course, the entire omission of the historic chapters of the book at this time would be possible. Indeed, much might be said in favour of this—since they will clearly appear under a handicap until the sources are found. The time for publication is, very plainly, *after* all the knotty points are straightened out.

The necessary thing is to throw the controversy back from yourself to the authorities from whom you derived your narrative. Then you will not be responsible for the weaknesses in the account. It seems to me very probable that these stories originated in mediaeval times, when the sense of history was slight, & critical standards lax. Close examination of the account discloses such a *theatrical* quality that one can hardly doubt the development *after* the wide popularisation of the original New Testament narrative. It very obviously *builds from* that narrative—adding a dramatic coherence & climax dependent upon the significance attached to the original tale. The element of *coincidence* involved in having the son of Pilatus tried before him is typical of the older school of dramatic construction. Now of course this was probably a natural growth over a long period—just like other folk-tales throughout the world. It may well recur in different mediaeval writings both Christian & Jewish—& Mohammedan also, for that matter—as do other apocryphal legends. But the genuineness of the tale *as legend* would of course form no guarantee of its genuineness *as history*. Still—this latter point need not bother you. Your purpose is *to shew that the legends exist*—& once you do that, you can let the critics tackle the original legends as best they may. But you can do that only by rediscovering & citing your sources. Without such backing, you yourself instead of your sources will have to bear the brunt of attack.

So my earnest advice is that you bend every effort toward the elimination of errors & rediscovery of sources *before* the account is again offered for publication. I'd recommend an easier & simpler course if I could, but I can't see any, try as I may. You may get further suggestions from your agent, or from the publisher to whom he has submitted the book. And more—when you reread the chapters in question more closely, you may recall the primary sources more readily than you could off hand. But remember also that the book would be quite suitable for submission *without* the debatable chapters. You could, if you wished, remove them for later investigation & verification.

Price certainly is busy, but I think he'll be available for at least a limited amount of collaboration before long. His success is truly remarkable—though he has earned it at the high cost of suspending his really literary efforts. Some day I hope he will have more leisure, so that he can resume his more serious writing.

I am still wrestling with piled-up work—the tasks before me being even heavier than I thought upon a first survey. Good luck with the book—& don't think I am cavilling when I point out matters which I believe absolutely essential to its acceptance.

All good wishes—
    Yrs most sincerely
      H P Lovecraft

[24]   [first leaf only: ALS, JHL; second leaf: American Jewish Archives, Cincinnati]

66 College St.
Providence, R.I.
Octr. 5, 1935

Dear Dr. de Castro:—

I am greatly interested in the researches you have made concerning those debate-filled historic chapters. I did not doubt but that the original sources would turn up in the end—after sufficient searching—& I trust that they will be duly cited in the final version of the text.

Vilmar[1] is an authority unknown to me—but as you see, his account (if it is literally the same as that presented in the text) is obviously legendary. The stubborn fact remains, that no Roman occupation of the Rhineland existed until about 8 or 9 years before the traditional date of the birth of Christ . . . which is 4 B.C., as commonly reckoned. Also—even if certain writers refer to a rebellion in Pontus during the Augustan period, it is obvious that the *Etruscans* had nothing to do with it—since Pontus lies far off on the Euxine, while the Etruscans had long been assimilated into the Roman fabric. Just how this connexion of Pontus & the Etruscans could have arisen—except through the inaccurately associative processes of mediaeval legend—I can't imagine . . . unless perhaps the revolt mentioned involved troops or colonists in whom the Etruscan element was strong. Furthermore—the *derivation of the name* "Pontius" from Pontus is obviously false. All agree that the name as borne by anyone in the Roman world must have come from membership in the ancient gens Pontia—the Samnite family so frequently encountered in the history of the Republic. An honorary cognomen or "agnomen" bestowed for exploits in *Pontus* could have but one form—PONTICUS—according to the linguistic laws governing such formations.

I'll look into Suetonius for the account of that *earlier* Syrian appointment of Pilatus.[2] Curious that I don't recall it—though it's fully 30 years now since I've read Suetonius—an author whom I unfortunately do not own. I really must pick up a copy when I find one reasonably priced. Regarding Tertullianus (yes—I recall his praise of Pilatus—"iam pro sua conscientia Christianum") & the Talmud—of course the *late dates* of these writings causes them to be open to legends arising out of the earlier Judaeo-Christian accounts . . . legends consciously or unconsciously built dramatically from the first crop of mingled fact & myth, & coloured with religious zeal or prejudice one way or the other. As you know, Pilatus was an especially favoured subject of myth-making—Eastern & Coptic traditions giving him a Christian wife (Claudia Procala or Procla) who is to this day a Greek Church saint, while the subjects of the just-now-limelighted Haile Selassie make Pontius himself a saint & martyr! Then there are of course the apocryphal *Acta Pilati, Epistola Pilati, Paradosus Pilati,* & *Mors Pilati* (probably Judaeo-Christian)—full of fantastic tales of Pilatus' sight

of the Resurrection, of his trial & sentence by Caligula, his penitent conversion to Christianity, his suicide to escape sentence (which contradicts another
legend that he was beheaded at *Nero's* order), the removal of his body to Vien-
na (where a structure* called "Pilate's Tomb" is still exhibited. The chronicler
naively traces the name VIENNA to VIAGEHENNAE![3] This place also figures in legend as the seat of Pilatus' banishment during is lifetime.) & later to a
mountain pool near Lucerne because the Tiber & Rhine both refused to harbour it. (The site of this pool is now called "Mt. Pilatus", & according to legend
the water displays strange agitation if anything is thrown into it. The devil removes the still-preserved body of Pilatus each year—on Good Friday—& forces it to go through a curious handwashing ceremony on a throne.) These
apocryphal books probably date from the 2nd century A.D. & afterward. Eusebius (circa 325 A.D.) in his famous Ἐκκλησιαστική Ἱστορία (& after exposure to all the current Christian legends) is the source of the statement (which
may or may not have a basis in fact) that Pilatus was banished to Vienna by
Caligula & committed suicide there because of various misfortunes. Regarding Talmudic sources—of which I have no knowledge—one may only point
out that later recordings of lost records are often coloured with legendry
which did not exist in the original versions. Obviously, only a profoundly erudite student of Jewish antiquities could form a just verdict on the extent to
which fragmentary transcripts & recensions of these early Palestinian Evan-
gels (themselves probably derived to some extent from purely oral legends of
a century's growth) can be accepted as historical. All that is beyond me. The
remarkable thing is, though, that the indicated origin of Jesus has not been
more widely accepted if the documents are generally regarded as dependable.
One could understand a wish to suppress these documents in the *Christian*
world—where the myth of divine paternity was to be sustained at any cost—
but I cannot see what reasons the *Jewish* world would have to suppress them.
The existence of a fanatical preacher of left-handed origin & wholly human
parentage would mean nothing one way or the other to the Jewish religion.
He would be grouped with other heretics who lived & founded false sects &
died—& there would be no object in concealing any facts pertaining to him.
And yet, so far as I know, the version here given is *not* endorsed by the main
stream of Jewish scholarship. Though I have no exact knowledge of the views
of Jewish historians, orthodox or otherwise, I seem to recall references here &
there which indicate a conflict of opinion—some regarding Christ as a local
impostor while a few accept the cult idea & disbelieve in his objective existence.
At any rate, I believe there is no attempt to take seriously the hostile & widely
conflicting Talmudic references (none of which, so far as I know, mentions Pi-
latic parentage) which influenced Judaism in the late imperial & mediaeval
periods. Just what modern Jewish scholarship thinks of Christ could make an

---

*actually part of the *spina* of a Roman circus.

interesting subject for study—I must look it up some day in the Jewish Ency-clopedia, which is generally accessible in libraries. But I feel very sure that the Pontian theory would be more widely noted & cited if it were accepted by any responsible body of Jewish scholars & historians. In the absence of such gen-eral acceptance one is forced to the provisional conclusion that the legends in question are vague & apocryphal. At least, that is the conclusion of one with-out special information based on near historical discoveries.

The whole matter is certainly highly interesting, & I would indeed be glad to use the notes you have so generously offered to send. I may not be able to follow them up at once, for my progamme is desperately crowded; but I would be grateful for a copy to have on hand for gradual following-up. Prob-ably most of the sources could be located in Providence libraries. I have Smith's Bible Dictionary—but unfortunately an old abridged edition which sheds no light on the points in question. Meanwhile I must get a look at Sue-tonius somewhere—for I can't recall any reference to the earlier service of Pilatus in Syria. The statement that he served under Archelaus is also puz-zling—insomuch as that tetrarch did not succeed to the Judaean throne till after the birth of Christ according to the received account. Archelaus' father Herod the Great (who may or may not have conducted the "slaughter of the innocents") was on the throne when Christ is said to have been born . . . . The Roman governor (legatus pro praetore) then being P. Quinctilius Varus, afterward so tragically overwhelmed by the Germans with his legion in the Saltus Teutoburgiensis (A.D. 9). Archelaus became tetrarch during the first year of Christ's reputed existence—Varus being then replaced as propraetor by the rather low-born P. Sulpicius Quirinius, an ex-consul who had been proconsul of Africa. Varus was such a close friend of Archelaus that Augus-tus didn't dare to trust them in the province together—between them they'd have doubtless looted it completely! Later Archelaus was banished to Vien-na—a circumstance which may or may not have some connexion with the tale that Pilatus also was banished thither. With him ended the tetrarchate—the region of Syria Palestina being then (A.D. 6-7) organised as the imperial province of Judaea under a procurator. When, then, did the young Pilatus first serve in Syria? Before the birth of Christ under Herodes the Great, or after it under Archelaus? Or did Archelaus have some minor office wherein he was Pilatus' chief prior to his accession to the tetrarchate? It is odd how every new angle of this legendry brings up some fresh problem! But I must get hold Suetonius & see what I have forgotten or overlooked.

I'm greatly interested to learn that you find grounds for believing the Christ reference in Josephus not interpolated. Hitherto the tendency to reject this—as well as a corresponding reference in Tacitus—has been well-nigh universal. An article on the subject alone, it seems to me, would be well worth writing.

Meanwhile, I wish you all luck with the book. It might be a good idea to send sections only for a continuance of the surface revision—although it really doesn't matter. As I said I can't very well promise speed. Such emendation ought to go only as far as the beginning of the chapters under dispute, since these sections will need a re-writing with the elimination of slips & the introduction of authorities. As for the material side of the arrangement—that hardly need be considered at this stage. If later on the book is accepted, I'd think a couple of free copies or something like that a sufficient reward. And regarding an introduction or anything like that—my share would really be too slight & superficial to warrant anything of the kind. But I hope that your agent's present attempt at placement will succeed—in which case the publisher will probably attend to the revision.

With every good wish, & thanks in advance for the notes mentioned, I remain

Yrs most sincerely,

H. P. Lovecraft

Notes

1. August Friedrich Christian Vilmar (1800–1868), historian of German literature who also wrote on the history of the German Christian church.
2. There is no mention of Pontius Pilate in Suetonius' *Lives of the Caesars*.
3. I.e., *Via Gehennae* (the road to Gehenna).

[25]   [TMs. transcription, JHL]

66 College St.,

Providence, R.I.,

Nov. 4, 1935.

Dear Dr. de Castro:—

Congratulations on the writing—which probably does much to increase the force & direct appeal of the book. Of course the ideal is to be accurate & *really* profound (i.e., sound & penetrating) without being [*sic*] the heavy *atmosphere* of conscious profundity obtrusively visible. Genuine scholarship testifies for itself in such details as precision & choice of facts, & acuteness of interpretation, even when the style is essentially simple & colloquial.

But I surely hope you will not let your activity abruptly cease upon the completion of "The New Way". Publishers of course are trying creatures to deal with, but the real reward of writing is simply the satisfaction of formulating & expressing what one has to say. I have known of many writers who do not feel that they worked in vain, even though their MSS have remained unpublished. My uncle translated the Æneid & Georgics of Virgil (he did not survive to read the Eclogues), parts of Lucretius,[1] &c., &c., & wrote many pieces of really important material & antiquarian research—& nothing ever saw the light of print save occasional magazine & newspaper articles. And yet he never felt in the least discouraged or prone to cease writing. Nor shall I ever stop dabbling in weird fiction even though all markets become closed to me.

Price certainly had a great time in Mexico. He visited Tenagua, Santa Cecelia, San Circula & other pyramids, the Temple of Quetzalcoatl at Teotihuacan, & picked up a most impressive range of sights. On the way back he was held up by a landslide, & had to take a rough, rocky detour which tore a hole in his gas tank. He mended the latter with *chewing gum* until he could get to a garage.

This has been a phenomenally mild autumn in New England, so that I've had a number of trips, & have spent considerable time in the open air. I visited New Haven Oct. 8, & on Oct. 16-18 our friend Samuel Loveman was here. We visited Boston & absorbed bookstalls, museums, & general antiquities. Hope you can get around on that 'bus trip! There's plenty in Providence to keep you interested.

All good wishes—

H P L

P. S. So rushed I haven't yet had a chance to get hold of Suetonius for a close inspection.

Notes

1. The translations are held by the Brown University Archives.

[26]   [ANS, JHL]

[6 August 1936]

Am living in Dryfus' Hotel. If you get this today don't go out in the rain.

De Castro

[27]   [TLS]

THREE ACROSTIC SONNETS
WRITTEN
IN A SEQUESTER'D PROVIDENCE CHURCHYARD
WHERE ONCE POE WALK'D[1]

I by H. P. LOVECRAFT

Eternal brood the shadows on this ground,
Dreaming of centuries that have gone before;
Great elms rise solemnly by slab and mound,
Arched high above a hidden world of yore.
Round all the scene a light of memory plays,
And dead leaves whisper of departed days,
Longing for sights and sounds that are no more.

Lonely and sad, a spectre glides along
Aisles where of old his living footsteps fell;
No common glance discerns him, tho' his song
Peals down thro' time with a mysterious spell:
Only the few who sorcery's secret know,
Espy amidst these tombs the shade of Poe.

II by R. H. BARLOW

Endless, the darkly printed tombstones rise;
Dim evening sunlight pours about them now,
Golden and pale, on path and grave and bough,
And furtively they stare with listless eyes,
Remembering ages lost beneath the years,
All silent now, with strife and love and tears
Like scattered leaves through which the autumn sighs.

Less than the leaves a century can grow
As tale and memory blend before the gaze;
No longer lost, these half-forgotten days . . .
Perhaps the shadows stir, perhpas [*sic*] they show
Outcast by life and death, the lonely form
Exiled, of Poe; the man of night and storm.

III by ADOLPHE de CASTRO

Enshrined within our heart remains thy name,
Dear Bard, unjoyed by lasting happiness
Great love bestows; but through the crushing stress,
A mystic spirit, dark, the Raven, came,
Revealed in horror stark and cold the sore
And trusting heart of gentle Leonore, [*sic*]
Lost Leonore, thou didst so well express.

Living thine art with endless horror chills
And shows ubiquitous malignity,
Nor knowing why grim fate with horror kills;
Perhaps thy spirit knew; it had brought to thee
On angels' wings the gift that's loved and feared,
Enranked to be a Monarch of the Weird.

NOTE:

Dear Fellow Sonneteers,

Likely you will deem it an unpardonable sin. So be it.
After reading your graceful lines, I felt that I could not let my screed stand as it

was. When I suggested an accrostic, [*sic*] I did not really think that we—or at least I—should write an acrostic sonnet, the most difficult composition in prosody, for of the thousand and one limitations of sonnet writing there is another—the initial letters. In copying, however, I tried to round off my own a bit. Naturally, you will say it is not cricket. It was meant to be spontaneous. There is one thing only I ever could do fairly well spontaneously—swear picturesquly [*sic*] and shoot from the hip. And even that was not wholly spontaneous, as the leather was greased and the point cut. So I worked my stuff over a bit, which I hope you will take with as much grace as you can muster. Au reste, I have to thank you for a liberal enducation [*sic*] and sore pedals. But it was fun. And the greatest fun was dear young Barlow. Bob actualllly [*sic*] desires to be old, not knowing what treasure he owns in his youth and brains and his overindulgence in imagination, and good memory of what he has read—so far. Encore, pardon!

Adolphe de Castro

Aug. 12, 1936

Notes

1. HPL has written his corrections on this typescript, but no corrections for AdC's poem. The overarching title given the three sonnets was that which HPL used for his own. AdC's poem was published under the title "Edgar Allan Poe"; Barlow's as "St. John's Churchyard."

[28]   [ALS; card nonextant]

66 College St.,
Providence, R.I.,
August 14, 1936.

Dear Dr. de Castro:—

Let me thank you most exceedingly for the new version of the acrostics. Surely it is justifiable to add a few refining touches after the original feat, & I congratulate you upon the finely polished result which you have now secured. In looking over my own attempt I have come across two things which I believe can be easily bettered, & have accordingly changed them in all available copies. May I ask you to embody them also in yours? They are as follows: (together with a third correction based on a misprint)

l. 4—for *Arching* read *Arch'd high*

[misprint in recent copy]   l. 5—for *scenes* read *scene*

l. 9—for *long past* read *of old*

Thanks in advance for making these changes. I'll see that all of yours are embodied in the copies here.

I trust your homeward journey was a pleasant one. Since Monday I've been working like the devil—partly outdoors & partly at my desk. Bob continues to haunt the bookshops with a wistful eye. Before long I hope to be able to shew him ancient Newport—as well as Salem & Marblehead. He sends his most cordial regards, as does my aunt—who received & appreciated your note.

With all good wishes, & renewed thanks for the revised copy of the acrostics, I remain

Yrs most sincerely,

H. P. Lovecraft

P.S. I enclose a card—which rather appeals to me—as a souvenir of your recent sojourn. You will doubtless recognise the church & the roofs & dome of the ancient hill.

[29] [ALS, JHL]

[A. Danziger De Castro
Former American Consul, Madrid.]

Aug. 20, 1936

My dear Lovecraft,

The enclosed letters, because of their contents and the cause back of them—altogether by your inducement—are sent to you for perusal and, if you will be so kind, return.

Something is the matter with my typing machine and so I am oblige[d] to inflict this scrawl upon you.

As always

Sincerely,

Adolphe de Castro

Kindest regards to Mrs. Gamwell

and to Robert Barlow.

Oh, dammit, how I miss you both.

[30] [TLS, JHL]

[A. Danziger De Castro
Former American Consul, Madrid.]
461 Port Washington Avenue
NEW YORK CITY

Aug. 23, 1936.

Amicus,

Am writing to thank you for the card of the beautiful church. It will remind me of the happy hours we spent in converse and sigh[t]-seeing.

The heat yesterday and today is enough to melt the most hard-boiled New Yorker. Fortunately my room is cool, and reading, undisturbed by noises and "Yidamer," a pleasure(*).

Kleiner called. We had a pleasant conversational and beery evening together. He took several short stories to read and see what, if any, arrangement we might make.

I am enclosing a clean copy of the acrostic sonnets, with the corrections you made in yours and the those [*sic*] I made in mine. For the reason I state in the foot note, Barlow's is left blank—for him to copy.

Please don't overwork and remember as kindly as you know how,

Your friend,

A. de Castro

Permit me to send greetings to your aunt Mrs. Gamwell.

[31]   [TMs. transcription, JHL]

66 College St.,

Providence, R.I.,

August 24, 1936.

Dear Dr. de Castro:—

Many thanks for the glimpse of the letters from Kuttner[1] & his mother. Almost simultaneously I had a long letter from K. himself, in which he expressed his delight at having encountered an old family friend so unexpectedly. It really is quite a coincidence that the infant of yesteryear should have become, at the time of his rediscovery, so closely connected with branches of literary endeavour similar to some of your own! I hope that Kuttner & his mother will be able to make the projected eastern trip—allowing you to become reacquainted with him, & permitting me to meet in person one of the most brilliant of my newer correspondents.

Barlow & I went to Newport Aug. 15—or possibly I mentioned that before. On Aug. 20—my 46th birthday—we explored ancient Salem & Marblehead, accompanied by friends whom we found in Lynn.[2] We saw most of the old museum houses, including the House of the Seven Gables (so-called—a house which Hawthorne knew, & which resembled the edifice described in the novel) & the "Old Witch House"—the latter the residence of Judge Jonathan Carver's, who in 1692 examined certain witchcraft suspects in the S. W. second-storey room. I enclose a view of this house—shewing it as it was about 75 years ago. Since then an unsightly commercial addition has been made to the eastern end of the structure.

Sorry to hear of the mishap to your typewriter, & hope it can soon be repaired. It certainly is an admirable machine when it works!

(*)Yidamer is my creation of Yiddish-American now the speech of all New Yorkers.

Barlow expects to move westward around Sept. 1st, but is uncertain about his ability to pause in New York. He sends you his best regards, & shares my regret that your stay in Providence could not have been longer. My aunt also sends her most cordial remembrances.

With every good wish, & renewed thanks for the sight of the Kuttner letters, I remain

Most sincerely yours,

H P Lovecraft

Notes

1. Henry Kuttner (1915–1958), weird fiction writer and late correspondent of HPL. For HPL's letters to him, see *Letters to C. L. Moore and Others*.
2. Kenneth Sterling and his friend (unidentified).

[32]   [ALS, JHL]

66 College St.,
Providence, R.I.,
Sept. 14, 1936.

Dear Dr. de Castro:—

Thanks very much for the prompt biographical response, which I forwarded at once to Moe. Our idle churchyard diversion surely is awaking an amusing extended series of echoes! I note with interest your version of Moe's lines. The word after *fancy's* was WINE. Pardon the poor script—the only possible clue, I fear, was the corresponding rhyme-word LINE. As to the name *Edgar* in the text—as I said last month, there is certainly no rule or even custom in English literature which excludes the spelled-out word from the body of the acrostic. Indeed, in Parker's Aid to Composition (the standard old-time work from which I learned rhetoric many a decade ago) the typical specimen acrostic given has the spelled-out word occurring in the text. Therefore no legitimate objection can be offered to the course followed by Moe, Barlow, & myself. Well—it will be interesting to see whether any further echoes are aroused by our late pastime![1]

Sorry that Kleiner couldn't handle the fiction—although it was the treatise material which I thought would be offered him. Hope he has landed a permanent position—which he certainly needed badly enough. Wish I could tackle the story you mention, but I don't see a chance of assuming anything new in 1936. I am utterly driven to the wall as it is—with a rhetorical textbook on my hands which must be done at a certain date,[2] & a discouraging waiting-list of other tasks after that. So much time was spent away from my desk during the summer social season, that I must plug like hell at the work which piled up during the lax period!

Glad you've heard again from Kuttner, & very much flattered to hear of his high opinion of my work. He is an extremely brilliant youth whose future course will be well worth watching.

Thanks for the interesting & tantalising Havana card. Wish we could all get down there—for I dread the coming winter. I never succeeded in reaching Cuba, although I expected to do so during a long trip in 1931. When, however, I reached Key West, I found I was too broke to continue. So I've been within 90 miles of the goal without making it. Whether I'll ever get there in the future rests with the gods.

Barlow left here Sept. 1ˢᵗ, & hoped to see you in N.Y. I don't know what digressions his programme included, but I trust he'll be able to include the call before he finally leaves the east. Had a pleasant visit from James F. Morton Sept. 11–12–13—he has now gone to Cambridge for the Harvard Tercentenary exercises.

Wright rejected the Barlow, Moe, & HPL acrostics when they were sent in, because he had already taken one. Now that the ball has stated rolling, we'll probably let one of the little "fan magazines" print the three efforts.

With all good wishes—& hoping that you don't dread the oncoming autumn & winter as badly as I do—

Yrs most sincerely,
H P L

Notes

1. Moe's poem was "In a Providence Churchyard." Henry Kuttner also wrote an acrostic (but not in "sonnet" form), "Where He Walked."
2. *Well Bred Speech*, revised for Anne Tillery Renshaw.

[33]   [ALS, JHL]

66 College St.,
Providence, R.I.,
Nov. 8, 1936.

Dear Dr. de Castro:—

Thanks exceedingly for sending me young Kuttner's letter, which sheds a highly interesting side-light upon my brilliant new correspondent. He seems to be a good deal like me in many ways—in that he is not very gregarious, not fond of spirits, & not much given to exercise or calculativeness. But he is a great deal more practical & versatile than I am—able to grind out saleable pulp material with a minimum of effort—& will undoubtedly get farther along in the world than I ever shall. I herewith return the letter—with renewed expressions of appreciation.

I read your altered version of my Poe acrostic with much interest, & feel flattered that you should have devoted so much attention to it. Did I tell you that my friend Moe's acrostic, with the comic last line removed (& the internal changes necessitated by this removal made), will be included in a Wisconsin Poetry Anthology which young August W. Derleth is editing for the N.Y. publisher Henry Harrison? And has Kuttner shewn you the Poe acrostic (in anapaests—not a sonnet) which he wrote in emulation of ours? Verily, an amusing series of echoes came from Little Bobby's idle notion of writing a Poe acrostic while seated on an ancient tomb on a summer's afternoon! Incidentally, Barlow & I will probably place our acrostics in one of the many weird-fiction "fan" magazines. As to the question of the two versions of mine—I may stick to my original in most essentials, for reasons which I'll list as per request. In line 3 I like the solemn effect of the two *spondees & pyrrhics* which replace iambics at the beginning of the line

<blockquote>¯ ¯ / ¯ ¯ / ˘ ˘   ˘ ¯   ˘ ¯
Great elms / rise sol / emnly   by slab   and mound</blockquote>

I also like the phonetic value (& associative value as well) of the word *solemnly*. In line 4 I want the *visual* image supplied by *Arch'd*. I also want the element of the churchyard's *hiddenness*—of its being a little elder world apart from the modern world—emphasised. More than that, I have a suspicion that the phrase *happy hearts* inclines too much toward the hackneyed & the sentimental. Even if it does not, it seems somehow not to blend with the keynote-mood of the verses. In the next line I do not want to lose the impression of the scene as a *single* one. In the line after that I do not want to lose the second spondaic foot, *leaves whisp—*, or the alliterative effect of *dead* & *departed*. Also, I dislike having an *inversion* (noun before adjective) if it can possibly be avoided. Coming down to the sestette & its second line—I do not want to lose the original image of the spectre's gliding along *all* the aisles of the churchyard instead of only *one*. That, though, is a very minor point—as is also the point of the slight repetitive effect of "*a* spectre . . . *a* path." Also rather minor is the fact that I'd like to keep the spondee at the opening of the line . . . . . although it *is* somewhat important to keep the constant "te tum, te tum" of pure iambics properly varied with occasional spondees & pyrrhics. The real point is that I do not wish to sacrifice the word *aisles** & the image that goes with it. A *path* is just a line of access. An *aisle* is a passage *between things*—with the added overtone of solemnity imparted by its being primarily a side-passage in a church of the traditional basilica type. Going down two lines more—if I retain the original form of line 11, it will be for two reasons. First, because I prefer the *intransitive* to the transitive use of *peal*. Second, because one ought to eliminate *pairs of adjectives joined with "and"* whenever possible. One might add as a third reason the now badly hackneyed nature of the word *weird*, whose over-use has almost rendered it ineligible for serious literary composi-

---

*I also want to save the phonetic value of the combination *aisles . . . old*—one of the two later insertions.

tion. However—one never can tell. Many of these points are mere matters of taste, & arbitrary opinions are rash. In any case I surely appreciate the attention & effort expended upon this impromptu half-hour's diversion, & I am grateful for the criticla [*sic*] exercise precipitated by the analysis. It may yet cause alteration in the text if I think the verses worth that much energy!

I'm sorry to hear that your health has not been unbrokenly good, but glad you are now feeling better. Don't over-exert, & I'm sure you'll find the winter a comfortable one—indoors, at least! My aunt's curve of recovery continues to be a steadily ascending one—& she sends you her sincerest regards.

The advance of autumn has terminated my outdoor reading & writing sessions, but occasional rural walks extended far into October. This autumn I acquired the custom of haunting a wooded hill—Neutaconkanut—on the western rim of the town, whence a series of marvellous views of outspread city & adjacent countryside may be obtained. I had often ascended it before, but have only recently examined & appreciated the exquisitely mystical sylvan scenery—curious mounds, flower-starred meadows, & hushed hidden valleys—beyond its crest. On a smaller scale, it is as attractive as those Quinsnicket or Lincoln woods which I shewed you last August—it will certainly become a favourite goal of mine next season.

Heard an interesting lecture on early R.I. astronomy the other night at the college—during which there was exhibited the old reflecting telescope used in observing the transit of Venus here on June 3, 1769.

All good wishes——Yrs most cordially——HPL

[34]   [ALS, JHL]

66 College St.,
Providence, R.I.,
Feby. 17, 1937.

Dear Dr. de Castro:—

Your news of Feb. 1st was just saved from being a surprise by a bulletin from our brilliant young friend Kuttner. As I told him, it was rather unfortunate that the West Coast had to welcome you with a spell of bad weather—but after all, a knowledge of climatic averages gives you the certainty that your move is indeed an advantageous one in the long run. I am very glad to hear that you are comfortably settled amidst familiar objects. Despite the element of pathos in the reminders of ampler days, I really think that they form a much more homelike & consoling environment than utterly strange objects could. At least, I have found it so in my own case. Our furniture, pictures, objets d'art, &c. here are only a last scrap of what we had at my birthplace; & yet I could not possibly exist in any other setting. I would be completely lost & adrift if I could not look about me & see at least a few of the accustomed objects at which I have gazed ever since I had consciousness.

I am glad that you still have some of the pictures & other things collected by yourself & Mrs. de Castro, & feel sure that their ultimate effect will be one of consolation rather than melancholy. I am glad, too, that you have unearthed some of your own scholarly MSS. Your linguistic experiments sound intensely interesting. One always has the feeling, when comparing the student's slow acquisition of a new tongue with his original quick grasp of his mother tongue in infancy, that there must be some natural linguistic method upon which pedagogy has not yet hit. Many attempts have been made to find such a method, but so far nothing very successful has seen publication. It is pleasant to know that some of your books are still with you—especially the classic poets. The Hawthorne item is surely an interesting treasure!

Kuttner was extremely glad to see you, & I am sure that you & he must have had some delightfully interesting conversations. He is certainly one of the most promising youths I have yet run across; & if he keeps up at his present rate, will certainly be heard from in the literary field. The worst obstacle in his way is of course the need to write cheap stories in the artificial technique demanded by such low-grade magazines as *Terror Tales* & *Thrilling Mystery;* but I think he has the energy & independence to do this in a sort of glibly inattentive way which will leave his real literary faculties free for more solid work. He is one of those fortunate persons who can concoct a saleable formula-story with almost no time or effort—so that his commercial work in that line will not injure his style as it would if more careful application were demanded. I am surely glad that his mother provides such a congenial & encouraging home setting—a vast asset in any literary career. He has spoken of the possibility of making an eastern trip during the coming year—in which case we shall all be abundantly glad to see him.

About our eternally-echoing acrostic series—I did not mean to imply that the rule of not mentioning the acrosticised name in the text might not be a good idea. I simply pointed out that such a rule has not been generally recognised in English literature, as attested by a wide variety of acrostics from responsible sources. Enclosed is Moe's mimeographed booklet containing our several effusions—a copy of which he asked me to send you. I fear that, through some error, the version of your text included is not the latest one; but I trust you can forgive this oversight in view of the booklet's limited circulation.

I trust you enjoyed a reasonably pleasant Yuletide. We had a tree & various other symbols of the season. Among my gifts the most distinctive was perhaps the yellowed & crumbling fragments of a long-interred human skull—exhumed from an Indian mound on the Maryland Eastern Shore by one of my correspondents.[1]

Our eastern winter has been phenomenally mild, but poor health has prevented me from being very active. A few exposures to cold weather in December started an old winter malady of mine—persistently swollen feet & ankles which force me to wear old shoes cut & stretched—& now I have a sort of lingering intestinal grippe which is proving very troublesome & debilitating. I barely have strength to keep up & get around, & have had to curtail many of my activities. My aunt has also suffered from a touch of grippe.

During recent weeks I have been trying to brush up on one of my old subjects—astronomy—after 20 or 30 years. The progress of the science has left me absurdly behind—but not long ago I received a request for some articles which forced me to cover the last decades as best I might.[2] Our public library has some excellent new books on the subject—the text book by J. C. Duncan & the layman's manuals by Bartky & Stokeley being apparently the best short cuts for the utterly non-mathematical amateur.

All good wishes, & hoping that the California climate will soon begin to live up to its reputation—
 Yrs most sincerely—
 H P L

Later—grippe has the upper hand at the moment. Doctor has me taking 3 different nostrums simultaneously, & am up only a little while each day. Shall have to curtail all activities for the balance of the winter.

Notes

1. Willis Conover, Jr. (1920–1996), editor of *Science-Fantasy Correspondent* and a late correspondent of HPL. For HPL's letters to him, see *Letters to Robert Bloch and Others*.
2. On this matter see HPL to August Derleth, [17 February 1937] *Essential Solitude* 768–69.

Alfred Galpin

Appendix

Alfred Galpin

Mystery

O Man! For what, through infinite aeons, hast thou been striving? For what toilest thou in the monastery, for what delveth thy Science? For what but hounding thy Supreme Lord and Maker, Mystery? What, in thy scale, is the lowest of Humanity? Is it not he, if indeed he exists, in whom there is no longing to *Know*—for whom MYSTERY has no charm? And who the highest, but he whose labors have been most nearly and effectively concentrated toward dispelling that rainbow cloud, Mystery? Truly the aim of thy overlapping days is following to their hidden and unthinkable lairs the greatest possible number of alluring, spectral mysteries.

And yet, what would be thy fate if thou shouldst attain the climax of thy advancing hopes? For what wouldst thou live, O Improphetic? What would thy brain, strained to its corporeal limits of development by the moiling struggle, aid thee? What would become of thy very soul, grown to its fulness of strength and beauty by the food of Perplexity and devouring starvation without it? O pity the Being, for whom there should be no Mystery, no life of mysteries, if, perchance, he should scratch the surface of one, and finding hidden therein the unsounded and immeasurable depths of the Infinite Mystery of LIFE, should find need to pass on.

Ah, Man! Thou art indeed bespoken for a sightless and lovable fool; toiling for the fascination of the toil, and vitally mortal without it; raising thyself against the revealing earth, only to find new breadths of panorama, only to meet with new and greater evils. And truly, it speaketh well for the Eternal Beneficience of Things, that the inevitable and omnipresent LAW checks thee, striving for Psychocide; that all things operate toward Good and toward Evil; that action equals reaction; that all Things have a use and a corresponding abuse; the Eternal and Omnipotent Balance.

So, toil on, O Man! With thy petty troubles of the hour; with thy delving science; with thy selfish, with thy fools, with thy wise, with thy noble. Toil on! What though Eternity; what though Infinity flow and heed thee not? *Strive blindly toward the light that kills, for the Eternal Hills and Valleys will preserve!*

Two Loves

(After, and with apologies to, Miss Elsie Alice Gidlow in the June *Vagrant.*)

I have two loves, who haunt me unceasingly.
Which shall I choose?

One is ugly to men's sight, and arouses repulsion in them;
Not so to me; for I know the true heart within.
Yes, he is ugly and repulsive to the many—
His robust mien and his plebeian companions dishonour him.
But they are as he:
For his heart is as pure gold, the gold
Scorned in sham by the would-be poetic, but ever true and useful.

He is constant, and I could love him forever;
Yea, with dishonour stamped on his brow by the mob, I yet do love him.
For his heart is as the heart of a thrifty and comely woman sought by all of thought.

He hath a hard skin, and is difficult of acquaintance;
But to him who searcheth beneath, he is a rich mine of delicious treasure.

In my sensuous dreams I behold him, and long for him;
When all the world is heartless and I am weary of it,
Then do I long for him.

The other I would shun; for he is traitorously fair and beauteous:
But he draws me to him inevitably, as the raft through many streams to the ocean.

His soul burneth as the hot torrents that prompt love—
Ever youthful and daring in heart, but changing ere ultimately carefree;
Inspiring hesitant fear at a distance, but enticing and ever victorious.

He is not constant,
Except as he forceth me to everlasting constancy;
For he is exacting.
He draws me to him and I drink of his luscious beauty—
But O the aftermath! The satient afterwhile!

He would destroy me;
He has become a part of my soul, and meaneth my ruin;
And yet I should die without him.

His beauty sparkles, and is given fastidious care.
His speech flows swiftly and fluently, and is the language of all who are
    subject to his sway.
Yea, him I long for passionately, and the other is only a comfort.

I have two loves who woo me unceasingly:
One is bologna and the other Scotch Whiskey:
Which shall I take?

Selenaio-Phantasma

Dedicated to the Author of "Nemesis"

In Elysium-fann'd fields of my slumber,
In the wild-tinted beauties of night,
I have feasted on sights without number,
Recreated all Heav'n with my sight:
And I wake to the sunrise at dawning, fit close to the dusk's mad delight.

Shadow'd visions of beauties unpainted,
Shifting sights of a Heaven beyond,
Primal nature in pureness untainted,
Without Man and his slave-making wand,
Meet my sight in procession uncanny, unorder'd, and link'd without bond.

Mingling phantoms above Man's poor notion,
Phantasmas obscure and unknown,
Undulations and waves of wild motion
Into infinite variance grown,
I behold in my slumbers of madness, from far shores of mad Cynthia blown.

I have seen things of cryptical meaning,
Hinting life far above mortal view;
Superstitions of primitive gleaning
Blend with fancy to forms strange and new;
And my fetterless brain leaps the mountain of Science and dreams 'tis not true.

All the hopes of a life are entwined
With the greed of a fancy unchain'd,
While my thoughts, by the sleep undermined,
Wander wordless, uncheck'd, uncontain'd
O'er unearthly expanses of Spiritland, haunting where once they had reign'd.

When, in midst of this immundane dreaming
Come effulgent the first rays of light,
Bringing back my rapt soul with their beaming,
Lending splendour to all within sight;
And I wake to the sunrise at dawning, fit close to the dusk's mad delight.

Remarks to My Handwriting

First form'd by Ibis in Egyptian mud,
Beside the hungry Nile's receding flood,
Thou next becam'st a sacred hieroglyph,
Awkward and cramp'd—gracelessly made and stiff.
Skipping the centuries and the Central Sea,
Latium and France, thou now inhabit'st me.

Yesterday's hen-tracks! Egypt, thou art curst!
Thy offspring's best is but a *pig*-pen's worst!
Could I but change the scrawl to fit my thoughts . . . .
But no—thou mak'st the same old row of blots.
My words are English, but the products strange
When stubborn Ibis waddles without change.
One blessing only lighteneth my load:
Thou art my language and my cipher code!

Marsh-Mad

A Nightmare

So stifling and oppressive had grown the dank, murkily thickening air of the swamp, that an overwhelming dread of the foul sentience of the vegetation and very atmosphere about me clutched clammily at my senses. The moon-streaked clouds to the north grew more spectrally dark and billowed on toward me. About me clung an all-pervading and indefinite stench that seemed a portent of some grim evil, hypnotic and dreadful. The sudden and unnatural darkness rendered every object in the gloomy swamp vague and ominous. There could be no doubt in my fear-harassed mind that these surroundings, so recently intended for the mere scene of a sportsman's lark, had assumed an aspect of mysterious, thaumaturgic terror.

The omnipresent silence of the place had long irked me strangely. In vain did I attempt to forget my surroundings. I struggled to concentrate my thoughts on the home I had left behind me, but no effort of mind could bring it any nearer than it actually, tantalisingly was; nor could it drive out the sight of this dismal marsh which threatened me at every hand. I tried to think over the many events of my active past, but I obtained only a dim recollection which seemed that of another man, who had lived and died long æons past. All pretense was now fast failing me, and I was forced to confront my situation, unpalatable as it might be, and to renew my long-abandoned efforts to find the path.

The rank vegetation, discolored and overgrown with masses of stagnant, creeping slime, yielded an odor indescribably reminiscent of all the horror of dead things; while the weird, glimmering light turned to a weirder shade under a forbidding canopy of exotic, distorted trees. I was indeed isolated from all that meant a normal state of life, in which Man reigned unhampered by the inexplicable; and the invisible terror of the fen crushed prostratingly upon me . . . . . . And now, as heavy clouds crawled overhead ill-bodingly, a new sense of dumb dread seized me. I felt that the dynamic silence and seeming-solitude of the swamp were soon to be rent asunder in the cataclysmic revelation of the unthinkably HORRIBLE.

How bitterly did I now regret the rashness which had sent me into the unexplored paludal recesses, notoriously teeming with goblindom—which had sent me unescorted and all but unprotected, with the warnings of those who should know dinning against my resolute deafness! . . . . . . I could barely ascertain, with the aid of my pocket compass, the northerly direction in which might lie the commonplace security for which I now so intensely yearned; but ere I might strike out thither a bursting clap as of the explosion of the gaseous atmosphere in that region, precluded the possibility of seeking refuge there. There was the rush of a devastating typhoon to the north, and I fled, panic-stricken, from that which I knew was now inevitable.

As I fled, new terrors made my frenzied path one of such utter fright, that I thought only of fleeing on and on, till flight was no longer possible; but at least till I should succumb in action, and not to the awful influences of the morass. Had I been calmer, I should have admitted the uselessness of this precipitation, and clung to some strong support until the storm had vented itself; but to hesitate, to seek shelter amongst all this—better by far a death of resistance, however mad and inutile! I fled on. The rush of stinking rain seemed a vast excretion which partook of the most noxious characteristics of the swamp. My legs dragged through rotten pools swelling to their angriest filth from the descending torrents. Vile animalculæ swarmed upon me, and my body was racked and torn in concert with my distracted mind.

A newly-impelled sheet of vivid rain swept over the marsh, and lashed its waters into torrents of seething destruction. I was picked up like a rotten log and hurried irresistibly onward.

Grasping all that might impede my course, as unwelcome as my voluntary flight had been relieving, I at first found nothing save yielding slime. At length, as my desperation reached its utmost, my outstretched hands encountered a low-bending limb of a gigantic tree, standing in sinister safety amid the wreck of all about it. A blast of wind seemed to make its branches twirl horribly upward, and I was tossed higher and higher, refused refuge until reaching a high limb I lost consciousness in its foliage. And such a sleep! . . . .

The huge trunk which sheltered me aroused in me an unutterable repulsion, a limitless loathing. Its vilely verdant bark impressed me as most closely resembling the scaly skin of an enormous lizard, and its tremendous limbs seemed to coil about me like savage serpents . . . . Assuredly I was mad! This monstrous organism must indeed be alive! Its great limbs I shed wildly—but against the path of the storm. I peered again. There could be no doubt of it. I heard delirious shrieks as its lesser limbs were torn from it. Its loathsome luxuriance nauseated me. I raved and shrieked in gibbering mania as the incredible Thing writhed and whirled in a world apart from that comforting, sanely furious storm.

I felt the slimy, murderous juices of the Thing eat into my soul. I fell into a lethal state of such pacific horror as no man can feel and remain sane. I felt within me the growing enslavement of the victim of the python, but mine—if it were possible, I shuddered—was of both mind and body. I visualized the unthinkable—saw ridiculous but blanching, revolting visions of the bull slowly succumbing to the gastric juices of the boa . . . . . . and always was that inward sense of grisly decay, a rapid leprosy which embraced my entire being. I screamed aloud in horror. My scream re-echoed and I screamed again. The universe had nothing in it but screams, echoes, screams and unending putrefaction. . . . .

I awoke to find the maggoty corpse of a huge buzzard upon my breast, cast there by the powerful wind of the previous night. Below me lay the swamp, ineffably wet but still navigable; but how prosaic a sight in the cheerful morning sun! I threw back my head and breathed in the pure air of dawn. All about me was the beautiful foliage of Nature; and beyond, not a quarter of a mile to the southeast, lay the fields that spelled home.

The Critic

Clarice is large and blonde, and somewhat dead;
　　But still not quite so dull as first she seems.
She's too self-conscious to be quite well bred;
　　Her face, though handsome, fails to haunt my dreams.

Peggy's a radiant thing, *petite* and gay,
　　As pink and plump and small as one might find;
Her nose is past conception retrousee,
　　Then, too, I fear she's shallow as her kind.

Marie's a puzzle: Prettiest of all
　　Or too anæmic? Innocent or wise?
She's cute and clever, slight but not too small,
　　But still, with her I'm never well at ease.

Then there are others—hosts of them, in fact,
　　Who take my eye—unknown more oft than not;
But I have no philandering, smooth tact,
　　And so the most of them are soon forgot.

So after all, in writing distant Syb
   That *cher enfant* of high society—
With her amusing genius for the fib,
   There's fun as much as flirting with the three!

Stars

The glow of youth was in his eyes as he rapped at the first door. A fair maiden appeared in the threshold. The sun glowed white with passion, low in the east.

"Observe the stars," spoke the maiden.

"Ah, there are none while the sun shines; none but your eyes," he replied. She smiled.

"Come in!" and he entered. The room was pink, and sweet with the odor of roses.

"Here will I abide forever with you," whispered the youth.

And when he had feasted upon her eyes, he said, "There are more stars. I must find them."

So he knocked at the second door. There was no answer; then the youth battered it down. The room within was set in golden colors, and filled with strange devices and hidden places. The sun without shone upon the room, and there were reflected the beams of innumerable stars. But the maiden was sorrowful at leaving the first room.

"Observe the stars," she warned, minding sad thoughts.

"Indeed, do they not shine brilliantly here!" exclaimed the man. So they labored with strange devices and searched the hidden nooks for many stars, until they were both gray and aweary with labor. When the dusk impended, they rested and sighed.

"The stars are of tinsel!" cried the man. "See, the dusk is near and they shine but leadenly. But look: is there not a marvelous light playing about next door! There indeed are real stars."

Gathering fair robes about them, he strode in dignity to the third door. It was broad open, and shut behind them. The room was dark with evening, and there were no stars within. When they looked forth, they saw that the glow came from the rooms behind them. They sat and regarded; but they were not comforted.

"There, assuredly, may be the stars; but we cannot reach them," he lamented. And as he sorrowed night came above, but it was not blackness. For far overhead stretched the ribbon of the Milky Way; and countless others, too, gave light.

"Behold! Observe the stars!" cried the woman; and "Behold!" echoed the man. So they drank in the sombre beauty of the infinite stars.

And as they looked, they saw in each other's eyes the gleaming of the brightest of stars.

Some Tendencies of Modern Poetry

Poetry, like everything else, is undergoing an upheaval. Democracy, a mere shadow in politics, is felt everywhere in the realm of art, corrupting whatever it touches. No longer is literature sacred; but rather it is a means of amusement to the reader, or profit to the writer. So vast is the sea of mediocrity, that each author strives for originality; not within himself, where only genius can look—but to strange forms, forbidden subjects, even to the unspeakably commonplace. To be an artist is unheard of—is it not better to revel amidst shattered idols than to do the things that others have done better before us? So they cry; and with their probings they have perverted the whole trend of English poetry.

Not but that such an upheaval may bring about some things of benefit. Of course the critical-minded iconoclast contributes his share to the progress of art; but he does not contribute art itself. Hence I propose to examine fairly, not the poetry it has produced, but the tendencies themselves that mark modern poetry. Loosely speaking, there are three general notions held by the various revolutionaries. They must ineluctably overlap, and sometimes they become as one; but the theoretical lines of demarcation nevertheless exist. They are, then: first, the cult of impressionism, or a revolution in poetic inspiration; second, the cult of realism, of the commonplaces and routine affairs of life—or a revolution in poetic subject matter; third, the cult of *vers libre*, or a revolution in poetic form. Each of these creeds, as expounded by its most vigorous enthusiasts, is extreme; yet each will no doubt contribute something fundamental to the thought and conceptions of succeeding generations.

Of these three creeds, the first is probably the least reasonable. The poet sits down to composition: Does he rack his brain for thoughts, or work himself into a "fine frenzy" of inspiration? No. The poet, with an effort which becomes easy with constant practice, goes to sleep, arrests himself in the process, and hastily jots down the discordant and disconnected thoughts of the moment. His impressions have but one virtue as poetry: they are indisputably sensuous. But are they simple? impassioned? musical? artistic? do they interpret life? Most emphatically do they fail. The reason obviously is that the "poet" negates intellect. He merely detaches his thinking faculties from his perceptive faculties, and allows the latter to run amuck over the printed page, adorned with rows of dots, dashes, and pretty irregular ripples of text division. So is Amy Lowell, descanting at painful length on her impressions of taking a bath. There is nothing of interpretation here. Even could the impressionist make his work musical and lend it some breath of poetic life, (as some quite frequently do,) there is that fundamental requisite of interpretation lacking. Less violently, impressionism consists in devotion to nothing but the superficial, ignoring basic facts, and the fault is therefore always the same. Like the realist, the impressionist takes out his notebook and copies down a fact or two, leaving the really vital part of the process to the reader. Literature is nothing if not an *interpretation of life;* and mental effort, artistic selection, artistic presentation, all enter primarily into interpretation. These the mere impressionist lacks.

What benefit, if any, may come then from this ephemeral fad? I doubt if anything substantial will result; but at least the great principle of the vividness, the necessity, of concrete detail, has been recognized. Seen through the transcending, imaginative eye of the future, there is wonderful raw material for poetry here. Then, too, imagism has called attention to that fascinating trick of dreaming into semi-consciousness, which may yet serve to the benefit of the poet. So far, it has been productive of much clever phrasing and occasional patches of quaint or even of beautiful imagery.

It is difficult to speak of the tendencies of realism without departing from poetry, which alone is our topic. The desire for lively detail, too, is at the core of all "strictly modern" letters. The extension of this principle into poetry, I believe, is a problem which will perplex critic and poet alike for decades; but it seems inevitable that Realism must, as representative of the whole age, conquer for that age at least. The whole problem must rest in the æsthetic tastes of the future. If there be anything beautiful, anything worthy of perpetuation in poesy, in Chicago or the life of the average American, Carl Sandburg and Edgar Lee Masters have certainly spied it; but their very means of communicating it introduces the vital question as to the possibility of adapting the exalted forms of poetry to such subjects. If one uses the forms of the past, shall they not be inappropriate? And if one invents new forms, shall they be poetry? It will be seen that this problem includes all that is really vital in the study of poetry today. If America is to contribute anything as individual to English poetry as the short-story to English prose, it will unquestionably be along such lines. But it is doubtful if even the most democratic public mind will long tolerate any great innovation in this respect; for the sublime notes of past centuries upon centuries of accumulating achievement cannot be forgotten—unless indeed our marked degradation in spoken language tells of a change that calls for a new Chaucer of the common people. Even then the foundations of art will not give way. Art must, after all is said and done, be based upon its effect; and the most profound arguments of those who argue principles rather than means, have been brought to naught by the operation of that one neglected principle.

To particularize, then: Realism can only endure as a vital force in poetry as far as it does not nullify the underlying precepts of poetic art. It is to be hoped that the more commonplace types of realism will be confined to prose; that life-as-it-is will not invade poetry of its own virtue, but only selectly, when it contains the loftiness, the beauty, the interest or the passion that is demanded by its vehicle. If hopes will not prevent mistakes at least the reasoning back of hope will force only the worthy to endure; and what endures is alone really worthy of consideration.

The final and most relevant topic of speculation today is in the matter of poetic form. Here there can be no absolutely set dogmas, and the only bounds to experiment can be those of our language and of good taste. Many projectors of inquiry into this field are mere untalented anarchists, making up in audacity what they lack in technique; but there are others who have based their productions upon thorough investigation and good authority. They cite Greek and Latin poetry, early alliterative verse, Japanese, Chinese and other Oriental odes, and could if they cared make much of English blank verse, which is most effective when least distinctively iambic pentameter. Propounding claims little dissimilar from those of Milton, they extend them with intention to revolutionize all poetic form. Their radicals are the inessentiality of rhyme and the independence of rhythm from mathematical, formal rules. This would appear to be a new field for the pioneer; but is it not merely starting anew from the ancient truth which, after centuries of development, have produced our present-day prosody? They forget that the Greeks, the Latins, the Orientals, were not lacking in definite rules; and that these rules were perfectly adapted to the language with which they dealt. So, too, have rules been built up for this language of ours—English, which is still American also. And what are the rules they would propose instead? (assuming that they offer rules, which the more reasonable would do). Fundamentally, they are merely these of simple rhythm, the simple rhythm of prose. The modernist would cast aside the "diagrams" of prosody, in the belief that the freer measures of prose are better suited to his art. [A quotation from *Poetry: A Magazine of Verse* of October, 1918, is typical:

"When . . . Mr. Masters touches on the iambic tetrameter of the *Spoon River* poems, it is hard to see how the term can be of more than faint interest to him. For one thing, it belongs to a lame science, one failing . . . to take note of the large delicate measures possible to prose. . . . Prosody at best provides the poet with but a set of diagrams more or less diverting, of which certainly a work of art, intact, complete, like the *Spoon River Anthology*, bears no trace."]

The selection goes on in painful obscurity, so I have quoted only the more intelligent portions. It would seem here that the modernist is sick of mathematical rules. Wishing to start out on his own resources, he scorns the products of finer tastes than his own. Viewing him thus, we can only tell him that if he prefers prose, let him use it. There is no subtlety in defending the intricate harmonies of prose; rather such a defense is sorely needed in this cacophonic age. And it is with prose, I believe, that this movement will ultimately deal the most; it is prose that will be enriched. If, however, we are to undergo a long period of experimentation with new forms, it is to be doubted whether the research will come to much. The pioneer will be followed by the perfecters; and perfection only comes with definiteness, which we certainly have already. Still, even if innovators are not the best of artists, it is possible that they may perform great services. The realm of blank verse—not of polyphonic prose—is comparatively unexplored beyond the classic heroic line; and if experimentation will serve only to illuminate the distinctions between prose and poetry, it will more than justify itself. Especially will this be so if it finds better means of adapting rhythm to the thought—the real aim of the entire movement.

However this may be, but one fact is evident: That the present age is one of speculation rather than of performance. I have endeavored to point out to what this speculation may eventually come. It will indubitably enrich prose; it should gradually open the way for new fields of expression in the domain of human events; it should clarify man's ideas on poetic form and poetic expression; it should act as a purgative of false notions and ignorant iconoclasm. When this shall have been done, the way will be open to an age that should immortalize American literature.

The Spoken Tongue

Have you ever stopped to consider what really terrible concessions you must make to spoken language? The man of any human contact must keep a dialect and a special grammar up his sleeve for every class he meets—and he who denies the existence of classes affirms that the section hand talks like a college professor. Such instability of course indicates constant changing of the language; and though my youth may be responsible for the impression, it seems to me that this change is progressing more rapidly every year. The tendency is in the age—together with the split infinitive, "Literary Digest" spelling (even though abandoned) and other amiable freaks.

The ridiculousness of the idea that English has any grammar was brought to me in the few weeks prior to my attendance at a fraternity "formal." My Professors, seniors, juniors, and even lower forms of college addressed me, others, and each other regarding their expected presence at this or some other one of the constituents of "formal" time. They all, with few exceptions, used the form "Who are you gonna take—?" The remainder, as I recollect, said "going" or even allowed themselves the luxuring of a "planning." But not one of this host used "whom." This is the more remarkable in an age in which reading plays so incomparably prominent a part; and the worst newspaper English seldom falls into such errors as the best of us use each day in conversation.

The French, of course, like being told what to say, and their language is the better for it. But all modern language shows a tendency toward monosyllabic expression and dependence upon word order or voice inflection rather than upon grammatical forms. If English is allowed to progress for another century at its present pace, we shall have an interesting product. Two-thirds of the verbs will be compounded with prepositions—even as the Ancient Romans, perhaps—but the prepositions will come after the verb. Witness the innumerable compounds of everyday speech—look out for, look after, look into, look down upon—I have chosen a bad verb for illustration but you may make your own mixtures. Where will our parts of speech be? Especially when the use of the same word in noun, verb and adjective form is becoming so prevalent. Then, too, if spoken language conquers we may have something like Chinese, where voice inflection tells the difference between profanity and a word of thanks. The necessity for some greater master of modern idiom, who shall yet be a scholar and a literary genius, is evident. Oh for another Shakespeare! Without him and his even more influential fellow, Chaucer, should we be speaking French, German, or low Latin today?

The World Situation

The League of Nations is dead; and its greatest supporter has linked his name with the greatest political tragedy of world history. Europe is in chaos. The pitiful council of powerless prestidigitators which still chooses to call itself a League of Nations, is doing nothing to check the plague of wars and uprisings that is sweeping over the recent battlegrounds. Russia, potentially the world's greatest power, is overrun with simple-minded children busy burning their fingers; while what effect she does have on the outside world is disastrous. Germany, sinned and now sinned against, is emulating Russia; and the only survivors seem to be many insignificant neutrals and the nations which seemed destined for the greatest things of the future—Japan, China, England and America.

This is a pessimistic picture; but the most contrarily opinionated person can deny but little of it. Still, I do not wish to be an apostle of desolate despair. Things are indeed in a pretty pass, but before the heyday of our little geoid, Satan demonstrated that wagons which are hitched to a star fall with exceeding force. Instead of placidly tending severally to their own affairs, nations chose in various ways to mix in the world. Some tried to conquer—too many. Others were defenders; others, though also partaking of the preceding classes, had world welfare in mind. From the sorry discord which has resulted, the only cure would seem to be that each large nation resume its own business, interfering only with occasional aid to the downtrodden. It is a disheartening enough end to such a grand affair as our recent World War; but though many refuse to see it, it would appear inevitable.

Here in America, there is less of suffering than of sheer folly. Political ties were forgotten—now they are back again, as bad as ever. Extravagance and other national peccadilloes are in turn asserting themselves; and the only survival of the wartime period seems to be profound hatred for those who don't believe the way we do. But withal we are not starving; the humble workingman, whose slum-born misery has so long been our leading recreation, seems to be enjoying himself; and our quadrennial festival, the Presidential Campaign, seems to be bringing out in all intensity the best and worst in our community existence. There is little to do but strive for sanity and decry the malignant abnormalities of the day. Never, however, ought we to lose sight of the fact that—however we may be interested in promoting our own affairs first—our "splendid isolation" is no more, and that inter-relation has not in the past meant inevitable friendship and amity. Sick as we are of war, it is no phantom which can be "boo-ed" away with disbelief, or considerate germ to be frightened away by the contagious sign of the day before. Adequate preparation to insure international standing in the great international business of war, is the one real lesson which comes to us out of the conflict.

The United's Policy 1920–1921

The ideal of pure literature paramount and unalloyed.

The conduct of the official organ as an exponent of the best in amateur writing, conservative but representative, and impartial in all controversies.

Assimilation of existing recruits rather than intensive recruiting. Promotion of local clubs according to the principles of earlier administrations, especially the Hoffman administration. Closer binding of clubs to the general association, and greater notice for the detached member.

Encouragement of open discussion of all matters concerning the amateur public, save that political contentions be avoided as far as possible. An impartial and receptive attitude toward all literary questions and disputes.

Encouragement of publishing both individual and co-operative, and recognition of mimeographed and circulated magazines on a basis of equality with printed magazines.

Recognition of the vital distinction between public and private criticism. Greater notice and enlarged personnel for the private bureau. Gradual development of the public bureau into a general topical review of important representative, current amateur literature. (Acknowledgment of current literary tastes as significant if only ephemeral. A. G. Jr.) (Preservation of sound literary ideals in defiance of contemporary decadence. H. P. L.)

Removal of verse and study laureateship classes, and removal of all restrictions regarding the number of entries necessary to ensure awards. Retention of the Literatus title and restrictions connected therewith.

Consolidation of Secretaryship and Treasurership into one appointive office, and consolidation of the two manuscript bureaux into one.

Elevation of entrance fee to one dollar, and dues to two dollars annually.

Maintenance of a special endowment fund for the official organ.

Attitude of amity toward other associations, neither proselyting nor permitting others to proselyte amongst us.

(Signed)
ALFRED GALPIN, Jr., Pres.
H. P. LOVECRAFT, Official Editor

Form in Modern Poetry

FOREWORD

In putting this essay before the amateur public more than a year after its composition, I feel it essential to declare that it does not represent my attitude at the present moment. I should re-write it, but I am unfortunately less dogmatic in my opinions now, and I should not be able to say so much about it. Briefly, I now regard poetry as rather the essence of all art, independent entirely of form. I should retain the distinction between the two kinds of form, but call poetic form rather VERSE. I am not sure that my conclusions would be essentially at variance with those below, but I am certain that I am now less dominated by professorial card-indices than I appear to be in the essay. The thing is interesting, to me at least, because it represents quite a definite landing-stage in the progress of my thought.

A. G., JR.

The study of form in poetry is to me the most fascinating of pursuits. Poetic distinctions lie at the root of character; and just as everyone feels them, so no one defines them. Every language has its own individual forms, specifically fitted to the national tongue and the national genius. The rude Hebrew sense-rhythm was perfectly adapted to the circumstances of scriptural inspiration; and the prosody of Greece, France or any other race has been a growth depending entirely upon the idiom of that race. In every case, there have been specific rules for imaginative composition, and in every case, these have been differentiated from the rules of plain or prose composition.

In English, twelve centuries of literary evolution have given us some of the most beautiful patterns of versification in any language. These forms have been infinite in possibilities of harmony; flexible, and supremely artistic. The rules lying back of them have not been compulsory. They have been evolved by our finest poetic tastes, and poor taste or bad may use them or leave them as it choose. No poet in the past has achieved immortality—at least as a poet—without employing these models either as he found them or as he was able to modify them. And now there is a widespread revolt against these "diagrams," with much iconoclastic experiment in new and strange fields.

This revolutionary tendency finds expression in a school popularly known as free verse, or *vers libre*. Representative of the modern spirit, there are many other novel fads in the air, and many have allied themselves with this, to its great detriment; but I shall treat only with that part of the movement which has in view an honest literary innovation. Here the claim is that the poet is unjustly restricted by mathematical canons of metre; that rhyme is inessential; and the problem is analysed down to a search for closer harmony between sense and rhythm. A profound task, this: To find for every nuance of thought or emotion, its rhythmical counterpoint!

Yet this seems to me to be the essence of the whole tendency, though it is often clouded over with contributory discussion. However well the aim may sound, I believe there is a serious fallacy back of it.

In the first place, contemporary writers seem to have forgotten the necessity for prose form. In this complex language of ours, both prose and poetry must ultimately recognise the laws of cadence. It is in losing sight of this fact that many have become converted to *vers libre*. Plato, Cicero, Milton, and in recent times Stevenson, Ruskin, De Quincey, Carlyle and all great French prose writers—all these represent a language which is definitely prose, but which is striking for its harmonious cadences. Reading any of these, one is quite likely to think of them as poetry, and in the more impassioned passages to read them as such. Just where the line can be drawn, no man can say save for himself. As a matter of fact, though, there are prose content and poetic content—prose form and poetic form. Just where anomalies like "Ossian" and the better moderns should be placed has always been perplexing, and refuge has frequently been taken in the convenient twilight zone of "prose-poetry." Accepting my rather categorical division, we may say that this generally includes poetic matter in prose form. Poetry should have both characteristics to be genuine. What the *vers libriste* seems to be guilty of, is ignoring the underlying truths of prose modulation.

"Granted," says he, "that innumerable artistic arrangements are possible outside present regulations, have we not therefore the nucleus of a new poetic vehicle, giving greater liberty to poetic inspiration, and yet adjusting sound to sense?" No, my dear sir. I must disagree. You forget that in the expression of any thought there must be a literary structure. Merely to express emotion or love of beauty in nondescript—however congruous—phrasing, is to deny that poetic form is distinct; and though I cannot for the life of me tell you just how it is distinct, I can only point out to you that my ancestors and yours have given us worthy examples for some generations.

Such a response, however, is based upon the assumption that there is no poetic quality in free verse forms. Whether or not this is so, is our real problem. I believe there are some more or less definite points of division in the highly specialised state which our language has attained. The indispensable requisite would seem to be *regularity*—not monotony, nor yet kaleidoscopic variety, but regularity such as constitutes rhythmical *unity*. The basic truth of this principle may be seen in every respectable piece of "irregular" verse in our literature. However mutable be the line-length or the rhyme, the fundamental rhythm never varies. In many long poems, notably the irregular ode of sustained length, there is a procession of patterns, which make together a more or less harmonious whole; but even then the original metric foot almost never changes. The *vers libriste* would abuse this prerogative of adjustment, of variety, until the original purpose of putting his work into verse is utterly forgotten, and the essential unity unrecognisable.

If the radical plead for "larger rhythms," I should have to suggest that any artistic effect of regularity is impossible beyond certain boundaries of the fundamental unit; the limits or nature of the unit depending on the language, and in our case being quite clear. Try as you will to read otherwise, you will find as a speaker of the English tongue that you cannot skip, at the most, more than three short syllables or two normal ones without indicating a beat or accent. Upon this fact is built our prosody. Here, then, is a further distinction. The unit in prose is the phrase, which leaves considerable freedom in interpretation; while the poetical unit must from the fundamental nature of the language depend upon a single vocal utterance, or stress. There is little danger of monotony or maladjustment here to the artist. He employs all the ornaments of melodious wording, well-placed pause and phrase, and the other beautiful subtleties that are first nature to him. Prose, on the other hand, has infinite possibilities of cadence or cacophony—every possibility but that of metrical regularity, which is verse.

Your "larger rhythms," then, are excellent prose; and thus you may flow to thought. In his rougher, freer medium, that is the task of the prose artist. The poet, however he may wish to rebel, must deal with certain pretty patterns. He may distort or re-arrange them at will, but by them he is eventually confined. These give the larger, the more sublime unity of poetry: such unity as is in the slow measures of Tennyson or in the torrential measures of Swinburne. What would these beautiful designs be, had their authors extracted that unity in an effort to fit every meaning to an appropriate but independent rhythm? Independent—that defines it. Poetry is supremely interdependent. The *vers libriste* pleads for larger units of independent rhythm—what is needed is larger groups of interdependent rhythm.

As to rhyme, there is less furore about that. It is a pretty ornament for the lyrist; but our most exalted works have been composed without it. Milton omitted rhyme for the same reason that the Greeks derogated undue embellishments: because his speech was rich enough without it. If the research attendant on the new movement accomplishes anything, it ought ultimately to increase other poetic beauties so that rhyme may be less essential. Blank verse, aside from the classic pentameter, is a realm comparatively unexplored, but fragrant with promise.

And the movement ought really to accomplish much. I have space merely to be theoretical, and in theory the case against free verse seems a bad one. But after all, viewed as an experiment, *vers libre* is a means of great revival of interest in the deeper truths of literature. By it, prose should indubitably be elevated—with the stabilisation, for instance, of "polyphonic prose." And its influence on poetic form should be notable. If any great upheaval is to be effected, it will perhaps go hand in hand with the growth of an independent American idiom. Otherwise, perfection comes only with definiteness, and that we assuredly have today. Many minor developments, perhaps a permanent reaction from some of the more binding restrictions culminating in the Victorian age; but greatest of all—enlightenment.

Picture of a Modern Mood

Outside, a subtle breeze deluded the spirit into warmth and comfort, while it wafted from the flesh all hot humours, all the sere flavour of the sun, all distress. Trees which had yesterday been unmoving skeletons, revealed today the clumsy new colouring of spring, and moved their fragrant twigs in strange rhythms. Nature was green, and red, and unknown browns. Leicester was sure that there had never been another spring like it, even within the domain of his faded infancy.

Inside, Leicester was even now putting together a few scant provisions for a stroll. Few indeed had he chosen thus far. Of the superior merit of Philip Morris cigarettes, he had no doubt, but he hesitated for a long time between "Dorian Gray" and "Le Crime de Sylvestre Bonnard." His indecision revived a doubt which had too long been dormant.

"Certainly I must take pen, paper and writing-board," he decided. "For months I have lounged unassertive about this college, a glutton for the new things it might afford me, for the cruel punishment of social striving—for mere impression. I have longed to write, until that longing has set up a permanent rainbow-future for me; now I must at least for a time seek to set down the strange thoughts I have felt, and cultivate expression."

As he set out, his long-legged gait was almost natural. His head no longer strutted over his right shoulder, but was suspended slightly forward and darted always from one side to the other, searching out some glimpse of undefiled mother earth, so alien in these streets of formless houses. Frequently he met those whom his waking self knew; then he gazed on them blankly or with a slight frown, and mumbled a guttural "H'lo" which would have been polite if it had sounded like English. Clutching the worn black boards of his dilapidated note-book, he strode evenly and swiftly forward, slowing down only occasionally as he deliberated at a crossroads.

It was almost purely an accident that he found a fit object to stay him; and I doubt if he recognised until long afterward how mad he had been ever to leave at all the immense choking wonder of that dam. Within him he was almost unconscious of self, save that he knew he must go somewhere far down the banks of the river and write of the things he saw while going there. This dim urge was almost irresistible, but as he saw the waters tumble insanely through the sluice-gates and converge into a rocky steeplechase, he reluctantly leaped the rampart and walked along the canal-bank until he stood above the sluice.

Never afterward could he tell just how long he stayed there, gazing at the endless permutations of millions of tiny water-drops. In the between states of his consciousness he formed sentences describing it, but afterward he re-

membered them only as a vague objective mist cast over the splendour of the
waters. . . . . . Nearest the bank the swollen river poured through three or four
gates, Leicester never noticed just how many. They rolled over the turn, sullen and green, then, like a fountain-head in some wild pagan god-land, burst
into a gorgeous eruption of iridescent whites and silvers and pale blue-tinted
creams. The foam from this volcano hurled itself backward, then rolled with
the undercurrent and came out in a thin stream two yards wide, still more furious than the body of the river, but lower and swifter than the lashed-up
crest whence it came. There were bubbles, supernally bright, on this current,
and the colours of it were not to be described, for Leicester was not a painter.
Other currents, similar, but each with its own beauty, flowed sinuously toward the common vortex; then they grew lower, steadier, more rapid. They
whipped through the irregular rock-bed like the weird dance of a far from ugly dragon, twisted around a final submarine promontory, and faded into the
shadowed green beneath the bridge. Some of it burst into foam again as it
came to the piers of the bridge, but from Leicester's position this was a weak
and uncourteous imitation, contributing only to prevent monotony.

Beyond, and sloping a trifle backward from the sluice-gates, was a long
stretch of undivided dam. The sun was diagonally over Leicester's head, high
enough not to displease his eyes and to imbue the whole vista with light. The
brilliant, yet not blinding reflection of the sun was almost all that Leicester
distinctly remembered of the broader background. But he never forgot the
margin between sluice and dam, where the waters seemed like white-hot
molten silver, gurgling in queer bubbles and splashes, and absorbing in some
supernatural manner the whole essence, but none of the dazzle of the sun.
This margin later united with the quiet places, imparting to them its turbu-
lence without its colour or its gleaming froth. Even this wide roadstead,
Leicester saw, was not free from a love of bubble-blowing, and there were
winding undercurrents which kept it never the same.

All this Leicester saw, and looked upon it for a long time. But words and
the restlessness of words still rang in his head, and he did not stay. Instead he
rose with the steadiness of a Philistine and continued plodding in the search
for seclusion. Even then he might have remained and tried to write there; but
he noted that there were many people of eminent practical curiosity about
him, who were gaping at the sight of a huge, black, ugly coal barge, caught by
the swirling currents and carried to the edge of the dam. So he went on. His
images of the flood were still too stupendous to occupy his mind, and he
commenced once more to look about him. He was now wandering in the
aisle of a forest of hewn and piled-up lumber, clumsy but immense and admirable. The path was of black cinders, pleasant to walk upon, and Leicester
smelt many faint odours of spruce, and pine, and woods he knew not by
name. He was still reeling in mind and unconscious of self, for when he made
a certain turn he was thrilled by a view of the opposite hillside, fresh with

awkward reddish saplings, shrubbery and unsullied greensward—all this seen in a curiously appropriate frame of thick logs, whose brown blended finely, and whose edges cut off just the proper piece of landscape.

But this was almost his last breath of what he remembered thereafter as his "Greek intoxication." He stumbled for nearly a mile along a river shore whose most charming sight, near at hand, was an occasional undwelt-on stretch of green. So in Leicester's mind came once more the daemon Will, with his mirroring attendants Effort and Self-Consciousness. Plain as was the path he walked upon, across the river there were catching panoramas, and the river itself was broad, and clear, and interesting. But he no longer used his eyes, for he had begun to think, and he was already beginning to destroy the beauty he had just experienced. He was moulding it into sentences, enlarging on some chance philosophy that had interjected, re-living the immediate past with the ulterior end of writing it on paper. . . . . . At length he reached a grotto where there was shade, and colour, and the loneliness of Pan.

Hitherto he had maintained the magic of his dying mood by the mechanical exercise of walking; it seemed to instil a rugged re-birth of emotional energy. The grotto was in the hollow of a hillside, overspread with stunted glorious trees, carpeted with moss and dry leaves and peeping wildflowers. Nothing was visible outside of it except an oval portrait of the opposite shore, outlined and gilded through the foliage about him. Leicester chose an inviting spot and sat down; but peace was not in his resting, for there remained the driving motive of pen and paper.

The sentences, pompous and metaphysical, which he had formed so brief a time ago, were confused and vague, and their music seemed mingled with the solemn crashing of the waterfall. The pen said, "Capitalise this scenery; it is very pretty." The trees muttered, "You are a fool, and should be sleeping now." His soul echoed, "You are a fool." Will, the voice of rhythm, interrupted to say, "You must choke back this bitter pessimism in the interests of Art." The old, old mockery of composition re-enacted itself: Leicester scribbled a few sentences, his enthusiasm waned, he knew the phrases were timid and discordant. His *empressment* became a cheaper and cheaper thing in the eyes of the growing monster Discontent. Beauty flew off on the wings of Mood, leaving the grotto sombre and menacing. . . . . . .

All this went on in Leicester's head until he had the grace to laugh.

"Poor striver after self-apotheosis," he told himself, "you are an artist reft of the power of expression. Hie you away, Hamlet; and pull your cap over your eyes, for the sun is low and stares you in the face."

The sun, in truth, was reddening; and as Leicester wandered on the return path, he found the discordant elements of his dead mood arranging themselves into a philosophy of decadence, strangely comforting. "It is *fin de siècle,*" he mused. "I was a Greek and loved beauty, now I am a modernist and I 'understand' it. This poor rivulet is now nothing other than the Styx. If it be lethal and perhaps lacking in proper illumination, it is at least beyond the ambitious pretence of the world; and it certainly endures longer than Homer himself."

Thus he consoled himself, reconciling the past with the future, which latter was to consist of insipid *bonhomie* and a healthy supper. The road was not long, and he was surprised when he found himself once more on the arched bridge below the dam. He leaned on the stone railing with a melodramatic air of compassion—whether for the insignificance of that bright but public panorama, or for the turmoil it had stirred in his soul, I can not say.

To satisfy a certain pose that grew within him, he took the scratched-up paper which represented his artistic production of the afternoon; crumpled it tightly, and threw it into the teeth of the current. It fell into the maw of a rising breaker, sank, and was seen no more.

"I suppose I shall be obliged to derive several very salutary morals from this experience," sighed Leicester. "Such valuable aids as 'One must have perspective' and 'Art should be spontaneous.' I can see plainly the comfort the English find in platitudes. On the whole, though, I cannot count the afternoon wasted."

A friend, who had been watching for hours the vain efforts of a large squad of coalheavers to extricate the barge from its predicament, slapped Leicester on the shoulder.

"They're going to have a hell of a time getting that thing out of there, aren't they?" said Leicester after a smile of greeting. The two set out for home; but Leicester did not talk much, for smile as he would, he could not shake from his ears the sullen and rapturous roaring of tons of faery-green waters, springing from the mid-stream geysers of Olympus.

Nietzsche as a Practical Prophet

The problem that Friedrich Nietzsche set himself was a double one. First, he intended to confound and overwhelm the forces of contemporary Christian morality; and then to propose a radical scheme of social organization and of individual aspiration which had as its supreme aim the creation of the superman.

To this problem he brought the genius of his own personality and its hitherto intensely conflicting elements. That is to say, he brought the hard sincerity which was derived from his personal struggle against centuries of tradition crystallized into the modern church. He had himself been a Christian, and a pious one, until his manhood; and yet there was in him that high seriousness of effort, that conscientious endeavor to solve in his own brain the problem of human ends, which refined itself gradually into a religion based on his own worldly and sensitive aristocracy.

Of the many influences which entered into his philosophy either as elements to be combated, or as elements to be absorbed, there were four which might loosely be chosen as the principal ones. H. L. Mencken* points out the two most obvious: Greek classicism and the new biology heralded by Darwin. I should choose two others, also, which were nearer to his home, if not to his heart: The scholasticism and ponderous romanticism of his German confreres, and the rather opposite influence of his master, Schopenhauer. The first involved him as a scholar and philologist, but the second opened up the vista of his thought and made possible Nietzsche's defiant emancipation from all the traditions about him.

His philosophy, then, was a revolt against all modern German traditions; it was a purely Nietzschean sublimation of the Schopenhauerian doctrine, a rather confused acceptance of Darwinism, and a straightforward defense of the classical spirit.†

To the solution of this problem Nietzsche directed his entire mental energy during the last fifteen years of his sanity. Reasonably enough, he started out with an attack on Christianity, the first bold step without which the remainder would be impossible. He showed that Christianity was a slave-religion, perpetuating the sick and botched while dragging down the strong, the healthy, and the courageous. He traced the origin of its morality and painted it, not as a divine and unquestioned edict, but as a mere perpetuation of customs, stupid customs and decadent at that. He mercilessly attacked the Oriental conception of a supernatural god, and proclaimed "on all walls—I have letters that even the blind shall see"—that since it asserts the supremacy of another world, the whole fabric of Christianity was a contradiction to life, a blasphemy to the soul of man, a stench in the nostrils of the seeing ones, a triumph of unreality, nihilistic pity, and a sickly and putrefied democracy. In the aphoristic books this was carried off with aplomb and a rather ironic analysis; by the time of "The Antichrist" this Oriental faith of Jesus and Paul became to Nietzsche the "one immortal blemish of mankind."

From this new point of view, which was much more penetrating and effective than the old rationalism of Voltaire and his school, Nietzsche practically rewrote the history of man. It seems to me that his most valuable contributions to modern thought are to be found in his piercing analyses of moral and historical problems of the past. Socrates and Christ as the great decadents, Luther and the Reformation as the worst catastrophe of modern times—men, philosophers and states were picked to scraps by his iconoclasm.

This was the achievement of his early aphoristic writings. Before this task should monopolize him or find complete expression, Nietzsche gave the world his constructive doctrines in the poetic testament "Thus Spake Zoroaster." The entire book is infused with the exalted spirit of a new aristocracy—an aristocracy of confident, honorable, ecstatic egoism. "This new table of

---

*"The Philosophy of Friedrich Nietzsche," by H. L. Mencken.
†Many of my facts are derived from the standard biography by Frederic Halevy.

values, O my brethren, I set over your heads: Become hard. . . . . Man is something that is to be surpassed." With these famous lines Zoroaster seeks disciples who will labor with him for the ultimate end and flowering of mankind in the superman. Zoroaster is very careful to warn off those who have not the inborn sense of honor necessary for this discipline. He is specific in preserving slave-morality for the slaves—that is, in preserving old moral values as the best protection for, and from, those who are incapable of welcoming his innovations. His is the most limited of aristocracies.

His ethical teachings may thus be summarized. His philosophy, therefore, can be arbitrarily divided into three essentials: (1) The will to power—his debt to Schopenhauer, whose will to live he turned from an abstract motive force of life to a conflict of individual wills, and made it not resigned, but vaunting and glorified. It is probably his most emphasized non-ethical idea. (2) The double morality—herren-moral and sclaven-moral. This presupposed a dual conception of society and was Nietzsche's most terrible weapon against modern democracy. (3) The superman, the quintessence of his prophecy, his most original and daring conception. Of his other novelties, only the eternal return is important, and that chiefly as an evidence of the uncontrolled passion which some call madness.

This, in brief, is the philosophy which, commencing about 1885 and gradually enlarging its scope, has been the horror of the conservative, the Bible of the revolte, the delight of the prose artist and poet. Perhaps no man has ever been more misinterpreted. He has been blamed, more or less justly, for German militarism, the sensual licenses of "modern moral degeneration," modern atheism, and, in general, for the failings of those cheaper souls whom he so well foresaw, playing the part of his disciple, proud of this high sanction for their sins.

But his influence was a greater and more positive thing than misconception and misrepresentation. He is one of the great prophets of this liberal age, and acquaintance with his writings has touched profoundly the lives of nearly all those leaders of men who have followed him. Today he is beginning to be understood.

In relation to his time, Nietzsche was obviously the enemy of everything most truly contemporaneous. He opposed democracy, scholasticism, romanticism, Christianity, and Christian ethics of all types. He attacked nearly every man who approached his eminence or who came into direct contact with his philosophy. He invented modern German prose and defied every rule of literary tact and coherence. From his mountainous isolation of thought he viewed the entire path of human history in a light that contradicted every current attitude. He arraigned every past philosopher, and when he borrowed an idea he infused into it the vigor and elevation of his own personality.

Back of this anachronism there is no mere perversity, still less reaction. There is rather the spirit of power, dynamic energy, of the glory in life and the striving for individual and social betterment. His time was "out of joint;" it worshipped abstractions, and Nietzsche held up vital energy as the a priori fact and the highest value. In this trait he was a true prophet and he anticipated with his quick and lively intuition much that is salt to modern minds. He saw directly into the workings of the human spirit, and made psychological advances informally which the technical and objective psychological schools were slower in reaching. For instance, in "Prejudices of Philosophers" he briefly analyzes the psychology of the philosopher, and then proposes that only psychological facts, not Greek abstractions, should be the basis of philosophy. Here and elsewhere he spoke vaguely of the "new psychology" as he did of "philosophers of the future." And he was partly justified in the appearance of Bergson and James, both of whom embody a great deal of the Nietzschean love of life. For example, Nietzsche anticipated James' pragmatism, his voluntarism in psychology and his temperamentalism in philosophy. Bergson's catchword "Creative Evolution" might be the very method for the superman, and Bergson also bowed to creative, vital energy. It is therefore quite likely that when Victorianism and its contemporaneous German culture have been forgotten, Nietzsche instead will be remembered as the very incarnate spirit of his time—not of the time in which he lived, but of the time with which he was pregnant. In the accidental timbre, the spectroscope test of his genius, he was in every sense a true prophet. So much for his greatness of soul: what of the logical fabric he created?

The most apparent thing about it is that Nietzsche had no metaphysical insight or logical subtlety—he could not leave the realm of life. I have been able nowhere in his works to find any clear statement of his metaphysics. He evidently accepted the biological data of Darwin, yet he attacked Darwin personally and tried to overthrow his theories. He did the same with Schopenhauer's will to live—altered it arbitrarily to fit into the pattern of his temperament. He spoke of will to power as a profound philosophical doctrine when it was merely the psychological fact of personal assertion, and when his own application of it rendered it futile as an explanation of the universe. Nothing is more evident than that he accepted evolution because it suited his love of the world, and the will to live because it suited his love of both will-power and life.

Even his ethical edifice will not stand the test of logic. The superman starts out by overlooking the conclusions of modern anthropo-biology, that man is incapable of development beyond his present biologic power* and that his future evolution must be selective and, more especially, social. One indication of this which everyone will recognize is illustrated by the fact of insanity, which is, in many cases, the result of mutations in the evolutionary

---

*"The Direction of Human Evolution," by Conklin, is a rather dull treatment of this point.

424 ❋ *Letters to Alfred Galpin and Others*

scale. The "sport" is abnormal, and is combated by the fundamental instincts of the race. More technically the conclusion is upheld by the fact of man's high degree of specialization, which brings about a decrease of adaptability. But even granting the possibility of a noble and select aristocracy, immune from the ordinary weaknesses of man, glowing with strength, a race of creators, of rulers—even this race is obviously not a surpassing of mankind, but an artificial culture separated from mankind in the mass by a long and arduous chain of sacrifice and peril, the product of which is its own negation. Nietzsche himself was the first to admit the immense labor necessary for the superman, but he had a passion for aristocratic perfection which overleapt all humanity. Going farther, Nietzsche knew too that the modern democratic freedman hated the aristocrat and would never sacrifice his own material interests for the fostering of genius. He would view the superman as a mere rhetorical tour de force, which in actual life could mean one of two things: Nobility, which he hates, and genius, which he leaves to chance.

I need go no farther on this via dolorosa to show what was already clear; yet I must admit the fascination of the idea, and the apparently powerful influence it is having on modern philosophies of evolution. The fault lay in the radical temper of its creator, not in the conception itself. This radicality of thought makes impossible a literal application of his dual morality, yet this also is valuable in theoretical ethics and may be applied, following Nietzsche's own example, to every factor of human progress.

Nietzsche was, therefore, as a thinker, a great prophet of revolt, a great iconoclast, a great innovator. If I may broaden the use of the ambiguous term "practical prophet" to include his influence in general on modern times, there remains a consideration of his personality, his artistic genius—its influence on his philosophy and on present-day thinkers and artists.

Probably the most emphasized trait of his personality was that unfortunate neuroticism which later led to his total insanity. I say unfortunate when I do not really mean it, because it is better to undergo savage derogation than to have written nothing worthy of such notice. And it is certainly obvious that we owe the superb literary finish, the whole bravura and fire of his philosophy, to that internal and agonizing emotional stimulus. He was like the nightingale and the thorn, like Shakespeare and his tragic passion for Mary Fitton.* He was in torture, but in exquisite torture. And it is a final and subtle shibboleth of one's taste, whether or not one is repelled by that beautiful instability which would wreck the efforts of the mediocre but which intensifies the purely instinctive thinking-in-words of genius.

It is to this insanity, such as it is, that we, therefore, owe his genius; but it will prevent his literal acceptance and make him rather a source than an

---

*I have this on the word of Mr. Frank Harris in his great book, "The Man Shakespeare."

authority. For him to win any significant literal disciples in practical affairs would mean that he must create aristocrats; and an aristocrat needs no Nietzsche. He was a philosopher, not a sociologist, and held always to the necessity of radicalism in thought.

And the final touch to his temperament was that hardness of soul, that revulsion which Chesterton calls a philosophy of "weak nerves." To me this shutting off of all but the emotions of personal glorification is the most vulnerable point in Nietzsche. I think Chesterton is almost justified when he says that truly great men are ordinary men. At least the really great man in my estimation is the man who accepts his own greatness without social prejudice, who has that overflowing soul which has no time for egoistic ecstasy, and who if he loves himself has love and pity to spare for those less fortunate beings whom he can by no honest interpretation avoid recognizing as his fellow men.

But this also is a fault in Nietzsche, and not in his glorious prophecy. No one with the artist soul to which he makes his strongest appeal can overlook the terrible soddenness, the weakness of will, the intrusive stupidity and filth of the modern mob autonomy. We must love mankind, but there must be discrimination. It is easier to love men from the cave of a hermit than from the window of a city apartment where the odor of democracy and the contemptible viciousness of the newspaper crying its wares offend the senses. Nietzsche teaches men the message that the soul of a strong man is precious and may not be poisoned with the conglomerate Freudian complexes of a herd. He was a poet, and will never lack hearers; his life was a tragedy, he will never lack sympathy. He possessed the essence of that noblest of all souls, the artist who can bear the brunt of truth and its pity; but he sacrificed everything in him that he thought was "soft" for the one purpose of perfecting his philosophy.

He pointed out the errors of our present democracy and opposed thereto an opposite equally fallacious. But life moves forward by opposites, and if he can gain hearers the future ought to tell how much of his proud and brave insight humanity can bear.

Voila tout.

To Sam L.

Ah, there are many ways to Arcady!
　Some purple-tinted in the evening haze,
　Some strewn with fresh-expired regrets, and some
That wind forever, with no destiny.

I, who have strewn too many of these with wan
　Dismemory'd ghosts and harsh-uprooted flowers,
　Knew that the search was vain, until there came
The fluted minstrelsy of fallen Pan

And cry of old Apollo in the night
  Of Beauty and the tyranny of fools.
  And I, too, raise my voice to hymn the pain
An ecstasy that *you* bring to the rite

Of your ancestral bacchanals—my friend,
  I'd never dare to call you that, but know
  Somewhere within that pagan heart of yours
The homely Nazarene is denizen'd.

Oct. 19, 1921

The Vivisector

An invitation to criticise the last two issues of *The Wolverine* gives one an excellent opportunity for evil-doing. One might in some cases take advantage of such openness, but this time one can't, because *The Wolverine* isn't that kind of magazine.

It is easily the best contemporary publication of the new typewritten sort, and is likely to remain so unless *Corona* or *Pine Cones* be resurrected. Indeed, if the last two numbers are an indication of those to follow, even these excellent veterans might have to yield first place. So much for praise, now for a little criticism.

"Facts Concerning the Late Arthur Jermyn and His Family", by Mr. Lovecraft, shows another phase of that writer's gloomy but powerful genius. It is perfect in execution, restrained in manner, complete, and marked by Mr. Lovecraft's uniquely effective handling of introductory and concluding portions. The legend is not so powerful as many of Mr. Lovecraft's dreamings have been, but it is unquestionably original and does not derive from Poe, Dunsany, or any other of Mr. Lovecraft's favorites and predecessors. Its affiliations are rather closer with Ambrose Bierce, and I personally should place it beside much of Bierce's best work without fearing for the fame of the United's representative. Mr. Lovecraft is unquestionably a man of distinguished genius in the short story, but he is unfortunate in coming rather late in the line of macabre writers, and in lacking many of those elements of sophistication which are so imperative in our times. For example, his critical faculty is poor and his stories are almost entirely at the mercy of his mood. Moreover, he is singularly lacking in psychological perception, a thing which is essential to immortalize any tale except that of the sheerest and most Shelleyan fiber. As a consequence of this latter lack the plot of the Jermyn tale is a trifle obvious, and its principal character is wooden. But with all these drawbacks Mr. Lovecraft is deserving of a fame much broader than he chooses to seek. For the power and persuasion of his style, and for the gripping, unearthly cast of his imagination, he is as great as any living author in his field and in the range of my acquaintance. He certainly excels Lord Dunsany in directness of narration and the whole realm of the horrible in imagination. If the reader be astonished at this praise, let him read "Polaris" and "The White Ship" for beauty of style, "The Doom that Came to Sarnath" or any of his temple or city fables for luxurious detail, or "Dagon", "The Statement of Randolph Carter", and "Nyarlathotep" for sheer wonder of imaginative power, and then he will merely have scratched the man's personality.

Next in importance to the serial tale are the editorials by Mr. Lawson. They are well-written, honest, and straightforward, thoroughly likeable without exception. I should, however, like to disagree with our editor on public criticism; for he suffers from the widespread and apparently ineradicable delusion that private criticism should be run in public columns. I say again, and would shout it from the housetops if I could, that when a writer wants personal, constructive criticism the place for him to seek it is the private critical bureau. Public criticism, I am weary of saying, should be of some decent literary caliber and should deal with works of public importance, not with infinitesimal details. Once admit private criticism into the public bureau and you have not only a repetitious series of admonitions, all about the same, but a troublesome obligation to include everything, entirely everything, or hurt someone's feelings.

For this occasion I continue in the old private-critic rut so well ploughed in *The United Amateur* by Mr. Lovecraft, and take up *The Wolverine* in detail. "At the Nadir" shows good writing ability on the part of a hard-working and earnest beginner, but the plot is very, very trite and the conclusion anticlimactic. Mr. Lehmkuhl knows better and will do good work later. My "Zoilian" colleague shows fine common-sense in the March number, but reveals prejudice in June: he seems on the one hand sadly bitten by Galpinitis, while on the other hand he is ridiculously unjust to Mr. Lovecraft's "Polaris", which is one of the best stories in amateur journalism.

The verse matter interests me a trifle less, but is of relatively high merit. "When Clover Blooms" is sincere, "Time" is excellently sentimental. "Appreciation" has a touch of exuberance about it, offset by the sly and pert correctness of Mr. Lovecraft's careless effusion in his favorite "Theobaldian" heroics, the instrument of his dull moments.

Another than Lovecraft had recourse to a pseudonym to cloak recent work. Like him a laureate in her department, Mrs. McMullen cannot help being graceful; but there is little substance in "Why" and the piece is impaired by mixture of archaic and modern verb-forms. "Afterwards" is of the same type—feminine and pleasing, but unimportant. Miss Pierce's poem may be put in the same category: it shows a certain plaintive sincerity but needs technical improvement.

So much for the two issues. Certainly, *The Wolverine* has amply proved its right to the laureateship bestowed by the National; and one can but hope that it will maintain an equally high standard in future numbers.

Four Translations from *Les Fleurs du mal* by Charles Pierre Baudelaire

Au Lecteur

Folly and error, lust and avarice,
Enwrap our souls, and vex our flesh amiss;
    As beggars their own vermin, so feed we
With sweet remorse our worn-out wickedness—

Pliant remorse, that yields to stubborn sin;
Time eases high resolves, and we begin
    Once more the gay and muddy pilgrimage,
Relying on vile tears to wash us clean.

On sorrow's pillow, Satan Trismegist
Enchants and slowly rocks our spirit to rest;
    And the rich metal of our will is molten
And vapouris'd by this wise alchemist.

It is the devil pulls our puppet-strings . . .
We are attracted by repugnant things;
    One step the nearer every day to Hell—
The horror wanes, but the hot odour clings.

Like a poor rake that in his wild unrest
Gnaws at some ancient harlot's martyr'd breast,
    We lie in wait and snatch clandestine pleasures,
And squeeze them dry, as oranges are prest.

Serried and swarming, like the Helminthes,
Ghouls in our brains wriggle in drunken sprees;
    And when we breathe, the unseen stream of death
Flows in our lungs, and leaves each hour his lees.

If club or dagger, poisoning or flame
Have not yet scroll'd the tokens of their fame
    On the bare canvas of our destinies,
'Tis merely that our spirits are too tame . . .

But with the panthers, jackals—with the lice,
The apes and serpents, scorpions, rats, and mice,
    The vultures, and the monsters of all shapes
In the menagerie that breeds all vice,

There's one the ugliest, wickedest of all;
He stirs not much; he makes but little brawl,

Yet is on leash to devastate the earth,
And with a yawn can make a god his thrall.

'Tis Boredom! Lost in some wild dream or other,
He weeps, and smokes his pipe—but why this pother?
    For well you know this dainty monster, Thou
Hypocrite reader—fellow man—my brother!

L'Ennemi

My youth was but a vagrant thunderstorm,
    Travell'd in some scarce moments by the sun:
Lightning and rain have made such ravage there
That all my garden's crimson fruits are gone.

Now I have reach'd the autumn of my thought,
    And soon—so soon!—must ply with spade and rake
To smooth again those riven furrows, where
The flood has left a graveyard in its wake.

And who knows? The new flowers that I dream
    May find this newly-laven soil, to teem
With unseen tonic for another start . . .

—O sorrow, sorrow! Time eats up our lives,
    And the obscure Enemy that gnaws each heart,
On our most precious life-blood feeds, and thrives!

Remords Posthume

At last, when you and your dark beauty sleep
    Beneath a black and marble monument;
    When you shall have for couch and tenement
A hollow grave, and vault with sides that weep;

When, with the stones that sift down through the heap,
    Your breast is batter'd, and your lithe flanks bent,
    And all the power of your heart is spent,
And these your wayward feet not even creep:

Then, in the waste of that great lonely night,
    Often the tomb will wail around your bed
With its deep homeless voice, mocking your plight.

And say, "What is it to you now, frail corse,
    That once you did not know the cry of the dead?" . . .
And the worm will still devour you, like remorse.

L'Ange Gardien

What are your thoughts tonight, poor solitary soul?
What do you say, my heart, that has been so wither'd,
To the most beautiful, the most good, the most dear,
At whose divine glance you have so suddenly blossom'd?

—We forsake all pride to sing his praises,
Nothing of ours can give you the sweetness of his direction;
His god-like flesh bears the perfume of the Angels,
And his eye clothes us in garbs of light.

Whether in the night and the solitude,
Or on the street, among the populace,
His ghost dances like a flame in the air.

Sometimes he sp`eaks, and says: "I am beautiful, and I command
That for love of me you love only the Beautiful;
I am the guardian Angel, the Muse, and the Madonna!"

Scattered Remarks upon the Green Cheese Theory

The moon, says a notorious cynic of the sixteenth century, is in the last analysis a large chunk of fibre, which has chipped off all sorts of ligneous splinters and carelessly left them to their own degeneration. Their decay into flesh-seeming substance, during which period the Old Block lost track of them, was followed by a pathetic assumption of directly solar origin on the part of the Matches, which a half-witted child of the demi-god Tyrrilongko had whittled, on a sunny day, from a fleshified spruce log. My authority explains the matter thus: Squeechum, a great bullying sort of spirit, who delighted in frightening children, came along as the poor child was seeking diversion in this already old-fashioned manner; and knowing the timid nature of his victim, he scared him half to death by imparting combustible Heads, or Skulls, to the newly shaven loglets. The child dropped his jaw in astonishment, and shivered like the wind-god on a cold autumn day. Squeechum was not half satisfied with this bit of diabolism, and went so far as to give the Skulls some special properties of his own contrivance. The chief of these was the necessity for friction, by which the creature's capital pieces might slowly be fretted into flame, to their great enjoyment and eventual dissociation. Thereupon the whole heap had in no time at all fallen to scraping one another; they were in danger of disappearing the next moment, but Squeechum—with that rare presence of mind which has preserved demons as a separate species even unto our day—endowed this union with a function, and behold! they rubbed off splinters even as did their distant ancestor, the Old Block. They then spent their burning-out years in rearing the splinters to maturity. It is from this epoch of Tinderkind that the great fear of inflammatory thoughts and contacts for the young, is first known to have swayed society.

When they were nicely spread out on the little boy's playground, Squeechum sneeringly left the latter to his own devices with them. The divine progeny, however, was as weary of the business as his crony, and was no longer even afraid of them. He found that their flame was harmless to his empyrean integument, and disgustedly sauntered off for a thrill at the hive of the Hybla Bees.

This carelessness properly redounded upon him, for the Tinderkind soon overspread his peninsula, and thence migrated to the remotest lunar caverns. The manufacture of Splinters was still a prime diversion, and had resulted in a dual differentiation of the species, but this manner of inciting combustion was soon found monotonous. They next turned to the Sun, and by their complete acceptance of his Ascendance received many sparks, which produced several fine bonfires and a great deal of eloquence. Like all civilised excrescences, they developed a language, but my authority hints slyly that Squeechum had an elbow in the affair. Be that as it may, it served to amuse the fire-seeking Splinters, and after some generations was employed to proclaim their direct filial importance to the Sun.

The gods and demons in this neighbourhood of space were a criminally negligent lot, and had not endowed their shavings with anything so clever as Squeechum's Skull; so pretty soon they waxed envious and quarreled among themselves about the right to set them on fire. While they were thus hotly engaged, Squeechum gathered up a plenteous handful and made Safety Matches of them. This he accomplished by squeezing their tops tightly and surrounding them with another layer of secret compound. This compound would inflame only through those portions of the natural environment which were sacred to Squeechum. He was making rapid headway with this cony-catching trick on his confreres when they discovered his absence and spied on him. By introducing variations of their own, they soon had the race divided into innumerable compartments, or Match Boxes.

"Within the last few centuries," says my cynical informer, "the Superhuman Powers have busied themselves in more cerulean employments, and the Tinderkind, following the empty-headed example of their first hewer, wander the globe in bewilderment. They have worn out their Patent Scratchers to the number of thousands; most of them, having lost the old spontaneity of the Lucifer Match, are content to frizzle out their existence on the first snitch of sand-paper they run across, endowing it with all the graces of language which have descended to them from a nobler epoch. Intermarriage between boxes has produced even more bewilderment, and the old standards of division by Scratching Shrines have disappeared almost even in name. Instead can be seen any number of single Matches, sick of poring over their genealogical tablets, who have found new uses for their top-pieces. They devote themselves to the collection of grains of sand, fretted from the old sand-paper of the race, or to speculation on the reaches beyond their globe. Their descent from the Sun is a favourite topic of argument, and has succeeded in inflaming a number of them; Squeechum and the unknown descendant of Tyrrilongko still figure in their folk mythology. But to me (continues the original narrator) the point of interest still lies in their uppermost Protuberance, for which they have discovered such various and novel uses. I was led into a deep maze of cogitation upon this unhappy race by hearing a vagrant member, whose red head showed signs of Luciferian atavism, complain as follows:

"'Great Spirit of the air, where are your lightnings? The sand-paper of our forefathers is uneven; it is rough, or it is smooth, and the dregs of the race have recourse to it. Great Spirit! You are not divine, you shall have no sawdust from me, if you can no longer circle this head with flame. Great Spirit! Our own altars inflamed us; but since you are quiet, even they no longer burn. The noble Match Box of my forbears is fallen and vanished, and I no longer know my own brethren. Give us, Great Spirit, a ball of fire from your hidden coffers, that our points may bow thereto and we may chant, united about it, something to our ashes of the song that inspired Tyrrilongko when first he made Match! Great Spirit!—'

"But I dissolved in tears, and heard no more.—"

My informer has carefully explained his cynicism on every page of his book; it was a rare attitude in those dark days. But poor old duffer! To weep at the aberrations of the merest of smoker's accessories shows indeed some deep well-spring of corruption in his soul; and I am forced to consider his cosmology a fabrication.

Department of Public Criticism

The third issue of Samuel Loveman's amateur magazine *The Saturnian,* which is known to several members of the U. A. P. A., contains more of magnificent poetry than any other publication which has ever been connected with the society. More in quantity; in quality it yields only to its own first issue, with Mr. Loveman's odes to Apollo and Dionysos, and the poem "Oscar Wilde."

The substance in the issue consists in the translations from the two French poets, Charles Baudelaire and Paul Verlaine. Such translations seldom appear. Judged simply as English poetry, they have a quality of beauty all their own; as renditions from a foreign tongue, they are almost beyond criticism.

The Baudelaire poems are the more numerous, and include some of the best translations ever made in the language. More than Verlaine, Baudelaire was susceptible of translation. He insisted upon music as a prime factor in his poetry, but the music is obtained with the old devices of smooth rhythms and richness of phrase which were not unknown before him in both English and French—indeed, his Alexandrines have much of the quality of English blank verse. This quality Mr. Loveman has rendered perfectly. In turning this highly polished and classical poetry into his own peculiar idiom, Mr. Loveman has lost some of its studious art; there are some overwrought phrases, touches of hectic colouring, and less regard than other translators have paid to the logical unfoldment of the thought. He has made it English rather than French, but all this is easily forgivable; for the faults are Baudelairian in their error. The poems are virile, alive, sensuously beautiful; and in not a single line or phrase is there the commonplaceness which Baudelaire so detested.

The versions are no more literal than was Baudelaire's translation of Poe. I can vouch, however, for Mr. Loveman's sureness of touch. He has altered much, but every alteration brings with it either idiomatic or imaginative force. More than once Mr. Loveman has actually improved upon the classical original. For example, the first four lines of "Exotic Perfume":

> When, with eyes closed, a sultry autumn night,
> I breathe the odour of thy vehement breast,
> I see myself upon strange beaches rest,
> Dazzled and charmed in the unsetting light.

I venture to say that there is a higher quality of imagination in this than in the original:

> Quand, les deux yeux fermes, en un soir chaud d'automne,
> Je respire l'odeur de ton sein chaleureux,
> Je vois se derouler des rivages heureux
> Qu'eblouissent les feux d'un soleil monotone.

Here the essential details of the image are strengthened in a shorter compass. The passage in question is one of the most musical in "Les Fleurs du Mal," but surely the translation has come as nearly as possible to equalling that factor.

Two other translations which equal or surpass the original are "Causerie" and "La Musique." The rich intensity and virile compression of the former make it a masterpiece purely as an English poem, yet the translator has taken fewer than his customary liberties. "Music," one of the most spiritual of "Les Fleurs," loses nothing in the translation.

I have carefully looked up the Modern Library Edition and the one or two other books where translations of Baudelaire are to be found. They are occasionally more faithfully literal, but without an exception mediocre in atmosphere and with scarcely a conception of phrase-making. I say with considerable assurance that every one of the *Saturnian* translations, down to the poorest, is superior to all that have preceded it.

The Verlaine poems are no less remarkable, but are rather an exhibition of virtuosity. Verlaine's music is purely French, and much of it derives more than half of its effect from intangible Gallic rhythms and assonances. The poems chosen for translation are among Verlaine's prettiest, and the renditions are amazingly skilful, but the results have much less poetic value than the more vital "Fleurs du Mal." Yet they contain many exquisite things; and in a completer volume of translations would be memorable. They recall the similar grace and sympathy of the Heine translations, in the second *Saturnian*, which suffered likewise from their fragmentary condition. One poem stands out particularly; a fragrant flower of a poem, commencing "La lune blance Luit dans les bois, "of which I recall seeing three other versions by more or less well-known poets, among them Arthur Symons. I refer the inquisitive to Mr. Symons' version in the appendix to his "The Symbolist Movement in Literature." The exquisiteness and grace of Verlaine live only in Mr. Loveman's version, which is short enough to quote entire:

> The moon of snow
> Shines in the wood;
> From every bough
> Thin voices brood
> That the green sprays cover. . . . .
> O my dear lover.
> The pool at our feet
> Profoundly traces
> The silhouette.
> Of the willow that faces
> The bleak wind's power. . . . .
> Muse on: it is the hour.
> A vast and far
> Content is given.
> And where we are
> Descends from heaven
> Air irised star, a flower. . . . .
> It is the exquisite hour.

To set off the exoticism of these poems, Mr. Loveman prints several simpler pieces of his own. They are less ambitious than some of his work, but are not entirely the losers for that reason. The poems are all quite brief, but are instinct with beauty and humanity, and show that Mr. Loveman, unlike any other who has ever been connected with Amateur Journalism, has something of infinity in him.

Intuition in the Philosophy of Bergson

The idea of intuition, while not the most novel of M. Henri Bergson's singular contributions to contemporary philosophy, appears to be fundamental to his entire system; and is indeed the key to understanding the methods by which this strange personality arrives at his notions. We find scattered throughout his writings several attempts to analyze it, more frequent references to its value as a new philosophical *method*, and a continual practice, quite consistent with his preaching, from which he derives many essentials of his philosophy.

This insistence upon mystical method is perhaps Bergson's most vital connection with contemporary thought, and therefore one of the chief causes of his now fading popularity. This is palpably an age in which mysticism, if not dominant, is at least an element to be reckoned with. Moreover, it makes acceptance of Bergson's system easier to the normal person, because it seems to lend an extra-intellectual plausibility to many of his vagaries.

While reference to it is so frequent in his works, particularly in his *magnum opus*, I have been unable to find a reasonable analysis of the method anywhere. In chapter two of "Creative Evolution," after stating that instinctive and intelligent life are two complementary directions of the central life stream, he says, "There are things that intelligence alone is able to seek but which, by itself, it will never find. These things instinct alone could find; but it will never seek them." There seems to be a difficulty here, which Bergson recognises even more explicitly a trifle later: "But a glance at the evolution of living beings shows us that intuition could not go very far. On the side of intuition, consciousness found itself so restricted by its envelope that intuition had to shrink into instinct."

The difficulty here is heightened by the difficulty of finding any experiential background for this analysis—it is another offspring of Bergson's "intuition." I have shown that his analysis of the functions of instinct and intellect, overlooking its other faults, seems unable to give us any clearer comprehension of intuition; but some of his other statements are superficially more satisfactory. In one place he says that intuition is "instinct that has become disinterested, self-conscious, capable of reflecting upon its object and of enlarging it indefinitely." The word "reflection" would seem to posit a certain co-operation of intellect in the process, and elsewhere Bergson recognises this. His view seems to be perfectly honest, and fairly consistent. He is in possession of a certain rather undefinable method of thinking, closely connected with the traditional sense of the word "intuition." He makes laudable efforts to explain this process, and manages to convey to us, in an indirect way, much of its essence.

Assuming, therefore, that Bergson is unable to give a scientific justification of his method, still is it not superior to that of the intellect? Bergson apparently thinks so. His whole analysis of the function of the intellect is a marvellously clever demonstration of his claim that intellect can not handle life, but is only at home in restricted spaces, with inert matter. But does his own method negate intellect? He is unable to define it, however nebulously, without including its expressed enemy. He admits outright more than once, that his "instinct" is by itself as helpless as intellect—indeed more so, for how can instinctive knowledge become conscious knowledge except through intellect? He does not say; therefore we may assume that instinct plays the initiatory role, but that it can only become knowledge when it reaches the higher thought centres.

There is, however, a vital contradiction to intellectualism, in that the intellect is not accepted as the ultimate source of knowledge, or judge between contradictory sources, and is discredited as far as possible from any participation in the knowing process. This is Bergson's mysticism; what does it mean?

The basic assumption in his plea for a new method, is that this "letting oneself go," this mystical *introspection,* can produce uniform results if philosophers apply themselves to it with proper zeal. There is something ludicrous about the vision that comes to my mind when Bergson pleads for a "new method" in philosophy. What a waste of perfectly good mathematical ability! Why not import spirit mediums into the profession, and be assured of fuller, if perhaps less accurate data? But that is beside the point, which is to find out what Bergson's intuition is and whether it will do all he thinks it will.

In the case of Bergson himself, there is apparently a large element of imagination, particularly of a *visual* sort, in his mentality. His figures of speech are distinctly pictorial; he has a habit of mistaking a particularly clear figure for a logical explanation. His picture of the vital impetus, of the evolution of life, is especially strong in imaginative quality. One is led to suspect, then, that his own "intuition," from which he apparently derives the general notion of the process in others, has a great deal of the poetic imagination in it.

Now, the difficulty about imagination, however well it be grounded in reliable "instinctive knowledge," is that it differs so markedly in the individual. It is an attribute of genius, perhaps the most inseparable of them all, but geniuses are notorious for following their own bent, and for being different from all who have come before. In Plato it gave the supra-sensible world, in Spinoza the "all," in Leibnitz the monad. And worst of all, it is impossible to argue with the authoritative visions of genius. The whole panorama is a vast postulate, no part of which will its parent allow to be argued from the rest. While intellect is a common meeting ground, in which all ideas must subscribe to the laws of logic and common experience; on the other hand, intuition is so indefinite that no two individuals can possibly have the same understanding of it, and it authorises the individual experience in sharp distinction from the common.

Reality, reached in this clandestine and subjective manner, becomes determined by the emotional association of the individual. And at this point Bergson seems to stop. He is effective from some points of view, in attacking the intellect; but his own vision is not of the sort which spreads, like that of Swedenborg or Bruno, or Plotinus. Intuition, as far as I can see it, becomes contradictory to real philosophy when it is emphasised in preference to reason. It necessarily gives the individual his data for speculation, and is a necessary attribute of great philosophy. But to seek the intuition rather than the why and wherefore, is an emotional process, which modern psychology is gradually showing to be merely one form of self-delusion. In persons of strongly imaginative temperament it means much; in art, literature, and the more refined contacts of life, this vague fellow-feeling is much more necessary than conscious syllogism. But it is not philosophy, and to ask philosophers to adopt it as a method is ridiculous.

The real effect of Bergson's plea is to make disciples of a certain cosmic temperament akin to his own, and to give them the groundwork of an inner mystical life. But it does not stimulate research into reality. If you care to agree with Bergson you will probably have little independent contribution to make. If you don't, more than likely you will reach a reality entirely distinct from the reality of Creative Evolution; or your introspection may lack the credibility of Bergson's, and you may be forced to abandon the method entirely.

The whole appeal, then, as I see it, is for people to sympathise with the opinions of this queer, this unique thinker. His philosophy is almost entirely without social connections, in essence or in presentation. Other philosophers feel themselves one of many, or at least recognise themselves as philosophers. Bergson seems to think of himself as an eye apart. He speaks disapprovingly of "metaphysics," "philosophers," "scientists," "the intellect," and even of his old occupation, mathematics. His intuition is personal, it places originality higher than consistency, and it seeks personal participation. For this reason it always seems to me that Bergson is persuading rather than convincing. He wants to wheedle one to his side, and he will use the most plausible argument at hand.

On the other hand, adopting a broader and sympathetic attitude, one may see much of value in the emphasis, at least, in Bergson's method. Like James, Nietzsche, and other typical modernists, he wants to inject *life* into philosophy. But Nietzsche puts life above truth; James makes life the criterion of truth, while Bergson has fundamentally nothing more to contribute than the mystics of the past. He wants, it might be put, to make philosophy interesting—he is in a certain sense a romanticist, even an impressionist. But I rather fear he is working in the wrong material. Philosophy is an ancient and sedate institution; break through it, like one of Bergson's rockets, and when the sparks have died down the eternal Logical Mind must analyse the light and bring it into focus with proved or accepted facts of past philosophers. His own most important additions to the stream of thought have been those in which he was most consistent, either within himself, or with experience. Apart from these isolated arguments; his temporalism, his conceptions of life and intellect, and so on, he is important only because of his spirit—his intuition. He had a gorgeous cosmic vision and he used every resource of argument, language, and feeling to make that vision common to mankind.

Ennui

When the earth blossomed and was green again, I denied the god of desolation and went among the trees. I breathed incense, and I knew that the gods of the forest were breathing their offerings to the implacable blue sky. I breathed of it as would the sky, had it any soul, and knowing that the sky had none, I was a god. For a moment joy was in me.

But the spirit of desolation was angry, and smote me. I did not see him; the grass, the flowers, sun and wind still moulded their evanescent palaces of warm perfume; but the will of my god is mighty, and he supplants these things. Then desire glistened in my brain, like a grey moon when the stars are out; I desired joy and lo! it had slipped away, and left not even sorrow in its place. And my desire grew strong, and I felt the strength of it through all my spirit; and I envisioned my dead sister Pain and would have sung to her in a high and melancholy voice. I would have sung to her of the cruel and moist lips of love, and of the agony that creates hope, of immeasurable fair gardens that mock the frenzy of fine words, of the ruin that comes to dreams in the morning; I would have chanted to the lonely bones of the desert the purity and exaltation that was once Pain. But the words were harsh, and the savour of their sickly passion suddenly cast me into despair. "Ai; Ai! Thou that dreamed of mountains and would be a God! Thou that spurned men and re-built fallen castles, and sang at night, in the desert, the anthem of your immemorial pride! Thy voice is pallid, it is not the voice of man, it is not the hymn of thy sister Pain; and as you speak you dishonour the crystalline vapours that are words, for your soul is empty, and its voice is hollow." And I beat my breast, and quaffed unspeakable red wines, and called to my garden the dancers of Eudemia, who danced before me with no garment, and were not ashamed, for they loved me. And I cried at them to go away, and pored over the beautiful mad parchments of old poets, and knew the thing that drove them mad. But in all this the voice of despair laughed always as men do not ever laugh, while it sucked the blood of my heart and sent it poisoned through strange channels in my breast.

Then I regained my voice, and it rose to the grey mansion of my God, saying, "Behold, you have taken away joy and beauty, give me now suffering, that I may feel one of men, and let me weep with the beggar at the cross-roads!" But my God spoke only in his old accents of despair. . . . . .

Then I grew angry, and denied again my God. And the mocking sharp voice of despair rose higher and became pale song. And this is what it sang, to the tepid sands of my little desert, as the sky was silent.

A Critic of Poetry

An article by one Michael White has been called to my attention, in which Mr. White, apparently one of Amateurdom's uncrowned Sainte-Beuves, makes some remarkable revelations about the poetry of my friend, Samuel Loveman. Mr. White marshalls a number of immortal names to crush his palpitating adversary—Barry Cornwall, Edgar Allan Poe, John Keats, and that distinguished critic Lord Macaulay. Mr. White is morally certain that these personages, in our modern age, would have joined the National Amateur Press Association, if only to deplore, with Mr. White, the decline of poesy. The companionship of Lord Macaulay has rendered him clairvoyant, and his rich comprehension of Keats has kindled in him a boundless store of friendly and paternal admonitions. He has theories of his own, like his predecessor in American scholarship, Mr. Poe.

"When he ceases to preach from Olympian heights and descends among men and women of the world, and interprets their heart songs, and adds his protests against the evils of the age," says Mr. White with prophetical benignancy, "then indeed shall he come into his own, a prophet and a teacher whose lips have been touched by the divine fire." He goes deeper than this. He reveals the secret springs of action which have brought upon us this masterpiece, his article; he is displeased that my friend, Howard P. Lovecraft, should have been enthusiastic about "A Triumph in Eternity"—such unscholarly methods lead astray the young men, now members of the National Amateur Press Association, whom Mr. White is going to make the prophets and teachers of the not too immediate future. As a critic of the modern—and quite un-Olympian—psychological school, Mr. White should be acquainted with the amiable and not too strictly discriminating enthusiasm of my good friend Mr. Lovecraft; but such oversights may be pardoned him, for with his great precursor, Matthew Arnold, Mr. White possesses "high seriousness." Poetry, and the criticism of poetry, are serious matters to Mr. White, who is pained at Mr. Loveman's "insincere misanthropic philosophy," and warns him that Poe dwelt among the morbid horrors of the tomb. Serious, Mr. White is not a mere impressionist in his criticism; he is something of a classicist, and a passionate advocate of good grammar and of the clear-cut, chiseled imagery of Alexander Pope and Edgar Guest. He does not allow the rapture of versification to seduce him from his conviction that the dead do not speak, particularly when their mouths are clogged with roots. He objects to one of Mr. Loveman's most simple and poignant pieces, after a medical examination of its tropes, with "there is no sequence—the closing lines leave us just where we were in the beginning." Alas! "This is the doctrine of Poe," who was not interested in politics. Like his contemporary rival, Mencken, Mr. White is interested in the doctrines and beliefs of his subjects. Mr. Loveman's theories are pernicious. He belongs to a school, and that school is dead, and I am ashamed of Mr. White's erudition that he didn't quote Swinburne to prove it—or disprove it. Alpheus and Arethusa, by the simple venom of their presence, will undermine, nowadays, the most exalted prophet, and seduce the reformer of society from his task. When the diapason of Mr. White's learned style has receded from the ear, one rests with the unbending conviction that Mr. Loveman is inferior to Keats and Milton, but that if he will follow Mr. White's directions, there is yet hope for him.

Let me do Mr. White justice—Mr. Lovecraft's criticism was "strictly Swinburnian," and I can agree with him that "A Triumph in Eternity" is rather exasperating. Beyond that point I should like to disagree with Mr. White but for his own rather unlyrical obscurity, which leaves me in considerable doubt as to his intentions. It would seem as if Mr. White did not know what he was talking about. And indeed, one does not criticise poetry by comparing it to Keats, or by resenting its syntax. Above all, one does not criticise poetry—of all things—by a series of negations. If Mr. White had any interest in writing articles, except perhaps to wield the dung-fork which his species are reported to bear in their hands at birth, he would at least have taken pains to find out something of Mr. Loveman's own type of mind and his reasons and methods in writing poetry. This is best done by putting, not Keats, but oneself, in the place of the writer, a suggestion perhaps a little malicious in the case of Mr. White. But it is rarely possible that his seer-like intelligence might then have divined that "A Triumph in Eternity" (although a legitimate subject, on account of Mr. Lovecraft's eulogy) was written very many years ago, and is no more representative of its author's mature creation than "Queen Mab" is prophetic of "The Sensitive Plant." Certain young persons, Mr. White, are often seized with a vicious and unphilosophical enthusiasm for good literature, particularly poetry. They have the atrocious and Nietzschean egoism to wish to emulate these productions; and if they be sufficiently young, and untroubled by vicious thoughts of their epoch, they are frequently known to imitate Milton, Swinburne, and even to poach upon our critic's preserves, and pay the "highest compliment" to Keats. Mr. Loveman, being a man of very profound sensibility to the best productions of the creative mind, has passed through that stage—very well through, I assure you, Mr. White. His personal and strictly original output since then has been small, but it has been sincere, intimate, poignantly felt, and exquisitely realized. And he has maintained his artistic integrity by attending strictly to his own affairs and leaving the evils of capitalism to Upton Sinclair, who has studied economics; and be it said, by leaving the heart songs of the men and women of the world, to Edgar Guest.

From the French of Pierre de Ronsard ("Amours"—Livre II.)

Aubade

Awake, my Mary, my fair indolent:
  Now the gay lark thrills, lyrically high,
  And Nightingale in rich-exhaling sigh
Murmurs, against a thorn, his love's complaint;—

Arise! over a pearl-embossed lawn
  Come with me: here's your pretty rosebush, red
  With opening buds; carnations, scarce have shed
The dew last night you fed them: it is dawn.

Last night you vowed, at bedtime, by your eyes,
  To wake before me; but Aurora's want
Still holds them in her veiling sorceries.

There there! a hundred kisses on them, and
  Upon your breasts a hundred, sweetly warning
My love to wake up early in the morning.
                    1924

Echoes from Beyond Space

Ebony and Crystal by Clark Ashton Smith (printed by *The Auburn Journal,* Auburn, Calif.) (1922).
The Star-Treader, and Other Poems by Clark Ashton Smith. (A. M. Robertson, San Francisco. (1912).

Here is a book, from an obscure newspaper office, which should be seen by every one who really cares whether good literature is written in America or somewhere else. For more than ten years Mr. Smith has been writing poetry of an amazing force and originality; has published three volumes, of which "Ebony and Crystal" is the latest; and our intensely occupied literati have never heard of him outside of his own state. This book challenges the reading public in more ways than one. Its chief poem "The Hashish-Eaters, [*sic*] or the Apocalypse of Evil" is the longest and most imaginative, to my mind unquestionably the greatest, poem in the literature of the grotesque. It does not stand alone. Line after line, poem after poem, is stamped with the idiom of a unique creative imagination. Obscurity has taught the poet to scorn contemporary notice and he has written with utter defiance of the unimaginative, critical minds that constitute the literary body politic. Why has he remained unknown? He has been closely contemporaneous, for one thing, with the intellectualised trend of ultra-modern writing, and his work makes no pretensions to analytical power or intellectuality. Then, connoisseurs of the grotesque are few; and the average man of culture, finding much of the book below the author's best level, turns away and loses the gold with the sand. But he has the examples of Bierce and Poe for company in his obscurity, both of whom have been powerful influences upon his writing.

I cannot attempt in this brief compass to justify my claims about Mr. Smith's ability, particularly since comparatively few amateurs have seen the works in question. But for a casual sample, here is the closing sestet from his sonnet, "To Life:"

> "Fair as the moon of summer is thy face,
> And mystical with cloudiness of hair. . . . . . .
> Only an eye, subornless by delight,
> Shall find within thy phosphorescent gate
> These caverns of corruption and despair
> Where the worm toileth in the charnel night."

But no single passage can give a notion of his sheer power and the surprising variety which it casts upon so limited a universe—it is a Baudelairian volume to the core, from that point of view.

The poet concentrates all the force of his imagination and of his immense and exotic vocabulary upon single lines, careless of the rules of perfect art, swooping through his unearthly outer world only to report, seldom to discriminate. Like Poe, he is the "haunted sot." But without Poe's superb art or his keen and versatile mentality, Mr. Smith is perhaps more naive; reading his volume gives me the same sort of delight that endears to me the minor Elizabethan drama—one can ramble on infinitely, now and then finding passages which repay an hour of drearier stuff. Naive, Mr. Smith is young. He writes as a schoolboy plays, with big words and big images and big effects which fail as often as they succeed—but succeed stupendously well. "The Hashish-Eaters" is a gigantic fib in which the events are very limited—the hero ascends into a universe of such processional horror and beauty as no one has painted before, and after a considerable fright, is left there with escape or awakening his only recourse. I would not have it well written for anything—the vocabulary is intolerably outlandish, and there is absolutely no conception of varied beat in his blank verse—it is too gloriously uplifting as it is and when there is a particularly good whopper, one can smile. It must be taken in its entirety, and so must the volume as a whole.

Mr. Smith was born in Central California in 1893, and has always lived in Auburn with his mother, writing poetry, making love, doubtless something of a local deity. He has never sought a "higher education." His first volume, "The Star-Treader," contains some of his finest work, written before his nineteenth year! He is certainly America's most prodigious boy-wonder, if one must collect such things. Perhaps his finest poem belongs to this early period, "Nero," which expresses with a horror that is truly and everlastingly sublime, a lust to be among the gods and to play sadistical tricks with the stars. This is Mr. Smith's province, the terrific and infinite void, which only such a whimsical imagination as his own can justly populate. But if you think he is powerless before other topics, read his love poems. He has written many, quite as astoundingly bad and good as the rest, with some which ought to outlast most of the American verse with which I am acquainted. But we cannot discuss his genius until some one has bought his books, and the professional haters of the new and daring in literature are likely to hold the field for some time yet.

Red . . .

My love's a blood-red-brilliant rose:
    My lady is a rubied wine,
A sparkling Burgundy, that glows
    With sunset-luster, crystalline.

Here on this hand, where I caressed
    That rose, are bitter flecks of red;
And the rich wine that thrills my breast
    Flows bitter, as if surfeited.

1930

En Route
(An American to Paris, 1931)

I. New York Harbor

Hail, thou Sea!
Liberator, Ocean, we hail thee!
Salt are thy waters,
Pungent the breath thereof,
Passionate thy striving—
Hail!

Strident ships and sailors,
Laughter, and sun, and wind
Congregate to greet thee—
Hail!

Quiver we before thee
Like beasts, wind-driven,
Seeking the open, the sunlight.
Grant us, O fathomless
Siren, breast unheeding,

Storm unending—sweep us
At last, to freedom!

II. On Deck

I wonder what the fish are doing
      'Way down there.
What a field for meditation
They must have; no noise or bustle,
      Free from care!

Fish, they say, are splendid brain-food.
      If that be so
The big chaps are in clover.
                    Perhaps not;
Nature's an inconsistent damsel,—
      They may not know.

Lord, if I had their chances, now,
      No more excuses!
No city din—no heartless public—
But scenery, quiet, isolation,
      All that conduces

To first-rate head-work. Of course, there's not
      Much atmosphere,
But then I'm from the Middle West,
I could survive.
             Yet . . . . for the present . . .
      I'll stay up here.

November

Above the plain sighs the evening wind,
      A cold breath,
Withering leaves, and grass, and the soul within me.
The slate-blue sky crawls against the sun,
      And freezes
The very wind that shudders now beneath it.
O wind! O sky! Night is coming after,
      And darkness,
And the clear naked limbs of trees . . .
                and silence.

Lament for H. P. L

Carl Fischer, Inc., New York.
No. 4 - 12 lines.

LAMENT FOR H.P.L.

Edward H. Cole

Some Words for Mr. Lovecraft

(Extracted from "The Reviewer's Club," *The Olympian* (vol. 7 no. 1) for October 1917.)

Although the *Conservative* is one of the best papers now published and presents the views of a man who has rapidly forged to the front ranks of this day's leaders, Mr. Lovecraft's peculiar prejudices, so rigidly adhered to and so forcefully promulgated, permeate the paper so utterly as to make it oppressive. Mr. Lovecraft is convinced that there was a time when English literature and the English language reached purity and perfection; accordingly, his mission in life is to return to that Johnsonian age and to lead others similarly backward. He believes in birth and blood. To him Socialism is anathema. He has strong anti-Semitic dislikes. In amateur journalism, he is convinced of the sordidness of politics, the uselessness of the National Amateur Press Association, and the eternal damnation of all those who do not seek the divine afflatus on the loftiest tips of the Johnsonian literary mountains. Of course, there is hyperbole in this characterization and several of the statements are rather strong. That, however, is just what Mr. Lovecraft drives a person to do. He uses hyperbole so often himself and so loves vigorous expression that he is a veritable gadfly. Now, in the July *Conservative*, Ira A Cole's poem "In Vita Elysium," would move the REVIEWER to hearty applause if only it were not expressed in that stately, regular eighteenth-century verse-form. How Ira Cole has developed! What rare gems of thought he has of late set forth in exquisite settings! But oh, that rigid, even—treading verse-form! What monotony, what inflexibility! If Ira Cole has become so accomplished a master of this form, what could he not do with the freer, lighter, flexible Romantic verse-forms? He is becoming merely a second edition of Mr. Lovecraft himself. Then there is Mr. McGavack's sturdy and bold statement of facts about the Genesis of the Revolutionary War. It takes courage to tell a democratic audience that the Revolution was really an act of unfilial selfishness, but Mr. McGavack sets forth the evidence succinctly and without patriotic gloss. Why did Mr. Lovecraft prefix the introduction in which his prejudices awaken prejudice and in which he shows sad lack of Mr. McGavack's historical knowledge and balance? Only in his editorials is Mr. Lovecraft at his best. His discussion of Mr. Tarkington's essay on Temperance is catholic-minded and fair, while his summary of the situation in the United Association stresses the one crying need of all amateur journalism.

For reasons of his own, Mr. Lovecraft has overlooked the REVIEWER on most of the *Conservative*'s publication days for the past two years. Will he not believe that he is a real stimulus to the REVIEWER and observe a more fraternal attitude on future mailing days?

Edith Miniter

Edith Miniter was one of the first with whom I became acquainted after I entered amateur journalism in 1905. Mere mention of that date reminds me how little fitted I am to write a biographical memoir of her, for at that time she was already one of the Old Timers whose very existence the Fossils were to thunder against within five years. I cannot attempt to write of her earlier years, despite knowing somewhat and having heard much; but from 1906 on, I came to know very intimately her admirable qualities, and later, too, to feel the lash of her criticism. Amateur journalism, indeed, was the greatest passion of her life. Life, I know, had hurt her. She received new acquaintances "on suspicion." Once they proved to share her love for our world of letters she gathered them to her heart and gradually admitted them to her circle of friends and opened to them a joyousness of conversation and companionship rare and precious. She seemed to find that Jacob Golden and I, who together

Edward H. Cole
Honorary Life Director
Emeritus

From *Fossil* (Summer 1965)

made her acquaintance as the young publishers of *The Hustler* were worthy of the privilege; and neither of us, I am certain, will ever lose from his heart the glorious days of the following five years. Her home at 17 Akron Street, Roxbury, was a Mecca to which came every amateur journalist visiting Boston. Together with her gracious and lovable mother, Lady Jane Dowe, Edith Miniter presided over a salon whose hospitality and brilliance were unforgettable.

She had created the Hub Amateur Journalists' Club in the nineties. That she was the heart which pulsated its life blood is obvious from the fact that although it lived to be one of the oldest organizations of amateur journalists, it ceased to exist after her departure from Boston, approximately ten years ago.

Edith Miniter became president of the National Amateur Press Association at the New York Convention in 1909. Unfortunately, her administration marks the transition from a somewhat Golden Age; and it is the unhappy fact that the convention at which she was chosen, and, indeed, the very fact of her election, gave rise to a bitter attack by the Old Guard (the Olympian Council) of the Fossils upon the participation of mature men and women in amateur affairs. Regardless of the merits of the case, it was indeed one of the ironies of life that the attack should have come in the administration of the one woman to whom amateur journalism was life itself and whose elevation to the presidency was a reward richly deserved and too long delayed. Though friendships of long standing were strained or destroyed, Edith Miniter met attack with ridicule and brilliant wit that kept many of the honors of the combat on her side. Nevertheless from that day there has been a cloud over anyone who has ventured to remain active, especially politically, in the National Amateur Press Association, beyond the period of youth. Although the New York convention of 1933 rather dissipated that cloud into nothing more than thin mist, and although, too, several of those who, over twenty years previously, had attacked her took occasion to mitigate their earlier severity, I feel certain that the injustices of the Young Blood Movement hurt Edith Miniter keenly.

The years that swiftly followed brought other unhappy consequences. Although there was the successful novel, or rather series of sketches, *Our Natupski Neighbors,* to mark the height of her professional success, there came with the World War a changed literary taste that prevented publication of the sequel upon which she was working. There came, too, the death of her loved mother, the break-up of her home, and several unsatisfactory attempts to live with one friend or another. Then, too, there was constantly the increase of asthma. So far as amateur journalism went, these years were marked by her unfailing efforts to keep alive the Hub Club, from which had departed, for one reason or another, most of the older members.

Ultimately she retired to Wilbraham, not far from Springfield, Massachusetts. There her family had property. There her relatives lived. There, in the happier days of her mother's life, there had been an annual vacation, shared infrequently but memorably by such amateur journalists as had the opportunity to make the trip. In the last years of her life she became a semi-invalid. At such times as she was able (infrequent, however) she welcomed short visits from friends; nevertheless, even writing letters became a task almost beyond her strength. She was compelled by reason of ill health to reject an opportunity to attend the convention in New York in 1933. For all that, she retained her lively interest in the affairs of our small world, and several who were fortunate to receive word from her in the past year will cherish the flashes of wit and the occasionally caustic comment on current affairs as well as the kindly and friendly interest and sympathy which characterized them.

Years ago, in the Akron Street days, a happy idea received animated discussion—the establishing of a Haven for amateur journalists, a colony to which we could retreat and hold communion with those we loved and with those, too, whom we fought but really cherished. We all realized, even as we painted the glad picture, how unlikely of realization it was in this mortal world. But none of us, I know, has ever quite despaired of the hope that in the world to which we shall go, each in his time, there will be a little corner apart where we who have shared bright golden hours in the fellowship of amateur journalism shall come together again for unending days. Should such a dream come true every one who knew her will look forward to joining that band and finding Edith Miniter as Presiding Genius.

Edith Miniter

Little Pilgrimages to the Homes of Amateurs

There is only one way to reach the home of E. H. Cole without climbing a hill and that is to climb another hill and come down the opposite side. This home is in Somerville, Mass., a city founded, I believe, in 1882, for the world in general, but not until 1905 for amateurs in particular, when Cole and Golden were discovered editing The Hustler.

As a preliminary to visiting here W. R. Murphy invariably rings up the House next Door, but this is not absolutely necessary. Whatever happens, however on being received at 36 Tower street you are asked to walk up stairs, and if you keep walking you get to the print shop where you see something absolutely peculiar to the place—type locked up top and bottom of page, with nothing to keep the sides from flying into space but a divinity that shapes our ends and the wind that is chastened to the shorn lamb.

The most prominent objects in the house are the Fossil Cup, the Gibson picture that looks like a lovely lady in some lights and a grinning skull in others, and Jacob Golden. The first two are fixtures and if the last doesn't show up in five minutes they think something has happened and send for him.

E. H. Cole has one of the best trained mothers in amateur journalism, she entertains amateurs at all hours without a murmur, and as a reward her son is sometimes so considerate as to give warning of their coming (for instance on fixed dates, such as the April and September club meetings.) Other times she is never caught napping. If forty amateur journalists with typical appetites walk in some evening just as she was planning for a quiet hour she rises equal to the occasion, orders the breaking open of the nearest grocery, and serves the results with sang froid and coffee.

Adolphe de Castro

Ambrose Bierce As He Really Was

An Intimate Account of His Life and Death

A people is as great as its literature. This has been said before, but it will not hurt to repeat it. Once in a while, a people strikes a balance of its literary "business" and the makers thereof. Without mental reservations, it says of one or another:

"This was a man!"

Ambrose Bierce undoubtedly was the master craftsman in literary art of his day. He wrought in an inimitable style the satire that required purely objective treatment and invented cutting invective in verse the meter of which has the rhythm of a veritable *danse du diable*. Bierce employed this sort of expression when fancy urged him to lash a sinner. Thoughts of mercy were as distasteful to him as a mess of herbs to a tiger.

Of course, he knew that he afforded amusement to many nude souls by his attacks against the soilure of others. But he grinned with satisfaction to know that those nude souls wondered when their own turns would come and trembled even as they smiled.

Survivors of a bygone day have lately revived a "Bierce cult," not so much for the sake of what he wrote as for what he is supposed to have been. Permit me to tell the story in brief of Bierce as I knew him rather intimately since 1886, and of his death in Mexico.

When I first met Bierce, I had been in San Francisco about two years, practising dentistry and endeavoring to write in the English language. Fortunately for my purpose, I became acquainted with Henry D. Bigelow—generally called "Petey" Bigelow—a real artist as a reporter and feature writer on the San Francisco *Examiner*.

Petey had introduced me to Robert Louis Stevenson, whom he greatly resembled physically. But as I had the merest bowing acquaintance with English literature, the name of the great Scotsman meant scarcely more to me than that of an Englishman who "wrote," was in delicate health and was exceedingly pleasant.

I even had the temerity to show Robert Louis Stevenson one of my short stories, translated from my own German, and the dear, wonderful fellow graciously praised it as "a very clever idea."

As Petey had spoken enthusiastically of "Mr. Bierce," whom he pronounced a marvelous genius, I begged him to bring Bierce to my office, which was already a rendezvous for a number of good fellows when they wanted a smoke, a drink and plenty of talk on many subjects.

Petey brought Bierce, and before long we were deep in conversation. Let me qualify this statement. The conversation was carried on by Bierce and Bigelow, with occasioned remarks directed at me. I spoke with extreme diffidence—the diffidence of a person whose trousers have ripped and who sidles along, so as not to show his back to the audience. Dropping the metaphor, I will say that I made my remarks mostly with nouns, fearing to employ conjunctions, adverbs, adjectives or even verbs, lest Bierce note my imperfect mastery of English. If Ambrose Bierce felt amused at my speech, he failed to show it; though once, when I said "idiocity" for idiocy, he stopped and looked at me pensively.

"Excellent word, 'idiocity.' Ought to be in the dictionary. But it is not, and the world will have to worry along with *idiocy*," he declared.

Physically, Ambrose Bierce lived up to my exuberant imagination of the literary tyrant. He was then near fifty years of age, easily six feet tall, broad-chested and lean bodied. His military shoulders were surmounted by a head which was beautiful and awe-inspiring. It was a fine, well-made head with a *mélange* of yellow-white hair of medium length which ran in all directions in curly wilfulness. His eyes, blue like sheer lightning, deep set and rather small, were overhung by long, shaggy, yellow brows, between which was "the thinker's furrow." His nose was straight, finely nostriled and fairly right-angular. A well-turned mustache covered a large, generous mouth with full lips and a strong chin that had the suspicion of a cleft. He had the red coloring of what is now called the Nordic type.

After the first visit, I saw a great deal of Bierce. My "sidling" in adjectives and prepositions gradually vanished. I read much under Bierce's guidance, and above all I read Bierce.

I delighted in his incisive remarks, in the cleverness of his versification, in the strength and beauty of his epigrams and the iridescent light shafts with which he bewildered his assailants.

Sometimes an adversary got under his guard, and then he'd spit like a cat. One such fencing foe was Frank Pixley, the editor of the San Francisco *Argonaut*, who wielded a wicked pen himself and of whom Bierce used to say:

"If the fellow had had an education, he would have become dangerous!" Which was great praise from Bierce.

When those two fighters were at it, literature of a superior sort was produced, which verified the talmudic adage that "the jealousy of authors begets learning." Pixley did not have the grace, the *savoir faire*, of Bierce, but he could lambast "the Pope's Irish," as he called the Catholics, in picturesque terms, and when he mentioned Bierce the ink in the pot sizzled.

Bierce retorted with epigrams, such as the one in which he cautions the heavy-booted muleteer walking over Frank Pixley's grave to "step lightly, stranger, everywhere but here."

Inexorable in his attack upon foes, he sometimes was tenderness itself with a friend—particularly when the friend was dead. He wrote of Ralph Smith:

Light lie the earth upon his dear dead heart,
And dreams disturb him never.

Yet he showed little of "the gleam of the Galilean," as one of his admirers expressed it, in speaking of Ralph Smith and others while they were in the flesh. "They may become backsliders, and I would have to use the lash," he would tell me.

I think of him as the American Heine; for like the great German poet, he planted asphodel in the dust of the literary incompetents he had slain.

Bierce and myself gradually assumed the relationship of master and pupil—with limitations, of course. He was busy with his writing, and I with the double task of attending to my professional duties and translating from many languages to sharpen my pen for English.

In 1888, Bierce had gone to Howell Mountain, Napa County, where he was singularly free from the asthma that tormented him so. Yielding to a temptation against which I had fought for a long time, I sent him a composition of mine which I believed, in my simplicity, to be blank verse. I received the "poem" back with a letter—the first handwriting of Bierce I had ever seen—in which he told me that the lines gave evidence of a poetic nature, but poetry in the accepted sense, and particularly blank verse, they were not. If I cared, though, to come to Howell Mountain, he would talk the matter over with me.

I had been overworking, and I do not exaggerate when I state that the thrill of receiving that invitation from Bierce was almost fatal to my weakened system. I telegraphed my acceptance, and on my arrival the biblical elder brother could not have manifested greater tenderness than Bierce showed me. He ordered me to take a shower, and—*mirabile dictu*—he personally gave me an alcohol rub, after he had seen how unhandy I was in the matter. He then put me to sleep.

During the next few days, I became a silent, spell-bound listener when Bierce talked. He was not only very eloquent, but he had a strong, singing quality in his voice, and I drank in his speech like precious nectar.

He would stop of a sudden and demand why I was silent. He would ask about my work. He would show especial delight in what I told him with reference to Semitic or Russian literature. He never could get enough of Mitchkievitch (it is spelled differently in Polish, but this is the way to pronounce it) and my renditions of Heine gave him great pleasure. He studiously corrected my literary errors. His information regarding English blank verse was so elucidating that I have never since attempted the form.

But Bierce instructed me in matters other than the merely literary, and his sentiments were in complete contradiction to his personal kindness to me. His sweeping assertion that "nothing matters" shocked me at first, then slightly amused me. He had probably read too much Schopenhauer—Nietzsche was not in vogue then—I told myself, and was willing to let it go at that. However, Bierce would not let it go at that. He wanted me to digest the fact that *nothing mattered.* It was not asserted with the gentle, philosophic intent of Emerson that "nothing is new, nothing's true and nothing matters." Bierce's grim dictum included the affections, the world's travail, its aspirations, its hopes, its beliefs, its hates and its loves.

"Some things matter—our friendship, for instance," I said.

"No, not even that. You are a sort of buffer. I can tell you what I will not put on paper. The skull here," he said, pointing to a hideously grinning skull, on the frontal of which Bierce had written 'One of my forgiven', "has served the purpose for some time. But it does not snap its eyes as you do. It has none to snap, but the point is the same—nothing matters."

"And love?" I asked.

"Satiety makes it immaterial."

"And children?" I inquired.

"Calves or companions. I don't blame the cuckoo hen for laying her eggs in other birds' nests. Wise bird the cuckoo. Take my word for it," he replied.

"And honor?" I persisted.

"The shadow of a shadow; the stuff fools' crowns are made of."

"And patriotism and civic righteousness?"

"Badges of fools and crooks—Johnson said it in more words, but it amounts to the same thing," he told me.

"And life and suffering and death? Do none of these count in the scheme of humanity?" I pleaded.

"They matter much to story writers. Personally I think there is nothing in death to seek or to fear. It is no more than life, and a good deal easier to maintain. One cannot die while alive, and when dead one does not know. So what's the hardship?"

No wonder they called him, "Bitter Bierce!"

As the years passed I became more and more his "buffer"; and it often came to me that Jesus was right when he told the Pharisees that they take the beam from their own eye before they would remove the mote from that of their fellowman, or words to that effect. There was absolutely no justice in his treatment of women, particularly those who refused to come under his personal sway. He branded one of the sweetest singers of California "an indecent liar and drunkard," simply because she had refused to receive him.

When I read this in Bierce's weekly "Prattle," I asked him if there were such a thing as "a decent liar." His answer was characteristic, "To hit a villain, one may lie decently." He soon after proved it to me. He had attacked a person, who believed the attack to have been inspired by me and had written Bierce so. Thereupon, Bierce not only published the man's letter and cut his character to shreds, but he wrote about me so loftily and exaggeratedly that I was constrained to ask him why he did it.

"To make his smart the keener," was Bierce's reply.

"Ah, then this is what you understand by decent lying?" I asked him.

He did not deem my question worth answering, and demanded to see the installment of *Oriental Aphorisms* I was then preparing for the *Overland Monthly* which Bierce did not like. After he had read the article he curtly remarked that it was too damned good for the *"Warmed-Overland."*

Bierce was not an academically educated man. He was, however, an assiduous reader of Brewer's *Phrase and Fable* from which he got his apt classical references. He had a rare contempt for all the old classics, and read extracts to steal their thunder, as he told me. He read Poe—I am quoting—"to avoid repetition and forestall comparison." He read Mark Twain, "to sharpen lethiferous wit against bovine humor." In these confidences he always made acrid sport of his literary friends. Jimmy Tufts, Bierce's worshiper and the dearest soul I have known, he named "a carrier of water and hewer of wood." Tufts had more than once helped put over a Biercean screed which the gentle and conservative managing editor, Henderson, would have blue-penciled or pigeon-holed.

Joaquin Miller, the Poet of the Sierras, was characterized "a sot, addicted to the drinking of the vilest rotgut, a fair poet but an abominable prose writer."

There are many persons living who believe that they enjoyed Bierce's friendship, but of whom the "buffer" heard much that was bitter. His friends were no more immune from attack than his enemies. He was a man to carry a grudge and spit his venom when least expected.

During the years in which he hurled his weekly shafts against pigmies, or trained a cannon on gnats, the readers of the San Francisco *Examiner* asked themselves the cause of Bierce's bitterness. Few could answer the question, but the "buffer" was of the few. There probably was one other, namely, William Randolph Hearst. But he was sure not to tell. Bierce undoubtedly brought more readers to the *Examiner* than all the other features combined, and yet Bierce received for his work—work that would today bring him a princely income—thirty-five dollars a week!

Now, why did Bierce labor for such a beggarly wage? Why did Bierce hate Billy Hearst with an inveterate hatred? Why, when Hearst wrote him a letter, did Bierce throw the letter on the floor and stamp on it? I witnessed this twice. Even in later years, Bierce wrote me that he was "nothing but a cog in Mr. Hearst's machinery." (The letter lies before me now.)

There are answers to all these questions. Bierce had been writing for the San Francisco *Chronicle*, then owned by Michael de Young, a Jew with an Irish-Catholic domestic establishment. De Young was an orthodox Jew when it came to circumcising the pay of his employees. Bierce did not like de Young; but necessity compelled him and expediency counseled Patience. He hoped to enter the service of the Southern Pacific Railway in higher capacity than W. C. Morrow, also a writer, who was a desk man in the "S. P.'s" offices. Bierce despised such low station. He submitted a plan to Senator Stanford, Vice-President of the railroad, by which the Company was to create the post of "General Counselor" at a salary of $25,000 a year. The Senator, who was a very progressive man, took the matter under advisement. However, C. P. Huntington knew no sentiment other than the music of his rolling stock, and he rejected the proposition.

William Randolph Hearst had just received the *Evening Examiner* as a birthday present from his indulgent father, who told him to make something of the paper and of himself. Hearst changed the *Examiner* to a morning paper, engaged the best talent he could find, and having in all probability heard of the failure of the Bierce deal with the railroad, he offered Bierce the post of a free lance on the *Examiner*. Hearst wanted a whip with which to lash the Republican Senator Stanford, and to wield against all and sundry who might be displeasing to him. Bierce, who had been writing under the pen-name of "The Town-Crier," was just the man for the work. Hearst sent Bierce a note, which did not find him at home. He was then returning, sadly disappointed, from the Southern Pacific's offices and he was going to collect the space rate for a little article he had written for the *Chronicle*.

He found Mike de Young playing the role of cashier. Bierce put in a slip, on which was written the amount coming to him as he had received it from the editor. But de Young found that there was a difference in his own favor of "thirteen and three-quarter cents." He shoved out four silver dollars, asking Bierce to give him the change. Bierce took the money and threw it in Mike de Young's face and "got his blood, anyhow," as he told me.

Bierce, almost hopeless, went to his lodging and found the Hearst note. He did not whoop, for he hated the world. But he was ready to accept the post offered to him. Now he had a chance to get even with "the thieves of the railroad," and he could at his leisure split the nerves of Mike de Young. This last he did in verse that scintillated and seared. Read *The Lifted Finger* and see the "bug in amber" that Bierce made of de Young.

Bierce did not wait until one sinned publicly or "exposed his mental vacuity" in the press. He voided his rheum upon the beards of all. He attacked the editors of other papers. If any one, to curry favor, sent him an effusion, he would print the worst part of it and put that person in the pillory. Few dared to reply to him. It is no overstatement to say that a great dread, mixed with grim satisfaction on the part of some, seized the community.

Yet Bierce himself was the prey of a gnawing grief. He believed in himself. He believed that he was of a mental stature to stand side by side with Horace, Juvenal and Dean Swift. He wanted to be so recognized by future generations, and he saw no way of realizing his one desire. His quotidain writing, his weekly "Prattle," his letters—and he wrote thousands of them—were all ephemeral. The only way to assure immortality, he felt, was to achieve a great book between covers.

He had written much and brilliantly in London under the name of "Dod Grile." He had received recognition from W. E. Gladstone. Then circumstances had compelled him to return to the United States and enter the field of hack writers at so much a line. He easily stood forth as the greatest, even in such a galaxy of good writers as California then had; but it was a beggarly existence at best, and no promise of eternal fame.

He sent his collected stories to every publisher in the country, but one after another refused to issue them. Then he sent out his verses to those lusty fellows "who drank wine from the skulls of authors," as Bierce said of the publishers. Again the rounds were made, and the poetry came back. He went so far as to separate the sheep from the goats; he submitted the milder ones, to no avail.

With each rejection, Bierce grew livid. He ground his teeth and swore at the "predatory wretches." He humbled himself to the point of asking William Randolph Hearst to publish his verses; but Hearst, too, refused. When E. L. G. Steele, an Englishman, magnanimously defrayed the cost of printing a volume of short stories, Bierce reviled the man to the "buffer":

"Who cares for prose? What lesson have I taught in my stories? None at all. It is my poetry that ought to go out in book form, and the idiot thinks he has done me a favor!"

My heart was wrung for his sake. This greatest of writers had poured out his grief and his bitterness to me, and I was helpless to do anything! I was then vacationing at Howell Mountain, and I often heard his complaints. On my return to San Francisco, I went to see Mrs. Phoebe A. Hearst and begged her to aid in the publication of Bierce's verses. "It is not advisable to perpetuate a curse between covers," said the wonderfully wise woman. It was the truth, but I felt sad beyond expression.

When I saw Bierce again I promised him I would publish his book if I lived. I knew nothing then of publishing. But when was true friendship lacking in courage? We were then in the blessed year 1889 and I would have given my life for Ambrose Bierce.

That same year I read a story in a German Magazine entitled, *The Monk of Berchtesgaden*. It was from the pen of Professor Richard Voss. It purported to be the diary of a monk, who on his transference to another monastery together with two other monks, passes a field in which is a gallows with a man hanging. The vultures gather to feast on the corpse, and the young and beautiful daughter of the hangman seeks to chase the birds of prey. Ambrosius, the hero of the story, falls in love with the girl. He shows his affection in many ways. His secret is discovered not only by the prior but also by a young fellow, a daring seducer, who wants to have his will of the girl. The monk becomes jealous, and in a fit of insane rage he kills the girl and is hanged.

Nothing I had ever read, not even *The Scarlet Letter,* by Hawthorne, had so gripped me. It was beautiful beyond the telling. The medieval, monkish style of the narrative made it doubly attractive, and it was just long enough—or short enough—to be right.

Not until I had translated the story into English did I become conscious of the fact that it would never do for American readers, twenty-five per cent of whom were Catholics and who this story would keenly offend.

I had written on the title page the exact origin of the story. For the time being, there was not the least thought in my mind of cabbaging the tale in any shape, form or manner. But I was keenly conscious that I must cut the literary cloth to suit the American wearer or else not do it at all. I therefore set about to make changes, slight indeed, yet in such a way as to enable me "to put it over." I wrote a version, almost exactly like the original, yet with a subtle change here and there that palliated the situation, but left the tragic element intact.

This done, I deliberately wrote another story, not omitting a jot or tittle from the central thought, only instead of being a monk, Ambrosius was a novice, intended for the Church through his own father's grief at the loss of the wife he adored. The girl was a changeling, and through a series of vicissitudes they finally won to a perfect state of happiness.

I had no choice between the two. My own story was enhanced by the tragic power of the original. Whatever stylistic blemishes or "Germanisms" adhered to my translation or to the rendition, could, I thought, be readily overcome by any person who pretended to write good English.

Accordingly, a Miss von Loevenfels was engaged to copy the story and was requested to eliminate all Germanisms. But the young lady, being German and the daughter of a German scientist, fell under the spell of the German and failed in what I desired to accomplish. A Dr. Gustave Glaser, graduate of Cambridge University, England, and writer for the *San Francisco News Letter,* copied the story, pocketed his fee, but did not change the result.

The impasse was doubly disheartening for the reason that I could trust none of the hack-writers and had not the courage to show the story to Bierce. His asthma prevented him from doing any lengthy writing, and he had often told me that he hated the long story. The manuscripts, therefore, reposed in my desk to be looked at occasionally. I could not submit them to a publisher because I did not want to be laughed out of the literary field as a poor translator.

One day a mutual friend of Bierce and myself—a stock broker by the name of Charles Kaufman—came to my office and picked up the manuscript. He laid it down only after he had read the last line.

"I wonder," he said at length, "how much you added to the work of the German?"

"Very little in this copy, but much in my own conception of how the ending ought to be for American readers," and I showed him the other copy, and also the German original.

"I like the tragic best. Has Bierce seen the story?" he asked.

"I would not molest Bierce with my writings," I replied.

"Nonsense. Bierce ought to read the story," he said and went away.

The following day Bierce came to my office.

"Kaufman told me you had written a good story. Let me see it," he demanded.

I gave him the two manuscripts and he took them home to read. A day or two after Bierce returned to my office, slammed the manuscripts on my desk and said:

"The tragic rendition is the better. This story will give you a good slice of reputation in the literary world."

"You don't say," I remarked, and bade him be seated and tell me more.

"And so, you damned sneak, you would have kept this story from me?" he cried, and his blue eyes shot glints of lightning from underneath his shaggy brows.

To say that his remark made me happy is to express it mildly. In a stride I was by his side.

"Dear, great Heathen Master, you do not for a moment think that I would have kept this from you. I feared to molest you," I told him, the tears running down my cheeks.

Of course, he was pleased and, putting his arm over my shoulder, he accepted a drink and entered upon the question of publication.

"I would not think of publishing the story with Germanisms in it," I protested.

"That's precisely what I intend to pencil," he told me.

"It will not do. You can no more escape the interest in the story than I or the others, and this very interest will make you a poor proof reader," I boldly told him.

"I plead guilty to the charge," he said.

"The only way to overcome it, is to copy it verbatim. When you actually copy the thing, your hand will not write a word that your taste will not confirm. Copy it," I pleaded.

"It is a luxury I cannot afford. If I do not write for the *Examiner*, I don't eat," he said, and I am quoting his exact words.

"I will give you fifty dollars a week, providing it does not exceed four weeks, for copying the story; and I will give you interest in the proceeds in whatever form the story is printed, providing again that you sign your name along with mine."

To this he consented. We at once went to our friend Kaufman who was a notary public. There Bierce himself wrote the contract in which he agreed *to revise* the story entitled *The Monk and the Hangman's Daughter*. He then and there also received the two hundred dollars cash. Each one got a copy of the paper (mine, alas, was burned in the San Francisco fire, but Bierce's copy certainly must be extant among his papers), and I at least went home happy as a lark. *The Monk and the Hangman's Daughter* would get the touch of a master hand.

It was finally finished in the strong, precise hand of Bierce. The revision, although slight, was nevertheless subtle and effective and the story was published in the *Sunday Examiner* of San Francisco. The prefatory note which set forth the exact origin of the story was signed by *myself and Bierce*—the three words are underscored to show that my name preceded that of Bierce in the first publication. Later, a publisher demanded that Bierce's name—as the better known—precede mine, and I reluctantly consented.

It was only after the Chicago publisher had failed and another offered to issue the story providing I would change the title to *Benedicta*, that Bierce and I broke. In a paragraph which attacked the proposed publisher in scathing invective, he wrote, "The story as it stands, I wrote myself."

When I called him to account, he abused me most picturesquely, not because I told him that he had lied, but because of the Hadrianic principle: "No one shall tell me how to destroy mine enemies!" The presumptuous publisher was his "enemy" and deserved annihilation.

Bierce always wanted the last word in an argument. He wanted to be right, though he were obviously wrong. He abused me, and desired to appear the injured party. Even when I not only published his verses, but through his "friendly advice" lost thousands of dollars, he heaped maledictions on my devoted head and warned our mutual friends to have nothing to do with me. In later years, when we had "made up," I once asked him why he had said such horrible things about me. "To forestall anything you might say about me," was his answer.

This glimpse of my association with Bierce is but a single page in the history. A book of many hundred pages might be written about the man, his work, his character or lack of character. The checkered pattern of our friendship included many side issues in which men and measures, nationally and internationally known, were involved. But all this will die with me. I was not a lamb myself. Down-at-the-heel scribes have more than once importuned me to give them details about Bierce's life, but I have always refused. One may defend his rights even against the King, but one need not be a tattle-tale.

If Bierce made me his "buffer" in my youth, he was perhaps quite certain that he could trust me. And, his faults apart, I still say that no other writer of his times possessed so wonderful a vehicle of expression, or wielded a wit so keen and cruel, as Ambrose Bierce.

With my hand on my heart, I say that it is my firm conviction, based upon much reading of the world's literature, that since the best period of remote antiquity, the world has produced no writer whose epigrams had the polish and the cutting quality—nay, the absolute matchlessness—of those written by Ambrose Bierce. Oscar Wilde and Bernard Shaw are children compared to this giant. Theirs is a diluted spirit, his is one hundred per centum.

Now as to his miserable end.

I am prepared at last to tell what I have hitherto deliberately withheld, or by equally deliberate misinformation have sought to conceal. Despite everything, Ambrose Bierce always was and always will be my hero, my master, and I have hated to admit that he was sordidly murdered in Mexico. But such is the case. Ambrose Bierce was shot to death by Villa soldiers a few weeks after Pancho Villa and Venustiano Carranza split.

Bierce, in his old age, had embarked on the quixotic adventure of participating in a Mexican revolution. He had joined the Villa forces and was with that General at the taking of Chihuahua, in 1913. After Villa was installed in Chihuahua City, there was virtually nothing for Bierce to do and he began to drink *tequila,* the vilest liquor that Mexico produces. Those who drink it for any length of time literally turn blue. In his ebriose condition, he committed the folly of criticising Villa.

Bierce had with him a peon who had worked a bit in Texas and understood a little English, even as Bierce understood a few phrases of Spanish. This man drank with Bierce and parroted Bierce's condemnation of Villa's methods. Becoming restless for action, Bierce suggested that they desert to the Carranza side. This was overheard and carried to Villa. The peon was forced to confess under torture, and Villa sardonically ordered him to lead the Americano out of Chihuahua City, to join Carranza. They left at night and had not gone a quarter of a mile when they were overtaken by a squad of soldiers and shot down like dogs. Their bodies were left where they lay, to be devoured by the vultures. I think that Bierce, burnt out, was bent on dying in Mexico, though doubtless he would have liked the circumstances of his exit to have been more glamorous.

Nearly ten years later, I wrote to Pancho Villa for an interview. I wanted to include him in my series, *Men in Mexico*. The General very politely, if lugubriously, declined to say anything for publication. But I would not stay refused, and went to see him. I was warmly received and told all I desired to know.

In the course of the conversation, I asked lightly if he had many American friends. The General expatiated upon the numerous trips he had made to Los Angeles with his brother Hipolito. I then asked if he recalled "Don Ambrosio," as I had been told he called Bierce. Villa's face became dark, and he frowned formidably.

That Gringo was this and was that, said Villa. For a time, he had paid no attention to him at all and had permitted him to souse himself with *tequila*. It was only after the Gringo had contemplated treachery that he was driven away.

"Driven away!" I came no closer than that to a confirmation of the murder from Villa's own lips. But I interpreted "driven away" quite differently from what we in America understand by the term. I had every reason to do so. It confirmed the evidence I had already pieced together, and which I have outlined above.

[Note:—Mr. Adolphe de Castro has recently won a law suit, which compels the publishers of a collected edition of the works of Ambrose Bierce to recognize him as the co-author of *The Monk and the Hangman's Daughter.*—EDITOR.)

Let There Be Light!

Half dreaming on the desert's edge I lay,
And saw the sun with tender touch caress
The sleeping palm to smiling wakefulness
And dow'r with golden tongues the fragrant bay.
Night spirits stole to crannied depths away
While distant mountains, clad in gloomy dress
Of seething vapors from the wilderness,
Raised flaming heads to greet triumphant day.

Low moaned the conquer'd spirit of the night
And called Simoom who, menace-breathing, slept
In fearsome vales, but quickly rose to fight
The nascent dawn; and, shrieking, crashing, leapt
On clouds of dust that whirled and, roaring, swept
The sky—but Allah said: "Let there be light!"

from "Had I Another Hundred Years"

The critics of my speech and acts,
Cannot arouse my ire;
But those who twist the truth and facts,
Are skunks that stink for hire

         *   *   *

And yet, with hundred years to live
And clarity of head,
I even might this skunk forgive
As soon as he were dead.

The Poe Acrostics

In a Sequester'd Providence Churchyard Where Once Poe Walk'd

Eternal brood the shadows on this ground,
Dreaming of centuries that have gone before;
Great elms rise solemnly by slab and mound,
Arch'd high above a hidden world of yore.
Round all the scene a light of memory plays,
And dead leaves whisper of departed days,
Longing for sights and sounds that are no more.

Lonely and sad, a spectre glides along
Aisles where of old his living footsteps fell;
No common glance discerns him, tho' his song
Peals down thro' time with a mysterious spell:
Only the few who sorcery's secret know,
Espy amidst these tombs the shade of Poe.

                    —H. P. Lovecraft

Edgar Allan Poe

Enshrined within our hearts is e'er thy name,
Dear Bard, unjoyed by lasting happiness
Great love doth yield; but through thy pain and stress
A messenger, the ghostly Raven, comes,
Revealing horror stark and cold; he bore

A tear that flowed from eyes of lost Lenore,
Light-glinting, and the shade of her caress.
Lo, then, thy genius flamed with art that chills
A grim, ubiquitous malignity.
Night-gloomed and pulsing with portending ills
Pernicious yet delightful, brought to thee
On angel's wings, a gift that, loved and feared,
Enranked thee greatest monarch of the weird.

                    —Adolphe de Castro

St. John's Churchyard

Endless, the darkly printed tombstones rise;
Dim evening sunset pours about them now,
Golden and pale, on path and grave and bough,
And furtively they stare with lifeless eyes,
Remembering ages lost beneath the years,
All silent now, with strife and love and tears
Like scattered leaves through which the autumn sighs.

Less than the leaves a century can grow
As tale and memory blend before the gaze;
No longer lost, these half-forgotten days . . .
Perhaps the shadows stir, perhaps they show
Outcast by life and death, the lonely form
Exiled, of Poe, the man of night and storm.
—Robert H. Barlow

In A Providence Churchyard

Elusive shadows flit about the close.
Dim-lighted windows of the church near by
Give back the orient of the sunset sky.
Around us, ranged in little scattered rows,
Rude forefathers of Providence repose,
A vanished crew, whose slender memory
Lives here alone in sorrow's chiseled cry,
Long past the love of friends or hate of foes.
And here may Edgar not have loved to dwell,
Now wan with woe, now rapt with Fancy's spell?
Perhaps a verse to Sarah Whitman's grace
Or words of matchless song to Annabelle
Evolved within this memory-haunted place!
—Maurice W. Moe

Where He Walked

Ever the quiet whisper comes. Sere as the falling leaf,
Dim and remembered faintly, like the pang of an ancient grief;
Ghost of a gray nostalgia that the kindred soul must know
As he walks by the lichened marbles that knew the touch of Poe.

Restless the chilly wind is, and restless the autumn leaves,
And they drift from the bowing maple as it trembles and sways and grieves,
Lifting its branches to sullen skies, drooping its branches low,

Low to caress the poet, many a year ago.

Ever the quiet whisper comes, stealing across the graves;
Night is within the whisper, and the silence of sunless caves,
Purple and onyx of Carcassonne, satyr and nymph of Pan,
Orcus, god of the underworld—the shadowed soul of man . . .

Ever the quiet whisper comes, the ghost of the lonely Poe.
                                              —Henry Kuttner

Glossary of Frequently Mentioned Names

Adams, Hazel Pratt (1888–1927), wife of A. M. Adams, both amateur journalists. She was official editor (1916–17) and president (1923–24) of the NAPA. Upon her death, HPL wrote the elegy "The Absent Leader."

Babcock, Ralph W., Jr. (1914–2003), a lifelong writer and printer (since the age of seven). Was active in amateur journalism (president [1934–35] and official editor [1939–40] of the NAPA), and publisher of the *Red Rooster, Scarlet Cockerel,* and other papers.

Barlow, R[obert] H[ayward] (1918–1951), author and collector. As a teenager he corresponded with HPL and acted as his host during two long visits in the summers of 1934 and 1935. In the 1930s he wrote several works of weird and fantasy fiction, some in collaboration with HPL. HPL appointed him his literary executor. He assisted August Derleth and Donald Wandrei in preparing the early HPL volumes for Arkham House. In the 1940s he went to Mexico and became a distinguished anthropologist.

Basinet, Victor L. (1889–1956), designer, longtime nurse, and artist. First president of the Providence Amateur Press Club.

Bradley, Chester P. (1917–1983), official editor of the NAPA (1934–35) and editor of the *Perspective Review.*

Bradofsky, Hyman (1906–2002), correspondent of HPL (1934–37). He was president of the NAPA (1935–36) and edited the *Californian* (1933f.), one of the most distinguished and voluminous amateur journals of the period.

Campbell, Paul J[onas] (1884–1945), amateur journalist and editor of the *Liberal, Bavardage,* and other amateur papers. President of the UAPA (1916–17).

Coates, Walter J[ohn] (1880–1941), amateur journalist, printer, editor of *Driftwind,* and staunch advocate of the literature of Vermont.

Cook, W. Paul (1880–1948), publisher of the *Monadnock Monthly,* the *Vagrant,* and other amateur journals; a longtime amateur journalist, printer, and lifelong friend of HPL. He first visited HPL in 1917, and it was he who urged HPL to resume writing fiction after a hiatus of nine years. In 1927 Cook published the *Recluse,* containing HPL's "Supernatural Horror in Literature."

Daas, Edward F. (1879–1962), amateur journalist who joined the UAPA within a year of its founding in 1895; was elected president in 1907 and served as official editor in 1913–14 and 1915–16. He recruited HPL to the UAPA in 1914. At the time of his death, he was serving as UAPA secretary. Editor of the *Lake Breeze.*

Davis, Edgar J. (1908–1949), young amateur journalist with whom HPL explored Newburyport and other locales in New England.

Davis, [Francis] Graeme (1881–1938), official editor (1917–18) and president (1918–19) of the NAPA. He wrote harshly of the rival UAPA in his amateur journal, the *Lingerer,* leading to HPL's essay "A Reply to *The Lingerer.*"

Dench, Ernest A[lfred] (1895?–?), British-born Brooklyn amateur, author of *Making the Movies* (1915) and other books about the cinema.

Derleth, August W[illiam] (1909–1971), author of weird tales and also a long series of regional and historical works set in his native Wisconsin. After HPL's death, he and Donald Wandrei founded the publishing firm of Arkham House to preserve HPL's work in book form.

Dowdell, William J. (1898–1953), amateur journalist, editor of *Dowdell's Bearcat,* who abruptly resigned as president of the NAPA in late 1922, leading the executive judges to appoint HPL as interim president.

Dryden, Wheeler (1892–1957), born George Dryden Wheeler, Jr., English actor and film director, half-brother of Charlie Chaplin, and father of rock musician Spencer Dryer.

Edkins, Ernest A[rthur] (1867–1946), longtime amateur journalist with whom HPL began corresponding in 1932. HPL persuaded him to rejoin the amateur journalism movement, and Edkins subsequently edited several issues of the journal *Causerie.*

Fritter, Leo (1878–1948), lawyer, amateur journalist, and member of the Woodbee Press Club. HPL supported Fritter's campaign to be president of the UAPA (1915), which Fritter won. (HPL was first vice-president.) He ousted HPL as official editor of the UAPA in the election of July 1922.

Gamwell, Annie E[meline] P[hillips] (1866–1941), HPL's younger maternal aunt, living with him at 66 College Street (1933–37).

Goodenough, Arthur H[enry] (1871–1936), amateur poet who resided in Brattleboro, VT. HPL visited him there on several occasions.

Greene, Sonia H[aft] (1883–1972), HPL's wife (1924–29). Born Sonia Haft Shafirkin in Ichnya (near Kiev), in Ukraine. Settling in the United States, she eventually joined the amateur journalism movement, publishing two lavish issues of the *Rainbow* and becoming president of the UAPA (1924–25). After her divorce from HPL, she moved to California and married Dr. Nathaniel Davis. *The Private Life of H. P. Lovecraft* (1985; rev. 1992) is her memoir of HPL.

Haggerty, Vincent B[artholemew] (1888–1943) amateur journalist associated with the NAPA in the 1920s and 1930s.

Hinrichs, O. W., official editor of the NAPA (1935), apparently responsible for the September 1935 issue. Removed from office by President Bradofsky and replaced by Helm C. Spink.

Hoag, Jonathan E. (1831–1927), an amateur poet. HPL, with James F. Morton, edited and published *The Poetical Works of Jonathan E. Hoag* (1923). The book contains HPL's annual birthday greetings to Hoag in verse.

Hoffman, Helene E. (1893–1919), president of the UAPA (1912–13), about whom HPL wrote the essay "Helene Hoffman Cole: Litterateur" and the poem "Helene Hoffman Cole: 1893–1919: The Club's Tribute." Wife of Edward H. Cole.

Houtain, George Julian (1884–1945), editor of the *Zenith*, amateur journalist who established the semi-professional humor magazine *Home Brew*, for which he commissioned HPL to write "Herbert West—Reanimator" (1921–22) and "The Lurking Fear" (1922) and CAS to illustrate the latter.

Jackson, Winifred Virginia (1876–1959), poet and amateur journalist who worked extensively with HPL during the period 1918–21; she was rumored to have amorous designs on HPL.

Kirk, George W[illard] (1898–1962), member of the Kalem Club. He published *Twenty-one Letters of Ambrose Bierce* (1922) and ran the Chelsea Bookshop in New York. For a time, he lived in the same apartment building in Brooklyn as HPL.

Kleiner, Rheinhart (1892–1949), amateur poet and longtime friend of HPL. Editor of *The Piper,* chairman of the Department of Public Criticism of the UAPA (1917–18), and president of the UAPA (1918–19). He visited HPL in Providence in 1918, 1919, and 1920, and met him frequently during the heyday of the Kalem Club (1924–26) in New York.

Kuntz, Eugene B. (1865–1944), Prussian-born poet, Presbyterian minister, and amateur journalist. HPL edited Kuntz's slim collection of poems, *Thoughts and Pictures* (Haverhill, MA: "Cooperatively published by H. P. Loveracft [*sic*] and C. W. Smith," 1932), probably revising the poems in the process.

Lawson, Horace L[owe] (1900–1980), amateur journalist who published several stories and essays by HPL in his journal, the *Wolverine.*

Leeds, Arthur (1882–1952?), an associate of HPL in New York and member of the Kalem Club.

Long, Frank Belknap (1901–1994), fiction writer, poet, member of the Kalem Club, and one of HPL's closest friends and correspondents. For a time he was the literary agent for Zealia Bishop, and he also did revisory work for Adolphe de Castro.

Loveman, Samuel (1887–1976), poet and longtime friend of HPL, Ambrose Bierce, Hart Crane, George Sterling, and Clark Ashton Smith. He wrote *The Hermaphrodite* (1926) and other works; member of the Kalem Club.

Lynch, Joseph Bernard (1879–1952), amateur journalist and member of the Hub Club.

McDonald, Philip B[ayard] (1888–1959), literary director of the Tesis Club of Toledo, assistant professor of Engineering English, University of Colorado, and assistant professor of English at New York University. Served as UAPA's chairman of the Department of Private Criticism. Husband of Edna Hyde.

McGeoch [Murch], Verna (1885–1949), official editor of the UAPA (1917–19).

McKeag, Ernest Lionel (1896–1974), British amateur journalist and later author of tales of adventure and science fiction.

McNeil, [Henry] Everett (1862–1929), author of historical and adventure novels for boys; member of the Kalem Club.

Merritt, A[braham] (1884–1943), writer of fantasy and horror tales for the pulps. His work was much admired by HPL in spite of its concessions to pulp formulae. His late novel, *Dwellers in the Mirage* (1932), may have been influenced by HPL.

Miniter, Edith (1867–1934), amateur journalist who also professionally published a novel, *Our Natupski Neighbors* (1916) and many short stories. HPL was guest at her home in Wilbraham, MA, in the summer of 1928.

Moe, Donald James (1914–1994), younger son of Maurice W. Moe.

Moe, Maurice W[inter] (1882–1940), amateur journalist, English teacher, and longtime friend and correspondent of HPL. He lived successively in Appleton and Milwaukee, WI.

Moe, Robert Ellis (1912–1992), one of Maurice W. Moe's two sons, who began corresponding with HPL in 1934 and met him on several occasions.

Morton, James Ferdinand (1870–1941), amateur journalist, author of many tracts on race prejudice, free thought, and taxation; longtime friend of HPL and member of the Kalem Club. In 1925 he became the curator of the Paterson (NJ) Museum.

Moloney, James Joseph, a typesetter at W. Paul Cook's printing establishment (the *Athol Transcript*), amateur journalist, and editor of the *Voice from the Mountains*. HPL cursed his typesetting of Samuel Loveman's *Hermaphrodite*.

Murphy, William R., fortieth president of the NAPA (1906–07). He won all the NAPA laureateships: poetry, essay, story, history, and editorial (twice). Editor of the *Pioneer*. Member of the editorial staff of the *Philadelphia Public Ledger*, specializing in dramatic and musical criticism.

Orton, Vrest (1897–1986), a late member of the Kalem Club. He was for a time an editor at the *Saturday Review* and later the founder of the Vermont Country Store. He compiled an early bibliography of Theodore Dreiser, *Dreiserana* (1929).

Parker, Charles A. A. (1880–1965), amateur journalist and editor of the little magazine *L'Alouette*, chiefly devoted to poetry, and *Bavardage*.

Price, E[dgar] Hoffmann (1898–1988), prolific pulp writer of weird and adventure tales. HPL met him in New Orleans in 1932 and corresponded extensively with him thereafter.

Renshaw, Anne Tillery (1890–c.1945), prolific amateur journalist, professor, second vice president of the UAPA (1915–16). Editor of the *Pinfeather* and *Ole Miss*. Late revision client of HPL, for whom he revised *Well Bred Speech* (1936) although much of the work HPL did for it was excised. She met HPL during the latter's visit to Washington, D.C., in April 1925.

Rimel, Duane W[eldon] (1915–1996), weird fiction fan and late correspondent of HPL, who revised some of his early tales.

Sandusky, Albert A[ugust] (1896–1934), amateur journalist whose use of slang amused HPL. HPL met him frequently during trips to the Boston area, member of the Hub Club. Editor of *The Hub Club Quill* and printer of early issues of HPL's *Conservative*.

Schilling, George S., editor of the *Badger*. First vice president of the UAPA (1914–15).

Smith, Charles W. ("Tryout") (1852–1948), longtime amateur journalist, editor of the *Tryout*, and friend and correspondent of HPL.

Smith, Clark Ashton (1893–1961), prolific California poet and writer of fantasy tales. He received a "fan" letter from HPL in 1922 and corresponded with him until HPL's death.

Smith, Edwin Hadley (1869–1944), a leading amateur journalist of the period, chiefly associated with the NAPA.

Spencer, Truman J[oseph] (1864–1944) of Hamden, CT, historian of the amateur journalist movement, author of *A Cyclopedia of the Literature of Amateur Journalism* (1891). Editor of the *Fossil*.

Spink, Helm C. (1909–1970), printer and official editor of the NAPA in 1930–31 and again in 1935–36 (with O. W. Hinrichs). He printed HPL's *Further Criticism of Poetry*.

Talman, Wilfred Blanch (1904–1986), correspondent of HPL and late member of the Kalem Club. HPL assisted Talman on his story "Two Black Bottles" (1926) and wrote "Some Dutch Footprints in New England" for Talman to publish in *De Halve Maen*, the journal of the Holland Society of New York. Late in life he wrote the memoir *The Normal Lovecraft* (1973).

Thrift, Timothy Burr (1883–?), editor of *Lucky Dog*, the *Aonian*, and the *Mailbag* ("the magazine of efficiency in advertising and selling"). Thirty-ninth president of NAPA.

Wandrei, Donald (1908–1987), poet and author of weird fiction, science fiction, and detective tales. He corresponded with HPL from 1926 to 1937, visited HPL in Providence in 1927 and 1932, and met HPL occasionally in New York during the 1930s. He helped HPL get "The Shadow out of Time" published in *Astounding Stories*.

Wandrei, Howard (1909–1956), younger brother of Donald Wandrei, premier weird artist and prolific author of weird fiction, science fiction, and detective stories; correspondent of HPL.

White, Michael Oscar, amateur journalist with whom HPL tangled over literary matters (specifically the poetry of Samuel Loveman) in the early 1920s. White compiled the booklet *In Memoriam: Jennie E. T. Dowe* (1921), to which HPL contributed a poem and a brief prose essay on Dowe.

Wright, Farnsworth (1888–1940), editor of *Weird Tales* (1924–40). He often rejected HPL's work of the 1930s, only to publish some of it after HPL's death upon submittal by AWD.

Wylie, Willard Otis (1862–1944), of Boston, noted philatelic editor and writer. Editor of *Our Compliments* and member of both the NAPA and UAPA.

Zorn, Ray H. (1910–1997), military postal worker in the 33rd Infantry Division in World War II, until he retired as postmaster of Troy Grove, IL in the early 1970s. He wrote poetry and music, published a literary magazine (*Nix Nem Quarterly Review*) and several other small-press items, including the *Lovecraft Collector* (1949).

Bibliography

A. Works by H. P. Lovecraft

Books

The Ancient Track: Complete Poetical Works. 2nd ed. Edited by S. T. Joshi. New York: Hippocampus Press, 2013.

Collected Essays. Edited by S. T. Joshi. New York: Hippocampus Press, 2004–06. 5 vols. [*CE*]

Collected Fiction. Edited by S. T. Joshi. New York: Hippocampus Press, 2015–17. 4 vols. [*CF*]

Dawnward Spire, Lonely Hill: The Letters of H. P. Lovecraft and Clark Ashton Smith. Edited by David E. Schultz and S. T. Joshi. New York: Hippocampus Press, 2017.

Essential Solitude: The Letters of H. P. Lovecraft and August Derleth. Edited by David E. Schultz and S. T. Joshi. New York: Hippocampus Press, 2008. 2 vols.

Further Criticism of Poetry. Louisville, KY: George G. Fetter, 1932. Text in *CE* 1.

H. P. Lovecraft in the Argosy: *Collected Correspondence from the Munsey Magazines.* Edited by S. T. Joshi. West Warwick, RI: Necronomicon Press, 1994.

Letters to Alfred Galpin. Edited by S. T. Joshi and David E. Schultz. New York: Hippocampus Press, 2003.

Letters to C. L. Moore and Others. Edited by David E. Schultz and S. T. Joshi. New York: Hippocampus Press, 2017.

Letters to Elizabeth Toldridge and Anne Tillery Renshaw. Edited by David E. Schultz and S. T. Joshi. New York: Hippocampus Press, 2014.

Letters to F. Lee Baldwin, Duane W. Rimel, and Nils Frome. Edited by David E. Schultz and S. T. Joshi. New York: Hippocampus Press, 2016.

Letters to Family and Family Friends. Edited by S. T. Joshi and David E. Schultz. New York: Hippocampus Press, 2020.

Letters to Rheinhart Kleiner and Others. Edited by S. T. Joshi and David E. Schultz. New York: Hippocampus Press, 2020.

Letters to Robert Bloch and Others. Edited by David E. Schultz and S. T. Joshi. New York: Hippocampus Press, 2015.

Looking Backward. Haverhill, MA: C. W. Smith, [1920].

Marginalia. Edited by August Derleth and Donald Wandrei. Sauk City, WI: Arkham House, 1944.

Selected Letters. Edited by August Derleth, Donald Wandrei, and James Turner. Sauk City, WI: Arkham House, 1965–76. 5 vols. [*SL*]

The Shunned House. Athol, MA: Recluse Press, 1928 (printed but not bound or distributed until 1959–61). Text in *CF* 1.

Fiction
"The Colour out of Space." *Amazing Stories* 2, No. 6 (September 1927): 557–67. In *CF* 2.
"Dagon." *Vagrant* No. 11 (November 1919): 23–29. *WT* 2, No. 3 (October 1923): 23–25. In *CF* 1.
"The Dreams in the Witch House."' *WT* 22, No. 1 (July 1933): 86–111. In *CF* 3.
"Hypnos." *National Amateur* 45, No. 5 (May 1923): 1–3. *WT* 4, No. 2 (May–June–July 1924): 33–35. In *CF* 1.
"The Lurking Fear." *Home Brew* 2, No. 6 (January 1923): 4–10; 3, No. 1 (February 1923): 18–23; 3, No. 2 (March 1923): 31–37, 44, 48; 3, No. 3 (April 1923): 35–42. *WT* 11, No. 6 (June 1928): 791–804. In *CF* 1.
"Nyarlathotep" (prose poem). *United Amateur* (November 1920).
"Pickman's Model." *WT* 10, No. 4 (October 1927): 505–14. In *By Daylight Only*, ed. Christine Campbell Thomson. London: Selwyn & Blount, 1929. 37–52. *WT* 28, No. 4 (November 1936): 495–505. In *The "Not at Night" Omnibus*, ed. Christine Campbell Thomson. London: Selwyn & Blount, [1937]. 279–307. In *CF* 2.
"The Tomb." *Vagrant* No. 14 (March 1922): 50–64. *WT* 7, No. 1 (January 1926): 117–23. In *CF* 1.
"The Tree." *Tryout* 7, No. 7 (October 1921): [3–10]. In *CF* 1.

Nonfiction
"Bureau of Critics." *National Amateur* 45, No. 4 (March 1923): 1–3 (unsigned). In *CE* 1.
"Bureau of Critics." *National Amateur* 56, No. 4 (June 1934): 7–8. In *CE* 1.
"Bureau of Critics Comment on Verse, Typography, Prose." *National Amateur* 56, No. 2 (December 1933): 1–2. In *CE* 1.
"Bureau of Critics." *National Amateur* 58, No. 2 (December 1935): 14–15 (as "Some Current Amateur Verse"). In *CE* 1.
"The Case for Classicism." *United Co-operative* 1, No. 2 (June 1919): 3–5. In *CE* 2.
"Chairman of the Bureau of Critics Reports on Poetry." *National Amateur* 57, No. 1 (5 September 1934): Sec. 2, p. 3. In *CE* 1.
"Commonplace Book." In *CE* 5.
"A Confession of Unfaith." *Liberal* 1, No. 2 (February 1922): 17–23. In *CE* 1.
"Department of Public Criticism." *United Amateur* 16, No. 2 (September 1916): 27. In *CE* 1.
"A Description of the Town of Quebeck in New-France, Lately added to His Britannick Majesty's Dominions." In *CE* 4.
"The Despised Pastoral." *Conservative* 4, No. 1 (July 1918): 2. In *CE* 2.
"European Glimpses." In *CE* 4.
"Finale." *Badger* No. 2 (June 1915): 17–16 [i.e., 20]. In *CE* 1.
"Helene Hoffman Cole—Litterateur." *United Amateur* 18, No. 5 (May 1919): 92–93. *Phoenix* 5, No. 4 (March 1946): 348–49. In *CE* 1.
"Homes and Shrines of Poe." *Californian* 2, No. 3 (Winter 1934): 8–10. In *CE* 4.

"H. P. Lovecraft: Letters to John T. Dunn." Edited by S. T. Joshi, David E. Schultz, and John H. Stanley. *Books at Brown* 28–29 [1991–92]: 157–223.

"In a Major Key." *Conservative* 1, No. 2 (July 1915): 9–11. In *CE* 1.

"In the Editor's Study." *Conservative* No. 12 (March 1923): 5–8 (unsigned). In *CE* 1.

"The Literature of Rome." *United Amateur* 18, No. 2 (November 1918): 17–21, 35–38 [partial]. In *CE* 2 [complete].

"A Living Heritage: Roman Architecture in Today's America." Californian 3, No. 1 (Summer 1935): 23–28 (abridged; as "Heritage or Modernism: Common Sense in Art Forms"). In *CE* 5.

"Looking Backward." *Tryout* 6, No. 2 (February 1920): [3–8]; 6, No. 3 (March 1920): [1–8]; 6, No. 4 (April 1920): [3–10]; 6, No. 5 (May 1920): [3–10]; 6, No. 6 (June 1920): [3–10]. *Boys' Herald* 63, No. 1 (1 January 1934): 7–8 (excerpt; as "Dr. Jekyll and Mr. Hyde"). *Aonian* 2, No. 3 (Autumn 1944): 146–51; 2, No. 4 (Winter 1944): 177–86. In *CE* 1.

"Lord Dunsany and His Work." In *CE* 2.

"Lovecraft Offers Verse Criticism." *National Amateur* 57, No. 4 (June 1935): 5–6. In *CE* 1.

"A Matter of Uniteds." *Bacon's Essays* 1, No. 1 (Summer 1927): 1–3. In *CE* 1.

"More 'Chain Lightning.'" *United Official Quarterly* 2, No. 1 (October 1915): [1–4]. *Lovecraft Studies* No. 8 (Spring 1984): 30–31, 36. In *CE* 1.

"Les Mouches Fantastiques." *Conservative* 4, No. 1 (July 1918): 7–8 (unsigned). In *CE* 1.

"[Letter to Edward H. Cole, 8 April 1919.]" In Sherman Cole, "The Olympian" part 4. *Fossil* (January 1979): 18.

"Nietzscheism and Realism." *Rainbow* No. 1 (October 1921): 9–11 (as "Nietscheism and Realism"). In *CE* 5.

"Notes on Verse Technique." Published as *Further Criticism of Poetry.* Louisville, KY: Printed on the Press of George G. Fetter Co., 1932. In *CE* 1.

"Old England and the 'Hyphen.'" *Conservative* 2, No. 3 (October 1916): [1–2]. In *CE* 5.

"The Pseudo-United." *United Amateur* 19, No. 5 (May 1920): 106–8. In *CE* 1.

"A Reply to *The Lingerer.*" *Tryout* 3, no. 7 (June 1917): [9–12]. In *CE* 1.

"Report of Bureau of Critics." *National Amateur* 57, No. 2 (December 1934): 1. In *CE* 1.

"Report of First Vice-President." *United Amateur* 15, No. 4 (November 1915): 56. In *CE* 1.

"Report of the Bureau of Critics: Verse Department." *National Amateur* 57, No. 3 (March 1935): 1. In *CE* 1.

"A Request." *Conservative* 2, No. 4 (January 1917): 4. In *CE* 1.

"Rudis Indigestaque Moles." *Conservative* 12 (March 1923): 6–8. In *CE* 2.

"Some Current Amateur Verse." *National Amateur* 58, No. 2 (December 1935): 14–15 (signed "H. P. L."). In *CE* 1.

"Some Dutch Footprints in New England." *De Halve Maen* 9, No. 1 (18 October 1933): 2, 4.

"Supernatural Horror in Literature." *Recluse* No. 1 (1927): 23–59. Rev. ed. in *FF* (October 1933–February 1935). In *CE* 2.
"To Mr. Lockhart, on His Poetry." *Tryout* 3, No. 4 (March 1917): [7–8].
"The Unknown City in the Ocean." *Perspective Review* (Winter 1934 [Fourth Anniversary Number]): 4–8. In *CE* 4.
"What Belongs in Verse." *Perspective Review* (Spring 1935): 10–11. In *CE* 1.
"The Work of Frank Belknap Long, Jr." *United Amateur* 23, No. 1 (May 1924): 1–4 (unsigned). In *CE* 2.
"The Youth of Today." *Conservative* 1, No. 3 (October 1915): 11–12. In *CE* 1.

Poetry (all items in *AT*)
"The Absent Leader." In *In Memoriam: Hazel Pratt Adams* ([ed. Anonymous] [Brooklyn, NY?: Blue Pencil Club?,] 1927: 11–12.
"An American to Mother England." *Poesy* 1, No. 7 (January 1916): 62, and reprinted in *Dowdell's Bearcat* No. 16 (November 1916): [12–14].
"Astrophobos." *United Amateur* 17, No. 3 (January 1918): 38 (as by "Ward Phillips"). *Fantasmagoria* 1, No. 1 (March 1937): 7–8.
"The Beauties of Peace: An Epistle to Henry F. Thomas, Esq., Author of 'A Prayer for Peace and Justice' in The Evening News for June 23, 1916." [Providence] *Evening News* 49, No. 123 (27 June 1916): 6.
"Ye Ballade of Patrick von Flynn; or, The Hibernio-German-American England-Hater." *Conservative* 2, No. 1 (April 1916): 3–4.
"Brotherhood." *Tryout* 3, No. 1 (December 1916): [7]; rpt. *National Magazine* 45, No. 3 (December 1916): 415.
"Brumalia." *Tryout* 3, No. 1 (December 1916): [1]; rpt. [Providence] *Evening News* 51, No. 152 (7 December 1917): Sec. 2, p. 2.
"Edith Miniter." *Tryout* 16, No. 8 (August 1934): [5–6].
"The Eidolon." *Tryout* 4, no. 10 (October 1918): [3–6].
"Fact and Fancy." *Tryout* 3, No. 3 (February 1917): [7].
"Gems from 'In a Minor Key.'" *Conservative* 1, No. 3 (October 1915): 8.
"The Feast: (Hub Journalist Club, March 10, 1923)." *Hub Club Quill* 15, No. 2 (May 1923): [13–15].
"Helene Hoffman Cole: 1893–1919: The Club's Tribute." *Bonnet* 1, No. 1 (June 1919): 8–9 (unsigned).
"In a Sequester'd Providence Churchyard Where Once Poe Walk'd." *Science-Fantasy Correspondent* 1, No. 3 (March–April 1937): 16–17 (as "In a Sequestered Churchyard Where Once Poe Walked"). *WT* 31, No. 5 (May 1938): 578 (as "Where Poe Once Walked: An Acrostic Sonnet"). In *Four Acrostic Sonnets on Poe* (1936), ed. Maurice W. Moe.
"In Memoriam: J. E. T. D." *Tryout* 5, No. 3 (March 1919): [6] (as by "Ward Phillips").
"Lines on Graduation from the R. I. Hospital's School of Nurses." *Tryout* 3, No. 3 (February 1917): [15–17], attributed to John T. Dunn.

"[Little Sam Perkins.]" *Olympian* No. 35 (Autumn 1940): 36.
"Medusa: A Portrait." *Tryout* 7, No. 9 (December 1922): 32–34; as by "Jeremy Bishop" and lacking the introductory letter.
"My Lost Love." *Crypt of Cthulhu* No. 21 (Eastertide 1984): 34–35.
"Ode for July Fourth, 1917." *United Amateur* 16, No. 9 (July 1917): 121; rpt. *National Magazine* 45, No. 10 (July 1917): 616 (as "Ode to July 4th: 1917"); [Providence] *Evening News* 51, No. 26 (3 July 1917): 3.
"[On Rheinhart Kleiner Being Hit by an Automobile.]" Unpublished in HPL's lifetime.
"The Simple Speller's Tale." *Conservative* 1, No. 1 (April 1915): [1].
"Sonnet on Myself." *Tryout* 4, No. 7 (July 1918): [2] (as by "Lewis Theobald, Jun.").
"The Spirit of Summer." *National Enquirer* 6, No. 13 (27 June 1918): 10. *Conservative* 4, No. 1 (July 1918): 1.
"To Alfred Galpin, Esq.: President of the United Amateur Press Association, on His Nineteenth Birthday, November 8, 1920." *Tryout* 6, No. 12 (December 1920): [7–8] (as by "L. Theobald").
"To Arthur Goodenough, Esq." *Tryout* 4, No. 9 (September 1918): [1–2].
"To Charlie of the Comics (With Profuse Apologies to Rheinhart Kleiner, Esq., Poet-Laureate and Author of 'To Mary of the Movies.')." *Providence Amateur* 1, No. 2 (February 1916): 13–14 (unsigned).
"To the Members of the Pin-Feathers on the Merits of Their Organisation, and of Their New Publication, *The Pinfeather.*" *Pinfeather* 1, No. 1 (November 1914): 3–4.

B. Works by Alfred Galpin

"The Critic." *Philosopher* 1, No. 1 (December 1920): 9 (as by "Consul Hasting").
"A Critic of Poetry." *Oracle* 4, No. 2 (August 1923): 8–10.
"Deep Sea Meditation." Nonextant.
"Department of Public Criticism." *United Amateur* 19, No. 5 (May 1920): 108–15.
"Department of Public Criticism." *United Amateur* 21, No. 2 (November 1921): 19–21.
"Department of Public Criticism." *United Amateur* 21, No. 5 (May 1922): 54–55.
"Echoes from Beyond Space." *United Amateur* 24, No. 1 (July 1925): 3–4.
"Ennui." *Conservative* No. 13 (July 1923): 10–11. As by "Anatol Kleinst."
"En Route." Unpublished.
"Form in Modern Poetry." *United Amateur* 20, No. 3 (January 1921): 34–36.
"Four Translations from 'Les Fleurs du mal' by Charles Pierre Baudelaire." *United Amateur* 21, No. 4 (March 1922): 39–40.
"From the French of Pierre de Ronsard ('Amours' Livre II)." Unpublished.
"Impromptu on Impromptus." *Pippin* 2, No. 1 (December 1918): [11].
"Intuition in the Philosophy of Bergson." *Conservative* No. 13 (July 1923): 5–9 (as by "A. T. Madison").

"Man and the Supernatural." *Voice from the Mountains* (July 1918): 12–13.
"Marsh-Mad: A Nightmare." *Philosopher* 1, No. 1 (December 1920): 7–8 (as by "Consul Hasting").
"Memories of a Friendship." In H. P. Lovecraft et al., *The Shuttered Room and Other Pieces*. Sauk City, WI: Arkham House, 1959. 191–201. In *Lovecraft Remembered*, ed. Peter Cannon. Sauk City, WI: Arkham House, 1998. 164–72.
"Mystery." *United Amateur* 17, No. 3 (January 1918): 40 (as by "Consul Hasting").
"Nietzsche as a Practical Prophet." *Rainbow* 1, No. 1 (October 1921): 4–7.
"Nolens Trahitur." *Silver Clarion* 2, No. 6 (September 1918): [1]–2.
"November." In *Poetry out of Wisconsin,* ed. August Derleth and Raymond E. F. Larsson. New York: Henry Harrison, Poetry Publisher, 1937. 100–101.
"Picture of a Modern Mood." *United Amateur* 20, No. 4 (May 1921): 61–64.
"Portrait of a Father." *Wisconsin Magazine of History* 63, No. 4 (Summer 1980): 263–77.
"Red . . ." Unpublished.
"Remarks on My Handwriting." *United Amateur* 19, No. 1 (September 1919): 4.
"Scattered Remarks upon the Green Cheese Theory." *United Amateur* 21, No. 4 (March 1922): 37–39 (as by "Anatol Kleinst").
"Selenaio-Phantasma." *Conservative* 4, No. 1 (July 1918): 3.
"Some Tendencies of Modern Poetry." *Philosopher* 1, No. 1 (December 1920): 10–11.
"Sonnet to Poetry." *Voice from the Mountains* (July 1918): 16.
"The Spoken Tongue." *Philosopher* 1, No. 1 (December 1920): 11–12 (unsigned).
"Stars." *Philosopher* 1, No. 1 (December 1920): 9.
"To Sam L." Previously unpublished. Ms. JHL.
"Two Loves." *Conservative* 4, No 1 (July 1918): 8 (as by "Consul Hasting").
"The United's Policy 1920–1921" (with H. P. Lovecraft). *Zenith* (January 1921): 1.
"The Vivisector." *Wolverine* No. 11 (November 1921): 16–18 (as by "Zoilus").
"The World Situation." *Philosopher* 1, No. 1 (December 1920): 12 (unsigned).

De Sanctis, Francesco (1817–1883). *De Sanctis on Dante*. Edited and translated by Joseph Rossi and Alfred Galpin. (Madison, WI: University of Wisconsin Press, 1957).
Fauriel, C[laude] C[harles] (1772–1844). *Fauriel in Italy: Unpublished Correspondence* (1882–1825). Edited by Alfred Galpin. Roma: Edizioni di storia e letteratura, 1962.
Galpin, Alfred Maurice, Isabella Panzini, and Marilyn Schneider. *Beginning Readings in Italian*. New York: Macmillan, [1966].
Galpin, Alfred Maurice. *French Prose: An Intermediate Reader.* New York: Macmillan, [1965].

"Lament for H. P. L: For Piano Solo." In H. P. Lovecraft, *Marginalia,* three leaves following p. 134. Recorded on *Fungi from Yuggoth: A Sonnet Cycle,* Nampa, ID: Fedogan and Bremer, 2015.

C. Works by Edward H. Cole

"An Appeal." *Tryout* 18, No. 9 (August 1937): [7–9].

"At Long Last." *Olympian* New Series 1, No. 35 (Autumn 1940): 36–38.

"Ausonius the Nature Lover." *Emissary* (July 1914): 11–15.

"Ave atque Vale!" *Olympian* New Series 1, No. 35 (Autumn 1940): 7–22.

"The Banquets I Ate in the Spring, Tra-La." *Olympian* 4, No. 4 (August 1911): 62–78.

"Books of Treasure." *Olympian* 4, No. 5 (April 1912): 92–102.

"Bureau of Critics." *National Amateur* 45, No. 4 (March 1924): [1]–2.

"Bureau of Critics Comment on Verse, Typography, Prose: Prose" *National Amateur* 56, No. 2 (December 1933): 3, 5.

"Bureau of Critics: Prose." *National Amateur* 56, No. 4 (June 1934): 6–7; 58, No. 2 (December 1935): 15–16.

"Bureau of Criticism: Prose Criticism." *National Amateur* 58, No. 4 (June 1936): 16–17.

"The Campaign." *Bema* (June 1913): 83–86.

"Chapters of History." *Olympian* 5, No. 4 (September 1913): 66–73; 5, No. 5 (December 1913): 77–108.

"Chapters of History: III. Three Years of Politics." *Olympian* 6, No. 1 (March 1914): 7–20, 32.

"Consolidation in Massachusetts." *Bay State Amateur.* 4, No. 3 (March 1915): [1–6].

"Constitutional Amendments." *Bema* (June 1913): 82–83.

"Convention Days and Nights." *Olympian* 5, No. 1 (September 1912): 3–18.

"Cook's 'Monadnock.'" *Olympian* 5, No. 3 (July? 1913): 47–54.

"Current Comment." *Bema* (February 1911): [13]–14.

"Cyrano." *Olympian* 5, No. 2 (November 1912): 30–34.

"The Current Year." *Bema* (January 1918): [7–8].

"Days That Are Past." *National Amateur.* (1912).

"A Definition of Policy and a Confession of Faith." *Olympian* 6, No. 6 (September 1914–February 1915): 109–17.

"Department of Literary Criticism: Prose Department." *Perspective Review* (Spring 1935): 9

"Edith Miniter." *National Amateur* 57, No. 1 (September 1934): 12; in *Dead Houses and Other Works*, ed. Kenneth W. Faig, Jr., and Sean Donnelly (New York: Hippocampus Press, 2008): 65–67.

"The Far Eastern Crisis." *Californian* 4, No. 4 (Spring 1937): 74–78.

"Favor and Prejudice." *Bema* (August 1912): 51–52.

"First Pages." *Olympian* 5, No. 4 (September 1913): 59–66; 5, No. 5 (December 1913):108–11; 5, No. 6 (January 1914): 115–19; 6, No. 4 (July 1914): 70, 72–73; 6, No. 5 (August 1914): 91–96.

"Five Sticks on Activity." *Bay State Amateur* 4, No. 2 (August 1914): [10–14].

"The Follies." *Bema* (August 1912): 57–58.

"Fraternal Follies." *Bema* (July 1912): 43–44.

"From the Bema." *Olympian* 6, No. 1 (March 1914): 1–5; 6, No. 2 (May 1914): 33–39; 6, No. 3 (June 1914): 49–53.

"Guide Books in General and One in Particular." *Bema* (August 1912): 53–54.

"Humor Lies in the Point of View." *Bema* (June 1913): 79–81.

"In Massachusetts." *United Amatur* 12, No. 5 (May 1913): 80.

"In Tribute: William R. Murphy." *National Amateur* 58, No. 4 (June 1936): 7–8.

"James Ferdinand Morton Jr." *Ghost* No. 5 (July 1947): 11–14. In H. P. Lovecraft, *Letters to James F. Morton* (New York: Hippocampus Press, 2011): 435–41.

"Jeffrey Farnol's Novels." *National Official* (June 1913): [20–22].

"John Milton Heins." *Face to Face with Amateur Journalists* 1, No. 1 (August 1919): [3–4].

"Laggards and Laureateships." *Bema* (August 1912): 53–54.

"Last Pages." *Olympian* 4, No. 3 (February 1910): 52–60; 4, No. 4 (August 1911): 78–82; 4, No. 5 (April 1912): 103–08; 5, No. 1 (September 1912): 19–22; 5, No. 2 (November 1912): 35–40; 5, No. 3 (July? 1913): 54–58.

"[Lovecraft Verse]." *Olympian* New Series No. 35 (Autumn 1940): 35–36.

"The Lover of Books." *Bema* (January 1913): [61]–62.

"A Medieval Saint." *Coagent* 3, No. 1 (March 1912): 24–29.

"A Middle West Quartette." *Bema* (August 1912): 58–60.

"Mutatis Mutandis." *Bema* (January 1918): [3].

"A National Bundle." *Bema* (August 1912): 56–57..

"The 'National Official.'" *Olympian* 5, No. 4 (September 1913): 74–81.

"New Year's Even in New York City." *Bay State Amateur* 4, No. 1 (January 1914): [1–2, 8].

"The 1917 Convention." *Tryout.* (1918).

"One Criterion of Value." *Bema* (January 1913): 66–74.

"Our Own 'Reviewers' 'Club.'" *Olympian* 6, No. 2 (May 1914): 41–43.

"Our Pulse." *Olympian* 6, No. 3 (June 1914): 5–64.

"Papers of the Past I. The Career of the 'Torpedo.'" *Olympian* 5, No. 6 (January 1914): 121–29.

"The Past Six Months." *Bema* (June 1913): 77–79.

"Personality in Amateur Literature." *United Amateur* 13, No. 2 (November 1913): 29–30.

"The Play Hour." *Olympian* 6, No. 6 (September 1914–February 1915): 121–23.

"A Play of Fancy." *Bema* (January 1913): 63–66.

"A Plea for Politics." *Coagent* 3, No. 1 (March 1912): [3]–5.

"The Point in Question." *Bema* (November 1910): 7–12.

"Presidential Qualifications." *Bema* (June 1913): [75]–77.

"Prize Papers and Others." *Bema* (July 1912): [37]–42.

"The Reviewer's Club." *Olympian* 5, No. 4 (September 1913): 81–83; 5, No. 5 (December 1913): 108–11; 5, No. 6 (January 1914): 131–34; 6, No. 1 (March 1914): 22–28; 6, No. 2 (May 1914): 45–6, 48; 6, No. 3 (June 1914): [68]; 6, No. 4 (July 1914): 85–6.; 6, No. 5 (August 1914): 104–08; 6, No. 6 (September 1914–February 1915): 124–25, 127–28.

"Some Words for Mr. Lovecraft" (extracted from "The Reviewer's Club"). *Olympian* 7, No. 1 (October 1917).

"Somerville in Brief." *Bay State Advocate* No. 11 (March 1912): [3–4].

"The Spirit of the Spanish Conquistadors." *Torpedo* 7, No. 6 (November 1913): [1]–9.

"Streets of Manhattan." *Brooklynite* 11, No. 2 (January 1920): 4.

"Sunset and Dawn." *Olympian* 6, No. 4 (July 1914): 75–84.

"Susan Brown Robbins." *Dowdell's Bearcat* 3, No. 2 ([December] Christmas number 1914): 2.

"The Thirty-Second Convention." *Olympian* (1908).

"The Thirty-Seventh Convention." *Bema* (July 1912): 44–47.

"The Trend of History." *Ghost* Spring No. 1 (1943): 36–38.

"These Smear Lads." *Leisure Hours* No. 23 (September 1937): [1–3].

"Trains." *Tick-Tock* (date not known): 21–23. In *Your Thoughts: The Story of Amateur Journalism*, comp. Ralph W. Babcock. [New York?]: Fossils, 1983, pp. [153–55].

"Truman Joseph Spencer: Biographical Notes." In Truman J. Spencer, *The History of Amateur Journalism*. New York: The Fossils, 1957, pp. [xv]–xvi.

"The Value of Amateur Journalism." *The Imp* 1, No. 1 (November [1913]): 5–6.

"A View behind the Veil." *Fossil* 55, Whole No. 157 (April 1958): [1], 61–63.

"William R. Murphy." *National Amateur* 58, No. 4 (June 1936): 6–7.

"With Stubborn Pen." *Bema* (April 1911): [25]–36.

"A Word with You, My Friend." *Bema* (July 1912): 47–48.

"Wreaths of Laurel." *Bema* (August 1912): [49]–51.

D. Works by E. Sherman Cole

"The Olympians." Part 1, *Fossil* 75, No. 4 (April 1978): 1–5; Part 2, *Fossil* 76, No. 1 (July 1978): 3–8; Part 3, *Fossil* 76, No. 2 (October 1978): 3–7; Part 4, *Fossil* 76, No. 3 (January 1979): 9–13; Part 5, *Fossil* 76, No. 4 (April 1979): 4–6.

E. Works by John T. Dunn

"Editorial." *Providence Amateur* No. 1 (June 1915): [7–8].

"On Acknowledgements." *Providence Amateur*. No. 1 (June 1915): [8–10].

"A Post-Christmas Lament." *Providence Amateur* No. 2 (February 1916): [6–7].

F. Works by Adolphe de Castro

After the Confession and Other Verses. New York: A. Danziger, [1908].

A Fair Plea. New York: [Allied Print Trades Council, 1904.]

Helen Polska's Lover; or, The Merchant Prince. New York: Adolphe Danziger, 1908; London: Henry J. Drane, 1909.

The Hybrid Prince of Egypt; Plus Song of the Arabian Desert. Los Angeles: Western Authors Association, 1950.

In the Confessional and the Following. New York: Western Authors Publishing Association, 1893.

In the Garden of Abdullah and Other Poems. Los Angeles: Western Authors Publishing Association, 1916.

Jewish Forerunners of Christianity. New York: E. P. Dutton, 1903, 1926 (rev. ed.; as *Jesus Lived: Hebrew Evidences of His Existence and the Rabbis Who Believed in Him*).

A Man, a Woman, and a Million. London: [n.p.], 1902.

The Monk and the Hangman's Daughter (with Ambrose Bierce). *San Francisco Examiner* (13 September 1891): 11–12; (20 September 1891): 13; (27 September 1891): 17–18. Chicago: F. J. Schulte, 1892. Translation of *Der Mönch von Berchtesgaden* (1890–91) by Richard Voss.

The Monk and the Hangman's Daughter; Fantastic Fables; [etc.] (with Ambrose Bierce). <1911> New York: Albert & Charles Boni, 1925. (*LL* 100)

The Painter's Dream. Los Angeles: Western Authors' Association, 1940.

Portrait of Ambrose Bierce. Preface by [Frank] Belknap Long. New York: Century Co., 1929.

The World Crucified: A Photoplay of the Mundane Activity of Christ in Six Apotheoses. Los Angeles: Western Authors Publishing Association, 1921.

"Ambrose Bierce as He Really Was." *American Parade* 1, No. 4 (October 1926): 28–44.

"An American Author Meets Shaw." *Mark Twain Journal* 9, No. 4 (July 1954): 5.

"The Automatic Executioner." *Crypt of Cthulhu* 10 (Yuletide 1982): 26–30.

"Edgar Allan Poe." *WT* 29, No. 5 (May 1937): 606. *Crypt of Cthulhu* 57 (St. John's Eve 1988): 27.

"The Electric Executioner" [orig. "The Automatic Executioner"]. *WT* 16, No. 2 (August 1930): 223–36.

"Had I Another Hundred Years." Nonextant. Extract contained in letter by de Castro to August Derleth (n.d., c. 1952), TLS, Wisconsin Historical Society.

"The Jews in San Francisco: The Last Half Century." *Overland Monthly* No. 148 (April 1895): 381–410.

"The Last Test" [orig. "A Sacrifice to Science"]. *WT* 12, No. 5 (November 1928): 625–56.

"Let There Be Light!" *Oriental Stories* 1, No. 4 (April–May–June 1931): 569; Mississauga, Ontario: Girasol Collectibles, 2005; Wildside Press, 2010; Fiction House, 2018.

"A Note concerning Joseph Pulitzer." *Mark Twain Quarterly* 9, No. 1 (January 1951): 21–23.

"A Sacrifice to Science." *Crypt of Cthulhu* 10 (Yuletide 1982): 31–46.

"The Story of Anti-Semitism: III. The Gospel of Hate." *Jewish Forum* (March 1931): 103–10.

G. Works by Others

Allen, Hervey (1889–1949). *Anthony Adverse.* New York: Holt, Rinehart & Winston, 1933.

———. *Israfel: The Life and Times of Edgar Allan Poe.* New York: George H. Doran Co., 1926. [HPL owned the 2nd. ed. of 1927.] (*LL* 27)

Appleton, John Howard (1844–1930). *The Young Chemist: A Book of Laboratory Work for Beginners.* Providence, RI: J. A. & R. A. Reid, 1876. (*LL* 47)

Barlow, R. H. "St. John's Churchyard." *Science-Fantasy Correspondent* 1, No. 3 (March–April 1937): 16.

Bartky, Walter (1901–1958). *Highlights of Astronomy.* Chicago: University of Chicago Press, 1935.

Baudelaire, Charles Pierre (1821–1867). *Lettres 1841–1866.* Paris: Société de Mercure de France, 1907. (*LL* 72)

Bulfinch, Thomas (1796–1867). *The Age of Fable; or, Beauties of Mythology.* <1855> Ed. J. Loughran Scott. Rev. ed. Philadelphia: D. McKay, [1898]. (*LL* 142)

Burritt, Elijah Hinsdale (1794–1838). *The Geography of the Heavens, and Classbook of Astronomy: Accompanied by a Celestial Atlas.* A New Edition, Revised and Illustrated by Hiram Mattison. New York: F. J. Huntington, 1853. (*LL* 150)

Bush, David Van (1882–1959). *Peace Poems and Sausages.* [Webster, SD: Reporter & Farmer Print, 1915.]

Collins, Wilkie (1824–1889). *The Moonstone: A Novel.* <1852> New York: A. L. Burt, 1868.

Cowper, William (1831–1800). *The Task: A Poem, in Six Books.* London: Printed for J. Johnson, 1785.

Derleth, August (1909–1971). *The Man on All Fours: A Judge Peck Mystery Story.* New York: Loring & Mussey, 1934. (*LL* 249)

———. *Place of Hawks.* Illustrated with wood engravings by George Barford. New York: Loring & Mussey, [1935]. (*LL* 250)

———. *Sign of Fear: A Judge Peck Mystery.* New York: Loring & Mussey, 1935. (*LL* 251)

———. *Three Who Died: A Judge Peck Mystery.* New York: Loring & Mussey, 1935. (*LL* 253)

Dexter, Timothy (1747–1806). *A Pickle for the Knowing Ones; or, Plain Truths in a Homespun Dress.* Salem, MA: Printed for the Author, 1802; second edition [n.p.], Printed for the Author, 1805.

Duncan, John Charles (1882–1976). *Astronomy.* New York: Harper & Brothers, 1926 (3rd ed. 1935).

Easton, Emily M. *Roger Williams, Prophet and Pioneer.* Boston: Houghton Mifflin, 1930.

The Encyclopaedia Britannica: A Dictionary of Arts, Sciences, and General Literature . . . , with . . . Revisions and Additions by W. H. De Puy. 9th ed. Chicago: Werner Co., 1896. 24 vols. (*LL* 318)

Ernst, James Emanuel (1893–1948). *Roger Williams, New England Firebrand.* New York: Macmillan, 1932.

Faig, Kenneth W., Jr. "Passion, Controversy and Vision: A History of the Library of Amateur Journalism." http://www.thefossils.org/laj_hist.pdf

Friedell, Egon (1878–1938). *A Cultural History of the Modern Age: The Crisis of the European Soul from the Black Death to the World War.* New York: Alfred A. Knopf, 1930–32. 3 vols.

Green, John Richard (1837–1883). *History of the English People.* New York: Harper & Brothers, [1878]–1903. (*LL* 400)

Hessler, John C. (1869–1944), and Albert L. Smith (1866–?). *Essentials of Chemistry.* Boston: B. H. Sanborn, 1902.

Hecht, Ben (1894–1964). *Erik Dorn.* New York: G. P. Putnam's Sons, 1921.

Homer (fl. 750 B.C.E.?). *The Iliad of Homer.* Translated by Alexander Pope <1715–20>. With Notes and Introduction by Theodore Alois Buckley. New York: A. L. Burt, [1902]. (*LL* 463)

———. *The Odyssey.* Translated by Alexander Pope <1725–26>. To Which Is Added *The Battle of the Frogs and Mice.* London: Printed for G. B. Whittaker, 1827. (*LL* 464)

Hutchinson, Alfred L. (1859–1930). *The Limit of Wealth.* New York: Macmillan, 1907.

Johnson, Fanny Kemble (1868–1950). *Silver Wings and Other Poems.* Philadelphia: Walter C. Chiles, 1891. (*LL* 509)

Krutch, Joseph Wood (1893–1970). *The Modern Temper: A Study and a Confession.* New York: Harcourt, Brace, 1929.

Lamb, Charles (1775–1834). *Complete Works in Prose and Verse.* Ed. with a preface by R. H. Shepherd. Boston: De Wolfe, Fiske, 1874. (*LL* 546)

Liddell, Henry George (1811–1898), and Robert Scott (1811–1887). *A Greek-English Lexicon.* Oxford: The University Press, 1843. (*LL* 569)

Lloyd, John Uri (1849–1936). *Etidorhpa; or, The End of Earth.* Cincinnati: John Uri Lloyd, 1895.

Lockwood, Sara E. H. (1854–?), and Mary Alice Emerson (1860–1936). *Composition and Rhetoric for Higher Schools.* Boston: Ginn & Co., 1901.

Long, Frank Belknap (1901–1994). *The Goblin Tower.* Cassia, FL: Dragon-Fly Press, 1935. (*LL* 580)

———. *A Man from Genoa.* Athol, MA: Recluse Press, 1926. (*LL* 581)

Lounsbury, Thomas R. (1838–1815). *History of the English Language.* New York: Henry Holt & Co., 1879. (*LL* 584)

Loveman, Samuel (1887–1976). *The Hermaphrodite: A Poem.* Athol, MA: W. Paul Cook, 1926. (*LL* 593)

———. *The Hermaphrodite and Other Poems.* Caldwell, ID: Caxton Printers, 1936. (*LL* 594)

Mather, Cotton (1663–1728). *Magnalia Christi Americana; or, The Ecclesiastical History of New-England, from Its First Planting in the Year 1620, unto the Year of Our Lord, 1698.* London: Printed for T. Parkhurst, 1702. (*LL* 645)

Matthews, Brander (1852–1929). *These Many Years: Recollections of a New Yorker.* New York: Charles Scribner's Sons, 1917.

———. *A Study of Versification.* Boston: Houghton Mifflin, 1911.

Maturin, Charles Robert (1782?–1824). *Melmoth the Wanderer.* <1820> London: Richard Bentley & Son, 1892. 3 vols. (*LL* 646)

Melville, Herman (1819–1891). *Journal Up the Straits, October 11, 1856–May 5, 1857.* Edited by Raymond M. Weaver (1888–1948). New York: Colophon, 1935.

Miniter, Edith (1867–1934). "Little Pilgrimages the Homes of Amateurs." *True Blue* 2, No. 2 (1 February 1910): [4].

———. *Our Natupski Neighbors.* New York: Henry Holt & Co., 1916.

The Modern Encyclopedia: A New Library of World Knowledge. Edited by A. H. McDannald. <1933> New York: Grosset & Dunlap, 1935. (*LL* 668)

Ovid (P[ublius] Ovidius Naso) (43 B.C.E.–17 C.E.). *Ovid.* Translated by Dryden, Pope, Congreve, Addison, and Others. [Edited by Samuel Garth.] New-York: Harper & Brothers, 1837. 2 vols. (*LL* 728)

Palgrave, Francis T. (1814–1897), ed. *The Golden Treasury: Selected from the Best Songs and Lyrical Poems in the English Language.* London: Macmillan & Co., 1861. (*LL* 736)

Parker, Richard Green (1798–1869). *Aids to English Composition, Prepared for Students of All Grades.* Boston: R. S. Davis; New York, Robinson, Pratt & Co., 1844. (*LL* 673)

Poe, Edgar Allan (1809–1849). *The Poems of Edgar Allan Poe.* Ed. Andrew Lang. London: Kegan Paul, Trench, 1881. (*LL* 767)

Powys, John Cowper (1872–1963). *Wolf Solent.* London: Cape, 1929.

Quackenbos, G. P. (1826–1881). *Advanced Course of Composition and Rhetoric: A Series of Practical Lessons on the Origin, History, and Peculiarities of the English Language.* New York: D. Appleton & Co., 1855. (*LL* 1083)

Remsen, Ira (1846–1927). *The Elements of Chemistry.* New York: Henry Holt & Co., 1887.

Roberts, Kenneth Lewis (1885–1957). *Rabble in Arms: A Chronicle of Arundel and the Burgoyne Invasion.* Garden City, NY: Doubleday, Doran, 1933.

Ryder, Melvin. *Rambles Round the Campus.* Boston: Sherman, French & Company, 1915.

Santayana, George (1863–1952). *The Last Puritan: A Memoir in the Form of a Novel.* London: Constable, 1935. New York: Charles Scribner's Sons, 1936.

Shaw, Thomas B. (1813–1862). *A History of English Literature.* With Notes and Illustrations by William Smith LL. D. London: John Murray, 1868.

———. *Outlines of English Literature.* <1849> With a sketch of American literature by Henry T. Tuckerman. New York: Sheldon & Co., 1852. (*LL* 862)

Smith, Clark Ashton (1893–1961). *The Double Shadow and Other Fantasies.* [Auburn, CA]: Auburn Journal, 1933. (*LL* 880)

Smith, Sir William (1813–1893). *Smith's Bible Dictionary.* Philadelphia: A. J. Holman Co., [1893].

Spalding, William (1809–1859). *History of English Literature; with an Outline of the Origin and Growth of the English Language.* Edinburgh: Oliver & Bod, 1853. or New York: D. Appleton & Co., 1853–89. (*LL* 1079)

Spencer, Truman J. (1864-1944). *A Cyclopedia of the Literature of Amateur Journalism.* Hartford, CT: Truman J. Spencer, 1891. (*LL* 899)

[State Street Trust Company, Boston.] *Towns of New England and Old England, Ireland and Scotland.* Printed to commemorate the landing of the Pilgrims. [Written by Allan Forbes (1874–1955).] Boston, 1920–21. (*LL* 907)

Stokley, James (1900–1989). *Stars and Telescopes.* New York: Harper & Brothers, 1936.

Teter, George E. (1877–1940). *An Introduction to Some Elements of Poetry.* Wauwatosa, WI: Kenyon Press, 1927. (*LL* 951)

Virgil (P. Vergilius Maro) (70–19 B.C.E.). *The Works of Virgil.* Translated by John Dryden <1697>. London: Henry Frowde/Oxford University Press (World's Classics), 1903–25. (*LL* 1002)

Weigall, Arthur (1880–1934). *Wanderings in Roman Britain.* London: Butterworth, 1926. (*LL* 1025)

Wells, Carolyn (1870–1942). *Faulkner's Folly.* New York: George H. Doran Co., 1917.

Index

Lightning Source UK Ltd.
Milton Keynes UK
UKHW020957070521
383312UK00013B/878